THE PERFECTIBILITY OF MAN

John Passmore

THE PERFECTIBILITY OF MAN

John Passmore

Third Edition

LIBERTY FUND

Indianapolis

This book is published by Liberty Fund, Inc., a foundation established to encourage study of the ideal of a society of free and responsible individuals.

The cuneiform inscription that serves as our logo and as the design motif for our endpapers is the earliest-known written appearance of the word "freedom" (*amagi*), or "liberty." It is taken from a clay document written about 2300 B.C. in the Sumerian city-state of Lagash.

© 2000 by Liberty Fund, Inc. All rights reserved
First published in 1970 by Charles Scribner's Sons
Printed in the United States of America
04 03 02 01 00 C 5 4 3 2 1
04 03 02 01 00 P 5 4 3 2 1

Library of Congress Cataloging-in-Publication Data

Passmore, John Arthur.
The perfectibility of man/John Arthur Passmore. — 3rd ed.
p.   cm.
Includes bibliographical references and index.
ISBN 0-86597-257-5 (alk. paper) — ISBN 0-86597-258-3 (pbk.: alk. paper)
1. Philosophical anthropology. 2. Perfection. 3. Mysticism. I. Title.

BD450   .P29   2000
128—dc21   99-087606

Liberty Fund, Inc.
8335 Allison Pointe Trail, Suite 300
Indianapolis, Indiana 46250-1684

*The Perfectibility of Man! Ah heaven,
what a dreary theme!*
D. H. LAWRENCE

Mortal things suit mortals best.
PINDAR

CONTENTS

PREFACE

Like any other author I should like my readers to read every word I have written. But this is a somewhat unusual book, covering three thousand years and delving into philosophy, theology, religions—Eastern and Western—political and social ideals, even theatre. I can excuse readers who sometimes find themselves at a loss. This preface is meant to help them find their way, to discover what particularly interests them, to avoid swamps—swamps which other readers, with a different training, will recognize as solid ground.

When I began to work on this book I soon discovered that the words *perfection* and *perfectibility* were used in a variety of ways. I set about distinguishing them. That effort takes up the whole of the first chapter. Those who are bored by the making and relating of distinctions, which others may enjoy as an analytical exercise, will do best to turn to pages 25–28, where the results are set out. Or they may turn back to the first chapter, if in their later reading they may be troubled by a reference to a particular form of perfectibility.

Chapters 2 and 3 are essentially devoted to that creator of so many of our ideas, Greek philosophy. On pages 94–95 the outcome of these chapters is summarized, and some readers, not all, will find it preferable to read that summary before they read the chapters. If they feel the need for more background information, the books mentioned in numbered notes on pages 38–94 may be of help. The chapters are of central importance.

The early Greek writers would not allow even the gods to be perfect. Christianity took God to be perfect. But a battle ensued about human beings. Was perfection possible for them, or could they do no more than lower their level of imperfectibility? Chapters 4 through 7 are devoted to this theme. It is by no means dead. There are those who turn to Eastern religions in search of perfection. Some understanding of these past debates is essential not only for the understanding of historical debates, but also of present-day aspirations. These chapters are summarized on pages 223–25.

If some readers are mainly interested in these religious disputes, others may think that we have reached the heart of the book only when we embark upon secular means of reaching perfection, as in the attempt to assist the course of history understood to be by nature progressive. I do not think any guidance is necessary for the readers of these chapters, 8 through 12. Occasional names may be unfamiliar, but very few; it was not thought necessary to introduce chapter summaries.

There have been plenty of perfectionists and some of them have been very persistent—just a few years ago in Moscow a famous physicist told me that the Soviet Union was bound to become a perfect country with perfect people; this was just, he said, a matter of logic. But even before the 1914–18 war and the depression, which not long afterwards emerged on a great scale, dystopians made their presence felt. The chapter entitled "Perfection Renounced" is in essence a critical look at tendencies in the twentieth-century intellectual world. It needs no special guidance.

The same is true of the final chapter, "The New Mysticism," but it introduces philosophical contrasts between play, games, and love that are, I think, vital to an understanding and critique of mysticism. It is perhaps worth noting that when this book first appeared in the United States a critic told the world that it would have been a good book if it had consisted only of the last three chapters. I hope that a new generation of readers will be conscious, as many earlier readers were, of the fact that our past is still alive in our present.

A final point. The extensive references are precisely that.

They can be left alone, except by those who want to check what I have written or to engage in further reading.

John Passmore

Professor Emeritus
Australian National University
Canberra
March 1999

Acknowledgments

My theme is a vast one, and I have traced it through three thousand years of man's intellectual history, from Homer to the present day. Inevitably, this is not in the fullest sense a work of scholarship; the fragments out of which I have tried to construct a mosaic were, in large part, excavated by other hands. In the process of writing this book I have learnt a great deal; I can only hope that my readers will learn if not as much, at least something, by reading it. If they do, it will be because I have succeeded in communicating to them what so many scholars have taught me, many more scholars than I have been able to particularize by name.

As for more personal acknowledgements, a number of my colleagues and post-graduate students have read, or heard as seminar papers, chapters of this book in one or the other of its many early versions. They have drawn my attention to a good many errors of fact, mistakes of judgement, and clumsiness in expression. For their critical attention to the opening chapters of the book, I should like particularly to thank Evan Burge and John Kleinig. (They have not, I should add in all fairness to them, seen the book in its final, or even in a near-final, form.) A considerable burden has fallen upon Mrs. Elizabeth Short in correcting my inveterate inaccuracy. Thanks are also due to Mrs. Glenda McIntyre, Mrs. Mavis Rose, Mrs. Estelle Haynes and Mrs. Diane Murray, for coping with the vagaries of my handwriting and the multiplicity of my interlinings, through innumerable retypings. My wife, as ever, has been called upon to contribute well beyond the normal limits of domestic responsibility. Finally, I should like to acknowledge once more my enormous indebtedness to the late Professor John Anderson. I have not found it possible to quote him; my indebtedness is to his lectures and to conversational remarks rather than to his publications. He would have profoundly disagreed with a great deal of what I have written, but it would never have been written were it not that I had the great good fortune to be one of his students.

JOHN PASSMORE
Australian National University,
Canberra
December 1969

THE PERFECTIBILITY OF MAN

PERFECTION AND PERFECTIBILITY

When, in everyday life, men are accounted perfect, this is most commonly in relation to their performance of a task or in a role. In such contexts, "perfect" acts as a superlative. A forger can be good, very good, excellent, or perfect at imitating signatures; an accountant can be good, very good, excellent, or perfect at drawing up balance-sheets. A perfect secretary, a perfect forger, a perfect accountant, all attain to the highest possible standards in the tasks they undertake. But this by no means implies that they are perfect in the performance of other tasks, in other roles. The perfect forger does not necessarily keep perfect accounts, nor is the perfect accountant always a perfect secretary. Even more obviously, he need not be a perfect man.

Indeed, it is a serious question whether perfection in this sense — let us call it "technical perfection" — has any intelligible application to man as such. That it has, Martin Foss, for one, denies. "Society," he writes, "simplifies and abbreviates its members to executors of their social purposes, their social professions. . . . If they are adequate to their purpose in the social scheme, they are called perfect. So we have perfect typists, perfect lawyers, perfect accountants. But are there also 'perfect men'? I do not think so."[1]* This is a pleasantly rapid way of rejecting the perfectibility of man.

1. Martin Foss: *The Idea of Perfection in the Western World* (Princeton, 1946; paperback ed., Lincoln, Neb., 1964), p. 9.

* Numbered footnotes refer quotations to their source or indicate the origin of a piece of information. They can safely be ignored except by those who wish to question the accuracy, or explore the context, of a quotation. Footnotes which are ancillary to the understanding of the text, or pursue a by-path, will be found, as here, on the page to which they refer. [In this edition, numbered notes have been moved to the page of citation.]

Being human is not a profession, nor does it by itself fulfil a social purpose. If, then, there is no other kind of perfection, or none applicable to human beings, except technical perfection, it is natural to conclude that *man as such*—as distinct from a secretary *qua* secretary or an accountant *qua* accountant—cannot, by the very nature of the case, attain to perfection.

This deduction admits of a number of replies. The nineteenth-century philosophical anarchist William Godwin, at least in his later writings, argues that if each man is perfectible in a task, then it follows that man as such is perfectible. "Putting idiots and extraordinary cases out of the question, every human creature," so Godwin maintains, "is endowed with talents, which, if rightly directed, would shew him to be apt, adroit, intelligent and acute, in the walk for which his organization especially fitted him." Each individual man, that is, has a set of talents which enable him to be trained to perform a particular task. And this makes it possible, Godwin continues, for each man to produce "something as perfect in its kind, as that which is effected under another form by the more brilliant and illustrious of his species." Each and every man, that is, can be so trained as to be technically perfect in some particular respect. And since man as such is a mere abstraction, since mankind is made up of individual men, to demonstrate that each and every man is perfectible is to demonstrate that *man* is perfectible.[2]

At first sight, however, there are two powerful arguments against deducing the perfectibility of man from the capacity of each man to perfect himself in some particular task. A man, we pointed out, can perfect himself in one role while being imperfect in another. He may be a perfect accountant but a dreadful public-speaker. There is an enormous gap, too, between his being a perfect accountant and his being

2. William Godwin: *Thoughts on Man* (London, 1831), pp. 36–37. For Godwin's earlier views see chs. 9, 10 below.

a perfect man. It is one thing to say, then, that each and every man can perfect himself at *something*, quite another to say that he can perfect himself in every task he is called upon, as a human being, to perform. Secondly, a man can perfect himself not only as a secretary or an accountant but as a forger, a blackmailer, a torturer, an informer. "All men are perfectible; for even the worst of men can perfect himself as a procurer." Something seems to have gone wrong with that argument. When moralists, theologians, philosophers, dispute about whether man is "perfectible," they take it for granted that the perfection in question does not include perfection in vice. To be perfectible in a task, it again follows, is not the same thing as being perfectible as a man.

Plato's republic is designed to meet both these objections. Plato allots to each man one task and one task only, that task in which his talents and skills enable him to perfect himself. "Each individual should pursue that work in this city," writes Plato of his ideal republic, "for which his nature was naturally most fitted, each one man doing one work."[3] So whereas in our society a man may be a perfect accountant but a failure as a father, in Plato's republic such a man will not be permitted to act as a father: that will be somebody else's task, somebody whose talents and skills enable him to perfect himself in the task of rearing children.

As for the second objection, Plato's republic is an ideal society. An ideal State will not contain forgers, blackmailers, or procurers. So although in our everyday imperfect States there are men whose talents and skills are wholly devoted to perfecting themselves in these deplorable occupations, in an ideal State each citizen will be allocated to a morally respectable task, chosen to accord with his talents. Perhaps, then, we need do no more than slightly modify Godwin's view: man is perfectible if and only if each man has talents

3. Plato: *Republic,* Bk. IV. 433, as trans. A. D. Lindsay, Everyman's Library (London, 1935; repr. 1948), p. 120.

and skills which would fit him for the performance of the task which would be allocated to him in an ideal society.

Obviously, however, to talk thus of an "ideal" society—a perfect society, that is—is to make use of another, and different, sense of perfection, not technical perfection. A perfect society cannot be defined as one which performs its social task perfectly: it *sets* social tasks, it does not *have* a social task. More concretely, in Plato's republic social tasks are set by a particular class of men—the "philosopher-kings" who act as its governors. No doubt, they are expert as rulers. But if they were only expert in a technical sense—good at keeping the society in order—it would be unsafe to rely upon them not to encourage such occupations as blackmailing, informing, torturing. Technically expert rulers, indeed, commonly provide more than enough employment for such skilled professions. The expertness of Plato's rulers is a by-product of, not the sole evidence for, their perfection. They are not perfect because they rule perfectly, they rule perfectly because they are perfect, as a consequence of their having seen "the form of the good." So, in the end, the whole structure of Plato's republic rests on there being a variety of perfection over and above technical perfection—a perfection which consists in, or arises out of, man's relationship to the ideal.

Even in the case of the ordinary citizen, indeed, technical perfection is not, for Plato, enough. There is, he no doubt says, an "image" of justice—of moral perfection—in "the principle that he whom nature intended for a shoemaker should attend to shoemaking and nothing else." But it is *only* an image. True justice "does not concern a man's management of his own external affairs, but his internal management of his soul, his truest self and his truest possessions."[4] In other words, technical perfection does not automatically carry human perfection with it; if men ought to seek technical perfection, this is only as an outward expres-

---

4. *Ibid.*, Bk. IV. 443, trans. Lindsay, p. 133.

sion of their moral perfection, their willingness to submit their passions to rational control.

A not dissimilar analysis of the relation between technical and human perfection is sometimes to be met with in Christian thought, especially, although not solely, in the Reforming tradition. "No one," Luther writes, "is without some commission and calling"—a set of tasks it is his responsibility to perform.[5] In most cases, this commission and calling is made clear to a man by the station into which he is born. "This means," Luther tells us, "that a servant, maid, son, daughter, man, woman, lord, subject, or whoever else may belong to a station ordained by God, as long as he fills his station, is as beautiful and glorious in the sight of God as a bride adorned for her marriage."[6] Men serve God best, Luther argues, by remaining in their vocation, however "mean and simple" it may be—although he does, somewhat inconsistently, allow that if a boy has *special* abilities it is the duty both of parents and of the State to make it possible for him to perfect those abilities by education.

At once, however, that difficulty arises which we have already met, although in a somewhat different context. Human beings may be born into stations which only a God considerably more broad-minded than the God of Christianity would find "beautiful and glorious." Luther himself gives a list of "sinful" callings: "robbery, usury, public women, and as they are at present, the pope, cardinals, bishops, priests, monks and nuns."[7] This list is no doubt somewhat controversial; not everybody would wish to include popes along with prostitutes. But the principle is what is impor-

---

5. *The Precious and Sacred Writings of Martin Luther*, ed. J. N. Lenker (Minneapolis, 1903), Vol. X: *Church Postil Gospels: Advent, Christmas and Epiphany Sermons*, p. 243, as quoted in D. R. Heiges: *The Christian's Calling* (Philadelphia, 1958), p. 50.

6. *Luther's Works*, American ed., Vol. XIII (St. Louis, 1956), p. 368, quoted in Heiges, *op. cit.*, p. 57.

7. *Luther's Table Talk*, trans. William Hazlitt (Philadelphia, 1873), p. 447, as quoted in Heiges, *op. cit.*, p. 58.

tant. Luther has to grant that the calling into which human beings are born—as a woman may be born, let us say, a temple-prostitute—is not necessarily the one, the perfect performance of which will make them "beautiful and glorious in the sight of God."

Furthermore, although he is so emphatic that men should work diligently at their calling—and Calvin emphasizes this even more strongly—Luther does not maintain, just as Plato did not maintain, that they will reach perfection *as men* in this way. Indeed, Luther vehemently rejects the view that, in their earthly life, men can achieve perfection. He draws, too, an important distinction between technical and vocational perfection. The Christian, according to Luther, must use his vocation primarily as a way of serving his fellow-men; technical expertness is desirable only as a means to that end.* So although technical perfection plays a part in Lutheran moral theology, it is only a small part; Luther would certainly not identify the perfectibility of man with his ability to perfect himself in any secular task or set of tasks.

A man's performance in his vocation, indeed, is to Luther important only because it demonstrates his obedience to God, and to God's plan for man—just as it is important to Plato because it demonstrates his willingness to submit himself to the rule of the philosopher-kings. This attitude is even more clearly expressed in the moral theology of Karl Barth. "Faithfulness in vocation," he writes, "means positively that in my vocation as it is I seek, either well or badly, to do satisfactory work to the best of my ability, skill and conscience, . . . giving myself to my own particu-

---

* The idea of a "calling," in its purest form, is crystallized in the Indian caste system. "And do thy duty, even if it be humble, rather than another's, even if it be great. To die in one's duty is life: to live in another's is death." So says the Gītā (2,33). Gandhi tried to introduce into the caste system the Lutheran conception of vocation as "service," rather than as the performance of tasks. He largely failed. See, on this theme, V. S. Naipaul: *An Area of Darkness* (London, 1964), Pt. I, ch. 2. Compare what is said below (pp. 455–56) about "aristocratic pride," nowhere better exemplified than in the caste system.

lar concern, remembering always that it is no accident but part of the plan and providence of God that it is my concern, and that God summons me to do justice to it."[8] In other words, technical perfection — in so far as perfection rather than conscientious application is what is called for — matters to Barth only as a special case of *obedientiary* perfection, absolute obedience to the will of God. This is man's real task, the task all men have to undertake: the practice of a calling does no more than exemplify it.

Obedientiary perfection, however, still has its problems: what guarantee is there that submission to God's will cannot lead men into imperfection? God, to judge from the Old Testament, makes strange demands upon men, bids them to act in ways which scarcely accord with our everyday ideas about moral perfection. Can the temple-prostitute really be confident that it is not God's will that she should continue in that station in life? But this, it might be said, is at worst the problem of determining in what God's will consists. There can be no denying that to do what God wills, once that will has been determined, is the path to perfection. But why should this not be denied? Some theologians, like the thirteenth-century Duns Scotus, have been prepared to reply that it is self-contradictory to suppose that God would ever will men to do anything except what is good. Nothing is *meant* by "good," on their view, except "action in accordance with God's will"; the supposition cannot intelligibly be entertained, therefore, that it might be good to disobey God.* But most theologians have been unhappy with the

---

8. Karl Barth: *Church Dogmatics*, Vol. III: *The Doctrine of Creation*, Pt. 4, ed. G. W. Bromiley and T. F. Torrance (Edinburgh, 1961), ch. XII, §56.2: Vocation, p. 642. This whole section on Vocation is highly relevant.

* Even Duns Scotus made one exception. "God is to be loved" and "God must be hated or dishonoured" are, he tells us, obligations from which even God cannot grant us a dispensation. Thus he hoped to forestall the obvious objection: if "That is good" simply means "That is what God wills," the question still remains why men should pay any attention to what God wills. William of Ockham found himself in difficulties on the same point. The articles by Allan B. Wolter on Duns Scotus and by Ernest A. Moody on William of

suggestion that "to do what God wills is good" means no more than "to do what God wills is to do what God wills." They have suggested, rather, that God is perfect, and must be obeyed just for that reason. But obviously, God's perfection is not obedientiary perfection; God obeys nobody, not even himself. So, if this view is to be maintained, perfection has to be defined, when it applies to God, as something other than obedientiary perfection. And the perfection of men's conduct when they obey God will then lie not in their obedience as such but in the fact that their conduct reflects the perfection of God.

Summing up, to identify the perfectibility of man with his capacity to perfect himself technically in a task is to encounter insuperable difficulties—unless perfectibility is wholly divorced from moral perfection. It is only if the task can be thought of as one set by a perfect Being or in a perfect society that there is any plausibility in supposing that a man can perfect himself as a human being merely by perfecting his ability in a task. Two consequences then follow. The first is that the perfection of such a Being or such a society does not itself consist in its perfect performance of a task. The second is that a man's perfecting himself in the performance of a task is not *in itself* sufficient to ensure his perfecting himself as a man: it is important only in so far as it bears witness to his perfection in some other, more fundamental respect, in obedience, in submission, in rational control.

Closely related to technical perfection, however, is a more philosophically complex concept of perfection—teleological perfection—which has often been invoked as the test of human perfectibility. This is the perfection which consists in a thing's reaching its "natural end." Its great ex-

---

Ockham in Paul Edwards (ed.), *The Encyclopedia of Philosophy*, 8 vols (New York, 1967), admirably sum up the points at issue. For a fuller discussion of the philosophical problems involved see J. A. Passmore: *Ralph Cudworth* (Cambridge, 1951), ch. iv.

ponent is Aristotle. Every form of activity, Aristotle argues, is directed towards an end. The art of sculpting, for example, has as its end the depiction of the human figure, the art of medicine has as its end health. It is impossible to suppose, Aristotle goes on to contend, that although sculptors and doctors each seek the end natural to the forms of activity they undertake, man as such has no end which he naturally seeks. The only question, for Aristotle, is in what that natural end consists. He identifies it with *eudaimonia*—"happiness" or "well-being." Man is perfectible, then, if and only if he is capable of attaining to well-being.[9]

The soundness of Aristotle's argument is more than questionable. Tasks are not set by Nature but by men, within particular forms of social organization: it would not be in the least surprising if man as such, unlike the sculptor or the carpenter, had no task to perform, no end to pursue. This, indeed, is precisely what we should expect. Tasks, forms of activity, differentiate men, diversify their responsibilities; there are sculptors, and sculptors who produce figures in marble rather than abstract arrangements of junk-metal as their "natural end," only in societies which call upon men to undertake, and encourage them to perfect themselves, in such activities.* No doubt there are natural differences be-

---

9. Aristotle: *Nicomachean Ethics*, 1, 7. For further details see ch. 3 below.

* I am not suggesting, of course, that at some point "society" says to itself: "Let there be sculptors and let them work in junk-metal." Men *set themselves* tasks. New types of tasks— or new views about the "natural" end of a task—commonly originate in this way. Some sculptor decides that he will no longer work in marble, or no longer seek to construct man-like figures. Once this novel point of view has been generally accepted, sculptors are trained in a different way, different demands are made upon them. The crucial point is that it is men who decide, whether about themselves or about other people, that there shall be, for example, computer-programmers and what shall count as the "natural end" of computer-programming, i.e. the end towards which it is directed. Aristotle's view is plausible only in a relatively simple society in which men and women have fixed and stable responsibilities. In such a society new types of tasks, or new views about the natural objective of a form of activity, do not arise or arise very seldom. In more rapidly changing societies, the theory of a "natural end" is often invoked as a polemical weapon by conservatives; so conservative art critics say "that is not sculpture" of some piece of work which is not the sort of thing sculptors have normally been accustomed to produce.

tween human beings; men cannot give birth to babies nor can women fertilize a womb. But even the "functions" of men and women, beyond this elementary point, are fixed by men, not by Nature. It is not Nature who decides whether women shall work in industry, in agriculture, or in the home, or what they shall take as their objective in those pursuits. The so-called "natural ends," indeed, should more accurately be described as "conventional" ends.

The distinction between technical and teleological perfection might at first sight appear to be a distinction without a difference. Technical perfection, it can plausibly be argued, is simply perfection in the methods necessary and sufficient to produce a particular end. A man is technically perfect in a task if and only if he is capable of attaining the objective to which that task is conventionally directed, i.e. its teleological perfection. But this is not quite the situation.

In some instances, no doubt, the two modes of perfection are but opposite sides of the same penny. We should not reckon a forger "technically perfect" unless he can actually produce a perfect imitation of a signature, the "conventional end" of forgery. But we might describe a sculptor as "technically perfect"—capable, that is, of perfectly performing such tasks as the carving of marble in the likeness of a human figure—and yet deny the perfection of the works he produces. He lacks, we say, "inspiration" or "genius." And on the other side, an artist might produce the works of art towards which his activity is directed without having perfected himself technically: technically rough, they yet delight the eye. A doctor might succeed in keeping his patients healthy only because they have an excellent constitution and are fortunate in the kind of work they undertake. Health can be a "natural gift," as distinct from the product of the doctor's skill, even when that skill is directed towards maintaining health. To sum up, whereas technical perfection entirely depends, as Kant argued, on

talent and skill,[10] men can achieve teleological perfection—
the end towards which their efforts are directed—as a gift,
or by luck, rather than as a result of effort.

This is a fact of great consequence for Christian theories of perfection. Aquinas took over the Aristotelian analysis of perfection and developed it systematically. Everything
whatever, he says, moves by its own nature towards a particular condition, the condition in which it can rest. That
condition is the thing's "perfection." The perfection of man
as such, according to Aquinas, lies in the vision of God—
or, more precisely, of the Divine Essence.[11] But at the same
time Aquinas argues that men can achieve that end only by
the grace of God, not by the mere exercise of talents and
skills. The vision of God is at once man's natural end and
a supernatural gift, just as it is the sculptor's natural end
to produce great works of art, and yet to do so requires a
kind of inspiration which is something over and above the
talents and skills he directs towards that end.* So technical perfection is not the same thing as teleological perfection, however closely the two are sometimes related to one

10. Immanuel Kant: *Critique of Practical Reason,* Pt. I, Bk. I, ch. I, §8, in the trans.
by T. K. Abbott, 6th ed. (London, 1909; photo. repr. 1948), pp. 129–30. Kant uses the
expression "practical perfection" for my "technical perfection."

11. Thomas Aquinas: *Summa theologica,* Pt. II, i, q. 3, a. 8, as trans. by Fathers of the
English Dominican Province (London, 1920).

* It does not follow, of course, that without some degree of technical skill the sculptor can achieve his end. In reaction against the view that the artist perfects himself by
perfecting his skills, critics are sometimes led to argue that skill is inessential, that the
artist can reach his objective only by completely rejecting the concept of technical perfection. This attitude, very common over the last half-century in Western Europe, is not
peculiar to it. So in seventeenth-century China Shih-t'ao, arguing against the current emphasis on technique, was led to conclude that "the perfect man has no method" or rather
"it is not that he has no method, but rather the best of methods, which is the method of
no-method." The flexibility Shih-t'ao is advocating is, no doubt, far from the extremes of
Western Romanticism. But his emphasis on genius and on a "mysterious depth which is
unfathomable" is very characteristic of those critics and artists who turn against the ideal
of "technical" perfection as means to achieving the painter's end. Shih-t'ao's essay is translated in Lin Yutang: *The Chinese Theory of Art* (New York, 1967). The quotations are from
p. 142 and p. 152.

another. A man can be technically perfect without attaining to teleological perfection; he can perform perfectly his religious and moral duties, so far as that involves the skilled use of his abilities, he can make himself expert in ritual and in Christian knowledge, without being vouchsafed the vision of God; and he can attain to that perfection without being technically perfect.

The presumption, as we saw, which lies beneath the concept of teleological perfection is that every kind of thing, including man, has a natural end in which alone it can find perfect satisfaction. There is another way of putting this metaphysical assumption. Everything, it may be suggested, contains unrealized potentialities; "becoming perfect" consists in actualizing the potentialities. A thing's "natural end" is to actualize, to realize, its potentialities. So in his *Critique of Judgement* Kant suggests that what he had previously called "practical perfection" — task-perfection — is more accurately described as "utility." To perfect oneself technically is to make oneself useful but not necessarily to perfect oneself. A thing perfects itself, he now says, only when it attains an end inherent in the thing itself, what it has it in itself to be, not merely an end which someone has chosen to set up as its objective.[12]

This explains some at first sight very odd philosophical remarks about perfection, as when Aquinas writes that "everything is perfect so far as it is actual" or Spinoza that "by perfection . . . I shall understand . . . reality."[13] The language, and the metaphysical presumptions, are Aristotelian. For Aristotle, what actually is must be better than what merely can be. To cite his examples, it is better actually to see than merely to possess the power of seeing, a build-

12. Kant: *The Critique of Judgement,* Pt. I: *Critique of Aesthetic Judgement,* Section 1, Bk. 1, §15; in the trans. by J. C. Meredith (Oxford, 1911), pp. 69–71.

13. Aquinas: *Summa theologica,* Pt. I, q. 5, a. 1; Spinoza: *Ethics,* Pt. IV, Preface, in the trans. by A. Boyle, Everyman's Library (London, 1910; repr. 1948), p. 144.

ing is better than the mere capacity to build.[14] In each case the merely potential, according to Aristotle, is incomplete, formless, imperfect. The actual is "perfect," then, in so far as it is the realization of, or the giving form to, a potentiality.

But there is something more than a little strange in thus identifying perfection with the realization of potentialities. Suppose a man is potentially a liar. When he actualizes that potentiality, has he thereby perfected himself? At this point, it is important to recall that the general concept of perfection does not have written into it any suggestion of *moral* excellence. A man can be a perfect scoundrel or a perfect idiot just as he can be a perfect saint; he can commit a perfect crime, be a perfect forger, or have a "perfectly rotten time of it." But, as we have already pointed out, when we speak of "perfectibility," as distinct from perfection *simpliciter,* the situation is different; to assert that man is perfectible is to assert that he can become, in some sense taken to be absolute, a better person. To the extent to which an analysis of perfection is directed towards helping us to answer the question whether human beings are, or are not, perfectible, it must not allow the response: "they are perfectible all right: there are plenty of men who are potential villains and who actualize that potentiality perfectly."

If perfection is to imply becoming better, and yet is still to be defined in terms of the actualization of potentialities, it must be supported by a very special theory of evil. Of any actual person—let us say, a repulsive bigot—it has to be said that "in so far as he is actual he is perfect." But what of his bigotry? This, it is then necessary to argue, is not actual. As Augustine puts the point: "Evil has no positive nature; what we call evil is merely the lack of something that is good."[15]

---

14. *Metaphysics,* 1049b–1051a.
15. *The City of God,* Bk. XI, chap. 9, abridged from the trans. by G. G. Walsh *et al.,* ed. V. J. Bourke, Image Books (New York, 1958), p. 217. On the issue as a whole, with

Similarly, Descartes takes it to be self-evident that blindness and error are not "real"; they are, he says, simply the lack or absence of a power which we possess by nature.[16] And Leibniz, so Bertrand Russell has suggested, makes his moral philosophy plausible only by moving backwards and forwards between a moral definition of perfection, for which evil is positive, and a teleological definition for which it is negative.[17]

On this view, then, the bigot does not actualize a human potentiality, he does not "realize his nature," by his bigotry. Rather, he fails to realize his nature, since he is deprived of some good which is potential in it. All potentialities, then, are for good. It is more than a little surprising how often perfectibilists have taken this for granted; the "release of potentialities" is calmly identified with the release of potentialities *for good.* In everyday life, of course, it is not in the least degree paradoxical to say of some particularly nasty child: "he is a potential criminal" or, even more specifically, a "potential murderer." Nor would it seem absurd, though the point might be disputed, to suggest that *all* men are potentially criminals. But if Augustine and Descartes and Leibniz are correct, all such judgements are mistaken: criminality is not a potentiality, capable of being actualized, but only a defect, the imperfect actualization of a potentiality. There are, indeed, a great many episodes in the history of perfectibilism which can only be understood by remembering that evil is assumed not to be "actual," and potentialities all to be for good.

So far, we have distinguished three different modes of human perfection: technical perfection, which consists in

special reference to Augustine, see John Hick: *Evil and the God of Love* (London, 1966), especially pt. II.

16. "Objections III with replies," Obj. XII, in *Philosophical Works of Descartes,* trans. E. S. Haldane and G. R. T. Ross, 2 vols (Cambridge, 1911–12; corr. repr. 1931–34), Vol. II, pp. 74–75.

17. *A Critical Exposition of the Philosophy of Leibniz,* 2nd ed. (London, 1937; repr. 1949), pp. 199–201.

performing, with the maximum efficiency, a specialized task; obedientiary perfection, which consists in obeying the commands of a superior authority, God or a member of the élite; teleological perfection, which consists in attaining to that end in which it is one's nature to find final satisfaction. Abstractly separable, they may, in the writings of a particular perfectibilist—or anti-perfectibilist—be variously conjoined and variously disjoined. All three rely, in some degree, on the concept of a function, an allotted task, an end to be pursued, whether set by other men, by society, by God, or by Nature.

Indeed, the Greek word *teleios,* commonly translated as "perfect," is etymologically related to *telos* (end)—the relationship between perfection and the achievement of an end is, as it were, written into it. The English word "perfect," however, ultimately derives, by way of Middle English, from the Latin word *perficere,* the roots of which, in turn, are *facere,* "to make," and a prefix *per* suggesting "thoroughly." The perfect, that is, is etymologically definable as the "thoroughly made," the "completed." Between the definition of perfection in terms of ends and the definition of it in terms of the "thoroughly made" or the "complete" there are, of course, close links. If a thing is badly made or incomplete, it may, in consequence, be unable to fulfil its function. A pair of secateurs may be useless because a screw has been put in crookedly or a spring is missing; a doctor may be unable to cure his patients because his sight is poor.

It is not necessarily the case, all the same, either that what fulfils its function must be well-made and complete or that what is well-made and complete must fulfil its function. We can say of a house: "The workmanship is poor, and we have never bothered to have the terrace completed, but it suits our purposes admirably." Or alternatively: "The workmanship is excellent, and the house is now complete, but as a place to live in, it is dreadful." In such judgements, we make use of criteria of good workmanship and of completeness which are independent of our criteria for suitability to an end. We can judge an Etruscan artifact, a bronze statue, to be well-made, complete, and so far perfect, without believing that it ever fulfilled its intended function, whether as a fertility god or as a funereal consolation to the dead.

The perfect, it might therefore be suggested, is best defined in Newman's manner as "that which has no flaw in it, that which is complete, that which is consistent, that which is sound."[18] Perfection is thus cut loose from any connexion with an end; one can simply look at a person and describe him as perfect by seeing him to be free of flaws. "Perfect," in this sense, is an adjective applying to objects, to persons, to States, not (necessarily) to the performance of tasks or to the ends towards which those performances are directed. By what criterion, however, are we to determine whether a characteristic counts as a flaw? The idea of a flaw, as it is normally employed, is a relative one, not absolute. So the English, but not the Greeks, consider it a flaw in food that it is lukewarm; the English, but not the Japanese, consider it a flaw in a garden that it lacks flowers; the English, but not all African tribes, consider it a flaw in a woman's beauty that she has pendulous ears. Not everyone would admit, even, that it is necessarily a flaw in a thing that it is unfinished, incomplete. "In everything, no matter what it may be," writes Yoshida Kenkō in his thirteenth-century *Essays in Idleness,* "uniformity is undesirable. Leaving something incomplete makes it interesting, and gives one the feeling that there is room for growth. Some one once told me, 'Even when building the Imperial Palace, they always leave one place unfinished.'"[19]

In Christian theology, however, it is ordinarily supposed that there are *absolute* flaws—moral and metaphysical. An

---

18. J. H. Newman: "A Short Road to Perfection" in *Meditations and Devotions* (London, 1894), pt. II, p. 382.

19. Yoshida Kenkō: *Essays in Idleness,* as trans. in *Anthology of Japanese Literature,* introd. and comp. by Donald Keene, rev. and enl. ed. (Harmondsworth, 1968), p. 229.

important form of absolute moral flaw is sin. About the nature of sin there are no doubt disputes, disputes about whether, for example, the mere experiencing of an illicit sexual impulse constitutes a sin, or only the "entertaining" of the impulse. When one Christian moral theologian asserts, and another denies, that men can ever, in this life, be free of sin, they may be disagreeing about the nature of sin rather than about man's moral capacities. But they would agree, at least, on one point: unless man can be sinless he cannot be perfect. So, in practice, disputes within Christianity about the perfectibility of man very often turn out to be disputes about the possibility of sinlessness. Let us call that sort of perfection which consists in freedom from moral flaw—including sin—*immaculate* perfection.

The idea of a "metaphysical" flaw is even more complex. Consider, for example, the following passage from Descartes, in which he sets out to show that a corporeal body cannot be perfect:

> When you talk of *a corporeal being of the highest perfection,* if you take the term "of the highest perfection" absolutely, meaning that the corporeal thing is one in which all perfections are found, you utter a contradiction. For its very bodily nature involves many imperfections, as that a body is divisible into parts, that each of its parts is not the other, and other similar defects. For it is self-evident that it is a greater perfection not to be divided than to be divided, etc.[20]

Descartes here takes it for granted that what in an immediately preceding passage he calls "simplicity and unity" are perfections, and that divisibility is an imperfection. Similarly, metaphysicians often presume that it is an imperfec-

---

20. "Reply to Objections II," in *Philosophical Works,* trans. Haldane and Ross, Vol. II, p. 37.

tion in a thing for it to be in any way dependent for its existence on anything else, to be complex, to be finite, to pass away. The possession of such characteristics is taken to demonstrate that the thing is not *really* complete. When it has a cause, or when it has distinguishable parts one of which might be taken away from it, something essential for its existence lies outside it. An article on perfection in the *Dictionnaire des Sciences Philosophiques*[21] will further illustrate the point:

> Do you want to discover absolute perfection? Leave to one side the imagination with its laborious combinations, lift yourself above man and the world; or rather, without leaving yourself, examine what reason reveals to you about each of your perceptions. Your consciousness tells you that your existence is a fugitive and borrowed one; at once, reason reveals to you a being absolute and eternal. Your consciousness teaches you that as a cause you are only a limited cause, i.e. effect and cause at once; reason elevates you to the first and omnipotent cause who has produced you and has produced everything else. It is just the same with infinite intelligence, infinite beauty, infinite justice. . . . Add to all this, not thousands of attributes (that would not be enough), not even thousands of infinite attributes, but—and this enfeebles the Reason compelled to confess it—an infinity of infinite attributes and that is the being to whom nothing is lacking, that is an absolutely perfect being.

The ideal of perfection, thus understood—*metaphysical* perfection or, as Kant calls it, "theoretic" perfection—removes it, we should at first be inclined to conclude, far be-

---

21. *Dictionnaire des sciences philosophiques*, ed. A. Franck, 6 vols (Paris, 1844–52). The article is by D. Henne. It is difficult for a translation quite to capture the rhetorical exuberance of the original.

yond human reach. For how can a man set out to become less finite than he is, or more of a first cause, or less of a temporal being? What hope has he of becoming "a being to whom nothing is lacking"? But human ambition is boundless. And so, under the influence of this metaphysical ideal of perfection, men have set out to become more like a first cause, in the sense of not allowing themselves to be affected or influenced by anything which happens to them; they have sought to become less finite and less temporal by freeing themselves from all concern with the changing and by uniting themselves with God; they have tried to persuade themselves that they "lack nothing" by rejecting as worthless all that this world contains. The achievement of perfection has thus been identified with the development of a capacity for standing aside from life, rising above it to union with a Being, or a Universe, supposed to be infinite and eternal. For only such a life, it has been supposed, can be metaphysically flawless, metaphysically immaculate.

The difficulty that to define perfection in such exalted terms removes it far beyond human aspirations has, however, often been recognized by less mystically-minded, more practical, moralists. When absolute perfection is defined in a manner which makes it no longer meaningful to suppose that any finite being could be absolutely perfect, it is commonly supplemented by a doctrine of "relative perfection," perfection relative to a humanly-attainable moral ideal, human as distinct from metaphysical perfection. The problem, then, is to determine what constitutes this ideal of perfect humanity.

Sometimes the ideal is made concrete as a person. Human perfection is taken to consist in imitating the example set by that person — *exemplary* perfection. For the Stoics, Socrates served as such an ideal; Christians have naturally turned to Jesus, considered as a human figure. The great problem, it has sometimes been supposed, is to choose between these two exemplary ideals: Joseph Priestley, for ex-

ample, wrote a book called *Socrates and Jesus Compared*.[22]
Kant, however, objects to any definition of perfection by reference to examples. "Nor could anything be more fatal to morality," he writes, "than that we should wish to derive it from examples. . . . Even the Holy One of the Gospels must first be compared with our ideal of moral perfection before we can recognize Him as such."[23] Why should this be so? Why should we not say, simply, that to be perfect is to be like such and such an exemplar, Jesus or Socrates?

The point Kant is making—it derives in the long run from Plato's *Euthyphro*—is that perfection cannot *mean* "being like such-and-such a person." For when we say: "Socrates is a perfect man" or "Jesus is perfect," this is not the empty tautology, "Socrates is Socrates-like," "Jesus is Jesus-like." We adjudge Jesus and Socrates perfect by comparing them with our ideal of moral perfection; in calling them perfect we mean that they perfectly exemplify that ideal. But if we are in possession of such an ideal, then it is only sensible to judge our own conduct, too, by direct reference to it. Contemplating the life of a particular person, no doubt, may help us to conceive our moral ideal more concretely, more vividly. In the end, however, it is by reference to the ideal that we must determine our own, or anybody else's, degree of perfection. "Examples," so Kant elsewhere argues, "serve for our encouragement and emulation. They should not be used as patterns."[24] To regard them as an inspiration, only, will serve to prevent us from thinking that we are obliged to imitate some personal peculiarity of the persons we take to be ideal—Jesus' habit of speaking in parables, for example, or Socrates' habit of falling into trances.

---

22. London, 1803. Franklin advised Americans to imitate *both*.

23. *Fundamental Principles of the Metaphysic of Morals*, Section II, as trans. T. K. Abbott in *Kant's Critique of Practical Reason and Other Works*, p. 25.

24. Kant: *Lectures on Ethics:* "Ethics: Example and Pattern in Religion"; in the reconstruction by Paul Mentzer, trans. Louis Infield (London, 1930; Torchbook ed., New York, 1963), p. 110.

But the problem Kant has here raised breaks out again at the level of ideals. We have still to decide between conflicting ideals of moral perfection, between, for example, the Buddhist ideal of disengagement and the humanistic ideal of involvement. How are we then to proceed? There is no higher ideal of moral perfection by reference to which men can decide whether their ideals of moral perfection are in fact perfect. Spinoza has argued, indeed, that the appeal to ideals is always arbitrary: we arbitrarily set up ideals—the perfect house, the perfect man—and then speak of things as perfect or imperfect in relation to these arbitrary notions of ours.[25] Approached in this way, the question whether man is perfectible has, as it stands, no answer. "Perfectible," we must ask, "in relation to whose ideal of perfection?"

Neither Plato nor Kant, however, would admit that ideals are arbitrary. For Plato, at least as he is commonly interpreted, ideals have an independent reality. Indeed, only the ideal is fully real. The triangle you or I might draw on a piece of paper is, in virtue of its imperfection, not a fully real triangle; the real triangle is the ideal triangle, the form of triangularity. Kant is not prepared, as he himself puts it, "to soar so high." Ideals, he grants, do not have objective reality. But they nevertheless have, he says, "practical power." They provide us with what he calls an "archetype," they "form the basis of the possible perfection of certain actions." "Although we cannot concede to these ideals objective reality (existence)," he writes, "they are not therefore to be regarded as figments of the brain; they supply reason with a standard which is indispensable to it, providing it . . . with a concept of that which is entirely complete in its kind, and thereby enabling it to estimate and to measure the degree and the defects of the incomplete."[26]

25. Spinoza: *Ethics,* Pt. IV, Preface; *ed. cit.,* pp. 141–42.
26. Kant: *Critique of Pure Reason,* Pt. I: "Transcendental Doctrine of Elements," Second Division, Bk. II, ch. III, Section 1: "The Ideal in General," as trans. N. Kemp Smith (London, 1929; corr. repr. 1950), p. 486.

But Spinoza's objection is not easily set aside; the content of such standards has still to be decided. To take an example from physical culture advertisements: must the "ideal specimen of a man" have bulging muscles? If perfection is defined teleologically, the mode of answering that question is clear. The perfect specimen must have bulging muscles if, and only if, bulging muscles are essential to the body's performance of its "true functions" or the pursuit of its "natural end." No doubt, this answer only postpones the day of reckoning: for it has still to be determined in what the natural end of the human body consists. But at least it *pretends* to provide us with an objective test by which the content of perfection can be determined. If, in contrast, the "ideal" is divorced from the concept of a function—as it is, for example, in the persistent Greek presumption that to have "an ideal shape" a thing must be spherical —then we seem to be left with no objective method by which to determine what can properly be incorporated in the ideal, whether, for example, the spherical is in fact the ideal form or, as some Japanese aestheticians argue, a form to be avoided.

Often enough, as we shall see, moralists change their minds about the perfectibility of man only because the ideal changes. Much will depend, for example, on whether the ideal man is defined as one who loves nothing but God for its own sake or as one who cares, above all, for the greatest happiness of the greatest number. It is not surprising that the ideal of perfection is so often made to rest on metaphysical rather than on merely moral grounds; to identify perfection with moral perfection leaves wide open the question how it is to be determined in what moral perfection consists. There is some solace—if perhaps, in the end, little intellectual satisfaction—in the view that Nature or God has settled that question for us, once and for all.

In the light of his general theory we should certainly have expected Plato, above all men, to argue that there is an ideal of humanity which men should try to copy in their pursuit of perfection, and that they are perfectible in so far as they can succeed in this task. But a momentous passage in Plato's *Theaetetus*—a passage which was to be much quoted in the centuries which followed—sets up God, not an ideal humanity, as the pattern on which man must model himself. "In the divine," Plato there writes, "there is no shadow of unrighteousness."[27] A man perfects himself morally—which, to Plato, is identical with perfecting himself *as a man*—by imitating the divine righteousness. To ask whether man is perfectible, then, is to ask how far man can be "like God." Aquinas carried this doctrine further by arguing that the perfection of *all* things consists in their being "like God."[28] Less metaphysically minded Christian philosophers have been content to define human perfection, and human perfection alone, in terms of likeness to God—*deiform* perfection. God, it is supposed, is at once a person and the ideal of moral perfection: a self-authenticating ideal in virtue of his supremacy. So there is no longer any problem in determining what man, or what ideal of man, is to be taken as the ideal. Man's ideal form is God. Exactly how God can be imitated, however, is another question and one which, to put it mildly, theologians have not found it easy to resolve.

If, in the *Theaetetus*, Plato identifies moral perfection with being "like God," a rather different ideal of perfection is suggested in his other dialogues, which identify it with harmony and order. This links it on the one side with immaculate perfection—freedom from flaw is defined as freedom from disorder—and on the other side with teleological perfection. Consider a "perfect clock." Then clearly this must keep time perfectly, thus fulfilling its function. The teleological perfection of a clock is perfect timekeeping. To

---

27. *Theaetetus,* 176 B–C, as trans. in F. M. Cornford: *Plato's Theory of Knowledge* (London, 1935), p. 87.

28. *Summa contra gentiles,* III. 19.

keep time perfectly its parts must be technically perfect. It must lack no parts and no part must be flawed, i.e. it must be immaculately perfect. But we could also define its perfection in still another way—by saying that the clock is a harmonious orderly arrangement of parts. Similarly, if we think of the soul as having parts—as Plato does in the *Republic*—then the perfection of the soul can be taken to consist in each of these parts harmoniously contributing to the perfection of the soul as a whole, playing its particular role in an ordered system. The nineteenth-century metaphysician Sir William Hamilton therefore defined perfection as "the full and harmonious development of all our faculties, corporeal and mental, intellectual and moral" and this came to be, for a time, the standard dictionary definition.[29]

It is in these terms that Plato defines the perfection of that ideal State, by reference to whose perfection the perfection of its individual citizens is to be determined. The ideal State is harmonious, orderly, stable, unified; the ideal citizen, by performing the tasks allotted to him, contributes to the total social harmony. Let us call this kind of perfection—the perfection of a system—*aesthetic* perfection. For it is often employed in the criticism of works of art, at its worst by critics like the German art historian Winckelmann for whom "perfection . . . was stately and harmonious form, almost anonymous in its regularity, unmarred by individual traits, frigid, devoid of emotions and showing no explicitly sexual characteristics."[30] I have already drawn attention to the links between aesthetic perfection, technical perfection, teleological perfection and immaculate perfection—aesthetic perfection involves the perfect performance of tasks in a flawless whole. It is no less closely related to metaphysical perfection: aesthetically perfect societies and aes-

29. *Lectures on Metaphysics*, ed. H. L. Mansel and J. Veitch, 6th ed., 2 vols (Edinburgh, 1877), Lecture II, Vol. 1, p. 20.
30. Luigi Barzini: *The Italians* (London, 1964), p. 33.

thetically perfect works of art are often described in language which reminds us of the metaphysically perfect—as unified, immutable, self-sufficient.

Once more, however, these various ideals of perfection, closely associated though they may be in many perfectibilist theories, are separable—not only theoretically, but in practice. That is why it has been necessary to distinguish them and give them different names. No doubt, as Hume points out, we particularly admire an object which is at the same time elegant and capable of performing its function efficiently. But, as he also goes on to suggest, some degree of aesthetic imperfection may be necessary if a thing is adequately to perform the task for which it was designed.[31] It was a leading tenet of the "functional" school of architects and designers that elegance and suitability for function must inevitably go together. But a chair which can be viewed with admiration as a harmonious shape is not necessarily the most comfortable of seats. More relevantly to our purposes, a society which values, above all else, unity, harmony, stability, may preserve an outward appearance of order only at the cost of suppressing human freedom and creative experiment. It may be by no means flawless, if we regard deception as a flaw; by no means perform its function, if we believe it to be part of the function of a society to foster enterprise. Plato's own republic is, indeed, a case in point.

Let us pause now to draw together the threads. When we describe a man as "technically perfect," we said, this is in relation to his efficiency in the performance of a task. But he cannot be technically perfect *as a man;* technical perfection applies only to a man's performance in a specialised role. This is so, at least, unless we suppose either that men have a

---

31. *Enquiry Concerning the Principles of Morals* (London, 1751), Section V, Pt. I, 172, in *Enquiries Concerning the Human Understanding and Concerning the Principles of Morals*, ed. L. A. Selby-Bigge, 2nd ed. (Oxford, 1902; repr. 1951), pp. 212–13.

task set for them by a supreme legislator, that of obeying his commands (obedientiary perfection), or alternatively that there is a task inherent in their very nature, their perfection consisting in the achievement of an "end" which is "natural" to them (teleological perfection). By somewhat devious metaphysical routes, the theory of "natural ends" leads to the identification of the perfect with the actual; for a man to be perfect is for him to realize what he has it in him to become. This carries with it the conclusion that a good deal of what we ordinarily count as actual is not "really" actual: sin and evil are defined as negation or privation, as a "lack" rather than as an accomplishment. By means of such arguments, teleological perfection is identified with the actualization of potentialities.

A somewhat different approach to perfection defines it as the "complete" or "well made." Perfection is then negatively defined (*immaculate* perfection) as the absence of flaw or imperfection—an imperfection sometimes identified with sin, sometimes with such metaphysical properties as complexity or self-sufficiency. Since in what is "complete" or "well made," or "immaculate," the parts fit together harmoniously, like the dove-tailed joints of a good piece of joinery, perfection is also defined as the harmonious working together of component parts (*aesthetic* perfection). Harmony and order are identified with perfection, conflict and disorder with imperfection. Finally, perfection may be defined in terms of conformity to a model, whether a model person (*exemplary* perfection), an ideal of *moral* perfection, or God (*deiform* perfection). God, in such instances, is usually taken to be both a person and an ideal—at once Plato's "God" and Plato's "form of the good."

It will by now be clear that the question "Are men perfectible?" does not admit of any easy straightforward answer. The reply, often merely obstructive, is for once justified: "It all depends on what you mean . . ." To assert that man is perfectible may mean either:

(1) there is some task in which each and every man can perfect himself technically;

(2) he is capable of wholly subordinating himself to God's will;

(3) he can attain to his natural end;

(4) he can be entirely free of any moral defect;

(5) he can make of himself a being who is metaphysically perfect;

(6) he can make of himself a being who is harmonious and orderly;

(7) he can live in the manner of an ideally perfect human being;

(8) he can become godlike.

Distinctions ought not to be made without necessity: the justification, if there is one, for distinguishing one from another these different ways of understanding perfectibility must be found in the story which follows. Two other possible sources of ambiguity should also be resolved. Christianity has sought to persuade men that they have two lives to live, one on this earth, the other in some infinitely more delightful, or inconceivably more horrendous, extra-terrestrial abode. When Christian theologians have denied, as they ordinarily have denied, that man is perfectible, what they have rejected as impossible is terrestrial, not celestial, perfectibility. The "perfectibility of man," in fact, normally means his perfectibility *on earth*. Heavenly perfection enters our story only in so far as it has been invoked as an ideal standard, in relation to which every human achievement must be adjudged imperfect.

A second ambiguity. The question: "Is man perfectible?" can be interpreted either as asking whether *any* man is perfectible or as asking whether *all* men are perfectible. Greek perfectibilists, and such Christians as have been perfectibilists, ordinarily ascribe perfectibility only to a very few men, endowed with exceptional talents or granted an extraordinary degree of divine grace. Not a few moralists, however, have been dissatisfied with such relatively modest aspirations. Each and every human being—assuming only that he is normally constituted—is capable, so Godwin argued, of being perfected. The doctrine that man is perfectible has, in consequence, two forms. Particularist perfectibilism ascribes terrestrial perfectibility only to an élite; universalist perfectibilism ascribes it to all men. The context will usually make it clear which variety of perfectibilism is in dispute.

FROM OLYMPUS TO THE FORM
OF THE GOOD

For the Homeric Greeks, the situation was clear. Not even the gods were perfect, if perfection entails freedom either from moral or from metaphysical defect. As the poet-sage Xenophanes complained, and Plato after him: "Homer and Hesiod have ascribed to the gods everything that is a shame and a reproach amongst men, stealing and committing adultery and deceiving each other."[1] Had Zeus laid down the commandment: "Be ye therefore perfect, even as your father in heaven is perfect" this would have been the sheerest hypocrisy, at least if the perfection in question is moral perfection.

In respect to metaphysical defects—or what Descartes, for example, took to be such—the Olympian gods were scarcely better off. They were, it is true, immortal and powerful, Zeus immensely so, but they were not self-created. They were born, even if sometimes by rather unorthodox mechanisms; they could suffer injury; there is not the slightest suggestion that they were indivisible or that they had an infinity of infinite attributes. Not even Zeus could stand alone in the Universe, a world complete in himself.

This is an important fact. There is a tendency nowadays to suppose it to be an *a priori* truth that what is divine must be perfect, both morally and metaphysically: that this is "part of what is meant" by being divine, or "part of the definition" of God. Sometimes this attitude is carried to the point of denying that the Olympian religion is "a religion

---

1. *KR*, fr. 169. All fragments from the pre-Socratics are as trans. in G. S. Kirk and J. E. Raven: *The Presocratic Philosophers* (Cambridge, 1957).

at all." That Homer should write of the gods as he does, in a tone which is unmistakably ironic, is particularly liable to shock and disturb the modern reader, persuading him that the Homeric gods were a mere literary convention who could not have been taken seriously, whether as objects of worship or as powers to be placated.

Such a view is clearly mistaken. It may be permissible to laugh at the gods; in a somewhat different sense, however, they have to be taken very seriously indeed. Some of the gods, it would seem, were more sensitive than others, more demanding, more insistent on their rights. But, in general terms, not to sacrifice to the gods, to neglect their rites, to profane their shrines, or to encroach in any way upon their privileges was to invite disastrous consequences, as Odysseus' men learnt to their cost. There were deeds the gods would not brook: sacrilege, a breach of the laws of hospitality, the killing of a blood-relation. In fifth-century Athens, certainly, to deny their divinity was a crime; Anaxagoras was charged with impiety for declaring that the sun was not a god, but a stone. The fact remains that it was by no means impious, let alone a contradiction in terms, to deny that the gods were perfect.

Nor, equally, was it at all obvious to the Homeric Greeks that men ought to imitate the gods, even in so far as the gods did approach perfection. Quite the contrary. To set out to imitate the gods was to exhibit *hubris,* to be arrogant, to get above oneself. "Do not try to become Zeus," the poet Pindar exhorted his readers. For, he continues, "mortal things suit mortals best." [2] In so far as men should guide their actions by models, it is the heroes, not the gods, on whom they should model themselves. [3] If the heroes are perfect, however, it is only as exemplars of how to confront a particular situation. When, in the *Odyssey,* Athena exhorts Telema-

---

2. Pindar: *Isthmian Odes,* V, lines 14–16.
3. W. Jaeger: *Paideia,* trans. G. Highet, Vol. 1 (3rd Eng. ed., Oxford, 1946), pp. 33–34.

chus to take Orestes as his model, she does not suggest that Orestes was a perfect man; he is, rather, a perfect example of how a man ought to act in a particular situation, a perfect revenge-taker. His perfection is a technical perfection, not an immaculate perfection.

The gods, indeed, will not tolerate men thinking of themselves as perfect in any but this limited sense. That this is so may not be apparent in the *Iliad,* where both Greeks and Trojans are conspicuously vainglorious. By the fifth century, however, the doctrine that the gods are, in the words of Herodotus, "envious and interfering" was established as traditional orthodoxy. The gods, Herodotus depicts Solon as saying, are "envious of human prosperity." Solon warns Croesus that "no man is ever self-sufficient; there is sure to be something missing." And Herodotus goes on to suggest that Croesus suffered his dreadful fate "presumably because God was angry with him for supposing himself to be the happiest of men."[4] Perfect happiness is for the gods alone; to set oneself up as being godlike, whether in respect to happiness or any other respect, was, to this way of thinking, the surest way to ruin. As the chorus in Aeschylus' *Agamemnon* warns us:

> In fame unmeasured, praise too high,
> Lies danger: God's sharp lightnings fly
> To stagger mountains.[5]

There was, however, no metaphysical problem, as distinct from a lack of common prudence, in a man's setting out to imitate the gods, in the sense in which there certainly is a metaphysical problem in understanding how any finite being could imitate the metaphysically perfect God of

---

4. Herodotus: *History,* Bk. I, 32, 34, as trans. Aubrey de Selincourt, Penguin Classics (Harmondsworth, 1954).

5. Aeschylus: *Agamemnon,* lines 467–69, as trans. Philip Vellacott in *The Oresteian Trilogy,* Penguin Classics (Harmondsworth, 1956; rev. repr. 1959).

Christian theology—eternal, infinite, unchanging and indivisible. A passage from one of Pindar's Odes is in this respect instructive. Men and gods, he says, both derive from the same mother, the earth-goddess Gaia. In intelligence and even in strength men therefore resemble the gods. If in comparison with the gods man is "as nothing," this is only because he lacks their power, and the security which derives from their immortality.[6]

Since they are of the same race, should some mortal attract the roving fancy of a god or goddess, they can interbreed—although it is rash, as Ixion discovered to his cost, for mortals, even royal mortals, to take the initiative in such matters. The same passions inspire both men and gods; Eros can shoot his darts at either. In their everyday behaviour, then, the gods can be imitated. To do so, however, was certainly not the path to moral perfection. Paradoxically, it is only after philosophers and theologians had attempted to set up a God who would be more worthy of imitation than the Olympian pantheon that the question arose how it is *possible* for men to imitate God.

Could man find perfection, if not by imitating the Olympian gods, then at least by obedience to them, by subservience to their will? That, too, was a difficult attitude for the Olympian religion to adopt, seeing that the will of the gods was seldom unanimous. In Plato's *Euthyphro*, Socrates draws attention to this problem. Euthyphro has defined piety as "doing that which is pleasing to the gods"; at the same time, he claims that he has acted piously in prosecuting his father for being responsible for the death of a slave. As Socrates points out, Euthyphro's action might well be "welcome to Zeus but hateful to Cronos or Uranus, and pleasing to Hephaestus but hateful to Hera."[7] Euthyphro's own action,

---

6. Pindar: *Nemean Odes*, VI, lines 1–10.
7. *Euthyphro*, 8B, trans. W. D. Woodhead in Plato: *Socratic Dialogues* (Edinburgh, 1953), p. 13.

that is, demonstrates how impossible it is to act in such a way as to please *all* the gods. To take another example, although in Aeschylus' trilogy, the *Oresteia,* Orestes obeys the express command of Apollo in killing his mother, that is no excuse in the eyes of "the servants of the old gods"— the Eumenides.

No doubt, the will of Zeus is supreme,* and if men knew what Zeus had decided, they would know what they had to do. But there is not the slightest indication that the will of Zeus seeks to perfect those it works upon. The events recounted in the *Iliad,* Homer begins by remarking, express the will of Zeus, but they do nothing to perfect the nature of Homer's human—or indeed, his divine—characters. If Helen shows signs of remorse, there is no suggestion that this is Zeus' doing.

Man, in relation to the gods, is often enough represented, indeed, as a mere victim: "Zeus controls the fulfilment of all that is," wrote the poet Semonides of Amorgos in the seventh century B.C., "and disposes as he will. But insight does not belong to men: we live like beasts, always at the mercy of what the day may bring, knowing nothing of the outcome that God will impose upon our acts."[8] In Sophocles' *Women of Trachis* the only explanation which is offered of Hercules' suffering is that Zeus chose to impose it upon him. "Mark the malevolence of the unforgiving gods." Thus it is that the play concludes. Perfection, so much is clear, was not to be sought in obedience to the will of such gods as these.

It is not surprising, then, that one can discern in sixth-century Greece a growing dissatisfaction with the Olympian

---

* Or supreme at least over the gods. Whether Zeus was also supreme over Fate—*moira*—is a much disputed question. There is an amusing dialogue by the satirist Lucian, *Some Awkward Questions for Zeus,* in which Zeus is asked to explain his relationship to *moira.* His complete inability to do so is matched by the inability of scholars to make up their minds on this same point.

8. As trans. in E. R. Dodds: *The Greeks and the Irrational* (Berkeley, 1951), p. 30.

religion—related perhaps to a fundamental change in the nature of Greek society, the decline of the heroic age. Men were no longer content with the typically military view that it is men's task to do or die, to endure or fight, not to question or understand. Their dissatisfaction might, in principle, have taken either of two forms: a moralizing of the traditional religion, which, while preserving the humanity of the gods, would more strongly emphasize that they, and especially Zeus, are on the side of goodness or, alternatively, a rejection of the Olympian pantheon in favour of some quite different conception of the divine.

It did, in fact, take both forms. In the plays of Aeschylus, for example, there is an obvious "moralizing" of the gods. No doubt, his *Agamemnon* depends for much of its dramatic force on the conception of *hubris*. On his return to Mycenae, Agamemnon is deliberately enticed by Clytemnestra to tread on a carpet suitable only for the gods and this prepares the way for his murder. But a different doctrine is also invoked, according to which human suffering has a moral purpose. "Man," intones the chorus, "must suffer to be wise." Prosperity, it is suggested—as an admittedly unorthodox doctrine—need not provoke calamity unless the prosperity is accompanied by sin: "sin, not prosperity, engenders grief." [9]

But the attempt merely to reform the Olympian religion was, in the very long run, destined to fail—although it is worth observing that its general effect was to make Zeus a figure more readily assimilable to, or replaceable by, Jahweh. Jahweh, like Zeus, made no pretence to metaphysical perfection, but he is depicted as being a righteous as well as an all-powerful God, even if his righteousness, as in his dealings with Job, sometimes takes a form quite incomprehensible to man. For our immediate purposes, however, the revolutionaries were more important than the reformers.

9. *Agamemnon*, lines 177, 758, trans. P. Vellacott, *ed. cit.*

One important source of the religious revolution was the new speculative cosmology, traceable back to the teachings of Thales at the beginning of the sixth century. Precisely what Thales meant when he pronounced that "All things are full of gods," it is now next-to-impossible to determine. But this consequence, at least, seems to follow: things can be divine which are not at all like human beings, which are not "of the same race as man." They can be divine, in the sense of being the supreme powers, ultimately responsible for things happening as they do. So, in order to understand, for example, what supports the earth, it is not necessary to suppose that it is held in position by a god; Thales' own conjecture was that it floats on water.

In Thales' successor, Anaximander, divinity is ascribed particularly to *to apeiron*—the "Boundless" or "Indefinite." The Boundless, indeed—except in respect to its material extension—begins to look very like what Pascal was to call "the God of the philosophers and the scientists," as distinct from "the God of Abraham, God of Isaac, God of Jacob." Aristotle sums up Anaximander's view thus: "Of the Boundless there is no beginning . . . but this seems to be the beginning of the other things, and to surround all things and steer all. . . . And this is the divine; for it is immortal and indestructible." [10] The Boundless, that is, takes over from the Homeric gods their power, their immortality, their indestructibility. But it is everlasting, not merely immortal— it has no beginning, whereas the gods were born. All things begin from it, and it controls all things; it has the power, that is, of a monotheistic God, not of a polytheistic god who must share his power with other gods. In short, it is like "the God of the philosophers" in its freedom from what philoso-

---

10. Aristotle: *Physics, Γ*4, 203b7, as trans in *KR*, fr. 110. I have, however, preferred the word "Boundless" to their "Infinite." There is some dispute whether, in spite of this remark of Aristotle, Anaximander actually called the Boundless "divine." See W. K. C. Guthrie: *A History of Greek Philosophy*, Vol. I (Cambridge, 1962), p. 89 n., for a defence of Aristotle on this point.

phers were later to think of as "metaphysical defect." If it is not simple, it is at least everlasting and uncaused. On the other hand, it does not in the least resemble the God of Abraham, Isaac and Jacob. There is no point in praying to the Boundless, or making sacrifices to it; if the Boundless is free of moral defect, this is only because moral predicates have no application to it. It is neither righteous nor sinful, good nor evil.

In the satirical poetry of Xenophanes the impact of these new cosmologies on the old Olympian religion is made explicit. Xenophanes, no doubt, was first and foremost a moralist. As we have already seen, he condemned Homer and Hesiod for having ascribed to the gods "everything that is a shame and a reproach amongst men." It is not unlikely that he influenced the "reformed theology" of Aeschylus. But Xenophanes was a revolutionary, not merely a reformer. Men everywhere, he says, have constructed gods in their own image: "the Ethiopians say that their gods are snubnosed and black, the Thracians that theirs have light blue eyes and red hair." If horses were capable of representing their gods in the form of images, he sardonically remarks, they would no doubt make their images look like horses, giving the gods bodies like their own bodies.

This anthropomorphic approach to the divine, Xenophanes argues, must be totally abandoned. In place of Homer's human-all-too-human Zeus, Xenophanes sets up "One god, greatest amongst gods and men, in no way similar to mortals either in body or in thought." Whereas Homer's Zeus left Olympus on a variety of missions and employed messengers and physical agents to work his will, Xenophanes' supreme god has no need either of travel or of subordinates. "Always he remains in the same place, moving not at all; . . . without toil he shakes all things by the thought of his mind."[11] And this for a particular reason: it is not fitting for him to move

11. *KR*, frs. 171–174, pp. 168–69.

about the universe.* Xenophanes' conception of a supreme God, then, is governed by ideas about what it is "fitting" for God to do. God is no longer just a power: he is, it is presumed, morally and metaphysically perfect. He will do nothing that is "not fitting"; this includes what is not metaphysically fitting as well as what is not morally fitting. Zeus is no longer to be depicted as committing adultery, not only because adultery is, morally speaking, "a shame and a reproach," but also because adultery implies both a degree of humanity and a degree of restlessness not appropriate to God.

Greek historians of philosophy, from Aristotle onwards, described Xenophanes as the founder of the Eleatic school of philosophy, and in particular, as the teacher of Parmenides. Modern scholars generally reject this view.[12] Yet there is a kind of rough justice in the Aristotelian "placing" of Xenophanes, even if little historical exactitude. From our present point of view, particularly, it is natural to think of Parmenides as carrying further Xenophanes' metaphysical perfecting of the divine.

Although the supreme God of Xenophanes is not like man either in bodily form or in his manner of thought, he still operates in ways which are at least analogous to human modes of action. God has neither eyes, nor ears, nor a brain, but the fact remains that "all of him sees, all thinks, and all hears."[13] He acts without toil, but he still acts. Parmenides,

---

* It is interesting to observe that the second-century pagan critic of Christianity, Celsus, argued in precisely Xenophanes' manner against the Christian conception of a God who took flesh. "Was he then unable to correct men merely by divine power," Celsus asked, "without sending someone specially endowed for the purpose?" From the point of view of philosophically-educated pagans, Christianity represented a reversion to the anthropomorphic pre-Xenophanes way of thinking about God. Compare Origen: *Contra Celsum*, IV. 3, as trans. H. Chadwick (Cambridge, 1953), p. 186.

12. See, for example, Kirk and Raven, *op. cit.* pp. 165–66, or, in more detail, W. Jaeger: *The Theology of the Greek Philosophers* (Oxford, 1947), ch. 3. Guthrie, in his *History of Greek Philosophy*, Vol. I, pp. 373–83, strongly emphasizes the points of resemblance between Xenophanes and Parmenides. Xenophanes, he argues, identifies God and the cosmos. My own statement of the case is a relatively "neutral" one.

13. *KR*, fr. 175, p. 170.

in contrast, ruled out all these ways of talking: the Parmenidean "Being" neither sees, nor hears, nor thinks, nor acts. So far Being is like Anaximander's Boundless; but unlike the Boundless, it must not be described as a power, as acting. "One way only is left to be spoken of," Parmenides concluded, "that it *is*." On our path to realizing this, however, we also come to see that Being is "uncreated and imperishable, for it is entire, immovable and without end."

Nor is Being only "imperishable" in the sense of everlasting. In Parmenides the eternal is for the first time distinguished from the everlasting. Being is eternal in the full sense that "it *was* not in the past, nor *shall* it be, since it *is* now, all at once, one, continuous."[14] Simple, indivisible, eternal, lacking nothing, devoid of all properties which involve negation or defect—for of negation, "what is not," it is impossible, so Parmenides argued, either to think or to talk—the Parmenidean Being represents the ideal of metaphysical perfection in the purest form it had so far assumed.

The modern reader may find it more than a little odd, when, having described Being in these terms, Parmenides goes on to say of it that it is spherical, "like the bulk of a well-rounded sphere."[15] He is liable to complain, like the spokesman for Epicureanism, Velleius, in Cicero's *The Nature of the Gods,* that he sees no reason for believing that the sphere is any more "perfect" than any other geometrical figure. However, the Greeks generally took it for granted that sphericity was essential to perfection. In the *Timaeus* Plato has no doubt that a Demiurge-creator, setting out to construct a universe which is as perfect as it can be, will make it

14. *KR,* fr. 347, p. 243. Like most other points in the history of Greek philosophy, this is disputed, as by L. Tarán in his *Parmenides* (Princeton, 1965). The idea of the eternal, it is sometimes argued, does not emerge until the neo-Platonists. See the references in John Whittaker: "The 'Eternity' of the Platonic Forms," *Phronesis,* Vol. XIII (1968), pp. 131–44. I have accepted the traditional account as recently presented, for example, in W. K. C. Guthrie: *A History of Greek Philosophy,* Vol. II (Cambridge, 1965), ch. I, p. 29. The point is not, for my purposes, a crucial one.

15. *KR,* fr. 351, p. 276.

"rounded and spherical, equidistant every way from centre to extremity—a figure the most perfect and uniform of all; for he [the Demiurge] judged uniformity to be immeasurably better than its opposite."[16] As the Stoic Balbus replies to Velleius in Cicero's dialogue: "What can be more beautiful than the figure that encircles and encloses in itself all other figures [since all the solid figures can be inscribed in a globe], and that can possess no roughness or point of collision on its surface, no indentation or concavity, no protuberance or depression?"[17]

This is an *aesthetic* sense of perfection. In the manner we normally take to be typical of classicism Parmenides and Plato and Balbus all presume that completeness, uniformity, evenness, regularity are obviously perfections, and that their opposites, the cragginess, irregularity, diversity so loved by romantics, are obviously aesthetic flaws.* To ascribe sphericity to Being, therefore, is to suppose it to be not only metaphysically but aesthetically perfect.

Even after this explanation we may still be puzzled by the sphericity of the Parmenidean Being. Is not to call Being a sphere at once to think, as Parmenides forbids us to do, of something as lying *outside* Being? But the Greeks, in a manner which was to have disastrous consequences for astronomy, were greatly struck by the fact that the circle is a continuous line. "The circle is of all lines," as Aristotle puts

16. *Timaeus*, 33B, as trans. F. M. Cornford in *Plato's Cosmology* (London, 1937; repr. 1952), p. 54.

17. *De natura deorum*, II, xviii, as trans. H. Rackham, Loeb Classical Library (London, 1933; rev. 1951, 1956).

* As late as the sixth century A.D. it was argued on similar grounds that the resurrected body must be spherical. In Buddhist thinking, the "perfected" man is often compared to the "well-rounded moon" or "the moon on its fifteenth day"; the moon in its perfectly rounded shape has reached maturity or completeness. The sphericity of the full moon may have had some influence on Greek thought, too. It is worth observing, that in spite of what is said above (p. 16) about the Japanese fondness for incompleteness, the word *maru* may mean either circular, or all-embracing, or perfect. The seventeenth-century Thomas Burnet in his *Sacred Theory of the Earth* argued that the earth when it was first created by God must have been "smooth and uniform, without Mountains or Sea" (Bk. I, ch. V). God could not make it craggy; it took the Flood to do that.

it, "the most truly one, because it is whole and complete."[18]
And they were no less struck by the fact that the sphere is
the only solid body which can move—by revolving—without
requiring any space outside of itself to move into. Aristotle
calls the sphere "perfect" just in virtue of this fact. So the
spherical nature of Being is presumed not to detract from
but rather to emphasize its perfection, in the sense of its
all-embracing completeness.

Now, if this perfect, spherical Being is identified with
God—and Parmenides seems to think of it in this way, to
judge from the religious atmosphere of the poem in which
he formulates his philosophical ideas—men cannot possibly imitate God or take him, or it, as a *moral* ideal, any
more than they can take Anaximander's Boundless as an
ideal. This conclusion was, of course, a consequence even
of Xenophanes' theology. For how can men imitate a God
"in no way similar to mortals, either in body or in thought"?
But it is even more obvious that no man can set out to imitate Parmenides' Being. As for praying to Being or seeking
its aid, that would be wholly absurd.

It might therefore be supposed that the Parmenidean
Being would be automatically rejected, as obviously irre-
ligious, by the adherents of any kind of religion for which
God is an object of prayer. In fact, however, particularly
by way of Plato's much-misunderstood discussion of Parmenides' Being—as "the One"—in his dialogue *Parmenides,* Being came to be regarded as a sort of philosophical
preview of the God of Christianity. So the Christian Boethius, writing his *Consolation of Philosophy* in the fifth century
A.D., felt free to describe God in what are explicitly Parmenidean terms: "For such is the form of the Divine Substance," he writes, "that it is neither divided into outward
things, nor receives any such into itself, but as Parmeni-

18. *Metaphysics, Δ*.6.1016b as trans. in *The Works of Aristotle,* ed. W. D. Ross, Vol. VIII,
2nd ed. (Oxford, 1928), based on trans. by W. Christ (Leipzig, 1895).

des says of it: "in body like a sphere well-rounded on all sides," it rotates about the moving orb of things, while keeping itself immovable."[19] It is one of the most extraordinary facts in the history of that most extraordinary phenomenon —Christian theology—that Parmenides' Being and Plato's "One" should be thus identified with the Christian God.* But the identification arises naturally enough, in a sense, out of the attempt to set up a God who would be metaphysically, as well as morally, perfect, when this is combined with a definition of perfection as freedom from any sort of negation (evil, as we have already seen, was defined as a special variety of negation). Of such a God we are obliged to say not only that he is characterizable by all those attributes which do not involve negation, but that these characteristics themselves are ultimately identical. For to distinguish is to negate, to say of one property, or of one part, that it *is not* another. (It is interesting to observe that Hindu religious thinkers reached the same conclusion: "As a unity only is it to be looked upon," according to the Brihadāranyaka Upanishad, " —this indemonstrable, enduring Being.")[20]

So Aquinas, having begun by arguing that God has to be immobile, eternal, simple, simultaneous in his existence— it is interesting to observe that he quotes Boethius on this point—not possessed of a body, infinite, and possessed of all

---

19. *The Consolation of Philosophy*, Bk. III, Prose XII, based on the trans. by I. T. (1609), rev. H. F. Stewart, Loeb Classical Library (London, 1918; repr. 1953). It is true that *The Consolation of Philosophy* is sometimes denied to be Christian. But the important thing, for our purposes, is that it was certainly read as such; indeed, early medieval philosophy is often called "the Boethian era." The issues are summed up in H. Liebeschütz: "Western Christian Thought from Boethius to Anselm" in A. H. Armstrong, ed., *The Cambridge History of Later Greek and Early Medieval Philosophy* (Cambridge, 1967), pp. 550–54.

* In medieval thought the "spherical" conception of God was, however, to be strangely transformed in an attempt to reconcile divine sphericity with divine infinity— an infinity which medieval theologians, unlike the Greeks, valued very highly. "God," it was said, "is an intelligible sphere, the centre of which is everywhere and the circumference nowhere." A very odd sphere indeed! Compare [anon.] A Benedictine of Stanbrook Abbey: *Medieval Mystical Tradition and Saint John of the Cross* (London, 1954), p. 68.

20. Brihadāranyaka Upanishad, IV. iv. 20, as trans. in S. Radhakrishnan and C. A. Moore, eds.: *A Source Book in Indian Philosophy* (Princeton, 1957), p. 88.

perfections, goes on to maintain that all these perfections must, in the end, be the same perfection. "God is simple," Aquinas writes, "but where there is simplicity, there can be no distinction among the perfections that are present. Hence, if the perfections of all things are in God, they cannot be distinct in Him. Accordingly, they are all one in Him."[21] No doubt men ascribe various names to God, but that is only because, Aquinas argues, they are in this life restricted to what Parmenides called "the Way of Seeming." When men come to see God as he really is, when they attain to the vision of the Divine Essence, their idea of God will be as simple as is God himself. And the essence of this metaphysically simple God is nothing other than his existence. It will be obvious how close this brings Aquinas's God to the Parmenidean Being, of which we can ultimately say only that "it is."[22] Of course, not only the great figures of Plato and Aristotle but Philo, Plotinus, Proclus and that ardent expropriator of neo-Platonism in the name of Christian theology, Dionysius the Areopagite, have intervened between Aquinas and Parmenides. Aquinas is quite convinced that, with Aristotle's help, he can take over a Parmenidean-type God while avoiding a Parmenidean-type monism. But that he can in fact do so, not all his critics have been convinced.

Parmenideanism was the culminating point in the revolutionary transformation of the Olympian religion by pre-Socratic philosophers. The Olympian religion, however, by no means exhausted the religious life of Greece. The cult of Dionysus, uniting God and man in the ecstasy of orgy, had only a loose association with the Olympian pantheon; the mystery rites, especially at Eleusis, involved a relationship

---

21. Thomas Aquinas: *Compendium of Theology*, trans. Cyril Vollert (St. Louis, Mo., 1947; repr. 1955), ch. 22, p. 24.

22. Compare R. Garrigou-Lagrange: *The One God: A Commentary on the First Part of St. Thomas's Theological Summa*, trans. Bede Rose (St. Louis, Mo., 1943; repr. 1959). Garrigou-Lagrange draws attention to Aquinas's criticism of Parmenides and his indebtedness on this point to Aristotle (p. 196).

with the divine much more intimate than the Olympian religion allowed. The initiated were promised, after death, entrance to the world of the gods. However widely it may have been believed that human beings ought not to aspire to be godlike, not everyone was prepared to accept so modest an estimation of what was humanly desirable.

In Empedocles' fifth-century poem, significantly entitled *Purifications,* a most un-Olympian view prevails. Man, according to Empedocles, is a demi-god, who, at the beginning of human history, committed a crime, involving the shedding of blood, for which all men since have had to pay the penalty.* Banished from their proper home among the gods, men must live, as a consequence of their guilt, in cycles of reincarnation, life after life defiled by sin until, by the exercise of purifying virtues, they finally return to earth, like Empedocles himself, as "prophets, bards, doctors or statesmen." Then at last they escape from the cycle: "I go about among you all," Empedocles therefore writes, "an immortal god, mortal no more."[23]

---

* The Homeric heroes sometimes feel ashamed of themselves; they can "lose face" by acting in an unworthy manner. But they do not feel "guilty" or "sinful." In his *The Greeks and the Irrational,* Dodds describes in detail the transition in Greek thought from "shame" to "guilt." Why Western man should develop, at this point of time, a sense of guilt—of guilt, even more remarkably, for a crime he has not himself committed—remains a mystery. It is highly likely that, as Dodds argues, these ideas originated outside Greece. But this still does not explain why they "caught on" or why they have continued to characterize Western society. The possibility cannot be ignored that what happened is that feelings of guilt were transferred from one form of activity to another rather than actually created *de novo.* Japan is usually quoted as the supreme example of a "guilt-free" society, a "shame" society, but some observers believe that the peculiarity of Japanese society lies in the fact that feelings of guilt are aroused in circumstances which are different from the "guilt-stimuli" of Western society. (See R. K. Beardsley: "Personality Psychology" in J. W. Hall and R. K. Beardsley: *Twelve Doors to Japan* (New York, 1965), pp. 369–71.) It would be rash, then, to conclude from the fact that the Greek heroes do not feel guilty when we would expect them to do so that the idea of guilt was quite unknown to the Homeric Greeks. It is related in complex ways to the idea of pollution, a pollution which can arise not out of a moral fault but an unwitting action—like the pollution which, in the Archaic version of the story, Oedipus incurs and which is passed on as a curse to his descendants. In the Homeric version of the same story, Jocasta kills herself but Oedipus continues to rule as a prosperous king.

23. *KR,* fr. 478, p. 354.

To what extent is Empedocles expressing views which circulated generally in Greece? This is a much disputed question. According to some scholars, there arose in fifth-century Greece a distinctive religious movement, the Orphic religion, with sacred books and dogmatic teachings, whose adherents, setting themselves apart from the Olympian religion, lived in Orphic communities, much as the Christians were to live in Rome—although with a greater willingness to make the traditional formal sacrifices to the Olympian gods. More sceptical scholars have argued that what is commonly called "Orphism" is at most an inchoate mass of popular beliefs, corresponding roughly to that body of superstition which persists in Christian communities and may, in some degree, affect the beliefs and the conduct of the most ardent Christians. Its supposed doctrines, they suggest, are in large part the invention of a much later day, of Christian Platonists and of neo-Platonists, constructing poetic myths for their own polemical purposes.[24]

Let us therefore say only this, that there circulated in fifth-century Athens, more or less widely diffused, a set of beliefs of which the most important ran somewhat as follows: the human being is latently immortal and divine; his latent divinity can be made manifest only if he purifies himself by ritualistic and ascetic practices. With this belief may have been associated a mythology, according to which man's nature is flawed and his divinity obscured as a consequence of his origins. The Titans dismembered and ate the god Dionysus; Zeus struck them dead with his thunderbolts and lightning; out of the ashes sprang the race of men.

So man is at once divine and earth-born. It is now his responsibility to free himself, by purifying rites, from the

24. For the "Orphic religion" view, see W. K. C. Guthrie: *Orpheus and Greek Religion* (London, 1935; 2nd ed. rev., 1952). Under the influence of I. M. Linforth's highly sceptical *The Arts of Orpheus* (Berkeley, 1941), Guthrie presents a more "minimal" account in *The Greeks and Their Gods* (London, 1950), ch. xi. See also E. R. Dodds: *The Greeks and the Irrational,* whose conclusions I have largely accepted.

element of earth he owes to his Titan origins and from the guilt arising from his share in the crime the Titans committed. Men can attain to such freedom from mortality and guilt only through a cycle of reincarnations, somewhat in the manner of Buddhist transmigration, from which they can finally escape only when they are sufficiently enlightened to see the need for purifying themselves. Then they become immortal gods. Whereas the Buddhist sects disagree amongst themselves about whether immortality or annihilation is the final consummation, for Orphic-type religions it was clearly the first. Godlike perfection, then, by no means lies beyond the reach of man: and purification is the path to it.

If it is a controversial question exactly in what Orphism consists, it is even more puzzling to know how to relate Orphism to the teachings of Pythagoras, which Herodotus explicitly linked with Orphism.[25] The Pythagoreans formed, it would seem, a kind of secret society; there were penalties for revealing Pythagorean doctrines to the uninitiated. To make matters worse, the followers of Pythagoras had the amiable, but historically disconcerting, habit of ascribing their own teachings to their master. Pythagoras himself wrote nothing, nor did his successors for some generations. Not surprisingly, then, it is difficult, almost to the point of impossibility, to determine what the historical Pythagoras taught.[26]

Some of the teachings which have come down to us as "Pythagorean" suggest the leader of a mystery religion rather than a philosopher—rules of prohibition, for example, which forbid his followers to step over a cross-bar or to allow swallows to nest under their roof. Yet there are also contemporary references to Pythagoras as a scientist,

---

25. Herodotus: *History*, Bk. II, 81.
26. For the evidence on which I have relied see Guthrie: *History of Greek Philosophy*, Vol. I, ch. IV, and Kirk and Raven, especially p. 228.

particularly a mathematician, with the strong suggestion that for him religion and mathematics were somehow allied. Amongst his successors, certainly, men proud to call themselves Pythagoreans, there were great mathematicians and great astronomers.

The two sides to Pythagoreanism, religious and philosophical, were linked by means of a set of ideas which were to be of very great importance in the subsequent history of perfectibility: the idea of contemplation, the idea of order or harmony, and the idea of purification by wisdom. Before the time of Pythagoras, *sophia* (wisdom) had no particular connexion with contemplation. It was possible to talk, as Homer does, of the *sophia* of a shipbuilder, as a way of referring to his practical ability. For Pythagoras, in contrast, *sophia* consists in looking on at the world: to him is ascribed—and although the ascription is doubtful, the general sentiment is certainly Pythagorean—the comparison of life to the festival-games at which "some come . . . to compete, some to ply their trade, but the best people come as spectators."[27] Here are the roots of the doctrine, which Aristotle was later to espouse, that the life of God is a life of pure contemplation—not a form of activity to which the Olympian deities were conspicuously devoted. The contemplation the Pythagoreans thus extolled is a contemplation of the order of the universe, and especially of its mathematical order. With the help of such contemplation, the soul, identifying itself with the order of the Universe, could purify and perfect itself and thus emerge from the cycle of transmigration.

If this account of Pythagoras—based on evidence, it must be confessed, which is both insubstantial in quantity and dubious in quality—is anything like the truth, then one sees how Pythagoreanism, Orphism and the teachings of Empedocles at once converge and diverge. For all three, the

27. *KR,* fr. 278, p. 228.

soul is involved in cycles of transmigration, from which it can escape only by purifying itself. But for the Orphics and for Empedocles, as not for Pythagoras, that cycle originates in a primeval deed, the guilt of which all men bear. All three agree that to escape from the cycle some form of bodily abstinence is essential. But for Empedocles and Pythagoras, as not for the Orphics, one must also become a person of a rather special sort — according to Empedocles, a poet, or prophet, or statesman, according to Pythagoras, a philosopher. And for Pythagoras alone, men are purified by contemplation of an ordered universe, achieving through that contemplation an orderly perfection in their own mind.

Now we are in a better position to understand the first systematic theory of perfectibility. This was worked out by Plato under Orphic-Pythagorean influence. But it was greatly influenced, too, by the Parmenidean analysis of metaphysical perfection and the Socratic identification of goodness and knowledge — the Socratic presumption that no one does evil willingly. As a deduction from Plato's general metaphysics, we should expect to find him arguing that no particular man can perfect himself, that only the ideal form of humanity can be perfect, just as he argues that no particular work of art, but only the ideal form of beauty, can be perfectly beautiful, or that no particular triangle, but only the ideal form of triangularity, can be perfectly triangular. But in the *Phaedo* Plato avoids this conclusion by making a sharp distinction between body and soul. The soul, he suggests, is more like a form than it is like a particular; in virtue of this fact a human being is perfectible.

What does "being more like a form" involve? The forms, so far as this is compatible with there being more than one of them, exhibit that metaphysical perfection which Parmenides took to be peculiar to Being. Whereas particular works of art — a particular painting, for example — may fade away, the form of Beauty, Beauty-in-itself, Plato tells us, can never be destroyed, nor can the form of Triangularity-in-itself or the form of Goodness-in-itself. The forms, that is, are eternal—or, at the very least, everlasting—and this, above all, is why Plato does not hesitate to call them divine.

That ordinary things—particulars—pass away is, he suggests, a necessary consequence of the fact that they are complex, composite, changeable. The forms, therefore, as eternal, must be simple, indivisible, unchangeable. The soul is "like the forms" precisely in respect to these metaphysical perfections. "The soul," Plato says, "most closely resembles the divine and immortal, intelligible and uniform and indissoluble and ever-unchangeable, while the body most resembles the human and mortal, the unintellectual and dissoluble and ceaselessly changing."[28] When Plato speaks in such contexts of "the soul" he does not mean the form of the soul—the soul-in-itself. It is *each individual soul* which possesses these perfections, or "something like them."

The conclusion might seem to follow that there is no question of perfecting the soul; it is already perfect, by its very nature. But the soul, Plato argues, does not ordinarily exhibit, in this life, its full perfection. This is because it is tainted by the body in which it is "imprisoned"—a metaphor he ascribes to Orphic origins.[29] The body, itself metaphysically imperfect, impermanent, mutable, corrupts the soul and drags it down to its own level.

This is a view which has obvious logical difficulties, partly concealed by Plato's use of the phrase "*like* the forms." In order to deduce the soul's immortality from its likeness to the forms, he has to treat this likeness as rather more than likeness, and as a likeness which applies equally to all souls. If souls have only *some* resemblance to forms, then it would not follow that they share with the forms the particular property of not passing out of existence—this could well be

28. *Phaedo*, 80B, as trans. Woodhead in *Socratic Dialogues*, p. 124. All quotations from the *Phaedo* are from this ed.
29. *Cratylus*, 400C.

one of the points on which they differed. And if only perfected souls are like the forms, then the conclusion would
seem to follow that only perfected souls are immortal. So
Plato's interest in demonstrating the immortality of the soul
leads him to insist on the close resemblance of each and
every soul to the forms—indeed, to describe souls in the
very same language he applies to the forms themselves.

On the other hand, his desire, as a moralist, to set before
men the care of their souls as a moral task leads him to describe the soul not as unchangeable but as capable of being
corrupted, not as simple but as capable of being "interpene-
trated by the corporeal." More than likely, it was Plato's own
uncertainty about the soul's nature which led Renaissance
Platonists to deny that the soul has *any* fixed metaphysical
nature, to think of it as capable of becoming either something like the divine or something like a material object, but
as in itself not belonging to either category. For Plato, however, the soul is naturally divine, even if it can only too easily
be corrupted. So perfection is a task, but a task in which
success can be hoped for—it is a task because most souls are
not in fact morally perfect, it is a task in which success can
be hoped for because the soul's metaphysical nature allies
it with the perfect.

Since the unwillingness of the body to submit to its authority is the principal cause of the soul's imperfection, the
path to perfection involves some measure of asceticism. The
philosopher, so Plato argues, will not be greatly concerned
with "such so-called pleasures as eating and drinking," or
"the pleasures of love," or the adornment of the body.[30] This
asceticism, however, by no means involves the mortification
of the body; there is in Plato no suggestion that in order to
achieve perfection the philosopher should, as Diogenes the
Cynic was to do, live in a barrel, or that like the Christian
hermits he should cut himself off from society, or that he

---

30. *Phaedo*, 64D–E.

should fast to the point of malnutrition, or that he should entirely eschew all sexual relations. The Socrates who in the *Phaedo* is depicted as bidding the philosopher not to devote himself to bodily pleasures is the very same Socrates who is a convivial guest in the all-night drinking party described by Plato in the *Symposium*. Simply, the philosopher is not "much concerned" with eating and drinking, or sexual relations, or personal adornment.

The crucial point for Plato, furthermore, is that the soul frees itself from the body not by asceticism as such—let alone by ritual incantations or ceremonial rites—but by acquiring knowledge. And knowledge, for Plato, consists in the apprehension of relationships between ideal forms; it is not to be acquired by any kind of empirical observation, involving the use of the bodily senses. "She [the soul] reasons best," he writes in the *Phaedo*, ". . . when most she is alone and apart, paying no heed to the body." When the soul tries to make discoveries by means of sensory observation "she is torn away by the body into the region of constant fluctuation, and she herself wanders about in confusion, reeling like a drunken man, because of her contact with things in similar confusion." When, on the contrary, the soul relies entirely on her own resources, forgetting the body, she "remains ever constant and changeless with the unchanging, because of her contact with things similarly immutable."[31]

What Plato says at this point obviously rests on the presumption that the human being becomes like what he perceives. There is, one might object, no reason why an orderly soul should become disorderly merely as a result of contemplating the disorderly, or a disorderly soul become orderly merely as a result of contemplating the orderly. But Plato, like the censors of our own time, thought otherwise. This presumption is even more important in the *Republic* where Plato introduces a supreme form, the form of the good, the

---

31. *Phaedo*, 65C; 79C–D.

knowledge of which he takes to be a sufficient and necessary condition of all wisdom. That it is a necessary condition, he explicitly argues: "This form of the good must be seen by anyone who hopes to act wisely, either in public or in private."[32] That it is a sufficient condition he takes for granted: to know the form of the good is to *be* good, indeed to be perfect.

It should be observed, however, that in the *Republic* he speaks of the philosopher not only as a knower, but as a lover: philosophers are, he says, "lovers . . . of that reality which always is."[33] And this is suggested by the etymological root of the word "philosopher," its derivation from *philein*, to love. He reaches the conclusion that by "associating with what is divine and ordered [a philosopher] becomes ordered and divine as far as mortal may," by relying on the principle that a man naturally imitates "that with which he lovingly associates."[34] Love and knowledge are, in Plato's thinking, closely associated, even if sometimes his stress is on knowledge and at other times, as in the *Symposium*, on love. So his fundamental presumption might be more plausibly put by saying that we become like what we lovingly-know; that presumption we shall observe, too, in Christian mysticism.

Plato described the form of the good in terms which readily lend themselves to a mystical interpretation. It is, he says, "the cause of knowledge and truth . . . but while knowledge and truth are both beautiful, you will be right in thinking it other and fairer than these." "It . . . transcends," he also writes, "even Being in dignity and power."[35] These are among the most influential statements in the whole history of human thought—the most disastrously influential,

---

32. *Republic*, Bk. VII. 517c. All quotations from the *Republic* are based on the trans. by A. D. Lindsay, but I have sometimes preferred a freer rendering.

33. *Ibid.*, Bk. VI. 485B.

34. *Ibid.*, Bk. VI. 500D.

35. *Ibid.*, Bk. VI. 508E, 509B.

we might say, considering how often they have been used to lend philosophical respectability to beliefs which are in spirit totally anti-philosophical.

In neo-Platonic thought, and in the writings of such Christian theologians as were influenced by it, the form of the good was not uncommonly identified with God. This is not altogether astonishing, considering that Plato described the form of the good as "the cause of all that is right and beautiful in all things." [36] Nor is it, I suppose, wholly surprising that the form of the good was also identified with the supreme Beauty of the *Symposium*. But what is surprising, on the face of it, is that the form of the good was also identified with "the One" of the first Hypothesis of Plato's *Parmenides*. For the context makes it perfectly clear what Plato was doing when he wrote: "The One neither is one nor is at all. . . . It cannot *have* a name or be spoken of, nor can there be any knowledge or perception or opinion *of* it. It is not named or spoken of, not an object of opinion or of knowledge, not perceived by any creature." [37] He was constructing a *reductio ad absurdum,* not defending "negative theology."

Yet if, as a scholar, one finds it surprising that Plato should have been thus interpreted, from another point of view it is not at all surprising. For what resulted from the conflation of the form of the good, the One, and Beauty was the conception of a Being in all respects perfect: per-

---

36. *Ibid.,* Bk. VII. 517c.

37. *Parmenides,* 142A, as trans. in F. M. Cornford: *Plato and Parmenides* (London, 1939), p. 129. For the neo-Platonic interpretation see pp. 131–35 of Cornford's commentary. Cornford is perhaps somewhat too hard-headed in his interpretation of Plato. But about the main point there can be no real doubt. This passage is a criticism of Parmenides, an attempt to show that the Parmenidean One is unintelligible. For an interpretation of Plato, which, without renouncing scholarship, emphasizes the mystical element in his thought, see A. J. Festugière: *Contemplation et vie contemplative selon Platon,* 2. éd. (Paris, 1950), and G. Vlastos: "A Metaphysical Paradox" in American Philosophical Association: *Proceedings and Addresses,* Vol. 39 (1966), pp. 5–19. Festugière defends the view that Beauty in the *Symposium* is, like the form of the good, "beyond all being." His arguments have not won wide acceptance.

fect in beauty, perfect in goodness, perfect in divinity, perfect in every metaphysical property. The Platonic forms, as
they were represented in the *Phaedo*, had, from the point of
view of the perfectibilist metaphysician, one great disadvan-
tage: they were a multiplicity. Even in the *Republic*, where
Plato came as close as he ever did to a Parmenidean monism, it is not suggested that the form of the good has the
kind of absolute metaphysical superiority possessed by the
Parmenidean One.[38] In none of his dialogues, indeed, does
Plato show himself fully prepared to put all his metaphysical eggs in one basket, by subordinating, for example, the
perfection of the forms to the perfection of God. Only by
taking that step for him, by identifying God, the form of the
good, Beauty and the One, could his authority be claimed
for so absolute a metaphysical amalgam.

The resulting inconvenience—a supreme Being which
"is not named nor spoken, not an object of opinion or
knowledge"—was easily borne by mystics, and even by theologians whom one might have expected to rebel against it.
So just as, by an exaggeration of a certain tendency in his
teachings, Plato came to serve as a principal authority for
ascetic doctrines of perfectibility, he also came to serve as a
principal authority for mystical doctrines of perfectibility,
according to which perfection has to be sought by rising
above the body, above any sort of knowledge or truth or
being, to a God describable only in negative terms. Mysticism and asceticism were, indeed, often allied: asceticism
was conceived of as the first stage on the process towards

38. It is possible, however, that Plato was in the *Republic* influenced by Eucleides, the
leader of those philosophers who tried to conjoin the teachings of Socrates and Parmenides. He taught, according to Diogenes Laertius, that "the supreme good was one, though
called by many names—sometimes wisdom, sometimes God, sometimes reason and so
forth" (*Lives of Eminent Philosophers*, Bk. II, 106, based on the trans. by R. D. Hicks, Loeb
Classical Library (London, 1925), Vol. 1, p. 235). This is roughly what Plato was taken, by
the neo-Platonists, to teach, and in the *Republic* he came as close to it as he ever did. On
this point see W. D. Ross: *Plato's Theory of Ideas* (Oxford, 1951), p. 44.

mystical perfectibility. The renunciation by the ascetic of his material possessions, his desires, his attachments to the world, served as a symbol of his final renunciation of his individuality, of all those predicates which made of him a distinctive human being.

For Plato himself, however, the situation was very different. For one thing, mysticism is essentially a doctrine of individual perfection. Individual perfection is no doubt the kind of perfection principally emphasized in the *Phaedo,* concerned as it is with the situation of a man confronting that essentially solitary experience—death. But even in that dialogue, Socrates is depicted as delighting in, and learning from, the company of his fellow-men. There is no sign whatever of the ascetic misanthropy of the early Christian *Sayings of the Fathers;* it is impossible to imagine Plato writing: "A man who avoids men is like a ripe grape. A man who companies with men is like a sour grape."[39] In the *Republic,* furthermore, Plato makes it perfectly clear that on his view no man can achieve perfection except by way of a perfect society, a society ruled by philosopher-kings. "Neither city nor constitution," he writes, "and not even any individual man, will ever be perfect, until philosophers . . . are in some way compelled to take charge of the state . . . or until those who now have charge of dominions and kingdoms are inspired by the love of true philosophy."[40]

Granted that the ideal city does not exist, the man who tries to perfect himself will nevertheless, so Plato suggests, try to live his life by its laws: the ideal city "is laid up in heaven as a pattern for him who wills to see, and seeing, to found a city in himself."[41] But only if the city can be actualized, it would seem, can men find the absolute perfection they are seeking. At the very least, this approach to perfec-

---

39. *Sayings of the Fathers,* II. 10, as trans. in *Western Asceticism,* ed. and trans. O. Chadwick, Library of Christian Classics, 12 (London, 1958), p. 42.

40. *Republic,* Bk. VI. 499B.

41. *Ibid.,* Bk. IX. 592B.

tion requires that men should think of themselves as citizens, not as engaged in a solitary pursuit of perfection.

No less important was Plato's insistence on education. This, above all, distinguishes him from the Christian mystic. Even if the final contemplation of the form of the good is, on Plato's view, a direct vision which defies all description and all analysis, the fact remains that in order to achieve that vision men, on Plato's view, have first to undergo a long and rigorous philosophical education. Education, not prayer and self-mortification, is the path to perfection.

Such an education, Plato adds, is not for all men. "A multitude cannot be philosophical."[42] Most men cannot achieve what Plato significantly calls "philosophical" goodness, for him the only true goodness. The most they can hope for is perfection in "civic" goodness, the sort of goodness they can acquire by obedience to the laws laid down for them by the philosopher-kings, by those rulers, that is, who in virtue of their knowledge of the good are capable of philosophical goodness. Men who live civically good lives, Plato suggests in the *Phaedo*, may return to earth, in a subsequent life, as "bees . . . or ants"—symbols of industry and order. They have no prospect, however, of joining "the company of the gods."[43]

Both Plato's emphasis on education as a means to perfection and his distinction between a perfectible élite and a non-perfectible multitude were to assume, in the centuries to come, a variety of shapes, religious and secular. Not that they were wholly peculiar to Plato. The Greek mystery-religions commonly drew a distinction between "beginners" and those who were, in virtue of a prolonged initiation, fit to be admitted to the highest mysteries. It is interesting to observe, too, that the highest mystery, at least at Eleusis, seems to have involved the vision of some object—perhaps

42. *Ibid.*, Bk. VI. 494A.
43. *Phaedo*, 82B–C.

a corn-ear. Plato, one might say, replaces initiation by education and the corn-ear by the form of the good.[44] But, by so doing, he greatly reduces the accessibility of the highest vision to the ordinary man.

In Plato's later thought, the theological impulse is more naked. In his earlier dialogues, the forms, in an extremely abstract sense, are rather like the Homeric heroes.[45] They act as exemplars: it is by reference to them that we are to judge ourselves and our own actions; they are the ideals we must try to match, the models to imitate. In his later dialogues, however, Plato came to lay the primary stress not on the forms but on the gods. Thus it comes about that perfection is defined in the *Theaetetus* as "likeness to the gods."

In the *Timaeus*—a dialogue which through the accident of its survival in a Latin version was to represent "Plato" to the medieval world—Plato described in more detail the relation between divine perfection and human perfectibility. He begins by entirely rejecting the view that the gods are in any sense jealous of men. The maker of the world or, as Plato calls him, the Demiurge—a word which literally means "craftsman"—was, he says, perfectly good, and in the perfect no jealousy can possibly arise. The Demiurge set out, therefore, to make a world in which "all things should come as near as possible to being like himself."[46]

The Demiurge is not, it should be observed, omnipotent. That is why not all men are in fact godlike. Although the Demiurge brought order into the world the material on which he had to work was too recalcitrant for him to construct a wholly perfect world. But as a result of the Demiurge's desire that all things should be as far as possible like himself, every man has within him a divine element, a "guiding genius." By cherishing this godlike element—as he can

---

44. In several places Plato deliberately formulates philosophical ideas in language borrowed from the mysteries. Compare *Symposium*, 210A, or *Phaedo*, 69C.

45. Compare W. Jaeger: *Paideia*, Vol. I, p. 34.

46. *Timaeus*, 29D, as trans. in Cornford: *Plato's Cosmology*, p. 33.

best do by contemplating the ideal harmony of the universe—man can bring himself into likeness with the gods. Here, then, the Pythagorean account of perfection receives a more explicit, Platonic, formulation. Man has a divine element in himself; he perfects that divine element by contemplating the ordered glory of the universe; in so doing he becomes "godlike."

THREE

THE GODLIKE MAN:
ARISTOTLE TO PLOTINUS

Aristotle was Plato's pupil; his indebtedness to Plato is obvious and extensive, so obvious and so extensive that the neo-Platonists write of Aristotelianism as if it were no more than a sub-branch of Platonism. Modern commentators, in contrast, tend to insist upon the points of difference between Aristotle and Plato. Plato the patrician, the idealist, the mystic, is contrasted with Aristotle the "philosopher of the common man," or at least of the educated citizen, not particularly imaginative but, in compensation, not easily persuaded into phantasy.

There is certainly one crucial point of philosophical disagreement between the two philosophers: Aristotle entirely rejects Plato's theory of forms and, more especially, that "form of the good" which was to be the corner-stone of neo-Platonic mysticism. A knowledge of the form of the good, even if there were such a thing, would, Aristotle argues, be practically useless to mankind. How will a doctor become a better doctor, or a general a better general, he rhetorically asks, as a result of knowing the form of the good? What the doctor needs to know is in what health consists, what the general needs to know is in what victory consists. A mere knowledge of the form of the good does not carry with it, as Plato seems to have presumed, a knowledge of the nature of, let alone an enhanced capacity to pursue, these highly particularized ends. One cannot perfect oneself in a particular task, that is, merely in virtue of a knowledge of the form of the good.

To perfect oneself, Aristotle suggests, is to achieve an end, a specific end. The general perfects himself as a general by achieving victories over his opponents, the doctor perfects himself as a doctor by achieving health in his patients. And, as we have already seen, Aristotle presumes that there must be an end appropriate to man as such, as distinct from man *qua* general and man *qua* doctor. The only problem is in what that end consists. Aristotle's preliminary answer is that the end for man is *eudaimonia*—traditionally, if somewhat misleadingly, translated as "happiness" or "well-being." This is not to be identified with pleasure. There are many things we would continue to desire, he says, even if no pleasure attached to them. We have still to discover, then, its precise character.

To settle this point Aristotle falls back, in a traditional Greek fashion, on the conception of a function.[1] Not only man *qua* sculptor or craftsman, he argues, but *man as such* must have a function peculiar to him. This cannot be "living," or "experiencing sensations," both of which men share with the beasts. Man's special function must involve the exercise of what is peculiar to man, his rationality, the highest part of his soul. And just as the specific task of *any* carpenter is identical with the specific task of a *good* carpenter, the only difference being that the good carpenter is better at performing that task, so similarly, if man's task is to exercise the highest part of his soul the good for man must consist in his exercising the highest part of his soul in the best possible manner. The good for man, then, is "an activity of soul in accordance with goodness or (on the supposition that there may be more than one form of goodness) in accordance with the best and most complete form of goodness."[2]

A problem still remains: to determine the nature of that "best and most complete form of goodness," by exercising

---

1. For a fuller account of Aristotle's views, which brings out their complexity, see W. F. R. Hardie: *Aristotle's Ethical Theory* (Oxford, 1968).

2. *Nicomachean Ethics* (*NE*), I. 7, as trans. J. A. K. Thomson (London, 1953; reissued in Penguin Classics, Harmondsworth, 1955), p. 39. All quotations from the *Nicomachean Ethics* are from this edition.

his soul in accordance with which the perfect man will excel. Further investigation reveals, according to Aristotle, that the "best and most complete form" of goodness is "speculative activity." For the man devoted to speculative activity has the most "complete" life; he is the most self-sufficient of beings; he is engaged in an activity which seeks no end beyond itself but is worth having for its own sake; he most fully realizes the nature of man—since "the intellect more than anything else is the man." Perfection, then, is only to be found in speculative activity.*

A man, Aristotle goes on to suggest, can live the speculative life only in so far as "he has a divine element in him," only in so far as he is capable of living like the gods. Like Plato before him, Aristotle puts himself in direct and conscious opposition to the Greek tradition, as expressed by Pindar, that it is wrong for men to try to imitate the gods. "We ought not to listen," Aristotle admonishes us, "to those who counsel us 'O man, think as man should' and 'O mortal, remember your mortality.' "[3] If, he admits in the *Metaphysics*,[4] there ever was a case where men might provoke the jealousy of the gods, it is when they attempt to achieve knowledge of the divine. But the poets lie, Aristotle assures us, when they say that the gods are capable of jealousy.

There is, it should be noted, an important ambiguity in Aristotle's conception of "speculative activity." When we read that the speculative life is an "activity" or that it con-

---

* It will by now be apparent how the neo-Platonists were able to amalgamate Platonism and Aristotelianism: by devoting all their attention to that relatively short section of the *Nicomachean Ethics* (Bk. X, 7–9) in which Aristotle extols the speculative life. If one looks elsewhere in the *Nicomachean Ethics* a rather different Aristotle emerges, who everywhere advocates moderation, the performance of one's civic duties, the use of "practical wisdom." This was the Aristotle whom in the fourteenth century the Renaissance "civic humanists" were to resurrect. But for Christian and neo-Platonic perfectibilists, uninterested in civic goodness, Aristotle is above all the exponent of the view that the highest good is contemplative, and that in contemplation man becomes like a god.

3. *NE*, X. 7; trans. Thomson, p. 305.
4. *Metaphysics*, A. 2. 983a.

cerns itself with "intellectual problems," we naturally identify it with the life of trying to find out, the life of the scientist
or the scholar or the philosopher. But what Aristotle sets
up as the ideal is not theorising but *contemplation*. "It stands
to reason," he writes, "that those who have knowledge pass
their time more pleasantly than those who are engaged in its
pursuit."[5] "Activity," it also turns out, does not imply actually
doing anything: "there is an activity not only of movement
but of immobility, like that of thought."[6]

Here, perhaps, Aristotle stands most at odds with the
general tendency of post-Renaissance thought, which tends
to value the journey more than the arrival, the process of
finding out more than the truth arrived at, the doing rather
than the having. "Our happiness will never consist," Leibniz
wrote in 1718, "and ought not to consist, in a full enjoyment, in which there is nothing more to desire, and which
would make our mind dull, but in a perpetual progress to
new pleasures and new perfections."[7] The contrast between
Aristotle and Lessing is even more startling: "If God held
enclosed in His right hand all truth," Lessing tells us, "and
in His left hand the ever-living striving for truth, although
with the qualification that I must for ever err, and said to
me 'Choose,' I should humbly choose the left hand and say
'Father, give! Pure truth is for Thee alone!' "[8]

Aristotle, or so his official doctrine suggests, would most
certainly choose the right hand. Some of his successors in
the Christian tradition—most notably perhaps Gregory of
Nyssa[9]—were to argue that the contemplation of God was

5. *NE*, X. 7; trans. Thomson, p. 303.

6. *NE*, VII. 14; trans. Thomson, p. 225.

7. Leibniz: *Principles of Nature and of Grace* (1718), trans. from *Philosophische Schriften*,
ed. Gerhardt, VI, 606, in A. O. Lovejoy: *The Great Chain of Being* (Cambridge, Mass., 1936;
repr. 1948), p. 248. Compare Lovejoy on this whole question.

8. Lessing: *Eine Duplik* (A Rejoinder: 1778), in *Werke*, ed. Julius Petersen and W. von
Olshausen (Berlin, 1925–35), Vol. 23, pp. 58–59, as trans. in H. B. Garland: *Lessing* (Cambridge, 1937; repr. 1949), ch. XI, p. 174.

9. Gregory of Nyssa, as quoted in A. H. Armstrong, ed.: *The Cambridge History of Later*

itself a "perpetual discovery" and that its delight consisted in that fact. But only in the eighteenth century did it come to be widely believed that man's aspirations should be unending, that his enjoyments do not lie in fruition but in action. (Just as for Newton, as not for Aristotle, a body will continue in uniform motion in a straight line unless it is brought to rest by an external force. Rest, that is, is not its "natural" condition.)

"We mistake human nature," writes Adam Ferguson in 1767, "if we wish for a termination of labour, or a scene of repose." When men seek "pure enjoyment, or a termination of trouble," he tells us, they "overlook the source from which most of our present satisfactions are really drawn"— the activity itself.[10] "Perfection," on this view, attaches to the performance of a task, not to the attainment of a state of repose. Aristotle's immediate successors, in contrast, condemned Aristotle for placing too much, not too little, emphasis on the value of mental activity. Indeed, in Aristotle's own theory of happiness—which makes of it at once an activity and an end—it is not too fanciful to detect a conflict between Aristotle the practising biologist, conscious of the joys of problem-solving, and Aristotle the metaphysician in search of a final end in which man can find rest.

Aristotle's conception of the speculative life as one of contemplation rather than of discovery is tied up with his view that the perfect life is god-like. It would be absurd, Aristotle says, to ascribe any of the practical virtues to God— justice, or bravery, or temperance or generosity. These are all of them virtues which make sense only in a secular situation, and they arise out of human limitations.[11] Continence

---

Greek and Early Medieval Philosophy, ch. 29, p. 456. See also the passages collected in John and Charles Wesley: *A Rapture of Praise;* hymns sel. and introd. H. A. Hodges and A. M. Allchin (London, 1966), pp. 22–33.

10. Adam Ferguson: *An Essay on the History of Civil Society* (1767), Pt. I, Section I and Pt. I, Section VII; in the ed. by D. Forbes (Edinburgh, 1966), pp. 7, 42.

11. *NE*, X, 8; trans. Thomson, pp. 307–8.

can no more be ascribed to God than adultery, honesty no more than theft. It would be equally absurd, presumably, to suppose that God could have intellectual problems, or that there is anything for him to discover. So by a process of exclusion Aristotle concludes that the divine goodness must consist in simple contemplation.

But now a new problem arises. What is there that God could find value in contemplating? Nothing less than the fully perfect, certainly, and nothing except God himself is fully perfect. Aristotle concludes, therefore, that God contemplates nothing but himself.[12] And by reflection back on man, relying on the premise that the perfect man will be godlike, this has the consequence that the true happiness, the perfection of man, too, must consist in the contemplation of "divine things"—a view which brings Aristotle very close to the Plato of the *Timaeus.*

It is not possible, Aristotle freely grants, for a man to live the wholly godlike life; only God can do this. "After all," Aristotle writes of the contemplative man, "he is a man and a member of society and, in so far as he is, he will choose to act on moral grounds. And this means that he will have need of external goods to permit him to live on the human level."[13] The speculative man, that is, still has to live the life of an ordinary citizen. In that sense, the best life for a man, as distinct from God, will inevitably be a "mixed life," in which contemplation is conjoined with purely moral excellences. But it is easy enough, all the same, to see how the mystics and the neo-Platonists could convert Aristotle to their own purposes.

For Aristotle's emphasis, at this point in the *Nicomachean Ethics,* is on the slight degree to which the contemplative man needs to participate in everyday life. If, like everybody else, the contemplative man depends upon the "ordinary

---

12. *Metaphysics, Λ.* 9. 1074b.
13. *NE,* X. 8; trans. Thomson, p. 307.

necessities of life," the fact remains that he requires, for his purposes, no more than a competence. Nor does he depend upon the existence of other men in order to exercise his goodness. It may sometimes be helpful to him, perhaps, to work with other men; but he does not *need* them. "He [the wise man] can speculate all by himself, and the wiser he is the better he can do it."[14]

This is one important difference between the perfect life of contemplation, and that wholly practical moral life which is, for Aristotle, the second-best life. A just man needs his fellow-men in order to exercise his justice upon them; a man cannot be generous with his money if he has no money to be generous with. Neither the just nor the generous man, that is, can be self-sufficient. It is the (almost entire) self-sufficiency of the theoretical life which is the supreme test of its perfection. Aristotle does not deny, of course—any more than Plato did—that to live such a life a man must first have been trained, initiated into the practical moral life. To that degree he is dependent upon other men. The contemplative man, furthermore, is not *metaphysically* self-sufficient. Man, unlike God, is not capable of metaphysical self-sufficiency; that, indeed, is why he is not wholly perfectible. But when he contemplates the divine, man comes as near to self-sufficiency as is humanly possible.

So, in Aristotle as in Plato, there is a contrast between philosophical and civic goodness—even if it is not as sharply defined in Aristotle as it is in Plato—and full perfection attaches only to the first. No doubt, Aristotle is prepared to describe a person with a high degree of civic goodness as possessing "a perfect character"—immaculate perfection, the sort of perfection displayed by such Old Testament exemplars as Noah and Job—but the mere fact that in order to display purely moral excellences a man with "a perfect

14. *NE*, X. 7; trans. Thomson, p. 304.

character" needs his fellow-men prevents him, in Aristotle's eyes, from attaining true, deiform, perfection.

Aristotle's reservations about the relationship between the contemplative life and the life of civic goodness were historically much less important than his description of the contemplative life as "godlike." The Hebraic ideal, like the older Greek ideal, was active rather than contemplative. When Christianity went in search of philosophical authority for the view that in contemplation men came closest to God, it had to seek it in Greek philosophy. And in Aristotle's doctrine that in order to live the contemplative life men, once they have been morally trained, need only the minimum of possessions and the minimum of contact with their fellow-men, Christians thought that they could find a philosophical justification for the monastic life—or even for the extremes of anchoritism.

The philosophers of the Hellenistic period took over the Platonic-Aristotelian suggestion that the best life, the life in which men achieve perfection, involves self-sufficiency. But activity, they argued, always involves the pursuit of some not-yet-achieved end. As against Aristotle, then, the life of contemplative activity could not be self-sufficient. The best life, the Hellenistic philosophers all agreed, was a life of *ataraxia* (peace of mind). The only question was how this could be achieved.

It is at first sight extraordinary that the three most influential Hellenistic schools of philosophy—the Sceptics, the Epicureans, the Stoics—should all agree, for all their notable differences on most other matters, that peace of mind was the supreme end to be sought after. This is one of the rare occasions on which the influence of social change on philosophy is direct and obvious. The third century was one of constant political struggle, in which the Athenians sought to throw off their Macedonian rulers. The old confidence had gone. One must not, of course, exaggerate.

The greatest period of Greek mathematics and astronomy was yet to come; Archimedes was only seventeen when Epicurus died in 270 B.C.; Hipparchus was born eighty years later. What had gone, at least for the time being, was not ability but audacity. And that is reflected, above all, in the writings of the philosophers. Even when, like Plotinus, they are actually developing original ideas, they pretend that they are not. "These teachings," he writes, "are, therefore, no novelties, no inventions of today."[15] No earlier Greek philosopher felt that he had to protect himself against the accusation of being original. One can see what had happened, almost equally well, by contrasting the comedies of Menander, their well-bred tolerance, their ingenious plots, with the unrestrained comic exuberance of Aristophanes. It is not surprising to discover that Menander learnt his philosophy from Epicurus.

The Epicureans agreed with Aristotle that the perfect life would be a life of happiness, but unlike Aristotle they identified happiness with pleasure, which, on their view, consists in freedom from fear and pain. They denied that speculative activity is valuable for its own sake. "Vain is the discourse of that philosopher," wrote Epicurus or one of his followers, "by which no human suffering is healed."[16] Here we observe that turning against science, against the idea that inquiry was valuable for its own sake, which is so notable and so disquieting a feature of the Hellenistic age. Science—in particular the atomic theory which Democritus had invented and Epicurus had developed—is useful, according to the Epicureans, only in that it helps to free men from their fear of the gods and from their fear of death, both

15. Plotinus: *Enneads*, V. 1. 8, as trans. Stephen MacKenna, 2nd ed. rev. B. S. Page (London, 1956), p. 376. All subsequent quotations from Plotinus are from this ed.

16. Trans. from H. Usener, ed.: *Epicurea* (Leipzig, 1887), p. 169. 14; in R. D. Hicks: *Stoic and Epicurean* (London, 1910), p. 191. For Epicurus generally, see C. Bailey: *The Greek Atomists and Epicurus* (Oxford, 1928); A. J. Festugière: *Epicurus and His Gods*, trans. C. W. Chilton (Oxford, 1955).

of which disturb their peace of mind. It destroys the fear of death by pointing out that death, as the cessation of sensations, is neither to be feared nor sought after; death lies "beyond good and evil." It destroys all fear of the gods by demonstrating that "a blessed and eternal being has no trouble himself and brings no trouble upon any other being; hence he is exempt from movements of anger and partiality, for every such movement implies weakness."[17]

At the same time, Epicurus is not, in the matter of the Olympian religion, a revolutionary; we can think of him, rather, as a reformer. At least he is a reformer in so far as he continues to think of the gods as persons; he is a revolutionary only in denying that the gods take any interest in human affairs, and more particularly, that they are "envious and interfering." The gods are immortal and their happiness is without blemish; they are perfect, then, but only in that Epicurean sense of perfection which identifies it with absolute happiness. It is fitting that they should be worshipped, because they possess such immaculate perfection, but to expect them to respond to prayers and sacrifices, or to fear their anger, would be wholly ridiculous.

Epicureanism, not uncommonly characterized as "swinish," has often been condemned as an ethic of self-indulgence. So in the Prologue to Chaucer's *Canterbury Tales* the Franklin is described as "Epicurus's own son" on the ground that

> Without baked meat was never his house,
> Of fish and flesh, and that so plenteous
> It snowed in his house of meat and drink.

Nothing could be further from the truth. Epicurus was, indeed, ascetic to a fault. "When we say," he wrote to Menoe-

---

17. Epicurus: "Sovran Maxims," 1, as trans. R. D. Hicks in the Loeb edition of Diogenes Laertius: *Lives of Eminent Philosophers*, Vol. 2, p. 663. All subsequent translations from Epicurus are from this volume.

ceus, ". . . that pleasure is the end and aim, we do not mean the pleasures of the prodigal or the pleasures of sensuality, as we are understood to do by some through ignorance, prejudice, or wilful misrepresentation."[18] Indeed, his ideal can most fairly be represented as a kind of secular monasticism. Peace of mind, according to Epicurus, can only be effectively secured in "a quiet private life withdrawn from the multitude."[19] Ideally, this will be withdrawal into a community of like-minded friends, the kind of community represented in its perfection by the life of the gods, as Epicurus had described it. The wise man will neither marry nor engage in politics, but neither will he, in the manner of the Cynics, live the life of a mendicant; he will seek an income sufficient to ensure that he is not dependent on others for the satisfaction of his simple needs.[20]

Once again, then, self-sufficiency emerges as a criterion of perfection, but now manifested in membership of a self-contained community rather than, as in the Cynic-Stoic tradition, in the individual man. The positive content of perfection lies in a pleasant calm, not in theoretic activity, which is only a necessary condition of our acquiring such calm. Can men achieve perfection, thus defined? They cannot, it would seem, since they cannot wholly free themselves from pain. On the other hand, Epicurus—himself a lifelong sufferer—explicitly says that "he who understands the limits of life knows how easy it is to procure enough to remove the pain of want and make the whole of life complete and perfect."[21] This is a consequence of the fact that "the term of evil is brief."[22] Provided men do not permit the fear of pain

18. "Letter to Menoeceus," trans. Hicks, Vol. 2, p. 657.

19. "Sovran Maxims," 14; trans. Hicks, Vol. 2, p. 669.

20. On the general idea of "retirement" in the Ancient World, compare A. J. Festugière: *Personal Religion Among the Greeks* (Berkeley, 1954), ch. IV.

21. "Sovran Maxims," 21; trans. Hicks, Vol. 2, p. 671.

22. "Sovran Maxims," 4; cf. Hicks, Vol. 2, p. 665. In this case I have not followed Hicks's translation.

to suffuse their life with anxiety they will find pain when it comes, Epicurus thought, easy enough to bear; the perfection of a life is not invalidated by an occasional, transitory, pain.

The great importance of Epicureanism in our story is that, for all that it does not deny the gods—publicly at least, although many of its critics alleged that it did so privately— it is a fully secularized analysis of perfection. By achieving a peaceful calm, men admittedly live a life which is "godlike." The "godlike" character of the good life is, however, in a sense accidental. Man's perfection is not defined by way of, nor does it in any sense depend upon, the gods. Were there no gods, the Epicurean analysis of perfection would be quite unaffected. It is for men to perfect themselves; the gods will neither help them to do so, nor hinder them from doing so. There is no suggestion that by perfecting themselves men will come to "live with the gods," or that they will cease to be human and become divine, or that they will acquire a higher metaphysical status, or that they will fulfil a function divinely laid down for them. Simply, the happy life is the best life; to perfect oneself is to live the best life. It is not in the least surprising that when men came, in the modern world, to look for a way of defining perfection which was independent of religion, they turned for that purpose to Epicurus. Modern utilitarianism is by no means identical with ancient Epicureanism; for one thing, it has served as an instrument of social reform. But it took over from Epicureanism its secular interpretation of perfection.

Stoicism, in contrast, is essentially religious in its attitude: in Rome, it came to be "the religion of educated men."[23] For the Stoics, there is no question that, in principle at least, man is perfectible. This is a direct consequence of

---

23. The best general account of Stoic moral ideals in English is E. V. Arnold: *Roman Stoicism* (London, 1911; repr. 1958), which is actually, for all its title, fuller on Greek than on Roman Stoicism.

the fact that he is rational and therefore godlike. The Stoics reaffirm the old Pindaric teaching that "men and gods are of the same race" but now in a new sense; the emphasis is not on their sharing the same passions—a Stoic god has no passions—but on their common rationality. "Reason . . . is a common attribute," writes Seneca, "of both gods and men, in them it is already perfected, in us it is capable of being perfected."[24] Man perfects himself, then, by becoming like God. The Stoic ideal of perfection, unlike the Epicurean ideal, is essentially God-centred, deiform, perfection. But in what does likeness to God, for a Stoic, consist?

It is not easy to answer this question briefly. Stoicism had a long history; some five hundred years separated Zeno, who founded the Stoic School in the third century B.C., from the last of the ancient Stoics, Marcus Aurelius. And its history was not only long but complex and diversified. The early Stoics were logicians and physicists; in their eyes a knowledge of logic and physics was essential to the perfected man. The Stoic Emperor, Marcus Aurelius, in the sharpest possible contrast, offered thanks to Providence that he was preserved, for all his addiction to philosophy, from "poring over textbooks and rules of logic or grinding at natural science."[25] But certain doctrines persist, lending unity to the long succession of Stoic thinkers, even if others were greatly modified when Stoicism broke its connexions with Greek cosmology and forged new relationships with the Roman state.

The Stoics always emphasize that Plato is their master. In Cicero's *De natura deorum,* for example, the Stoic Balbus appeals to the authority of "Plato, that divine philosopher" and the Epicurean Velleius refers sneeringly to "your master

---

24. Seneca: *Epistulae morales,* 92, as trans. R. M. Gummere, Loeb Classical Library (London, 1917–43), Vol. 2, p. 465. All quotations from Seneca's *Letters* are from this ed.

25. Marcus Aurelius: *Meditations,* I, 17, as trans. Maxwell Staniforth, Penguin Classics (Harmondsworth, 1964), p. 42. All quotations from Marcus Aurelius are from this ed.

Plato." [26] This can seem very strange to the modern reader, if he comes to the Stoics from the *Phaedo* and the *Republic*. But the Plato the Stoics so greatly admired is the cosmological Plato, the Plato of the *Timaeus,* and the ethical Plato, the Plato of the early Socratic dialogues, rather than the metaphysical Plato.

In the *Timaeus,* Plato describes the manner in which this world "came to be, by the god's providence, in very truth a living creature with soul and reason." [27] This conception of the world, as "a living creature with soul and reason," the Stoics took over from Plato, although they modified it in two respects. In the first place, their world-soul is corporeal, as Plato's is not. In the second place, they thought of Providence not as creating the "world-soul" but as being the ruling principle within it. (Some commentators, indeed, have taken this to be Plato's real view, as distinct from his mythological fancies.) "All this universe which encompasses us is one," writes Seneca, "and it is God: we are associates of God; we are his members." [28] Nature, as the Stoics conceive it, is a fiery world-soul in perpetual change—their cosmology is a curious mixture of Plato and Heraclitus. To speak of it as being "governed by providence" is to draw attention to the fact that this change is rationally determined for the benefit of the rational beings the world contains— gods and men.

The arguments by which the Stoics defended their position, arguments which Cicero ascribes to Zeno, begin from the assumption that Nature must exhibit all perfections, since it is the most excellent of all things. Therefore, Zeno argued, it must be not only eternal, but wise, blessed and divine. Since its parts are sentient, it must be sentient; since

26. Cicero: *De natura deorum,* II, xii and I, viii, trans. Rackham, Loeb ed., pp. 153, 23. Quotations are from this ed.

27. *Timaeus,* 30ʙ, as trans. Cornford: *Plato's Cosmology,* p. 34.

28. *Epistulae morales,* 92; Loeb ed., Vol. 2, p. 467.

it gives birth to beings which are animate and wise, it must itself be animate and wise.[29] Here are the beginnings of arguments which were to play a very large part in Western theology, even when it made a radical distinction between the Creator and the created Universe—arguments which take it as their point of departure that God is the most perfect of all things, and that the less perfect cannot give rise to the more perfect.[30] But the peculiarity of Stoicism, from the Christian point of view, lies in its identification of God with Nature.

So "likeness to God" is for the Stoics a very complex notion. It involves conformity to God's will, but not, in an Hebraic sense, obedience. "I do not obey God," writes Seneca, "but I assent to what he has decided."[31] (One is reminded of a famous remark and an equally famous comment: Margaret Fuller's "I accept the Universe" and Carlyle's "Gad, she'd better!") So far as God is thought of as a legislator his laws are not specific commands, of the type represented in the Ten Commandments: they are laws of nature. (No doubt the Stoics, like many another after them, sometimes succumbed to the temptation to play upon the ambiguity of "natural law," to think of laws of nature as at once universal and irresistible and as something which a wicked man can break, just as he can break the law of the land.) The sage, the perfected man, sees how things happen and conforms his will to that course of events, not to a commandment. But since God is rational we can also make the same point by saying that the sage lives "in accordance with reason."

"The end may be defined," so Zeno taught, "as life in

29. *De natura deorum,* II, viii; Loeb ed., p. 145.

30. For a discussion of this argument and a bibliography, see David Sanford: "Degrees of Perfection" in *The Encyclopedia of Philosophy,* Vol. 2.

31. *Epistulae morales,* 96; cf. Loeb ed., Vol. 3, pp. 105–6: "Non pareo deo, sed adsentior." In this case I have not followed the Loeb trans.

accordance with nature, or, in other words, in accordance with our own human nature as well as that of the universe, a life in which we refrain from every action forbidden by the law common to all things, that is to say, the right reason which pervades all things, and is identical with Zeus, lord and ruler of all that is."[32] To live in accordance with nature, to be rational, to conform to what God wills, to be godlike, are all identified, since God, Nature, Reason, Providence can be distinguished only by abstraction; in substance they are identical. "For what else is Nature," Seneca asks rhetorically, "but God and the Divine Reason that pervades the whole universe and all its parts?"[33]

The Christian critics of Stoicism were quick to point to what they took to be a contradiction within Stoicism, between the conception of God as Providence and the conception of God as Nature. "Although they [the Stoics] say that the providential being is of the same substance as the being he directs," writes Origen, "they nevertheless say that he is perfect and different from what he directs."[34] But for the Stoics there was no incompatibility in saying both that God and man were "of the same substance" and that God directs all things. Men differ from God, in their view, only in so far as a particular natural event differs from Nature as a whole; man, to use one of the favourite Stoic metaphors, is "a particle of God." Since God is a fiery spirit, man is a "fiery particle," and since he is a particle of God, perfection lies in principle within man's reach.

Undoubtedly, however, the Stoics had a difficulty to face. If man is a particle of God, why is he not automatically perfect? Imperfection, according to the Stoics, arises from

32. Diogenes Laertius: *Lives of Eminent Philosophers,* VII, 88; Loeb ed., Vol. 2, pp. 195–97.

33. *De beneficiis,* IV, vii, as trans. J. W. Basore in the Loeb Classical Library ed. of *Moral Essays,* Vol. 3 (London, 1948), p. 217.

34. Origen: *Commentary on St. John,* XIII.

the fact that men fail to see things as they are, and therefore "give their assent to false judgements." Avarice, for example, is simply the false judgement that money is good;
correct that judgement, by bringing men to see how little
value attaches to the ownership of pieces of metal, and their
avarice will be conquered.

Marcus Aurelius sums up thus: "The good life can be
achieved to perfection by any soul capable of showing indifference to the things that are themselves indifferent. This
can be done by giving careful scrutiny first to the elements
that compose them, and then to the things themselves;
bearing also in mind that none of them is responsible for
the opinion we form of it."[35] (Compare the Buddhist teaching that "people are tied down by a sense-object when they
cover it with unreal imaginations; likewise they are liberated
from it when they see it as it really is.")[36] In other words, if
we look carefully at those things which are "indifferent"—
unworthy of a rational man's concern—we shall see at once
that they are of no importance in themselves. If, however,
we fail to look at them carefully we may wrongly suppose
that they demand action on our part; that they must be
pursued, or desired, or regretted. So Marcus Aurelius is continually urging himself, in a manner which came to be familiar in the writings of the Christian moralists, to look in detail
at fame, or sexual love, or power, and thus to see it for what it
is, and how little worthy it is of a rational being's attention—
to see, in T. S. Eliot's words, "the skull beneath the skin." The
irrational man fails to do this. As a result of bad training,
or the promptings of instincts which "blind the understanding," he is attracted by the superficial appearance of things
and therefore attaches to them an importance they do not
possess.

35. *Meditations*, XI, 16, trans. Staniforth, p. 171.
36. See *Buddhist Scriptures*, sel. and trans. Edward Conze, Penguin Classics (Harmondsworth, 1959; repr. 1968), p. 104.

It is still anything but clear how "a particle of God" can exhibit even this degree of irrationality, how he can fail to see things as they are. In a metaphor which the medieval church was to apply to heretics, Marcus Aurelius suggests that a man can estrange himself from Nature, cutting himself off from it like a branch from a tree, but a branch which still retains sufficient life to be grafted on again "by grace of Zeus the author of all fellowship."[37] This way of looking at man's relationship to Nature, however, ascribes to him a kind of free will quite incompatible with the Stoic view of Nature as a system of providentially-governed changes. Indeed, the problems which came to be most characteristic of Christian theology—the problem of explaining the existence of moral evil in a providentially governed universe, the problem of explaining how man can exercise any freedom whatever in such a universe, the problem of explaining how man can be at once an image of God and corrupt—all broke out for the first time in their full force within Stoic theology. Insist too strongly on the providential government of the universe, and the conclusion seems to follow that man has no need of moral effort. Insist on man's capacity to "cut himself off" from Nature and it is no longer possible to argue that all things form part of a single providentially-governed Nature. Insist that man is a "particle of perfection," an "image of God," and the natural inference is that he has no need to strive for perfection; insist that he constantly goes astray and the perfection of the universe as a whole is threatened.

Putting these metaphysical problems aside, it has still to be determined in what the perfection of the individual soul consists. Marcus Aurelius is fond of describing the perfected soul by means of a geometrical metaphor. It is, he says, a soul which has attained a "perfectly rounded form." To perfect oneself is to become a "totally rounded orb, rejoicing in

37. *Meditations*, XI, 8, trans. Staniforth, pp. 168–69.

its own rotundity." [38] If we approach the Stoics by way of Parmenides, these remarks no longer surprise us. The soul, like Being, to be perfect must be rounded. And we recall our own metaphors: "a well-rounded personality," "an all-round education." Roundedness implies, above all, completeness. The "rounded-soul" contains in itself whatever is valuable, and therefore does not need to move outside itself. When a cricketer is described as an "all-rounder," this conveys that he is good in every department of cricket, at bowling, batting and fielding. Similarly, the "rounded-soul" will be good in every department of virtue.

But there is a great difference between the two cases, according to Stoic teaching. A man can be a good cricketer either because he is an all-rounder or because he is exceptionally good in some one department of cricket; he can be an excellent batsman even although he is a poor bowler. There is no analogy to this, so the Stoics argue, in the case of virtue. Virtue is a general condition of the soul, which no doubt finds expression in a particular way on a particular occasion—as justice, let us say, rather than as courage—but which a man either has or lacks *as a whole*. (It is more like "health" or "physical fitness" than it is like "being good at cricket.")

It had been a Platonic doctrine, deriving from Socrates, that the various virtues are so inextricably entangled that one cannot exist without the other. It is impossible for a man to "specialize," as it were, in a particular virtue. For the Stoics, too, virtue is essentially one—although it can be diversely manifested, in different circumstances, as prudence, or temperance, or justice. "Virtue," according to the Stoic Ariston, "when it considers what we must do or avoid, is called prudence; when it controls our desires and lays down for them the limits of moderation and seasonableness in our

---

38. *Meditations*, XI, 12; XII, 3, trans. Staniforth, pp. 170, 180. In the latter case I have not followed Staniforth exactly.

pleasures, it is called temperance; when it has to do with men's relations to one another and their commercial dealings, it is called justice." [39] Either, then, a man has a virtuous soul, or else he is wholly devoid of virtue. We cannot properly say of him that, for example, "he is a just man but imprudent."

This explains the notorious Stoic paradox: a man is either perfect or he is bad. For if a man lacks *any* virtue he altogether lacks virtue. If virtue is treated as the performance of an external act, then, of course, a man can be virtuous in one respect and not in others; he can, for example, be cowardly and yet be a temperate drinker. But to the Stoic what matters is not the external act, but the condition of the soul, the possession of a certain kind of will, or moral intention. The coward's will is infected, and so, therefore, is his temperance. On the one side stands the Sage, the perfected man, the man whose will is unblemished; on the other side the mass of unregenerate humanity.

Since the Sage possesses perfect virtue, his soul is also "rounded" in the sense of "lacking nothing which is valuable." No doubt, the Stoics agreed with Aristotle, however godlike a man is, he is still human; even a Sage must eat, must seek public office, must acquire a reasonable competence. But whereas Aristotle described health and wealth as "goods," i.e. as having value in themselves, this the Stoics wholly denied. Even less were they prepared to accept the Epicurean view that pleasure is good. Cicero quotes Zeno as asserting that "virtue is the only desirable good"; [40] that became the official Stoic doctrine. Although health and freedom from pain are "advantages" they are not goods. The perfected man will in general pursue them, as Nature instructs him to do, but he remains "indifferent" to them; it

---

39. Ariston of Chios, quoted in Plutarch: *Moralia*, 441A, as trans. W. C. Helmbold, Loeb Classical Library, Vol. 6 (London, 1939), p. 21.

40. *De officiis*, III, viii, 35; cf. trans. by J. E. Higginbotham in *Cicero on Moral Obligation* (London, 1967), p. 148.

will not matter to him if he loses his health, or is racked
by pain. His perfection is unaffected by such losses, just because health and freedom from pain are not, in any proper
sense of the word, "goods."

In a loose sense, the Stoics were prepared to admit, goodness attaches to health and wealth, and virtue to doing what
is civically appropriate, but this is only because the pursuit of advantages and the maintenance of decorum are for
the most part rational. "When I don suitable attire," writes
Seneca, "or walk as I should, or dine as I ought to dine, it is
not my dinner, or my walk, or my dress that are goods, but
the deliberate choice which I show in regard to them"[41]—
not the character of my action, as such, but the rationality
of my choice.

If health and wealth were goods in any but this deriva-
tive sense, so the Stoics argued, no man could preserve his
equanimity, his peace of mind. Health and wealth he may
lose at any moment, for reasons which lie completely outside his control. Virtue is the one thing attachment to which
is compatible with serenity, since perseverance in virtue lies
entirely in the power of man's will. So the Stoic view that only
virtue is good is a deduction from the Platonic principle to
which Aristotle had found it impossible wholly to commit
himself: that the man who possesses the good stands in need
of nothing else, that he is wholly self-sufficient, perfect in
a metaphysical sense. Their ideal of virtue is regularly described by the Stoics in the now familiar language of metaphysical perfection: Cicero tell us that virtue for Zeno was
simple, unique and one;[42] Stoic writers constantly speak of
virtue as that which is complete in itself, which requires no
supplement, which contains no defect.

In many respects, indeed, the Stoic ideal of perfection

---

41. *Epistulae morales,* 92; Loeb ed., Vol. 2, pp. 453–55.
42. *Academica,* I, x; cf. trans. by H. Rackham, Loeb Classical Library (London, 1933;
rev. 1951), p. 445.

resembles the ideal of perfection incorporated in some sections of the Bhagavad-Gītā, in which the sage is represented as a being who "is the same to friend and foe," who "puts away both pleasant and unpleasant things," who "has no expectation," who is "free from exultation, fear, impatience and excitement."[43] Similarly, the Stoic wise man, according to Diogenes Laertius, is "passionless"; he will never feel grief; he is not "pitiful" and makes "no allowance for anyone."[44] It is not simply a matter, as it was for Plato, of subduing the passions, of controlling them by reason. Sometimes, influenced by Plato, the Roman Stoics talk in this way. But for orthodox Stoicism the Sage must not only control but destroy his passions. No surprise need be felt that the Stoics found it difficult to nominate examples of a Sage.

If Sages are so rare, however, and if, short of perfection, there is only badness, the ordinary man may well despair—he may turn away from the pursuit of virtue on the ground that it is wholly unattainable. The imperfect man, the Stoics point out in reply, may in certain respects do what the perfected man—the Sage—does; the imperfect man, too, may serve his fellow-man and may act so as to preserve his health and wealth. In a sense, he is then a "better man" than those who seek what the Sage would avoid or act in ways which he would find unsuitable. The fact remains that since such men do not act with perfect detachment, they cannot properly be described as being morally good. Many Christian theologians have argued, in the same spirit, that although a pagan is in some respects "better" if he acts justly rather than unjustly, he nevertheless lacks true moral goodness since his just act is not motivated by a love of God. As the Westminster Confession puts it: "Works done by unregenerate men—although, for the matter of them, they may be things which

---

43. *Bhagavad-gītā,* XII, §15–19, as trans. in *Hindu Scriptures,* sel., trans. and introd. R. C. Zaehner, Everyman's Library (London, 1966), p. 302.

44. *Lives,* VII, 117, 118, 123; Loeb ed., Vol. 2, pp. 221, 223, 227.

God commands . . . are sinful and cannot please God. . . . And yet their neglect of them is more sinful and displeasing unto God."[45]

Men who without themselves being Sages act as the Sage would act, must not, on the Stoic view, be thought of as possessing a measure or degree of perfection—any more than, for the Westminster Confession, a virtuous pagan possesses a degree of Christian perfection. For the Stoics, as we said, a man is either completely perfect or completely imperfect. Until the very moment he achieves perfection, he should be regarded as wholly vicious. If we can speak of a man as "making progress" towards perfection, this should not be taken to mean that perfection is no more than the final stage in a gradual progress, in which perfection is more and more nearly approached. At the end, there is a sudden leap, quite unlike anything that has gone before, somewhat as if a blinded man whose eyes had been gradually healing behind a bandage were suddenly to have the bandage removed.

The contrast, and comparison, with what were to be orthodox Christian doctrines is an interesting one. The contemporary critics of Stoicism laughed at the Stoic doctrine that there was, in the end, a sudden leap into perfection. Did this mean, they asked, that a man might go to bed on Sunday night perfectly bad and wake up on Monday morning a perfected sage? Perfection, they argued, could only be achieved, in so far as it could be achieved at all, as the culmination of a steady progress.

For Christianity, however, there are two sudden breaks in a man's moral development; one is his experience of divine grace, the other is death. In general, Christian theologians have argued that only after death can men achieve perfection, that in this life the best they can hope for is

---

45. Westminster Confession, Section XVI, quoted from H. Bettenson, ed.: *Documents of the Christian Church*, World's Classics (London, 1943; repr. 1946), p. 346.

moral progress. But many of them have also argued that men can be suddenly transformed—and, some have said, perfected—by divine grace. The question whether perfection is the culminating point in a gradual progress or involves a sudden leap from sinfulness to a totally different condition of the soul—involving what Plato called "a conversion of the soul"[46]—was, indeed, to be a principal point at issue between optimistic secularists and their theological opponents.

How is individual perfection related, for the Stoics, to social perfection? The Stoics were greatly influenced by the Cynics, and the Cynic Diogenes had already announced that he was a "citizen of the world." The early Stoics, in particular, thought of themselves as members of a single society, passing beyond all national boundaries, a society united by its conformity to reason. Zeno wrote a *Republic* which was, in part, a criticism of Plato's *Republic*. Where it departed from Plato was in its universality. It was a "world-state" which governed all men, without distinction between Greek and barbarian, slave and free men. "For what is a Roman knight," Seneca was later to write, "or a freedman's son, or a slave? One may leap to heaven from the very slums."[47] There is more than a little appropriateness in the fact that of the two great Roman Stoics, one, Epictetus, was a slave, the other, Marcus Aurelius, an emperor.

Zeno's republic contained nothing corresponding to the Platonic classes: all its members had an equal responsibility to be fully rational. Merely in virtue of his perfect rationality, a Stoic was a member of such an ideal state, a community of Sages, much as for Plato a philosopher governed his life by the law of the ideal republic. And difficult as it was to construct such a society, it was not, so the Stoics argued, impossible in principle. The Stoic also admitted, it is true, his

46. *Republic*, 518D.
47. *Epistulae morales*, 31; Loeb ed., Vol. 1, p. 229.

allegiance to that particular state in which he was born, as, in the words of Epictetus, "a small image of the Universal state." But if later Stoics did particular service to the Roman State, the most cosmopolitan of actual states, Stoicism was in its first beginnings a doctrine which had revolutionary import, a movement towards perfection in human society as in the human individual. This sharply distinguished it from Epicureanism, or from any form of solitary asceticism.

In the event, however, what was secondary in Stoicism, the performance of those acts which the Sage would think it "proper" to perform, came to assume a central position. Stoicism was converted into a practical morality, a way of living in the State as it existed and making the best of one's life as an ordinary citizen. Moral progress, rather than the ideal of total perfection, was in Roman times the ideal which the Stoic moralist set before men, as Epictetus does in his *Discourses*.[48] It was still argued that only the Sage was perfect, and that all other men were bad. But since the condition of Sagehood was excessively rare, properly ascribable only to remote Greek heroes like Hercules and Odysseus—the *Odyssey* was read as a moral allegory, a kind of Pilgrim's Progress of the Sage—or perhaps to Socrates, to Diogenes the Cynic, or to such Stoic Fathers as Zeno and Cleanthes, the best thing to do was to concentrate on persuading men, however imperfect, to perform those kinds of acts which the perfect Sage would also, if so differently, perform. Duty and rationality, rather than detachment and self-sufficiency, came to be the everyday Stoic ideals. This was not the last time that an impossible ideal of perfection was to be replaced, for all practical purposes, by a humanly attainable objective; much the same thing happened in the seventeenth century in reaction against the rigorous moral ideals of Augustinianism.

The great importance of the Stoics, however, was that

48. Epictetus: *Discourses.* See especially Bk. IV.

they put before men a human exemplar of perfectibility, the Sage. He was a godlike being, in virtue of his rationality, but he was not a metaphysically remote being; he was *human,* and his perfection was, in principle, accessible to human beings. "Set before your mind the question," writes Epictetus, "what would Zeno or Socrates have done?" And again: "If you are not yet Socrates, you still ought to live as one who wishes to be Socrates."[49] When men moved away from theological ideals of perfection, they turned to Stoicism, just as they turned to Epicureanism, in search of an ideal which was humanly attainable. They turned, however, to Roman rather than to Greek Stoicism—to an ideal of conduct which emphasized rationality rather than absolute self-sufficiency, which exhorted men to seek civic responsibility, impartiality and justice rather than to seek absolute detachment. For Augustinian Christians, in contrast, the attractiveness of Stoicism lay in its very absoluteness, in its insistence that man must try to be godlike, and that to do this he must first release himself from all human concerns.

"The history of Christian philosophy," writes Henry Chadwick, "begins not with a Christian but with a Jew, Philo of Alexandria, elder contemporary of St. Paul."[50] Philo read the Old Testament, and more particularly the Pentateuch, in the light of Greek philosophy. His God is at once the personal God of Abraham and Jacob and the God of Xenophanes and of Greek speculation after him, immutable, infinite in perfection, sufficient to himself. He set theologians on that path which was to lead to the definition of God laid down, for example, by the Vatican Council: "There is one true and living God, Creator and Lord of heaven and earth, almighty, eternal, immense, incomprehensible, infinite in

49. *Manual(Encheiridion),* 33, 51; I give a rendering freely based on the trans. by W. A. Oldfather, Loeb Classical Library (London, 1926–28), Vol. 2, pp. 521, 535.

50. In A. H. Armstrong, ed.: *The Cambridge History of Later Greek and Early Medieval Philosophy,* p. 137. See also, for Philo generally, H. A. Wolfson: *Philo: Foundations of Religious Philosophy in Judaism, Christianity and Islam,* 3rd ed. rev., 2 vols (Cambridge, Mass., 1962).

intelligence, in will and in all perfection, who as being one, sole, absolutely single and immutable spiritual substance, is to be declared as really and essentially distinct from the world, of supreme beatitude in and from Himself, and ineffably exalted above all things beside Himself which exist or are conceivable."[51]

For Philo converts the "unchangeable Jahweh" of the Old Testament—unchangeable only in the sense that he is steadfast, not given to changing his mind—into a God who is unchangeable in the Greek, metaphysical, sense of that word. And at the same time he converts a Jahweh who is "one" merely in having no competitors into a God who is simple and indivisible, as Parmenides understood simplicity and indivisibility. "It is one of the facts that go to make His blessedness and supreme felicity," Philo writes, "that His being is apprehended as simple being, without other definite characteristic."[52] It is this God, at once Jahweh and a metaphysical being, in relation to whom man's perfection is defined.

The path to perfection, as Philo envisages it, begins with faith, a faith in God comparable to Abraham's. This is a point at which Philo breaks sharply with the Greek tradition. There is nowhere in Greek thought any suggestion that faith is a virtue, let alone that it is "the queen of virtues,"[53] to quote only one of Philo's ecstatic descriptions of it. In a sense, it is true, the Stoics exhort us to have faith in the Universe, in its providential ordering, but Philo means by "faith" more than that: it involves, also, faith in the teachings of a revealed religion.

The next step on the path to perfection consists in de-

---

51. *The Decrees of the Vatican Council*, ed. Vincent McNabb (London, 1907), Decree I, pp. 18–19.
52. *On the Unchangeableness of God*, 55, as trans. F. H. Colson and G. H. Whitaker in the Loeb Classical Library ed. of Philo's works, 10 vols (London, 1929–62), Vol. III, p. 39. All quotations from Philo are taken from this ed.
53. *On Abraham*, XLVI, 270; Loeb ed., Vol. VI, p. 133.

stroying the passions, so as to achieve a Stoic freedom from desire. (Of the passions, the most fatal, according to Philo, is spiritual pride, the lust to be equal to the gods—the Greek *hubris*.) As the soul ascends still further towards God, it recognizes in the body a fatal obstacle. Only by divesting itself of all that belongs to the body can the soul achieve perfection. "The soul that loves God," Philo writes, "having disrobed itself of the body and the objects dear to the body and fled abroad far away from these, gains a fixed and assured settlement in the perfect ordinances of virtue."[54] This does not imply extreme asceticism, of which Philo disapproves; it does imply a Stoic "lack of concern" for the body. But even the Stoic Sage has not, according to Philo, reached true perfection. In the end, triumphing over the sensuality of the body, the soul can hope to perfect itself by achieving a vision of God—or, at least of one of the "powers" or "manifestations" of God. The most important of these powers is what Philo calls "Logos," the "Word," the main means by which God communicates with the world: it is God as Thought, as distinct from God as pure Being.[55] But the manifestations of God also include the world itself. That is why a man can arrive at a vision of God through "philosophy," i.e. an understanding of the nature of the world, seen as an emanation of God's light—although he may also arrive at such a vision directly, as Moses did.

Of God, according to Philo, nothing positive can be said. Except in so far as he vouchsafes to give men a revelation of his nature, he is in detail unknowable—the vision of God is a blinding light, not the clear sight of an articulated object. The God seen in such a vision has no properties in common with man; we can say of him only that he is eternal, self-existent, omnipotent, omniscient, for these predicates

---

54. *On the Allegorical Interpretation of Genesis*, II, xv, 55; Loeb ed., Vol. I, p. 259.

55. For comparable Rabbinical views see Charles Guignebert: *The Jewish World in the Time of Jesus* (1935; Eng. trans. 1939; repr. New York, 1959, 1965), Bk. II, ch. 1, pp. 83–95.

belong to himself alone, and place him outside of every genus. We cannot possibly ascribe to him, as the Stoics did, such properties as rationality, let alone, as the Old Testament seems to do, wrath and anger. If the Old Testament is divinely inspired, even although, read literally, it ascribes to God attributes which are quite unworthy of him, this is only to say that it is quite wrong to read the Old Testament literally: it should be read as allegory.* The Old Testament stories "are no mythical fictions . . . but modes of making ideas visible, bidding us resort to allegorical interpretation."[56]

By such means, Philo does for the Old Testament what Greek philosophy had done for both the Olympian religion and the mystery religions; he dehumanizes it, converts it into a metaphysics. The consequences of this dehumanizing were to be incalculable.

Can all men, in principle, hope to achieve such a degree of perfection as is involved in the vision of God? At this point, Philo's position is in some degree predetermined by the existence of a sacred book, conceived of as "revelation"—even if it has to be interpreted allegorically—and of prophets, conceived of as men especially inspired by God. Since only some men have been chosen by God to receive his revelations, it is impossible to argue that all men have the same possibility of perfecting themselves. Without a revelation, faith can only be a truncated faith. For philosophy, by itself, can demonstrate nothing more than the existence of God; only by revelation can man pass beyond that point to a knowledge of God's plans for man. By this argument Philo preserves the authority of the Old Testament as the

---

* Philo did not invent the allegorical method. It had been practised by the Greeks themselves on the writings of Homer; the Stoics made great use of it, especially in its etymological form; Philo inherits an Alexandrian rabbinical tradition which had already been forced into allegorizing in order to defend the Old Testament against Greek criticisms that it was nothing more than a collection of outdated myths.

56. *On the Creation*, LVI, 157; Loeb ed., Vol. I, p. 125.

principal source of revelation; philosophy can interpret, but cannot contradict, its teachings about God's relationship to man. Revelation acts as a bridge, as it were, between God and man, a bridge metaphysics is unable to construct.

This is an exemplification of Philo's more general doctrine that to strive is not enough. When a man has achieved as much as he can by his own efforts, he realizes his own insignificance; only with the aid of divine grace can he take the final step, to the ecstasy of direct contact with God. "And the man who has despaired of himself is beginning to know Him that IS."[57]

In the *Republic* Plato had suggested that "the form of the good is seen last and with difficulty";[58] he had compared seeing it with looking at the sun: he had argued that the sight of the form of the good was not for all men. But Plato was none the less convinced that if men cannot achieve the vision of the form of the good this is only because they do not have the right sort of soul or have not had the right sort of training. For Aristotle, too, this is why not all men are capable of living the contemplative life. Philo is the first explicitly to argue that human effort to reach perfection, however talented and skilled, is not enough. Perfection is, in the last resort, God's gift, even if, for Philo, that gift is bestowed, not arbitrarily, but only on those who have made themselves ready to receive it. "Strictly speaking," he writes, "the human mind does not choose the good through itself, but in accordance with the thoughtfulness of God, since He bestows the fairest things upon the worthy."[59]

The doctrine of grace, it is true, was not a wholly unfamiliar one. In Plato's *Ion*, it is suggested that the "rhapsode"—

---

57. *On Dreams,* I, X, 60; Loeb ed., Vol. V, p. 329.
58. *Republic,* 517.
59. A fragment from the lost fourth book of his *Legum Allegoria* (*On the Allegorical Interpretation of Genesis*), as trans. H. A. Wolfson in his *Philo,* Vol. 1, p. 442. This fragment is not included in the Loeb ed., but the text may be found in *Fragments of Philo Judaeus,* ed. J. R. Harris (Cambridge, 1886), p. 8.

the public reciter of Homer's poetry—achieves his effects not by the exercise of skill but because he is possessed by a god. And in Homer himself, it many times happens that a character feels himself to be divinely assisted so as to be able to act "beyond his powers." But there is no suggestion in Homer or Plato that perfection can be reached in this way. Ion's imitative art is, in Plato's eyes, a very lowly one; the divine assistance offered to the heroes in Homer is temporary and precarious.[60] The importance of Philo was that he made of God's working in man a fundamental condition of man's perfectibility.

Philo's influence on such fellow-Alexandrians as Clement and Origen was extensive. However, for all that their ways of thinking so often ran parallel, he does not seem to have directly influenced Plotinus or Plotinus's neo-Platonic followers.[61] Unlike Philo, Plotinus does not have the problem of reconciling Greek with Hebrew ideas; he may—there is considerable disagreement among scholars on this point —have felt the influence of India, but he is extraordinarily remote from those mystery religions, each with their Redeemer and many with their "special revelations," which flourished in Plotinus's third-century Rome. There is no sign in his writings of contact with orthodox Christians, not even with the Platonized Christianity of Justin Martyr or Clement of Alexandria. He regarded himself not as a "neo-Platonist," as we now describe him, but as a Platonist, pure and simple,

60. For some other examples of the workings of divine grace in Greek religious thought, see E. R. Dodds: *Pagan and Christian in an Age of Anxiety,* Wiles Lectures, 1963 (Cambridge, 1965), p. 90 n.

61. Interpreting Plotinus is a very difficult task; his principal work, the *Enneads,* is a collection of essays, rather than a systematic book, written over a long period of time, and arranged for publication by Plotinus's pupil Porphyry. It may well incorporate important changes in ideas. The inner tensions in Plotinus are particularly stressed in Philip Merlan's article on Plotinus in *The Encyclopedia of Philosophy,* Vol. 6. See also Emile Bréhier: *The Philosophy of Plotinus,* trans. from the French ed. of 1952 by J. Thomas (Chicago, 1958); A. H. Armstrong on Plotinus in *The Cambridge History of Later Greek and Early Medieval Philosophy,* pp. 195–268; and, for a rather different view, J. M. Rist: *Plotinus: The Road to Reality* (Cambridge, 1967).

although his Plato was a very special and limited one, the Plato of isolated passages, scattered through his dialogues, which could be read in a quasi-mystical way.

Plato had suggested in the *Republic* that the soul has three parts; in the *Timaeus* he calls them "three distinct forms of soul."[62] Plotinus, however, distinguishes in man two *different* souls, the true or "upper" soul and the embodied or "lower" soul. The embodied soul is, for Plotinus, to be controlled but not ignored; it is, as we might express the matter, entitled to its rations. There is, too, a kind of "civic goodness" appropriate to it; its demands in this regard have to be respected. The fact remains that to achieve his true end, to discover what he has it in himself to be, man must identify himself, not with his embodied soul, but with his immaterial or "true" soul. Sin and suffering belong only to the embodied soul, the true soul is by nature divine. But to become divine men must first, as it were, rediscover their true soul and identify themselves with it; that is the only way in which they can follow the precept, laid down in the *Theaetetus,* to become like God. To be virtuous, in the sense of "civic goodness," is not enough, seeing that, Plotinus agrees with Aristotle, it is impossible to ascribe temperance, for example, to the godlike; "temperance" is a quality possessed by men who are not wholly free of the body they have learnt to control.

The object of the true soul, according to Plotinus, is to repair that relationship with "the One" which is natural to it; that is its proper end, and only in such a relationship can it find perfection. What Plotinus meant by "the One," however, it is difficult to the point of impossibility to say. Like the form of the good in Plato's *Republic* it "transcends even being."[63] For a being, Plotinus argues, must always be a being *of a certain form,* and that implies limitation. So not

---

62. *Republic,* 435 B–C; *Timaeus,* 89E, trans. Cornford, p. 353.
63. *Republic,* 509B.

even Parmenides went far enough, in Plotinus's eyes, in his denial of distinctions, in so far as he identified the One with "Being." The One is certainly not to be identified with the supreme intellect, because intellect involves a distinction between the mind and its objects, and no distinctions are admissible within the simplicity of the One. "Think of The One as Mind or as God," Plotinus writes, "you think too meanly." [64] Sometimes, Plotinus calls the One the Good, with a reference back to Plato, but this is only to remind us that it is the supreme end or aim. He even calls it—as well as the simple, the unconditioned, the transcendental—"the father." In some sense, it "begets all things" but certainly not with a father's love, nor even by any causal means. It creates by the overflow of its perfection. "Seeking nothing, possessing nothing, lacking nothing," Plotinus writes, "the One is perfect and, in our metaphor, has overflowed, and its exuberance has produced the new." [65]

It is easy enough to understand the fascination of Plotinus for Greek-educated Christians. He sets up a perfect "One" as something which lies above good, or being, or intellect, but which is at the same time, by its very nature, creative. It is a One which is wholly non-finite, undetermined, and yet inconceivably rich and comprehensive in nature. It is a "One" which "takes flesh" in the sense that it embodies itself, but which does so by an "overflow," i.e. without losing anything of its original nature. And what is thus embodied can return, without loss, to the One from which it emerged.

When we look more closely, no doubt, we can see the impossibility of reconciling Plotinus's metaphysics either with Christian morality or with Christian theology—an impossibility arising from the fact that the "One" is in no sense a personal or a providential God, a source of grace or re-

64. *Enneads*, VI. 9. 6, trans. MacKenna, 1956, p. 619.
65. *Enneads*, V. 2. 1, trans. MacKenna, p. 380.

demption or revelation, and can be none of these things without losing its character as the "One." But we need not, all the same, feel any surprise that neo-Platonism provided Christianity with so much of its metaphysical framework, especially when it was conjoined, naturally if not altogether consistently, with the similar, but more Hebraic, theology of Philo.

To return now to our special concern, the progress of the individual soul. The individual soul "finds itself," achieves perfection, by a process of "cutting away" whatever ties it to the bodily. Plotinus takes over the Orphic-Platonic metaphor of the imprisoned soul; the soul has to free itself from the body and only in that process can discover its own true nature. It finds itself, that is, by excluding what is not itself. It establishes its supremacy over the merely bodily, in the first place, by the exercise of such virtues as temperance; by these means it can achieve what the Stoics, but not Plotinus, understood by perfection. To reach a higher level, the level of the Intellect, it must engage in strenuous intellectual activity—Plato's dialectic; to achieve its final perfection, it must move above the level of the intellect to a purely intuitive contemplation of the One.[66]

In Aristotle, we suggested, the ideal of the contemplative life is in some degree dissociated from the rest of his ethics. No doubt, the contemplative life is the supreme good, the final end for all men. But Aristotle draws a distinction between the moral and the intellectual life, the first being the characteristically human life, the second a life man can live only in virtue of the fact that he possesses something divine within him. Much that Aristotle says on this point was certainly taken over by Plotinus. The contrast Plotinus draws between the "true" and the embodied self, for example, is more than hinted at when Aristotle says that the "divine particle" which makes it possible for us to

---

66. *Enneads*, IV. 8. 4; cf. MacKenna, pp. 360–61.

live the contemplative life "is superior to man's composite nature." But it is characteristic of Plotinus that he seeks to unify at the same time as he seeks to distinguish. The composite self is in the end divine, too; the practical life is also theoretical. And, in particular, contemplation is not an end which only the divine particle in man seeks, it is the end which *everything* seeks.

So, according to Plotinus, "all things are striving after Contemplation, looking to Vision as their one end," not merely all animate beings but "even the unreasoning animals, the Principle that rules in growing things, and the Earth that produces these." They do not all, of course, achieve contemplation in the same manner or to the same degree, but each comes to possess it "in its own way and degree," even if it is only as an image or a "mimicry" of the contemplation at which the perfected soul arrives.[67]

It is difficult, without plunging into the intricacies of Plotinus's metaphysics, to understand how he defends this conclusion. But Plotinus's metaphysics, at this point, may be thought of as a particular manner of interpreting and developing that gnomic utterance of Thales from which philosophy begins: "All things are full of gods." In the subsequent history of Greek philosophy, such gods had been replaced by atoms in motion; the atomic theory of Democritus has no need of gods. Plotinus rejects the conception of mechanical explanation. All action, he argues, mechanical action as well as human action, must be governed by an idea, or a particular "Vision." Fundamentally, then, action is contemplation coming into material embodiment.

The difference between the most primitive mechanical action and the highest perfection of the human soul—the contemplation of the One—is, in other words, a difference in degree only. Each is a form of contemplation, the difference lying in the kind and degree of contemplation. Simi-

67. *Enneads*, III. 8. 1, trans. MacKenna, p. 239.

larly, even the most "practical" of men, the least contemplative by our ordinary standards, seek the material goods they pursue, according to Plotinus, only in order that they can grasp them in thought, in contemplation. Merely to possess them materially would be no satisfaction; to be satisfied by them, men must be aware of them.

The effect of this approach is that the whole of Nature appears as a "great chain of being," to use the phrase Lovejoy has made familiar.[68] Perfection involves climbing a ladder, advancing in grade, and in the process freeing oneself from the limits imposed on contemplation by one's embodied individuality—kicking away, as it were, the ladder on which one has climbed up. In part, this is the language of the mystery religions, with their initiations, their "beginners" and "perfected," their grades of illumination. But for Plotinus, as for Plato before him, entrance to a higher grade does not depend on initiation into rites and ceremonies, on participation in sacraments or on faith in the revelations of a sacred book, but rather on moral and intellectual activity. And the final effect is not that, as in the sacraments of the mystery religions, God enters into the worshipper, but that man approaches the One. During his long progress, man has to rely upon his own efforts; the One, unlike Philo's God, is not the sort of thing which could take an interest in the soul's strivings or help it by an exercise of grace. "It is not that the Supreme reaches out to us seeking our communion: we reach towards the Supreme."[69] It is true that Plotinus also tells us that "the higher cares for the lower and adorns it," but this is a care for the Universe as a whole, not a grace granted to individuals.

About the exact nature of the final stage in perfection it is hard to be confident. Some passages in Plotinus suggest that the soul, when it contemplates the One, at the

68. See note 7 above.
69. *Enneads,* VI. 9. 8, trans. MacKenna, p. 622.

same time discovers its identity with it; other passages that it always preserves its individuality. Nor is this uncertainty surprising. If the One is defined as an immutable, eternal being, how, it is natural to ask, can a particular man, a being in time, enter into relation with the One except by ceasing to be man, becoming the One? But how, on the other hand, can it then be said that a man "loves and embraces" the One, a phrase which certainly suggests that he retains some measure of independence? Plotinus says of himself that he "cannot help talking in dualities . . . instead of, boldly, the achievement of unity."[70] So it would seem that in truth we unite with the One, although our speech betrays us into saying that we "love" or "see" or "have a vision of it." The problem here involved—the problem of at once differentiating the perfected being from God and uniting him with God— was constantly to break out in Christian mysticism which, by its very nature, teeters on the brink of a pantheism quite incompatible with the Hebraic ingredient in Christianity.

What then was the Greek legacy? First and foremost the establishment of the idea of metaphysical perfection, and the ascription of that perfection to a Supreme Being, whether the Being was distinguished from or identified with Nature. Secondly, the view that human beings, or some human beings, could share, even if in a modified form, the metaphysical perfections of the Supreme Being—all his perfections except those which define his supremacy, such as his all-embracingness. Thirdly, the view that perfection involves knowledge, in some sense of the word. Even if, at its highest point, this is a knowledge that passes all understanding, it nevertheless must be, so the Greeks generally argued, based on knowledge in a more ordinary sense, involving a rational understanding of the Universe. Fourthly, a strong suggestion that this knowledge, and consequently perfection, could only be achieved by withdrawal from the world.

---

70. *Enneads*, VI. 9. 10, trans. MacKenna, p. 624.

But this was contradicted by the suggestion that it might be achieved in an ideal society. Fifthly, an attempt to set up a lower level of morality, short of perfection, which could serve as a practical aim for the ordinary citizen and, perhaps, as a preliminary stage on the path towards perfection. In what diverse ways these ideas were incorporated into, and rejected by, the manifold varieties of Christian teaching we must now turn to consider.

FOUR

CHRISTIANITY REJECTS PERFECTION: THE ELEMENTS

The crucial text is in Matthew, from the Sermon on the Mount: "Be ye therefore perfect, even as your Father which is in heaven is perfect."[1] Nothing could be more explicit, more uncompromising. Jesus here lays it down that men are to perfect themselves.* Since he would not behave so absurdly as to command men to become what they are in fact incapable of becoming, it follows, on the face of it, that men

---

1. Matthew 5:48.

* Albert Schweitzer has argued that the more stringent of Jesus' precepts were only an "interim ethics," directed to a community living in daily expectation of a Second Coming and called upon to live "separated" lives until that day arrived. Whatever be thought of the accuracy of this view as a description of Jesus' intentions, Christians have generally presumed that Jesus' teachings were meant for all men at all times or, at the very least, at all times for a spiritual élite. The Early Church, a small group of fervent believers living in an intensely eschatological atmosphere, was perhaps more ready, however, than the Church of Augustine's day to believe that men *could* be perfect, immaculately perfect at least. The Epistle to the Hebrews (6:4–6) was read as asserting that no Christian could expect forgiveness should he sin *even once* after he has been cleansed by baptism. Many early Christians, for that reason, did not seek baptism until they believed death to be near. In the second century the Apostolic Father, Hermas, permitted one, although only one, post-baptismal sin. From the point of view of less accommodating Christian moralists, such as Tertullian after he became a Montanist, this was the thin edge of the wedge. For Hermas, see "The Shepherd" in *The Apostolic Fathers*, trans. K. Lake, Loeb Classical Library, 2 vols (London, 1913), Vol. II, pp. 83–85, and for examples of early Christian perfectibilism— not necessarily typical—see the article on "Perfection (Christian)" in James Hastings, ed.: *Encyclopaedia of Religion and Ethics*, Vol. 9 (Edinburgh, 1917). As so often, the statements ascribed by Matthew to Jesus can be matched in the Old Testament (Deuteronomy 18:13 and Leviticus 19:2). But, in the more anthropomorphic and legalistic atmosphere of these utterances, the problems we are discussing in this chapter did not arise. In fact, both Noah and Job are called "perfect." If the prophets tend to emphasize the imperfection of men, there were Jewish writers who affirmed that all men can and ought to be perfect. See, for example, Ben Sira in Ecclesiasticus 15:12, 15. It is now sometimes argued that the exhortation to be perfect is not a genuine saying of Jesus but a summing up by Matthew of what he took to be Jesus' demand upon men. This, like Schweitzer's "interim ethics," is an interpretation of the situation which could only be maintained in comparatively recent times and has not affected the main historic tendencies of Christian teaching.

must be *able* to perfect themselves. So Pelagius was to argue. But Pelagius has been almost unanimously condemned as a heretic, the arch-heretic. With relatively few exceptions, Christians have denied that men are capable of becoming perfect, even with the aid of divine grace. Why this unusual degree of unanimity?

The explanation is in part metaphysical, in part moral —or more accurately, perhaps, "anthropological," in that older sense of the word in which it means "relating to the nature of men." On the metaphysical side, once Christian theologians took over what Karl Barth has called "the pagan tradition of describing God as 'simple, absolute Being,'"[2] they found it impossible, on metaphysical grounds, to ascribe godlike perfection to man. On the "anthropological" side—and much more importantly from the point of view of everyday Christian teaching—the Christian emphasis on guilt and sin, on human corruption, already strong in Paul, greatly intensified in the troubled, demon-ridden, world of North Africa and Hellenistic Rome. Man, it came to be argued, was through-and-through corrupt, by his inborn nature. This denigration of man had the effect of increasing the moral, as distinct from the metaphysical, distance between God and Man. Man begins his life with so heavy a moral handicap that it becomes ridiculous to suppose that he can attain to perfection before death overtakes him.

First, let us look at the influence of Greek metaphysics. Originally, many Christians were suspicious of Greek culture and, more particularly, of Greek philosophy. Paul had written: "Beware lest any man spoil you through philosophy and vain deceit." Celsus, writing in the second century, accuses the Christians of enjoining men thus: "Let no one

---

2. *God Here and Now,* trans. P. M. van Buren (New York, 1964), p. 13. Just when Hellenization set in I shall not attempt to say; some recent scholars think of Paul, even, as a Hellenizer, or suggest that Christianity was from the very beginning a Hellenistic sect. See, for example, Jacob Neusner, ed.: *Religions in Antiquity,* Studies in the History of Religions, XIV (Leiden, 1968).

educated, no one wise, no one sensible draw near." In his
reply to Celsus, Origen does not deny that this is an apt
enough description of a good many Christians, although
Origen's own view is that "the gospel wants us to be wise."[3]
Tertullian's outburst is notorious: "What is there in common between Athens and Jerusalem, between the Academe
and the Church? . . . For us, we have no need for curiosity,
after Jesus Christ, nor for investigation, after the Gospel!"[4]

Tertullian, however, was an extremist. And his outburst,
significantly enough, was provoked by the fact that by the
end of the second century attempts had already been made
to construct what Tertullian scornfully calls "a Christianity
of the Stoic, of the Platonist, of the Dialectician!" Once
Christianity set out to convert the educated Graeco-Roman
world it had to explain itself intellectually; at the very least,
its new converts, Greek-like, felt impelled to explain their
conversion to themselves in intellectual terms. It was em-
barrassing, no doubt, after having extolled Christianity as
"the Word," a once-and-for-all complete revelation of God
to man, to appeal for intellectual support to Plato. But there
were ways out of this difficulty. Philosophy, so Clement of
Alexandria argued, "prepares the way" for the New Testament; it was the Schoolmaster to the Greeks, just as the Old
Testament was the Schoolmaster to the Jews, and no less a
revelation.[5] In the end, indeed, the two revelations, Hebraic
and Greek, are identical: "For what is Plato," Clement asks
after Numenius, "but Moses speaking in Attic Greek?" Even
in the seventeenth century there were many who argued,

3. *Contra Celsum*, III. 44–45, trans. Chadwick, pp. 158–59.

4. *De Praescriptione Haereticorum*, vii, quoted in P. de Labriolle: *History and Literature
of Christianity from Tertullian to Boethius*, trans. H. Wilson (London, 1924), pp. 18–19, which
should be consulted generally on this question.

5. *Miscellanies* (*Stromateis*), I.28; II.18.2. See E. F. Osborn: *The Philosophy of Clement of
Alexandria* (Cambridge, 1957), pp. 122–23. "Schoolmaster" is the traditional translation
but "moral guardian" would be more accurate. The Oxford "moral tutor" is perhaps the
nearest equivalent. Clement's quotation from Numenius is in *Miscellanies*, I. 150, trans.
Osborn, p. 123.

as there is still an occasional diehard who argues, that not only Greek philosophy, but the whole of modern science, lies concealed in the revelation granted to Moses.[6] By such arguments Greek philosophy could be made respectable, not a rival but an ancillary to Revelation.

The assimilation of Hebraic thought and Greek philosophy once made, God came to be thought of not merely, in the Hebraic manner, as an immensely powerful, absolutely reliable, perfectly righteous, perfectly just, perfectly merciful Being, but as also, in Philo's manner, metaphysically perfect, as "the God of the Philosophers," identifiable with Plato's "form of the good," the "One" of Plato's *Parmenides* and the "ideal" Beauty of his *Symposium*. Then the difficulties which lie in ascribing to man a perfection like that of his Father in Heaven, while still remaining within the ambit of Christian thinking, are only too obvious. Consider, for example, Augustine's deliberately paradoxical description of God as "good without quality, great without quantity, a creator though He lacks nothing . . . in His wholeness everywhere, yet without place, eternal without time, making things that are changeable, without change of Himself, and without passion."[7] How could any man be perfect as such a God is perfect?

Indeed, under post-Platonic influence, theologians began to argue that no predicates can be applied, with the same significance, to both God and man. We have already met this view in Philo; Clement of Alexandria, writing his *Miscellanies* about the end of the second century, applied Philo's arguments to the God of Christianity. Strictly speaking, he says, even names like "the good" or "the perfect" do not apply to God. To be perfect as God is perfect, then, is

6. Harry Rimmer: *The Harmony of Science and Scripture* (Grand Rapids, 1936). In the seventeenth century this view was strongly maintained by the Cambridge Platonists, especially Henry More.

7. *De Trinitate*, V.i.2, as trans. A. W. Haddan in Vol. 7 of the 15 vols collected ed. by M. Dods (Edinburgh, 1872–76).

quite impossible; so far as God can properly be called "perfect," this cannot be in any sense in which man is capable
of perfection. The Stoics, according to Clement, were altogether mistaken in believing that human goodness could be
identical in character with divine goodness. To those who
would quote against him Jesus' command to men that they
should be perfect, Clement replies with another passage
from Matthew: "there is none good but one, that is God:
but if thou wilt enter into life, keep the commandments."[8]
The "perfection" which is demanded of all men, Clement
concludes, is not godlike perfection but to "keep the commandments"—obedientiary perfection.

Yet how differently Clement sounds when later in the
Miscellanies he writes his chapter "On Spiritual Perfection"![9]
We no longer hear how different man is from God, or how
impossible it is for man to share God's perfection. The ordinary Christian, no doubt, may have to content himself with
keeping the commandments. But "the perfected gnostic,"
the man who has reached the heights of Christian knowledge, is "assimilated to God," he has "undisturbed intercourse and communion with the Lord," he is "translated
absolutely and entirely to another sphere." There could
scarcely be a neater illustration of the two opposing tendencies in Hellenized Christianity: the one to make God so different from man that it becomes impossible to understand
how man could ever be "like God," the other so to exalt
man that complete assimilation to God lies well within his
powers—or at least within the powers of a spiritual élite.

More than a thousand years later, Aquinas reaffirmed
Clement's principle that "no name is predicated univocally

8. Matthew 19:17.
9. *Miscellanies*, VII. 3, as trans. J. B. Mayor in *Alexandrian Christianity*, ed. J. E. L. Oul-
ton and H. Chadwick, Library of Christian Classics, 2 (London, 1954), pp. 100–101. For a
discussion of the earlier argument from Bk. V of the *Miscellanies*, see Osborn: *The Philosophy
of Clement of Alexandria*, pp. 25–37.

of God and of creatures."[10] But he, too, still wanted to assert that men can, in some sense, be "like God." He tried to reconcile the two opposing tendencies in post-Platonic theology—one to insist on God's unlikeness to man, the other to insist on the possibility of man's becoming like God—in a somewhat remarkable way. Human beings can be like God, he argues, even although it "can in no way be admitted that God is like creatures."[11] Aquinas denies, that is, that likeness is a symmetrical relationship. "A statue," he says, "is like a man, but not conversely."* The outcome of this argument is that although man can achieve a perfection which is in some analogical sense "like" God's perfection, he cannot be perfect *as* God is perfect; he cannot even satisfy that less ambitious injunction of Luke's to be merciful as God is merciful.

God's goodness, as Aquinas sees the matter, is unified in a way in which human goodness cannot be unified; Aquinas ascribes to God alone that unified goodness which the Stoics allowed to the Sage. Men achieve their goodness, so Aquinas argues, not, as God does, simply by being, but "through many things"; a man, unlike God, can be good in one respect and not in others. The human being, too, cannot stand alone; he is "incomplete" without his relationship to God. He lacks, that is, the self-sufficiency which Aquinas, Greek-wise, assumes to be essential to perfection.[12] In short, if men are ever to be accounted perfect, they certainly cannot be perfect as their Father in heaven is perfect; the Stoics

---

10. *Summa theologica,* Pt. I, q. 13, a. 5.

11. *Ibid.,* Pt. I, q. 4, a. 3.

* We may well be dissatisfied with Aquinas's argument on this point, which confuses, on the face of it, between the relation "is a likeness of," which is admittedly asymmetrical, and the symmetrical relationship of likeness. A man, no doubt, is not "a likeness of" a statue—something made in order to be like a statue—but it does not follow that he is not *like* a statue. "How like he is to that famous bust of Socrates" is a remark we might well make of a man. But Aquinas is working with a very strange semi-causal concept of "likeness," derived from "Saint Dionysius."

12. *Summa contra gentiles,* III. 20.

were wholly mistaken in supposing that they could achieve that level of perfection.

There was, on the face of it, one obvious way of preserving, when confronted by this difficulty, something at least of the force of the commandment to be perfect as God is perfect. Jesus did not say: "Be ye perfect even as *I* am perfect." But once he was taken, in however obscure a sense, to *be* God,* it might have seemed reasonable enough to think of Jesus, himself a man, as the pattern which, except in so far as his behaviour involved the use of supernatural powers, men should attempt to imitate. The idea of such a perfect exemplar was a quite familiar one, both to Hebrew and to Greek thought; Jesus could take the place of Abraham or of Socrates. And does not Jesus speak of himself as setting an example?[13]

The idea of imitating Jesus, of following his example, certainly plays a central part in Christianity. One of the most highly esteemed of medieval Christian devotional writings bears the title *The Imitation of Christ;* the imitation of Christ is, for its author, the task all men are called upon to undertake, their way of acquiring merit in the eyes of God. "The imitation of Christ," on this view, gives content to the concept of "task-perfection," it sets the task. And although Calvin, to take an example of a very different kind, entirely rejects the central assumption of *The Imitation of Christ*, denying that the Christian can "acquire merit," whether by imi-

---

* I do not know how to state the Christian view on this matter. To take too literally John's "I and my Father are one" (10:30) is clearly heretical. The Sabellian doctrine that monotheism can be preserved only on the supposition that God the Father died on the cross forms no part of Christian orthodoxy. The reader must interpret for himself my assertion that Jesus was taken to *be* God; I shall not venture to explain to him what, if anything, it means. Let him turn for that purpose to the theologians, to Augustine on the Trinity, to Aquinas, or to a host of modern commentators. The expression "Jesus was taken to be the Eternal Word" can, if any reader thinks it more perspicuous, be substituted without harm to my argument for "was taken to be God."

13. John 13:15. For a detailed discussion of "Jesus Christ, the Pattern" see James M. Gustafson: *Christ and the Moral Life* (New York, 1968), pp. 150–87.

tating Christ or by any other means, the imitation of Christ continues to be of central importance to him. Through our sufferings and tribulations we come to an assurance, according to Calvin, that we are at one with Christ, are living Christ's life. "We share Christ's sufferings," he writes, "in order that as he has passed from a labyrinth of all evils into heavenly glory, we may in like manner be led through various tribulations to the same glory. . . . The more we are afflicted with adversities, the more surely our fellowship with Christ is confirmed." No one, he elsewhere asserts, can properly claim to be a disciple of Christ unless he is prepared to imitate Christ. For Calvin, however, such imitation, which is not a means to salvation but a consequence of it, is restricted to self-renunciation and "the voluntary suffering of the Cross"; there is no question of man's being able to imitate Christ's moral perfections.[14]

There are, indeed, great difficulties in the idea of "becoming perfect as Jesus was perfect," if this is taken to mean anything more than imitating him by "taking up our cross." Some of them are theological. One has only to read Aquinas's account of the relationship between Jesus and God—Jesus having, for example, two intellects, two wills and, in general, two natures while remaining one person*—to see what theological problems can arise in setting up Jesus as a model suitable for humanity to follow.[15] To say that man must be perfect as Jesus' human nature is perfect is to abandon the ideal of being perfect as God is perfect; to say

14. For the first passage from Calvin see *Institutes of the Christian Religion*, III. viii. 1, trans. F. L. Battles, 2 vols, Library of Christian Classics, 20, 21 (London, 1961), Vol. 1, p. 702. For the second reference see *Commentary on Matthew*, 16. 24, as quoted in F. Wendel: *Calvin*, trans. P. Mairet (London, 1963; paperback ed. 1965), p. 250.

* The opposite, "monophysite," doctrine that Jesus had only one nature, and that divine, was, however, extremely powerful in the fifth-century Church, especially in Alexandria. Formally condemned by the Council of Chalcedon in 451, it remains the official teaching of the Coptic and the Armenian Church. On this view the imitation of Jesus would, quite unambiguously, be the imitation of God.

15. *Compendium of Theology*, ch. 212, as trans. C. Vollert, pp. 235–39.

that man must be perfect as Jesus' divine nature is perfect merely revives the original difficulties. In any case, these "two natures" are not, for orthodoxy, to be thought of as wholly disconnected. Even Jesus' earthly body is "divinized" in a way which makes him inimitable; his actions, too, are informed by a degree of charity which lies beyond man's reach. In the thirteenth century Bonaventura argued, indeed, that considered as external actions capable of being imitated by men, many of Jesus' actions are imperfect. It would be quite wrong, on this view, for men to take them as their standard.[16]

That view of Christianity which takes the path to perfection to lie in the "imitation of Christ" very easily leads, furthermore, to heterodoxy.* A modern Roman Catholic theologian, Louis Bouyer, has remarked that however Christian its intentions, it leads to "a view of Christ in which the divine would appear as nothing more than the ideal of perfection that could be readily conceded to exist in a human nature conceived of exclusively within the lines of our own experience."[17] It suggests, that is, that Jesus' divinity is merely con-

---

16. For details see Gordon Leff: *Heresy in the Later Middle Ages,* 2 vols (Manchester, 1967), Vol. 1, pp. 85–86.

* A less extreme view is that the imitation of Jesus is no more than a preliminary stage on the path to true Christian virtue. So although Bernard of Clairvaux begins by insisting on the need for imitating Christ as "a man meek and lowly of heart, kind and collected, chaste and pitiful, conspicuous for all goodness and sanctity" he goes on to argue that "although such devotion to the flesh of Christ is a gift, . . . nevertheless I call it carnal in comparison with that love which does not [so much] regard the Word which is Flesh, as the Word which is Wisdom, Justice, Truth, Holiness." Man cannot *perfect* himself, that is, by imitating Jesus. See R. N. Flew: *The Idea of Perfection in Christian Theology* (Oxford, 1934; repr. 1968), pp. 220–22. Views which to a theologically unsophisticated observer look very similar to this have, however, been condemned as heresy. See R. A. Knox: *Enthusiasm* (Oxford, 1950; corr. repr. 1951). The path of orthodoxy is, indeed, a narrow one. Mystics have disagreed about whether even the image of Christ on the Cross is, at the last stages in mysticism, a distraction. Teresa denied that it was, but knew that she stood somewhat alone on this point.

17. The quotation is from the article "Jesus Christ" in Louis Bouyer: *Dictionary of Theology,* trans. C. U. Quinn (New York, 1966), pp. 250–51. For a fuller discussion of the effects of devotion to a *human* Jesus, see L. Bouyer: *Liturgical Piety* (Notre Dame, Ind., 1955), espe-

tingent: as if it would be proper to compare him with Buddha, with Socrates, with Confucius, and ask which is the morally better man, and which, therefore, it will be better to imitate. An unorthodox modern theologian, P. M. van Buren, has asked, indeed, whether a humanist might not speak of himself as being "in Socrates" just as an evangelical does of being "in Christ."[18]

Matthew Arnold might no doubt write in his *Antidesperation:*

> Was Christ a man like us?—Ah! let us try
> If we then, too, can be such men as he!

But Arnold's definition of religion in *Literature and Dogma* as "morality touched by emotion" would satisfy few Christians. (It is interesting to observe just how often Arnold refers to *The Imitation of Christ.*) Abelard thought that Christ died on the Cross to set men an example of how they should behave, rather than as a sacrifice on their behalf. But Abelard was condemned as a heretic. John Stuart Mill wrote that "it is Christ, rather than God, whom Christianity has held up to believers as the pattern of perfection for humanity." But the advantage he sees in this, that Christ serves as a model "even to the absolute unbeliever," is unlikely to recommend itself to orthodox Christians.[19] Criticizing Teilhard de Chardin, a Roman Catholic theologian has discovered in his system "a certain aroma of Pelagianism" on the ground that for Teilhard "Christ is a guide, a model, a trainer," rather than "the Saviour, the Source of grace, the only Mediator between

---

cially pp. 247–50. Compare, for a similar Protestant view, Karl Barth's discussion of D. F. Strauss in *From Rousseau to Ritschl,* trans. B. Cozens (London, 1959), ch. x, pp. 362–89.

18. See P. M. van Buren: *The Secular Meaning of the Gospel* (London, 1963; repr. 1965), pp. 138–39.

19. *Three Essays on Religion: Nature, The Utility of Religion, Theism* (London, 1904), p. 106.

God and Man."[20] When heterodox theologians pronounce that "God is dead" all they sometimes mean is that although the Christian story "may manage to stay on as merely illuminating or instructing or guiding, . . . it no longer performs its classical functions of salvation or redemption."[21] And indeed Christianity, if not God, is dead, if "the Christian story" is merely a guide to behaviour. To become perfect, for orthodox Christians, it is not enough to look with admiration at the human life of Jesus as any secularist might do, and then set out to imitate him: it is to be redeemed by his sacrifice, and then perfected by his grace. Jesus is not a "hero" in the Greek sense; he is God, or "the Word made flesh," come to earth to save men from their sins—a most un-Olympian conception.

There was another possible way out for Christianity, a way of preserving, as intelligible, the commandment that men should make themselves perfect as God is perfect. Christianity might have gone the whole way and neo-Platonized itself. It might have emerged as the view that man can perfect himself by ceasing to be man, by absorbing himself into the Deity. Jesus could easily enough have been fitted into this picture, by means of the Graeco-Jewish conception of the Logos.* He is, it might have been said, the Logos made flesh—serving to demonstrate to all men, by way of example, that although they are in the flesh they can still hope, if only by the sacrifice of that flesh, to become God.

This was a real temptation for Christianity. Just how real can be seen by considering the case of "Dionysius the Areopagite" or, as he is sometimes called, "pseudo-Denys." Dio-

---

20. Nicolas Corte: *Pierre Teilhard de Chardin*, trans. M. Jarrett-Kerr (London, 1960), p. 94, referring to the criticisms of the abbé Louis Cognet.

21. T. J. J. Altizer and William Hamilton: *Radical Theology and the Death of God* (New York, 1966), p. x.

* There was a time, not long ago, when it was generally presumed that the doctrine of the Logos was entirely Greek in origin. It is now recognized that there was a late-Jewish Logos doctrine. The Greek and the Jewish doctrines were not identical but they were eventually assimilated to one another, if not by John then at least in subsequent theology.

nysius was a Christian neo-Platonist of the fifth century, author, amongst other works, of a *Divine Names* in which he examines the nature and attributes of God, and a *Mystical Theology* which describes the ascent of the soul to mystical union with God. He was wrongly identified—or identified himself, there is some disagreement on this point—not only with that Dionysius whose conversion to Christianity by Paul is recorded in the New Testament[22] but with Denys, the French martyr.

After his translation into Latin by John Scotus Erigena in the ninth century,[23] Dionysius exerted an extraordinarily powerful influence on medieval theology, especially in its mystical and negative forms. Not until the sixteenth century was it generally recognized, and even then by no means universally admitted, that Dionysius was, in fact, a fifth-century heretic. In his *Summa theologica*—and especially in the section entitled "Treatise on God"—Aquinas refers to him constantly. Dionysius, indeed, is his principal "Platonic" source. Without Dionysius' authority, it would have been far more difficult for Christian mysticism to maintain its orthodoxy; his writings were, as it has been put, "the charter of Christian mysticism." When, as we shall see later, the Spanish mystic, John of the Cross, was denounced to the Inquisition as a heretic, his defender, the Professor of Theology in the University of Salamanca, appealed to "Saint Dionysius" as compelling evidence that John's mysticism did not pass beyond the limits of orthodoxy.

22. Acts 17:34.

23. There may have been earlier translations but it was Erigena who did most to bring Dionysius to the attention of theologians. His own *De divisione naturae* is profoundly influenced by Dionysius. For a detailed study of the influence of Dionysius on a particular Christian mystic see F. von Hügel: *The Mystical Element of Religion as Studied in Saint Catherine of Genoa and Her Friends,* 2 vols (London, 1908; repr. 1961), Vol. II, pp. 90–101. Dionysius himself can be read in *Dionysius the Areopagite on the Divine Names and the Mystical Theology,* trans. and ed. C. E. Rolt, 2nd ed. (London, 1940; repr. 1957). All references are to this translation. The historical detail on the role of Dionysius derives, in part, from the *Oxford Dictionary of the Christian Church,* ed. F. L. Cross (London, 1957).

God, for Dionysius, is "super-essential," transcending all "Discourse, Intuition and Being." We achieve a knowledge of "It," in this super-essential character, only by "unknowing," by mystical apprehension. (One of the most famous of English mystical writings is called *The Cloud of Unknowing;* it appeals to Dionysius as an authority who "clearly endorses all I have said, or will say, from beginning to end.")[24] The Scriptures, Dionysius admits, appear to describe God's nature in everyday language, but they do not speak of God as he is revealed to the mystic. They describe God in language which is suitable for the limited comprehension of the ordinary, unenlightened, man—as when they speak of God as the "Cause and Origin and Being and Life of all creation." In contrast, "any lover of that Truth which is above all truth" must not "celebrate [God] as Reason or Power or Mind or Life or Being, but rather as most utterly surpassing all condition, movement, life, imagination, conjecture, name, discourse, thought, conception, being, rest, dwelling, union, limit, infinity, everything that exists."[25]

The Scriptures use symbols, material symbols, to convey to an élite what cannot be said directly. By means of symbols they tell men, in particular, that God is "a Principle of Perfection to them that are being perfected; a principle of Deity to them that are being deified."[26] Dionysius is prepared to assert, that is, that men can be perfected and even deified. Man, in the neo-Platonic style, is one of the "emanations" of Dionysius' super-essential God. And as an emanation of God he can finally return to God. There is, according to Dionysius, "a perpetual circle for the Good, from the Good, in the Good, and to the Good . . . perpetually advancing and remaining and returning to Itself"—an ethical

---

24. From the translation into modern English by Clifton Wolters (Harmondsworth, 1961), ch. 70.

25. *Dionysius on the Divine Names*, pp. 55, 60.

26. *Ibid.,* p. 55.

procession which was to haunt the imagination of medieval mystics.[27]

It is not necessary to continue. The general character of Dionysius' thinking is by now sufficiently clear. Equally clear, in consequence, is the temptation of neo-Platonic ideas for Christians. If we ask: "Why did not Christianity convert itself into a variety of neo-Platonism?" one possible reply is that, in the writings of many of its theologians, it did so. But that reply would not be wholly accurate. Reading Dionysius, and recalling that for centuries no difficulty was felt in supposing his writings to be the work of a saint of the Roman Catholic Church, reading John Scotus Erigena and recalling that his orthodoxy was for long unquestioned, reading Aquinas, even, on the names of God, we may be inclined to conclude, with so many Protestants, that Roman Catholic orthodoxy allowed itself to be wholly overwhelmed by an essentially non-Christian neo-Platonism.* It is not surprising that Martin Luther exhorted his followers "to detest as a veritable plague this *Mystical Theology* of Dionysius and

---

27. *Ibid.,* p. 107. See the extraordinary diagram from the fourteenth-century mystic Heinrich Suso in A. Nygren: *Agape and Eros,* trans. P. S. Watson, rev. 1-vol. ed. (London, 1953; repr. 1957), facing p. 616.

* On this point, it is illuminating to read the account of Dionysius (Pt. I, ch. ix) and of Erigena (Pt. II, ch. xii–xiii) in the Jesuit historian F. Copleston's *History of Philosophy,* Vol. II (London, 1950). He admits that what Dionysius says about the Trinity is "questionable" and that he has very little to say about the Incarnation. Quite without irony, however, he goes on to remark that it does not seem possible to reject Dionysius's views on the Incarnation as "definitely unorthodox" unless "one is prepared also to reject as unorthodox, for example, the mystical doctrine of St. John of the Cross, who is a Doctor of the Church" (p. 92). In the end, however, Copleston is prepared to admit that there is a tension in the thinking of Dionysius between his neo-Platonism and his genuine Christianity. He expresses doubt, too, whether his writings would have exercised the influence they did exercise, had it not been for the supposition that he was Paul's Dionysius. Copleston finds a similar "tension" in Erigena. He does not dispute Erigena's condemnation by the ecclesiastical authorities—this was not until 1210, three and a half centuries after the publication of his *De divisione naturae*—but writes of him with sympathy. Indeed, to condemn Erigena outright and *in toto* would be to condemn, at the same time, a great body of Roman Catholic mystical writings. And Copleston is perfectly correct in saying that neither Dionysius nor Erigena allow themselves to go completely over to neo-Platonism, close though they come to doing so.

similar works," condemning it as "pure fables and lies" and "sheer nonsense," the work of a man who is quite obviously a disciple of Plato, not of Christ.[28] (It is important to remember that Luther himself greatly admired the mystical *Theologia Germanica,* a work which appeals to "Saint Dionysius" as one of its principal authorities and in its opening chapter describes God, in Dionysian terms, as "Nothing." Luther knew what he was rejecting.)

Yet, even at its most Platonic, Christianity does not wholly neo-Platonize itself. For Christianity, however Hellenized, is a Jewish religion. Against paganism, Clement of Alexandria sets not philosophy but "the voice of the Divine Word," the Jewish lesson that men "could not be saved in any other way but by believing."[29] To think of Christianity as a whole as a misshapen offshoot of Greek philosophy is quite to misunderstand its nature as a religion—however accurate a description that may be of a good deal of Roman Catholic theology.

The Jews were not philosophers; they were quite devoid of that speculative curiosity which characterized the Greeks, their habit of asking how and why. No Xenophanes arose amongst the Jews to rebuke them for ascribing to Jahweh acts which would be accounted a shame and a disgrace amongst men;* no Socrates to ask them to define righteous-

---

28. The relevant passages are collected in A. Nygren: *Agape and Eros,* pp. 705–6. Calvin's attitude was very similar.

29. *Exhortation to the Greeks,* trans. G. W. Butterworth in the Loeb Classical Library selection of his works (London, 1919), pp. 189–91.

* It is by no means surprising, however, that many Christians were perturbed over this point. To read the Old Testament literally, Origen argued, as a record of God's actions would be to conclude that God is worse than "the most savage and unjust of men" (*De principiis,* IV, ii, I). In the second century the Marcionite heresy spread like wildfire through the Christian world; it is sometimes suggested, indeed, that had it not forbidden marriage, and hence reduced the number of its adherents, it would have conquered the world. It rejected the Old Testament as describing the deeds of a God who was not a God of love, and therefore not the Christian God. Indeed, it admitted as truly Christian only—and then in an expurgated form—Luke's gospel and the Pauline Epistles, with their characteristic antitheses between Law and Love. Had Marcion succeeded, there would have been no obstacle to the Hellenizing of Christianity. But the Old Testament was too

ness, or justice, or to explain why Noah and Job should be accounted perfect; no Parmenides, in particular, to inquire how God stood in relation to the world. The Jews were innocent of systematic theology, of ethical theory, of cosmology. Philo, writing in the first century in cosmopolitan Alexandria, was their first philosopher—although admittedly his thinking, in part, grew out of post-Exilic Rabbinical speculation—and their last for a thousand years. Philo's influence, certainly, Christianity was to feel. But in the Old Testament writings as they stood, read literally, not allegorically as Philo read them, there were no philosophical theories to be found.

There were, however, doctrines of a kind to be extracted from the Old Testament. If there was not an ethical theory, there were certainly moral reflections; if not a cosmology, then at least a creation story; if not a theology, then at any rate a special assumption about God and his relation to man. These reflections, stories and assumptions had a permanent effect on Christian theories of perfectibility, however much, in the outcome, they were to be modified and reinterpreted in the light of Greek speculations and the sacramental practices of the mystery religions.

In some ways, the most influential Jewish idea of all, and the least Greek, was the idea of a sacred book, holy scriptures, a solitary and complete source of revelation, given by God to Moses—or at least, for there is dispute on this point, to Moses and his successors. This was to act as a permanent restraint on Christian, as on Muslim, theological speculation. No doubt, there were Greek analogues. The writings of Homer and Hesiod were usually regarded, Xenophanes and

---

valuable as a source of prophecies to be lightly discarded. The point, above all, which distinguished Christianity from its alternatives, the manifold mystery-religions of the Hellenistic world, was that its God-Man had been *prophesied*. Compare Justin Martyr's use of the prophecies—for all that Jews might grumble that the lion had not lain down with the lamb—in his speech to the Emperor Hadrian. "The First Apology," trans. E. R. Hardy, in *Early Christian Fathers*, ed. C. C. Richardson, Library of Christian Classics, I (London, 1953), pp. 260–77.

Plato notwithstanding, with special veneration; Plotinus was unwilling to disagree outright with Plato. The fact remains that Greek speculation was never seriously restrained by the belief that the final truth, about the perfectibility of man or about anything else, must somehow be contained in a special revelation. Aristotle's famous dictum that he could not love Plato so well, did he not love the truth more, may stand as representative of the attitude of the best Greek thinkers. In the teachings of the Bible, in contrast, it is necessary to have faith, utter and uncritical confidence, a conception quite alien to the spirit of Greek philosophy.*

Christian disputes about perfectibility, therefore, are in part—in a manner very disconcerting to a philosopher—a battle of texts. The true view, it is presumed, must at least be consistent with what has been revealed in Scripture, and ought, in so fundamental a matter, to be deducible from it. Thus internecine Christian controversies move within a kind of "Biblical space," its limits determined by Biblical texts. The boundaries of this Biblical space, to make matters even more awkward, are themselves contested. The meaning of individual texts is anything but clear; their right to be accounted a genuine part of the sacred writings may be a matter of dispute. Some Christians, furthermore, are prepared to read Biblical texts allegorically in the manner of Philo and Origen, as symbols rather than as historical records; others, not going so far as this, reserve the right to read them in ways which, they freely admit, were not specifically intended by their authors; for still others the

---

* For classical Greek philosophy, as for Plato, faith (*pistis*) is the lowest form of belief, characteristic only of the wholly uneducated, who fail to reflect critically on what they experience or are told. The Jewish-inspired Christian emphasis on faith struck educated pagan observers with astonishment; it represented, in their eyes, the extreme of anti-intellectualism—"foolishness." It was not long, no doubt, before Christianity itself began to place more stress on intellectual argument, to a degree which eventually provoked the Lutheran counter-reaction, with its emphasis on the primacy of faith. But at its most intellectual, Christianity still has to appeal to faith, to have recourse to "mysteries." Compare E. R. Dodds: *Pagan and Christian in an Age of Anxiety*, pp. 150–53.

Bible must be taken literally, read in a manner which rules out special interpretations or allegorizing. But however subject to adjustment, the Biblical boundaries act as a restraint upon every Christian—and for the Greeks there were no comparable boundaries.

The second important fact about the Hebrew religion is that its God is a person, a person it is appropriate to describe as merciful, just, righteous, wrathful. The general tendency of Greek philosophy was, in contrast, to depersonalize the idea of divinity: at first, as in the Ionian physicists, the Olympian Gods; eventually, as in Plotinus, the God of the Orphic-style religions. Something of the same kind happened, no doubt, within the Hebrew religion, especially after the Exile and not impossibly under Greek influence. In Rabbinic speculation God is progressively de-anthropomorphized; he no longer acts upon the world directly but rather—in the manner Philo described—through his "Spirit" or his "Word." But he remained a *person,* the Father of his people, providentially active in their history. "Wholly remote from Jewish thought," as G. F. Moore puts it, "is the idea of God as pure and simple *being,* in his proper nature an unknowable and unnamable Absolute." [30]

The depersonalization of God, towards which Christian theology is certainly tempted, can take either of two forms—"substantial" depersonalization or "conceptual" depersonalization. "Substantial" depersonalization consists in converting God into "the One," the substance of substances, entirely self-sufficient, wholly unified, absolutely simple. This is the path taken by Parmenides and Plotinus. "Conceptual" depersonalization consists in turning God not into a substance, but into an abstract concept, a pure quality. So Augustine said of God that we must think of him not as

---

30. *Judaism in the First Centuries of the Christian Era,* 3 vols (Cambridge, Mass., 1927–30; repr. 1962), Vol. I, p. 361. For the post-Exilic "metaphysicalising" of God see Charles Guignebert: *The Jewish World in the Time of Jesus,* Bk. II, ch. 1.

merciful but as Mercy. The awkwardness in asserting of God
both that he *is* Being and that he *is* Mercy or Justice is met
by denying that the substance-quality distinction applies to
God. But the total effect is, to say the least of it, confusing in
the extreme. It is not at all clear what precisely we are being
asked to do when we are told "to think of God as Mercy."

The source of the conceptualizing of God is Plato, although Plato did not himself conceptualize God; he speaks
of him not as a Form but as knowing or apprehending
Forms. But "the form of the good" looked, to Christian
theologians, like their God, and they were even more impressed, as were the neo-Platonists, by Plato's account of
Beauty in the *Symposium*. Plato there describes, professing
to quote Diotima, priestess of the mystery religions, man's
yearning for Beauty and the way in which it finally finds satisfaction. Beginning from the love for one particular body,
the man in search of beauty rises, according to Plato, from
that particular object to a love of beautiful bodies in general. From that point he rises still further to "set a higher
value on the beauty of souls than on that of the body," and
then, higher again, to admire the beauty of human society
and of human knowledge. Even at that point he cannot find
rest; he must pass on, rising still higher on the ladder of
being, until he is able to contemplate "essential beauty entire, pure and unalloyed; not infected with the flesh and
colour of humanity." By that means he can come to achieve
immortality and "win the friendship of Heaven."[31]

There is not the slightest suggestion in this passage that
Beauty is to be identified with, or even that it characterizes,
God; as in the *Phaedo*, men become like the gods by contemplating the forms, but *the forms are not themselves gods*. Yet
when a modern Thomistic theologian, Garrigou-Lagrange,
quotes this passage he does so in order to illustrate what
he calls "the natural love for God" and he imports into his

---

31. As trans. W. R. Lamb, Loeb Classical Library (London, 1925), 210c–212.

translation a reference to "a man who attains to the contemplation of God" which has absolutely no place in the text.* So attached are theologians to this most un-Christian, most Platonic, description of human perfection! Of persons it is proper to say that they are merciful, just, loving, but certainly not, except as an extravagant metaphor, that they are mercy, justice, love. Indeed, if it were true that "God is Love" then God ceases to be loving; love cannot love, any more than justice can be just, or mercy merciful. Only people, not concepts, can love. If God is a person, then it is necessary to abandon any attempt to identify him with concepts.

Even although Christianity tended—in its theology as distinct from its religious practices—to depersonalize God, it is normally pulled back from the verge of describing God as suprapersonal, in the neo-Platonic manner, just in virtue of its adherence to Revelation. So for all that Aquinas so often writes of God in neo-Platonic terms he still argues that the "proper name" of the supreme being is "He-who-is," not "the One." Clement may write of the problem of naming "It"—not "Him"; Dionysius may speak of our "super-essential understanding of 'It' "; God may be described by Anselm as "id quo maius cogitari nequit"—"that *thing* than which nothing greater is thinkable." But Aquinas is on more orthodox, if perhaps less consistent, ground in describing God as "He." In the long run Revelation conquers neo-Platonism. "Being like God" or "entering into union with

---

* *The One God, ed. cit.,* p. 329. Garrigou-Lagrange or his translator, it is fair to add, brackets the passage in question, but in round, not square, brackets which do not make it clear that it is an interpolation. And even if it is only intended as a gloss, the fact remains that there is nothing whatever in the text to justify the gloss. Theologians now generally agree—it is interesting to observe—that Augustine's mystical visions were Platonic rather than Christian. There are some dissentients on this point, as is only to be expected since Augustine is not the only Christian to express his vision in Platonic terms, but the point is difficult to controvert, in the light of the language Augustine uses. Compare Gerald Bonner: *St. Augustine of Hippo* (London, 1963), and, on the other side, Cuthbert Butler: *Western Mysticism,* 2nd ed. (London, 1926).

God" consists in perfecting oneself *as a person,* not in ceasing to be a person. But the opposite view—that personality must be cast off—is by no means unknown in Christianity; classical mysticism, to say the very least, has trouble in avoiding the Buddhist and neo-Platonic view that so long as I remain "I," I cannot achieve perfection.

Thirdly, Christianity took over from the Old Testament a conception of God and his relationship to the world which has no precise parallel in Greek thought, which denied, indeed, what seemed to the Greeks obvious—that "out of nothing nothing can be made." Not that the Old Testament ever made so metaphysical a remark as that "the world was created out of nothing." But this is how Christian theologians, at least from the second century on, interpreted such texts as "God said, Let there be light: and there was light." "Thou didst speak," wrote Augustine, "and they [heaven and earth] were made." [32] The neo-Platonic doctrine that men and the world are created by a mere overflow of God's goodness as distinct from a divine act, the Orthodox Christian must condemn as heresy.

The Hebraic view, thus understood, raises in a particularly acute form the question: "Why are not men perfect?" The imperfection of men can no longer be explained, as Greek thinkers explained it, either as a consequence of the bungling incompetence of God's coadjutors, since he had none, or the imperfections of the materials on which he had to work, since he created out of nothing, or his own limitations as a creator, since he was omnipotent. Dissident theists, like William James, have sometimes been attracted by one or the other of these Greek hypotheses—the view that God's powers are limited had quite a run among philosophers in the latter half of the nineteenth century— but they certainly lie on the remotest periphery of Christian thinking. The alternative, Zoroastrian, hypothesis that

---

32. *Confessions,* XI. v. The text is Genesis 1:3.

all the world's evils are the work of Satan and his minions came to the fore in post-Exilic Jewish thinking, and was profoundly to influence Christianity. But it threatened, if taken too seriously, to weaken God's supremacy. It came to be associated, too, with heresy, with such powerful heresy as Manichaeanism. Satan could be allowed some influence over men, but it would not do to explain their imperfection solely by reference to his wiles.

God, Christians also learnt from the Old Testament prophets, exercises a constant watchfulness not only over the world as a whole, but over each and every individual it contains, a doctrine to which even the Stoics were hesitant to commit themselves. "For the ways of man are before the eyes of the Lord and he pondereth all his goings."[33] In Jewish thought, the point of this remark was moral, not metaphysical; men cannot hide their sins from God. But why then, it is natural to ask, does he not save men from themselves? Why, even if men are born imperfect, does he not take steps to ensure that they will perfect themselves?

Christian theologians tried to solve this problem by taking over and refashioning another Old Testament idea— the idea of an elect. In the Old Testament, the elect were a nation, the Jewish nation, chosen not because they possessed any special merit but simply because God had picked them out as his own: "Not for thy righteousness, or for the uprightness of thine heart, dost thou go to possess their land."[34] For the Greeks, in contrast, if men—individuals or a nation—were "elect," this was as a consequence of their merits. Even Philo, as we have already seen, describes grace as a reward for merit.[35]

In the later prophetic writings, the idea of a chosen nation is transformed into the idea of a chosen people—

---

33. Proverbs 16:2.
34. Deuteronomy 9:5. See also Deuteronomy 7:6–8.
35. See pp. 87–88 above for grace in Greek thought.

who need not form part of a single national group. It is in this form that it was taken over by Christianity: the "chosen people" is the Church, the Body of Christ. And that in turn was converted into the idea of chosen "individuals," granted a special grace by God, over and above the grace granted to all Christians. The importance of this fundamentally Jewish idea of "election" can scarcely be overestimated, particularly when it was interpreted as implying that men could make progress towards perfection *only* as a consequence of such divine election. God saves men from themselves, and in no other way can they be saved. If he does not save everybody this is either because—there is dispute on this point— he has chosen to save only a few, or because some men refuse the grace he offers them. Whether he ever carries his "saving" even of his elect to the point of perfecting them in this life is, as we shall see, also a matter of dispute. But certainly, on the Christian view, if he does not, men have no hope of perfecting themselves.

The God of the Old Testament is not only an elective but a "jealous" God, not only supreme but solitary in his divinity. Man, therefore, cannot perfect himself, on the Hebraic view, by becoming divine, by being transformed into a lesser god, as even relatively monotheistic Greek philosophers were prepared to allow. For the Greeks, the characteristic of "being divine"—"being deathless"—was the important one; it was a matter of detail to how many persons that predicate is applicable. For the Jews, as the Christians ordinarily understood the Old Testament, the central presumption was that there was *one particular person* who alone could properly be called God.*

---

* There is considerable argument as to whether, or from what point on, Judaism was strictly monotheistic. "Thou shalt worship no other God but me" certainly does not imply "there is no other God but me"—it suggests the contrary. This is what G. F. Moore calls "practical monotheism," as distinct from "theoretical monotheism." (Compare, too, "for the Lord your God is God of gods" in Deuteronomy 10:17.) My sole concern is with what Christians thought they read in the Old Testament, not with the complex history of Judaism. For Christians, until very recently, the Old Testament was essentially one book, even

Of course, a man might become a saint. No doubt, too, saints in the Roman Catholic Church performed many of the functions which the Greeks ascribed to minor deities, serving, for example, as the "household gods" of churches, communities, or individual persons, and taking over particular minor responsibilities, as Antony of Padua takes a special responsibility for the return of lost property. But a saint, all the same, is not a god—even if he may play a larger part in the religious consciousness of, let us say, a Neapolitan than the more austere figure of God himself. (For the French peasant, it has been said, the Trinity consists of Mary, Joseph and Jesus. In describing Roman Catholic "orthodoxy" one is often a long way from describing what the majority of Roman Catholics actually believe.)

The Old Testament God, furthermore, is a God who stands alone, and is eternally distinguishable from his creation. Men cannot in any sense become part of God, or unite themselves with God in a single Being: God and his creatures remain for ever distinct. No doubt, there have been temptations, on this point, to heterodoxy. The ideal of unity with God reasserts itself within Christian mysticism. Even Charles Wesley, though certainly no pantheist, could permit himself to write in a hymn:

> Till all my hallow'd soul be thine;
> Plung'd in the Godhead's deepest sea,
> And lost in thine immensity!

But the main tendency of Christianity remains resolutely Hebraic in its separation of God from his creatures.

---

although the word "Bible" derives from the plural Greek "biblia"—books. The idea that it was the history of a *developing* religion is a relatively new one, which the Jews themselves would have entirely rejected. If Christians noted the plural "us" of Genesis 3:22—"And behold the man is become as one of us"—or observed that "Elohim," generally translated "God," has a plural form, they either concluded that this is a "royal plural" or else, in Eusebius's manner, that it was the Trinity who were being thus plurally referred to. (Astonishingly enough, Eusebius takes almost all his Biblical evidence for the Trinity from the Old Testament.)

If we ask, then, why Christianity did not become neo-Platonic, one answer is that it was committed, by its adherence to Revelation, to a set of beliefs which were essentially opposed to neo-Platonism: the belief in a personal God, creating the world by an act of will, wholly distinct from it, and exercising within it his grace. So far as it was faithful to these teachings, Christianity could not accept a neo-Platonic theory of perfection, a perfection which men could achieve by their own strivings and which consisted in returning to the One from which they had emanated.

There was a particular reason why Christianity found it necessary to take a determined stand against perfectibility. It had to distinguish itself from Gnosticism. The exact relationship of Gnosticism to Christianity is still a matter of dispute. It used to be supposed that Gnosticism was a form of Christian heresy; the sects which the Church Fathers attack as "gnostic" certainly incorporated Christian doctrines. But gnostic *ideas* ante-date Christianity, perhaps as Jewish heresies, even if it is only after the rise of Christianity that gnosticism took shape, in the teachings of Valentinus or Basileides, as a mythological system.[36] Clement of Alexandria opposed it with particular vigour, as did Plotinus—with the more vigour because they stood so close to it in so many respects. Certain members of Plotinus's own intellectual circle were, it would seem, gnostic; there are ideas in the *Enneads* which it is not easy to distinguish from Gnosticism. As for Clement, he, as we have already seen, had been prepared to employ the word "gnostic" to describe the fully-fledged Christian. Indeed, Christianity of the Platonic sort was very liable to find itself confused with Gnosticism, or to be unconsciously influenced by it, and found it all the more necessary sharply to distinguish itself from it.

36. See R. McL. Wilson: *The Gnostic Problem* (London, 1958) and, for an indication just how little can, in discussing Gnosticism, be taken for granted, Ugo Bianchi, ed.: *Le Origini dello Gnosticismo,* Studies in the History of Religions, XII (Leiden, 1967)—a symposium containing essays in German, French, Italian and English.

Over the last two thousand years, Gnosticism, under a variety of influences, has assumed a number of different forms—as Manichaeanism, Catharism, the Brotherhood of the Free Spirit, to say nothing of twentieth-century sects. What in all these versions it has insisted upon is that men *can* be perfected and that to achieve perfection they must purify themselves by complete aloofness from the flesh, from whatever is material, with the help of a higher knowledge—"gnosis"—accessible only to true believers. "Born of light and of the gods," runs a Gnostic poem, "I am in exile and cut off from them . . . I am a god, and born of gods, shining, sparkling, luminous, radiant, perfumed and beautiful, but henceforth reduced to suffering"—to suffering through presence in the flesh.[37]

This was an uncomfortable doctrine for Christianity, because its own attitude to the flesh and, more generally, to "the world" was by no means unambiguous.[38] No doubt Christ had taken flesh; it followed that the flesh could not be intrinsically evil. But many Christians found this hard to believe. The first centuries of Christianity abound in heresies, influential heresies, according to which Christ's flesh was an illusion, not true flesh but a way in which he made himself visible to men. Some "Docetists"—to name one such heretical sect—went so far as to deny that it was Christ who died on the Cross; Judas, they said, changed places with him at the last moment. (According to the Gnostic Basileides it was Simon of Cyrene who died on the Cross.) Even for orthodoxy, Christ took flesh by very special means, which preserved him from contamination. He was not conceived by the ordinary processes of generation; Joseph was no more

37. Quoted in J. Guitton: *Great Heresies and Church Councils*, trans. F. D. Wieck (London, 1965), p. 65.

38. For details see, for example, Rudolf Bultmann: *Primitive Christianity in Its Contemporary Setting*, trans. R. H. Fuller (London, 1956), pp. 189–95, "The Situation of Man in the World." The complexities are nowhere better brought out than in the First Epistle of John. On this see K. E. Kirk: *The Vision of God*, 2nd ed. (London, 1932; repr. New York, 1966), p. 83.

than his foster-father. He was born in such a way as to preserve his mother's virginity. As for human relationships of
a fleshly kind, if Christians were permitted to marry, it was
certainly better for them to make "themselves eunuchs,"
as Origen literally did. Paul has no doubt that the world
would be a better place if everybody was like him, in respect to continency. If he concedes that it is "better to marry
than to burn," his tone of contempt is unmistakable.* As
for the material world in general, there are relatively few
signs in Christianity—although the attitude is by no means
unknown—of the spirit exhibited in the Rabbinical saying
that "a man will have to give account on the judgement day
of every good thing which he might have enjoyed and did
not." [39]

Gnosticism could not easily be fought off by emphasizing, when this emphasis was so hedged around with reservations, the value of the flesh and the world. The flesh, the
world and the devil were too uncomfortably allied in Christianity itself: "Love not the world, neither the things that
are in the world. If any man love the world, the love of the
Father is not in him. For all that is in the world, the lust of

---

* Elsewhere, no doubt, Paul attacks those false teachers who would forbid marriage
entirely (I Timothy 4:3); he urges that married men should love their wives; he compares
the relation between Christ and the Church to the relationship between husband and wife
(Ephesians 5). But the apocryphal Acts of Paul make it perfectly clear that by the middle
of the second century Paul was regarded as doing what he could to discourage matrimony.
Christian attitudes to marriage, taken over the centuries, have been extraordinarily complicated. Mystics have delighted in the imagery of bride and bridegroom to describe their
relationship to God, while at the same time condemning marriage as an obstacle to perfection and attempting to scourge themselves free of all sexual desires; Roman Catholicism has extolled the virginity of Mary while counting marriage as a sacrament; Puritans
have limited marital relationships in the oddest of ways. Paul's attitude in I Corinthians 7,
quoted above, has, however, been typical of Christian asceticism: marriage, on that view,
is a second-best relationship, a concession to the flesh. "To avoid fornication," as Paul puts
it, "let every man have his own wife."

39. Quoted in G. F. Moore: *Judaism*, Vol. II, p. 265. Calvin, however, urges us to appreciate the good things of this world—even if, at the same time, he tells us to despise the
world and this earthly life. (Compare *Institutes*, III. xx. 42 and III. x. 2–4.) D. S. Wallace-
Hadrill in *The Greek Patristic View of Nature* (Manchester, 1968) has emphasized the enthusiasm for nature displayed by the Greek fathers.

the flesh, and the lust of the eyes, and the pride of life, is not of the Father, but is of the world."[40] What Christians could and did deny, however, is that matter as such, as distinct from man's worldly attitude to it, was evil, and that, in consequence, men could perfect themselves by cutting themselves free from whatever is material. The doctrine of the resurrection of the body—as against the Gnostic view that salvation belongs to the soul alone, since the body is by nature subject to corruption—was one way of insisting on that point. The doctrine of the Eucharist was another. "Vain in every respect," writes Irenaeus, staunch critic of the Gnostics, "are they who despise the entire dispensation of God, and disallow the salvation of the flesh, and treat with contempt its regeneration, maintaining that it is not capable of incorruption. But if this indeed do not attain salvation, then neither did the Lord redeem us with His blood, nor is the cup of the Eucharist the communion of His blood, nor the bread which we break the communion of His body."[41] In spite of all these theological points, Gnosticism has been a constant temptation to Christianity: the view, at least, that Christians could perfect themselves, if once they were prepared to withdraw from the world, to mortify the body, and thus to soar above the flesh is one which constantly recurs in Christian thinking.* The easiest way of meeting it boldly

---

40. I John 2:15–16.

41. Trans. in *A New Eusebius*, ed. J. Stevenson (London, 1957; corr. repr. 1968), pp. 123–24.

* Paul explicitly attacks asceticism in Colossians 2:20–23, a passage which, interestingly enough, is translated in the Authorized Version in a fashion which is obscure to the point of unintelligibility. But there can be no doubt that he was widely read as an ascetic. In the apocryphal Acts of Paul Paul is reported as teaching: "Blessed are they that keep the flesh chaste; blessed are they that abstain; blessed are they that renounce the world; blessed are they that possess their wives as if they had them not; blessed are the bodies of virgins." At the same time, Paul was to be extensively quoted by antinomians: phrases like "there is nothing unclean in itself" (Romans 14:14), "to the pure all things are pure" (Titus 1:15) and "every creature of God [everything that is created by God] is good" (1 Timothy 4:4) were obviously extremely convenient for those who wished to argue that any form of conduct was permissible to the sanctified. Antinomianism and asceticism are the extreme poles of Christian thought. But each of them is particularly important, as we

is to deny, as Luther did, that man is perfectible *whatever he does.*

Most fundamental of all, however, in forming Christian attitudes to perfectibility is that feeling which underlies so much Christian teaching, that man is by nature guilty, sinful, in such a way and to such a degree that not even Christ's sacrifice, although it saved man from the worst consequences of his sin, could wholly perfect him. "In the course of justice," as Portia puts it in *The Merchant of Venice,* "none of us should see salvation; we do pray for mercy." To pray for perfection would be to ask altogether too much. The merits of Jesus, according to Luther, might be "imputed" to man, but man himself was, although not beyond redemption, certainly beyond perfection. If for Roman Catholicism Christ's merits were in some degree imparted, as distinct from imputed, to man, this was still not to the extent necessary to secure man's perfection.

At this point, too, Revelation was crucial—the Genesis story of the Fall of Man. That story has a double importance for the history of perfectibility. Christians of the more optimistic sort have read it as asserting that men were once perfect, so that imperfection is not, as it were, inseparable from man's nature. And on this belief—as on the Marxist belief in "primitive Communism"—was often based the hope that men might again achieve perfection. "Time will run back," in Milton's words, "and fetch the Age of Gold." On the other side, when the Genesis story was pressed into the service of the theory of "original sin," it acted as a bulwark against Gnostic, and neo-Platonic, doctrines of perfectibility.

The Greeks had invented myths not dissimilar to the Garden of Eden story. Hesiod described a Golden Age in which "men lived like gods, free from worry and fatigue," and contrasted that Golden Age with the rigours of the Age

---

shall see, to the Christian perfectibilist. The passages from the Acts of Paul are to be found in *The Apocryphal New Testament,* ed. M. R. James (corrected ed. Oxford, 1955), p. 273.

of Iron, in which we now live.* Empedocles, as we have already seen, traced back men's sufferings to a primaeval sin, the guilt of which all men inherit, and, in so doing, he may have been giving expression to a commonly-held religious belief. Plotinus—read and admired by Augustine—ascribed the imperfection of the soul, in its embodied form, to its having fallen away, as a result of the attractions of the material Universe, from the One to which it properly belongs. "It has fallen:" he writes, "it is at the chain: . . . it is a captive; this is the burial, the encavernment of the Soul." He associated his view, one may note in passing, with "the Empedoclean teaching of a flight from God, a wandering away, a sin bringing its punishment."[42] But no Greek believed that man was corrupted once and for all by his having fallen away from God; he could still hope, in this life, to regain his godlike state.

The Christian doctrine of "original sin," as resulting from the Fall, is not made explicit in Genesis, where it is the suffering rather than the sinfulness of man which derives from Adam's Fall. Even after Paul had written in his Epistle to the Romans—in a passage the meaning of which is anything but obvious—that "by one man sin entered into the world, and death by sin; and so death passed upon all men, for that all have sinned," the doctrine of original sin was by no means firmly established in the Christian Church. Paul,

---

* As early as the second century, Irenaeus, with an ingenuity worthy of a better cause, tried to weave the Garden of Eden and the Golden Age into a single narrative. Josephus in his *Antiquities of the Jews*, written about A.D. 94, had already introduced into his account of the Garden of Eden many details derived from the classical "Golden Age." Thus it is that the extremely bare Biblical narrative was converted into the Garden of Eden of the popular imagination. For Josephus see L. H. Feldman: "Hellenizations in Josephus's Portrayal of Man's Decline" in Jacob Neusner, ed.: *Religions in Antiquity*, pp. 336–53.

42. *Enneads*, IV. 8. 4–5, trans. MacKenna, 1956, p. 361. E. R. Dodds, in his *Pagan and Christian in an Age of Anxiety*, pp. 24–26, argues that, although Plotinus first thought of the "fall" as the result of sin, he finally came to the conclusion, by the time he came to write *Enneads*, IV. 3.13, that it was no more than an inherent biological necessity. In the light of this reference to Empedocles, I am inclined to doubt whether Plotinus ever finally made up his mind on this question. Dodds draws attention to similar neo-Pythagorean teachings, in which, as for Augustine, the sin is a kind of *hubris*.

indeed, was not an influential figure in the Early Church; for a time Christianity swung away from Pauline doctrines.

"In all the writings of the Apostolic Fathers," according to Boas, "the name of Adam occurs but once and the Earthly Paradise and the fatal tree are not mentioned at all."[43] Not until the end of the second century did the Fall come to be discussed in detail by Christian writers, and even then, in the writings of Theophilus, the penalty of the Fall is still "labour, pain, grief and death" rather than sin. The struggle against Gnosticism, however, led Irenaeus to suggest that man's sin arose out of Adam's Fall; this provided an alternative to the Gnostic view that it arose either as a direct consequence of man's materiality, or as a result of the operations of an Evil One. Origen, Athanasius, Tertullian and Ambrose took this doctrine further, and Ambrose, in particular, explicitly laid it down that all men must take the responsibility for Adam's sin. But it is only in Ambrose's pupil, Augustine, that the doctrine of original sin, as a product of the Fall, is promulgated with its full severity. "God, the Author of all natures but not of their defects, created man good," he wrote in his *City of God,* "but man, corrupt by choice and condemned by justice, has produced a progeny that is both corrupt and condemned. For, we all existed in that one man, since, taken together, we were the one man who fell into sin through the woman who was made out of him before sin existed."[44]

On the nature of Adam's sin Christian theologians have been unable to agree. Gluttony, disobedience, egoism, spiritual pride, have all had their advocates. Some theologians, indeed, have ascribed to poor Adam every possible form

---

43. Quoted from George Boas: *Essays on Primitivism and Related Ideas in the Middle Ages* (Baltimore, 1948), p. 15. The historical detail which follows in the main text is derived partly from that source, partly from the *Oxford Dictionary of the Christian Church,* article "Original Sin."

44. *The City of God,* Bk. XIII, ch. 14, in the abridged trans. ed. V. J. Bourke, pp. 278–79.

of sin, all inherent in his single act of eating the forbidden fruit.* Empedocles had suggested that man's original sin was some form of bloodshed. But the Garden of Eden story, flexible though it is, would scarcely admit of *that* interpretation. On the whole, indeed, the Christian Church has been much less interested in bloodshed and violence, as forms of sin, than in sexual desire, or in pride, in the attempt by man to achieve that self-sufficiency and independence which the Greeks took as their ideal, to become what the Lord God of Genesis describes as "one of us." Pride and sexual desire have sometimes been conjoined—as in the doctrine, which seems to have been Augustine's, that Adam's sin originated as pride but revealed itself as, and is passed on to his successors through, sexual desire, the desire involved in the very act of generation.

The formal ground of original sin, too, has been disputed, whether all men suffered from Adam's crime merely because he was their ancestor—as on the archaic view, which Hesiod had affirmed and against which Euripides had protested, that pollution was inherited—or because all men are in some sense "part" of Adam, or because Adam entered, as the legal representative of his descendants, into a covenant with God and for Adam's breaches of this covenant all men must take responsibility. But that there had been a sin, and that all men must endure the consequences of that sin was to become, for all its obscurity, standard Christian doctrine.[45] And in its more rigorous form—al-

---

* So Milton writes: "What sin can be named which was not included in this one act? It comprehended at once distrust in the divine veracity, and a proportionate credulity in the assurances of Satan; unbelief; ingratitude; disobedience; gluttony; in the man excessive uxoriousness, in the woman a want of proper regard for her husband, in both an insensibility to the welfare of their offspring, and that offspring the whole human race; parricide, theft, invasion of the rights of others, sacrilege, deceit, presumption in aspiring to divine attributes, fraud in the means employed to obtain the object, pride and arrogance." (*De doctrina christiana*, Bk. I, ch. XI; as trans. in *The Works of John Milton*, ed. F. A. Patterson, 20 vols [New York, 1931–40], Vol. 15, pp. 181–83.)

45. See F. R. Tennant: *The Sources of the Doctrines of the Fall and Original Sin* (Cambridge,

though not all Christians have been prepared to accept this interpretation—it is not merely the consequence of Adam's sin but *its actual guilt* which all men inherit.

As a consequence of Adam's sin, "There is no question," so Augustine wrote, "of man's meriting a place in God's City." This, it might seem, is all that need be said about Christianity and perfection. "The whole mass of mankind is cankered at the roots"; it has not the slightest prospect of perfecting itself. The best an individual man can hope for is that, by God's grace, he will turn out to be one of that "fixed number of saints" by which God will fill his City. There were other lines of argument, too, which led to the same conclusion. One might call them empirical in the sense that they rest, unlike the doctrine of original sin, not on a supposed Revelation but on a knowledge of human nature, a knowledge of its incapacity fully to obey the commands which God laid down for all men.

The commands of perfection, it has generally been agreed, were summed up in Matthew 22:37–39. The first and foremost commandment is that "Thou shalt love the Lord thy God with all thy heart, and with all thy soul, and with all thy mind"; the second commandment that "Thou shalt love thy neighbour as thyself." A number of questions* arise immediately in the attempt to interpret these

---

1903) and, for controversy in the United States since 1750, H. Shelton Smith: *Changing Conceptions of Original Sin* (New York, 1955). The relatively small "coverage" of Shelton Smith's book lets one see more clearly how difficult Christians find it to agree about the nature and transmission of original sin. F. R. Tennant's article on "Original Sin" in J. Hastings, ed.: *Encyclopaedia of Religion and Ethics*, Vol. 9, is a good summary. See also N. P. Williams: *The Ideas of the Fall and of Original Sin* (London, 1927; repr. 1938).

* There are deeper questions which we have to avoid. What is meant by "love" in these contexts? Is the love of God, of self, of the world, of neighbours, the same or a different kind of love? See on this topic A. Nygren: *Agape and Eros;* John Burnaby: *Amor Dei* (London, 1938; repr. 1960) with Augustine as its central theme; M. C. D'Arcy: *The Mind and Heart of Love* (London, 1945, repr. 1946); R. G. Hazo: *The Idea of Love* (New York, 1967), Pt. I, ch. 3. D'Arcy, in particular, brings out very clearly the enormous complexity of the idea of love. But if after reading these books one then goes back to Plato's *Symposium*, it becomes apparent how much there is still to be said. In earlier versions of this chapter,

commandments, and it is largely because they answer them differently that Christian sects can disagree so profoundly about the conditions, and the limits, of human perfectibility. The most fundamental question can be put thus: on the face of it men love a great many things and this seems to be part of their nature. How can they, then, ever bring themselves into, or be brought into, a state of mind in which they love God with *all* their heart, and *all* their soul, and *all* their mind? Will not their other loves always interfere with the complete dedication of their heart to God?

A second question is a special application of this more general question: if men are to love God with their whole heart, how is it possible for them also to love their neighbours? Do not these two commandments conflict? And how, in the light of the first commandment, can Paul write, "For *all* the law is fulfilled in one word, even in this; Thou shalt love thy neighbour as thyself"?[46] For surely what the Law puts first is that we shall love not our neighbours, but God.

Thirdly, what is the force of the phrase "love thy neighbour as thyself"? Does this imply a third commandment: "Thou shalt love thyself"? And if, once more, to be perfect a man must love himself, then how can he love God with *all* his heart?

Three different tendencies within Christianity arise out of different answers to these questions: we may characterize them, respectively, as theocentric, egocentric, and (to coin an etymologically somewhat barbarous but self-explanatory adjective) fratrocentric. For a *theocentric* Christian, to be perfected a Christian must love God with all his heart, even if that means the entire destruction of his own happiness. Should it be true, to take the extreme instance, that by loving God he will wreak his own damnation, God still ought

---

I tried to discuss these issues, but they refused to be confined within manageable limits. To a restricted degree, I return to them in the last chapter.

46. Epistle to the Galatians 5:14.

to be loved. This was the view taken by Fénelon in a famous eighteenth-century French controversy. The soul, according to Fénelon, should be able to say to God, "If thou
wouldst condemn me to the eternal pains of hell, without
losing thy love (although the supposition is impossible) I
would love thee none the less."[47] For *egocentric* Christians,
in contrast, a man perfects himself by achieving his own
happiness; to this everything else is subordinate. If he loves
God this is because God offers him happiness; if he loves
his neighbours, this is because such love is a path on the
way to happiness. So, arguing against Fénelon, Bossuet was
led to maintain that "to love God is simply to love our own
beatitude more distinctly."[48] And Aquinas had already laid
it down that: "assuming what is impossible, that God were
not men's good there would be no reason to love him."[49]
For the *fratrocentric* Christian the foundation of perfection
is the love of neighbours; to this, self-love must be wholly
subordinated, and it is only through the love of neighbours
that God can be loved. Contrast Aquinas, for whom the love
of our neighbour is not *essential* as the love of God and self-
love are essential: "if there were but one soul enjoying God,
it would be happy though having no neighbour to love."[50]
Ascetic Christianity of the extreme sort, indeed, saw in a
neighbour nothing more than an occasion of sin.

Most Christians, however, would seek to avoid the absolutism of, in their different ways, a Fénelon or a Bossuet or
an anchorite. The question: "Ought we to love God even
if he cared nothing for our happiness?" is, they would argue, an abstract one, which need not be faced. In practice,
the three loves, of God, of self, of neighbour, entirely co-

47. Quoted in R. N. Flew: *The Idea of Perfection in Christian Theology*, p. 267. Francis de
Sales taught a similar doctrine. See R. A. Knox: *Enthusiasm*, pp. 254–58.

48. *Instruction sur les états*, 10, as quoted in K. E. Kirk: *The Vision of God*, p. 458.

49. *Summa theologica*, Pt. II, ii, q. 26, a. 13. I have not followed the Dominican version
here.

50. *Ibid.*, Pt. II, i, q. 4, a. 8. Compare Aristotle on the speculative life, which stands
in no need of others, pp. 62–63 above.

incide and must, considering their nature, do so. This was certainly Augustine's view. "Scripture," he writes, "enjoins nothing except charity . . . I mean by charity that affection of the mind which aims at the enjoyment of God for His own sake and of one's self and one's neighbour for God's sake. By lust I mean that affection of the mind which aims at the enjoyment of one's self and one's neighbour without reference to God."[51] Anything other than God, on this view, must be loved only as a way of loving God. The things of this world ought to be "used"—as instruments of salvation—not enjoyed. Neighbours were somewhat of a problem for Augustine. It was clear that they must not be loved for their own sake—this is a variety of lust—any more than one's self ought to be loved for its own sake. His conclusion was that neighbourly love is a missionary love; the true love for neighbours consists in "bringing them in" to God—a doctrine which was to be invoked, in later times, to justify a good many forms of conduct which it is otherwise not very natural to include under the heading of "neighbourly love," from wars to inquisitions. Augustine himself defended a policy of "dragging men to salvation" and asserted the Church's right to "compel men to good."[52] When the beggar calls, "Alms for the love of God," he displays his Augustinian orthodoxy; to give alms for the love of man is not to give them as one should. It is to act out of "cupidity," not out of "charity." For the seventeenth-century Jansenists, devotees of Augustine, all alms-giving had to be carefully scrutinized, to ensure that its true motive was the love of God.

Augustine's theology is certainly *theocentric,* then, in so far as he firmly maintains that nothing but God ought to be loved for its own sake—the love of God, he says, "suffers not a tricklet to be drawn off from itself, by the diversion of

---

51. *De doctrina christiana,* III. x. 15, 16, as trans. in *An Augustine Synthesis,* arranged E. Przywara (London, 1936; repr. 1945), p. 347.

52. *Epistle* 173. Cf. his *Select Letters,* trans. J. H. Baxter, Loeb Classical Library (London, 1953), p. 285.

which its own volume would be diminished."[53] There is no love "left over," as it were, to be directed towards the world, or towards our neighbours, or towards ourselves. But this is not inconsistent, according to Augustine, with my loving myself because self-love, rightly understood, is not a distraction from loving God, but is equivalent to it. "The love wherewith a man truly loves himself is none other than the love of God. For he who loves himself in any other way is rather to be said to hate himself."[54] For a man to love himself in this sense, to seek his own true good, is to cherish the image of God within, to love God. To raise the question, then, whether Augustine's theology is fundamentally egocentric or fundamentally theocentric is to ask a question which cannot be answered; for on his view a theocentric and an egocentric theology, properly understood, will coincide.

Luther will have no truck with such concessions to self-love. His theology is resolutely theocentric. Those who truly love God, he says, "submit freely to the will of God whatever it may be, even for hell and eternal death, if God should will it, in order that his will may be fully done; they seek absolutely nothing for themselves."[55] "Love your neighbour as yourself" does not imply, as Augustine had also recognized, "you *ought* to love yourself"; it rests only on the observable fact that every man does love himself; it is the equivalent of Jesus' other precept: "All things whatsoever ye would that men should do to you, do ye even so to them."[56] Men ought not to love themselves but hate themselves, hate themselves precisely because they love themselves. By hating themselves, they can both love God and love their neighbours. For the medieval doctrine, as expressed, for example, by Bernard of Clairvaux, that men can attain to perfection

53. *De doctrina christiana*, I. xxii. 21, as trans. in A. Nygren: *Agape and Eros*, p. 503.

54. *Epistle* 155. 15, quoted in John Burnaby: *Amor Dei*, p. 121.

55. Luther: *Lectures on Romans,* ch. IX, trans. W. Pauck, Library of Christian Classics, 15 (London, 1961), p. 262.

56. Matthew 7:12.

by beginning from self-love and gradually arising above it, Luther has nothing but contempt.[57] According to Luther, then, the sign that a man loves God with his whole heart is that he hates himself, and is prepared, even to damnation, wholly to submit himself to God's will—not that Luther believed that such a man would be damned! Augustine, in contrast, saw as the perfected man one who loved himself, in the "higher" sense of self-love, but who loved nothing in the world for its own sake. They agree, however, on the crucial point; neither kind of perfection is possible to men.

Augustine's *Confessions* is in this respect a very revealing document. Up to a point, it follows a common pattern, if in an unusually distinguished manner: the story of a pagan sinner saved, saved by conversion to Christianity. But Augustine does not end his story at this point: the curtain does not fall on a triumphant note with his conversion; he describes in detail his state after his conversion and the agonies which still beset him.

And what is his problem? It can be put thus: he is still unable to love God with his whole heart. He still finds in himself a longing for food and drink; he sometimes "sins criminally" by caring more for the musical beauty of a hymn than for its religious content; the sins of the eyes still trouble him; from the malady of curiosity he is by no means free, nor from the love of praise, nor from the desire to be loved by men. Only in one case does he feel ready, perhaps, to confess himself sinless, achieving the indifference of a Stoic Sage. "With the attractions of odours," he writes, "I am not much troubled. When they are absent, I do not seek them; when they are present, I do not refuse them; and I am always prepared to be without them."[58] We breathe a sigh of relief on Augustine's behalf. But wait! "Perhaps I am deceived."

---

57. On Bernard, see A. Nygren: *Agape and Eros,* p. 646.

58. *Confessions,* X. 32. The trans. is adapted from that by A. C. Outler, Library of Christian Classics, 7 (London, 1955), p. 230.

Only God knows the secrets of a man's heart. Perhaps after all, Augustine reflects with anxiety, he is merely deluding himself in supposing that he is no longer susceptible to the charm of perfume. Perhaps he has turned aside without necessity, merely to enjoy the sweet scent of a summer garden; perhaps he has dreamt nostalgically, in a Roman winter, of the smell of the hot earth in his native Carthage; perhaps, most abominable sin of all, he has unconsciously lingered as he passed in the street a girl, fresh from the bath, to savour the sweetness of her skin.

Augustine, it is worth observing, tries to steer clear of the wilder shores of Puritanism; even Puritanism, indeed, becomes in his eyes a temptation, an occasion for sin. "Sometimes I err out of too great preciseness," he rebukes himself, "and sometimes so much as to desire that every one of the pleasant songs to which David's Psalter is often set, be banished both from my ears and from those of the Church itself."[59] There are times, indeed, at which he writes for the moment like the Platonist he also was, and is prepared to enjoy the beauty man creates in so far as it emanates "from that Beauty which is above our minds, which my soul sighs for day and night."[60] But "Beauty," in this context, is a synonym for God. Whereas in aesthetic appreciation we fasten our eyes on the attractive object as it is in itself, to enjoy it for its own sake, Augustine permits us to enjoy the beauty of physical objects only as an expression of God.

The final outcome of Augustinianism, then, is reasonably clear. In the first place, no man ought ever to claim that he is perfect, since only God can be sure that he is not deceiving himself. And, secondly, it is highly unlikely, to say the least of it, that any man will be perfect, that he will succeed in achieving that degree of detachment from any form of sensuality, any form of secular love, which Augus-

---

59. *Ibid.*, X. 33, adapted from Outler, pp. 230–31.
60. *Ibid.*, X. 34, as trans. Outler, p. 233.

tine demands of the morally perfect man. Augustine does not assert that it is actually impossible for a man to achieve perfection; to say that would be to limit God's omnipotence. But he is quite sure that God has not in fact chosen to bestow upon any man that degree of divine grace he would need in order to be wholly perfect.

Luther came, by a very different route, to the same conclusion. Augustine had been a "great sinner," Luther had been a monk. Like Paul before him, he thought he could speak out of his own experience in laying it down that no man could hope to be perfect by his own efforts. As a monk he had been a perfectionist: "When I was a monk," he writes, "I thought . . . that I was utterly cast away, if at any time I felt the concupiscence of the flesh." It was with a sense of relief that he abandoned such a monkish ideal of perfection and concluded: "Martin, thou shalt not utterly be without sin, for thou hast yet flesh."[61] Unlike Augustine, it does not appal Luther that he is still subject to human frailties: such sin, he thought, "nothing hindereth . . . holiness"[62] provided only that the man who committed it had faith in God and was repentant. What is more important, even if a man could succeed in freeing himself from all "lusts of the flesh," *he would still not be perfect;* to suppose otherwise was, for Luther, the mistake of mistakes. Luther, we said, had been profoundly influenced by the *Theologia Germanica;* the leading tenet of that centre-piece of fourteenth-century devotion was that egoism, taking "myself to be my own," is the root of all evil.[63] It is just because men cannot overcome

61. *Commentary on Galatians* 5:17, rev. trans. by P. S. Watson (London, 1953, 1956), quoted in *Martin Luther: Selections from His Writings,* ed. J. Dillenberger (New York, 1961), pp. 148–49.

62. *Ibid.,* 5.19. See Dillenberger, p. 160.

63. Trans. S. Winkworth, corr. version, ed. W. R. Trask (New York, 1949; London, 1950). See, for example, ch. XXXVI: "Adam, I-hood and self-hood, self-will, sin, or the Old Man, the turning away or departing from God, all these are one and the same" (p. 178). Augustine sometimes spoke of pride as the root of all evil, a pride which is closely related to this kind of egoism, when a man "lets God go and loves himself," as Augustine puts it.

their egoism, cannot wholly submit to God's will, so Luther argues, that they cannot hope to achieve perfection. "Love God," for Luther, came to mean "Have complete faith in God," "Place your entire trust in him." Sinful man cannot hope to reach such heights.

To sum up, then, Christ's command to be "perfect, even as your Father in heaven is perfect" is, according to that orthodox Augustinian view which has predominated in the Christian Church, impossible for men to obey. Impossible for metaphysical reasons, since human perfection, so far as it can be attained at all, is the perfection of a finite temporal being, with all the limitations this involves. Impossible for moral reasons, since man, even when granted God's grace, has been so corrupted by Adam's Fall that he is incapable of achieving, even, that degree of moral perfection which his metaphysical nature permits.

It is interesting to observe that when American Unitarian transcendentalists set out, in the nineteenth century, to challenge the view that man cannot perfect himself, these are precisely the points they seized upon. Channing's discourse on "Likeness to God," is, in this respect, particularly striking.[64] He rejects, in the first place, the doctrine of original sin. Man, on Channing's view, is not born corrupt, and must not allow himself to become corrupted. But that is only his starting-point. The perfections of God, he argues, are human perfections, raised to a higher power. "God is another name for human intelligence, raised above all error and imperfection, and extended to all possible truth."

Nevertheless, it might be replied, the fact remains that God's perfections are infinite, man's finite; the insuperable gap between God and man persists. To this objection Channing answers, first, that an attribute does not change its

---

But even if pride is the original cause of man's sin, that sin now consists in the "lusting of the flesh." (Compare Burnaby: *Amor Dei*, pp. 188–91.)

64. Delivered in 1828. Reprinted, in part, in George Hochfield, ed.: *Selected Writings of the American Transcendentalists* (New York, 1966). The quotations are from pp. 57–58, 60.

nature by becoming infinite. Secondly, and more fundamentally, Channing rejects the view that man is finite: "there
are traces of infinity in the human mind . . . in this very respect it bears a likeness to God." Channing sees what has
to be argued if it is to be said that men can perfect themselves by being "like God"; God must be converted into a
being much more like man than traditional Christian metaphysics allows him to be, and man must at the same time
be elevated to a moral and metaphysical status considerably
more exalted than Christianity would allow to him. So long
as man is thought of as a being at once finite and corrupt
and God as a being who is perfect in a sense quite other
than the sense in which man could, with any degree of intelligibility, be described as perfect the Christian cannot avoid
concluding that he is by nature incapable of being perfect
as God is perfect. At best he has to think of the injunction
in Matthew, and the Sermon on the Mount generally, as expressing an ideal, or as a challenge to complacency, rather
than as a precept to be obeyed.[65]

65. Compare A. Boyce Gibson: *The Challenge of Perfection* (Melbourne, 1968). This is
a brief essay but it brings out the main issues.

FIVE

PELAGIUS AND HIS CRITICS

Not all Christians were satisfied with Augustine's conclusion that, in this life, perfection lies beyond men's reach. The most direct, the most far-reaching, attack on Augustine was initiated in the fifth century by that sturdy British lay-monk Pelagius and his younger, more outspoken disciple — also a layman — Coelestius. Like many another religiously-minded Englishman after him, Pelagius made his way to Rome; like many other religiously-minded Englishmen after him, he was appalled by the moral laxity, to his northern eyes, he there encountered. And a large part of the blame, so Pelagius thought, attached to Augustine. If men were told that they could not conform their lives to the teaching of the Gospels, try as they might, this was bound to weaken their moral fibre.

The Christian's duty, according to Pelagius, is clear and unambiguous. God has commanded men to be perfect; God would not have commanded them to do what lies beyond their powers. It is, he wrote in his *Letter to Demetrias,* "blind folly and presumptuous blasphemy" for men to tell God that they cannot do what he has commanded them to do, "as if, forgetting the weakness of men, his own creation, he had laid upon men commands which they were unable to bear."[1]

---

1. Quoted from H. Bettenson, ed.: *Documents of the Christian Church* (London, 1943; repr. 1946), p. 74. See also the article by R. G. Parsons on "Pelagianism and semi-Pelagianism" in James Hastings, ed.: *Encyclopaedia of Religion and Ethics,* Vol. 9, and the works on Augustine by E. Portalié, trans. R. J. Bastian (London, 1960); Peter Brown (London, 1967); and especially Gerald Bonner (London, 1963), along with John Ferguson: *Pelagius* (Cambridge, 1956). There is a slightly more technical, very thorough, discussion of the Augustine-Pelagius controversy in Nigel Abercrombie: *The Origins of Jansenism* (Oxford,

To suppose that God would punish men for not doing what they cannot do, furthermore, is to ascribe to him "unrighteousness and cruelty." Pelagius sums up thus: "He has not willed to command anything impossible, for he is righteous; and he will not condemn a man for what he could not help, for he is holy."*

In developing his anti-Augustinian thesis, Pelagius was led entirely to reject the concept of original sin. "Everything good, and everything evil," he argued, "on account of which we are either laudable or blameworthy, is not born with us but done by us: for we are born not fully developed, but with a capacity for either conduct; and we are procreated as without virtue, so also without vice."[2] At birth, that is, men are neither perfect nor corrupt. They are born, however, with a capacity for perfecting themselves or corrupting themselves, by the exercise of their free-will. It is up to them to employ that capacity aright—although once God sees that they are intent upon perfecting themselves he will no doubt lend them a hand. Sin is not inherent in man's nature; it is nothing more, Pelagius assures us, than a bad habit. "There is no other cause of the difficulty we find in doing well, but the long-continued customs of sin, which begin to grow upon us in childhood, and little by little corrupt us."[3] And bad habits can always be broken by a deliberate act of will, although a long-standing habit, Pelagius is prepared to admit, can be difficult to eradicate.

1936). See also, for a critical view of Pelagius, G. de Plinval: *Pélage, ses écrits, sa vie et sa reforme* (Lausanne, 1943).

* The story runs—it has been disputed—that Pelagius first made his way to Rome in order to study law. Coelestius was certainly a lawyer. Pelagius's approach is in any case a lawyer's: what kind of legislator would he be who set up laws nobody could obey and then punished his subjects for not obeying them? Compare J. N. L. Myres: "Pelagius and the end of Roman rule in Britain," *Jnl. Rom. Studies,* Vol. 50 (1960), pp. 21–36.

2. As quoted in Augustine: *On the Grace of Christ and on Original Sin,* II. xiv, trans. P. Holmes in *The Works of Aurelius Augustinus,* Vol. XII (Edinburgh, 1874), repr. in modernized version in *Basic Writings of Saint Augustine,* ed. W. J. Oates, 2 vols (New York, 1948), Vol. 1, p. 628.

3. *Ad Demetrias,* 8, quoted in N. Abercrombie: *The Origins of Jansenism,* p. 22.

Not a few modern readers will sympathize with Pelagius in this debate, seeing in him the blunt Englishman cutting through the tortuosities of North African sensuality and sensibility. It is worth noting, however, that Pelagianism carried with it a Stoic-like severity of judgement. Since sin can always be avoided by the exercise of will, a man deserves eternal damnation, Pelagius concluded, should he fall into the slightest sin. On his view, the Church was, and only ought to be, a community of saints, of men intent on perfecting themselves. It was not a school for sinners; it ought to cast sinners from out of its body, as God would most assuredly cast them into Hell. Such severity is only too characteristic of "universal" perfectibilists. If all men can be perfect, given only that they seriously try, it is a short step to the conclusion that they deserve damnation—or execution—for not being perfect.

The immediate effect of Pelagianism was to provoke Augustine to write a long series of anti-Pelagian tracts, in which he developed the typical Augustinian themes of human corruption and the free bounty of divine grace. The problem which faced Augustine, as it has faced so many Christian thinkers after him, is neatly expressed in a letter he wrote, about 426, to Valentinus, the abbot of a Tunisian monastery. The monks, disturbed by Augustine's anti-Pelagian teachings, had divided into two factions, one faction "extolling grace to such an extent that they deny the freedom of the human will," the other faction maintaining that our free will "is aided by the grace of God so that we may think and do what is right." The second faction, Augustine tells Valentinus, is correct: God co-operates with man's free will. He goes on to formulate the Christian dilemma thus: "If then there is no grace of God, how does He save the world? And if there is no free will, how does He judge the world?" Free will must be granted, to justify God's condemnation of man; man is condemned by God because he has wrongly used his freedom. But without grace, Augustine is emphatic, the world could not be saved. For it is "a thing . . . utterly impossible" that "without it we could by any means think or do anything well-pleasing to God."[4]

Plato thought that men could be perfected by intellectual activity; Augustine was convinced from his own experience that neither education nor any other form of human effort could save men from sin. Had he not been well-educated? And had he not tried desperately, and failed, to overcome by his own efforts the power of sexual desire? Paul, for rather different reasons, had been equally certain that human efforts are powerless. No one could have been a better Jew than he was; no one could have adhered more strictly to the precepts of the Law. And where had his righteousness led him? To persecute Christians, to deny the one true faith. "It is by this grace of God through Jesus Christ our Lord," so Augustine expressed the faith he shared with Paul, "that all those who are delivered, are delivered, since no one can be delivered in any other way than through it."[5]

Whereas, then, Pelagius called upon men to reform themselves by their own efforts, Augustine, convinced that this was impossible, sought in God's grace the solution to the problem how men could be saved. They could love God and love their neighbours, only *because God chose to love them.* "When God crowns our merits, He crowns nothing but His own gifts." To suppose otherwise is "perverted and sacrilegious." Augustine is not, of course, inventing these views. "Herein is love," he quotes from John, "not that we loved God, but that he loved us." And again, "We love him, because he first loved us."[6]

To Plato, love is a lack, a yearning, a desire to possess an object. The object itself is indifferent to this yearning. If a

---

4. *Epistle* 214, to Valentinus, in Augustine: *Select Letters,* trans. J. H. Baxter, pp. 405–7.

5. *Epistle* 179, as trans. J. H. Baxter in *Select Letters,* p. 313.

6. I John 4:10, 19, quoted by Augustine in *On the Grace of Christ and on Original Sin,* I. xxvii. See *Basic Writings,* Vol. 1, p. 602. See also *Epistle* 194. 19, as quoted in J. Burnaby: *Amor Dei,* p. 238.

Platonist "loves beauty," he yearns to possess it, but he does not expect Beauty to reach out and try to possess him. The idea of a God who creates love in his worshippers, the idea that it is only through God's efforts that man can love him — these are what give Christianity its peculiar flavour, when it is contrasted with Greek philosophy.* That is why Christianity is sometimes described as "a religion of love, not of Law." Christ's "commandments," many Christians would say, are better described as promises, indicating the nature of the gifts God freely bestows upon men rather than the demands he makes upon them. Not that this has been by any means the sole, or the consistent, teaching of Christianity. The lawyers and the moralists, of whom Pelagius was certainly one, have seen to that.

The Augustinian theory of grace had two immediate consequences for perfectibility: the first, that men cannot achieve perfection by their own efforts; the second that in so far as in this life they can progress towards perfection, it is only with the help of God's grace. These conclusions still leave it an open question how far that progress can be carried, to what degree a man can, before death, be perfected by God's grace. At first, as a good Platonist, Augustine seems to have supposed that Christianity would perfect him. In a sermon delivered in A.D. 394 he was quite confident that men can live "the life of the consummate and

---

* Similar theories of grace, however, are to be found in the Hindu religion and in certain varieties of Buddhism. Within the history of Buddhism, indeed, one can distinguish something very like the Augustinian-Pelagian controversy. On the comparison between Christianity and Hindu teachings see Sabapathy Kulandran: *Grace: A Comparative Study of the Doctrine in Christianity and Hinduism* (London, 1964). On the situation in Buddhism, and for the suggestion that this kind of antithesis between an "optimistic" and a "pessimistic" view of human effort breaks out quite generally within religion, see H. D. Lewis and R. L. Slater: *World Religions* (London, 1966), reprinted as *The Study of Religions* (Harmondsworth, 1969), especially ch. III. Some commentators maintain that the older Platonic view of love persists even in Augustine. See especially A. Nygren: *Agape and Eros*.

perfect man of wisdom." Six years later, however, he was no less confident that anyone who thinks that "in this mortal life a man may so disperse the mists of bodily and carnal imaginings as to possess the unclouded light of changeless truth" only too clearly demonstrates that "he understands neither what he seeks, nor who he is who seeks it."[7]

Not only his own personal experience but his experience, as bishop, of his fellow Christians led Augustine to change his mind on this point. Men, he admitted, might perhaps, like Paul, be "blameless, as touching the righteousness which is of the law." They can perhaps achieve, that is, "external" righteousness. This, however, is but "dung" in comparison with that "perfect state of righteousness," that absolute perfection, that immaculate love of God, which men hunger after.[8] And God has not chosen, in his wisdom, so to love men that they can, in this life, love him with their whole heart.

A third consequence is less direct. Grace is God's gift to men. Some men have been granted this gift, and others not: the number of the elect is, indeed, predetermined.[9] God knows beforehand who will reject the grace he offers them, even although it is by their own free will, Augustine usually suggests, that they do so.[10] Not only, then, are men unable to achieve perfection in this life; only in certain cases, predetermined, does God give them the degree of grace necessary for salvation. There is, for Augustine, nothing un-

7. Trans. in Peter Brown: *Augustine of Hippo*, p. 147. The first quotation is from *De sermone Domini in monte*, I. ii. 9, the second from *De consensu evangelistarum*, IV. x. 20. There is a useful discussion of this issue in the French ed. and trans. of Augustine's *Retractiones* (*Oeuvres de Saint Augustin*, vol. 12: *Les Révisions*, ed. Gustave Bardy, Paris, 1950, pp. 200–16).

8. *On the Grace of Christ*, I. liii, in *Basic Writings*, Vol. 1, p. 617. The Biblical refs. are to Philippians 3:6, 8.

9. Romans 8:29–30.

10. Augustine-scholars disagree on this point. Augustine sometimes seems to suggest, like the Jansenists after him, that grace can be irresistible. Compare J. Burnaby: *Amor Dei*, pp. 226–34.

just in this: men should thank God for his mercy, that he has chosen to save the few. It would have been entirely just had he left all men to endure, unredeemed, the effects of Adam's, and their, sinfulness.

These doctrines, thus given shape by Augustine, were in the future history of Christianity to constitute the orthodoxy of the main streams of Christian thought, Roman Catholic and Protestant. The Council of Carthage, meeting in the year 418, accepted, in their essentials, the Augustinian teachings. It anathematized the proposition that men could, without special grace from God, fulfil the commands of God by the exercise of their own free will. It rejected the view that when the saints pray "forgive us our trespasses" they are praying for others, not for themselves, or that they utter these words "out of humility and not because they are true." Not even the saints, the Council agreed with Augustine, are, or can be, immaculately perfect. "Causa finita est," Augustine announced triumphantly to his Carthage congregation.

There were, however, dissentients. Many bishops subscribed unwillingly to the decisions of the Council of Carthage; no less than eighteen were deposed, amongst them Julian of Eclanum. Julian's teachings will serve to illustrate what, until 418, a Roman Catholic bishop had been free to teach. Everything God creates, Julian argues, must be good; since each man is created by God no man can be intrinsically corrupt. Although Adam sinned he did not, in so doing, modify the moral character of his descendants. Julian entirely rejected, that is, the idea of a transmitted original sin. In virtue of their possessing free will, Julian went on to maintain, men are "independent of God, free to make their own decisions." God's grace, for Julian, is chiefly manifested in the "grace of creation," in the fact that God created men so that they are *capable* of goodness. Some pagans, in virtue of this grace, have, Julian says, "lived lives as perfect as any Christian."* For the rest, God's grace is made apparent, according to Julian, in the "grace of revelation," offered to men in the Holy Scriptures, and in the sacrifice of his own son—a grace made, if not strictly necessary, at least highly desirable by the fact that men had fallen into a "bad habit" of sinning, out of which the Scriptures and Christ's sacrifice helped to shock them.[11]

Other theologians sought to compromise between the Pelagians and the Augustinians. John Cassian was a warm admirer of Augustine, fully prepared to accept his doctrine of original sin. But he has come to be regarded as the founder of "semi-Pelagianism"—or, as some scholars prefer to call it, on account of its remoteness from the teachings of Pelagius, "semi-Augustinianism"—because he diverged from Augustine's teachings on certain crucial points. Man, he maintained, makes the first movement towards God. When he seeks God's grace, this is from his own natural resources and not because God has given him the "prevenient" grace to do so. Cassian knew his monks; he feared that they might be tempted by Augustinianism into spiritual laziness, sitting back to await God's call, or else might lapse into spiritual despair, if the call did not come. Nor is it true, Cassian argued, that God has chosen his elect in advance. No doubt, since God is omniscient, he must know who will be saved. It is none the less his will that all men should be saved—not merely, as Augustine had glossed "Christ came to save all men," all *sorts* of men, but each and every man.

For a time it looked as if Cassian, or Cassian's spirit,

---

* Augustine complained that Julian seems to take a positive delight in "praising these pagans," praise which, Augustine said, would be "more bearable" if Julian were prepared to recognize that pagan virtue, in so far as it has ever existed, is the fruit of a *special* grace from God.

11. Julian's views, like Pelagius's, are known only through the quotations of his adversaries. I have followed the summary in R. G. Parsons' article on "Pelagianism and semi-Pelagianism" (see note 1 above). On Augustine's relation to Julian, see E. Portalié: *Guide to the Thought of Augustine, passim,* and P. Brown: *Augustine of Hippo,* ch. 32.

might triumph. Some sixty years after the Council of Carthage, about the year 473, the Synod of Arles promulgated, as against the more ardent proponents of predestination, the principle that "man's freedom of will is not extinct but attenuated and weakened." It declared anathema the view that "Christ has not undergone death for the salvation of all men." [12] It asserted that "man's effort and endeavour is to be united with God's grace" and that "he that is saved is in danger, and he that has perished could have been saved." The wording of the synod's resolution can often be matched in Augustine's writings, but the emphasis, the spirit, is Cassian's. For the suggestion, certainly, is that God's grace is granted to those who with "effort and endeavour" seek it out. In more technical language, grace is co-operative rather than prevenient.

But Augustine was finally to be the victor. In the year 529, without reservation and in Augustine's own words, the Council of Orange reasserted that original sin corrupted the whole human race. It rejected Cassian's view that God's grace can be bestowed on men in response to their prayers —that, in the formula characteristic of the asceticism of the Eastern Church, "grace springs from the desire for it"—except where the power to invoke it has already, by God's prevenient grace, been granted to them. It anathematized the Pelagian teaching that "by the force of nature we can rightly think or choose anything that is good." At one point only did the Council deviate from what may have been Augustine's teachings—his interpreters disagree on this point. It rejected outright the doctrine of "dual predestination," the doctrine, that is, that some men are predestined to be saved and others to be damned. [13] "Not only do we not believe," the Council affirmed with conviction, "that some have been predestinated to evil by the divine power, but also, if there

12. See H. Bettenson, ed.: *Documents of the Christian Church*, p. 85.
13. *Ibid.*, pp. 86–87.

be any who will believe so evil a thing, we say to them with all detestation, anathema." It has remained the orthodox Roman Catholic view that although the number of the elect is predetermined, no man is predestined to be damned.* As the Council of Quierzy-sur-Oise expressed the official view in 853: "To those who are saved salvation is a gift of God; but those who perish are lost through their own fault."[14]

The fluctuations of the century which passed between the Council of Carthage and the Council of Orange were to be repeated again and again in the history of Christianity. The history of Christianity—at least on the intellectual side —could be told as a long controversy in which Christians have swung between the extremes of Pelagianism and the extremes of dual predestination. Some Christians have been prepared to rest at the extremes, but most have tried to find a *via media* between them. They have sought to preserve the freedom of the will while still affirming that men are initially corrupt, to maintain predestination—on the face of it, one of the fixed boundaries of "Biblical space"—while reserving the right to exhort men to moral action.

The reason is obvious. On the one side, Christianity must insist that man is wholly dependent on God. Once accept Julian's view that in exercising his free will man achieves "independence of God" and the path to secularism lies wide open. Yet, on the other side, Pelagius's initial objection to Augustinianism could not be entirely passed over. There is a serious risk, many Christians have felt, that if it be too strongly emphasized that men are wholly dependent on God's grace for their power to act morally, that they cannot, of their own unaided free will, "choose anything what-

---

* The examiner, as we might paraphrase this in the language of John Barth's novel *Giles Goat-boy*, not only knows how many are to pass but has already determined *who* is to pass. All the same, if people fail it is entirely their own fault. Not everybody finds this reasoning satisfactory.

14. Quoted in H. Daniel-Rops: *The Church in the Seventeenth Century*, trans. J. J. Buckingham (London, 1963), p. 341.

ever that is good," this may lead to a weakening of their moral effort. In his *Spiritual Exercises* Ignatius Loyola laid it down that Jesuit preachers should not "make a habit of talking about predestination" and that "if we have to talk about it to some extent on occasion, our language should be such as not to lead ordinary people astray, as can happen if a man says: "It is already settled whether I am to be saved or damned; my good or bad conduct cannot make any difference." So they lose heart and cease to bother about the activities which make for their souls' health and spiritual profit." [15] Many Protestants, however, reject this policy of silence as something not far short of an insult to God, "as if," in Calvin's words, "he had unadvisedly let slip something hurtful to the Church." [16]

In the modern Christian Church, so it is often said, the hymns may assume predestination, but the sermons are Pelagian. The Pelagian (or Benjamin Franklin) view that God helps those who help themselves has nowadays a wider appeal to the Christian in the street—especially in those societies in which, however mistakenly, it is generally believed that careers lie "open to the talents"—than any doctrine which emphasizes man's powerlessness to improve his own conditions by his own efforts. In a slave society, or even in a feudal society, it is very easy to believe that if a man is to rise in the world spiritually this can only be because he is extended some special grace; that is an accurate enough description of what happens at the level of civil society. It is only by his master's grace, not as an inevitable consequence of merit, that a slave secures his liberty. But once success is related, or is thought to be related, to merit, Pelagianism acquires a greater degree of plausibility.* Yet on the

---

15. *Spiritual Exercises*, §367, rule 15, as trans. Thomas Corbishley (London, 1963), p. 123.

16. *Institutes of the Christian Religion*, III. xxi. 4, trans. Battles, Vol. 2, p. 926.

* Calvinism is in this respect a strangely intermediate doctrine; it is not surprising that there has been so much controversy, ever since Max Weber's *The Protestant Ethic and*

other side, the doctrine that *anyone* may be saved—whatever his merits—has been one of the great attractions of Christianity. That Christian thinking has fluctuated, therefore, in its views about moral effort and its relationship to divine grace need occasion no astonishment.

Let us look briefly at some of the episodes in the Pelagian-Augustinian controversy. To turn first to Aquinas. Aquinas was greatly influenced by Augustine. But he was also an Aristotelian, and a close student of Dionysius; he found it impossible to believe that man is wholly corrupt. In his characteristic way, Aquinas sought to solve his problems by "distinguishing," in this case between human nature as it was "in its integrity," i.e. before the Fall, and human nature as it now is, after the Fall.[17] Before the Fall, according to Aquinas, men could so far perfect themselves as to be able, without special grace, to perform works of justice, fortitude and other virtues. In that sense they could fulfil all the commandments of the law. But, as Augustine had also explained, there is a deeper sense of "fulfilling the law," peculiarly Christian, in which it is required of men not only that they do what the law commands, but that they obey the law from the motive of "charity"—the spiritual love of God—in contrast with a merely natural gratitude for God's blessings. Even before the Fall, so Aquinas teaches, men needed special supernatural grace ("elevating grace") to fulfil the commandments of the law in this spirit of charity.

Since the Fall, Aquinas continued, men are unable, with-

---

the Spirit of Capitalism (1920; trans. T. Parsons, 1930), about the exact relationship between Calvinism and capitalism. On the one side, no one could more rigidly insist than Calvin that no man has merits in the eyes of God. On the other side, Calvin—or at least the Calvinists after him—also suggest that worldly success can serve as a sign that a man has been "elected" by God. The elect ought, in the words of 2 Peter 1:10 to "give diligence to make [their] calling and election sure." Although, then, success is not a consequence of merit, it is a sign of election, which ought to be confirmed by diligent effort. Thus it is that Calvinism opens the way to a secular version of Pelagianism. Take away the idea of election, and it is easy to reinterpret Calvin thus: "Show your merit by diligent application to your vocation, and success will follow."

17. *Summa theologica*, Pt. II, i, q. 109, a. 2.

out the aid of yet another kind of grace, "healing grace," to fulfil the commands of the law even in an external sense. But how far, so much granted, can grace carry them? At this point, Aquinas appeals to the authority of Paul's Epistle to the Romans. Speaking as one already healed by grace, according to Aquinas, Paul there writes: "With the mind I myself serve the law of God; but with the flesh the law of sin."[18] This means, Aquinas argues, that grace can so repair the mind of those to whom it is granted that they will commit none of the sins which arise out of the reason. And reason is the source, according to Aquinas, of all mortal sins, all sins which, if not forgiven by God, will bring upon the sinner eternal damnation. For it is the essence of such sins that they involve a *deliberate* turning away from God. But "because of the corruption of the lower appetite of sensuality" men cannot, even with the aid of divine grace, avoid all *venial* sin. So they can never, Aquinas concludes, live a wholly sinless life, even with divine aid; the Fall has made that impossible.

So far, then, as perfection is taken to be equivalent to sinlessness, to "freedom from blemish," men cannot, if Aquinas is right, achieve perfection. But human perfection, for Aquinas, means much more than sinlessness. It involves being "like God" in that special way in which man can be "like God," i.e. by contemplating him. Aquinas quotes with approval from the *Nicomachean Ethics* Aristotle's view that man's ultimate perfection lies in contemplating the highest object of contemplation, and conflates it with Matthew's "Blessed are the pure in heart: for they shall see God."[19] Since the principal commandment of Christianity is to love God, and since God is often described as *being* love, it might have

---

18. Romans 7:25.
19. Matthew 5:8. For a detailed treatment of this theme, see K. E. Kirk: *The Vision of God.* There is a special problem for Aquinas: the vision of God comes to man only through God's grace. How then can it be man's natural end? For the complexities of scholastic argument on this point, see, for example, Nigel Abercrombie: *The Origins of Jansenism,* pp. 63–65. See also p. 11 below.

been expected that human perfection, for Aquinas, would consist in the absolute love of God. But it is extraordinary how many Christian theologians have accepted the other, the typically Greek, view that perfection consists in the contemplation, rather than the love, of God. It is "through this vision," Aquinas specifically argues, "that we become most like God." [20]

It would be very easy, he admits, to conclude from the fact that men attain to God by loving him that their "last end and happiness," too, consists "not in knowing God, but in loving him, or in some other act of the Will towards him." [21] But this, he says, is clearly wrong. Reason is the highest part of man's nature. Therefore human perfection must lie in an act of intellect, not of the will, in contemplation, not in love. Then, too—again the argument is Aristotelian—to find is better than to seek: the vision of God is the possession of God, whereas the love of him does not imply possession. Aquinas goes on to give a great many other reasons, of the same Aristotelian kind; the fact that he gives so many, indeed, may suggest that he feels the strength of the opposing case.*

The vision of God, according to Aquinas, comes only in eternity; the kind of knowledge of God men have in this life, whether by faith or by demonstration, does not amount to seeing God [22]—or at least not to seeing God except im-

20. *Summa contra gentiles,* III. 51.

21. *Ibid.,* III. 26.

* Contrast Duns Scotus for whom "thinking of God matters little if he be not loved in contemplation." Aquinas, it is worth noting, did not even *consider* the view that the ultimate perfection for man might lie in his being able to love in heaven, as never before, his fellow human beings. But a nineteenth-century Roman Catholic theologian, Baron von Hügel, does discuss this possibility. He tells the story of the soul who is informed on entering heaven that now it will be able "throughout eternity . . . [to] serve its fellow-souls, those down there still on earth, as well as these here in heaven." The soul, says von Hügel, is deeply disappointed. Let it rather, the soul pleads, be absorbed in God. See "The Difficulties and Dangers of Nationality" in F. von Hügel: *Essays and Addresses on the Philosophy of Religion,* Second Series (London, 1926; repr. 1951), p. 275. Von Hügel takes this story over from a German theologian, Paul de Lagarde.

22. *Ibid.,* III. 38–47.

perfectly, "through a glass darkly." Scripture presents some difficulty for Aquinas on this point. In the *Summa theologica* he finds himself obliged to admit that Moses and Paul had a direct vision of God, in an "ecstasy" which took them out of their body.[23] But in every other case in which someone is said to have "seen God," what he must actually have experienced, Aquinas tells us, is not a vision of God as he is but only an image of a sensory kind, which somehow stood for or represented God.* Forgetting Moses and Paul, indeed, this is all that in his *Summa contra gentiles*[24] he allows to be possible. The consequence is that since absolute perfection lies in the vision of God, no man can achieve perfection in this life, however hard he tries and however much God helps him. The most he can do is to achieve that lower, "evangelical" perfection, which consists in loving God before all else and being free of all mortal sin. So much, but only so much, Aquinas allows to man—if he be granted God's grace.

The immediate effect of Aquinas's teaching was to increase the Christian emphasis on free will and diminish the emphasis on grace. Aquinas, we may well feel, has not departed far from Augustine on this point. But Augustine can be interpreted—and often has been interpreted—in a man-

---

23. *Summa theologica*, Pt. I, q. 12, a. 11.

* At the very end of his life, perhaps under the influence of his neo-Platonic friend and assistant William of Moerbeke, Aquinas may have changed his views on this point. He is reported as saying of his theology that it was "worthless," in the light of spiritual experiences which had, late in life, come his way. But, whatever the truth of this story, the lesson of his purely philosophical writings is that man should not, in his present life, attempt to pass beyond the limitations imposed by the fact that all his knowledge has its origins in sensory experience. In this case, too, the peculiar relationship between Jesus and God causes difficulties. John reports Jesus as saying: "he who sees me sees him who sent me" (12:45) and again, "he who has seen me has seen the Father" (14:9). Nevertheless, Aquinas does not count seeing Jesus as "seeing God"; it is not seeing God's essence. Jesus, as the Scholastic formula has it, is God but not the *whole* of God.

24. *Summa contra gentiles*, III. 47. The reader should be warned that some interpreters of Aquinas would read him as allowing more to the mystical perfectibilist than I represent him as doing.

ner which concedes much less than Aquinas reads him as conceding to free will. And Aquinas certainly rejected the view that man is morally helpless except when God chooses to grant him the grace to act well. Even without special grace, he says, man can do "some particular good" even although he "cannot do all the good natural to [him]" — nor, of course, display the "supernatural good" of *caritas*.[25] Not a great concession, perhaps, but enough to alarm more ardent anti-Pelagians.

Some of Aquinas's successors carried his emphasis on freedom and merit a little further. In the fourteenth century that devoted Augustinian, Thomas Bradwardine, thought he could detect a Pelagian beneath every academic gown. "I rarely heard anything said of grace in the lectures of the philosophers . . . ," he writes in the preface to his *De causa dei contra Pelagium*, "But every day I heard them teach that we are the masters of our own free acts, and that it stands in our power to do either good or evil, to be either virtuous or vicious, and such like."[26] In the manner of his time, Bradwardine does not name his "new Pelagians" and he is almost certainly exaggerating the extent of their Pelagianism. That his "new Pelagians" were fourteenth-century Julians, or even fourteenth-century Cassians, is highly improbable. But differences of emphasis that now look minor to us, the slightest concessions to the power of the human will, were to Bradwardine fraught with disastrous consequences.

Whatever the situation in Roman Catholic theology, Renaissance neo-Platonists certainly extolled the powers of the human will to a degree unprecedented since Pelagius's condemnation. Pico della Mirandola's fifteenth-century *Oration*

---

25. *Summa theologica*, Pt. II, i, q. 109, a. 2. See also Pt. II, i, q. 85, a. 2 and Pt. II, ii, q. 23, a. 2.

26. Trans. in H. B. Workman: *John Wyclif*, 2 vols (Oxford, 1926), Vol. 1, p. 121. On Bradwardine see especially G. Leff: *Bradwardine and the Pelagians* (Cambridge, 1957).

will serve as an example of Renaissance Pelagianism.* God, he says, had created the whole universe before he created man—everything with its own nature and in its own place. Then God decided to produce a being capable of contemplating the beauty of the universe he had created. But he faced a difficulty: he had already exhausted every possible "nature." "There was not among His archetypes that from which He could fashion a new offspring, nor was there in His treasure-houses anything which He might bestow on his new son as an inheritance." So God created man, uniquely in the universe, as "a creature of indeterminate nature." Man, and man alone, according to Pico, has the power to choose what place in the universe he shall occupy, whether to "degenerate into the lower forms of life" or "to be reborn into the higher forms, which are divine." Man is born, that is, without a nature, but with the capacity to choose what nature he will adopt—as Sartre was also to argue in the twentieth century.[27] The French humanist Charles Bovillé (Carolus Bovillus) carried matters even further.[28] At birth, he agrees with Pico, man is neither innately corrupt nor innately good, nor has he, indeed, any nature whatsoever. But in virtue of this fact—because he is himself of no

---

* Pico's *Oration* is generally, but not quite accurately, referred to as "Oration on the Dignity of Man"; properly speaking, this is the title only of the first section. There has been a good deal of controversy about this oration. Pico was in many respects—for example, in his attitude to scholastic philosophy—one of the more conservative of the humanists. Many commentators have found it hard to believe that he "really meant" his *Oration*, with its complete ignoring of divine grace, to be taken seriously. But whatever Pico "really meant" to say, the *Oration* as it stands can only be read as, for its century, a startling defence of human dignity, human powers, human possibilities. Compare P. O. Kristeller's article: "Pico della Mirandola, Count Giovanni" in *The Encyclopedia of Philosophy*, Vol. 6, esp. pp. 309–10 and, of the works there referred to, especially the report of the 1963 conference on Pico: *L'opera e il pensiero di Giovanni Pico della Mirandola nella storia dell'umanesimo*, 2 vols (Florence, 1965).

27. For Pico's oration see *The Renaissance Philosophy of Man*, sel. and ed. Ernst Cassirer, P. O. Kristeller, J. H. Randall, Jr. (Chicago, 1948; paperback ed. 1956, repr. 1965), pp. 224–25. On Sartre see John Passmore: *A Hundred Years of Philosophy*, 2nd rev. ed. (London, 1966), ch. XIX.

28. See the account of Bovillus in E. F. Rice: *The Renaissance Idea of Wisdom* (Cambridge, Mass., 1958), pp. 106–23.

fixed essence—he can perfect himself by appropriating the whole of nature to himself.

In comparison, such innovations as the sixteenth-century Jesuit Molina introduced into the traditional teachings were modest in the extreme, for all that the Dominicans, faithful to the memory of Aquinas, tried to secure their condemnation. Molina sought only to establish that divine grace is not what immediately acts in man; that it operates in man not in virtue of its own power but because (as God foreknows) those to whom he grants it will choose freely to accept it.[29] To Pelagian eyes, certainly, this was no more than a tiny crack in the Augustinian façade, if so much as that, but the Reformers were to think very differently.

A reaction was only to be expected; when it came, at the hands of Luther and Calvin, it was with unprecedented violence. Luther, as we have already seen, wholly rejected not only the Pelagian view that man could perfect himself by his own efforts but the more modest doctrine that he could be perfected by God. Man's corruption lies too deep for that. So Augustine had argued, too, but Luther went much further than even Augustine had gone; he entirely rejected the psychological mechanism which had so far been presumed by Pelagians and anti-Pelagians alike. He denied that men possess a free will which, with or without the aid of God's grace, can choose the good. He did so, not reluctantly, not as an unintended consequence of taking Revelation seriously, but with an enormous sense of relief. "I frankly confess," he wrote in his *Bondage of the Will*, "that, for myself, even if it could be, I should not want 'free will' to be given me, nor anything to be left in my own hands to enable me to endeavour after salvation." And that is because no matter how desperate his efforts, he would still be left with no certainty that he had done all that he might have done. "If I

29. For a fuller account of Molina, see N. Abercrombie: *The Origins of Jansenism*, pp. 93–114. His principal work was *Concordia liberi arbitrii cum gratiae donis*, publ. 1588.

lived and worked to all eternity, my conscience would never reach comfortable certainty as to how much it must do to satisfy God." [30] The only final way of overthrowing the belief that one ought to be perfect was to reject that mechanism which alone, it had generally been agreed, could make it *possible* for men to perfect themselves.

Free will, Luther argued, is a term properly applicable only to God—Luther, it must be remembered, had been taught by disciples of William of Ockham, that redoubtable defender of divine omnipotence. Only God can do whatever he chooses to do. "If 'free will' is ascribed to men," Luther significantly remarks, "it is ascribed with no more propriety than divinity itself would be—and no blasphemy could exceed that!" [31] Man's attempt to think of himself as "free," that is, is just another manifestation of his attempt to think of himself as godlike. The truth of the matter is that he is absolutely impotent, at least in all matters relating to his spiritual welfare.

In his *Freedom of the Will* Erasmus had displayed some alarm about the consequences of men's believing that when they act well, it is because God acts in them. "Let us assume," he writes, "that it is true, as Augustine has written somewhere, that God causes both good and evil in us, and that he rewards us for his good works wrought in us and punishes us for the evil deeds done in us. What a loophole the publication of this opinion would open to godlessness among innumerable people. . . . How many weak ones would continue in their perpetual and laborious battle against their own flesh? What wicked fellow would henceforth try to better his conduct?" [32] In reply, Luther thunders against "that pru-

30. Martin Luther: *On the Bondage of the Will*, VII, xviii (Weimarer Ausgabe, XVIII, 783) as trans. J. I. Packer and O. R. Johnston (London, 1957), p. 313.

31. *On the Bondage of the Will*, II. ix (Weimarer Ausgabe, XVIII, 635–38); ed. cited, p. 105.

32. Erasmus-Luther: *Discourse on Free Will*, trans. and ed. E. F. Winter, Milestones of Thought (New York, 1961), pp. 11–12.

dence of yours . . . by which you are resolved to hold to neither side." You admit, he says to Erasmus, that the power of free will is small, and that it is quite ineffective, in its pursuit of the good, without the aid of God's grace. But to say that the will is "free" although it is none the less devoid of power is, Luther argues, a contradiction in terms. The most that can properly be said is that there is something about human beings which makes them fit to be granted God's grace—"God did not make heaven for geese." To describe this quality in men which makes them attractive to God as their "free will" is hopelessly to confuse the issue.[33]

Turning from Luther to Calvin, the perfectibilist is unlikely to find fresh grounds for hope.[34] "Whatever is in man," Calvin tells us, "from the understanding to the will, from the soul even to the flesh, has been defiled and crammed with concupiscence. Or, to put it more briefly, the whole man is of himself nothing but concupiscence."[35] Just as for the Stoics the Sage is good through-and-through; so for Calvin man is corrupted through-and-through; he is incapable of performing any action which is not in some degree corrupted. He is not bad merely because he commits particular bad acts, any more than the Stoic Sage is good because he commits particular good acts. Such specific acts, Calvin writes, as "adulteries, fornications, thefts, hatreds, murders, carousings"—in this *mélange*, with its extraordinary anticlimax,[36] the Calvinist sense of values is very obvious—are more properly to be called "the fruits of sin" than "sins." The sin lies in the corruption, the perversity, from which these "works of the flesh" flow, a perversity which "never ceases in us, but continually bears fresh fruits." It is not simply that we

33. *On the Bondage of the Will,* II. ix; ed. cited, pp. 104–5.
34. But compare the last note on pp. 148–49 above.
35. *Institutes,* II. i. 8, trans. Battles, Vol. 1, p. 252.
36. No more extraordinary, of course, than Augustine's *Epistle to Alypius* (Ep. 29, in *Select Letters,* trans. Baxter, pp. 69–91) and Paul (I Corinthians 5:11 and, more especially, Galatians 5:19–21). The Calvin passage is *Institutes* II. i. 8, Vol. 1, p. 251, in Battles' trans.

now lack what Adam had—complete innocence. Our corruption is a positive corruption: "our will is not only destitute and idle of good, but so fruitful and fertile of sin that it cannot be idle." To suppose otherwise, according to Calvin, is at once to deprive God of his rights and to encourage man to *hubris*. "Nothing, however slight, can be credited to man without depriving God of his honor, and without man himself falling into ruin through brazen confidence." [37]

Yet if only in order to counter the "complacency" of the unrighteous, Calvin finds himself compelled to grant that there is still in man, in however perverted a form, something of the image of God. After his Fall man retains "some sparks of understanding," however "choked with dense ignorance" they may be; he has "some desire for truth," even if that desire, "such as it is," is soon destroyed by vanity or carelessly turned to idle and unimportant topics; he still has some capacity in regard to "earthly things"—government, household management, mechanical skills and the liberal arts; he is not entirely without "universal impressions of a certain civic fair dealing and order." So whereas Calvin will write at one time that "there is more worth in all the vermin of the world than there is in man, for he is a creature in whom the image of God has been effaced," [38] he will at another time insist that although "miserably deformed" the image of God still persists in man. No doubt "righteousness and rectitude, and the freedom of choosing what is good, have been lost"; nevertheless "many excellent endowments, by which we excel the brutes, still remain." [39] In Luther's terminology, man is a member of the Earthly as well as of the Heavenly Kingdom, and in the first capacity can properly deploy his reason and his will. It is only when it comes

---

37. *Institutes,* II. ii. 1, as trans. Battles, Vol. 1, p. 255.

38. *Sermon on Job,* 2:1f, as trans. in T. F. Torrance: *Calvin's Doctrine of Man* (London, 1949; repr. 1952), p. 88. The earlier argument may be found in *Institutes,* II. ii. 12–13: the trans. is adapted from Battles, Vol. 1, pp. 270–72.

39. *Commentary on James,* 3:9, as trans. Torrance, *loc. cit.*

to spiritual questions that reason, according to Calvin, is "as blind as a mole"—or, in Luther's words, is "the devil's whore."

No doubt, even in spiritual matters, reason retains certain powers. It is quite capable of deducing God's goodness, providence and justice, so Calvin argues, from a consideration of the nature of the world and of human history. Men are blameworthy if they do not recognize God's supremacy; they cannot excuse themselves on the ground that they have not been granted a special revelation. As the Westminster Confession puts it: "the light of nature, and the works of creation and providence, do so far manifest the goodness, wisdom and power of God, as to leave men inexcusable." Reason is capable, too, of distinguishing between good and evil. So pagans are blameworthy for not behaving morally. But the fact remains that man's corruption is such that without the aid of the Holy Spirit he is "stupid and senseless" in all spiritual matters. The most Reason can attain to, in fact, is a very general recognition of God's existence and goodness—of the sort one finds, let us say, in Plato—and a power of acting in a way which, judged externally, is righteous.*

At this point, however, Calvin still finds himself troubled. He cannot forbear regarding as morally excellent, at

---

* The problem which here confronts Calvin, and not Calvin uniquely, is a particularly acute one. He can scarcely deny that Plato, without benefit of Revelation, taught moral lessons which Christianity also wishes to teach; he admits, as we saw, that "natural reason" is capable of distinguishing between good and evil. Yet on the other side, such doctrines as that salvation and damnation are unrelated to moral effort, that some men are predestined to be saved and others to be damned, that a Revelation which is necessary for salvation has been granted to some people and not to others—so that Australian Aborigines, let us say, had for almost two millennia no possible access to it—are, from the standpoint of "natural reason," nothing short of morally abominable. In the theological sphere, too, "reason" has to be allowed a certain power, if only reason in the form of historical investigation—for Roman Catholic doctrines have to be rejected and Revelation harmonized—yet it must not be allowed to question Revelation itself. So Reason has to be kept, like a savage dog, on a leash; praised so long as it acts as a watch-dog, but feared lest it bite the wrong people or turn on its master. The very large number of passages in Calvin which bear on the powers of Reason have been brought together, under various heads, by Leroy Nixon in *John Calvin's Teachings upon Human Reason* (New York, 1963).

a more than "external" level of morality, the Roman patriot Camillus, and as morally despicable, at a more than ordinary level of corruption, the Roman conspirator Catiline. But they were both "natural men," ignorant of the true God, and therefore, on the face of it, equally and utterly corrupt. So Calvin finds himself forced to suppose that God sometimes bestows special grace even on men who do not belong to the elect—a grace which enables them to perform noble and heroic deeds.

From his point of view, of course, what are ordinarily called "natural gifts" are all of them God-granted endowments, part of that "general grace" which is God's gift, at their creation, to all men. Calvin cannot allow, however, that this "general grace" is ever sufficient to save a man. For if it were, then men, once created, could seek their own salvation from their own resources; to that degree, they would be independent of God. Such a Pelagianism is inherent, as Calvin sees the situation, in the theology of Aquinas, which allows, from Calvin's point of view, altogether too much power to such "natural gifts" as reason. Yet, on the other side, men are blameworthy for not having fully used the grace God has granted them at their creation; they can rightly be blamed for not becoming what they still, corrupt though they are, "have it in themselves to be." When he wants to emphasize how blameworthy men are, Calvin emphasizes what they are capable, even without special grace, of becoming; when he wants to emphasize how dependent on God they are, he stresses their utter corruption.

Calvin cannot bring himself to say that science, art, extraordinary heroism, are all of them, as infected by the corruption of self-love, entirely valueless. They are corrupted, certainly, but not wholly corrupted. If, on the one side, to allow any "natural gifts" to man is to cut across that conviction of man's utter dependence at every moment of his life on God which lies, so Calvin thought, at the heart of all religion, yet on the other side to allow him no such "natural gifts" is to turn all "natural" men, equally, into villains. And Calvin, a cultivated man, a scholar, cannot bring himself to say this either. So we find him writing: "I do not so dissent from the common judgement as to contend that there is no difference between the justice, moderation, and equity of Titus and Trajan and the madness, intemperance, and savagery of Caligula or Nero or Domitian . . . and — not to tarry over individual virtues and vices — between observances and contempt of right and of laws." Yet at the same time, he goes on, "what Augustine writes is none the less true: that all who are estranged from the religion of the one God, however admirable they may be regarded on account of their reputation for virtue, not only deserve no reward but rather punishment, because by the pollution of their hearts they defile God's good works."[40] Not all his successors were to be convinced that, if Titus and Trajan are really better men than Caligula and Nero, it can at the same time be true that "they deserve no rewards but rather punishment." But to Calvin this is essential; man himself has no merits; in the eyes of God he is worthless. Calvin was not even prepared to admit, as Aquinas did, that man can, with God's help, be wholly free of "mortal" as distinct from "venial" sins. The whole distinction between mortal and venial sins, indeed, he rejected as untenable.

The Council of Trent had accepted Aquinas's teaching on this point. It anathematized "whoever shall say that the commandments of God are impossible of observance even to a justified man." "They admit," Calvin writes in reply, "that even the most holy sometimes fall into light and daily sins. First I ask, whether there be any sin, however light, that is not inconsistent with the observance of the law? For what vicious thought will creep into the mind of man if it be wholly occupied with the love of God?"[41] On this question,

40. *Institutes,* III. xiv. 2–3, trans. Battles, Vol. 1, pp. 769–70.
41. John Calvin: *Tracts and Treatises,* trans. H. Beveridge, 3 vols (Edinburgh, 1958,

then, Calvin's position is quite straightforward. We are commanded to love God with our whole heart, and mind, and
strength. If we do, then we shall not commit any sin whatsoever; our mind will be wholly free of any "vicious thought."
And if—as is in fact always the case—we do not, then we
cannot pretend that we are keeping God's commandments.

Perfection in however limited a degree, it must therefore
be concluded, lies quite beyond the reach of man: "He who
has come nearest to perfection has not yet advanced half-
way." [42] For "no man ever lived who satisfied the law of God,
and . . . none ever can be found." [43] So it is not only that men
cannot be perfect in some special metaphysical or theological sense, involving, let us say, the direct vision of God. They
cannot even succeed in obeying God's commands; they cannot be free from sin, in the most obvious, straightforward
sense of that word. The human will is so corrupted that not
even God can wholly release it, in this life, from its bondage
to sin. "God commences so to reform his elect in the present
life, that he proceeds with this work little by little and does
not fully achieve it until death, so that they are still guilty
before his judgement." [44] The elect are *justified* once and for
all, and wholly, but they do no more than make progress
towards sanctification.

It would be an extremely complex task to trace the history of Pelagianism and anti-Pelagianism through the centuries that followed the Reformation.[45] Let us look rather
to our own century, to 1912, when there appeared a book

---

repr. from ed. of 1851), Vol. 3: *In Defence of the Reformed Faith,* p. 132. The Canon of the
Council of Trent is on p. 105 of the same vol.

42. *Ibid.,* p. 145.

43. *Ibid.,* p. 130.

44. *Institutes,* III. xi. 11. On this complicated question see F. Wendel: *Calvin,* trans.
P. Mairet, pp. 255–61, whose version of this passage I have followed.

45. We shall meet other varieties of Pelagianism in subsequent chapters. See also
Benjamin B. Warfield: *Perfectionism,* 2 vols (New York, 1931). The 1-vol. ed. (Philadelphia,
1967) restricts itself to Oberlin perfectionism and its German successors. The original ed.
includes a good deal of material on nineteenth-century perfectionists.

which will serve to sum up what Pelagianism, in the period preceding that great turning-point in human history, the First World War, had finally become. This is F. R. Tennant's *The Concept of Sin*, which Reinhold Niebuhr, a hostile critic, once described as "the most elaborate of modern Pelagian treatises."*

The main objections to Pelagianism—apart from the supposition that the Christian has to believe that men are born corrupt because this is the Biblical teaching, a view Tennant contests at length—have arisen, according to Tennant, because immaculate, sinless, perfection has been confused with what Tennant calls "absolute" perfection. The two ideas, he says, are wholly distinct. A young child may be sinless but he cannot be absolutely perfect. To be absolutely perfect, according to Tennant, a man needs a type of disposition, a degree of knowledge, a kind of temperament, the absence of which in a child or in a man is in no sense a sin. For Tennant defines absolute perfection in *aesthetic* terms, as involving the possession of a harmonious, easily-flowing goodness, not within the reach of the will. Sin, in contrast— for Tennant as for Schleiermacher—is by its very nature a deliberate act of will, a conscious rejection of moral principles.

Man's animal condition carries with it, Tennant freely admits, elements of discord, which are incompatible with absolute perfection. To be good, men have to struggle— to struggle with their animal impulses, to struggle against temptations. But it is quite improper, according to Tennant, to call man sinful or "imperfect" (in the relative sense),

---

* It is not a particularly original book. Its indebtedness to Kant, to Ritschl, to Schleiermacher, is obvious; many of its teachings can be matched in nineteenth-century America, in the writings of the "Oberlin perfectionists." More remotely, its roots lie in the third century, in Irenaeus, who argued that what was wrong with Adam and Eve was immaturity, and that mankind is still growing to moral maturity, as opposed to the view that the history of humanity is the history of a Fall from an ideal moral condition. But it is precisely its representative character which makes *The Concept of Sin* so important for our present purposes.

merely because he has certain "propensities" which an aesthetically perfect man would lack. The "elemental blind impulses of our nature" are in themselves not "sinful." To regard them as such, according to Tennant, is "to perpetuate the Manichaean heresy and to encourage sanctimonious prudery." They are "the material of sin" only because in the course of human evolution it is particularly these impulses which have to be "restrained, modified, or stifled, by the morally enlightened will."[46] They persist in man as temptations, but to be tempted is not to sin. Their existence explains why, however, man cannot be perfect either as Jesus is perfect or as "our Father in heaven is perfect"; to achieve such perfection men would have to become "like gods," a condition to which it is impossible for them to attain. "The content of perfection for man," Tennant therefore writes, "is necessarily circumscribed by man's nature, by what he is and what he is capable of becoming."[47] So "perfection for man" does not consist in living in accordance with the example set by Jesus, let alone the example set by God; the only ideal which has any relevance to men is a human ideal, within reach of human beings.

But is not such an ideal by its very nature, as Spinoza had argued, merely relative? Tennant accepts the consequence. It is and must be relative, relative to the state of human development, relative to society, relative to the knowledge and capacity of the individual. To demonstrate that a man is "imperfect," then, in the only sense of imperfection which is relevant to moral judgement, it is not enough to argue that he is imperfect as compared with God or, even, that he is imperfect as compared with some ideal which future generations may set up; the only question is whether he is imperfect in relation to *the ideal which is accessible to him*. In spite of his indebtedness to Kant's *Religion Within the Limits of*

---

46. *The Concept of Sin* (Cambridge, 1912), pp. 144, 149.
47. *Ibid.*, p. 79.

Reason Alone Tennant breaks with Kant completely on this, a crucial, point. On Kant's view the moral law is, and must be, absolute; for Tennant, influenced by evolutionary biology and comparative anthropology, the question "*Whose* moral law?" is a proper and relevant one.

It will be obvious what has happened. Tennant has lowered his sights for man. He has remained a Pelagian, in his emphasis on what a human being can achieve by the exercise of his will, while abandoning the absolute perfectionism of the Pelagians. To the Augustinian-Lutheran answer to Pelagius: "Man cannot be perfect, as God is perfect, by the exercise of his will," Tennant replies: "That is so, but he can be perfect as *he* can be perfect, judged by the criteria which are applicable to him." He can be adjudged perfect, that is, as a being who at that time and in that place is, in regard to some action, "in a position to recognize within himself the moral imperative 'I ought' with regard to it" and to conform his will wholly to that "ought."[48]

The question still remains whether men can attain to *complete* "perfection" in this sense, sinless perfection, the avoidance of any breaches of the moral law they recognize. This, for Tennant, is an empirical question. There is no reason in the nature of the case, certainly, why men should not be sinless and "the ideal has been approached perhaps more often and more nearly than we think."[49] But since man's tendency, as Kant had also pointed out, is to make greater and greater demands upon himself as he develops morally, it is not surprising that even the saints should feel themselves to be sinners.

One could scarcely expect Tennant's views to win universal acceptance. From the point of view of more orthodox Christians, he at once demands too little of men and

---

48. *Ibid.,* p. 96. Compare Charles G. Finney: *Lectures on Systematic Theology,* 2nd ed. (London, 1851), pp. 748–49, quoted in B. B. Warfield: *Perfectionism* (1967), p. 146, n. 306.
    49. *The Concept of Sin,* p. 270.

expects too much from them. On the one side, he allows
men to lower their standards, not to feel guilty, as Augustine did, because they cannot reach absolute perfection,
because they cannot love God with their whole heart and
whole soul and whole mind. On the other side, he expects
men to reach that moral standard which lies within their
capacity merely by the exercise of their own wills. His concept of sin, Tennant elsewhere assures us, is not incompatible with Christian teachings about Grace and Redemption.
But how astonishing it is, from an Augustinian standpoint,
to encounter a whole book on the nature of sin which does
not so much as mention grace!

Not surprisingly the counter-reaction to nineteenth-
century Pelagianism was as violent as the Augustinianism
and the Calvinism which it substantially reinstated. The
counter-reaction was no doubt precipitated by the First
World War. Karl Barth, for one, tells us that this was the
decisive event in his intellectual history—not so much the
war as such, perhaps, as the failure of liberal theologians to
remain Christian in the face of it, their ready surrender to
nationalistic patriotism.[50] But Barth himself suggests that,
important though the First World War was to him, it was
only one of a series of factors contributing to the same outcome: a complete dissatisfaction with what had happened to
moral theology, the sort of theology we have exemplified by
the admittedly extreme instance of Tennant's *Concept of Sin.*

Barth is certainly the most important, and the most systematic, of modern Augustinians. But let us look first at
a slightly more moderate, considerably more "accessible,"
theologian, Reinhold Niebuhr. For Reinhold Niebuhr, as for
Bradwardine, there are Pelagians everywhere. Aquinas, according to Niebuhr, carried semi-Pelagianism to a point at

---

50. For the effect of the War as a whole on the belief that human beings could moralize themselves by their own efforts, compare Otto Piper: *Recent Developments in German
Protestantism* (London, 1934).

which it is indistinguishable from Pelagianism. Even Calvin is suspect. He allowed too much sanctity to the righteous; he encouraged self-righteousness, so Niebuhr suggests, by over-emphasizing sensuality—which men can learn to control—rather than the much more fundamental sin of pride.

The essence of sin, for Niebuhr, is pride; it lies in the fact that "the self lacks the faith and trust to subject itself to God." And this is a consequence of the human condition, a condition which Niebuhr describes in terms which owe a great deal to Kierkegaard. Man is made anxious, Niebuhr argues, by his ontological position. He is a being who is at once involved in Nature and stands outside it, foreseeing, unlike the brute beasts, its caprices and perils. Almost inevitably, in the attempt to overcome this anxiety, he seeks to strengthen himself, to convert his dependence, by the exercise of reason, into independence.[51] And in so doing he sins.* "Original sin," then, lies not in the inheritance of a trait, not in concupiscence, but in man's refusal to accept his ontological status; sin is "man's unwillingness to acknowledge his finiteness."[52] It at once follows that man cannot hope to conquer his sinfulness by independent action, by the exercise of freedom; independence and freedom are the very source of his sinfulness. Only by complete trust in God's grace, only by surrender to God's love, has the soul any prospect of escaping finitude and, with it, sin. As for the belief that man can perfect himself by his own efforts, this is of the very essence of sinfulness, of man's refusal to "acknowledge his finiteness."

---

51. *The Nature and Destiny of Man*, 2 vols (London, 1941; repr. 1945), pp. 266–70.

* This is not, it should be observed, a peculiarly Protestant view. Compare the Roman Catholic theologian Baron von Hügel's essay on "The Facts and Truths concerning God and the Soul which are of most importance in the Life of Prayer" included in *Essays and Addresses on the Philosophy of Religion*, Second Series. Von Hügel rejects the taint theory of original sin, argues that "the central sin, for the Christian, is Pride and Self-sufficiency" and derives pride from "the delicate poise of our imperfect freedom" (p. 236). Nor does von Hügel stand alone among Roman Catholics in holding these doctrines.

52. *Faith and History* (London, 1949), p. 133.

Niebuhr is, all the same, relatively optimistic about human beings and their destiny. Man has still left to him, he thinks, a relic of his original righteousness, and that relic constitutes his point of contact with God. Karl Barth, at least in his earlier writings, goes much further than Niebuhr in his condemnation of humanity, in denying to man any sort of natural goodness. "We are sinful creatures," he writes, "we are unfit for its [the Word of God's] service. We cannot in our own strength become either believers or witnesses. In the light that falls upon us when we are taken into its service we have to discover and confess that we are not only useless, but inexcusably recalcitrant."[53] Nor is it only the human being who is thus condemned; it is life as a whole. No Manichaean could be more insistent on this point. "God has come into our life in its utter unloveliness and frightfulness"—he has come into "this frightful world."[54]

There is no question, for Barth, of the human being's having any value in himself; Scripture speaks of man, he says, only as sinful. "Man as such has no dignity of his own, nor has the fellowship of man with man."[55] The belief, so often supposed to be peculiarly Christian, in "the infinite value of the individual soul" is in fact, according to Barth, pagan. There is nothing in man to attract God's attention to him; the doctrine of an arbitrary election reaches in Barth its supreme point. It in no way, he says, lies "in the nature of man or in some capacity of his own that he among all creatures may belong to God." That heaven is made for men rather than for geese is purely and simply "an inconceivable gift." Man's sin consists, on Barth's view, in the fact that he "despised grace"; he "wanted to be as God"—to become, as the Book of Genesis puts it, "one of us"—and "in wanting

---

53. *Church Dogmatics*, Vol. I: *The Doctrine of the Word of God*, 2, trans. G. T. Thomson and Harold Knight (Edinburgh, 1956), p. 702.

54. *Dogmatics in Outline*, trans. G. T. Thomson (London, 1949; repr. New York, 1959), ch. 16, p. 109.

55. *Church Dogmatics*, Vol. I, 2, p. 404.

that he sinned . . . he broke the relationship which bound him to God and his fellow-man." So what was for the Greek philosophers and for Greek-inspired Christians the noblest of human aspirations, to become like God, is, for Barth, the root of all evil.[56] We are back where we started, in archaic Greece; *hubris,* for Barth as for Niebuhr, is the sin of sins.

The great mistake of traditional Christian theology, as Barth sees it, is that it was persuaded to substitute the God of the philosophers, a "simple absolute being," for Jahweh. The Bible, according to Barth, speaks of the sovereignty "of a quite different God." No doubt the "simple absolute Being" was presumed by theologians, and by the Greek philosophers themselves, to be in some sense sovereign. But its sovereignty was merely a logical or ontological supremacy, not the sovereignty of a God that "can do wonders." It is only in its relationship to the sovereignty of that wonder-working God and his free elective grace—a sovereignty and a grace exhibited above all else in Jesus Christ—that a man, according to Barth, can discover what sort of being he himself is. That kind of biologico-anthropological "understanding" of the self which Tennant attempts is useless. And what man comes to discover through Revelation is his own valuelessness, his own helplessness, before God.

When Emil Brunner dared to suggest that, although corrupted by sin, men could at least answer when God calls to them, Barth replied in a bitter pamphlet *Nein! Antwort an Emil Brunner* (1934).[57] In no possible way, he argued, can man progress towards God unless God enables him to do so. There is only one thing which "comforts" and "sets up" the Christian and that is the forgiveness of sins. Everything men do, everything they achieve is, in Barth's eyes, "subject to the judgement that it is sin." Men have no merits with

56. See Karl Barth: *God Here and Now,* trans. P. M. van Buren, pp. 4–7.
57. See the English trans. in E. Brunner: *Natural Theology,* comprising "Nature and Grace" by E. Brunner and the reply "No!" by Karl Barth, trans. P. Fraenkel (London, 1946). Barth's *Nein!* was originally publ. in Munich.

which to plead before God; they are saved only by being "Jesus Christ's property," and belonging for that reason to the kingdom of God's "inconceivable mercy."

Even Barth, however, did not remain wholly faithful to his original severity. In 1956, he delivered a lecture on "The Humanity of God" which represents, he freely admits, a change in the direction of his "evangelical theology." Forty years ago, he says, what he was emphasizing "was not so much the humanity of God as His *deity*—a God absolutely unique in His relation to man and the world, overpoweringly lofty and distant, strange, yes, even wholly other."[58] This was essential, he suggests, in order to make a sharp break with the theology of the preceding three centuries, which had become anthropocentric, laying its principal stress, as Schleiermacher did, on human piety rather than on divine command. In such a theology, so Barth sums it up, "man was made great at the cost of God." But his critics were perhaps right, Barth now admits, in complaining that what he had done was to stand Schleiermacher on his head, to make God great at the cost of men. "What," Barth asks, "if the result of the new hymn to the majesty of God should be a new confirmation of the hopelessness of all human activity?"

To remove that risk it is now necessary, Barth thinks, to emphasize not God's "otherness" but his "humanity," as revealed in the Incarnation, where God reveals his humanity in his "concern" for man. And from the fact that God has this "concern" for man, it follows, after all, that man has a *peculiar* distinction, "as one to whom Jesus Christ is Brother and God is Father." Man, Barth still argues, is not "elected to intercourse with God" merely in virtue of being human. But he is elected as "the being especially endowed by God." This is evident, Barth feels ready to affirm, even in man's

---

58. Included in Karl Barth: *The Humanity of God,* trans. J. N. Thomas and T. Wieser (London, 1961), pp. 37–65.

culture. Admittedly, he at once hastens to add, "culture testifies clearly in history and in the present to the fact that
man is *not* good but rather a downright monster." But still . . .
"one could not . . . say that culture speaks only of the evil
in man." In culture man attempts, even if he so often "runs
aground," to put to good use "the good gift of his humanity."
And it is this man, the man who participates in culture, who
"interests God." Barth allows himself, indeed, to speak with
approval of the slogan, "You men are gods." Even more star-
tlingly, he is not prepared to rule out *a priori* Origen's hypothesis that God's mercy is such that in the end all men will
be saved, that God will reconcile all things to himself. There
could scarcely be a better illustration than Barth's essay of
the permanent tension in Christianity, between a depreciation and an exaltation of man. It is interesting to observe
that Niebuhr, too, has come to feel that he was too severe
in his "rather violent, and sometimes extravagant, reaction
to what I defined as the 'utopianism' . . . of a Protestant and
bourgeois culture."[59] In general terms, indeed, the tide of
twentieth-century Augustinianism seems to have passed its
peak.

What are we to conclude from this brief sketch—it is no
more than that—of Pelagianism within Christianity? This
much, I think, that any movement towards Pelagianism is
bound in the end, so long as Christianity survives, to be re-
sisted. For to allow that man can do anything to perfect himself is to diminish his utter dependence on God; to allow
that *even for one moment* he does not need God is to make of
God at that moment a supernumerary. And if at that moment, why not at other, or at all, moments?

Yet on the other side to assert that man is helpless, without God's grace, to take even the first step towards perfection is, on the face of it, to discourage men from moral
action. It involves the risk that should men once feel them-

---

59. *Man's Nature and His Communities* (New York, 1965), p. 21.

selves alienated from God, there will be nothing to restrain them. It is true that there are various ways of meeting this contingency—by insisting on the endless resources of divine forgiveness, by arguing that "civic" goodness, although not supernatural goodness, is still, in some measure, attainable even by the corrupted man, by setting up, as Calvin tried to do at Geneva, a state so rigorously governed by "the saints" that men did not dare to lapse into crime. But even these methods do not in the end suffice.

Perry Miller has described in detail what happened in one small New England community, the way in which Pelagianism gradually developed out of the internal difficulties of the community—its incapacity to find any way of disciplining those who sat back and waited for God's grace to fall, or not to fall, upon them. If God can, if he chooses, lift a saint from a dunghill, why not be warm and cosy in the dunghill, awaiting his grace? It had to be argued, in opposition to such practical antinomianism, that a Christian could do something to *prepare* himself for salvation, as distinct from simply standing still and waiting "for Christ to do all for him." That Cassian-like concession to Pelagius gradually led, at the hands of Cotton Mather, to the even more Pelagian doctrine that if men would only do whatever it lies within their own power to do "there would be a greater likelihood (I say not a certainty, but a likelihood) that God would grant them that higher power" [his grace]. How Augustine and Calvin must have shuddered in their graves! Thus it was that the United States gradually made its way, from being the most Calvinist, to being the most Pelagian of Christian nations.

More generally, there is within Christianity, just as there was within Stoicism, an internal conflict between Christianity the religion and Christianity the system of moral precepts. As a religion, Christianity emphasizes above all else the omnipotence of God and his spiritual monopoly as the sole source of all goodness and righteousness. Man is, in contrast, wholly ineffective, spiritually null and void. In this mood, Luther can write that: "So man's will is like a beast standing between two riders. If God rides, it wills and goes where God wills. . . . If Satan rides, it wills and goes where Satan wills. Nor may it choose to which rider it will run or which it will seek; but the riders themselves fight to decide who shall have and hold it." [60] But as a set of moral precepts, Christianity tells man to what rider it should run and which it should seek. The philosophical difficulties which arise within both Christianity and Stoicism—the impossibility of reconciling divine omnipotence with human freedom—flow out of and reflect this deep conflict between the religious and the moralistic impulse.

60. *On the Bondage of the Will*, II. viii (Weimarer Ausgabe, XVIII, 635–38), trans. Johnston and Packer, pp. 103–4.

PERFECTIBILITY WITHIN CHRISTIANITY: THE ASCETICO-MYSTICAL TRADITION

The gospel according to Matthew tells a story which was to be at once an embarrassment and an inspiration to Christianity. An embarrassment to such Christians as have sought to convince themselves that Christianity and worldly prosperity are perfectly compatible, an inspiration to those Christians who have refused to believe that, in this life, perfection lies beyond men's reach. A rich young man came to Jesus and asked him: "What good thing shall I do, that I may have eternal life?" Jesus' first answer was that the young man should keep the commandments, to which the young man replied, with remarkable insouciance, that he had kept them all his life. What else, therefore, must he do? And Jesus replied: "If thou wilt be perfect, go and sell that thou hast, and give to the poor."[1]

In his *Miscellanies,* Clement of Alexandria had sought to demonstrate that a man need not abandon philosophy in order to become a Christian; in his sermon, *The Rich Man's Salvation,* he set out to show that the Christian need not abandon his wealth, either. Jesus' exhortation must not, Clement argues, be taken literally. What Jesus "really means" is not that men should *literally* abandon their riches —it was only necessary to look around the crowded streets of Alexandria, Clement told his congregation, to see that there was no virtue in poverty as such—but that they should banish from the soul "its excessive desire, its morbid excitement over them, its anxious cares."[2] In other words, it is the

1. Matthew 19:21.
2. Trans. G. W. Butterworth in *Clement of Alexandria,* Loeb Classical Library (London, 1919), p. 293.

passions so often attaching to the possession of wealth, not the wealth itself, that the Christian must discard.

By such means, room was found within the Church for those who were not prepared to sacrifice their worldly goods in the interests of Christian perfection.* But not all Christians were satisfied thus to soften the teachings of Jesus. The story of the rich young man was, on the face of it, straightforward enough; it purported to be a historical record, not a parable. And it held out to Christians the hope of perfection—to such Christians, at least, as were prepared to accept the arduous discipline of poverty. There were other similar texts: that text, for example, which praises those who "made themselves eunuchs" for heaven's sake; those many texts which insist that men must wholly submit themselves to God's will. Brought together as the significantly-entitled "counsels of perfection," these texts were read as laying down a path which Christians could follow to perfection, the path of poverty, chastity and self-abnegation.

Even if in the long run what men had to seek was de-

---

* Clement's views were destined to have a long life; they are expounded in Lawrence Lipton's *The Holy Barbarians* (New York, 1959, paperback ed., 1962) by a young Roman Catholic member of the "beat generation" to explain why he does not feel it necessary to give up his riches: "The circumstances of one's own personal wealth . . . are of little importance. I mean, the thing that is important is the detachment from one's own possessions" (p. 55). One is at once reminded of Stoicism. But Clement's interpretation can be lent Biblical support by reference, for example, to 1 Corinthians 7:29–30: "it remaineth, that both they that have wives be as though they had none; And they that weep, as though they wept not; . . . and they that buy, as though they possessed not." On the basis of a pious forgery, it was for long believed that Seneca got his ideas from Paul. Whether the true situation is that Paul got them from Seneca—or at least from the Stoicism of Tarsus—is still disputed. See J. N. Sevenster: *Paul and Seneca* (Leiden, 1961) which tends, however, to exaggerate the difference between Paul and Seneca. Pelagius was unconvinced by the Clementine argument; it was one of Augustine's objections to Pelagius that he threatened by his moralistic intransigence to drive out of the church the landowners essential to its institutional life. A modern commentator on Augustine (Portalié) denounces Pelagius's "wild error"—that the wealthy cannot hope to be saved. In the thirteenth century Francis of Assisi narrowly escaped ecclesiastical condemnation, and some of his friends were less fortunate, for taking the virtues of poverty too seriously. The great Church of Assisi is one of the most ironical of all ecclesiastical memorials, almost as if a modern multiversity were set up in honour of Socrates. See Peter Brown: *Augustine of Hippo*, pp. 347–52 and Gordon Leff: *Heresy in the Later Middle Ages*, Vol. 1, Pt. 1.

tachment from the world, it is not humanly possible, many
Christians decided, for a man to be fully detached from
earthly goods so long as he still remains in full possession
of them. Should a Christian genuinely seek to perfect himself, they concluded, the only safe thing for him to do was
entirely to divest himself of all that he owned. "The deserts
are full of mourners," Basil wrote in the fourth century.
What the desert anchorites were mourning was the growing worldliness of Christianity as it was slowly transformed
into the Roman Church and took over from Rome its imperial splendour. But it was not only the snares of property,
of power, of high office, which the mourners sought to escape, whether in the sands of the desert or within the walls
of the monastery. "The glance of a woman," so one of them
wrote, "is a poisoned dart." The glances of women fell harm-
lessly in the desert wastes and spent their force against the
monastery wall. In pious tales about the sanctity of monk or
hermit, one point is constantly emphasized: never, never,
did he risk being poisoned by the darts of a woman's glance,
however holy, however ancient, however closely related she
might be. Self-will, too, was an obstacle to perfection; in
the desert or the monastery self-will could be tortured into
submission.[3] For such was the path to perfection.

Asceticism, of course, was no new thing. It was opposed,
we suggested, to the general tendency of Judaism, which
emphasized the goodness of the world God had created
rather than the need to sacrifice its pleasures. But even the
Jews had their ascetics. In his essay on *The Contemplative
Life* Philo described the manner of life of certain Jewish
monastic communities; reading this description, the fourth-
century Christian historian Eusebius quite naturally con-

---

3. For details of the extremes to which these practices were carried, especially, but
not only, in the Eastern Church, see H. B. Workman: *The Evolution of the Monastic Ideal*,
2nd ed. (London, 1927), pp. 45–54. *The Sayings of the Fathers* make it sufficiently clear what
counted as preparation for perfection. See also P. F. Anson: *The Call of the Desert* (London,
1964).

cluded that Philo was referring "plainly and unquestionably to members of our Church."[4] The discovery of the Dead Sea Scrolls has increased our knowledge of these Jewish ascetic Essene sects: it was already well-known from Josephus's *The Jewish War* that the Essene sects "renounced pleasure as an evil," and saw virtue in "continence and poverty."

Among the Greek philosophers, too, the Pythagorean brotherhoods called upon men to subdue the flesh; the Cynics taught men to despise the body; the Stoics proclaimed that, in order to become godlike, men must rise beyond the passions and be indifferent to material goods; the Platonists sought to ascend to the One by way of a renunciation of the flesh and the passions. So in Christian anchoritism and Christian monasticism a number of traditions in Western thought—to say nothing of Oriental influences—converged in a single powerful stream, restrained only, so far as it was restrained, by the fear of falling into Gnosticism, with its contempt for the body as the work of the Evil One. The object of the anchorite and the monk was, in the first place, to bring themselves to a state of sinlessness, of immaculate perfection, by renouncing the world. And that implied, not only a physical sundering from the ways of man, whether in the deserts sought out by the anchorites or in the monasteries of the monks, but the achievement of an absolute "freedom from desire." For any form of secular passion, it was presumed, must be a subtraction from the love due to God; the hermit had achieved his spiritual aim if he could truly say: "Only I and God are in the world."

Basil autobiographically described a pattern of life which was typical of a not inconsiderable number of his fourth-century contemporaries.[5] He wasted his early years,

4. *History of the Church*, 2. 17. 14; trans. G. A. Williamson (Harmondsworth, 1965). The relevant extracts from Philo can be conveniently read in A. Dupont-Sommer: *The Essene Writings from Qumran*, trans. G. Vermes (Oxford, 1961), pp. 21–26.

5. See particularly Letter 223 in Saint Basil: *The Letters*, trans. R. J. Deferrari, Loeb Classical Library, 4 vols (London, 1926–34), Vol. III, pp. 293–95.

he tells us, on the acquisition of "that wisdom made foolish by God," i.e. the teachings of the philosophers. Not until he turned again to the Gospels, and in particular to the story of the rich young man, did he discover how to achieve what he was really seeking, a path to perfection. So Basil sold all his possessions and gave them to the poor, resolving that in future he would live "entirely without thought of this life," in such a manner that his soul "should have no sympathetic concern with the things of this world." Thus determined, he wandered through Egypt and Mesopotamia, encountering on the way many Christians who were already living the life he desired to live, "not concerning themselves with the body, nor deigning to waste a thought upon it, but as if passing their lives in alien flesh." That phrase—"passing their lives in alien flesh"—has the root of the matter in it; for ascetic Christianity, as for Orphic-type religions, whatever is fleshly is "alien"; only by recognizing its foreignness can man achieve perfection. But Basil finally turned against the life of the solitary hermit—solitary, so far as discipline is concerned, even when the hermit lived in a community of hermits. It encouraged men, he thought, prematurely to suppose themselves perfect; it offered them no opportunities to practise the Christian virtues. So the monk, rather than the anchorite, came to represent Basil's ideal.

John Cassian was one of the first founders of Christian monasteries. He had no doubt, he tells us in his *Conferences,* that "life in a hermitage is a finer life than that in a monastic community," that to learn how to live as a hermit is to "learn the rules of the perfect life."[6] But men ought, he argued, first to purge themselves by living in monasteries. Otherwise there is the risk that when they go to live alone in the deserts they will find themselves like Jerome "boiling with desires

---

6. His *Conferences* are included, in part, in *Western Asceticism,* ed. O. Chadwick. They purport to give an account of the teachings of Egyptian ascetics. But we can safely presume that Cassian approved their teachings. The reference is to p. 194.

in a frozen body, in which there raged a conflagration of passions"—Jerome who "sat alone in the company of scorpions and wild beasts and yet was in the company of dancing girls."[7] It is impossible to "run away from one's sins." But once purged, it was only in solitude that men could achieve "the sublime vision." The perfect life, Cassian emphasizes, is not to be achieved merely by giving away one's possessions; renunciation is necessary but not sufficient. Asceticism is to be practised only as a rung on the ladder to "purity of mind," the achievement of a condition of mind in which one is wholly dedicated to God and "free from every earthly distraction."

In support of his view that the endless contemplation of God, rather than the practice of good works, is the Christian's ultimate objective, Cassian quotes from Luke that story of Mary and Martha which was to provide scriptural support for so many varieties of Christian asceticism and Christian mysticism: the busy Martha, actively serving Jesus and his disciples, does not realize, unlike the contemplative Mary, seated at Jesus' feet, that "we need few things, or only one thing," that it is wrong "to be troubled about many things." The "one thing" which men need is to contemplate and listen to God, as Mary did. That passage in Exodus[8]— "For there shall no man see me, and live"—which is generally taken to mean that only after death is it possible to see God, has in fact, according to Cassian, a very different, more hopeful meaning: to see God men need only be *dead to this world.*

What of the love of our neighbour as distinct from God? In the more extreme forms of anchoritism, this fades out of the picture. So far as human beings are to be loved, it is only in the same sense that Nature may be loved—as a reflection of God's power and glory. "Who can contemplate

7. Jerome: *Epistles* (Letter 22).
8. Exodus 33:20.

the immeasurable blessedness of heaven," Cassian asks, "at that very moment when he is welcoming visitors with gracious hospitality, when he is concerned with caring for the needs of his brethren?" Essentially, the soul intent on perfection must be alone with God. "A man who avoids men," to repeat a passage already quoted from the *Sayings of the Fathers*, "is like a ripe grape. A man who companies with men is like a sour grape." Or again: "Say also to your soul, 'What do I want with man?' "[9] Anchoritism, that is, carries egocentric Christianity to its extreme point, a point at which it becomes, in the words of a Christian critic, "nauseatingly self-interested."[10]

In the more communal type of monasticism, the position was rather different; one's neighbour was a fellowmonk. Precisely for this reason Augustine preferred the monastic to the solitary life. It provided, he thought, an opportunity for the exercise of Christian virtues. Basil's *Longer Rules* make the same point. Christ's precept of charity, he says, does not permit the individual to consider nothing except his own salvation. "Whom, therefore, will you wash, to whom will you minister, compared to whom will you be the lowest, if you live alone?"[11] Christian charity must infuse the monastery, and might in some measure be reflected in works of charity directed to the world outside the monastery. But love did not, must not, include any disinterested affection for a fellow human being as such.

Christianity, as we said, is often described as "the religion of love." But it is worth observing that love, in the ordinary human sense of the word, has found among Christians its severest critics. "The best insight into our religion,"

9. Pts. I–XVI of Rosweyde's ed. of *The Sayings of the Fathers* are included in *Western Asceticism*, ed. O. Chadwick. The references are to pp. 42 and 47. The passage from Cassian is from his *Conferences*, XXIII. 5. 1, quoted in O. Chadwick: *John Cassian*, 1st ed. (Cambridge, 1950), pp. 105–6.

10. Chadwick: *John Cassian*, ed. cited, p. 180. These passages have been omitted from the 2nd ed. (1968) of this work.

11. Quoted in G. B. Ladner: *The Idea of Reform* (Cambridge, Mass., 1959), p. 341.

wrote the Jansenist Jacques Esprit, "shows that love, far from being innocent, is guilty of the most enormous crimes; since it cannot exist in man without depriving God of his right. For by stifling his love for God, it hinders him from paying that due honour, admiration and service which his creator requires."[12] Nor is this attitude surprising, or ascribable to some merely personal, pathological, attitude of mind. Love is the great secularizer; it is our loves which make life worth living, which hold us to this world, which illuminate and enliven it. In that sense, love—not least but not only the love of man for woman—must appear the great enemy to those who wish to deny the world. That is why Teresa of Avila was so alarmed to discover that she loved her sister above other women and was deeply concerned about her unhappiness. In Teresa's eyes, this was a sure proof that she was still not perfect, still not "entirely detached," still not wholly given to God.[13]

A passage in the writings of the Franciscan mystic Angela of Foligno, beatified by the Roman Catholic Church, illustrates this attitude in an even more uncompromising form. Angela had been married and had produced children; within a few days her husband, her children and her mother all died. She writes of their death thus: "In that time, and by God's will, there died my mother, who was a great hindrance to me in following the way of God; my husband died likewise; and in a short time there also died all my children. And because I had begun to follow the aforesaid [mystic] way, and had prayed God to rid me of them, I had great consolation of their deaths, although I also felt some grief." From a secular point of view, this is monstrous heartlessness—"I had prayed God to rid me of them." But such heartlessness is only too characteristic of perfectibilists, secular

---

12. *Discourses on the Deceitfulness of Humane Virtues*, trans. W. Beauvoir (London, 1706), p. 264.
13. *Life*, ch. 31.

or religious. Jesus himself had asked: "Who is my mother? and who are my brethren?"; he had made it plain that "he that loveth son or daughter more than me is not worthy of me."[14] It was easy enough for Christians in search of perfection to conclude that it was better not to have parents or husbands, sons or daughters. Only thus can one be wholly protected against loving them for their own sake, in a way which subtracts from the love of God.

The ideal of perfection as renunciation of every form of human love in the quest for the vision of God involved, as with Stoicism, a distinction between an élite and the bulk of the population. The bulk of the population were to obey the commandments, as the rich young man had done; but the élite, the "salt of the earth," should seek to tread the path to perfection. This distinction between the élite and the ordinary Christian—corresponding to Plato's distinction between philosophical goodness and civic goodness— appears very early in Christianity. In the *Didache*—dating, most likely, from the second century—we read: "If you can bear the Lord's full yoke, you will be perfect. But if you cannot, then do what you can."[15] "In a great house," wrote Jerome in a similar spirit, "there are also vessels of wood and earthenware, as well as vessels of silver and gold."[16] Indeed, a contrast between the ordinary Christian and the élite was written into the distinction between clergy and laity, as soon as that distinction had established itself. The layman has not fully dedicated himself to God; if he loved God with his whole heart, he would cease to be a layman. In his *Concerning Perfection* Aquinas goes so far, like Dionysius before

14. Matthew 12:48 and 10:37. The passage from Angela is from *Visionum et instructionum liber*, cap. ix, trans. M. G. Steegmann as *The Book of Divine Consolation of the Blessed Angela of Foligno* (London and New York, 1908), p. 5.

15. In *Early Christian Fathers*, ed. and trans. C. C. Richardson, Library of Christian Classics, 1 (London, 1953), p. 174. On the question of date, see the translator's introduction.

16. Quoted in H. B. Workman: *The Evolution of the Monastic Ideal*, pp. 57–58.

him,* as to form a hierarchy of perfection, with bishops first, the religious orders second, parish priests and archdeacons third—although he grants, of course, that even bishops can be defective in charity.[17] It is impossible to escape the conclusion that a man has, to say the least, small chance of attaining even to moral perfection who does not become a member of the clergy. (Pelagius, that indomitable layman, had refused to accept this conclusion.)

As for absolute perfection, the vision of God, there were always those amongst the hermits and monks who asserted that the élite, if only for passing moments, could "see God face to face," and to that extent could achieve perfection, if only momentarily, in this life. This was certainly the case in Greek and Syrian monasticism, as represented, for example, in the fourth-century *Book of Grades,* with its sharp distinction between "the perfect," who knew heaven even while still alive, and the "righteous," who did their duty as worldly Christians, but could not expect to achieve the highest blessedness whether on earth or after death. Even Basil suggests, for all his criticism of the anchorites as too wont to consider themselves perfect, that it is possible to perfect oneself in this life—to "break through to another world." Benedict laid down his *Rules,* he told his monks, in order that those who kept to them should live righteous lives as monks. "But men aspire to the perfect life." To reach this life, he says, the monks must turn to Cassian and Basil, and through them hope "under God's protection to climb to those greater heights of knowledge and virtue to which the holy fathers beckon you."[18] In general, the Greek fathers,

---

* Dionysius, interestingly enough, had set priests and deacons well above monks in "the ecclesiastical hierarchy"; in his hierarchy, indeed, bishops stand immediately next to angels, but monks only just above ordinary baptized Christians. The religious orders had obviously come up in the world since Dionysius wrote.

17. *De Perfectione,* ch. XII.

18. *Rule of Saint Benedict,* 73; as trans. in *Western Asceticism,* ed. O. Chadwick, pp. 336–37.

most notably Gregory of Nyssa, stood closer than did, say, Augustine to the neo-Platonic concepts of perfectibility.* Whereas in the Upanishads it is suggested that "there is no difference between a desire for sons and a desire for riches; and there is no difference between a desire for riches and a desire for [exalted] states of being: all of them are nothing more than desire"[19]—and as desire to be rejected—the desire for "exalted states of being" certainly played an important part in the growth of monasticism.

What of sinlessness, immaculate perfection, as distinct from that sort of perfection which consists in catching a glimpse of God? Cassian discusses this question at considerable length and, on the face of it, denies that men can be sinless.[20] But he grants that an ascetic can conquer not only his vices, but even his moral imperfections. If he cannot properly be called "sinless," this is only because he cannot all the time concentrate all his mind on God. It is a sin to think about anything but God, and such thoughts will recur even when all desire has been destroyed. By the ordinary standards of the active life, then, men can be sinless; only in relation to the very special standards of the mystic are men incapable of immaculate perfection.

It would be a mistake, of course, to suppose that all Roman Catholic teachers have seen in monasticism, in asceticism or in mysticism the sole, or even the best, path to perfection. Whereas Teresa, writing of a "diligent and holy

---

* A fuller study of Christian ascetico-mysticism would have to pay much greater attention to the Greek fathers and, more generally, to the Eastern Church. In particular, Gregory of Nyssa is a central figure, who almost certainly influenced Dionysius and independently re-entered Western thought when he was translated by Erigena. For Gregory see Jean Daniélou: *Platonisme et théologie mystique: essai sur la doctrine spirituelle de saint Grégoire de Nysse* (Paris, 1944), or for a greater emphasis on Gregory's philosophical ideas, H. F. Cherniss: *The Platonism of Gregory of Nyssa* (*University of California Publications in Classical Philology*, Vol. 11, No. 1, 1930).

19. Brihadāranyaka Upanishad, III, v, as trans. in *Hindu Scriptures*, ed. R. C. Zaehner, Everyman's Library (London, 1966), p. 51.

20. *Conferences*, XIII. See the discussion of this *Conference* in O. Chadwick: *John Cassian*, ed. cited, pp. 126–34.

man," says that "his life seems to be as perfect as the married state permits,"[21] with the implication that the married state limits his perfection, Francis de Sales condemned as "a heresy" the attempt "to banish the devout life from the regiment of soldiers, the shop of the mechanic, the court of princes or the home of married folk."[22] All men, he argued, are capable of contemplating the divine.

From Augustine on, indeed, moral theologians have sung the praises of "the mixed life." Augustine had no doubt that the contemplative life is the best life—he constantly reverts in his *Sermons* to the contrast between Mary and Martha—but he none the less lays it down in *The City of God* that "no man has a right to lead such a life of contemplation as to forget in his own ease the service due to his neighbour," even if it is also true that no one "has . . . a right to be so immersed in active life as to neglect the contemplation of God."[23] But this concession to the active life is associated in Augustine with the doctrine that the contemplative life cannot be carried to its full perfection by corrupted human beings.[24] That is what full-blooded Christian perfectibilists are not prepared to accept. On their view, the active life is bound to be a distraction; the Christian ought to, and can, achieve perfection here and now by wholly absolving himself from the daily round of distracting obligations, such obligations as preaching.

For Newman, in contrast, perfection "does not mean any extraordinary service, anything out of the way." That man is perfect, he writes, "who does the work of the day perfectly."

21. *Life,* ch. 23.
22. *Introduction to the Devout Life,* Pt. I, ch. 3, trans. J. K. Ryan (London, 1953), p. 8. Francis is writing, it should be observed, *after* the Reformation. His *Devout Life* was not published until 1607. Compare what is said about Teilhard de Chardin at p. 400 below.
23. *City of God,* Bk. XIX, ch. 19, trans. M. Dods (Edinburgh, 1872). Compare what Plato says in the *Republic* about the responsibility which lies on the philosopher who has seen the form of the good to return to play his part in the State. In the *Philebus* Plato introduces the concept of a "mixed life."
24. *Tractatus in Joannis evangelium,* CXXIV, 5 on John 21:19–25.

If he were asked what a man should do to be perfect, New-man continues, he would reply: "Do not lie in bed beyond the due time of rising; give your first thoughts to God; make a good visit to the Blessed Sacrament; say the Angelus devoutly; eat and drink to God's glory; say the Rosary well; keep out bad thoughts; make your evening meditation well; examine yourself daily; go to bed in good time, and you are already perfect." This somewhat governess-like conception of perfection lies far from the ideals of the Syrian monasteries, with their incessant search for a life which would lead them out of life.[25] It is as if Benedict's *Rules* were to be thought of, not as rules for righteousness, but as rules of perfection. But the ascetic element in Roman Catholicism still persists, even if nowadays somewhat diminished.

The Reformers directed their fire, with particular zeal, against ascetic ideals. Martin Luther had been a monk. As a monk, he came to think, he had gone in search of a degree and type of perfection which man neither can, nor should, hope to achieve. "The saints of the Papists," Luther writes in his *Commentary on Galatians,* "are like to the Stoics, who imagined such wise men, as in the world were never yet to be found. And by this foolish and wicked persuasion . . . the schoolmen brought both themselves and others without number into [horrible] desperation."[26] Christians who try to bring themselves to such a state of perfection as to be "without all feelings of temptations and sins" are trying to reduce themselves, Luther argues, to the state of "sticks and stones."

Calvin was no less hostile to monasticism. Officially, he admitted, the monks claim no more for monasticism, as Aquinas claimed for it in his *Apology for the Religious Orders,* than that it is the best preparation for the life to come.

25. *Meditations and Devotions, ed. cit.,* pp. 382–83.
26. Quoted in *Martin Luther: Selections from His Writings,* ed. John Dillenberger, pp. 158–59, from rev. ed. by P. S. Watson (1956), pp. 508–18.

But in practice, Calvin maintains, the monks thought of themselves as being *actually* in a state of perfection, a state which, according to Calvin as to Luther, no man can hope to achieve in this life. And it was entirely wrong of the monks, Calvin adds, to suggest that the monkish life was intrinsically superior to any other, even as a preparation for heaven.

Calvin, indeed, completely rejected what he calls a "double Christianity," one variety for the spiritual élite, one variety for ordinary people. All Christians, on his view, are equally bound by "every little word uttered by Christ"; there is no ground for distinguishing between "commands" and "counsels" of perfection. The only effect of monasticism, he argues, is to make men vainglorious, as if by their own efforts they could attain to perfection.[27]

It is interesting to observe, in this connexion, that Pelagius was a lay-monk, and that Cassian, the monastery-founder, was also the founder of semi-Pelagianism. The ascetic life was by its nature a deliberate attempt to attract the grace of God, by living a life of peculiar sanctity. Benedict, recognizing this, tried to temper the Pelagian implications of monasticism by exhorting his monks to remember Paul's "By the grace of God I am what I am."[28] But it is impossible to read Benedict, or Cassian, except as a set of exhortations to human effort. That is what Luther and Calvin observed with detestation.

But was not Calvin a Puritan, the Puritan of Puritans? How, then, could he condemn asceticism? Puritanism and asceticism, however, are by no means the same thing. Asceticism attempts to withdraw from the world as a whole; Puritanism condemns the world only in so far as it is sinful, not, for example, commerce, or political service, or marriage, but, characteristically, the theatre, the consumption of alco-

---

27. *Institutes of the Christian Religion*, IV, xiii, 11–14, trans. F. L. Battles, Vol. 2, pp. 1265–69.
28. I Corinthians 15:10.

hol, any form of sensual delight.* Within Christianity, asceticism and Puritanism are normally conjoined and it is the easier to confuse them. The world is at once, for the ascetic, unworthy of his attention and an occasion of sin. But Buddhism is ascetic without being Puritanical; it rejects "the flesh" not because sensual delights are wicked but because they are transitory. And to recognize their transitoriness those who wish to reach perfection through enlightenment "must first of all know the taste of the pleasures which the senses can give."

The Buddha Shakyamuni, whom, in the West, we think of as Buddha, at first lived a life of complete sensuality—entertained by "soft words, tremulous calls, wanton swayings, sweet laughter, butterfly kisses, and seductive glances."[29] What converted him from the sensual life was not the belief that such sensuality was wicked but the realization that its joys are transitory: "It is not that I despise the objects of sense," he told his counsellor when he resolved to abandon sensuality, . . . "But when I consider the impermanence of everything in this world, then I can find no delight in it. . . . If only this beauty of women were imperishable, then my mind would certainly indulge in the passions."[30]

---

* Calvin's own attitude is anything but straightforward. At times, he writes in the manner of an ascetic: "there is no middle ground between these two: either the world must become worthless to us or hold us bound by intemperate love of it." But he also writes that God has provided the world "not only . . . for necessity but also for delight and good cheer." (*Institutes*, III, ix. 2; III, x. 2.) Perhaps his most general view is that what God creates—the world—may properly be delighted in but that men often delight in it in the wrong, fleshly, manner. Recent commentators tend to emphasize Calvin's "humanism" and to blame the Puritanical excesses of Calvinism on his disciples. But this is perhaps an over-correction. For the older view see Williston Walker: *John Calvin* (London, 1906), pp. 304 ff., for the newer view G. E. Duffield, ed.: *John Calvin* (Abingdon, 1966). Perhaps the best-balanced account is in François Wendel: *Calvin*, trans. P. Mairet (London, 1963). From the point of view of the history of perfectibility what Calvin actually taught is much less important than what his disciples represented him as teaching, and that, quite certainly, was a kind of Puritanism. Those readers who feel that my account of Calvin is unfair to him are at liberty to think of me as writing about Calvinism.

29. *Buddhist Scriptures*, sel. and trans. Edward Conze (Harmondsworth, 1959), p. 38.
30. *Ibid.*, pp. 40–41.

This, we might say, is a *metaphysical* criticism of sensuality, characteristic of asceticism in all its forms, very obviously of Platonism, and it is quite distinct from that *moral* criticism which is the essence of Puritanism, for which "wanton swayings" and "seductive glances" are intrinsically sinful. The Puritan, too, does not expect to reach perfection by renouncing sensuality—such a renunciation, for him, is at most a *sine qua non* of salvation. It need not even be related to salvation, for Puritans may, like Shaw, be secularists, with a horror of sensuality which has no theological roots. The Bodhisattva, in contrast, is in search of perfection. He hopes to become "a fully enlightened Buddha, perfect in knowledge and conduct"[31]—and to achieve that end by an ascetico-mystical renunciation of the world.

Asceticism, indeed, is usually associated with mysticism, understood (in its Christian form) as the view that we can in this life attain to that "vision of God" or "union with God" in which perfection consists. Buddhist mysticism is, in principle, bound to state its objective differently, since Buddhism is not, in its classical versions, committed to belief in God. For Buddhism, what the mystic seeks is a foretaste of Nirvana, the entire extinction of the self. But in practice the two forms of mysticism are not always so different as one would suppose. The great temptation, at least, of Christian mysticism is a form of pantheism, for which the individual soul entirely disappears in an undifferentiated unity. Such a pantheism lies at the heretical border of Christian asceticism, just as Manichaeanism lies at the heretical border of Christian Puritanism.

Take the case of Dionysius the Areopagite, whose *Mystical Theology* had so crucial an influence on Christian mysticism. Dionysius begins with a prayer to "Trinity, which exceedeth all Being, Deity, and Goodness." The "Trinity" is orthodox enough, but what about the phrase "which ex-

31. *Ibid.*, p. 24.

ceedeth all Deity"? Dionysius goes on to warn us that what he has to say is directed only at the "initiated." Only the "initiated," indeed, are likely to understand what Dionysius means when he says of "the Good Cause of all things" that it "is revealed in Its naked truth to those alone who pass right through the opposition of fair and foul" and are prepared to "leave behind them all divine enlightenment." Only the initiated will recognize, when the time comes, that he has finally reached that "Darkness of Unknowing wherein he renounces all the apprehensions of his understanding . . . and . . . through the passive stillness of all his reasoning powers [is] united by his highest faculty to Him that is wholly Unknowable, of whom thus by a rejection of all knowledge he possesses a knowledge that exceeds his understanding."[32] The uninitiated may well imagine that what they are being urged to do is to cast aside all morality—for how else are they to move beyond "fair and foul"?—and all the teaching of the Christian Church. For what else can be meant, in such a context, by the "divine enlightenment" which is to be "left behind"? If "all knowledge" is to be rejected, this must surely include the knowledge gained by Revelation.

It is sometimes said, indeed, that all mysticism is identical, that the idea of a "Christian mysticism" is a contradiction in terms, since the mystical experience, by its very nature, consists in union with an "undifferentiated One," which can no more be the specifically Christian God than it can be the specifically Muslim God or the Buddhist Nirvana. If Christian mysticism is to be contained within the bounds of orthodoxy it has somehow to avoid this conclusion, but it is not at all clear how it is to do so. Angela of Foligno, for example, professes to arrive at a condition in which she beholds as something higher than God's power "a *Thing*,

---

32. Quotations are as trans. C. E. Rolt in *Dionysius the Areopagite on the Divine Names and the Mystical Theology*, pp. 191–94.

as fixed and stable as it was indescribable." A Parmenidean One, perhaps, but certainly not a personal God. Yet Angela's orthodoxy is not suspect.[33]

Roman Catholic mysticism, although active enough from the early days of the Church, reached its peak in the thirteenth to the sixteenth century, first in England and Germany and then in Spain. For the most part it has been accepted as orthodox, but Meister Eckhart, the founder of the German mystical school, had some twenty-eight of his principal theses condemned as heretical—although his disciples, and some modern commentators, allege that they are heretical only when torn from their context.[34] "The Father himself begets his Son," wrote Eckhart, "and what is more, he begets me as his son—the self-same Son! Indeed, I assert that he begets me not only as his Son but himself as myself, begetting me in his own nature, his own being. At that inmost source I spring from the Holy Spirit, and there is one life, one being, and one action." Here the temptations of mysticism to identify are clearly exemplified: God, the Father, the Son, and the mystic soul are amalgamated into one. Whereas for Aquinas perfection resides in the *vision* of God, for Eckhart the perfect soul is converted into *being* God. "We are not wholly blessed," he writes, "even though we are looking at divine truth; for while we are still looking at it, we are not in it. As long as a man has an object under consideration, he is not one with it." [35]

If Eckhart was eventually condemned, his pupils Heinrich Suso and John Tauler were not, and from Tauler's *Sermon on the Hunt of the Sun* we can see the limits of what

33. Compare Evelyn Underhill: "The Blessed Angela of Foligno" in Paul Sabatier *et al.: Franciscan Essays* (Aberdeen, 1912; republ. Farnborough, 1966), pp. 88–108. The reference is to p. 104.

34. See, for example, Gordon Leff: *Heresy in the Later Middle Ages*, Vol. 1, pp. 281–82, 293–94.

35. Quotations are from Sermon 18 and Sermon 22 in *Meister Eckhart: A Modern Translation* by R. B. Blakney (New York and London, *c.* 1941).

was permissible.[36] Tauler draws the classical distinction between two classes of Christian—the "noble souls" and the
ordinary, unenlightened Christians. The ordinary Christian, according to Tauler, when he is touched by grace either
tries to respond to it, in the manner of the theologians,
"with rational concepts and high speculation," or else, in
the manner of the conventionally devout, "he seeks satisfaction in self-chosen observances, devotions, meditations."
Such men have not really "arisen," Tauler argues, and this
is manifested in the fact that they still display such faults as
pride, solicitude, spitefulness.

The noble ones are very different. They put themselves
completely in God's hands, abandoning themselves entirely
to his will. Those men who have reached this height Tauler
freely describes as "supernatural men." He goes so far as to
say, indeed, that "they, in a sense, *are* no longer, but God
is in them." They have reached a height in which "there is
no longer sin, because they enjoy a godlike freedom." No
doubt, he adds, even when they have achieved the highest
degree of perfection they must still watch themselves, "lest
God should find something in [their] soul to hinder the accomplishment of the Divine purpose." The fact remains that
man is in principle perfectible, perfectible here and now,
capable of becoming both immaculate and godlike.

Roman Catholic mysticism achieved its completest expression in sixteenth-century Spain, at a time and a place,
interestingly enough, which also witnessed a violent reaction against mystical teachings, under the leadership of
that resolute Dominican Melchior Cano. Cano's hostility
was particularly directed against the Alumbrados or, as they
are more often called, the "Illuminists" (both names have
the same significance—"the Enlightened ones"). It is not
at all clear whether the Illuminists, most of them Francis-

36. My references are to the trans. by D. Attwater included in C. J. Barry, ed.: *Readings
in Church History*, Vol. 1 (Westminster, Md., 1960; repr. 1965), pp. 593–95.

cans or Jesuits, constituted a loosely-associated group of like-minded Christians or whether "Illuminist" was no more than a convenient label which the Inquisition could attach to any Christians who incurred their displeasure by emphasizing mystical religious experience rather than the formally-organized devotions of the Church.

This much is certain however: the Inquisition cast its nets widely. Men as high in rank as the Cardinal Archbishop of Toledo, intellectuals as distinguished as the poet Luis de Leon, were condemned to lengthy periods of imprisonment—the latter for translating into Spanish the Song of Songs, which was, of course, universally read as a mystical poem, symbolizing the delights of mystical union. Even Ignatius Loyola incurred the displeasure of the Dominicans, and was accused of fleeing Spain to escape their investigators.

The shadow of imprisonment and the stake—there was a notable *auto-da-fé* of Illuminists at Llerena in 1579—lay across both Teresa of Avila and her follower, John of the Cross. Teresa's confessor was asked to report on her teachings; although his report was favourable, it is hedged about with reservations. One of her spiritual advisers, the Jesuit Balthasar Alvarez, was to find himself condemned by his own Order, suspected of Illuminism. John of the Cross was denounced to the Inquisition.[37] If, then, scholars have found it impossible to bring to entire consistency what either Teresa or John says, this may in part be because they were neither of them logicians, in part because, a common difficulty with mystical writings, they profess to be describing the indescribable and can scarcely be expected to do so with clarity, but in part because to have made claims of

---

37. For the Spanish anti-mystical movement see K. E. Kirk: *The Vision of God, ed. cit.*, pp. 431–33. The report on John can be read in *The Complete Works of St John of the Cross*, ed. and trans. E. Allison Peers, rev. ed. (London, 1953; 1 vol. repr. 1964), Vol. 3, pp. 355–404. See also Friedrich Heer: *The Intellectual History of Europe*, trans. J. Steinberg (London, 1966), pp. 272–80.

too large a kind could easily have involved them in serious difficulties with the Inquisition.

The general pattern of their mysticism, however, is clear enough for our present purposes. It was a quest for perfection, which rested on an asceticism of the severest kind, characteristic of the Carmelite order to which they both belonged and which they sought to restore to its primitive austerity. In her *Life* Teresa refers to the body as the "evil guest" of the soul; she describes herself as a "foul and stinking dunghill"; it is, she says, a sign of spiritual progress "to hold the world in profound contempt." From the age of twenty, she tells us—and this is a sure sign of the ascetic as distinct from the Puritan—she already pitied those who followed the ways of the world "even in its lawful pursuits."

John of the Cross wore underclothes of knotted ropes,[38] and was as emphatic as any anchorite on the need for avoiding "evil communications," i.e. his fellow-men. "The Lord," he writes to a nun, ". . . loves you to be quite alone, desiring to be Himself your only companion."[39] Nuns and monks, he thought, should live in their convent or monastery "as if they lived alone." Both Teresa and John accepted Augustine's interpretation of "love your neighbour as yourself"; to love one's neighbours meant to try to bring them to God. In offering spiritual advice they were indefatigable. But as we have already seen, even Teresa's natural affection for her sister appeared to her as a sin. As for John, the imperfections from which men must try to purify themselves include, he says, any attachment, however slight, to "a person, a garment, a book, a cell, a particular kind of food, tittle-tattle."[40] So attachments to persons are ranked with attachments to places, to food, or, even, to tittle-tattle. All affections must

38. For a heart-rending description of the mortifications the mystics thought fit to impose upon themselves see, for example, Heinrich Suso: *The Life of the Servant*, trans. J. M. Clark (London, 1952).
39. *Works*, Vol. 3, p. 260.
40. *Ibid.*, Vol. 1, p. 50.

be killed, however desirable they may be in the eyes of the world.*

No Hindu or Buddhist has ever preached more forcibly than John the need for securing "the detachment and annihilation of that [natural] self."[41] Men, if they hope to be perfect, must, he says, first pass through a period of darkness, a condition in which "the spiritual and the sensual desires are put to sleep and mortified, so that they can experience nothing, either Divine or human; the affections of the soul are oppressed and constrained, so that they can neither move nor find support in anything; the imagination is bound and can make no useful reflection; the memory is gone; the understanding is in darkness, unable to understand anything; and hence the will likewise is arid and constrained and all the faculties are void and useless; and in addition to all this, a thick and heavy cloud is upon the soul, keeping it in affliction, and, as it were, far away from God."[42] Only in such a "dark night of the soul," devoid of all human faculties and therefore wholly dependent on God, can the soul "walk securely." It is tempting to ascribe much of what John has to say about the dark night of the soul to the Spanish love of suffering and death. And it is worth noting that both for Teresa and for John: "Take up thy cross and follow me" is the principal command of perfection, and that both wrote poems in which the recurrent theme is a longing for death.

There was, it is true, nothing unfamiliar in the idea that

* One is naturally reminded once more of Stoicism. It is interesting to note that Seneca, himself a Spaniard, was very widely read in fifteenth-century Spain. Teresa's nickname for John of the Cross was "my little Seneca." For all the austerity of their life and even more of their teachings, both Teresa and John of the Cross were a good deal more human than their doctrines would have allowed them to be. But the fact remains that they thought they *ought* to cast off all attachments to persons, at least attachments for their own sake. On Seneca in Spain, see A Benedictine of Stanbrook Abbey: *Medieval Mystical Tradition and Saint John of the Cross, ed. cit.,* p. 68.

41. *Ibid.,* Vol. 1, p. 85.
42. *Ibid.,* Vol. 1, p. 421.

a "dark night of the soul" is an essential stage in the progress towards mystical enlightenment. When this very passage from John was denounced to the Inquisition, John's learned defender could point to a comparable suggestion in the writings of Bernard of Clairvaux. The first chapter of Dionysius's *Mystical Theology* bears the title, "What is divine gloom?" The author of *Theologia Germanica* tells us that the righteous man must, like Christ, descend into hell before he can ascend into the heaven of perfection—a hell in which he feels unworthy, even, of divine punishment.[43] Even that cheerful, energetic, English mystic who wrote, in the fourteenth century, *The Cloud of Unknowing*, was insistent that the mystic must pass through "darkness, a cloud of unknowing." But this "darkness," this "gloom," is described by John with a peculiar horror, only to be matched by his Spanish disciple Molinos who, in his *Spiritual Guide*, describes the contemplative soul as "seeing itself deserted by God, surrounded with temptations, with darkness, with difficulties, with afflictions, with troubles, with a hard discipline of dryness . . . being in such affliction that its tortures seem nothing other than a long death, and a continual martyrdom."* John sums up thus: "the road of suffering is more secure . . . than that of fruition and action." He does not deny that action, as distinct from contemplative worship, can be "profitable," but it is unsafe, he thinks, because in acting "the soul is practising its own weaknesses and imperfections."[44] The road to perfection, then, is paved with bitter sufferings. Only by such sufferings, it is presumed, can self-love be mortified, every affection which binds men to

---

43. *Theologia Germanica*, ch. XI.

* Molinos was to find himself imprisoned, allegedly for immorality. But the charges against him were based on his private letters rather than the *Spiritual Guide*, a work which had been widely distributed, translated and recommended by highly-placed ecclesiastical authorities. The quotation, from the *Spiritual Guide*, iii. 5, is as trans. in R. A. Knox: *Enthusiasm*, p. 291.

44. *Works*, Vol. 1, p. 425.

the world destroyed, and the soul made ready to be entirely filled with the love of God. How far, thus prepared, can the soul reach towards perfection?

Much now depends on what is to be understood by "perfection." Take first impeccability, "immaculate perfection." John would have been free, without taint of heresy—or so his counsel assures us—to maintain that at the highest reaches of contemplation the mystic can, for a time, be free of sin. But John, his defender argues, does not even claim so much, because he grants that the soul, even when it has achieved union with God, is not wholly free from temptation.[45] In fact, however, John admits no more than that what he calls "the natural desires" are not in this life "wholly mortified." It is only if the mere existence of natural desires in "the sensual part of the soul" constitutes a sin, even although the rational soul is quite undisturbed by them, that John's defender can be acquitted of the charge of being disingenuous. For John certainly maintains that the soul can be free not only from mortal sins, not only from venial sins, but even from "imperfections."[46] Indeed, if "The Points of Love" records his teachings correctly, as it professes to do, John explicitly asserted that "the soul that is in the union of love has not even the first movements of sin."[47] And how could it be otherwise, if it has entered into full union with God?

Aquinas, it will be remembered, defined perfection, at the purely human level, as first, "the removal from man's affections of everything that is contrary to the love of God, such as mortal sin," and secondly, the removal of "whatever hinders the mind's affections from turning wholly to God." Together these constitute what John calls "evangelical perfection." There can be no doubt, on his view, that

45. *Ibid.*, Vol. 3, p. 393.
46. *Ibid.*, Vol. 1, p. 49.
47. *Ibid.*, Vol. 3, p. 231.

such a degree of perfection lies within man's reach; it is, indeed, the highest level of perfection for which a spiritual adviser should consciously strive, the highest point which can be reached by human effort without the aid of very special grace. But if such a degree of perfection already carries human beings far beyond what the Reformers would allow to mortal men, it is still not enough for Teresa, for John, or any other mystic; it is no more than a stage on the ladder of perfection.

What of the vision of God? Even this, John allows to the perfected mystic, who can reach, indeed, to such a degree of illumination that he sees all created things through the eyes of God. As the Islamic mystic Avicenna had already suggested, he contemplates all things as God contemplates them, because "God is contemplating in him."[48] He is no longer obliged, that is, to achieve his knowledge of God's nature through his knowledge of created things. It is true that God is still not known fully "in his essence"; he appears to the enlightened soul, for example, to be in movement, although God is in fact unmoving. (John's "vision of God" owes more to Aristotle than to the Bible.) But at least this much can be said: that God "draws back . . . some of the veils and curtains which are in front of [the soul] . . . and it is able to see (though somewhat darkly, since not all the veils are drawn back) that face of His that is full of graces."[49] So a partial, though not a complete, vision of God is available to man in this life, made possible, as the vision of God was made possible to Moses, by God's protective grace, shielding man from the full sight of God's glory. The comparison with Moses is revealing: John is obviously not prepared to accept the view that the case of Moses was exceptional, that it was not a standard of what men should hope to achieve.

48. Avicenna (Ibn'Sina): *Stages of the Mystical Life,* in M. Smith, ed.: *Readings from the Mystics of Islam* (London, 1950), p. 49.
49. *Works,* Vol. 3, p. 190.

The second stage in the progress towards perfection—"illumination"—certainly lies within men's reach.

As for the final stage, "union with God," here, particularly, heresy was to be feared. John was acquainted with the mystical writings of the Arabs; they, certainly, had sometimes passed beyond the bounds of Muslim tolerance. Some members of the Sufi sect, indeed, had achieved martyrdom by proclaiming, *simpliciter,* "I am God," or, "There is nothing inside this clothing but Allah." Christians were certainly no more tolerant than Muslims of such pretensions to be God made flesh.

In its perfected condition, according to John, "the soul lives the life of God," a life in no respect animal. Its understanding is enlightened by God, it is no longer dependent for its knowledge on the senses; its will is one with God's will; its memory is of "the eternal years," not only of its own past; its desire is God's desire; its movements are God's movements. But does it not, if this is so, become God? Metaphysics saves John from pantheism. The *substance* of the soul, he argues, is not changed into the *substance* of God, even although the soul, in respect of all its activities, is "united in Him and absorbed in Him." Teresa makes little use of scholastic terminology, but when she writes that the mystic achieves "a most definite union of the whole soul with God," in which "two things become one,"[50] it is presumably this sort of union she has in mind. A theology created in an attempt to make some sense of the Incarnation could thus be deployed in aid of mystical perfectionism.

How does mysticism stand in relation to the Pelagian controversy? It is very hard to say. Such theological concepts as original sin play no part at all in John's thinking; no doubt he accepted the orthodox teaching on this point, but he does not let original sin dominate his thinking as it dominated the thinking of Augustine or the Reformers. One sees

50. *Life,* ch. 17.

why the twentieth-century Calvinist theologian, Emil Brunner, complains that "the mystic dodges the question of guilt and forgiveness."[51] Indeed—a true ascetic—John has very little to say about sin of any kind; his emphasis is the Stoic one, on the need for becoming detached from the world, rather than the more characteristically Christian emphasis on being saved from sin. No doubt, this is in his eyes a false antithesis, as it was for Augustine. Any kind of attachment to the world is itself a "sin," as involving the misuse of a love which properly belongs only to God. For him, as for the rich young man in Matthew's story, it is relatively easy to keep the commandments; the disciplines which interest him *begin* at that point.

Up to a certain level, one might say, Christian mysticism is Pelagian, or semi-Pelagian; beyond that point it veers sharply to the opposite extreme. In the Roman Catholic world of the counter-Reformation, John of the Cross found himself denounced for assigning too little importance to good works, and for suggesting, or so it was alleged, that in its higher states of union with God the will is no longer free. Such twentieth-century anti-Pelagians as Niebuhr and Barth, in contrast, see in mysticism one of the forms assumed by Pelagianism. In virtue of its insistence on the need for mortification, for detachment, mysticism is bound—however much it may officially acknowledge that nothing can be achieved without God's help—to emphasize the importance of human effort. Once a measure of perfection has been achieved, however, the soul can only pray, and hope, and wait, in a quite un-Pelagian way. Even its prayers must not be petitions but exercises of love, forms of worship. And if the union with God should finally be achieved, it comes not as a result of human efforts but as "an interior assault of the Holy Spirit," as "the supernatural assault of love." So whereas man achieves evangelical perfection, immaculate

51. *The Word and the World* (New York, 1931), p. 50.

perfection, by an exercise of will, co-operating with God's grace, he achieves absolute perfection, the union with God, only by wholly surrendering to that grace.

In seventeenth-century French "Quietism," it is worth observing, this anti-Pelagian "waiting" occupies the very centre of mysticism. "My desire is to desire nothing," wrote the Quietist Marie-Rosette, "my will is to will nothing, to remain attached to nothing. . . . But I do not even desire to desire nothing, because I think that would also be a desire."[52] Asceticism—the "Pelagian" element in mysticism—was, on the Quietist view, not only unnecessary but a positive distraction. What the Christian had to learn to do was to wait, to wait until God moved him; if he busies himself with the practice of mortifications he is demonstrating a quite un-Christian impatience.

John's favourite metaphor, which he develops at great length and in extraordinarily sensual detail, is the Song of Songs metaphor of the bride and the bridegroom—John is, of course, the bride, and the bride of the Christian tradition, wholly passive, entirely dominated by her groom.* It is perhaps not surprising that, although women have made no contributions whatever to "intellectual" theology, so many of the leading mystics, up to the twentieth-century Evelyn Underhill, have been women; the language of mysticism—especially of what is often called "nuptial" mysticism as distinct from the "speculative" mysticism of Eckhart and his followers—comes more easily from their lips.

---

52. For the Quietist controversy see H. Daniel-Rops: *The Church in the Seventeenth Century*, pp. 368–93 (the quotation from Marie-Rosette is on p. 369), and R. A. Knox: *Enthusiasm*. Compare the Hindu doctrine quoted on p. 122 above.

* The soul, according to Zaehner, must realise that "If it is to commune with God, its role can only be that of the bride, it must play the woman." He quotes Eckhart as saying that to become fruitful a man must necessarily be a woman; he reminds us that Suso in his autobiography always refers to himself in the feminine gender. (R. C. Zaehner: *Mysticism: Sacred and Profane*, Oxford, 1957, p. 152.)

SEVEN

PERFECTIBILITY WITHIN CHRISTIANITY: PROTESTANT AND HERETICAL

For orthodox Protestantism, God has revealed himself, once and for all, in Christ. The mystic, in trying to rise above the world in order to achieve the vision of God, wilfully hurries past God, as Karl Barth puts it, God "who descends in His revelation into this world of ours."[1] The Scriptures belong to this world. To that degree, Barth suggests, the Quakers were correct in calling them, in contrast with the direct workings of the Holy Spirit, "carnal." But in them alone, according to Barth, can men meet God as he is, objectively; the mystic substitutes subjective impressions of God for that objective knowledge which Christ, through the Scriptures, has revealed to men. Nor does orthodox Protestantism allow that by means of a direct vision of God, or by any other means, men can achieve in this life even "immaculate perfection," let alone the kind and degree of perfection envisaged by John of the Cross. Human corruption is too profound to be entirely healed, as distinct from being graciously forgiven. The true Christian can be "perfected" only in the sense, that through his faith in Christ, Christ's merits are "imputed" to him. But this imputation does not free him from sin.

Yet in certain important respects the seeds of Protestantism, or at least of German Reformation Protestantism, were first planted within the fertile soil of medieval mysticism, in Tauler, in the anonymous *Theologia Germanica*—of which Luther said that it meant more to him than any other

---

1. Karl Barth: *Church Dogmatics*, Vol. II: *The Doctrine of God*, Pt. 1 (Edinburgh, 1957), ch. V, §25. 1: Man before God, p. 11.

book except the Bible and the writings of Augustine—and in *The Imitation of Christ.* For all such mystical works of devotion teach the same three lessons. First, that the knowledge of God is not to be achieved by theology, but by listening to God's Word. "What have we to do with quiddities and qualities?" asks the author of *The Imitation of Christ.* "If a man listens to the eternal Word, he is delivered from a multitude of opinions."[2] Secondly, that men must be prepared to "yield to God," that they must not count anything good as their own work, but rather as God's working in them. Thirdly, that if in the end men are to arrive at an inner peace, they must first be prepared to "descend into hell," enduring a deep conviction that they are unworthy even that God should deign to punish them. And these lessons, quite certainly, were also the lessons of the Reformation.

Mysticism of this kind is essentially anti-Pelagian. Such mystically-inspired Protestant perfectibilists as the Quakers and the Methodists do not question that men are entirely dependent for their perfection on the exercise of divine grace. There is no suggestion in either George Fox or John Wesley that men can so much as prepare themselves for grace by mortification or "detachment"—although they agree, of course, that the devout Christian will live a simple "unworldly" life. What the Quakers and Wesley do question, however, is Augustine's conviction that as a matter of empirical fact God never gives men sufficient grace to make them perfect, or, at the very least, sinless. That had already been denied by certain of the sixteenth-century Anabaptists, and by a number of earnest minor sects after them. But we shall concentrate our attention on the two perfectibilist varieties of Protestantism which have had a special historical importance: the Quakers and the Methodists.

2. *Imitatio Christi,* I. 3. ii, as trans. Justin McCann (London, 1952). The *Imitation of Christ* is traditionally ascribed to Thomas à Kempis, but this ascription has been questioned. "Quiddities and qualities" could be paraphrased as "scholastic jargon."

In the year 1659 George Fox, the first of the Quakers, was taken before a magistrate and examined.[3] Asked whether he was sanctified, he tells us in his *Journal,* he replied, "Yes, for I was in the Paradise of God." Was he then free from sin? " 'Sin,' said I, 'he has taken away my sin (viz: Christ my saviour) and in him there is no sin.' " Orthodox Protestantism allowed, of course, that men's sin could be, by the grace of God, forgiven; Calvinists, at least, maintained that men might come to a full assurance that they would be saved. But Fox is saying much more than this: that Jesus came to earth to *destroy* sin, and that when he dwells in a man, there is no room in that man for sin. Not unnaturally, his conclusions were disputed. Some clergymen came to see Fox, so he tells us, "to plead for sin and imperfection." For "they could not endure to hear of purity, or being made pure here [in this life]." But Fox was unconvinced. They were merely "babbling about the Scriptures," he told them, unless they saw that the Scriptures were directed towards making us holy.

Still worse, from the orthodox point of view, was the case of James Nayler. In 1652, appearing before Judge Fell on a charge of blasphemy, Fox had been asked to meet the accusation that he had claimed to be equal with God. He replied without hesitation: "My Father and I are one." James Nayler, a disciple of Fox, intervened with a question to the judges which was intended as an explanation: "Dost thou ask him as a creature or as Christ dwelling in him?"[4] Fox was no theologian, but that he recognized a distinction of the sort Nayler is here suggesting emerges from a somewhat remarkable letter he wrote to Oliver Cromwell in 1654. There he speaks of himself as being "called of the world by the name George Fox" but as also having "a new name . . . which the

---

3. For this story, see *The Journal of George Fox*, ed. N. Penney, 2 vols (Cambridge, 1911), Vol. 1, pp. 2–3. I have modernized the text.

4. *Ibid.*, Vol. 1, p. 66. The letter to Oliver Cromwell may be found on pp. 161–62.

world knowes not." Since he has experienced a rebirth, he is no longer that sinful man born George Fox; now he has Christ dwelling in him, he is a new and sinless man. And that "new man" deserves a new name, but a name by which the world ought not to call him.

The distinction between "I am Christ" and "Christ dwelleth in me," between George Fox the creature and Fox the new-born, Fox the renamed, is a subtle one, easily missed by enthusiasts and scarcely convincing to critics. When James Nayler was released from Exeter prison in 1656, he was greeted by a small band of enthusiastic devotees; surrounded by their hosannas, he rode to Bristol in a manner too reminiscent of Jesus' entrance into Jerusalem. Charged with blasphemy, he said of his worshippers that they were to blame if they were worshipping the visible James Nayler, but not if they were worshipping the invisible Christ within. The court was unimpressed, and Nayler was severely punished.

The Quaker cause suffered too. It was obviously dangerous to talk too freely of "the Christ within," just as it had been dangerous for the Sufi mystics to proclaim that Allah lay within them. No doubt, all men were sons of God. They all had the seeds of Christ within them, they all "participated in" Christ—to use the metaphor which Plato had applied, to meet a not entirely dissimilar problem, in order to explain how a number of beautiful objects could all be said to have Beauty within them.* But to say that they *were*

---

* This links with what was said above about the imitation of Christ. Plato found it extremely difficult to give any satisfactory account of the relationship between "forms" and particulars. To say that particulars imitate forms, as he sometimes does, is not enough: it does not suggest the ontological dependence of particulars on forms. So, similarly, to say that men should imitate Christ does not make clear their dependence on Christ. Plato sometimes talks, therefore, about particulars as "participating" in the forms; Christians suggest, in the same spirit, that men are to participate in Christ, that this is the "real meaning" of imitation. Precisely in what this participation consists is in both cases very obscure; Plato himself in the *Parmenides* draws attention to the extreme difficulty of making any sense of the metaphor.

Christ, however this expression was intended, was to encourage the James Naylers of this world.

Surely there was another alternative. Could it not be said, simply, that Christ by his grace transformed men's nature rather than that he lent them his own nature? The difficulty was that the Quakers were still, in part, Calvinists. Man's nature was corrupt; he had to be reborn; he had to acquire a *new* nature, and that, on the face of it, could only be Christ's nature.

The doctrine that men could become sinless persisted within the Quaker movement, even if the mechanism was better left obscure. The theologian of the movement, Robert Barclay, is obdurate on that point in his *Apology for the True Christian Divinity*. If men experience the "new birth," he says, "the body of death in sin comes to be crucified and removed, and their hearts united and subjected to the truth; so as not to obey any suggestions or temptations of the Evil One, but to be free from actual sinning and transgressing of the law of God, and in that respect perfect." He grants, no doubt, that "this perfection still admit[s] of a growth" and that the *possibility* of sinning remains. But this last admission can scarcely be reconciled with what he also says, namely, that the grace of Christ is able "to counterbalance, overcome and root out the evil seed, wherewith we are naturally, as in the Fall, leavened."[5] It is very easy to understand why Barclay wanted to maintain that new-born men could still sin; if men are told that they are now incapable of sinning they are only too likely to draw the conclusion that they have a perfect liberty to do as they please. But it is less easy to see *how* they can sin, if the evil seed within them is wholly rooted out. No doubt, as William Penn especially emphasized, full perfection—the achievement of complete

---

5. Robert Barclay: *Apology for the True Christian Divinity,* Proposition VIII: Concerning Perfection: Thesis; 8th English ed. (Birmingham, 1765), p. 204, and Proposition VII, p. 171.

wisdom, complete glory, complete happiness—has been reserved, on the Quaker view, for the after life. On the face of it, however, immaculate perfection, of a kind which makes it impossible for men to sin, was available here and now.

Quakerism was destined not to become the popular religion it set out to be; its immediate history, indeed, was to be a history of sects within sects. But the Methodism which Wesley founded did become a popular religion. And Wesley firmly asserted that Christians can and ought to attain to perfection. Methodism did not always remain faithful to Wesley's teachings. His perfectibilism was not attractive to all Methodists; George Whitefield, the most powerful preacher of the Methodist movement, was a Calvinist and there soon grew up, within Methodism, a minority Calvinist wing, with resulting schisms.[6] But it is his perfectibilism which makes Wesley so significant a figure in the history of Christian ideas—as distinct from the history of ecclesiastical organization or of evangelical preaching.[7]

In his *Plain Account of Christian Perfection*[8] Wesley describes the progress and development of his teaching on perfection from 1725 until 1777. He tries to show, as against those who accused him of unorthodoxy and inconsistency, that he was both orthodox and—with some few reservations—consistent. Wesley's religious history, as he relates it, is like Paul's, or like Luther's, in contrast with Augustine's. He had always been, in the eyes of the world, a devout, righteous man, but his reading of Jeremy Taylor's *Rules and Exercises of Holy Living and Dying* convinced him that, for all his devoutness, he was only "half a Christian." There was no

6. See, for example, John Leland Peters: *Christian Perfection and American Methodism* (South Nashville, Tenn., 1956).

7. Compare James B. Mozley: *Lectures and Other Theological Papers* (London, 1883), Lecture XI, "The Modern Doctrine of Perfectibility," and R. N. Flew: *The Idea of Perfection in Christian Theology*.

8. John Wesley: *A Plain Account of Christian Perfection*, in *Works*, 16 vols (London, 1809–13), Vol. 11, pp. 158–250. The page references hereafter are to this ed.

half-way house, he now came to think, between dedicating *every* part of his life to God, and devoting it "to myself; that is, in effect, to the devil." Four years later he read *The Imitation of Christ*. This showed him, Wesley tells us, that not only his life, but his whole heart must be dedicated to God; a year or so later, in 1729, William Law's *Christian Perfection* convinced him "more than ever, of the absolute impossibility of being half a Christian." [9] For it is the central point of Law's argument that every Christian must take literally Christ's command to be perfect—a perfection defined by Law as "the right performance of our necessary duties" and "the exercise of such holy tempers as are equally necessary and equally practicable in all states of life." This, Law argues, is at once the highest degree of perfection Christianity demands and the lowest it allows. No Christian can be satisfied with less.[10] Wesley's belief in perfectibility, then, is grounded in a long tradition of devotional writing, Anglican and Roman Catholic.

In 1733, Wesley preached his first perfectibilist sermon at St. Mary's Church, Oxford. He explicitly lays it down, in that sermon, that the Christian must seek "holiness" (immaculate perfection), a holiness which frees the soul from all sin and endows it with Christ's virtues, so that it can truly be said to be "perfect as our Father in heaven is perfect." This perfection Wesley further defines, in an Augustinian manner, as a love of God so absolute that it wholly excludes any love of the creature, except in so far as by loving the creature we may express our love for its Creator. That is the sense, he argues, in which God is a "jealous God"; God will permit nothing else to be loved for its own sake.

From the general attitude expressed in this early sermon, so Wesley maintains, he never departed. But he car-

---

9. *Ibid.*, pp. 158–59.
10. William Law: *A Practical Treatise upon Christian Perfection* (London, 1728), Introduction, p. 3.

ried his perfectibilism to a higher pitch—a pitch he came eventually to think of as altogether too high—in the preface to the collection of hymns he published in 1741.[11] Only the Stoics have ever claimed so much for man as Wesley there claimed, and then only for their ideal Sage. The perfected Christian, Wesley says, will want for nothing; he will not even ask for ease from pain; he will never doubt what to do; he will never be troubled by temptation. It would be wrong to hold Wesley to these judgements, in the light of the reservations he later expressed about them. They represent, all the same, the ideal he would have liked not merely to lay before, but to regard as realizable by, the Christian. If he came to think of such an ideal as set too high, this was in the light of experience, not because he came to be critical of the ideal itself. (He is, incidentally, usually careful not to claim that he has himself been perfected.)

In the following year, by way of preface to a new volume of hymns, Wesley returned to the subject of perfection, in a manner designed to remove misapprehensions. He does not claim for men in this life, he now says, "freedom from ignorance, mistake, temptation, and a thousand infirmities necessarily connected with flesh and blood."[12] Secondly—and this against the antinomian sects—there is no perfection of a kind which would raise men "above the law," which would have the effect that the "perfected ones" need no longer take the sacraments, or live simple lives, or pray. Thirdly, to say that the Christian can perfect himself does not imply that he will be infallible—he may still, Wesley grants, whether through ignorance or mistake, go against God's will "in things not essential to salvation." Elsewhere, in his 1740 sermon on "Christian Perfection," Wesley had mentioned another thing he does not mean; he does not mean that men can make themselves, even with the aid of

11. *A Plain Account of Christian Perfection, ed. cit.*, pp. 172–76.
12. *Ibid.*, pp. 178–79.

God's grace, perfect in the aesthetic sense of the word—in all respects graceful, imaginative, quick in understanding.

What then *does* Wesley mean? "We mean [by perfect]," Wesley tells us, "one in whom is the mind which was in Christ, and who so walketh as Christ also walked: a man that hath clean hands and a pure heart, or that is cleansed from all filthiness of flesh and spirit; one in whom is no occasion of stumbling, and who accordingly does not commit sin." Such a man is "sanctified throughout," his "soul is all love," he "loveth the Lord his God with all his heart," he "loveth his neighbour, every man, as himself; yea, as Christ loveth us."[13]

Wesley's view, it might be thought, makes the Atonement unnecessary. Not so, Wesley argues. For although they are not properly to be called sins, men's involuntary transgressions, arising out of their ignorance, are still faults, and need to be atoned for. In this sense, even the perfected Christian still needs to pray: "Forgive us our trespasses." Indeed, Wesley was reluctant to use the phrase "sinless perfection" in case the conclusion was wrongly drawn that a Christian could be free even from such involuntary transgressions.

At first Wesley denied that perfection once achieved can ever be lost—he accepted the Calvinist doctrine of "inamissable" (unlosable) grace, with the consequence, on his view of grace, that the perfected man is sinless for ever. As one of his hymns described the perfect Christian:

He walks in glorious liberty,
To sin entirely dead.

But his experience of the Methodist movement persuaded him otherwise. "Formerly we thought," he writes, "one saved

---

13. *Ibid.*, p. 179.

from sin could not fall. Now, we know the contrary. We are surrounded with instances of those, who lately experienced all that I mean by perfection. They had both the *fruit* of the Spirit and the *witness.* But they have now lost both."[14]

The three great dangers for the Christian, according to Wesley, are pride, enthusiasm, in the eighteenth-century sense of the word, and antinomianism. Insensibly, a man convinced that he has entirely surrendered himself to God can come to be proud of himself just for that reason; his egoism reasserts itself as spiritual pride. As for "enthusiasm" —the belief that, as a perfected man, the believer has had special revelations from God over and above what Scripture reveals to all men—that, said Wesley, was a "daughter of pride." And closely linked with "enthusiasm" is antinomianism; the perfected man comes to think of himself as "above the Law," no longer subject to normal judgements on his conduct.

That these were real dangers is only too abundantly illustrated in the history of Methodism and the Quaker movement. Fletcher of Madeley, close friend of Wesley, felt constrained to admit that "Antinomian principles have spread like wildfire among our societies . . . I have seen them, who pass for believers, follow the strain of corrupt nature; and when they should have exclaimed against Antinomianism, I have heard them cry out against the *legality* of their wicked hearts; which, they said, still suggested that they were to *do* something for their salvation."[15] The Quaker-educated, Methodist-attracted, Hannah Whitall Smith has made it clear in her "Personal Experiences of Fanaticism" just how, in their search for "spiritual baptism" and guided by the "Inner Light" beloved of the Quakers, men and

14. *Ibid.,* p. 228. The hymn is quoted on p. 182.
15. J. W. Fletcher: *Second Check Against Antinomianism,* 3rd letter (*Works,* Shebbear, Devon, i, p. 63), as quoted in K. E. Kirk: *The Vision of God,* p. 419.

women could be led to interpret sexual experiences as the highest forms of sanctity.[16] She describes, for example, the agonies of mind of a young woman who had allowed herself to be persuaded by a Methodist clergyman that she had been chosen to be the mother of children who were to be born—with some degree of carnal assistance from the clergyman—to the Holy Ghost. Becoming pregnant, "she dared not admit the idea that it was a delusion, for her whole spiritual life seemed to depend upon believing that she had been rightly guided; for if she could think that in the most solemn moments of consecration, the Lord could allow her to be so deceived, she would feel that she could never trust Him again."[17] Similarly, men, once persuaded they were "perfect," could not bring themselves to believe that they had fallen away from perfection; it was necessary to suppose, rather, that what they found themselves doing, however at odds with conventional moral standards, was, in some mysterious way, the work of the Lord.

To see antinomian perfectibilism in its most developed form, we must turn our attention to the history of Christian heresy, to those sects which lie on the periphery of Christendom. For long periods in the history of official Christianity, indeed, there has run parallel with it a competing religious movement—we have met it already as Gnosticism—sometimes manifested only in the form of isolated sects, sometimes living a powerful, but underground, existence as a secret community of believers, sometimes emerging publicly as a potent rival to the established Church. From the twelfth to the fourteenth century, it took the form of Catharism—better known, perhaps, as "the Albigensian heresy." We can sum up the Cathar objection to orthodox Christianity thus: Christianity allows too much value to the flesh,

---

16. Publ. in Hannah W. Smith, *Religious Fanaticism*, ed. with introd. by Ray Strachey (London, 1928).

17. *Ibid.*, p. 191.

too little power to the spirit. Every material thing, so the Cathars maintained, is the creation not of God but of Satan.

Christianity, or so we have suggested, is ambiguous in its attitude to the world; the Cathars sought to put an end to that ambiguity. If the Cathars maintained—like the early Gnostics—that Jesus had only "passed through" Mary, not being made flesh by her, this was a more extreme expression of those very same feelings that lay behind the Christian emphasis on Mary's virginity. But the official Christian Church, so the Cathars argued, had compromised with the Devil; it had succumbed to the temptations of wealth and worldly power; it had failed to insist with sufficient force on celibacy, as a pre-requisite of salvation. For the Cathars, there could be no compromise; any concession to the flesh was a concession to the Devil. The perfected man must wholly reject the flesh and all its ways.

Christianity, the heretics also argued, had at the same time allowed too little to the spirit; the human spirit, they claimed, is capable of so perfecting itself, so freeing itself from the flesh, that it can become one with God. At this point, too, there were precedents for their teachings in the earlier history of the Church. The second-century Montanists were completely convinced that men can become Gods. Their leader Montanus had no hesitation in proclaiming, "I am the Lord God, the Almighty present to you in man's form," just as, a little later, Paul of Samosata was to announce, "I too, if I wish, shall be Christ, since I and Christ are of one and the same nature." [18] If Christians whose heterodoxy was by no means obvious could write thus—Montanus was condemned by Pope Zephyrinus only after much hesitation and Paul was bishop of Antioch—it is not surprising that bolder heretics so often laid claims to divinity.*

---

18. Both quotations are from Steven Runciman: *The Medieval Manichee* (Cambridge, 1947; repr. 1955), pp. 18–20.

* It must be remembered that as late as the end of the second century Christians

Was it merely a libel when their opponents accused the Cathars of using their hostility to the flesh as a mere cloak for libertinism? Charges of this same kind, it is well to remember, were levelled against the early Christians; Christian "love-feasts," many of their pagan critics alleged, were sexual orgies in disguise, their communion service a form of cannibalism, their fraternal relationships a cover for incest. All these charges early Christian apologists like Athenagoras felt it necessary to rebut at length. But it is easy to see how the Cathar teachings could produce the consequences Wesley so greatly, and so justifiably, feared—pride, enthusiasm, antinomianism. Can a man say of himself, without pride, that he is "perfected"? Convinced that he is perfect, is he not liable to think of himself as no longer subject to merely human laws?

The "perfected" Cathar, no doubt, claimed to have passed beyond the point at which men are capable of sinning. But in this claim there is a crucial ambiguity. It may mean that "perfected" men will, once perfect, no longer perform acts of the kind men commonly call sinful. Or it may mean that after they have been perfected, nothing they do subsequently, however immoral in the eyes of men, counts for the fully sanctified as a sin. The enemies of perfectibilist heresies have always alleged the second interpretation and sometimes, it would seem, with justification.

In the case of medieval sects, it is, of course, difficult to be at all certain what they taught, even when, as so often happened, they placed great emphasis on "sacred books." It was the medieval habit to burn their manuscripts along with the offending heretics, and it was not a medieval habit, any more than it is a modern habit, to refrain from slander, when

---

were still claiming the power, in Christ's name, of raising men from the dead. So, writing in the second century, Irenaeus tells us that "dead men have actually been raised and have remained with us for many years" (quoted in Eusebius: *History of the Church*, 5, 7, 4; trans. cit., p. 210). It is not surprising that men felt themselves to be Christ, when they believed themselves to possess such powers.

it serves the interests of orthodox piety. So our only source of information is, in many cases, the highly suspect expositions of their opponents. But thanks to the assiduity of Norman Cohn,[19] we are able to examine in some detail the teachings of those Brethren of the Free Spirit who, under a variety of names, flourished in Europe from the twelfth until the sixteenth century, when—as the "Spiritual Libertines"—they aroused the wrath of Calvin.

Metaphysically, the brethren were deeply influenced, like Augustine before them, by neo-Platonism, which they interpreted in a pantheistic fashion. More important than their general metaphysics, however, was their view of the human soul and its relation to God. "From eternity," wrote one of them, "the soul of man was in God and is God,"[20] they were, that is, pantheists of a somewhat irregular sort. Not things as such, but only their essences, were in God; but even transitory beings *sought* to be God. In the manner to which we have become only too accustomed, they drew a distinction between the ordinary believer, the "crude in spirit," and the élite, the "subtle in spirit." In the end, admittedly, both the crude and the subtle would become God, but only the subtle could become God here and now, possessing all the divine perfections. The bull of Clement V, issued in 1311 and directed against the Brethren, specifically condemns the proposition that "a man in this life can attain to such perfection that he is incapable of sinning or surpassing his present degree of grace, since to do so would make him more perfect than Christ."[21] But the more spiritually ambitious of the Brethren were not content to rest even at this point; they had, they claimed, advanced in perfection beyond God, of whom they no longer had any need.

19. See his *The Pursuit of the Millennium* (London, 1957), together with Gordon Leff: *Heresy in the Later Middle Ages*, Vol. 1, pp. 308–407, which develops and corrects Cohn's account of the Brotherhood.

20. Cohn, *op. cit.*, p. 181.

21. Leff, *op. cit.*, p. 314.

In this paranoiac mood, they were scarcely likely to pay much attention to merely human claims upon them or to restrictions imposed upon their conduct. "One can be so united with God," an "adept" wrote, "that whatever one may do one cannot sin."[22] Their favourite Biblical text was Paul's "To the pure all things are pure."[23] The English Ranter, Laurence Clarkson—the Ranters were the English branch, as one might express the matter, of the Brethren of the Free Spirit—quotes this text in defence of his view that honesty (in its seventeenth-century sense of "chastity") and adultery are indistinguishable. "For," he says, "with God they are but one, and that one Act holy, just, and good as God . . . what Act soever I do, is acted by that Majesty in me . . . there is no act whatsoever, that is impure in God, or sinful with or before God."[24]

This was in a book which bore a somewhat odd-sounding title—*A Single Eye All Light,* with a reference to Matthew: "The light of the body is the eye: if therefore thine eye be single, thy whole body shall be full of light."[25] The title brings out, in a metaphorical way, the essence of the Ranters' teachings. It refers obliquely to a metaphor much favoured by patristic and medieval theology in order to indicate the condition of man: man, according to this metaphor, has "two eyes," one spiritual, fixed on heaven and one, secular, on the earth. What the Ranters stood for, in contrast, was "a single eye all light"; the human being was to be entirely spiritual, entirely filled by the divine light, with no eye fixed on the merely worldly.* And in such a being, they

---

22. Cohn, *op. cit.,* p. 187.
23. Titus 1:15.
24. Cohn, *op. cit.,* pp. 348–49.
25. Matthew 6:22.
* Compare the mock-advertisement in the newspaper of the Oneida community (for which see p. 221 below). "It is known that many persons with two eyes habitually 'see double.' To prevent stumbling and worse liabilities in such circumstances, an ingenious contrivance has been invented by which the *whole body* is filled with light. It is called the '*single eye,*' and may be obtained by applying to Jesus Christ." (Charles Nordhoff: *The Com-*

argued, there could be no sin. What Wesley was prepared to admit—that some of his followers had been perfect and had then fallen—was in the eyes of the Brotherhood a monstrous absurdity. Once a man was wholly possessed by God, once his will was wholly subordinated to the divine will, how *could* he fall? Teresa had been puzzled by the same difficulty, but had been prepared to set it aside as "a mystery." The Ranters were bolder. It was logically impossible for a perfected man to sin; his actions were God's actions; if what he did seemed to be sinful, this could only be because it was so regarded by the sinful eyes of men. It is easy to understand why George Fox was so anxious to distinguish himself from the Ranters.

The Ranters' views were sufficiently widespread to provoke, in 1650, the English House of Commons to pass an act for "the Punishment of Atheistical, Blasphemous and Execrable Opinions" which laid down penalties for those who professed that "acts of adultery, drunkenness, swearing . . . are in their own nature as holy and righteous as the duties of prayer, preaching, or giving of thanks to God" or that "whatsoever is acted by them, (whether whoredom, adultery, drunkenness or the like open wickedness) may be committed without sin."[26] The Brethren's attitude to property was no less uncompromising: the noble spirit had a right to keep whatever he could lay his hands on. For did not the idea of "mine and yours" belong to the realm of the Devil as distinct from the realm of God?[27] A fact of great historical importance, this doctrine was generalized—all property, so it was argued, was held by man in common. Utopian communism and the doctrine of sinless perfection were thus conjoined in a single stream.

---

munistic Societies of the United States, New York, 1875; repr. 1960, p. 267.) The doctrine of the single eye can also be found in mediaeval mystical writings, e.g. *Theologia Germanica,* ch. VII.

26. Cohn, *op. cit.,* pp. 325–26.

27. Compare *Theologia Germanica,* ch. XXII and *passim.*

To treat such doctrines as mere aberrations, as Cohn tends to do, is to miss their true significance, as a set of doctrines by which, as their recurrence suggests, Christians can be not implausibly tempted. Paul's own Church at Corinth, it would seem, had understood him, and not altogether unnaturally, as freeing them by his teachings from the governance of any kind of law. (Paul writes of himself, rather, as substituting a new law, the law of faith or the law of love, for the old law.)[28] And certainly there are passages in Luther which could be read with approval by any of the Brethren of the Free Spirit. "Our freedom," he writes, ". . . is freedom from the demands and obligations of the law," or again: "inasmuch as he is a Christian, he is above the law and sin. For he hath Christ the Lord of the law present and inclosed in his heart."[29] Anxious to oppose every form of "moralism," for which righteousness matters more than faith—"There is no one," Luther wrote, "who would not prefer to be without perfect righteousness than without the grace of God"[30]—Luther not uncommonly expressed himself in ways which could encourage antinomianism. It was Luther himself, no doubt, who first used that word as a form of condemnation. But he did so in reply to a friend and fellow worker, Johannes Agricola, who, in explicitly maintaining that the Ten Commandments are no longer of any importance to Christians, thought of himself as an orthodox Lutheran. (To Luther himself they were a kind of moral lifebuoy, to which Christians might properly cling in times of great moral distress.)

It is always a temptation for Christian thinking, we have already suggested, so to emphasize the inability of man to act of his own accord that all his acts must be thought of

28. See especially I Corinthians, 5, and Henry Chadwick: *The Early Church* (Harmondsworth, 1967; London, 1968), pp. 33–34.

29. *Preface to Romans* and *Commentary on Galatians,* as trans. in *Martin Luther: Selections,* ed. Dillenberger, pp. 30, 112.

30. *Adversus Latonum* (*Werke,* Weimarer Ausgabe, VIII, 106) as trans. in Kirk: *The Vision of God,* p. 418.

as God's. And then it is no longer possible to regard any of his acts as sins. The Augustinian view that evil is essentially privative and so far negative, a view designed to reconcile its existence with God's omnipotence, also has its dangers for the Christian: it can easily be pushed into the stronger view that evil exists only for those who have failed to see the world as it really is, who lack that divine illumination in the light of which the unreality of sin is made clear.

Again, the doctrine that the flesh must be subdued can readily be so reinterpreted as to lead to the conclusion that no fleshly act is of any importance.* The Christian, it might even be concluded, ought deliberately to engage in, for example, sexual acts in order to prove to himself how little they matter to him. The story told of Clement of Rome, that, finding himself jealous of his wife, he offered her to his fellow clergy as a way of overcoming that jealousy, reflects this feeling that a sexual act, immoral in itself, can be a test of strength; enthusiasts of a rather different sort have lain with other men's wives to prove that it left them spiritually unmoved. "To kiss women and embrace them," so the French Béghards are said to have maintained, "provided they did not consummate the carnal sin, was greatly meritorious, and an argument of fortitude and abstinence, and of a strong and acceptable love of God, and the truest proof that each party was resolutely virtuous."[31] Would not consummation, more ardent enthusiasts naturally asked, be an even stronger proof of virtue, provided only that in that consummation the saints retained their absolute detachment?

We have so far left aside the question how, for Christian

---

* Compare "Expecting nothing, his heart and mind disciplined, having relinquished all possessions, *performing action by the body alone, he incurs no sin.*" (The Sage, as described in *Bhagavad-Gītā*, ch. IV, verse 21, in the trans. by Maharishi Mahesh Yogi, Harmondsworth, 1967—my italics.) It is significant, however, that in other translations this passage appears in a much less antinomian form. Christians are not the only ones who know how to turn scriptures to their own purposes.

31. Quoted in R. A. Knox: *Enthusiasm,* p. 103.

perfectibilists, individual perfection is related to social perfection. There can be little doubt that the early Christians expected that Christ would return to earth and rule over a perfect kingdom wholly comprised of his saints. These millennarian ideas derive from Hebrew sources, the Book of Daniel and such apocryphal books as Enoch. They retained their fascination for many centuries; Ralph Cudworth, Isaac Newton, Joseph Priestley all devoted themselves to the interpretation of the Book of Daniel. Millennial sects persist in our own time, ranging from the (relatively) orthodox Seventh Day Adventists to the highly heterodox Jehovah's Witnesses. Not infrequently, the presumption is that men can live now as saints in preparation for that second coming; in Seventh Day Adventism, millennial aspirations are linked with a considerable degree of asceticism.

Augustine substituted for millennial hopes a City of God, conceived of, in terms which echo Plato's *Republic,* as "a shadow of the eternal city"[32]—the eternal city which, for Augustine, is the Kingdom of God in heaven. The city of God is "a communion of saints." For Augustine, that does not mean that it is a city of the perfected, since no one on earth can be perfected. But it is a city of those who love God and who are predestined to join God's kingdom in heaven, as distinct from the city made up of those who love not God but the world. Men are divided, not in terms of what perfection they have achieved, but in terms of what they love— God or the world. It is easy to see, however, how this doctrine of two cities could be converted into another one, for which the city of worldly men is identified with the secular city and the city of those who love God with a community of perfected saints, owing no allegiance to the temporal order.

We can then put the matter thus: the idea of a perfect society composed of perfect men, a society existing here on

---

32. Augustine: *The City of God,* Bk. XV, ch. 2, in the abridged trans. ed. V. J. Bourke, p. 325.

this earth as distinct from a kingdom of heaven, entered into Christian thought in two ways. First as millennialism, the belief in a Second Coming — presaged by calamities and the emergence of anti-Christ on earth — after which Christ will reign on earth over a kingdom of saints. Secondly, as the idea of a City of God composed of men who are already perfected and living on earth in a perfect community in the midst of a secular state to which they owe little or no obedience. The two ideas were often conjoined; the saints, it is then suggested, were to live now in a city of God in preparation for Christ's second coming.

To particularize the variety of forms which these ideas have assumed in the history of Western Europe would be a task of immense complexity. One example will have to serve — the nineteenth-century Oneida community in the United States. Its solution of the problem of reconciling perfected sinlessness with the impulses of the flesh was unusually ingenious and, as it would appear, more than ordinarily successful.[33] John Humphrey Noyes, the Founder of the Oneida community, was a student of theology at Yale. In the course of his Biblical studies, he lit upon a momentous discovery: the Second Advent had already taken place, in the year A.D. 70 when Jerusalem fell. The Ten Commandments were at that same time abrogated; but not the New Testament commandments of love. The New Testament showed men how to perfect themselves through faith. Noyes made it clear that he was himself perfected in this way, and therefore incapable of sinning, as other men could also be, if they had sufficient faith. The Gospel, he claimed, "provides for complete salvation from sin."

Noyes interested himself in the quasi-communist societies which were springing up throughout America, under the influence of such Utopian reformers as Fourier. They

---

33. The details that follow are in part derived from chapter VII of Ray Strachey's introduction to Hannah W. Smith: *Religious Fanaticism*, pp. 100–117.

failed, with dismal regularity; and Noyes thought he knew why. They failed because they were unable to solve "the problem of marriage"—a "problem" he had already encountered in the lives of his perfected friends. Noyes's own solution was "complex marriage." There was no doubt that men and women must love one another, and the more they loved one another the better; with the freedom to love, marriage must never be allowed to interfere. Yet Noyes wished to retain what was essential in ascetic Christianity—the need for *detachment*. Paul had told the Corinthians that a married man inevitably "careth for the things that are of the world, how he may please his wife."[34] Some Christians had sought to avoid this deplorable consequence by avoiding all sexual relationships; others, of the more antinomian sort, by allowing themselves none but irregular relationships. But Noyes had a different solution: marriage with a wife one did not too much care for.

Men and women must not be allowed to "form attachments"—whether to persons or to possessions; this was the unforgivable crime. If a man felt himself becoming attached to a particular woman, so that he could love only her, this was a derogation from the love due to all women; he must at once separate himself from her and allow another man to take his place. The same was true of a mother's love of a child or, of course, of any attachment to private possessions. So the perfect could be preserved from temptation: the temptation of "egoism." Thus it was that Noyes carried to their logical conclusions the teachings of such sixteenth-century Moravians as Ulrich Stadler. On property Stadler had written: "*Mine, thine, his, own* divides the Lord's house and is impure. . . . For everything has been created free in common. . . . Whoever appropriates them (creaturely things) for himself and encloses them is a thief and steals what is not

34. I Corinthians 7:33.

his."[35] As Proudhon was later to put the same point: "Property is theft." Ordinary marriage, to Noyes, was simply one form assumed by the property-relationship.

Noyes did not claim, it should be observed, that all the members of his community were sinless. Once more we encounter the distinction between the sinless perfected ones, the leaders of the community, who set the standards for the community as a whole, and the ordinary practising believers. And when Noyes spoke of "sinless perfection," he did not mean that the perfected ones lived in accordance with "the law"; the Ten Commandments were gone, and with them the law. ("Notice is hereby given that all claims made by the old firm of Moses and Law were cancelled 1800 years ago.") The perfection he had in mind was a mystical perfection, involving a "daily and familiar intercourse with God," an intercourse which destroyed all selfishness. Selfishness, understood as the desire to own or possess, is, for Noyes, the only form of evil; the whole community was designed to ensure that such selfishness would not arise, or, once arisen, would not endure.[36]

Under the dictatorship of Noyes, the Community flourished to an unparalleled degree. But the Presbyterian Synod of New York took alarm and Noyes thought it expedient to abolish its central feature—its system of "complex marriage"—after which the community decayed. The great interest of the Oneida Community lies in the fact that it preserved the ascetic ideal of detachment without any trace of the Puritanism with which, in Christianity, it has almost invariably been allied.

Let us now try to sum up the lessons of the last three

35. Ulrich Stadler: *Cherished Instructions on Sin, Excommunication, and the Community of Goods,* in *Spiritual and Anabaptist Writers,* ed. G. H. Williams, Library of Christian Classics, 25 (London, 1957), p. 278. The order of the sentences has been modified.

36. This quotation is taken from *The Circular,* the paper of the Community. See Charles Nordhoff: *The Communistic Societies of the United States,* p. 267.

chapters. Christianity has been, in its major official sects, opposed to the view that men can, in this life, live flawless lives. Of course, it did promise perfection in a future life, sometimes to all men—Origen expressed the belief that in the long run even Satan will be saved—sometimes to all men who diligently seek after it, sometimes only to an elect. But in this life, according to the central stream of Christian thinking, nothing more can be achieved than *progress* towards perfection.

To the degree to which progress towards perfection is possible, it is dependent, according to the main Christian tradition, upon the assistance of God's grace. This was the sense in which, as Origen argued in his *Contra Celsum,* Christianity was for all, Platonism only for the few. According to Plato, perfection lies open only to men of a certain nature and a certain education; Christianity offered the hope of ultimate perfection to all sorts and conditions of men, by making it dependent on God's grace. But at the same time it made it impossible for a man to achieve perfection by his own efforts. There were disagreements about the degree of terrestrial perfection to which even God's grace could carry men, but it was generally admitted that not even God's grace made men perfect, although this, of course, lay within God's power; God has simply, as Augustine thought, chosen not to bestow so much grace on men in this life.

Many Christians, however, have been dissatisfied with this conclusion. They have sought complete perfection, whether by renunciation of the world, or by direct union with God, or by an overwhelming conversion, or by placing themselves entirely in God's hands, or by an exercise of will. And often enough they have tried to live within a small community of believers, as Epicurus set up the ideal of a community of friends in a garden, where perfection would be achieved in a fellowship of the perfect. That perfection, in this life, lies open to all men, not many Christians have believed since Pelagius was condemned, but that it is impossible even for an élite, many Christians have refused to admit. Conquer the flesh, overthrow egoism, and God will take possession. Such Christians, however, have differed greatly about what is meant by "conquering the flesh," or by "overthrowing egoism," to say nothing of their disagreements about how, and to what degree, God can take possession of the individual, and what the evidence is that he has done so.

EIGHT

PERFECTING BY SOCIAL ACTION:
THE PRESUPPOSITIONS

Pelagius and Augustine agreed on one point—the alternatives were clear, at least at the extremes. Either man could perfect himself, by the exercise of his own free will, or else he could be perfected only by the infusion of God's grace. These were the poles between which Christian controversy fluctuated. In the seventeenth century, however, a third possibility began to be canvassed, cutting across the ancient quarrel between Pelagians and Augustinians. Perhaps men could be perfected not by God, not by the exercise of their own free will, not even by some combination of the two, but by the deliberate intervention of their fellow-men.

So long as the Platonic or the Augustinian way of defining perfection was taken for granted, this possibility could be ruled out of court. No man—however clever, however wise, however technically well-equipped—could, purely as a consequence of his own efforts, bring his fellow-men to a condition in which they were able to contemplate the form of the good, or unite themselves with the One, or love nobody and nothing except God. He could, no doubt, assist them in their attempts to attain those ends. In his *Republic,* Plato described a course of education which, undertaken by a selected few, could help them to reach a point at which they were ready to contemplate the form of the good; Plotinus can tell such men as are fit to undertake an arduous quest what steps are necessary to achieve union with the One; her spiritual advisers can advise Teresa in her search for spiritual perfection. The fact remains that for Plato and for Plotinus natural endowments, for Christianity the grace of God, are essential prerequisites for the attaining of perfection; the educator, the spiritual adviser, have an important but only an ancillary role to play in the perfecting of men.

But must perfection be conceived of in such ambitious terms? There are two programmes of education in Plato's *Republic,* one designed for ordinary men, who could not hope to achieve perfection but could attain to "civic goodness," the other restricted to such civically good men as gave promise, in virtue of their qualities of temperament and intellect, of being incipient philosopher-kings. Suppose Plato were to abandon the idea that, to be perfect, men must first contemplate the form of the good. Then perfection could be described in wholly non-metaphysical terms, as the attainment of the maximum possible civic goodness together, perhaps, with such a degree of "philosophical goodness" as education could ensure. It is then as if Aristotle's *Ethics* had contained no reference to the theoretical life, or had described that life in purely secular terms as a life of scientific investigation, or as if the Stoic ideal of the perfected Sage had been abandoned but the Stoic account of moral progress retained.

This is the kind of perfection which, towards the end of the fourteenth century, the Florentine "civic humanists" began to extol.[1] Whereas the neo-Platonists and their Christian successors had, so we suggested, amalgamated Plato and Aristotle into a single, metaphysical, philosopher, the civic humanists brought into prominence the Aristotle of the *Politics* and of those books of the *Nicomachean Ethics* in which he describes the life of the ordinary citizen. They read Lucretius and rediscovered the ethics of Epicurus; they read Epictetus and Cicero's *De Officiis* and admired the moral out-

---

1. See especially H. Baron: *The Crisis of the Early Italian Renaissance,* 2 vols (Princeton, 1955). The complexity of Renaissance thought is brought out in P. O. Kristeller's essay on "Philosophy and Humanism in Renaissance Perspective" in B. O'Kelly, ed.: *The Renaissance Image of Man and the World* (Athens, Ohio, 1966). See also J. A. Mazzeo: *Renaissance and Revolution* (London, 1967), ch. I.

look they found expounded there, Stoicism without metaphysics. Refusing to admit the superiority of the contemplative over the active life, they at the same time redefined
both kinds of life.

For most Christian moralists the active life meant what
it had meant for Cassian—that part of the life of a monk or,
at most, of a secular priest which was devoted to works of
charity and mercy or to ecclesiastic administration. There
were isolated exceptions, like the fourteenth-century English mystic Walter Hilton, who were prepared to allow that
a layman, as well as a priest or a member of a religious order,
could live that "mixed life" of action and contemplation
which Augustine had advocated.[2] But not even such dissentients were prepared to count the ordinary virtues of the citizen—"civic goodness" as distinct from the peculiarly Christian virtues—as the "active" ingredient in a mixed life. The
civic humanists, however, at once extolled the active life,
as contrasted with either the purely contemplative or the
mixed life, and identified it with the "civically good" life of
free, enterprising, community-minded citizens. Theirs was
essentially a city-centred view of life, reminding us of the
etymological origins of such words as "urbane" and "civilized." They totally rejected that ideal of retirement which
Epicurus had advocated and monasticism had carried into
practice. In many ways, indeed, their attitude represented
a resurgence of the ideals of ancient Athens, the Periclean
City-State.

On the other side, the "contemplative" life gradually
came to be identified not with the life of the monk or the
hermit, withdrawn in silence from the ways of man, but with
the vigorous, inquiring life of the scholar, the philosopher,
the scientist, typified by Leonardo da Vinci but no less manifest in the burning, inexhaustible zeal of the Renaissance

2. See Joy Russell-Smith: "Walter Hilton" in James Walsh, ed.: *Pre-Reformation English Spirituality* (London, 1965), pp. 182–97.

classicist. The traditional sharp distinction between the contemplative and the active life was thus blurred. Florence, city of businessmen, scholars, statesmen, artists and scientists, prepared the way for that eighteenth-century alliance between commerce and philosophy which did so much to encourage men's hopes that they not only could be, but would be, perfected.

It is true that for the time being the civic humanists were defeated. Florence itself, as it lost its civic freedoms, came to be dominated by the Platonic Academy, by philosophers like Ficino who carried neo-Platonism to vertiginous extremes. But the new spirit, once aroused, could not be entirely destroyed. It carried over, in important respects, into Lutheranism and Calvinism; it continued to survive, as a thin but continuous line, until the time was ripe for it once more to expand at the Enlightenment.

The Renaissance break with the past was not, of course, absolute and decisive. Such breaks never are. One of the most notable expressions of the new attitude is Pietro Pomponazzi's sixteenth-century *On the Immortality of the Soul.* This is the work of a Paduan Aristotelian, more than suspect, it is true, to ecclesiastical authorities, but well-versed in, and amicably disposed towards, the Thomistic tradition. Pomponazzi does not for a moment deny that in so far as men can become godlike this can only be through the cultivation of their "theoretical intellect." What he does deny is that the perfection of this intellect is man's natural end, or that men can properly be described as "perfect" only in so far as they are wholly devoted to the contemplative life.

Taking over an Aristotelian classification, Pomponazzi distinguished between three forms of intellect: the theoretical, the practical, the productive. All men, he says, possess these three forms of intellect in some degree. They possess some knowledge, however rudimentary, of fundamental theoretical truths—such truths as that nothing can both be and not be at the same time. They are "productive," they can create and build. They are "practical" in Aristotle's sense of the word, capable, that is, of making moral and political decisions. But only the "practical" form of intellect, according to Pomponazzi, is proper and peculiar to man, and this is the only form of intellect which all men must attempt to develop to its full perfection. It is neither possible nor desirable for all men to perfect themselves as metaphysicians or as builders. But it is both possible and desirable, according to Pomponazzi, for them all to perfect themselves morally. "As to the practical intellect," he writes, "which is proper to man, every man should possess it perfectly. . . . For the whole would be most perfectly preserved if all men were righteous and good, but not if all were philosophers or smiths or builders."[3]

Pomponazzi's reference to "the whole" is particularly significant. By "the whole" he means "mankind" or "the human race." There was nothing new in thinking of mankind in this way as a single whole; the Greeks had not done so, but Augustine had. What is novel in Pomponazzi's approach is that he takes as his point of departure the *perfecting* of "the whole"—of mankind—rather than the perfecting of the individual. In so doing, he anticipated the characteristic approach of modern perfectibilism, at least since the eighteenth century. The individual is to be perfected only as part of the perfection of mankind. And if mankind as a whole is to be perfected then—unless within the framework of a Buddhist-type theory of reincarnation—the ideal of perfection has to be set at a level which men can, in their present life, hope to achieve. And this is the case, Pomponazzi is suggesting, if perfection is identified with moral or "practical" perfection.

If it be objected that the perfection of the practical intel-

---

3. Quotations are based on the trans. by William H. Hay, rev. by J. H. Randall in *The Renaissance Philosophy of Man, ed. cit.*, pp. 355–57. For a fuller discussion of Pomponazzi's views see A. H. Douglas: *The Philosophy and Psychology of Pietro Pomponazzi* (Cambridge, 1910), ch. x.

lect will not of itself bring men perfect peace, Pomponazzi's answer is that men are not to expect perfect peace. Were, indeed, a human being to arrive at a state in which, like the Stoic sage, he was entirely free of anxiety, he would cease to be human. Nor should men repine at the fact that they will never know all that they might wish to know, and will never be secure in an eternal happiness. A mortal being ought not to desire eternal happiness, "since the immortal is not fitting for a mortal." He should abandon his desire to be like God, whether in knowledge, in security or in happiness. "It is characteristic of the temperate man to be content with what suits him and what he can have." A few men, no doubt, should try to perfect themselves as philosophers, a few men as builders or as sculptors. But it is not necessary to the perfection of mankind that they should do so. What *is* necessary is that all men should perfect themselves as active, moral, beings. Perfection, then, is not metaphysical perfection but task-perfection, and man's task is a moral one.

We are back at last, in spirit, with Pindar, with Pindar's exhortation to "think mortal thoughts." Contemplating in retrospect the long history of Graeco-Christian thought, to say nothing of the Eastern religions, what strikes us most of all is the extravagant nature of the objectives it sets before men, and what goes with this, the severity of the conditions it lays down for their perfection. To be a philosopher-king or a Stoic sage, to love nobody and nothing except God for his own sake, to make oneself worthy of eternal happiness, to achieve union with the One, to attain to the vision of God or the form of the good—what vaulting ambitions these are! But now Pomponazzi exhorts men to forget the ambition to be godlike. "The bliss of man . . . ," as Pope was to put it, "is not to think or act beyond mankind."[4] Man is neither god nor beast: let him recognize this fact, and be content with the perfection proper to him. "All men can and ought to be

4. Alexander Pope: *Essay on Man*, Epistle I, lines 189–90.

of good character." That is the kind of perfection, perfection of character, which men should therefore take as their objective.

In his *Of Wisdom,* published almost a century later in 1601, that enigmatic but influential philosopher-theologian Pierre Charron adopted a still more worldly attitude.* His object, he tells us, is not to "prepare men for a cloister" but rather to set down the right method of "training a man up for the world, and forming him for business and mixed conversation"[5]—a most un-Augustinian ambition, very characteristic of the eighteenth-century world to come, not least in its reference to the delights of "mixed conversation."[6] Charron's heroes, his exemplars, are neither Stoic sages nor saints and martyrs. He sets up as "ideal types," rather, such practical men of affairs as Aristides the Just, Pericles, Alexander, Camillus, Scipio. The ideal wise man, he says, can properly be compared with a perfect piece of workmanship "which hath all its parts entire, and is finished according to the nicest rules of art." He has been so educated that "every part within and without, his thoughts, and words and actions, and every motion is graceful, and noble, and what is for the honour of his nature." It is obvious what is hap-

---

* Charron's own intentions are still disputed. He was accused by one of his more violent Jesuit opponents of being a secret atheist, intent on destroying religion. His own expressed view, sincere or not, is that he was teaching men how they should live even in the absence of divine revelation. What he was rejecting, he said, is not God, but the idea of a rational theology. In other words, he was a disciple of William of Ockham. Whatever his intentions, the effect of his teachings was to set up a concept of moral perfection which is entirely independent of theology. "The true science and the true study of man is man"— in saying this, Charron anticipated the preoccupations of the eighteenth century. Man, not God, is moving into the central position. Calvin had begun his *Institutes* by laying it down that what wisdom men possess is concerned either with God or with man. In fact, Charron is suggesting, man's wisdom is entirely about man. See R. H. Popkin: *The History of Scepticism from Erasmus to Descartes* (Assen, 1960), especially ch. 3.

5. All quotations are from the preface (pages not numbered) of *De la Sagesse* in the trans. *Of Wisdom,* by George Stanhope (London, 1697).

6. Compare H. Davis: "The Conversation of the Augustans" in R. F. Jones, *et al.: The Seventeenth Century* (Stanford, 1951; repr. 1965), pp. 181–97.

pening. The teleological concept of perfection, for which to be perfect is to attain some remote end, has been replaced by an aesthetic concept, for which to be perfect is to possess a harmoniously developed moral character, a character which men can, in principle, be so educated as to possess here and now. The perfect man is a work of art, the harmonious realization of an educator's ideal; education, not God, is the source of grace.* This was a typically Renaissance attitude to the human being and human perfection, carried over by Charron into the early seventeenth century and made central by Shaftesbury.

But are not men so bedevilled with lust, so tarnished with egoism, that such a moral character lies wholly beyond their reach? Not even Calvin, as we have already seen, was prepared to go quite so far: however violently he reacted against the Renaissance picture of man, he admitted, like Augustine before him, the merits of a Camillus and a Scipio. What is wrong, for an Augustinian, with a Camillus or a Scipio is not their actions, not the mode of life they live, but their motives. It is not enough, on Calvin's view, for a man's life to be as harmonious as a work of art; if it is not infused by the love of God it is through-and-through corrupt.

One thing that happened in the seventeenth century was that men began to question whether motives are of such overwhelming importance. Augustine himself had drawn attention to the fact that actions performed out of pride could be quite indistinguishable from actions performed out of charity. "All the good works that are willed and done by charity," Augustine wrote, "may be set in motion by its

---

* It is interesting to observe the *Shorter Oxford English Dictionary* gives as the main meaning of grace "attractiveness, charm, now usually the charm belonging to elegance of proportions or (especially) ease and refinement of movement, action, or expression." The other meaning of "grace," as "a favour granted," is treated as secondary and the specifically theological sense as a technical variant. There could scarcely be a better illustration of the degree to which the Renaissance has overcome the Augustinian attitude to life.

contrary pride." "Charity," to take one of Augustine's examples, "clothes the naked, so does pride."[7] Taking his cue from Augustine, the eighteenth-century moralist Pierre Nicole was even more explicit about what could be achieved by men's natural motives, without spiritual aid. "Entirely to reform the world," he wrote, "that is to say, to banish from it all vices and all the grosser disorders . . . one would only need, given the absence of charity, that men should possess an enlightened self-interest. . . . However corrupted such a society might be within and to the eyes of God, there need be nothing lacking to it in the way of being well regulated . . . and what is even more wonderful is that although it would be entirely animated and moved by self-love, self-love would nowhere appear in it; and although it would be entirely devoid of charity, one would see everywhere only the form and characteristics of charity."[8] If enlightened self-interest could produce a society so much better than any in which men were now living, it was more sensible, some of Nicole's readers were to conclude, to try to develop in men a greater degree of enlightened self-interest rather than to wait until God, so unpredictable in his ways, should choose to infuse them with charity.

"We shall have to transform it [virtue] into the idea of doing good and vice into the idea of doing ill," says the materialist Bordeu in Diderot's dialogue *D'Alembert's Dream*.[9] Diderot's dialogue was written in 1769 — although not published until 1830 — and Bordeu is not so much laying down a programme for action as describing what, very largely, had by that time already been done. Virtue, it had come to be

7. *Ten Homilies on the First Epistle General of St John*, 8th Homily, §9, as trans. by John Burnaby in Augustine: *Later Works*, Library of Christian Classics, 8 (London, 1955).

8. "De la charité et de l'amour propre," ch. xi, in *Essais de morale*, first publ. Paris, 1671–78 (Mons, 1707 ed.), Vol. 3, pp. 197–98. On this theme see also Gilbert Chinard: *En lisant Pascal* (Lille, 1948), pp. 97–118.

9. Quoted from *Rameau's Nephew*, trans. J. Barzun and R. H. Bowen (New York, 1956), p. 168.

widely agreed, consists in "doing good," even if that "doing of good" flows from self-love rather than from the love of God. Provided the poor are clothed, does it really matter whether this is out of vanity or out of charity?

Naturally enough there were dissentients from this novel attitude. Traditional Augustinians—and even Christians of a less severe kind—continued to argue that actions not performed out of a love of God were worthless. But as the century wore on, the disfavour attaching to "self-love" generally diminished. Pascal's "God alone is to be loved, self alone to be hated" was generally condemned as what Dr. Johnson called "monastic morality." Bishop Butler, preaching in 1726, was prepared to maintain that "self-love in its due degree is as just and morally good, as any affection whatever."[10] The important thing, it was more and more commonly argued, is that a man shall so act, whatever his motive, as to bring happiness to his fellow-men. "Charity" no longer had, as its principal meaning, "the love of God"; it came to be identified, by clergy and laymen alike, with disinterested benevolence, good nature, usefulness to others. "The highest merit which human nature is capable of attaining" is conveyed, Hume tells us, by such epithets as "sociable, good-natured, humane, merciful, grateful, friendly, generous, beneficent."[11] The novels of Henry Fielding teach the same lesson, implicitly. In *Joseph Andrews,* Mr. Barnabas is depicted as telling Joseph that "he must divest himself of all human passions," but Fielding makes it clear what he thinks of Mr. Barnabas. He greatly prefers Tom Jones, who is scarcely a model of Christian virtue. No doubt Tom Jones needs to reform, but his generosity and warm-heartedness make his "sins" venial, not mortal.

10. Blaise Pascal: *Pensées,* No. 617; James Boswell: *Life of Samuel Johnson,* 1778, Everyman's Library (London, 1906), Vol. 2, p. 210; Joseph Butler: *Fifteen Sermons Preached at the Rolls Chapel* (London, 1726), Preface, §34.

11. David Hume: *An Inquiry Concerning the Principles of Morals* (1752), Section II, pt. 1; in the ed. by C. W. Hendel (New York, 1957), p. 9.

The moral guide-books, such books as *The Whole Duty of Man*, gradually shift their emphasis. Man's primary duties for seventeenth-century moralists are directed towards God, for their eighteenth-century successors towards man. The very word "bienfaisance" had to be invented in France to convey the new moral attitude. As for those who feared that self-love and the love of man might be in conflict, Pope, following Shaftesbury, had the answer: "Thus God and nature linked the general frame, And bade self-love and social be the same."[12] Just as Augustine was convinced that "true" self-love and the love of God would coincide, so Pope was convinced that "true" self-love would coincide with "true" benevolence.

To an intransigent Christian like Kierkegaard what happened was a tragedy. Morality, he says, was cut off from its roots in the infinite, in divine grace, reduced to what Kierkegaard calls "finite good sense," to a "flat, self-indulgent mediocrity." Man said to God, "No thank you; I should prefer to have none of this help, and salvation, and grace"; he set out to perfect himself only by the criteria of the "finite understanding" and in so doing he cut himself off from his "natural tendency" towards the eternal.[13] But by the end of the seventeenth century even churchmen were tired of disputes about grace and free will, and both tired of and frightened by fanaticism—or what they called "enthusiasm." Metaphysics had fallen into disrepute; Revelation had proved to be too controversial a guide. Only a few bold spirits went so far as to deny the existence of God—an act which still required physical as well as spiritual courage.

12. Pope: *Essay on Man*, Epistle III, lines 317–18. For fuller details and a demonstration that this transition dates back to the late seventeenth century, see R. S. Crane: "Suggestions Toward a Genealogy of the 'Man of Feeling'" in *The Idea of the Humanities*, 2 vols (Chicago, 1967), Vol. 1, pp. 188–213. For the persistence of the older view see A. O. Lovejoy: *Reflections on Human Nature* (Baltimore, 1961).

13. Søren Kierkegaard: *The Last Years: Journals, 1853–5*, ed. and trans. R. Gregor Smith (London, 1965), pp. 280, 290.

It was sufficiently obvious, however, that a morality based on theology would be an endless source of wrangling. All men seemed to agree, in contrast, that benevolence was, at the secular level, the key virtue; the Scriptural injunction to "love one's neighbour" made it possible for broad-minded Christians, forgetting for the nonce that this was no more than the second commandment, to feel themselves at one with Deists or secularists on this point.

In the sixteenth and seventeenth centuries not only the Reformers — and Calvin, it must be remembered, was a humanist compared with some of his followers — but within Roman Catholicism the Jansenists had carried the Augustinian emphasis on human impotence and human worthlessness to a new pitch of intensity. The reaction is already manifest in seventeenth-century Cambridge. The Cambridge Platonists had all of them been educated as Calvinists. To a man they rejected Calvinism, reviving against it the neo-Platonism of the Renaissance.[14] Men, they argued, were rational beings, endowed with free will, and it is as rational, freely-choosing beings that they must live their lives, moral and religious. Mere submission to the divine will, a blind faith in revelation, a passive waiting for grace were not enough. One of them, Ralph Cudworth, condemned with particular vigour that "merely legal state" when "men are only passive to God's law, and unwillingly subject to it for fear of wrath and vengeance, [which] must needs be a state of miserable bondage and servility, distraction and perplexity of mind."[15] And this is what, in practice, Calvinism had come to advocate.

The new tendencies of thought, both in France and in England, can be seen even more clearly outside philosophy,

14. For details see J. A. Passmore: *Ralph Cudworth* and articles on "Cambridge Platonists" and the individual Cambridge Platonists in *The Encyclopedia of Philosophy*. See also Ernst Cassirer: *The Platonic Renaissance in England*, trans. J. P. Pettegrove (Edinburgh, 1953).

15. Second Sermon, reprinted in Ralph Cudworth: *The True Intellectual System of the Universe*, 2nd English ed. by T. Birch (London, 1743; repr. 1820), IV, 382. Compare J. A. Passmore: *Ralph Cudworth*, ch. VI. p. 70.

in, for example, Molière's *Tartuffe*. Professedly, of course, Molière's satire was directed only against religious hypocrites. But his ecclesiastical opponents, who succeeded for some years in preventing its performance, were not deceived. Implicit in *Tartuffe* there is a moral and religious outlook quite opposed to Augustinianism. "He has taught me," says his dupe-disciple Orgon of Tartuffe, "to have affection for nothing; he has detached my soul from every friendship; were I to see die my brother, my children, my mother, my wife, I should regard that as a matter of no importance whatever."[16] To which Cléante, spokesman for what Kierkegaard was so indignantly to call "finite good sense," replies no less indignantly, "What humane sentiments you profess!"

A little later, Cléante expounds more directly his own convictions. Truly devout men, he says, display "a devotion which is human, which is gentle." They are not censorious; it is in their action, not in their judgements on their fellowmen, that they make it clear what kind of person they are. The same emphasis on action is involved, implicitly, in Tartuffe's own self-defence; it is Tartuffe who argues that he must be judged not by his deeds but by his "heart," i.e. by his motives and his intentions. He is more than ready, he says, to forgive his enemies "in his heart" but it would be "a cause for scandal" if he were to enter into further communication with them. For Molière, then, religion must be "sensible," humane, not unduly censorious, not destroying human affections in the name of the love of God. And morality must be manifested in men's deeds; Valère, generously offering his wealth to facilitate Orgon's escape from his persecutor, is the truly moral man. We do not need first to ask ourselves whether he has acted out of "love for God" in order to settle that point.

16. Molière: *Tartuffe*, Act I, Scene 5. Literally: "Que je m'en soucierais autant que de cela." In actual performances, a piece of stage business is used to bring out the force of "cela," e.g. Orgon blows away a puff of smoke.

Let us forget about the older metaphysical definitions of perfection, let us concentrate on exhorting men to perfect themselves in their relations with their fellow-men—that, Pomponazzi's and Charron's injunction, looked for a time as if it might be acceptable to all men, or to all but a few "enthusiasts." One can still feel, as one reads the seventeenth- and eighteenth-century moralists, the sense of relief with which they set their sights on these comfortable, finite objectives, and still share the exhilaration, too, with which some of them set out to remake the world in the image of universal benevolence, to perfect it in secular charity.

Such an ideal of perfection differs from the classical Graeco-Christian ideals not only in its metaphysical unambitiousness, but in another fundamental respect: it suggests that perfection is incremental. Men can be brought little by little, and to an unlimited degree, to care for their fellow-men. In classical theories of perfection, perfection involves a sudden breaking-through to a new life. Consider, for example, how John of the Cross describes the path to perfection. Our ordinary, secular life must be thought of, he says, as a web. What the soul prays for is that this web should be broken, "broken by some encounter and supernatural assault of love." Spiritual acts, according to John of the Cross, "are performed in the soul as in an instant."[17] No doubt a long discipline has to precede mystical experience—just as, for Plato, it had to precede the vision of the form of the good or, for Plotinus, union with the One. The fact remains that men are finally perfected, as the Stoic sage was perfected, in an instant, by an immediate act.

Calvin had taken a different view of God's manner of action. "God," he wrote, "abolishes the corruptions of the flesh in his elect in a continuous succession of time, and indeed little by little."[18] What men have to hope for in this

---

17. *Complete Works, ed. cit.,* Vol. 3, pp. 123–24.
18. *Institutes,* III. iii. 9, as trans. in F. Wendel: *Calvin,* trans. P. Mairet, p. 243.

life, according to Calvin, is not to be suddenly raised up to perfection but rather to grow "little by little." Calvin's emphasis on gradual improvement, at least during man's earthly life, is only one of the ways in which he prepared the ground for that eighteenth century he would so whole-heartedly have detested. It was important, too, that Calvin, like Luther before him, was so bitterly opposed to the ideal of a special "religious life," so emphatic that a man's "spiritual growth" must be exhibited in his daily work, that men will not grow towards perfection by turning their backs on the world. In arguing thus, Calvin inherited the spirit of the Renaissance "civic humanists"—sometimes to be found, of course, in New Testament epistles—and carried it on into modern times. Moral philosophers, then, had an audience partly prepared for them when they argued that the per-fectibility of man consists in his capacity to be morally im-proved rather than in his capacity to enter into relation with some higher metaphysical Being, and that this capacity is exhibited in his purely secular activities.

"Perfection," that is, is no longer thought of as a peculiar spiritual experience, to be sought after in the monastery or convent; it consists, rather, in the daily practice of morality. No doubt the older idea of a cataclysmic break-through, in the form of a political and social revolution, continued to haunt the imagination of men, combining itself in a variety of ways with a gradualist perfectibilism. But such break-throughs, it was generally agreed, did no more than prepare men for greater perfection; men are perfected gradually, even if only after a revolution, whereas on the traditional view, the preparation was gradual, the break-through to per-fection sudden. Even the traditional idea of heaven as a place where perfection would be experienced at once and for all time is replaced by the idea of a heaven where, as Joseph Addison puts it, the soul "is to shine for ever with new accessions of glory and brighten to all eternity . . . still adding virtue to virtue and knowledge to knowledge." When

Joseph Priestley's son died, Priestley expressed the hope, in a similar spirit, that he "had the foundation of something in his character, on which a good superstructure may be raised hereafter."[19]

What happened, indeed, is that the idea of perfectibility came to be entirely divorced from the idea of absolute perfection. In the 1796 edition of *Political Justice* Godwin could write: "By perfectible . . . is not meant . . . capable of being brought to perfection. But the word seems sufficiently adapted to express the faculty of being continually made better and receiving perpetual improvement." And he continues thus: "The term perfectible, thus explained, not only does not imply the capacity of being brought to perfection, but stands in express opposition to it. If we could arrive at perfection, there would be an end to our improvement."[20]

The final outcome of this view is that there is no such thing as perfection, understood as a condition to be achieved once and for all, in which man can finally rest; the very idea of absolute perfection, Godwin himself suggests, may turn out to be "pregnant with absurdity and contradiction." If that still has to be demonstrated, he is sure of this much at least: the very nature of man excludes it, since man is so constituted that so long as he survives, he will learn. There is no such thing as a "perfect man" if by this we mean a man who has no longer any potentiality for improvement. There is, however, such a thing as *perfecting* men, bringing about moral improvement, and such a thing as *perfectibility*, the capacity for being morally improved. The doctrine of the perfectibility of man can now be reformulated thus: *all men are capable of being perfected, and to a degree that has no limit.*

19. *The Theological and Miscellaneous Works of Joseph Priestley*, ed. J. T. Rutt (London, 1817–32), Vol. 1, p. 328, as quoted in *Priestley's Writings on Philosophy, Science and Politics*, ed. J. A. Passmore (New York, 1965), p. 18. The passage from Addison may be found in *The Spectator*, No. 111 (Saturday, July 7, 1711).

20. *Enquiry concerning Political Justice*, Bk. I, ch. 5, in the facsimile of the 3rd ed. by F. E. L. Priestley, 3 vols (Toronto, 1946), Vol. 1, p. 93. This whole chapter was added to the 3rd ed.

Or, as Robert Owen spelled it out in more detail, to assert that man is perfectible is to assert the possibility of "endless progressive improvement, physical, intellectual and moral, and of happiness, without the possibility of retrogression or of assignable limit." [21] The classical ideal of perfection identified it with something which could not possibly be gone beyond; a man who had once seen the form of the good or achieved union with the One had no greater perfection left to hope for. The new perfectibilist looked forward, rather, to an infinitely extensible moral improvement.

Suppose we then go on to ask how this perfecting is to be brought about. The obvious candidate—obvious since the time of Plato—is education, and it is in education, or in education supplemented, as in Plato's *Republic*, by such other forms of social control as legislation, that eighteenth-century perfectibilists placed their trust. But it had first to be shown that education, as distinct from divine grace, was capable, even, of leading men to virtue. The great turning-point, in this respect, is Locke's *Some Thoughts Concerning Education*, first published in 1693.

"Of all the men we meet with," Locke there writes, "nine parts of ten are what they are, good or evil, useful or not, by their education. It is that which makes the great difference in mankind." [22] Notice that Locke is talking about men's moral character; education, he is saying, makes men "good or evil, useful or not." For Locke, indeed, education is essentially moral education. "It is virtue then," he maintains, "direct virtue, which is the hard and valuable part to be aimed at in education." [23] The Augustinian denied that men can be educated into virtue; man's corruption is too deep-seated to be corrigible by any merely human means. That is the view which Locke is rejecting.

---

21. *The Book of the New Moral World* (London, 1836), p. iv.

22. John Locke: *Some Thoughts Concerning Education*, §1. Compare *The Educational Writings of John Locke*, ed. J. L. Axtell (Cambridge, 1968), p. 114.

23. *Ibid.*, §70. Compare *Educational Writings*, p. 170.

He exaggerates, Locke confesses at the very end of *Concerning Education,* whenever he writes, as he often does, as if the young child were "white paper, or wax, to be moulded and fashioned as one pleases."[24] "Few of Adam's children," he is quite prepared to admit, "are so happy, as not to be born with some bias in their natural temper, which it is the business of education either to take off, or counter-balance."[25] Notice, however, the implicit presumption—the bias is always of a kind which education can "take off" or counter-balance. Like Robert Owen after him, that is, Locke denies that there is any innate "bias" which education is powerless to correct. Some men are harder to educate than others—they are slower to learn or too hasty in their judgements: that is all. With this fact in mind, let us look again at Locke's concession, at first sight granting so much to the Christian tradition: "few of Adam's children are so happy as not to be born with some bias in their natural temper . . ." Surely, Augustinian Christians would protest, *all* Adam's children have "a bias in their natural temper," a bias towards evil, the effect of original sin. This bias, furthermore, cannot be "taken off" or "counter-balanced" by any merely natural means, and certainly not by education.

In fact, Locke is entirely rejecting, as he does more explicitly in *The Reasonableness of Christianity,* the doctrine of original sin. He reverted to an old heresy, condemned by the Council of Orange in 529, to the effect that, in the Council's words: "Only the death of the body, the wages of sin, was transmitted through one man to the whole human race, and not sin also, the death of the soul."[26] He admits that, as a result of Adam's sin, men are born mortal; he denies, how-

---

24. *Ibid.,* §216. Compare *Educational Writings,* p. 325.
25. *Ibid.,* §139. Compare *Educational Writings,* p. 244.
26. Council of Orange, Canon 2, quoted in H. Bettenson, ed.: *Documents of the Christian Church,* p. 86. For *The Reasonableness of Christianity* see *The Works of John Locke,* 12th ed., 9 vols (London, 1824), Vol. 6, p. 6. In his *Paraphrases on the Epistles of St Paul* (*Works,* Vol. 7, p. 323) Locke argues that his view of original sin is identical with Paul's.

ever, that they are born with an innate inclination towards depravity. That is the point at which modern perfectibilism, in all of its forms, most sharply separates itself from the orthodox Augustinian tradition.

Nor yet, on the other side, are men born, according to Locke, with an inclination towards goodness, endowed by nature with "propensities of benevolence to each other." Some of Locke's immediate predecessors, especially the Cambridge Platonists, had taken this view. "There is . . . ," Ralph Cudworth had argued, "a principle of common sympathy in everyone."[27] Another Cambridge man, Richard Cumberland, although no Platonist, is even more positive on this point. "There are in mankind," he wrote, "*considered as animal beings only,* propensities of benevolence to each other."[28] Even without the aid of divine grace, that is, human beings are inclined by nature to love one another.*

---

27. British Museum Add. MSS. 4983, 83, quoted and discussed in J. A. Passmore: *Ralph Cudworth,* p. 72.

28. *A Philosophical Enquiry into the Laws of Nature,* first publ. in Latin in 1672, trans. John Towers (Dublin, 1750), p. 211. My italics.

* It is interesting to observe that in China, as early as the fourth century B.C., Mencius had already committed himself to the view that "Man's nature is naturally good just as water naturally flows downward" (*Book of Mencius,* 6A:2). He explicitly rejects the Lockian doctrine that it is education which makes men virtuous: "Humanity, righteousness, propriety, and wisdom are not drilled into us from outside. We originally have them with us" (6A:6). This came to be the standard Confucian doctrine. Confucius himself had been by no means so explicit. "By nature," he is reported as saying, "men are alike. Through practice they have become far apart" (*Analects* 17:2). This could well be interpreted in a Lockian sense. But Confucianism, as a religious movement, came to be committed to the view that man is naturally good. There could scarcely be a greater contrast than there is between the Augustinianism which governed European thinking for over a thousand years and the Confucianism which reigned in China—although by no means without competition from Taoism and from Buddhism—for some two millennia. In many respects Confucianism stands very close to the characteristic teachings of the eighteenth century, which was, it is worth noting, fascinated by Chinese civilization. Confucius, like the eighteenth century, seeks the perfection of man through the exercise of virtue, a virtue with two aspects, knowledge and "humanity" (*jen*). Knowledge, for Confucius as for the eighteenth century, is first and foremost knowledge of mankind (*Analects* 12:22). He defines "humanity" as "earnestness, liberality, truthfulness, diligence and generosity" (17:6)— typical eighteenth-century virtues. The "heavenly law" of Confucianism, furthermore, is very like the God of the deists, an impersonal governor of the Universe. What happened in the seventeenth and eighteenth centuries, one might almost say, is that European thought

This, according to Cumberland, is a matter of everyday experience. By the latter part of the seventeenth century, indeed, the native goodness of man was a clerical commonplace, insisted on by innumerable Latitudinarian divines.[29]

Locke will have none of it. In a marginal note to his copy of a tract by Thomas Burnet, a friend of Cudworth's, Locke succinctly rejects the Cudworth–Cumberland picture of human nature. "Men have a natural tendency," Locke writes, "to what delights and from what pains them. This, universal observation has established past doubt. But that the soul has such a tendency to what is morally good and from evil has not fallen under my observation, and therefore I cannot grant it."[30] Then what is the situation? Men are born with one, and only one, natural impulse—the morally neutral impulse to pursue what gives them pleasure and avoid what gives them pain. Apart from that one natural tendency their minds are entirely devoid of any impulses whatsoever.

The continuity, as well as the contrast, with traditional Christian doctrines is very striking. Christian perfectibilists commonly laid down as the first step on the road to perfection what they called purgation. As Charron sums up: "Theology, even like mysticism, teaches us that to prepare the soul properly for God and his work . . . we must empty it, cleanse it, strip it and denude it of all opinion, belief, inclination, make it like a white sheet of paper . . . so that

---

became Confucianised. Not, of course, that this is a correct historical account of what happened, if we are thinking in terms of "influences." Confucian-type ideas—originating, as we have suggested, in Greek sources, Platonic, Stoic or Epicurean—were already abroad before Confucius was translated. But Confucianism served as a living proof that the love of neighbours was not a peculiarly Christian doctrine and that morality could be separated, as Shaftesbury argued, from religion. Compare Virgile Pinot: *La Chine et la formation de l'esprit philosophique, 1640–1740* (Paris, 1932), Bk. 2, ch. III. Confucius and Mencius are quoted from Wing-tsit Chan: *A Source Book in Chinese Philosophy* (Princeton, 1963).

29. See, for example, R. S. Crane in *The Idea of the Humanities*, Vol. 1, pp. 188–213.

30. Cited in A. C. Fraser's ed. of Locke's *Essay Concerning Human Understanding* (Oxford, 1894), Vol. 1, p. 67 n., quoting from Noah Porter's "Marginalia Lockeana," *New Englander and Yale Review*, July, 1887. See also pp. xliii–iv of Fraser.

God may live and operate in it."[31] And this is because, in the words of the eighteenth-century Quaker poet Matthew Green:

> For so divine and pure a guest
> The emptiest rooms are furnished best.[32]

But, Locke is now saying, when men are born their minds are already "empty rooms"—"furnished best," in consequence, for the intervention of the educator. So the newborn child does not *need* to go through a period of purgation. He is already in that condition to which, according to the mystics, he could bring himself only by a prolonged discipline; he is already "denuded of all beliefs, opinion, and inclinations" with the important exception of his inclination towards happiness and aversion from pain. The educator can move into that empty room and furnish it with habits, thereby bestowing upon the child his moral character.

For virtue, according to Locke, consists in having good habits; moral education, therefore, is essentially habit-formation. Such habits can be inculcated in many different ways. Essentially, however, the educator appeals to that original impulse towards pleasure and aversion from pain with which Locke endows the new-born child. This does not mean that the educator should depend on blows and sweetmeats. Quite the contrary: to proceed in this way, Locke argues, is so to shape the child that he will respond only to physical pain and physical pleasure. Shame is the form of pain to which the educator must principally appeal, and reputation the form of pleasure. "If by these means," Locke writes, "you can come once to shame them out of their

---

31. *Petit traité de sagesse* (Paris, 1646), pp. 46–48, as trans. in Louis I. Bredvold: *The Intellectual Milieu of John Dryden* (Ann Arbor, Mich., 1934; repr. 1956), p. 35.
32. Matthew Green: "On Barclay's Apology for the Quakers" in *Minor Poets of the Eighteenth Century*, ed. Hugh l'Anson Fausset, Everyman's Library (London, 1930), p. 234.

faults, (for besides that, I would willingly have no punishment) and make them in love with the pleasure of being well thought on, you may turn them as you please, and they will be in love with all the ways of virtue."[33]

At a certain level, there is nothing original in Locke's analysis of moral education. A similar doctrine is to be found in Plato, at the beginning of the second book of his *Laws*. A child's first consciousness, Plato there says, is of pleasure and pain. "This is the domain," he goes on to suggest, "wherein the soul first acquires virtue or vice"; he will acquire virtue if and only if he is subject to "early discipline in appropriate habits."[34] To that extent Plato and Locke — and many other educators, like Quintilian, in the centuries that separated them — are at one. But for Plato *true* virtue, "philosophical" goodness, must rest on knowledge, not on habit. Locke's contemporary, Leibniz, took the same view. "The practices of virtue," he wrote in the preface to his *Theodicy*, "as well as those of vice, may be the effect of a mere habit, one may acquire a taste for them; but when virtue is reasonable, when it is related to God . . . it is founded on knowledge."[35]

Scholastic theologians, basing themselves on Aristotle but modifying his views in the interests of Christianity, had a great deal to say about habit. They admitted that "acquired habits" — acquired by "education," in a broad sense of the word — could carry man a certain distance. The fact remains, they argued, that "infused habits," conferred by the grace of God, are essential for "true" goodness. The Calvinists, too, were confident that virtues founded on habit, virtues available to pagan and to Christian alike, could only be a simulacrum of true virtue. Locke, in contrast, is suggesting that *true* virtue is a matter of habit. He grants that, at a

---

33. *Some Thoughts Concerning Education*, §58. Compare *Educational Writings*, p. 154.
34. Plato: *Laws*, §653, as trans. A. E. Taylor (London, 1934), p. 29.
35. *Theodicy*, Preface; in the ed. by Austin Farrer, trans. E. M. Huggard (London, 1952), p. 52.

later stage in his development, the child should be brought to understand how virtue and religion are related, but he denies that this knowledge is essential to virtue.

Even more shocking than the elevation of habits, derived from education, to being both necessary and sufficient for virtue in the fullest sense of the word was Locke's belief that shame and reputation were the instruments by which men were to be educated into virtue. "Shame and reputation"—in short that *amour propre,* that concern for one's position in the world, which Christian moralists united in denouncing. Contrast the reformer Zwingli, whose ideal educator must forbid "all desire for fame," must persuade his pupils that "ambition is a deadly poison," and above all must root out "self-pleasing," which Zwingli identifies with the devil.[36] Contrast, too, Pascal for whom "admiration ruins all from childhood"; in his eyes it is only another sign of human depravity that "children . . . who lack this spur of emulation and glory fall into indifference."[37] (He is opposing the educational practices of the more worldly-wise Jesuits.)[38] The idea that children could be morally educated by an appeal to such spurs would have been, in his eyes, quite monstrous.

It is clear enough what Locke is doing. Not only enlightened self-interest—*amour de soi*—but even a concern for reputation—*amour propre*—were to lose their old terrors.* In some ways, indeed, we are back in the atmosphere of Homeric Greece. Reputation and shame are the important things; if a man can learn to feel ashamed at the right moments there is no need to fear for his virtue.

---

36. Ulrich Zwingli: *Of the Education of Youth,* as trans. G. W. Bromiley in *Zwingli and Bullinger: Selected Translations,* Library of Christian Classics, 24 (London, 1953). See especially pp. 105–13.

37. Pascal: *Pensées,* No. 142.

38. See Ian Cumming: *Helvetius* (London, 1955), p. 13.

* This distinction was made famous by Rousseau. But it has its roots in Aristotle and had been Gallicised by the Protestant philosopher Jacques Abbadie in his *L'art de se connoistre soy-même* (1692). Abbadie spent some years in England.

Of course, nothing is ever quite as it was before. Locke is a Christian. In the long run, he freely admits, it is the law of God which determines what is virtue and what is not. But the law of God is sometimes difficult to determine, and remote from the affairs of men. The actual, day to day, test of virtue and vice, so Locke argues in his *Essay*, is that "approbation or dislike . . . which by a secret and tacit consent, establishes itself in the several societies, tribes, and clubs of men in the world." [39] Fortunately, he says, the rules established by such societies largely coincide with the laws which God has laid down for men. (Locke knew Nicole well, having translated him, indeed, into English.) We can therefore safely take them as our guide. And it is quite unrealistic, he thinks, not to recognize that "commendation and disgrace" are the strongest incentives to conformity. So an Augustinian might with melancholy have reflected. But to Locke the power of commendation and disgrace is rather a reason for optimism: it provides the educator with a weapon for forming men's moral character.

Let us look now at what Locke thought he had shown and its relevance to perfectibilism. Locke has argued, first, that there is nothing in men, no innate depravity, to prevent them from being morally improved. Secondly, that there are secular processes, controllable by men, by which they can bring about the moral improvement of their fellowmen, particularly the processes of education. (Locke uses the word "education" very broadly, to cover, for example, the control of diet and "toilet training.") Thirdly, that secular reformers can achieve their end by manipulating pleasures and pains, especially the pleasures of reputation and the pains of blame. It will at once be obvious that Locke has opened up, in principle, the possibility of perfecting men by the application of readily intelligible, humanly control-

---

39. *Essay Concerning Human Understanding*, Bk. II, ch. xxviii, in the ed. by A. C. Fraser, Vol. 1, pp. 477–79.

lable, mechanisms. All that is required is that there should be an educator, or a social group, able and willing to teach the child what to pursue and what to avoid.

A great deal of detail had still to be filled out. Locke's own moral theory is notoriously obscure; he is by no means a consistent utilitarian. Only relatively late in the eighteenth century was moral action unambiguously defined—by Francis Hutcheson and after him by Helvetius, Priestley and Bentham—as the pursuit of the greatest happiness of the greatest number, and moral education, in consequence, as the process of ensuring, by the judicious application of pleasures and pains, that men will pursue this end. The fact remains that Locke laid the foundations of what was to be one of the most influential forms of eighteenth- and nineteenth-century perfectibilism, according to which men can be morally improved to an unlimited degree by education and other forms of social action.

Locke's *Some Thoughts Concerning Education* was an immensely popular book. By the end of the eighteenth century it had been reprinted at least twenty-one times; almost immediately translated into French, it was reprinted in that language at least sixteen times.[40] At first, however, it was read, for the most part, as a manual for mothers rather than as incorporating, or suggesting, a revolutionary theory of human nature and the formation of moral character. It is interesting to observe the tenour of the protests which, even so, were raised against it. In general, they were protests that Locke had underestimated the importance of men's innate tendencies and, in consequence, had exaggerated the influence of education. Thus began that controversy between the proponents of "nature" and the proponents of "nurture" which was to prove as persistent and as obdurate as the controversy between Pelagians and Augustinians, of which, in important respects, it is the secular echo.

40. For details see *The Educational Writings of John Locke*, ed. Axtell, pp. 98–104.

In his *Man a Machine*—first published in 1747, just before Hartley and Condillac had carried Locke's teachings
to new extremes—La Mettrie distinguished what he calls
"the outstanding excellence" (*premier mérite*) of man from
his "second excellence." The "outstanding excellence" derives from man's natural constitution. "Whence comes skill,
science, and virtue," La Mettrie asks, "if not from a disposition which makes us fit to become skilful, wise and virtuous?
And whence comes this disposition, if not by Nature? We
have admirable qualities only from her; we owe her all that
we are."[41] Only the "secondary excellences," according to
La Mettrie, derive from education—such excellences as the
social graces. And what, he asks, "would be the fruit of the
most excellent school, without a matrix open to the entry
or to the conception of ideas?" Some people, La Mettrie
admits, might be reformed by education, but very few. In
general, he thought, "it is easier for the good to become
wicked, than for the latter to improve."[42] So if La Mettrie is
correct, there are important limits to the possibility of perfecting men by education, limits set by man's inherent physical constitution, a constitution varying from one person to
another. Locke had admitted, as we saw, native differences
in temperament but not, what La Mettrie contends for, a
native difference in moral capacity.

In Great Britain the "nativists" emphasized innate psychological impulses rather than innate physiological structures. The eponymous heroine of Samuel Richardson's
Pamela, minx turned matron, expounds at considerable
length Locke's advice on the training of children and for the
most part does so with complete approval. But on one point
she demurs: in laying down principles for the training of
children, Locke did not, she says, pay sufficient attention to

41. Trans. from the critical ed. by A. Vartanian: *La Mettrie's L'Homme machine* (Princeton, 1960), p. 166.

42. *Anti-Sénèque, ou Discours sur le bonheur* (1748), quoted in Lester G. Crocker: *An Age
of Crisis* (Baltimore, 1959), p. 208.

their "little innate passions." This was the characteristic re-action.[43] There were, no doubt, exceptions. In his *Concerning Virtue or Morality*, first published in 1731, John Gay set out to demonstrate, in a manner which to an extraordinary degree anticipated the utilitarianism and associationism of the century that was to follow, that what Pamela called "little innate passions" were in fact not innate but the product of experi-ence, experience acting upon that impulse towards pleasure and away from pain to which even Locke had been pre-pared to allow innateness.[44] But Gay was for a time ignored or dismissed.

David Hume, however, had read Gay; it is Gay he has in mind, almost certainly, when he condemns the attempt to reduce all other passions to complications of the desire for pleasure and aversion from pain, describing this attempt, forgetting his own blackened pots, as a striking illustration of "that love of simplicity which has been the source of so much false reasoning in philosophy." "I should desire to know," Hume asked rhetorically, "what can be meant by as-serting, that self-love, or resentment of injuries, or the pas-sion between the sexes is not innate."[45] For Hume, in conse-quence, education has only a limited role in forming man's moral nature; it strengthens, but certainly does not create, the moral tendencies of men—those moral principles "most deeply radicated in our internal constitution," principles like "the desire of punishment to our enemies, and of hap-piness to our friends," which, he says, arise in our minds di-

---

43. The *Pamela* quotation is from Letter XCI. For a fuller account of the reaction to Locke see J. A. Passmore: "The Malleability of Man in Eighteenth-Century Thought," in Earl R. Wassermann, ed.: *Aspects of the Eighteenth Century* (Baltimore, 1965), pp. 21–46.

44. John Gay's "Dissertation concerning the fundamental principle of virtue or mor-ality" can most easily be read in L. A. Selby-Bigge, ed.: *British Moralists*, 2 vols (Oxford, 1897), vol. II, pp. 267–85, where the text is of the fifth ed. of 1781. The title of the first ed. is "A dissertation concerning the fundamental principle and immediate criterion of virtue and the origin of the passions."

45. *Enquiries Concerning the Human Understanding and Concerning the Principles of Morals*, ed. L. A. Selby-Bigge, §2, p. 22 n.

rectly, "from a natural impulse or instinct, which is perfectly unaccountable."[46] In short, education, if Hume is right, is in some measure the secular equivalent of co-operative grace, but it is neither essential to nor does it precede the moral tendencies of man. It is not, therefore, as it is for Locke, the secular equivalent of "prevenient" grace, the grace without which men cannot even *begin* to be moral. Nor can it perfect men, whose innate passions already irresistibly incline them, before education begins its work, to particular courses of action.

But in 1749, just one year after Hume had rhetorically asked what could be meant by asserting "that self-love, or resentment of injuries, or the passion between the sexes is not innate," David Hartley took that question as a genuine one and answered it in painstaking detail—freely acknowledging his indebtedness to Locke and to Gay. Neither self-love, nor resentment of injuries, nor "the passion between the sexes," nor even the pursuit of happiness, is, according to Hartley, innate. Each of them derives from the working of associative mechanisms upon our original experiences of pleasure and pain.

The child stretches out his hand and touches the fire; he feels a painful sensation. Thereafter, as a purely mechanical consequence of his action, he "fears to touch it." In other words, he associates touching the fire with pain and avoids doing so. Hartley, then, explains human actions by invoking the "association of ideas" whereas Locke had contented himself with the everyday language of "habit." But Hartley thinks of himself as doing no more than pointing to the mechanism which underlies habit formation, a mechanism suggested to him, indeed, by Locke's own psychological analyses. "All that has been delivered by the ancients and moderns, concerning the power of habit, custom, example,

---

46. *Treatise of Human Nature*, Bk. III, pt. II, §3 and Bk. II, pt. III, §9; in the ed. by L. A. Selby-Bigge (Oxford, 1888; repr. 1951), pp. 501, 439.

education, authority," he writes, "goes upon this doctrine [of association] as its foundation and may be considered as the detail of it in various circumstances."[47]

In France, very similar views were worked out by Condillac. In his *Treatise on Sensations*—which was published in 1754, five years after Hartley's *Observations on Man,* but derives directly from Locke—he set out to demonstrate that man is no more than the sum of all he has learnt. Even those intellectual powers and differences in temperament which Locke had admitted to be innate were no more, Condillac tried to show, than habits formed as a result of experience. It was Hartley, however, who deduced from this picture of man those social and educational conclusions which are our more immediate concern; in his work the basic psychological assumptions of a Locke-based perfectibilism appear for the first time in a fully-developed form.

"If beings of the same nature," Hartley tells us, "but whose affections and passions are, at present, in different proportions to each other, be exposed for an indefinite time to the same impressions and associations, all their particular differences will, at last, be overruled, and they will become perfectly similar, or even equal. *They may also be made perfectly similar, in a finite time, by a proper adjustment of the impressions and associations*" (my italics).[48] So, it would seem, not only can children be educated to think and feel alike, but also men can be re-educated to the same effect, and in a finite time. This practical intention is never far from Hartley's mind. "It is," he says, "of the utmost consequence to morality and religion, that the affections and passions should be analysed into their simple compounding parts, by

---

47. *Observations on Man*, Pt. I, ch. 1, §2, Prop. X, in the 5th ed. (London, 1810), Vol. 1, p. 67. Locke had drawn attention in his *Essay* to the importance of the association of ideas although he describes it only as a source of error and confusion. See J. A. Passmore: *Hume's Intentions*, rev. ed. (London, 1968), pp. 106–7, for a fuller discussion of what Hartley learnt from Locke on this point.

48. *Observations on Man*, Pt. I, ch. 1, §2, Prop. XIV, Cor. 6; in the 5th ed., Vol. 1, pp. 84–85.

reversing the steps of the associations which concur to form them. For thus we may learn how to cherish and improve good ones, check and root out such as are mischievous and immoral." Even our power of willing, of governing our passions derives, he suggests, from the automatic operations of associative mechanisms.[49] As Locke had put the same point, our power of willing the good is both "got and improved" by practice, as a result of experience. Or as Locke's French disciple Morelly had expressed the matter: "we are habituated to willing just as we are habituated to thinking."[50] Willing is one of our habits—not, as Pelagius had thought, the work of an innate faculty which can cut across our habits.

Admittedly, the possibility of remaking men, so Hartley agrees with Locke, is subject to a certain condition: it is "beings of the same nature" who can be educated, or reeducated, in this way. But this is not to Hartley, any more than it was to Locke, an important distinction. He has bodily differences in mind, and these, he thinks, profoundly affect a few persons—absolute idiots, for example—but only a few. He is prepared to sum up his conclusions, conclusions on which he bases his hope that all men will eventually be perfected, in the most general terms: "association tends to make us all ultimately similar." Thus, given only that association is in good hands, human or supernatural, the operations of association can, and will, make all men happy: "if one be happy, all must."[51]

Although it was an eighteenth-century creation, associationism had its hey-day in the middle of the nineteenth century at the hands of James Mill and Alexander Bain; towards the end of that century it came under attack on a variety of grounds. Galton and his fellow-geneticists, like

---

49. *Observations on Man*, Pt. I, ch. 1, §2, Prop. XIV, Cor. 5; in the 5th ed., Vol. 1, p. 84.

50. *Essai sur l'esprit humain* (1743) quoted in L. G. Crocker: *An Age of Crisis*, p. 119. For the Locke reference see *Some Thoughts Concerning Education*, §38. Compare *Educational Writings*, p. 143.

51. *Observations on Man*, Pt. I, ch. 1, §2, Prop. XIV, Cor. 12; in the 5th ed., Vol. 1, p. 87.

the eighteenth-century French materialists before them, sought to demonstrate the crucial importance of innate differences in intellect and character; MacDougall and Freud raised instinct-psychologies, which at no time had wholly succumbed to associationism, to a new pitch of sophistication; Bradley, Ward, Stout, the Gestalt psychologists, in their very different ways, attacked associationism's underlying psychological and philosophical assumptions; "behavioural" psychologists forcefully contended that "ideas," the fundamental Lockian units, ought to play no part in psychological explanations, which should confine themselves, solely, to overt behaviour.

Yet the spirit of associationism lived on, and nowhere more vigorously than in the writings of these very same behavioural psychologists. A conditioned response, no doubt, is importantly different from an associated idea; the language and the procedures of behavioural psychologists bear little resemblance to the language and the procedures of their associationist predecessors. But the behavioural psychologists still maintained, like the Lockians before them, that human behaviour can be explained only by supposing it to be a complication of single units, united under the influence of the environment; they still argued that innate differences are of no real significance in the formation of character; they still expressed the conviction that men can be improved to an unlimited degree by controlling the formation of their habits. It is not surprising that, under Pavlov's influence, such a psychology won official approval in the Soviet Union and wide acceptance in the United States, both of them countries which are deeply involved in the technological "management" of human beings, and both of them committed to the belief that, in some ill-defined sense, "all men are equal."

"All healthy individuals . . . ," proclaims J. B. Watson in his *Behaviorism,* "start out *equal.* . . . It is what happens to individuals after birth that makes one a hewer of wood and a drawer of water, another a diplomat, a thief, a successful business man or a far-famed scientist."[52] Men are born, that is, "blank sheets," to be furnished with behavioural responses. Their moral defects do not originate in the perversity of their instincts—Watson is a vigorous critic of "instinct" psychologies—but rather in the fact that they carry over into adult life the "organized habit systems" they have formed as children. These habit systems can, in principle, be reconstructed by deconditioning—the behavioural equivalent of Hartley's "reversing the steps of the association."

Watson admits that he does not yet fully know how this is to be done. He is convinced, nevertheless, that "some day we shall have hospitals devoted to helping us change our personality, because we can change the personality as easily as we can change the shape of the nose." This belief in the possibility of transforming personality by psychological means is linked, in Watson as in the associationists, with perfectibilist ideals—"perfectibilist" in the modern sense in which it means "admitting of unlimited improvement." "I wish I could picture for you what a rich and wonderful individual we should make of every healthy child," Watson writes, "if only we could let it shape itself properly and then provide for it a universe in which it could exercise that organization —a universe unshackled by legendary folk-lore of happenings of thousands of years ago; unhampered by disgraceful political history; free of foolish customs and conventions which have no significance in themselves, yet which hem the individual in like taut steel bands."[53] This is the unmistakable, the clarion, voice of eighteenth-century perfectibilism, ringing out in twentieth-century America. When the Founding Fathers of America, inspired by Enlightenment ideals, laid it down that all men are equal, they were wrong, Watson willingly admits, if they meant that men as they are

---

52. J. B. Watson: *Behaviorism*, rev. ed. (Chicago, 1930; repr. 1957), ch. XII, p. 270.
53. *Ibid.*, pp. 302–3.

at present constituted are equal. But they were correct on the fundamental point; men are born equal even if they now everywhere live in hierarchies.

When Christianity was still young, it was possible for a Christian to hold views not very different from Watson's. In his *Contra Celsum,* Origen ascribed to the pagan Celsus the view that "no one could entirely change people who sin by nature and habit" and Origen retorted against Celsus that "every rational soul is of the same nature" even if "many men have become evil by upbringing and by perversion and by environment."[54] But once Christianity was committed to the conception of original sin, the doctrine that the source of human wickedness lies in man's environment rather than in his nature had to be abandoned to the opponents of Christianity. To Watson, indeed, Christianity is the outstanding example of that folk-lore which prevents men from understanding and improving their modes of conduct—from constructing for themselves a better society by building better men.

The "behavioural scientist" B. F. Skinner has written a Utopia in the form of science fiction, bearing the name of *Walden Two,* which will serve to illustrate his perfectibilist hopes. Some of Skinner's disciples have found inspiration in *Walden Two,* so much inspiration that they have set out to establish a similar colony in which to live and work; others among his readers have seen in it cause for desperation, a frightening reflection of the kind of world behavioural science may make not only possible but actual.

The founder of Skinner's colony, Frazier, expounds a full-blown Locke-Watson theory of human nature—or, rather, of human *non*-nature, at least as far as moral differences are concerned. Although he is prepared to allow, if reluctantly, that there are innate differences in intelligence, Frazier has found, he tells us, no such differences in moral

---

54. Origen: *Contra Celsum,* III, 67–69, trans. Chadwick, pp. 173–74.

tendency. "We have no truck," he says bluntly, "with phi-losophies of innate goodness—or evil, either, for that mat-ter. But we do have faith in our power to change human behaviour." His leading principle, as he elsewhere expresses it, is that "men are made good or bad and wise or foolish by the environment in which they grow."[55] Experiment is still needed, he admits, in order to determine exactly how men's environment can be so modified as to ensure that they will be good rather than bad, wise rather than foolish. But that such experiments can be made to succeed Frazier, like Skinner himself in his *Science and Human Nature*, does not for a moment doubt.

In the omnipresence of experiment, Skinner's Frazier sees the special virtue of his Utopia as compared with its classical predecessors and its superiority, too, over the So-viet Union. The Soviet Union, he is ready to concede, started well; it failed because it abandoned the spirit of social ex-periment in favour of a static orthodoxy. It is not only in-dividuals, according to Frazier, who can be improved by experiment; the State—the "superorganism"—is no less subject to experimental manipulation. Our present-day so-cieties, he tells us, operate at an "efficiency of the order of a fraction of one per cent"; the possibility of improve-ment, therefore, is practically unlimited. So Frazier conjoins a boundless confidence in experiment with the Lockian be-lief in the malleability of man in order to construct a Utopia which is not, on his view, an impracticable ideal but a real-izable society.

Once again we note the characteristic modern emphasis on change, novelty, improvement as opposed to the char-acteristic Graeco-Christian-Buddhist yearning for eternity, for a state of perfect rest in which change could only be a disruption to perfection. H. G. Wells had already drawn

55. B. F. Skinner: *Walden Two* (1948; repr. in Macmillan Paperbacks, New York, 1962), pp. 196, 273.

attention to this contrast in his *A Modern Utopia,* first published in 1905. The classical Utopias were all of them, he pointed out, "perfect and static States," whereas "the Modern Utopia must be not static but kinetic, must shape not as a permanent state but as a hopeful stage leading to a long ascent of stages."[56] Perfection is dead, long live perfectibility!

The time has come to sum up. Beginning with the Renaissance, but with increasing confidence in the seventeenth century, men began to maintain that in their relationships to their fellow-men, rather than in their relationships to God, lay their hope of perfection. "Perfection" was defined in moral rather than in metaphysical terms, and came gradually to be further particularised as "doing the maximum of good." It was no longer supposed that in order to act morally men must abjure self-love; self-love was harnessed to the improvement of the human condition. "Perfectibility" meant the capacity to be improved to an unlimited degree, rather than the capacity to reach, and rest in, some such ultimate end as "the vision of God" or "union with the One." If men are to be able to perfect one another without divine assistance, however, it has to be presumed that they are not invincibly corrupt. Hence perfectibilists, following in Locke's footsteps, rejected original sin. Indeed, they agreed with Locke that men have no inborn moral tendencies, no innate tendency to act well or to act badly, but only a tendency to pursue pleasure and avoid pain.

This new "moral psychology" opened the way to the suggestion that men could be to an infinite degree improved by the use of appropriate social mechanisms—in the first place, education. Education, Locke suggested, consists in forming moral habits in children by associating certain of their activities with pleasure, especially pleasure in the form of commendation, and others with pain, especially in the form of blame. Hartley developed Locke's innovations into

56. *A Modern Utopia* (London, 1905), ch. 1, §1.

a systematic perfectibilism by working out in detail an associationist psychology, according to which men could be not only educated but re-educated to any desired pattern.

In the twentieth century "behavioural" psychologies have taken the place of associationism, but the fundamental assumptions remain. Innate differences are unimportant; men can be moulded to any desired shape by employing the appropriate psychological procedures. The road to infinite improvement lies open, on this view, to man: the only question is whether he is prepared to seize the opportunities which psychological science now offers him.

NINE

GOVERNMENTALISTS, ANARCHISTS AND GENETICISTS

The classics of education—Rousseau's *Émile* as much as Locke's *Some Thoughts Concerning Education*—normally take as their point of departure an educational situation which involves but a single pupil, living in an artificially purified society, carefully designed to preserve him from the temptations inherent in everyday social relationships. The implementation of such an educational ideal raises obvious problems. It is based on the presumption, never more strongly emphasized than by Rousseau, that society, as it is at present constituted, inevitably corrupts. That is why the child ought not to encounter its effects until he has reached maturity, when his education will act as a prophylactic.

On the face of it, however, the teacher himself, as a member of society, is already corrupted and therefore quite the wrong person to teach the child. The University of Oxford, in the days when the University controlled the town, came nearest to exemplifying a system of education in which a single pupil confronts a tutor, in an artificially isolated social situation. Its teachers, too, were Oxford-trained celibate clergymen. But not even they, as the history of Oxford all too vividly reveals, would have satisfied the moral ideals of a Locke or a Rousseau.

Rousseau was not unaware of this problem. "How can a child be well educated," he asks in *Émile,* "by one who has not been well educated himself?" And his answer is by no means confident. "Can such a one be found? I know not."[1]

---

1. *Émile,* trans. Barbara Foxley, Everyman's Library (London, 1911; repr. 1918), p. 17.

But he certainly did not grasp its full significance, as Marx did when he accused Locke and his followers of having forgotten "that the educator must himself be educated."[2] It is not merely that uncorrupted teachers are hard to find. If Rousseau is right in believing that society, as it now exists, inevitably corrupts, then it is impossible *in principle* to discover an uncorrupted teacher.

Watson and Skinner attempt a solution. If each generation concentrates on giving a better education to its successor, then men can look forward in the long run, Watson suggests, to a society infinitely superior to any they have yet created. Skinner goes out of his way to make it clear that the founder of his ideal colony, Frazier, does not possess the virtues he is attempting to inculcate in others. "Isn't it enough," says Frazier, "that I've made other men likeable and happy and productive? Why expect me to resemble them?" The explanation of his defects is simple: "I'm not a product of Walden Two." But this, he contends, does not matter: "Must the doctor share the health of his patient? Must the ichthyologist swim like a fish? Must the maker of fire-crackers pop?"[3]

Frazier is confident that he knows what ought to be done to produce successors who will be better men than he is— successors, indeed, who will not only be better men but can be relied upon to train their successors to be better men still. The assumption remains, however, that this training can only take place in an enclosed situation. Skinner's Walden Two is as remote from city life as Thoreau's Walden, which, for all Skinner's scientific up-to-dateness, it imitates in its rurality. "Crowds are unpleasant and unbeautiful." But the question is whether such an indefinite progress, based

2. Karl Marx: "Theses on Feuerbach" in *Writings of the Young Marx on Philosophy and Society,* ed. L. D. Easton and K. H. Guddat (New York, 1907), p. 401.

3. B. F. Skinner: *Walden Two,* pp. 249–50.

on a chain of improvement from teacher to taught, can be guaranteed, or even reasonably anticipated, in the midst of a society which remains for the most part unchanged. Frazier's successors will not be ideal men; they will not have been selected by ideal men; the community in which they live is but an island in a sea of social inefficiency. The risk that his successors will have precisely those defects which would render them liable to external corruption is a very real one. For this reason many social reformers have argued that widespread social changes must precede reforms in the system of education, or must at least run parallel to them.

Such reformers fall into two groups: let us call them "governmentalists" and "anarchists." The governmentalists see in government—and, more particularly, in legislation—the principal agent of perfection; the anarchists, in the sharpest possible contrast, rest their hopes on the destruction of the State and its replacement by a completely different form of social organization. Helvetius, a convinced Lockian, is the founding father of modern governmentalism. At first sight, his emphasis, like Locke's own, is on education rather than on legislation, as when he writes that "to be happy and powerful is only a matter of perfecting the science of education."[4] But Helvetius uses the word "education" in an unusually broad sense.

"Everyone," he writes, "has for teachers both the form of government under which he lives and his friends and mistresses, and the people around about him and books he reads."[5] So "education" includes not only the processes by which a teacher develops in his pupils new capacities, habits, and tastes, but also the processes by which a state modifies the behaviour of its citizens, in order to make them conform to higher moral standards. This is the kind of "education"

---

4. C. A. Helvetius: *De l'Homme et de son éducation,* Introduction, ch. II, in *Oeuvres,* 5 vols (Paris, l'an II [1794], Vol. 3, p. 11).

5. *De l'Esprit,* Discourse III, ch. I, in *Oeuvres,* Vol. 1, p. 346.

which Helvetius came particularly to emphasize. Laws, he maintains, are "the soul of empires, the instruments of public welfare," instruments which are admittedly "still imperfect" but which can "from day to day be made perfect."[6] It is by means of laws that men are to be taught to prefer the public good to their own interests; it is laws which are to "extinguish the torches of fanaticism and superstition."[7] These are the doctrines which the theologians of the Sorbonne particularly selected for condemnation: that "it is by good laws that men are to be made virtuous" and that "one should complain less of the wickedness of men than of the ignorance of legislators, who have always put in opposition particular interests and the general interest." The Sorbonne theologians knew a revolutionary idea when they saw one.[8] Laws, of course, were no novelty, but to ascribe to them such extraordinary social functions was to go far beyond the traditional expectations of loyal subjects.

Helvetius dedicated his *De l'Homme* to Catherine and to Frederick the Great, "enlightened despots" both of them. It is through the efforts of such rulers, he thought, that "the universe must be enlightened."[9] Critical though he was of traditional despotisms, he seems to have had no fear of absolute authority—as Diderot, no Frederick-lover, complained[10]—provided only that it was "enlightened," basing its actions, that is, on his ideas. That is one of the many respects in which Helvetius resembles Plato. He thought he knew how to solve the awkward question: "Who, in a corrupted society, shall frame the laws?" "Enlightened despots"

---

6. *De l'Homme et de son éducation,* Section VII, ch. XII, in *Oeuvres,* Vol. 4, p. 235.

7. *De l'Esprit,* Discourse II, ch. XVII, in *Oeuvres,* Vol. 1, p. 249.

8. Anonymous: "Essai sur la vie et les ouvrages d'Helvetius" in *Oeuvres,* Vol. 1, pp. 30–31.

9. *De l'Homme et de son éducation,* Préface, in *Oeuvres,* Vol. 3, p. 7.

10. D. Diderot: *Réfutation suivie de l'ouvrage d'Helvetius intitulé L'Homme.* This was written between 1773 and 1774 although not published until 1875, in *Oeuvres complètes,* ed. J. Assézat, 20 vols (Paris, 1875–77), Vol. 2.

is his answer—the modern equivalent of philosopher-kings. If only as a result of the laws of probability, such a despot, he confidently affirms, is bound to turn up occasionally, the white marble in a bag of despots who are otherwise uniformly black. But Helvetius did not pause to explain precisely how, in a world where all other men are governed by their private interests, a legislator could arise who would be wholly dedicated to the general interest, prepared to devote himself to ensuring that everybody else's private interests would coincide, as his own automatically did, with the general interest.

One must remember that, by the very nature of eighteenth-century French society, the *philosophes* had little opportunity of acquiring any experience of political activity, its problems, its potentialities. "Living as they did quite out of touch with practical politics," as de Tocqueville points out, "they lacked the experience which might have tempered their enthusiasms. Thus they completely failed to perceive the very real obstacles in the way of even the most praiseworthy reforms, and to gauge the perils involved in even the most salutary revolutions." Their natural tendency, furthermore, was to think in terms of absolute authority: they "despised the public almost as heartily as they despised the Deity."[11] "The people," wrote Diderot, "are the most foolish and the most wicked of all men"; D'Alembert described "the multitude" as "ignorant and stupefied . . . incapable of strong and generous actions"; Condillac once went so far as to describe "the people" as a "ferocious animal."[12]

Yet even Joseph Priestley, for all that his political ex-

11. *The Old Régime and the French Revolution*, Bk. III, ch. 1, as trans. Stuart Gilbert (New York, 1955), p. 140.
12. See Diderot's *Essai sur les règnes de Claude et de Néron*, Bk. II, Des Lettres de Senéque, XXXVI (1778–82), in *Oeuvres complètes*, ed. Assézat, Vol. 3, p. 263; D'Alembert's article "Multitude" in the *Encyclopédie*, cf. *Oeuvres complètes de Diderot*, ed. Assézat, Vol. 16, p. 137; Condillac: *Cours d'études pour l'instruction du Prince de Parme: l'Histoire ancienne*, Bk. IV, section 3, Des Lois, ch. XVI, in *Oeuvres philosophiques*, ed. Georges Le Roy, 3 vols (Paris, 1948), Vol. 2, p. 126.

perience was very different—it is impossible to imagine him dedicating any of his works to a despot, however enlightened—was prepared to affirm that "the great instrument in the hand of divine providence of this progress of the species towards perfection, is society and consequently government."[13] It is with the help of government that Providence will prepare men for that "glorious and paradisaical" future which Priestley so confidently predicts for them—although for Priestley, of course, it must be a government which "knows its place" and does not act except when the general interest demands that it do so.

Jeremy Bentham, writing in the same utilitarian tradition but without Priestley's lively confidence that Providence would guide government to its proper ends, worked out in detail the code of laws which an ideal legislator would enforce. Bentham was much more conscious than Helvetius had been, however, that legislation has its limits as a moralizing agent; so much so that his *Essay on the Influence of Time and Place in Matters of Legislation* may fairly be described as anti-perfectibilist. It is not only that Bentham explicitly denies that perfection, which he equates with perfect happiness, lies within men's reach. "Perfect happiness," he writes, "belongs to the imaginary regions of philosophy, and must be classed with the universal elixir and the philosopher's stone." So much modern perfectibilists have, for the most part, been prepared to admit.

Bentham went further than this: it is unreasonable, he thought, to expect that the improvement of the human condition will be perpetual. Artistic creation, for example, might simply disappear, once artists had produced all that it is possible for art to encompass.* As to moral vices, Ben-

---

13. *An Essay on the First Principles of Government,* 2nd ed. (London, 1771), §1, p. 1, excerpted in *Priestley's Writings,* ed. Passmore, pp. 197–98.

* In his *Autobiography* (Ch. V), J. S. Mill describes the depths of melancholy to which he was reduced when it suddenly occurred to him that since musical combinations are limited in number, music would sooner or later come to a standstill. To be so concerned

tham did not believe that they could be wholly legislated out of existence. "It may be possible," he wrote, "to diminish the influence of, but not to destroy, the sad and mischievous passions." For legislation, as Bentham envisages it, cannot equalize talents and should not try to equalize possessions; envy, jealousy, and hatred, therefore, it cannot destroy.[14]

Other governmentalists were less restrained. The fiery revolutionary conspirator Babeuf was an unrelenting critic of that post-Revolutionary French Republic which executed him in 1797, no less than of the regime it had overthrown. Yet few men have ever held out greater hopes for a new form of government, an administration which would be dedicated to the common welfare. "This form of government," he said in his defence before the court at Vendôme, a defence in which he proclaimed himself an inheritor of the ideas of the *philosophes,* "will bring about the disappearance of all boundary lines, fences, walls, locks on doors, trials, thefts, and assassinations; of all crimes, tribunals, prisons, gibbets and punishments; of the despair that causes all calamity; and of greed, jealousy, insatiability, pride, deception and duplicity—in short, of all vices." It will put an end as well—and now Babeuf anticipates the "welfare state"—to "the gnawing worm of perpetual inquietude . . . about what tomorrow will bring, or at least what next year will bring, for our old age, for our children and for their children."[15] Helvetius, to whom Babeuf explicitly refers, might have lis-

---

about the possible exhaustion of music in the future as to lose all capacity to enjoy Mozart in the present is an attitude of mind only too characteristic of anxiety-ridden perfectibilists. But once it is admitted that whole spheres of human life, by their very nature, can permit only limited prospects for improvement, the suspicion is naturally aroused that this might be true more generally—that human activity, in virtue of its very finiteness, is bound eventually to exhaust its capacity for improvement.

14. *Essay on the Influence of Time and Place in Matters of Legislation,* ch. 5, §2, first publ. in *The Works of Jeremy Bentham,* ed. John Bowring (Edinburgh, 1843), Vol. I, p. 194.

15. F. N. Babeuf: Defence at his trial at Vendôme, 1797, quoted in A. Fried and R. Sanders, eds.: *Socialist Thought: A Documentary History* (Edinburgh, 1964), ch. II, §4, p. 68.

tened to him with sympathy, but Bentham would have done so with scepticism.

Bentham has yet another, more decisive, argument against perfectibility by legislation. By its very nature, he points out, the modification of behaviour by legislative acts inflicts pain; legislation improves human conduct by associating penalties with actions which men would otherwise have found it pleasant to perform. Only thus can it create that identity of interests which is essential, on Bentham's view, to a smooth-running society. So evil, in the form of pain, will be a permanent feature of a legislation-governed society. Helvetius had envisaged a system of government which employed rewards as well as penalties, allotting, for example, sensually attractive young women to men of great achievement, as a sort of Nubile Prize.[16] The sterner Bentham has no such delights to offer. Punishments, not rewards, are to attract men to virtue; and "all punishment in itself is evil."[17]

Bentham's general attitude, then, is like Pomponazzi's: "Let us seek what is attainable." If the "attainable" does not include perfect happiness or indefinite progress, it is still set, however, at a far from despicable level. By perfecting their legislative system, men can create for themselves, Bentham assures us, "a most delightful abode, compared with the savage forest in which men have so long wandered."[18] Legislation opens up a Promised Land—Bentham's own analogy—even if that land has still to be worked by the sweat of men's brows.

There are other factors at work, too, which tend to perfect men and which are not subject to the limitations of legislation. Bentham will not admit education to be such an

16. Helvetius: *De l'Esprit,* Discourse III, ch. XV, in *Oeuvres,* Vol. 2, pp. 66–74.

17. *Introduction to the Principles of Morals and Legislation,* ch. XV, in *Works,* Vol. I, p. 83.

18. *Essay on the Influence of Time and Place in Matters of Legislation,* ch. 5, §2, in *Works,* Vol. I, p. 194.

independent factor; it is no more, he says, than a particular form of government—"government acting by means of the domestic magistrate"[19]—and is therefore subject to exactly the same limitations as government in general. The teacher, like the legislator, cannot but impose pain, in however spiritualized a form.

By the time he came to write his *Deontology,* however, Bentham had come under the influence of his independently-minded disciple, James Mill, who took as his fundamental principle, so his son J. S. Mill informs us, "the formation of all human character by circumstances, through the universal Principle of Association, and the consequent unlimited possibility of improving the moral and intellectual condition of mankind by education."[20] In his *Analysis of the Phenomena of the Human Mind,* James Mill tried to describe in detail the way in which, as a result of the operation of associative mechanisms, men can gradually develop a love for humanity which will thereafter direct their conduct;[21] at Bentham's hands this piece of psychological analysis was converted into a law, the "law of the progress of sympathy."

As society develops under the influence of commerce men are involved, Bentham points out, in an increasingly large number of distinct social groups. Where once they lived their lives in private, their home a castle protected against the influence of government, now they find themselves obliged, as a result of the responsibilities inherent in the growth of commerce, to live more and more of their lives in public, in a manner, therefore, which is subject to the moral pressures of their fellow-men. Thus it must happen, according to Bentham, that they daily become more virtuous and "will continue to do so, till, if ever, their nature

19. *Principles of Penal Law,* Pt. III, ch. XX, in *Works,* Vol. I, p. 569.
20. J. S. Mill: *Autobiography,* 3rd ed. (London, 1874), ch. IV, p. 108.
21. James Mill: *Analysis of the Phenomena of the Human Mind* (1829), ch. XXI, Section II, Subsection II; in the ed. by J. S. Mill, 2 vols (London, 1869), Vol. 2, pp. 214–30.

shall have arrived at its perfection." Bentham's argument finally issues, indeed, in a dramatic conclusion worthy of the most convinced perfectibilist; "Shall they stop? Shall they turn back? The rivers shall as soon make a wall, or roll up the mountains to their source."[22] The pressure of public opinion completes that moralizing task which the legislator cannot carry to perfection. It does not even occur to Bentham, revealingly enough, that the pressures of public opinion might be corrupting rather than moralizing. Such was his confidence in the moral effects of commerce.

Bentham's enthusiasm for the potentialities of legislation was, in the outcome, to be more influential than his recognition that it needed to be supplemented. If legislation could make a garden grow where there was now a wilderness, that was quite enough for the less ambitious sort of perfectibilist. John Stuart Mill's reaction, as a young man, to Bentham was by no means untypical. Bentham, he noted, was "studiously moderate, deprecating and discountenancing as reveries of vague enthusiasm many things which will one day seem so natural to human beings, that injustice will probably be done to those who once thought them chimerical." But this apparent "superiority to illusion" only served, Mill tells us, to strengthen Bentham's influence; here was no fanatic, no dispenser of cure-alls, but a man who actually underestimated the potentialities of his own discoveries. Furthermore "the vista of improvement which he did open was sufficiently large and brilliant to light up my life."[23] It was only too easy, then, for enthusiastic Benthamites to discount Bentham's reservations and to be overwhelmed by the prospect of perfecting men by legislation.

Thus it is that Mill could become a socialist without feel-

---

22. *Deontology*, ed. J. Bowring, 2 vols (London, 1834), Vol. 1, p. 101, as quoted in Elie Halévy: *The Growth of Philosophical Radicalism*, trans. M. Morris (London, 1928; new ed., 1934), p. 471.
23. *Autobiography, ed. cit.*, ch. III, p. 67.

ing himself to be wholly unfaithful to Bentham's teachings and that a Fabian socialist like Graham Wallas could take Bentham as his mentor.[24] "There is nothing in Bentham's character, in the principle of utility . . . ," a recent commentator has remarked, "to suggest that he could not have been a supporter of Fabian Socialism had he lived a hundred years later."[25] The Fabian Socialists, of course, completely rejected the *laissez-faire* economics which Bentham took for granted; they greatly extended the range of activities to which, in their judgement as compared with Bentham's, it was appropriate that legislation should be applied; they emphasized—as, so we have pointed out, Bentham also went on to emphasize—the degree to which human behaviour is "moulded by the social pressure."[26] But their basic assumption that legislation, backed by administration, could be employed to make private and public interests coincide, derives its inspiration from Helvetius and from Bentham.

Nowadays, indeed, "there ought to be a law about it" has come to be, in England, a cant phrase. The anarchist Kropotkin has summed up this attitude to law in a manner which only verges on parody. "Instead of themselves altering what is bad, people begin by demanding a *law* to alter it. . . . A law everywhere and for everything! A law about fashions, a law about mad dogs, a law about virtue, a law to put a stop to all the vices and all the evils which result from human indolence and cowardice."[27] For the anarchists, in contrast, to have recourse to law is the mistake of mistakes. The impartial legislator, wholly detached, disengaged from

---

24. For Wallas on Bentham see his *Men and Ideas* (London, 1940), pp. 19–48. Of course, the Fabians were also, and importantly, influenced by Comte, by Marx, by Ruskin. See A. M. McBriar: *Fabian Socialism and English Politics, 1884–1918* (Cambridge, 1962).

25. D. J. Manning: *The Mind of Jeremy Bentham* (London, 1968), p. 97.

26. Sidney Webb: "The History of Socialism" in *Fabian Essays*, ed. G. B. Shaw, Jubilee ed. (London, 1948), p. 57, as quoted in Anne Fremantle: *This Little Band of Prophets* (London, 1960), p. 82.

27. Peter Kropotkin: "Law and Authority" in *Kropotkin's Revolutionary Pamphlets*, ed. Roger N. Baldwin (New York, 1927; repr. 1968), pp. 196–97.

his own interests, whose existence both Helvetius and Bentham have to presume, is, on their view, a dangerous myth. In practice, just as Helvetius dedicated his *De l'Homme* to the "enlightened despots" and Bentham sought to interest Catherine the Great in his Constitutional Code, so the State Socialist—it is interesting to observe the admiration of such Fabians as the Webbs and Bernard Shaw for the Soviet Union—is committed, so the anarchists argue, to the support of tyranny. Law, on the anarchist view, is no more than an exercise of force, an evil, as Bentham had admitted, but not, as he had thought, a necessary evil.

Anarchists come in many different shapes and sizes. There are individualist anarchists, co-operative anarchists and communist anarchists, anarchists who expect mankind to be saved by its passions and anarchists who expect it to be saved by its reason, atheistic anarchists and Christian anarchists, reforming anarchists, anarchists who commit themselves to a detailed blueprint of the new stateless society and anarchists who believe that it is of the essence of anarchism to abandon all programmes, all blueprints for the future. Yet at the same time, anarchists share a common set of beliefs; we can sum up these beliefs by saying that they all take literally Rousseau's cymbal-clashing slogans. From the opening of *Émile*, "everything is good as it comes from the hands of the Creator, everything degenerates at the hands of man"; from the opening of the *Social Contract*, "man is born free and is now everywhere in chains." In the context of Rousseau's own political thought, these slogans do not mean quite what the uninstructed reader would take them to mean. Rousseau himself was not an anarchist; the society which had been man's downfall could also, on his view, be man's saviour. Sometimes, indeed, as in his *Treatise on the Government of Poland*, Rousseau writes as if he were a pure Helvetian; in his *Social Contract* an obscure figure "the Legislator" plays a vital part; his less sympathetic critics have detected in his theory of the "general will" to which individual wills must be subordinated the roots of modern totalitarianism.[28]

The British anarchist, William Godwin, profound admirer of Rousseau though he was and convinced that his *Émile* was "one of the principal reservoirs of philosophical truth, as yet existing in the world," was equally emphatic that Rousseau's genius deserted him in his purely political writings.[29] Perhaps the most influential of all anarchists, P. J. Proudhon, attacked Rousseau with particular venom: "Never man," he wrote, "united to such an extent intellectual pride, aridity of soul, lowness of tastes, depravity of habits, ingratitude of heart. . . . His philosophy is all phrases and covers only emptiness, his politics is full of domination; as for his ideas about society, they scarcely conceal their profound hypocrisy."[30]

The fact remains that much else in Rousseau besides his resounding slogans anticipated the teachings of the anarchists; Proudhon himself certainly felt his influence. There are, for example, the Anabaptist-reminiscent opening sentences to the second part of Rousseau's *The Origin of Inequality:* "The first man who, having enclosed a piece of ground, bethought himself of saying *This is mine,* and found people simple enough to believe him, was the real founder of civil society. From how many crimes, wars and murders, how many horrors and misfortunes might not any one have saved mankind, by . . . crying to his fellows, 'Beware of listen-

---

28. See, for example, J. L. Talmon: *The Origins of Totalitarian Democracy* (London, 1952). The recent literature on Rousseau is for the most part designed to prove that he was a great deal more consistent, more sensible and more coherent than either his disciples or his critics have commonly believed. It is summed up in Peter Gay: *The Party of Humanity* (New York, 1964), Pt. III, ch. 8. The new Rousseau is succinctly described in Ronald Grimsley's article "Jean-Jacques Rousseau," in *The Encyclopedia of Philosophy*, Vol. 7. For references to Rousseau's criticism of Helvetius see Joan McDonald: *Rousseau and the French Revolution, 1762–1791,* University of London Historical Studies, XVII (London, 1965), p. 35, n. 1.

29. *Enquiry Concerning Political Justice,* Bk. V, ch. 15; ed. Priestley, Vol. 2, pp. 129–30.

30. P. J. Proudhon: *General Idea of the Revolution in the Nineteenth Century,* trans. J. B. Robinson (London, 1923), pp. 120–21.

ing to this impostor; you are undone if you once forget that the fruits of the earth belong to us all, and the earth itself to nobody.' " [31] This, certainly, was a doctrine the anarchists could respond to with enthusiasm.

Mandeville had caused more than a little stir by arguing in his *Fable of the Bees* that the practice of virtue was incompatible with the development of a prosperous commercial society. Commerce can flourish, he had said, only where men are proud, avaricious, emulative. Rousseau could easily be read as making a similar point, that virtue and commercial progress do not go together. "As the conveniences of life increase," he wrote, "as the arts are brought to perfection, and luxury spreads, true courage flags, the virtues disappear." [32] The anarchists were ready to draw from their reading of Rousseau the conclusion that society as it now exists must be destroyed, to be replaced by a simpler society where virtue could be practised without danger.

Then, too, there was the suggestion in Rousseau's *Émile*, and even more in *La Nouvelle Héloïse*, that the human being has innate potentialities which must be allowed to flower, as distinct from being forced into a predetermined mould. "Each individual," according to Rousseau's mouthpiece Julie, "brings with him at birth a distinctive temperament, which determines his spirit and his character. There is no question of changing or putting a restraint upon this temperament, only of training it and bringing it to perfection." Furthermore, this temperament is never of a kind which would, if properly trained, lead men to evil. "There are no mistakes in nature," Julie tells us. "All the faults which we impute to innate disposition are the effects of the bad training which it has received. There is no criminal whose tendencies, had they been better directed, would not have yielded

---

31. *The Social Contract and Discourses,* trans. with introd. by G. D. H. Cole, Everyman's Library (London, 1913; repr. 1938), p. 207.

32. Rousseau: *Discourse on the Moral Effects of the Arts and Sciences* in *The Social Contract and Discourses,* trans. Cole, p. 145.

great virtues."[33] That doctrine was destined, through Froebel, Pestalozzi, Dewey to have a long intellectual history. The artist-anarchist-educator Herbert Read looks back to Rousseau as his intellectual ancestor, as the first, he says, to develop the theory of "freedom as the guiding principle of education"—even if, Read also thinks, Rousseau failed to carry it "to its democratic limits" and worked out, on the contrary, "a doctrine of sovereignty which was elaborated in a totalitarian direction by later philosophers."[34] In general, it was easy enough to extract from selected passages in Rousseau the thesis that moral development is not a matter of conforming to pre-established standards but of realizing one's inner potentialities, potentialities at present stifled by the established institutions of society, private property, the Church and, above all, the State.

Only by careless reading, however, could the anarchists extract from Rousseau the doctrine that man is bound to perfect himself. Man's perfectibility, he certainly says—and it was Rousseau who brought into vogue the word "perfectibilité"—is precisely what distinguishes him from the animals. But this faculty, he goes on to add, "is the source of all human misfortunes . . . which, successively producing in different ages his discoveries and his errors, his vices and his virtues, makes him at length a tyrant both over himself and over nature."[35] In other words, there is nothing in man's "perfectibility," his capacity for improving his position relative to Nature and to his fellow-men, to give promise that he will progress morally. His "perfectibility" can as readily

---

33. Rousseau: *Julie, ou La Nouvelle Héloïse* (1761), Cinquième Partie, Lettre III. Julie is represented as expressing the ideas of her philosophical husband M. de Wolmar, but Rousseau's own note shows that at this point he is in agreement with them. Another note, which Rousseau at one time proposed to add, makes it clear that he thinks of these observations as a refutation of Helvetius. See *Oeuvres complètes de Jean-Jacques Rousseau,* ed. Bernard Gagnebin and Marcel Raymond, Vol. II (Paris, 1961), pp. 563 and 1672(d).

34. *Education Through Art,* 3rd rev. ed. (London, 1958; paperback repr. 1961), pp. 6–7.

35. *Discourse on the Origin and Foundation of the Inequality of Mankind,* in *The Social Contract and Discourses,* trans. Cole, p. 185.

lead him into vice as into virtue; the successful criminal makes use of his "perfectibility" to a greater degree than does the virtuous patriarchal farmer of Rousseau's imagination. That men will certainly, some day, perfect themselves morally is not, then, a doctrine the anarchists could learn from Rousseau. But he helped to teach them, whether or not this is what he wanted to teach, that man is naturally good and naturally free, and that social institutions, as they now are, are the source of all his corruption. So, for all the violence with which Proudhon elsewhere attacks Rousseau, it is to Rousseau that he turns in order to justify his claim that "man—as Rousseau has told us—is virtuous by nature," that all man needs in order to act virtuously is to be free.[36]

Of the peace-loving, individualist, unrevolutionary philosophical anarchists, William Godwin is the outstanding example. No one could be more remote from the popular stereotype of the anarchist as a man of violence. Although his views altered in other respects, he remained firmly committed throughout his life to the basic principle he laid down in his *Political Justice:* there is only one method of social reform, by gradually improving social institutions in a manner which moves step by step parallel to "the illumination of the public understanding."[37]

In the main text of the first edition of *Political Justice,* Godwin was prepared to concede that new political institutions, along democratic lines, might produce the desired effect on men, by "cherishing in their bosoms a manly sense of dignity, equality and independence."[38] But this, he soon

---

36. P. J. Proudhon: *De la Justice dans la révolution et dans l'église,* Neuvième étude, Préambule; in the 4 vols ed. by C. Bouglé and J.-L. Puech (Paris, 1930–35), which is part of the unnumbered set *Oeuvres complètes,* nouvelle éd. (Paris, 1923–), this may be found in Vol. III, p. 483.

37. *Enquiry Concerning Political Justice,* Bk. IV, ch. 2; ed. Priestley, Vol. 1, p. 273. Compare on this theme David Fleisher: *William Godwin: A Study in Liberalism* (London, 1951), pp. 84–85, 126–31.

38. *Enquiry Concerning Political Justice,* 1st ed. (London, 1793); ed. Priestley, Vol. 3, p. 144.

came to feel, was altogether too generous a concession, since "government by its very nature counteracts the improvement of individual intellect."[39] In his later revisions of *Political Justice,* Godwin set out to expunge from his work all remnants of the Helvetian doctrine that man can be perfected by legislative means. "With what delight," he wrote, "must every well-informed friend of mankind look forward to the auspicious period, the dissolution of political government, of that brute engine, which has been the only perennial cause of the vices of mankind."[40]

It was not by legislation that men were to be perfected, but rather by the unfettered exercise of their reason, its liberation from the restrictions now imposed upon it by government, private property and marriage. Godwin entirely rejects that conception of morality on which the ideal of perfection by legislation rests. The imposition of punishments, he says, cannot moralize a man; nothing arouses Godwin's indignation to more fervent heights than the penal systems Bentham sought only to make more efficient. A man is not morally improved, in Godwin's eyes, when, solely in order to avoid judicial penalties, he is coerced into preferring the interests of the community to his own interests. He acts morally only when he is *intellectually* convinced that, other things being equal, he must prefer the welfare of twenty men to the welfare of one man, it being wholly irrelevant that the "one man" is himself.[41]

If we ask which is to come first, the liberalization of social institutions or the enlightenment of men's reason, Godwin's answer, as we have already seen, is that the two must run parallel. A little more enlightenment and men will begin to liberate themselves from their irrational institutions; that degree of liberation will in turn make them more rational

---

39. *Enquiry Concerning Political Justice,* Preface to 3rd ed.; in Priestley, Vol. 1, p. viii.
40. *Ibid.,* Bk. V, ch. 24; ed. Priestley, Vol. 2, p. 212.
41. *Ibid.,* Bk. II, ch. 6; ed. Priestley, Vol. 1, pp. 172–73.

and so on indefinitely to an earthly paradise. For by such a process of gradual, rational improvement, inspired by an enlightened few, men can finally become godlike, not only fearless and courageous, truthful, honest, and intellectually advanced but more than that: "They will perhaps be immortal." Only then, as immortals in a community of fully adult beings, no longer obliged to act as pupils to their predecessors, no longer subject, as children, to the authority of parents, can Godwin's society of rational men achieve its full fruition. "Man is a godlike being"—in Godwin the old ambition to be like God re-establishes itself.[42]

The paradise to come will be, above all, a community of individualists. Godwin's hostility is particularly directed towards the force and fraud inherent in all government: his ideal is a man who, in any situation, is competent to exercise, in perfect freedom, his own judgement. Indeed, he carries his individualism to grotesque extremes. In Godwin's paradise, there will be no theatrical performances and no orchestras, since both plays and symphonies necessarily involve "an absurd and vicious co-operation."[43] About the propriety of reading other men's books, even, he was doubtful. Rousseau had already suggested that society began to decline morally when men were no longer content with what they could create with their own hands. Godwin carries matters much further. "Every thing that is usually understood by the term co-operation," he goes so far as to suggest, "is, in some degree, an evil."[44] That is his great objection to marriage: it is "a monopoly, and the worst of monopolies," the source of "despotic and artificial" rights of possession, involving, inevitably, self-deception, the shutting of one's eyes to realities, the subordination of one's own rationality to the

---

42. *Thoughts on Man*, p. 9.
43. *Enquiry Concerning Political Justice*, Bk. VIII, ch. 8; ed. Priestley, Vol. 2, p. 504.
44. *Ibid.*, Bk. VIII, ch. 8; ed. Priestley, Vol. 2, p. 501. For a fuller discussion of this topic see B. R. Pollin: *Education and Enlightenment in the Works of William Godwin* (New York, 1962), pp. 83–90.

wishes of another.[45] This does not mean that human beings should separate themselves off from one another, retreating to a Syrian desert. But their relationships, in the ideal society of Godwin's imagining, will be at all points free, at all points rational, and never carried so far as to threaten that individuality which is "of the very essence of intellectual excellence"[46] — and, therefore, of moral excellence, too.

Godwin, then, is completely at odds with such of his anarchist successors — Kropotkin, for example — as have sought to substitute a society based on co-operation for a society based on force. The most conspicuous exponents of co-operation in the early nineteenth century were not anarchists; one does not know, indeed, quite how to describe a social reformer like Charles Fourier — "socialist" is as misleading as anarchist. Like the anarchists, and in more formidable detail, he is merciless in his attacks on contemporary civilization. "Civilization," he wrote, "is . . . a society that is contrary to nature, a reign of violence and cunning."[47] But Fourier was no less critical of classical perfectibilists, who, he says, in their treatises on "perfectible perfectibility" absurdly and monstrously sought to persuade men to govern their lives by reason.[48] For Fourier, men's passions have to be taken as given. "Ferocity, the spirit of conquest, robbery, concupiscence, and many other unsavory passions," he wrote, "are not vicious in the seed; only in growth are they rendered vicious by the civilization that poisons the mainsprings of the passions, which were all considered useful by God, who created none of them without assigning to it a place and a purpose in the vast harmonious

---

45. *Enquiry Concerning Political Justice*, Bk. VIII, ch. 8, ed. Priestley, Vol. 2, p. 508.
46. *Ibid.*, Bk. VIII, ch. 8; ed. Priestley, Vol. 2, p. 500.
47. Charles Fourier, quoted in F. E. Manuel: *The Prophets of Paris* (Cambridge, Mass., 1962), p. 215, from unpubl. papers. Manuel should be consulted generally on Fourier.
48. *Théorie de l'unité universelle* (1822), in *Oeuvres complètes*, 6 vols (Paris, 1841–45), Vol. 5, pp. 153–63, excerpted in Charles Fourier: *L'Attraction passionnée:* textes choisis par René Schérer, Coll. Libertés 56 (Paris, 1967), p. 185. The original title of Fourier's work was *Traité de l'association domestique-agricole, ou Attraction industrielle*.

mechanism. As soon as we wish to repress a single passion we are engaged in an act of insurrection against God. By that very act we accuse Him of stupidity in having created it." [49] This comes closer to the popular impression of what Freud said than anything Freud ever wrote, but it is not difficult to discover its roots in the Rousseau of *La Nouvelle Héloïse.*

Fourier advocated the setting up of a form of social organization, the "phalanx," so organized that within it the passions of every different kind of man could be satisfied. Whereas classical perfectibilists had hoped to reform men, Fourier sought to reform society, to make of it a form of organization suited to the satisfaction of man as he actually is, as distinct from man as the moralists pretend that he could be. Up till the present, he argues, "in love as in commerce every progress in civilization is nothing more than progress in social hypocrisy." [50] Philosophers—Fourier's *bête noire*—who have boasted of "the perfecting of reason" have in fact been boasting of the perfecting of hypocrisy. The destruction of this so-called "progress," the destruction of hypocrisy, is the first step towards the perfecting of man.

There was no problem, Fourier thought, in "educating educators." Let but one phalanx be set up, and that would be enough; its immense superiority to existing forms of social organization would at once be apparent; all men would be convinced. Such an experiment, it is sometimes said, has been tried and can be seen to have failed in, for example, Hawthorne's Brook Farm. But what must rather be questioned is whether Fourier's experiment *could* be attempted; men corrupted by hypocrisy cannot so lightly shake off their burden in order to create a brave new phalanx. Into an ideal society they carry with them their accumulated guilt, their anxieties, their corrupted passions.

---

49. F. E. Manuel: *The Prophets of Paris,* p. 235, quoting from Fourier's unpubl. mss.
50. Fourier: *Publication des manuscrits,* 4 vols, 1851–58, excerpted by R. Schérer, *op. cit.,* p. 199.

Fourier is beloved by the surrealists for the exuberance of his imagination; André Breton wrote an *Ode* in his honour. And certainly a man who could anticipate—along with a good deal else, like air-conditioning, which has turned out to be not so fantastic—a time when the seas would run lemonade, can easily be transformed into a figure of fun. The sexual freedom of his phalanxes, with their readily-available women, carefully matched by an organized system prophetic of "computer-dating," is no doubt the fantasy, as Manuel suggests, of a frustrated travelling salesman.[51] Yet there is a sense, perhaps, in which Fourier is the most humane of all social reformers; he is the least inclined to take as his ideal a society suited only for Man, ideal, rational, godlike Man, as distinct from a society in which human beings as they actually are could live, and breathe freely, in their diverse and complicated ways.*

To return to the anarchists proper, Proudhon is as wary of Fourier's "association" as he is of any form of government, any legislative act. "I have always regarded Association in general—fraternity—as a doubtful arrangement," he writes, "which, the same as pleasure, love and many other things, concealed more evil than good under a most seductive aspect." Indeed—and the hit at Fourier is obvious—"I distrust fraternity as much as I do passion."[52]

Contracts, not fraternal relationships, were Proudhon's ideal, contracts entered into on rational grounds, as distinct either from laws, imposed by force, or fraternal relationships, based on passion rather than reason. He converted

---

51. F. E. Manuel: *The Prophets of Paris*, p. 225.

* One of the nicest things about Fourier is his attitude to women, whom he seems genuinely to like, to care for, and to seek to emancipate. This attitude comes as a particular relief after a prolonged reading of Christian perfectibilists, for so many of whom woman has the choice of being the Virgin Mary or Mary Magdalene—unreformed. One begins to sympathize with Oliver Gogarty's comment on Ireland: "It's high time the people of this country found some other way of loving God than by hating women."

52. *General Idea of the Revolution*, trans. Robinson, p. 79.

laissez-faire economics, indeed, into a universal social policy. Not only economic relationships, but every form of social relationship, should, on his view, be left to the free operation of freely contracting groups and individuals. That is why he could write that in his ideal society "commerce, the concrete form of contract, . . . takes the place of law."[53]

Proudhon's object, he tells us in *The Philosophy of Progress,* is to strengthen men's belief in progress while destroying their belief in the Absolute. Indeed the idea of progress, as Proudhon there presents it, is little more than the simple negation of the classical idea of the Absolute, of the metaphysically perfect. "Progress," he says, ". . . is the affirmation of universal movement, the negation, in consequence, of every immutable form and formula, every doctrine of eternity, irrevocability, impeccability, etc., when applied to any being whatsoever; of all permanent order, even that of the universe; of any subject or object, empirical or transcendental, which does not change."[54] His critics were not slow to point out, however, that perpetual movement is by no means the same thing as progress; the movement might be cyclical, temporary advances being followed by retrogressions.

In the Ninth Study of his immense work *On Justice,* Proudhon returns, therefore, to this theme, but in a rather different spirit. He now defines Progress as progress in justice, brought about by the free acts of free men. Up till his own time, he admits, society has not exhibited a progressive advance: it has been subject to decline, to retrogression. The explanation of society's defects—and no less the explanation of the defects of individual men, their sins—is, he says, that actual justice has failed to coincide with men's ideal of justice. In consequence, men have been led to defy justice,

53. *Ibid.,* p. 244.
54. *Philosophie du progrès,* ed. Th. Ruyssen in *Oeuvres complètes,* nouvelle éd. (Paris, 1946), pp. 49–50.

entangled as it is, to take over Pope's phrase, in the "net of law."[55] Or alternatively, recognizing the defects of legalistic "justice," they have set up as their ideal something other than justice, some Absolute object, such as God. And every society which takes permanence as its ideal is bound to be unjust; it can sustain itself only by the exercise of force, force directed against the natural tendency to change. In the long run its efforts are bound to be unavailing; its inevitable fate, then, is to decline.

The situation is very different when justice and the ideal coincide. "In a society based on pure right, where justice and liberty are constantly advancing, it implies a contradiction," according to Proudhon, "for time to bring with it a falling-off at any point." By the very nature of the case, such a society must progress for ever; every year of virtue adds to its social capital and its productive forces; "the collective being . . . enjoys through justice a perpetual regrowth of health, beauty, genius and honour." Whereas the age of religion, which is now ending, has been an age of endless struggle, the age to come, the age of justice, will, Proudhon has no doubt, be an age of "universal fraternity, human unity, a general harmony between the powers of man and the forces of the planet."[56]

In the end, then, Proudhon is swept away by his own enthusiasm into the very Utopianism he elsewhere attacks so severely; the familiar ideals of unity and fraternity are too much for him, for all his suspicion that they are nothing more than a cloak for tyranny. It is impossible to derive from the writings of Proudhon, in fact, a consistent theory about man's perfection and its conditions. Occasionally he writes as a Utopian; he regularly asserts that man is infinitely perfectible; he commits himself to the view that progress is in-

55. Pope: *Essay on Man*, Epistle III, line 192.
56. P. J. Proudhon: *De la Justice*, Neuvième étude: Progrès et décadence, ch. IV; *ed. cit.*, Vol. III, pp. 541–42.

evitable. And yet, at other times, he writes as one convinced that conflict is man's eternal lot. "Man's life," he then suggests, "is a permanent war, war with want, war with nature, war with his fellows, and consequently war with himself. The theory of a peaceful equality, founded on fraternity and sacrifice, is only a counterfeit of the Catholic doctrine of renunciation of the goods and pleasures of this world, the principle of beggary, the panegyric of misery."[57]

There is a similar ambiguity in his attitude towards revolution. He had been sufficiently influenced by the German metaphysics of progress to be prepared to write, sometimes, as if a society based on justice *must* come into being, as if the revolution he advocates *must* succeed. "Revolution," he argued in his *General Idea of the Revolution in the Nineteenth Century,* "is a force against which no power, divine or human, can prevail: whose nature it is to be strengthened and to grow by the very resistance which it encounters."[58] For the most part, however, he exhorts men to action. He tells them that it is only through their active concern, as free men, for justice, that the revolution will come about. Nor does he, generally speaking, expect the revolution to be a violent one. The bourgeoisie are coming to realize, he thinks, the growing weakness of their own position; they can be persuaded that it is better to surrender their present privileges. Reason, then, will lead men to the just society.

As Marxism gained in strength, indeed, Proudhon came to be more and more opposed to the idea of violent revolution. "It is folly and injustice," he wrote, "to knock the walls of authority with your democratic and socialist battering ram. Turn it rather against the inertia of the masses, against the governmental prejudice which arrests all popular force

---

57. *Système des contradictions économiques* (1846), trans. as *Economic Contradictions* by B. R. Tucker (Boston, Mass., 1888), Vol. 1, pp. 234 f., and quoted in Atindranath Bose: *A History of Anarchism* (Calcutta, 1967), p. 125.

58. *General Idea of the Revolution,* trans. Robinson, p. 15.

and let despotism fall by its own uselessness."[59] "Prejudice" is here the key phrase; in the typical Enlightenment manner, Proudhon is suggesting that the task before men is to destroy prejudice rather than to combat authority. Prejudice once destroyed, the Bastille will fall of its own accord.

What is particularly important in Proudhon, for our purposes, is his thorough-going rejection of the idea of perfection through legislation, no less than the idea of perfection through God. "God is stupidity and cowardice; God is hypocrisy and falsehood; God is tyranny and misery; God is evil."[60] God, law and even "fraternity," understood as a binding force, are all in the same boat; all of them collapse in the face of moral criticism, criticism from the standpoint of freedom and justice—the only things that Proudhon cared deeply about. Man can perfect himself only through the destruction of such idols, which moral criticism proves to be worthless; then he can face the world as a free man in a society governed neither by God nor by man but by the spirit of justice.

Of the anarchists who come nearer than either Godwin or Proudhon to the popular stereotype of the anarchist as an angel of destruction the most influential, perhaps, was Bakunin. He was a revolutionary, but he feared above all the sort of revolution which consists merely in the transfer of power. Like Proudhon before him, he had no doubt that Marxism, just because it thought in terms of a transfer of power, could only lead to tyranny. Acton's declaration that "power tends to corrupt and absolute power corrupts absolutely" he, like Proudhon, would have been prepared to nail to his mast-head.

The State, according to Bakunin, is "the most flagrant negation, the most cynical and complete negation of hu-

59. *Les Confessions d'un révolutionnaire* (1849), as trans. in A. Bose: *A History of Anarchism,* p. 139.

60. *Système des contradictions économiques,* trans. Tucker, Vol. 1, p. 450 and quoted in Bose: *A History of Anarchism,* p. 140.

manity."[61] Or as he also puts it, it is "by its very principle an immense cemetery in which all manifestations of individual and local life . . . come to sacrifice themselves, to die and to be buried."[62] Like theology, it presumes that man is bad by Nature and that it has the task of making him good; the State, indeed, is nothing but a terrestrial Church—"the altar on which the real liberty and the well-being of peoples are immolated to political grandeur."[63] Once power is in the State's hands it stays there. It is ridiculous to suppose that a dictatorship might deliberately bring about conditions in which its own power would wither away. "No dictatorship can have any other aim but that of self-perpetuation, and it can beget only slavery in the people tolerating it."[64] The only way, therefore, in which men can become free moral beings, the only way of ensuring "the triumph of justice, that is, the complete liberty of everyone in the most perfect equality for all"[65] is first to destroy the State, by a revolution which will not be a transfer of power but the abolition of power.

It is interesting that Bakunin should compare the State to a Church; his own thinking is rich in religious metaphor. The French Revolution was, he says, a "Revelation" which brought down to the masses its new Gospel—"not the mystic but the rational, . . . not the divine but the human Gospel, the Gospel of the Rights of Man."[66] And although Bakunin here contrasts the "mysticism" of the old Gospel with the "rationality" of the new Gospel, there is something more than a little mystical in that destructive anarchism into

61. Bakunin's works are numerous and scattered. My references are mostly to *The Political Philosophy of Bakunin,* comp. and ed. G. P. Maximoff (Glencoe, Ill., 1953; paperback ed., 1964). The quotation is on p. 138.

62. From a series of articles written in 1869 for the journal *Le Progrès,* Geneva, trans. in A. Fried and R. Sanders, eds.: *Socialist Thought,* ch. VII, §2, p. 343.

63. *The Political Philosophy of Bakunin,* ed. Maximoff, p. 208.

64. *Ibid.,* p. 288.

65. *Ibid.,* p. 155.

66. *Ibid.,* p. 192.

which, especially under the influence of the Russian nihil-
ist Nechaev, he was finally driven.[67] Let everything be destroyed—the mystics' "purgation"—and the spirit will at last
be able to work freely. Like the mystic, the revolutionary
must rid himself of every sentiment which might attach him
to the world as it now is. "All soft and enervating feelings of
relationship, friendship, love, gratitude, even honour, must
be stifled . . . by a cold passion for the revolutionary cause."
He must concentrate his attention on one thing and one
thing only—"merciless destruction."[68]

The difference, of course, is that it is to be the spirit of
man, not the Holy Ghost, which is to have the way prepared
for it by the destruction of society. But why, it is natural to
ask, should the new Phoenix, thus born from the ashes of
the old, be more glorious than its predecessor? The mystic
did not have to demonstrate that a God-infused man would
be perfected by God's entrance into him: that followed from
the very definition of God. But only if it be presumed that
man is "naturally good" and yet has nevertheless gone hopelessly astray in a manner he will not, given a fresh start, repeat, is there any ground for expecting that the new society
which is to arise out of the ashes of the old will be any better
than its predecessors. In a reborn society man may well re-
forge the chains that bind him. The Christian is confident
that after death he will be transfigured. The anarchist, quite
as devoutly, but without the aid, however limping, of Revelation, shares the Christian's faith in the possibility of "making
a new start," of beginning afresh, as if the past could simply
be destroyed without persisting to haunt the imagination
of the present; or as if, as Pelagius also thought, by a sheer
act of will the established network of habit could be wholly

67. For Nechaev one cannot do better than read Dostoievsky's *The Possessed*, where
Nechaev appears as Verkhovensky. See also Bazarov in Turgenev's *Fathers and Sons*. For a
straightforward account of nihilism see A. Bose: *A History of Anarchism*, pp. 221–47.

68. M. Bakunin and S. G. Nechaev: *Revolutionary Catechism*, as quoted in E. H. Carr:
Michael Bakunin (London, 1937), p. 380.

destroyed, once and for all. The myth of the fresh start is, indeed, one of the most persistent, if one of the least convincing, of myths; Mr. Micawber may have migrated to Australia but he is still waiting for something to turn up.

There is yet a third variety of modern perfectibilism, flowing neither from Locke nor from Rousseau, perfection by genetic control. This has had a long history; genetic controls were invoked by Plato in his ideal Republic. Christianity, however, did not encourage Platonic Utopianism. It was even less attracted by the idea of genetic controls. If men's moral improvement is dependent on the exercise of divine grace, then it was impious to suggest that they might, by more careful breeding, improve the moral character of their descendants. In our time, admittedly, the Jesuit Teilhard de Chardin has described it as "indispensable" that "a nobly human form of eugenics, on a standard worthy of our personalities, should be discovered and developed." But this is only one more reason, in the eyes of his critics, for denying that Teilhard's evolutionary theology is genuinely Christian.[69]

When, with the Renaissance, the Utopian impulse reasserted itself, the Utopia-makers were soon to be found maintaining, as Campanella did in his *City of the Sun*, that eugenic controls were, in any ideal society, essential; Campanella's wise and good rulers "distribute male and female breeders of the best natures according to philosophical [scientific] rules."[70] Among the disciples of La Mettrie, too, Cabanis was a warm advocate of selective breeding. It was not until the nineteenth century, however, that the enthusiasm for eugenics came fully into its own.

The general tendency of nineteenth-century thought

---

69. *The Phenomenon of Man*, trans. B. Wall and others (London, 1959; repr. 1960), pp. 282–83. See the highly adverse criticism of this passage in Thomas Molnar: *Utopia—the Perennial Heresy* (New York, 1967), p. 128.

70. Campanella: *Civitas Solis* (1623), trans. as *City of the Sun* in *Famous Utopias*, introd. Charles M. Andrews (New York, 1937), p. 292.

had been Pelagian, in the sense that salvation, secular and eternal, was presumed to depend on a man's own efforts, in accordance with the spirit displayed in Samuel Smiles' *Self-Help*. When, in 1869, Francis Galton published his epoch-making *Hereditary Genius*, Charles Darwin wrote to him to confess that he had "always maintained that, excepting fools, men did not differ much in intellect, only in zeal and hard work." [71] Galton shook that egalitarian faith. Galton was not content to argue that genius was, in large part, hereditary; he drew practical, social engineering, conclusions from that fact. "There is nothing either in the history of domestic animals or in that of evolution," he wrote, "to make us doubt that a race of sane men may be formed, who shall be as much superior mentally and morally to the modern European, as the modern European is to the lowest of the Negro races." [72] (Note the association, even in Galton, of eugenics with that racialism which has, in the post-Nazi era, done so much to bring it into disrepute.)

The only question was how that transformation could be brought about. Two methods, in Galton's time, were commonly suggested: "negative" eugenics sought to breed out defects by, for example, sterilization; "positive eugenics," in Plato's manner, sought to improve the human stock by matching males and females in accordance with "philosophical principles." In the twentieth century, new biological techniques, in part already developed, in part envisaged—such techniques as artificial insemination and the modification of genetic tendencies by physio-chemical means—have encouraged more highly-coloured prospects of eugenic control. So the eugenicist H. J. Muller has been led to maintain that "by working in functional alliance with our genes, we may attain to modes of thought and living

71. Charles Darwin: Letter to Francis Galton, in Karl Pearson: *Life of Francis Galton*, 3 vols in 4 (Cambridge, 1914–30), Vol. I, p. 6.
72. Francis Galton: *Hereditary Genius*, 2nd ed. (London, 1892), Prefatory chapter, p. x.

that today would seem inconceivably godlike."[73] That now-familiar ambition—to become godlike—can now, if Muller is right, at long last be achieved. Not, however, by philosophical reflection, not by mystical contemplation, but by the manipulation of genes.

Muller's leading assumption is that the "positive" eugenicist, however he operates, first determines what qualities he wishes to see more widespread or developed to a higher degree, just as a dog-breeder might decide to breed for longer ears, and then selects from amongst the available stock the appropriate parents or the appropriate genes. In sharp contrast, Medawar has argued that a population which is genetically so designed as to strengthen a predetermined characteristic or set of characteristics will tend to die out, to be less "fit" in a purely biological sense, less capable of surviving, than a more heterogeneous population. "There seems no doubt," he writes, "that some large part of human fitness is vested in a mechanism which provides for a high degree of genetic inequality and inborn diversity, which makes sure that there are plenty of different kinds of human beings." And he goes on to draw a conclusion highly relevant to our present theme: "This fact," he says, "sets a limit to any purely theoretical fancies we may care to indulge in about the perfectibility of men."[74] It sets a limit, because if we deliberately try to breed for perfection, we shall breed a population which will die out.

In a way, Medawar's criticism of genetic perfectibilists is reminiscent of Malthus, of what Malthus argued in his *Essay on the Principle of Population*, first published in 1798 and intended as a reply to the perfectibilist hopes of Godwin. Malthus was a clergyman, horrified at the suggestion

73. H. J. Muller: "Man's Place in the Living Universe," an address at Indiana University, in Indiana Univ. Publs., 1956, p. 24; quoted in Paul Ramsey: "Moral and Religious Implications of Genetic Control" in *Genetics and the Future of Man*, Nobel Conference Discussion, 1965, ed. J. D. Roslansky (Amsterdam, 1966), p. 127 n.

74. P. B. Medawar: *The Future of Man*, Reith Lectures (London, 1960), p. 53.

that men might perfect themselves or their society by their own efforts, without supernatural aid. If men try to improve society, he argued, they can do so only by weakening the natural checks on population growth, such checks as poverty, disease, war, plague, and famine. Population growth will then outstrip the means of subsistence: a society which weakens these natural checks will inevitably die out. So, one might say, the penalty for *hubris,* for trying to make man's condition godlike, is death. And that is true whether the *hubris* takes the form of social revolution or of genetic control.

In 1911 Galton wrote a Utopia, under the not very enticing name of *Kantsaywhere;* it was rejected by his publisher and Galton decided to destroy the manuscript. By chance, however, it has been in part preserved. It is a somewhat remarkable Utopia, as the remaining fragments make clear, in which, for example, only those who receive sufficiently high marks at public examinations are permitted to marry. Those who fail their examinations have the option of emigrating, or living under a constant surveillance designed to ensure that they do not propagate their kind.[75] Such an unbounded faith in examinations may strike us as being more than a little pathetic, but Galton's *Kantsaywhere* enables us to see, at least, what a rigorously controlled society a eugenic Utopia would have to be. Inevitably, eugenic controls can only be imposed within an authoritarian society.

For the most part, therefore, modern eugenicists allot an important but nevertheless only a subsidiary role to eugenics. It is to be only one method of social control. This comes out very clearly in Frederick Osborn's *Preface to Eugenics,* first published in 1940, when the Nazi example had made more obvious the dangers of eugenic policies. The first task, Osborn suggests, is the general improvement of the environment. Only after that has been achieved should

75. Compare Karl Pearson: *Life of Francis Galton,* Vol. IIIA, pp. 411–25.

positive steps be taken to encourage births amongst those who have shown themselves capable of responding to the stimulus of improved environment and to discourage births amongst those who have shown that they cannot respond to environmental improvements.[76] Thus the effects of environment can be fully allowed for before the eugenicist embarks upon his task.

The implication, nevertheless, is that however extensively the environment is improved, eugenic measures will still be necessary. That view has been challenged in the Soviet Union. The biological battle of the 1940's in which Michurin and Lysenko set out to destroy "bourgeois genetics" turns around the question whether the environment is, in this respect, the decisive factor. Michurin and Lysenko are in the Locke-Hartley tradition; environmental differences, in their eyes, are all-important. No doubt, they admit, there are, at the present stage of human history, genetic differences between men. These differences can be destroyed, they nevertheless maintain, by suitable modifications of the environment. "Pseudo-scientific formal genetics," according to E. M. Chekmenev, "is used by the ruling classes of capitalist countries to prop up their metaphysical and idealistic notions."[77] For to suppose otherwise would be to set limits to the perfectibility of individual men under communism, limits set by their genetic constitution.

The great problem, in any case, remains: who shall do the controlling? As Rousseau pointed out and as we have all come more and more to recognize, men may be degraded by the same means which could be used to elevate them. Let us assume that conditioning, education, genetic controls are as effective as their proponents maintain. Then men may be

76. Frederick Osborn: *Preface to Eugenics*, rev. ed. (New York, 1951), pp. 241–42.
77. C. P. Blacker: *Eugenics—Galton and After* (London, 1952), p. 276, quoting from *Situation in Biological Science:* Proceedings of the Lenin Academy of Agricultural Sciences of the U.S.S.R., July–August, 1948. Complete stenographic report [reports by T. D. Lysenko and others] (Moscow, 1949; distrib. Collets, London), p. 279.

conditioned to be indifferent to suffering; they may be so educated that they spontaneously submit to tyranny; they may be bred to conform, as helots, to the commands of their masters.

If we are to see in the idea of perfecting by social action ground for hope about the future, rather than for despair, we need to have some good reason for believing that the perfecting mechanisms will be employed in the interests of freedom rather than in the interests of absolute authority. Without that ground for hope, Marx's question "Who shall educate the educators?", a question which can be extended to "Who shall reform the reformers?", remains unanswerable. It is one thing to say that the mechanisms for perfecting men are now at our disposal; it is quite another thing to say that they will in fact be used in order to perfect men. This is what the anarchists pointed out. But they themselves rely upon what one can only regard as myths: the myth of man's natural goodness, the myth of rebirth. Perfection is no more to be expected from the destruction of existing social institutions than from their extension and their strengthening. The chains which men bear they have imposed upon themselves; strike them off, and they will weep for their lost security.

THE PERFECTING OF MAN BY
SCIENTIFIC PROGRESS

At the very most, the Lockian, the Benthamite, the geneti-
cist, can plausibly claim to have established that man is *in
principle* perfectible, and by natural, as distinct from supernatural, means. So as against that picture of man which
ascribes to him an all-pervasive corruption they have produced arguments to show that nothing in man's nature prevents him from being perfected. And as against the view that
he can be perfected only by divine grace, they have demonstrated to their own satisfaction that he can be perfected
by the judicious use of educative, legislative or genetic controls. But they often write as if they had established much
more than this: that man can in fact look forward to an endless history of constant improvement. Very obviously, however, there is a vast gap between demonstrating that man *can*
be perfected and demonstrating that he *will* be perfected.
How, if at all, can the gap be bridged?

The French Enlighteners were almost completely blind
to the prospect that education, legislation, genetic control,
might all of them be used to pervert men rather than to
perfect them. In England, where the perfectibilists were
politically much more sophisticated than their French colleagues, there was a higher degree of alertness to this possibility. Thus, for all his confidence in Providence, Hartley
wrote of his associationism that it "cannot fail both to in-
struct *and alarm* all such as have any degree of interested
concern for themselves, or of a benevolent one for others."[1]

---

1. *Observations on Man*, Pt. I, ch. 1, §2, Prop. XIV, Cor. 5 (my italics); in the 5th ed.
Vol. 1, p. 84.

Even more significant is the unanimous opposition of English associationists to State education.

From Priestley to J. S. Mill, the associationists were all of them radicals, both in politics and in religion. They valued diversity: the last thing they wanted to see was the imposition of uniformity on human society. Yet, if, as they believed, all men are equal at birth and if, as they also argued, education can mould them to whatever shape is desired, the State is at once supplied, in the mechanisms of education, with an effective method of destroying every kind of radical dissent. Priestley had no doubt, therefore, that a system of State education would be "prejudicial to the proper design of education";[2] J. S. Mill more forthrightly condemned State education as "a mere contrivance for moulding people to be exactly like one another." "The mould in which it casts them," he went on to say, "is that which pleases the predominant power in the government . . . ; in proportion as it is efficient and successful, it establishes a despotism over the mind, leading by natural tendency to one over the body."[3]

The English associationists were convinced, however, that the sole precaution needed in order to avoid this danger was to keep education in private hands. It must be remembered, of course, that in England State and Church were one; keeping education out of the hands of the State also meant keeping it out of the hands of the Established Church. But even if by this means they could have preserved diversity, it is far from clear that the perfectibilists would thereby have achieved any of their wider aspirations for education. A set of private educators may each of them exercise his private despotism: what are called "private schools" may be nothing more than the instruments by which minorities

2. Joseph Priestley: *An Essay on the First Principles of Government* (2nd ed., 1771), Section IV, excerpted in *Priestley's Writings*, ed. Passmore, p. 306.
3. J. S. Mill: *Utilitarianism, Liberty and Representative Government*, introd. A. D. Lindsay, Everyman's Library (London, 1910; repr. 1944), p. 161.

try to enforce uniformity on their members; private schools, indeed, may be more despotic, more authoritarian, than their State counterparts.

The French associationists were well aware of that fact. Many of them had been educated at Jesuit schools; the effect, as in Helvetius's case, was to make them ardent advocates of State education. Helvetius never seriously faces the practical question how a State system is to be prevented from establishing a despotism over the mind; at most, he tries to circumvent this objection by suggesting a degree of decentralization. This is not as surprising as it might seem. Helvetius had plenty of experience of a State which ignored education, which saw in it a threat to autocratic government; he had no experience of a State which used a system of education deliberately to further its own despotic purposes. In England, in contrast, both Mill and Priestley greatly underestimated the difficulties of setting up educational institutions which should be at once privately controlled and genuinely devoted to free inquiry. The Dissenting Academies, in which Priestley himself had placed such hopes, survived for only a few years.

Even if, in respect to perfectibility by education, it is necessary to distinguish between the position of the French and the English Enlighteners, the fact still remains that the English Enlighteners, too, were to modern eyes surprisingly ready to presume that now the means of perfecting men had been discovered, it could confidently be expected that they would in fact be perfected. This attitude survived well into the twentieth century. Fifty years ago, as the biologist Luria has pointed out, the prospect that methods will be found for directly controlling human heredity would have been contemplated not only without alarm but even with enthusiasm. "The culture of enlightenment," he goes on to say, "had fostered in them [men] the comfortable conviction that human progress and the ideals of brotherhood were advancing monotonously at a steady, if often uneven, pace."[4] This "comfortable conviction" carried with it the belief that scientific discoveries would always fall into "the right hands" and were certain, therefore, to be used for the benefit of mankind.

On what was this belief grounded? In the first place, the Enlighteners were tremendously impressed by their own emergence as, so they thought, a new and distinct social class. To a striking degree they formed, for all their squabbles, a single, self-conscious, community. It might seem ridiculous to his French admirers that Priestley should continue to defend Christianity; Hume and Rousseau might find themselves at odds. The fact remains that Hume felt himself morally obliged to care for Rousseau in England when local hostility drove him out of Switzerland. And the French revolutionaries elected Priestley a citizen of the Republic. "The philosophers of different nations," wrote Condorcet, "who considered the interests of the whole of humanity without distinction of country, race, or creed, formed a solid phalanx banded together against all forms of error, against all manifestations of tyranny, despite their differences in matters of theory."[5] In short, they made up the secular equivalent of Augustine's "City of God," a Republic of Letters, devoted not to God but to truth and humanity.

It was their responsibility, the Enlighteners thought, at once to keep themselves remote from the intrigues of political life and yet to be the true governors of the people. "Happy are men of letters," so D'Alembert summed up, "if they recognize at last that the surest way of making themselves respectable is to live united and almost shut up among themselves." D'Alembert is not suggesting that the Enlighteners should ignore the world; it was only that they should

4. S. E. Luria: "Directed Genetic Change: Perspectives from Molecular Genetics" in *The Control of Human Heredity and Evolution*, ed. T. M. Sonneborn (New York, 1965), p. 16.

5. A. N. de Condorcet: *Sketch for a Historical Picture of the Progress of the Human Mind*, trans. June Barraclough, Library of Ideas (London, 1955), p. 141.

exert their influence on government indirectly, through their teachings, rather than directly, by the exercise of political power. It is by this means that they would, D'Alembert thought, promote "the too rare art of good government."[6] Charles Duclos was no less convinced that the true role of the intellectual was to be "the power behind the throne," the actual, although not the overt, governor of men. "Of all empires that of the intellectuals," he wrote, "though invisible, is the widest spread. Those in power command, but the intellectuals govern, because in the end they form public opinion, which sooner or later subdues or upsets all despotisms."[7] In short, the Enlighteners hoped, in Churchill's famous phrase about journalists, to exercise "the privilege of the harlot in every age: power without responsibility."

There is no need to worry, for example, lest State education should fall into the hands of the wrong people. Condorcet was quite clear how this possibility was to be avoided: the State would pay the teachers, but Enlighteners would select them. It does not occur to him for a moment that the State might not acquiesce in this arrangement. If the French Enlighteners could happily envisage a State-controlled education, it was because they were convinced that they would do the controlling. Priestley and Mill, in contrast, were only too aware that their influence on a State-controlled system would be negligible.[8] Helvetius's optimism was no doubt at times subdued, but only because he felt constrained to admit that the number of enlightened men prepared to devote their attention to the problems of government is limited: that fact might delay, but could not for ever hold back, he is still confident, the perfecting of government

6. Quoted by Charles Frankel: *The Faith of Reason* (New York, 1948), p. 10, from the trans. by John Morley in *Diderot*, I, 129.

7. Quoted in M. Roustan: *The Pioneers of the French Revolution*, trans. F. Whyte (London, 1926), p. 265.

8. For details see J. S. Schapiro: *Condorcet and the Rise of Liberalism* (New York, 1934; repr. 1963), ch. XI, pp. 211–12.

and, through the perfecting of government, the perfecting of mankind.

The Enlighteners also thought they knew who was bound to come to overt power in the State—the commercial classes. And there was, they were convinced, a natural alliance between the new governors and the spirit of enlightenment. Overt power to the middle class, actual power to the intellectuals—that was the future of society as they envisaged it. The "honest man," the merchant, the "civically good" man, replaced the aristocrat and the hero—in England especially—as the "ideal type" of humanity. The merchant class, it began to be argued, was the true nobility. Molière might have his fun at the expense of "le bourgeois gentilhomme," but Molière's seventeenth-century "cit turned gentleman" is for Steele and Addison in the eighteenth century the "new master," entitled by his enterprise and diligence to take the place of the aristocrat, turned lazy and effete.[9]

Whereas the twentieth-century radical is normally hostile not only to "Big Business" but, often enough, to commerce in general, that was not at all the situation in the eighteenth century or in the early years of the nineteenth century. Commerce and liberty, so Voltaire maintained in his *Philosophical Letters,* are intimately associated. The close link between literature and finance was, he thought, one of the glories of the eighteenth century.[10] No Rotarian could be more enthusiastic about the benefits of commerce than was Joseph Priestley. By bringing the merchant into contact with other places and people, he tells us, commerce "tends greatly to expand the mind and to cure us of many hurtful

---

9. Compare Paul Hazard: *La Crise de la conscience européenne, 1680–1715* (Paris, 1935), Pt. III, ch. vii, pp. 339–47, and Voltaire: *Lettres philosophiques,* Letter X.

10. The first reference is to the tenth of Voltaire's *Lettres philosophiques* (1734). For the second reference see Voltaire: *Oeuvres complètes,* ed. Moland, 52 vols (Paris, 1877–85), Vol. XXII (1879), pp. 364–65, quoted in Mario Einaudi: *The Early Rousseau* (Ithaca, N.Y., 1967), p. 37.

prejudices"; it encourages benevolence and a love of peace; it develops such virtues as punctuality and "the principles of strict justice and honour." The small shopkeeper, Priestley was prepared to admit, may be grasping and avaricious; large-scale commerce, trade, he remained convinced, is a powerful influence for the good. "Men of wealth and influence," so he sums up, "who act upon the principles of virtue and religion, and conscientiously make their power subservient to the good of their country, are the men who are the greatest honour to human nature, and the greatest blessing to human societies."[11] Condorcet, more realistically, was fain to admit that commerce did not seem, as yet, to have spread liberty and enlightenment through Asia and Africa. He was nevertheless confident that "the moment approaches when, no longer presenting ourselves as always either tyrants or corrupters, we shall become for them the beneficent instruments of their freedom."[12] For, the assumption is, commercial interests are "naturally" enlightened; once the influence of the Church was destroyed, their enlightenment would develop apace.

Of course, there were dissentients: this is one of the many respects in which Rousseau, with his mistrust of commerce and his yearnings for a simple life, was odd man out. Holbach, too, argued that agriculture, not commerce, must be the basis of a sound social order; he was once moved to observe that "there is no more dangerous creature alive, than the businessman seeking his prey."[13] But well into the nineteenth century social reformers still looked to the in-

---

11. The first quotation is from *Lectures on History and General Policy*, 4th ed. (London, 1826), Lecture LI, pp. 412–25, included in *Priestley's Writings*, ed. Passmore, pp. 267–68. The second quotation is from *Lectures on History and General Policy* (London, 1788), p. 423, as quoted in Basil Willey: *The Eighteenth-Century Background* (London, 1940; Penguin ed. Harmondsworth, 1962), p. 193.

12. Condorcet: *Sketch of the Progress of the Human Mind*, p. 176.

13. Quoted in Ian Cumming: *Helvetius*, p. 112. For his general view see Baron d'Holbach: *Système sociale*, 3 vols (Londres, 1773), Vol. III, ch. VII. For Rousseau see Einaudi, *loc. cit.* and pp. 109–10.

dustrialists for support.* The socialist Saint-Simon anticipated a form of society in which industrialists and scientists
would be joint governors; the anarchist P. J. Proudhon addressed himself to "you, businessmen" who "have always
been the boldest, the most skilful revolutionaries"; the Utilitarians exhorted the middle classes to cast off those aristo-
cratic-inspired illusions which prevented them from recognizing that it was in their own interest to pursue the general
interest.[14]

Only gradually did nineteenth-century thinkers come to
be disillusioned with the middle classes. In the nineteenth
century there was a gradual lowering of the social classes to
whom reformers appealed: Godwin, primarily, to farmers
and "small men," Marx to the industrial proletariat, Bakunin to peasants and unskilled labourers. It had become apparent, Marx argued, that the middle class would not permit itself to be enlightened beyond a certain point. But it
was still presumed that there was *some class or other* which
could be relied upon to speed enlightenment.

Helvetius, as we have already seen, rested his hopes not
so much on a social class as on individuals—"enlightened
despots." Not many of the Enlighteners were happy with this
solution. Diderot directed against Helvetius what he called
*A Sustained Refutation of the Book of Helvetius entitled "Concern-
ing Man."* One point he made in his "refutation" is that at

* The attitude of the Enlightenment on this matter is by no means wholly absurd. It is
only in middle-class societies that the Enlightenment ideals of freedom, justice, tolerance,
have been, however imperfectly, realized. But the presumption that the commercial state
would be content to act as the executive of the intelligentsia is, of course, an extraordinary
fantasy. (Sometimes it was defended by reference to the example of China, where, so it
was supposed, the philosophers decided, and the Emperors transformed their decisions
into actions.) Enlightenment ideals die hardest in the United States; both the Roosevelt
and the Kennedy Presidencies sought to put into practice the ideal of a "natural alliance"
between intellectuals and an enlightened middle class.

14. For Saint-Simon see J. L. Talmon: *Political Messianism: The Romantic Phase* (London,
1960), p. 59; for Proudhon, his *General Idea of the Revolution in the Nineteenth Century*, trans.
Robinson, p. 5; for the Utilitarians, see Elie Halévy: *The Growth of Philosophic Radicalism*,
trans. M. Morris, Foreword to Pt. III, pp. 313–15.

best, since the despot is not omniscient, there is no assurance that he will select as his successor a man of capacity and benevolence. And if once freedom dies out, Diderot warns, it is not easily recovered; the "benevolent despot" may do no more than prepare the way for a malignant tyranny. His very "benevolence," indeed, is a menace to human society.[15]

Skinner and Watson, or so we have suggested, are faced with the same problem. Neither the admittedly imperfect parent nor the admittedly imperfect leader can be wholly confident of producing precisely that kind of successor who can be trusted, when the time comes, to select his successor with the same care and the same good fortune. "The authoritarian," as Karl Popper has argued, "will in general select those who obey, who believe, who respond to his influence. But in doing so, he is bound to select mediocrities."[16] It is perhaps significant that in his *Republic* Plato envisages the final collapse of his ideal state as arising in a not dissimilar way: mistakes are made in breeding, as a result of which men are appointed to office who are unworthy to rule.

The God of traditional Christian theology does not have this problem; God has no successor, and he is endowed with omniscience and omnipotence. (To judge from the Christian story of the fall of the angels, however, even God's choice of ministers can leave something to be desired.) But a secular perfectibilist cannot plausibly, even if he sometimes comes very close to doing so, ascribe immortality, or omniscience, or omnipotence, to his legislators, his psychologists, or his geneticists. Secular perfectibilism, as we have so far described it, lacks that metaphysical underpinning which lends what plausibility it possesses, for all its vulnerability to philosophical criticism, to the idea of perfection by divine action. If men are to be perfected by educators or

---

15. *Réfutation suivie de l'ouvrage d'Helvétius intitulé L'Homme* in *Oeuvres complètes*, ed. Assézat, Vol. 2, p. 381.

16. *The Open Society and Its Enemies*, 4th ed., rev. (London, 1962), Vol. 1, pp. 134–35.

legislators or geneticists, this can only be by a series of fortunate chances, as a result of which the right sort of men
come to power and choose the right successors. There is
nothing to guarantee, or even faintly to suggest, that these
conditions will be fulfilled.

If, however, human history is so designed as to *guarantee*
that man will continue to improve his condition, then occasional mistakes in the selection of educators, or legislators,
or psychologists, or geneticists, can be dismissed as unimportant. In the long run men are bound to be perfected,
whatever setbacks they may suffer as the result of errors
of judgement. That was what the economist-statesman Turgot argued in his famous lecture at the Sorbonne, delivered
almost precisely midway through the eighteenth century,
on December 11, 1750: "Manners are gradually softened, the
human mind is enlightened, separate nations draw nearer to
each other, commerce and policy connect at last every part
of the globe, and the total mass of the human race, by alter-
nating between calm and agitation, good and bad, marches
always, however slowly, towards greater perfection."[17]

The idea of progress,[18] thus conceived, is a peculiarly
modern one. It is scarcely to be met with, if at all, before
the first decades of the eighteenth century, in the optimistic
prophecies of the Abbé de Saint-Pierre. Greek thought, for

17. Turgot was an abbé, and the discourse was originally delivered in Latin. It can be
read complete in *Oeuvres*, ed. Gustave Schelle, 5 vols (Paris, 1913–23), Vol. 1, pp. 214–38.
The passage trans. above is on pp. 215–16. A partial trans. is included in the Appendix to
The Life and Writings of Turgot, ed. W. W. Stephens (London, 1895), pp. 159–73, where this
passage occurs on p. 160.

18. See, for a laborious analysis of the manifold varieties of progress theory, C. Van
Doren: *The Idea of Progress* (New York, 1967). F. J. Teggart, ed.: *The Idea of Progress: A Collection of Readings*, rev. ed. by G. H. Hildebrand (Berkeley, 1949), contains most of the leading documents; J. B. Bury: *The Idea of Progress* (London, 1920; repr. 1924) is still the most
important historical study. But see also Morris Ginsberg: *The Idea of Progress: A Revalua-
tion* (London, 1953). For a Protestant version see John Baillie: *The Belief in Progress* (London, 1950; repr. 1951) and, for a Roman Catholic version, Christopher Dawson: *Progress
and Religion: An Historical Enquiry* (London, 1929; repr. 1945). For details about French
theories of progress, in particular, consult the bibliography in Henry Vyverberg: *Historical
Pessimism in the French Enlightenment* (Cambridge, Mass., 1958).

the most part, was committed either to the belief that men had declined ever since the Golden Age and would continue hereafter to do so or else, as with the Stoics, to the belief that human history was cyclical in character, progressing only to a point at which it reaches its climax. Then it must start again, perhaps passing once more through the identical course of history, perhaps through a course of history which is essentially similar but differs in detail. On the first interpretation of the cyclical view—maintained, for example, by the Stoic Posidonius—Socrates, snub-nose and all, would be born again, would teach precisely the same doctrines and would again be put to death; on the second interpretation, someone very like Socrates in a society very like Athens would suffer a very similar fate. Neither form of cyclical theory, it will be obvious, held out to men any hope of infinite improvability.*

No doubt, this is not the whole story. In the fifth century B.C., men were by no means indisposed to pride themselves on the degree to which they had improved on their predecessors. The musician-dramatist Timotheus boasted in a manner which is nowadays only too familiar: "I do not sing ancient melodies, my own are better by far; . . . ancient muse, begone."[19] The mere fact that in the *Republic* Plato was so emphatic that novelties must be prohibited testifies to his conviction that if not restrained they were inevitable. Aristotle, writing a little later, was fully confident that he had improved on his predecessors; later still, in his *Naturales quaestiones*, Seneca expressed his conviction that his succes-

---

* One sometimes runs across the cyclical theory in the eighteenth century—Vico's *Scienza nuova*, first published in 1725, is the most notable example. But Vico was very little read in his own century; not until the mid-nineteenth century was he at all widely referred to. He did not come fully into his own until the present century. It is interesting that he should have provided the central philosophical framework for James Joyce's *Finnegans Wake* which, in so many respects, rejects Enlightenment ideals.

19. As trans. on p. 35 of Ludwig Edelstein: *The Idea of Progress in Classical Antiquity* (Baltimore, 1967), the most thorough-going case for the belief in progress in the Graeco-Roman world.

sors will solve many scientific problems to which he did not himself know the answer. So much must be admitted. But it is one thing to assert that over a limited period of time the human situation has improved, or will improve, whether in knowledge or in artistic achievement, quite another thing to assert that mankind as a whole is gradually perfecting itself—not only in some particular respect but universally—and that it will continue to do so throughout the course of human history.

In its more orthodox forms, Christianity did not encourage such hopes. At first, indeed, Christians lived in the immediate expectation of a Second Coming, to be followed, many early Christians believed, by the establishment of God's Kingdom on Earth. But that was a cataclysmic occurrence; the idea of a Second Coming lends no support to a doctrine of gradual secular progress, in which all mankind would participate. Quite the contrary. It was only Christ's saints who would participate in God's Kingdom, and they would be perfected in an instant, by divine grace.

Origen tried to incorporate the cyclical theory of history into Christianity. He saw no reason why the Word should not be made flesh once more, once more to save mankind from their sins, or why individual Christians, once judged, might not find themselves forced to re-enter life, to win salvation.[20] But Augustine wholly rejected this possibility. "Once Christ died for our sins," he wrote, "and, rising from the dead, he dieth no more. . . . We ourselves after the resurrection shall be ever with the Lord."[21] Augustine's rejection of the cyclical theory "left room," as a cyclical theory does not, for in-

---

20. The contrary is often asserted. But compare Origen: *De Principiis*, Bk. II, iii. 1–5 and Bk. III. v. 2 f., trans. as *On First Principles* by G. W. Butterworth (London, 1936; repr. New York, 1966), pp. 83–89, 238 f. He denied, however, that *identically the same world* might recur.

21. *The City of God*, Bk. XII, ch. 13, as trans. M. Dods (Edinburgh, 1872), repr. in *Basic Writings of Saint Augustine*, ed. W. J. Oates, Vol. 2, p. 192.

terpreting history as progressive. But it is one thing to maintain, as Augustine did, that history is lineal, quite another to assert that history is working towards the perfection of all men.

On Augustine's view, men progress towards perfection only if God so chooses. And although the number of perfected saints, members of God's chosen few, will increase throughout history until the appointed number has been reached, this does not carry with it any suggestion that there will be a corresponding improvement in secular society. Augustine was prepared to concede, even, that secular society had actually declined since the birth of Christ; his main anxiety was lest the Fall of Rome should be interpreted as proof that God was not at work in history.

Some early Christians, impressed by the fact that the birth of Jesus had taken place during the age of Augustus, were attracted by the hypothesis that mankind had now set out upon a progressive path, in which Caesar and God would conjointly assure man's temporal and spiritual welfare. Eusebius went so far as to proclaim that the prophecies of Isaiah had been fulfilled, and swords could now safely be beaten into ploughshares. The Fall of Rome, in these circumstances, came as a tremendous shock to Christian opinion. For this very reason Augustine was the more concerned to show that Christianity did not set its hopes for man on secular progress.[22]

He did not deny, in fact he argues at length, that men have shown themselves ingeniously inventive, and have so far added to the richness of human society. But even when, for his own special reasons, he is particularly emphasizing the munificence of God in endowing men with rationality and inventiveness, he is quick to point out that human in-

22. See especially Theodor E. Mommsen: "St. Augustine and the Christian Idea of Progress," in *Journal of the History of Ideas,* Vol. XII, No. 3, pp. 364–74, repr. in P. P. Wiener and A. Noland, eds.: *Ideas in Cultural Perspective* (New Brunswick, N.J., 1962), pp. 515–43.

ventiveness is often enough employed for purposes which are "superfluous, . . . dangerous and destructive," as when it is displayed, for example, in the ingenious arguments by which heretics defend "errors and misapprehensions." Man's inventiveness, as distinct from his grace-infused supernatural virtue, is always double-edged.[23] As Socrates was fond of pointing out, the art of medicine, normally directed towards healing, can also be made use of by a murderer. In the mere fact of human inventiveness, there is nothing to justify any confidence in the future of mankind.

The very idea of a "future for mankind" is, however, Augustinian in its inspiration. The Greeks did not for the most part think in terms of "mankind," as distinct from freemen and slaves, Greeks and barbarians. Augustine did. All mankind, he often emphasizes, descends from the same pair— from Adam and Eve. And God arranged matters in this way, he says, so as "to give unity to mankind by the likeness of nature." If we think of mankind as a unity, with a history, then it is also natural to think of that history as being parallel in certain respects to the history of individual human beings. And this might well lead us to suppose that just as a child must by its nature—short of dying—develop into an adult human being, so a society must finally grow to the perfection of maturity. Augustine himself suggested that with the birth of Christ mankind has entered into what corresponds, in the individual, to full maturity; it has finally achieved that degree of spirituality which man's earthly condition permits.[24] No fundamental change is to be expected until the Second Coming.

In the early seventeenth century, as one manifestation of the general depreciation of man and the world so characteristic of that period, it was not uncommonly argued

---

23. *The City of God,* Bk. XXII, ch. 24, as trans. M. Dods, in *Basic Writings,* Vol. 2, p. 649.

24. *De Genesi contra Manichaeos,* Bk. 1, ch. xxiii–xxiv, in J. P. Migne: *Patrologia latina* (Paris, 1845), Vol. 34, col. 190–94. The doctrine of "ages" is discussed in R. L. P. Milburn: *Early Christian Interpretations of History* (London, 1954), pp. 79–80.

that the world was now in a state, not of maturity, but of senility. The extravagance with which this view was sometimes expressed is scarcely credible. In a sermon delivered in 1625, the poet-clergyman, John Donne, saw "the age and impotency of the world" clearly revealed in the irregularity of the seasons, the diminished warmth of the sun, the shortening of man's stature and the annual appearance of "new species of worms, and flies, and sicknesses, which argue more and more putrefaction of which they are engendered."[25] Although this gloomy picture of human history did not go unchallenged, its challengers commonly admitted that they were writing against the mainstream of contemporary thought. As late as 1741, when David Hume published his essay *Of the Populousness of Ancient Nations,* his immediate motive was to dispute the view that the modern world had fallen into a state of decline, as evidenced by the fact that it had been greatly reduced in population.

Bacon, however, had already taken a very different view, and as so often he was the harbinger of the new age. Men are misled, he says, because they speak of Greece and Rome as "antiquity" or as "the world in which the ancients lived" and ascribe to that world, therefore, the wisdom proper to maturity. But in fact, paradoxical though this may sound, it is the moderns who are the ancients, it is they who have achieved, as a result of the long history of mankind, a "greater knowledge of human things and a riper judgement" than the relatively young "ancient world" could have at its disposal.[26]

There were obvious dangers, however, from the point of view of the proponents of progress, in this way of looking

25. John Donne: *Sermon* XXXVI of the ed. of 1640, as quoted in R. F. Jones: *Ancients and Moderns,* 2nd ed., rev. (St. Louis, 1961), p. 25, which should be consulted generally for a fuller account of the whole controversy about mankind's age.

26. Francis Bacon: *Novum Organum,* aphorism LXXXIV, as trans. in *The Works of Francis Bacon,* ed. J. Spedding, R. L. Ellis, D. D. Heath, 14 vols (London, 1857–74; facs. repr. Stuttgart, 1962), Vol. IV, p. 82. Pascal uses the same argument in his *Fragment d'un traité du vide.* It was generally agreed that "antiquity" in human history did not carry with it senility but maturity.

at the situation. Perhaps men had reached maturity in the great achievements of the seventeenth century, the century of genius, perhaps nothing more could now be expected except a gradual slide into senility. Writing at the end of the seventeenth century, Charles Perrault, more interested in literature than in technical innovation, suggested that his own century had "arrived in some sort at the highest perfection." Progress had recently been slower; it could scarcely be pretended that the new writers were serious rivals of Molière or Racine—oddly, if typically, Perrault identifies the fate of France with the fate of mankind. There was some consolation in this fact: "I have the further joy of thinking that we shall probably not have much to envy in those who will come after us."[27] In the end, indeed, Perrault was led to suspect that mankind might at last be passing into senility, as "the distaste which one often finds nowadays for the best things" may seem to indicate.[28]

Fontenelle, in his essay *On the Ancients and Moderns,* took a rather different view. All men, he suggests, are naturally equal; modern man has the same brains, the same nervous system, as the ancients possessed. There is nothing they could do which men can no longer do. As it happens, however, circumstances in the ancient world were particularly propitious to the development of eloquence; perhaps modern men will, in this respect, only equal and not surpass the ancients. But the situation in science, he argues, is very different; science requires a degree of maturity into which mankind had only recently grown. "A good cultivated mind contains, so to speak," he writes, "all the minds of preceding centuries; it is but a single identical mind which has been developing and improving itself all this time." In its infancy it was wholly devoted to keeping alive; in its youth

---

27. *Parallèle des anciens et des modernes en ce qui regarde les arts et les sciences* (Paris, 1688–97), Vol. I, p. 99.
28. *Ibid.,* Vol. I, p. 54.

to eloquence and poetry; now is the time for the exercise of reason and intelligence in science.

What of the fear that senility may come? At this point, Fontenelle suggests, the analogy must be abandoned: once such a mind has reached maturity it need have no fear of decline — "men will never degenerate, and there will be no end to the growth and development of human wisdom."[29] But to argue thus, very obviously, is to try to have it both ways: to make full use of the analogy between the development of individual men and the development of mankind in order to establish the "necessity" of progress while abandoning the analogy as soon as its consequences turn out to be uncomfortable. Not unless it could be maintained, as Saint-Pierre maintained in his 1737 *Observations on the Continuous Progress of Universal Reason,* that mankind was still only in its infancy, could it safely be concluded that unlimited progress still lay ahead of him.[30]

This controversy, on the face of it, could have gone on for ever. (It still in fact goes on. In a contemporary "philosophical novel" it is solemnly argued that mankind is now at "mid-adolescence.")[31] What possible grounds were there for maintaining that mankind was now in its infancy, its manhood, or its second childhood? Saint-Pierre, and after him Turgot and Condorcet,* were convinced, however, that there were excellent grounds for believing that mankind was only now seriously setting out on its long march towards perfection.

29. B. le B. de Fontenelle: *On the Ancients and the Moderns,* excerpted in F. J. Teggart, ed.: *The Idea of Progress,* p. 184. Pascal's *Preface to a Treatise on a Vacuum,* written about 1647, takes the same view that all mankind can be considered as a single mind. Compare Teggart, pp. 164–69.

30. For Fontenelle and Saint-Pierre see J. B. Bury: *The Idea of Progress,* chs. V and VI.

31. John Barth: *Giles Goat-Boy* (New York, 1966), Vol. I, Third Reel, ch. 3, pp. 254–55.

* The choice of names is important. By no means all Enlightenment thinkers, especially in France, were convinced that progress was inevitable, even if for the most part they at least granted it to be possible. Compare Peter Gay: *The Party of Humanity* (London, 1964), pp. 270–73.

In part, they based their arguments on purely inductive grounds. Perrault, they said, was wrong: in every respect human culture was still advancing, and therefore could properly be expected to continue to do so. "Anybody who has read Locke," wrote Voltaire, "is bound to find Plato merely a fine talker and nothing else. From the point of view of philosophy a chapter from Locke or Clarke is, compared with the babble of antiquity, what Newton's *Optics* are compared with those of Descartes."* Two points strike us in Voltaire's observation: not only has mankind progressed from the babbling of a Plato to the intellectual grandeur of a Samuel Clarke, but, more striking still, it has progressed, with the same great steps and in less than a century, from Descartes to Newton. The human mind, it is clear, was on the march.

But there were great difficulties in a purely inductive argument for progress. No one could be more contemptuous than were the eighteenth-century perfectibilists of the Dark and the Middle Ages. "The triumph of Christianity," according to Condorcet, "was the signal for the complete decadence of philosophy and the sciences." The Arabs saved mankind, taking over the torch of science from the Greeks. This fact, Condorcet suggests, ought to preserve us from "anxiety about the future." But if Arab science, as Condorcet also argues, was "only a temporary exception to the general laws of nature which condemn servile and superstitious nations to ignorance and degradation,"[32] it has rather

---

* Voltaire, however, is by no means a consistent exponent of progress. No Frenchman with any literary perception could fail to realize that Perrault was right: eighteenth-century French literature had fallen far below the levels set in the seventeenth century by Racine and Molière. In defence of his own age, Voltaire sometimes suggests that what the eighteenth century lacks in genius it more than compensates for in enlightenment. But at other times he writes with unrelieved gloom about the cultural decline of his own age. It was much easier to be optimistic if one forgot about art and literature and concentrated on science. Compare Vyverberg: *Historical Pessimism*, pp. 183–85.

32. *Sketch of the Progress of the Human Mind*, pp. 72, 87. On Voltaire's opinion of Plato,

the appearance of a miracle than anything it would be safe to count upon. What grounds are there for believing that the torch of knowledge will not flicker once more, this time to be finally extinguished?

The first ground for this belief, Enlightenment philosophers replied, was that mankind had in the seventeenth century lit upon a method of discovery, a method which would guarantee future progress. The emphasis on method, indeed, was one of the leading characteristics of seventeenth- and eighteenth-century thought. Bacon, if only for controversial purposes, was prepared to allow that the ancients had more native genius than the moderns: if he nevertheless held out great hopes for the future of the world, this was because he thought he had discovered a new method, by which scientific investigation and the improvement of human life—prospects dear to Bacon's heart—could be advanced to heights previously unheralded. Descartes took the slightly different view that all men were substantially equal in genius, but that he himself had advanced beyond other men because he had hit on the right method of inquiry. (The original title he had proposed for his *Discourse on Method,* it is worth observing, was *The Prospect of a Universal Science which can Elevate our Nature to its Highest Perfection.*) Leibniz made claims for his "art of inventing" which now strike us as being little short of fantastic; it would solve, he was convinced, all the major problems not only of geometry and physics but of medicine, morals, law, theology and metaphysics. Any qualms there might still have been about the practical usefulness of the new methods were speedily removed by the scientific triumphs of Newton, widely hailed as a compelling demonstration of the riches to be hoped for from a combination of the "inductive" method in which

---

compare the article "Platon, section II" in his *Dictionnaire philosophique,* 2e éd. (Paris, 1826), Vol. VII, pp. 367–69 (*Oeuvres complètes,* Vol. LVII).

Bacon had placed his faith and the mathematical method on which Descartes had relied. "God said, Let Newton be, and there was light," as Pope so eloquently turned a commonplace.

The new scientific method was the break-through, the revelation men needed to ensure their future progress; now the way lay clear ahead to the unremitting growth of enlightenment. Even so, even granted that physical science was now embarked upon a triumphant path, it still had to be shown that scientific progress would do anything to improve men morally or to remedy the ills of human society. Pascal had been one of the first to argue that science must, by its very nature, progress, but that sturdy Augustinian would certainly not admit that scientific progress was bound to bring with it an amelioration of man's moral condition.* Fontenelle, for all his optimism about the progress not only of science but of literature, was not prepared to conclude that in virtue, too, man must constantly improve his condition. "The heart," he wrote, "changes not at all, and the heart is the whole man." On no part of the earth's surface, he thought, are enough rational men likely to be born "to establish a fashion for virtue and uprightness."[33]

The first step towards arguing the contrary was to demonstrate that the new methods could be applied as much to the study of human nature and human society as to the study of the physical world. So much both Hume and Hartley thought they could demonstrate. In its subtitle, Hume described his *Treatise of Human Nature* as "an attempt to in-

---

* Even Gibbon shows some hesitancy on this point. He concludes the thirty-eighth chapter of *The Decline and Fall of the Roman Empire* thus: "We may therefore acquiesce in the pleasing conclusion that every age of the world has increased and still increases the real wealth, the happiness, the knowledge, and *perhaps the virtue*, of the human race" (my italics).

33. *Dialogues des morts anciens et modernes*, in *Oeuvres de Fontenelle* (Paris, 1790–92), I, 239–40, as trans. in H. Vyverberg: *Historical Pessimism in the French Enlightenment*, pp. 44–45. This book should be consulted generally as a corrective to the view that eighteenth-century writers were unanimously optimistic about the future.

troduce the experimental method of reasoning into moral subjects"; Hartley set out, with equal confidence, to apply to the study of the mind "the method of analysis and synthesis recommended and followed by Sir Isaac Newton." In the eighteenth century, indeed, it was a poor-spirited moral and political philosopher who did not aspire to be "the Newton" of his speciality. Helvetius described himself as the Newton of legislation; Bentham was convinced that *he* was the Newton, and Helvetius only the Bacon.

There were obvious objections, nevertheless, to any attempt to Newtonize the social sciences. Superficially, at least, human behaviour and social change display a species of complexity which does not lend itself to being reduced to a deductive mathematical pattern, of the type Newton had employed in his *Principia Mathematica*. No doubt Hobbes and Spinoza attempted to apply the geometrical method to the study of human nature and Locke expressed his conviction that moral conclusions are as capable of being demonstrated as mathematical conclusions. But in the eighteenth century philosophers came to be more and more suspicious of purely deductive philosophical systems; the moral sciences, it was generally agreed, had to rely upon "probable reasoning."

What saved the day was the recognition that "probable reasoning" could itself be reduced to a mathematical form. Leibniz had drawn attention to the resemblance between the situation of a man who is called upon to make a practical decision and the situation of a gambler who is trying to determine where to place a bet; he had complained that logicians, putting all their emphasis on demonstration, had failed to realize that probabilities could be accurately estimated.[34] Once Laplace and de Moivre had worked out their calculus of probabilities, philosophers were even more con-

34. "New Proposals" in *Selections*, ed. P. P. Wiener (New York, 1951), pp. 578–79, trans. from Louis Couturat: *Opuscules et fragments inédits de Leibniz* (Paris, 1903), pp. 224 ff.

vinced that practical decisions could be made rational with the help of a calculus which would reduce them to mathematical form. If, as Bishop Butler maintained, "probability is the guide of life," the calculus of probability would enable men to follow that guide with more confident steps.

Hartley is characteristic in fixing his hopes for the further development of the social sciences on de Moivre's theory of chances and Newton's differential calculus. "Future generations," he was prepared to anticipate, "should put all kinds of evidences and inquiries into mathematical forms . . . so as to make mathematics and logic, natural history and civil history, natural philosophy and philosophy of all other kinds, coincide *omni ex parte.*"[35] If it is possible in principle, as Hartley here suggests, to reduce even history to "mathematics and logic"—Kant, too, was to look forward to the emergence of a "Newton of history"—there were certainly the best of reasons for believing that mathematical analysis was the royal road to the understanding of human nature and human society. In a similar spirit, Condorcet, trained as a mathematician, tried to show in detail how the calculus of probabilities could be used as a way of determining not only the social laws by which human history was governed, but the wisest political policy to adopt in a given situation.[36] If the calculus of probabilities could be successfully employed in the analysis of gambling—the very paradigm of chance and uncertainty—there was no reason why it should not be employed with equal success in the analysis of political decisions.

In our own century the mathematical "theory of games" has aroused similar hopes. It has been recommended not only as a tool for understanding economic behaviour and international relations but even as a reliable method of de-

---

35. *Observations on Man,* Pt. I, ch. 3, §2, Prop. LXXXVII, in the 5th ed., Vol. 1, p. 363.
36. For fuller details see J. S. Schapiro: *Condorcet and the Rise of Liberalism,* pp. 116–18. In his *Sketch of the Progress of the Human Mind,* p. 191, Condorcet admits that such a calculus is still "in its earliest stages" but emphasizes its tremendous potentialities.

termining what moral policy it is best to adopt.[37] In the light of our own experience, it is easy to understand why the eighteenth century was so enthusiastic about the calculus of probabilities as a guide to political decision-making. As for moral decisions, Francis Hutcheson had already suggested that these could be made rational by the application of a mathematical method, a line of approach which Bentham more systematically developed in his "hedonic calculus."[38]

Let us suppose, for the sake of argument, that these hopes were well-founded, that social and moral problems can be solved by mathematical analysis. Let us suppose, in other words, that it is possible by mathematical means to determine what, in a Benthamite sense, "is the best thing to do." Two obvious gaps have still to be filled, before we can conclude that the way now lies open to the perfectibility of man. It has first to be shown that the truths thus mathematically arrived at can be communicated to the ruling powers, and secondly, that once they are thus communicated, the ruling powers will govern their actions by them.

On the first point, a striking feature of eighteenth-century thought is its belief in the possibility of designing an ideal language. In his *Essay Towards a Real Character and a Philosophical Language,* written as early as 1668, Bishop Wilkins had set out to construct such a language. Not only would it facilitate commerce, he promised in his "Epistle Dedicatory"—it would also greatly help in diffusing the knowledge of true religion "by unmasking many wild errors, that shelter themselves under the disguise of affected phrases." Leibniz went even further. "Once missionaries are able to introduce this universal language," he wrote, "then also will the true religion, which stands in intimate harmony with reason, be established, and there will

---

37. Compare, for example, R. B. Braithwaite: *Theory of Games as a Tool for the Moral Philosopher* (Cambridge, 1955).

38. For the history of this idea see Louis I. Bredvold: "The Invention of the Ethical Calculus" in R. F. Jones *et al.: The Seventeenth Century,* pp. 165–80.

be as little reason to fear any apostasy in the future as to fear a renunciation of arithmetic and geometry once they have been learnt."[39] The Enlighteners substituted "true science" for "true religion" while otherwise retaining the optimistic expectations of Wilkins and Leibniz. Science, Condillac suggested, is nothing but a well-made language; once the newly-acquired truths about human society are set out in a well-made language men's "wild errors" about human society would disappear, and there need be no fear of scientific apostasy.[40] It is only "the inexactitude of language," Condorcet similarly maintained, which makes it impossible for ordinary men to understand the great truths of science. "The perfection of scientific language, which is at present so vague and obscure" will solve, he thinks, the problem of communication.[41]

So much granted—granted, that is, that the governors will be able to understand the mathematically-derived conclusions of the scientists—a problem still remains. Suppose the moral scientist can communicate to his fellow-men, clearly and unmistakably, and in a form they cannot help understanding, a set of fundamental truths about human society and human nature. Suppose, even, he is able to demonstrate, on the basis of these truths, that a particular policy is the best policy to adopt. There is surely still the risk that men will not act as the moral scientist would advise them to act. Understanding does not necessarily bring with it agreement, and men do not always do what it is best for them to do.

---

39. "Towards a Universal Characteristic" (1677), as trans. in *Selections*, ed. P. P. Wiener, p. 25, from *Philosophische Werke*, ed. A. Buchenau and Ernst Cassirer, Vol. 1: *Hauptschriften zur Grundlegung der Philosophie* (Leipzig, 1924). For predecessors of Wilkins and Leibniz, see Jonathan Cohen: "On the Project of a Universal Character" in *Mind*, Vol. LXIII, 1954, pp. 49–63.

40. Compare Charles Frankel: *The Faith of Reason*, pp. 53–56. Condillac did not, however, approve of the attempt to set up a *universal* language. See I. F. Knight: *The Geometric Spirit* (New Haven, 1968), p. 175.

41. *Sketch of the Progress of the Human Mind*, p. 191.

At this point in the argument, the seventeenth-century secularization of the moral ideal comes to be of the first importance. So long as the doctrine prevailed that what it is best for men to do is to see God, or unite with the One, or love God with their whole heart, there is an obvious gap between knowing what it is best to do and actually doing it. That is precisely why Augustine and his successors were so convinced that men cannot possibly do what is best without the aid of God's grace. But once doing what is best is identified with being as benevolent as possible—or, in the language of utilitarianism, pursuing the greatest happiness of the greatest number—the situation is transformed.

In the first place, it is now a technical problem to determine what it is best to do; advice on how to act, it would seem, can properly come only from men who are expert in calculating consequences. Secondly, the pursuit of the greatest happiness of the greatest number is, at first sight at least, an attainable ideal, which men have no excuse for not pursuing: the new perfectibilism is to this degree Pelagian. (Although it is un-Pelagian in so far as it tends to regard bad environment and the consequential formation of bad habits as an absolute barrier to moral action, not something which a person can overcome by an act of will.) Finally, and more relevantly, whereas there is no plausibility whatever in Aquinas's view that what every man really seeks after is to "see God," there is at least a superficial plausibility in the doctrine that what he "naturally" seeks is the greatest happiness of the greatest number.

Only a superficial plausibility, to be sure. Bentham, for one, was well aware that men could be persuaded to seek the general interest only if, by the imposition of sanctions, it was made to coincide with their own interest. But there were many others who agreed with Shaftesbury and Pope that private and public interest coincide by nature, as a direct consequence of the Providential government of the world, the "guiding hand." It is always and inevitably in the individual's own interest, on this view, for him to pursue what is best for the greatest number. Once he is told what this "best" is, the conclusion was then drawn, he will at once be persuaded to act accordingly.

To a striking degree, then, the Enlighteners accepted the Socratic doctrine that vice is always a form of ignorance, that if a man once learns what it is best for him to do, he will necessarily act in that way. Even Thomas Hobbes, scarcely the most optimistic of men, expressed his conviction that if only "the moral philosophers" had made the same progress as the physical philosophers so that "the nature of human actions [were] as distinctly known" then "the strength of avarice and ambition, which is sustained by the erroneous opinions of the vulgar, as touching the nature of right and wrong, would presently faint and languish; and mankind should enjoy such an immortal peace, that . . . there would hardly be left any pretence for war."[42] Avarice and ambition, that is, are special varieties of ignorance; banish that ignorance and perpetual peace lies near at hand.

A mistaken sense of interest, Condorcet similarly suggested, is "the most common cause of actions contrary to the general welfare"; the violence of our passions is the result either of habits we have adopted "through miscalculation" or of our not knowing how to restrain them, and so in either case has its origin in ignorance. The growth of physical sciences, he pointed out, has certainly led to an improvement in technology. "Is it not also part of the necessary order of nature," he went on to ask, "that the moral and political sciences should exercise a similar influence upon the motives that direct our feelings and our actions?"[43] Diderot, to take yet another case, was convinced that "we are criminals only because we judge wrongly"; it is neither their passions nor

42. *De Cive*, ed. S. P. Lamprecht (New York, 1949), p. 3.
43. *Sketch of the Progress of the Human Mind*, p. 192.

the corruption of their will but their mistaken judgements which lead men morally astray.[44]

This line of thought reached its apotheosis in Godwin. In his perfectibilism, everything depends upon it. Not for him, Helvetius's trust in enlightened despots or Bentham's in an ideal legislator. "To dragoon men into the adoption of what we think right, is," he says, "an intolerable tyranny."[45] If men are to be perfected, then, it cannot be by legislation, backed by sanctions, but only by changing their opinions, convincing them by rational argument.

Godwin had read his Hume, as few of his contemporaries had done. He accepted Hume's argument that "reason alone can never produce any action, or give rise to volition," that reason "is, and ought only to be the slave of the passions."[46] But this did not perturb him, or alter his conviction that opinions are the source of all our volitions. For Hume had also admitted that "the moment we perceive the falsehood of any supposition, or the insufficiency of any means, our passions yield to our reason without any opposition."[47] Reason is no doubt the slave of our passions, in that reason cannot act except by means of the passions. The passions are nevertheless governed by reason in the sense that if reason shows them "things as they are"—Godwin's favourite, Stoic, phrase—then the passions are bound to pay heed to its conclusions. So it is possible to govern men's passions by changing their opinions. Their passions the reformer cannot alter; men will continue, whatever he does,

---

44. Denis Diderot: *Introduction aux grands principes*, in *Oeuvres complètes*, ed. Assézat, Vol. 2, p. 88.

45. *Enquiry Concerning Political Justice*, Bk. IV, ch. 1, ed. Priestley, Vol. 1, p. 257.

46. David Hume: *A Treatise of Human Nature*, Bk. II, Pt. III, Section III, ed. Selby-Bigge, pp. 414–15.

47. *Ibid.*, p. 416. For evidence that Godwin had, at an early date, read Hume, see B. R. Pollin: *Education and Enlightenment in the Works of William Godwin*, pp. 41–44, 58. For a substantial philosophical discussion of the points at issue see D. H. Monro: *Godwin's Moral Philosophy* (London, 1953), chs. 2, 6.

to pursue pleasure and avoid pain. But by argument, by pointing to the truth, the direction of their passions can be altered. The manner in which men act and even—what is for Godwin, as not for a pure Utilitarian, very important—the way in which they feel can be profoundly modified. They can come to love what they previously hated, and to hate what they previously loved. "I may desire," Hume had said, "any fruit as of an excellent relish; but whenever you convince me of my mistake [in believing it to taste well] my longing ceases."[48] And what is true of fruit is equally true of more fundamental objects of desire.

If we ask why men, for all their rational powers, are nevertheless imperfect, why it is that their history is, as Godwin freely admits, "little else than a record of crimes,"[49] the answer, according to Godwin, is quite simple: the opinions which now govern their voluntary actions are mere prejudices, deliberately fostered, as often as not, by "sinister forces," especially by Church and State. The philosopher can rid men of these prejudices if only he is free to argue with them; if his arguments sometimes fail this must be because they are not sufficiently "laborious, patient and clear." That is Godwin's ground for believing that men are perfectible; their "vices and moral weakness" can always be dispelled by reason and replaced by "nobler and more beneficent principles in their stead." So, he felt free to conclude, "every perfection or excellence that human beings are competent to conceive, human beings, unless in cases that are palpably and unequivocally excluded by the structure of their frame, are competent to attain."[50] Granted, then, that science, our knowledge of "things as they really are," was bound indefinitely to improve, it immediately followed that men's "vices" and "moral weakness" would gradually be

---

48. Hume: *A Treatise of Human Nature*, Bk. II, Pt. III, Section III, *ed. cit.*, pp. 416–17.
49. *Enquiry Concerning Political Justice*, Bk. I, ch. 2; ed. Priestley, Vol. 1, p. 6.
50. *Ibid.*, Bk. I, ch. 5; *ed. cit.*, Vol. 1, pp. 88–93.

dispelled—unless "sinister forces," "vested interests," succeeded in placing a barrier between the Enlighteners and the to-be-enlightened.

These hopes for science persisted into the nineteenth century. In Thomas Love Peacock's novel *Headlong Hall*, first published in 1816, the perfectibilist, Mr Foster, has no hesitation in asserting that "men are virtuous in proportion as they are enlightened and that, as every generation increases in knowledge, it also increases in virtue."[51] This is the source of nineteenth-century Utopianism. For if in order to improve themselves men only need to know what is best, then Utopias have a practical utility: show men what it is best for them to do, appeal to their reason, and nothing more is necessary in order to perfect them. Or nothing except to persuade "vested interests" not to interfere.

Robert Owen's *The Book of the New Moral World* is in this respect typical. It bears the subtitle "containing the rational system of society, founded on demonstrable facts, developing the constitution and laws of human nature and of society," and was addressed to William IV, King of England. Owen's perfectibilist claims were unrestrained: his book "opens to the family of man," he says, "without a single exception, the means of endless progressive improvement, physical, intellectual, and moral, and of happiness, without the possibility of retrogression or of assignable limit." Human society so far, according to Owen, had rested on "fundamental errors of the imagination"; that explained why it was so corrupt. But from now on things were going to be very different: "Under your reign, Sire, the change from this [corrupt] system, . . . to another founded on self-evident truths, ensuring happiness to all, will, in all probability, be achieved." The time was ripe; as a consequence of their experience of the Napoleonic Wars men could not but see that a new kind of society must be established. William

51. Ch. IV; in the one-volume collected ed. by David Garnett (London, 1948), p. 25.

the Fourth, with the British Empire behind him, had the power to act. What he had to do was to institute an alliance with only two clauses: "The first, That the contracting parties shall abandon, by the most public declaration, the fundamental error on which society has hitherto been based: and second, That they shall adopt the opposite truth for the base of all their future measures."[52] Let not William the Fourth imagine that he can side-step his responsibilities. "The progress of knowledge," according to Owen, "now renders this revolution, in the general condition and character of mankind, so irresistible, that no earthly power can prevent, or much retard its course."[53] The only real question is whether it was to be brought about by William the Fourth or by violence.

If we now ask what are the truths, at last discovered, which are so momentous to mankind, it turns out that there are some twenty-five of them. But they can be summed up thus: all men are made what they are by their characters and their circumstances. The great error which "the allied powers" had to forswear is the belief that man has free will; the great truth is that his "feelings, thoughts, will and actions are predetermined for him by the influence of external circumstances acting upon his original constitution." To those who maintain that the belief in free will is the foundation of morality, Owen replies that it is only necessary to look around to see what dire consequences that belief has had for the world; we need have no doubt that the universal acceptance of the opposite belief, emphasizing the fundamental importance of education, will enable men to train their descendants "to be . . . a race of superior beings physically, intellectually and morally."[54]

Owen was by no means a mere visionary. He was a busi-

52. Quotations from R. Owen: *The Book of the New Moral World,* pp. iv–vii.
53. *Ibid.,* p. xi.
54. *Ibid.,* pp. 20, 24.

ness man of considerable practical competence, whose model community at New Lanark was, for once in the history of such communities, a financial success. His belief in the power of knowledge to bring about moral change is not the dream of an intellectual, hungry for power. It is a testimony, rather, to the fact that able, practical men could think it self-evident that by a simple alteration in men's beliefs a new world could be brought into being. Let men once see that everything depends on education, and they would immediately introduce the best possible education and could thus perfect men and their society.

The nineteenth-century Utilitarians were not prepared to allow as much as Godwin had allowed to the passions. Describing his own youthful attitude, J. S. Mill tells us he was hostile to any praise of, or favourable reference to, feeling. He was a thoroughgoing Utilitarian who, quite unlike Godwin, regarded only actions as worthy of praise or blame; feelings, or any sort of motive, were morally irrelevant.[55] It was the opponents of the Utilitarians who appealed to feelings, denouncing utilitarianism as "cold" or "hard-hearted." The Utilitarians, for their part, condemned any reference to feelings as "sentimentality." "What we principally thought of," Mill writes, "was to alter people's opinions; to make them believe according to evidence, and know what was their real interest, which when they once knew, they would, we thought, by the instrument of opinion, enforce a regard to it upon one another." By altering men's opinions mid-Victorian Utilitarians sought to secure "the regeneration of mankind."[56] Mill himself, attracted by the "developmental" theories of progress to which he was introduced by Saint-Simon and Comte, moved somewhat away from this absolute reliance on the power of opinion. But it by no means entirely ceased to influence him, or his contemporaries.

55. J. S. Mill: *Autobiography, ed. cit.,* ch. II, pp. 48–49.
56. *Ibid.,* p. 111.

There gradually developed, then, in the eighteenth century a chain of inference which ran thus: Man had until that time been a mere child in respect of knowledge and, in consequence, of virtue; he was now at last in a position, as a result of the development of science, to determine how human nature develops and what is the best thing for human beings to do; this new knowledge could be expressed in a form in which all men would find it intelligible; once they knew what it is best to do, men would act accordingly and so would constantly improve their moral, political and physical condition. Provided only, then, that "sinister interests" did not prevent the communication of knowledge, the development of science was bound to carry with it the constant improvement of the human condition, to a degree which would be, like the growth of science itself, unlimited.

Similar views are still with us. It is not uncommonly presumed that what is wrong with the world is that, as it is put, "the social sciences have failed to keep step with the progress of the physical sciences." Elton Mayo's comment is typical of a thousand others: "If," he writes, "our social skills had advanced step by step with our technical skills, there would not have been another European war."[57] Often enough, indeed, the exponents of such a view express it more naïvely than Godwin ever did. Godwin certainly believed that once men came "to see things as they are" they would act in such a manner as to increase the happiness of their fellow-men. But no one could be more conscious than he was of the force of prejudice and the degree to which it is fostered by social institutions like the State and the Church. He was more than prepared to concede that men are for the most part swayed by sentiment and governed by habit rather than directed by rational opinion. Were they to see "how empty are the claims of birth and privilege," they would

57. Elton Mayo: *The Social Problems of an Industrial Civilization* (Cambridge, Mass., 1945; London, 1949), p. 21.

assuredly demand their overthrow; of that much Godwin was confident. But he was not at all optimistic that vested interests would ever permit men to attain to such clarity of vision. Something more is needed, then, some additional argument, if we are to have good grounds for believing that humanity will in fact be perfected—as distinct from being, in principle, perfectible.

Sometimes that "something more" was derived from Biblical prophecies. There was, for example, that prophecy of Isaiah which looks forward to a time when, under the guidance of Providence, men "shall beat their swords into ploughshares, and their spears into pruninghooks: nation shall not lift up sword against nation, neither shall they learn war any more."[58] And then there were the darker prophecies of the apocalyptic books, and especially the Book of Daniel, with the help of which men sought to predict the stages by which "the whole creation moves" towards what Tennyson called that "one far-off divine event." It is often supposed that speculation about the future, based on Biblical prophecy, attracted only the credulous monk or the no less credulous Protestant sectary. But in the seventeenth and eighteenth centuries this was far from being the case. The Cambridge Platonist, Ralph Cudworth, wrote a *Commentary on the Seventy Weeks of Daniel* which his fellow-Platonist Henry More described as "of as much price and worth in theology as either the circulation of the blood in physic, or the motion of the earth in natural philosophy."[59] Newton devoted much of his life to the interpretation of prophecies. In that section of the *Observations on Man* in which Hartley described the calculus of probabilities and the differential calculus, he set alongside these meth-

58. Isaiah 2:4.

59. Henry More: *Explanation of the Grand Mystery of Godliness*, Preface, as quoted by T. Birch in R. Cudworth: *The True Intellectual System of the Universe*, 2nd ed. (London, 1743; repr. 1820), I, Preface, xiii.

ods, as of equal worth, the methods of prophetic interpretation introduced by Joseph Mede, teacher of Cudworth and Henry More.*

The most interesting example of the way in which secular and prophetic arguments for progress were combined is to be found in the writings of Joseph Priestley, often described as the founder of modern perfectibilism. About his confidence in the future, certainly, there can be no doubt. "Whatever was the beginning of this world," he once wrote, "the end will be glorious and paradisaical, beyond what our imaginations can now conceive."[60] If we ask, however, on what evidence he based these optimistic forecasts, no simple answer can be given.

In the first place, Priestley enthusiastically accepted Hartley's associationism, as a mechanism for perfecting. In principle, then, men could be perfected by education. Secondly, he saw in the history of science an exemplification of what in the preface to his *The History and Present State of Electricity* he called "a perpetual progress and improvement," which could be expected to continue, he thought, to heights which are "really boundless and sublime." The growth of science was a living demonstration that progress was not only possible, but actual. Thirdly, such secular changes as the French and the American Revolutions, and more generally the rise of commerce, increased Priestley's confidence

---

* The apocalyptic books of the Bible had been very important to Luther and his Protestant successors; Luther identified the Pope with Antichrist and sought to explain by means of the Revelation of St. John the Divine why God's Church had for so long been ruled by anti-Christ. The Cambridge Platonists, characteristically, looked at the Book of Revelation in an optimistic spirit, as promising a millennium which, in Milton's words, "shall put an end to all earthly tyrannies, proclaiming thy [Christ's] universal and mild monarchy through Heaven and Earth." For the relation of these millennial views to the theory of progress see E. L. Tuveson: *Millennium and Utopia* (Berkeley, 1949; Harper Torchbook ed., 1964). The quotation from Milton is on p. 92.

60. *An Essay on the First Principles of Government,* 2nd ed. (London, 1771), Section 1, pp. 1–10, excerpted in *Priestley's Writings,* ed. Passmore, p. 198. See also the passage from Priestley's *Letters to the Right Honourable Edmund Burke,* 3rd ed. (London, 1791), pp. 143–55, there excerpted, pp. 251–58.

that governments everywhere would gradually be liberalized. Fourthly, he believed that if once vested interests, as a result of these political developments, lost their force, truth was bound to prevail. But finally and in the last resort, his expectations for the future were based on his belief in the providential government of the world, and on the prophecies of Scripture.

A time *must* come, he was convinced, when "the common parent of mankind will cause wars to cease to the ends of the earth, when men shall beat their swords into ploughshares."[61] He had to confess that when he looked at human history, as distinct from the history of science, he found it difficult to extract from that history any support for his belief in the inevitability of progress. But if ever his belief in progress faltered, he had only to remember God's promises to men: it is Providence who perfects man through associative mechanisms, Providence who gives its energy to science, Providence who is gradually perfecting human society by advancing trade and commerce, Providence who will ensure, in his own good time, the destruction of vested interests.* If then we ask, "Who shall perfect the perfecter?" Priestley's answer is—"Providence." Not God the grace-infuser working directly on the soul of the

---

61. *Letters to Edmund Burke*, p. 148, as excerpted in *Priestley's Writings*, p. 255.

* This use of the word "Providence" as a synonym for "God" dates back, according to the *Oxford Dictionary*, only to 1602. Before that time it was no doubt possible to speak of "God's providence," meaning by that his providential care, but not to use "Providence" as a kind of personal noun. Written into this novel use is the conception of a God whose whole concern it is to care for the felicity of mankind; "providential care" is no longer, that is, only one of God's activities but the function which constitutes, if we can put the matter thus, his whole reason for existing. God is that which so governs the total scheme of things as to ensure that it will serve men's—which are also God's— interests. And God's objective is not, primarily, to redeem men, to forgive them, or to mete out justice to them but to secure their final felicity, their ultimate perfection. He is, in short, a most un-Augustinian God. For a general survey of the role of Providence in eighteenth-century thought, see Norman Hampson: *The Enlightenment*, The Pelican History of European Thought, 4 (Harmondsworth, 1968), Pt. I, chs. 2–4. See also Basil Willey: *The Eighteenth-Century Background: passim,* and compare pp. 53–55 below.

individual believer, but God as Providence working through associative mechanisms, through science, through revolutions.

God—as Hartley had also maintained—will perfect not only human society but each and every individual man. Hartley and Priestley share Origen's belief, generally accounted heretical, that in the end all men, however sinful, will be saved.[62] Origen's views had been revived in the seventeenth century by the Cambridge Platonists.[63] They incorporate a concept of God which accords with the new moral temper of the age: God is beneficence, universal benevolence, or in Shaftesbury's words "the best-natured Being in the world." That is why he must finally save all men, and produce on earth a better world for them to live in. As Godwin was to define him, God is "abounding in benevolence, without the slightest cloud of frustration or passion . . . forever active and seeking at all times and in every direction for opportunities of doing good."[64] No other God, and certainly not the Calvinist God, could satisfy Priestley's and Hartley's and Godwin's moral demands. If he worked rather slowly to achieve his ends, this was because men had first to be disciplined, to be educated, so as to be worthy of perfection. The apparent evils in human history were, for Hartley and Priestley, part of that education. But, in saying so much, Hartley and Priestley were feeling their way towards a theory of progress as "natural development," not as a mere consequence of the growth of knowledge, but as inherent in

---

62. See Origen: *De Principiis*, Bk. III. vi. 5, as trans. G. W. Butterworth, pp. 250–51, together with Butterworth's note 3, p. 250 and note 1, p. 251. For the subsequent history of Origen's doctrine see C. A. Patrides: "The Salvation of Satan" in *Journal of the History of Ideas*, XXVIII, 1967, pp. 467–78.

63. See especially George Rust (?): *A Letter of Pleasant Resolution Concerning Origen*, anonymously publ. in 1661. For a discussion of its authorship see D. P. Walker: *The Decline of Hell* (London, 1964), pp. 125–26.

64. William Godwin: *Essays Never Before Published* (London, 1873), p. 248, as quoted in B. R. Pollin: *Education and Enlightenment in the Works of William Godwin*, p. 48.

the very nature of the Universe. Will this fill the gap between the doctrine that man is, in principle, perfectible and the promise that he can look forward, in fact, to the constant improvement of his moral character, his degree of happiness, and his social relationships?

ELEVEN

PROGRESS BY NATURAL DEVELOPMENT: FROM JOACHIM TO MARX

Of those many Christians, of varying degrees of heterodoxy, who have sought to make use of Biblical prophecies in order to predict the future course of human history, one was of exceptional importance: the twelfth-century monk Joachim of Flora. "The knowledge of things past," he wrote, "is the key of things to come."[1] Only if they can find such a key can men be sure that in the long run they are bound to be perfected, by the mere onward flow of history.

Although, in an age much given to numerology, the advent of the year A.D. 1000 had for a time revived men's hopes that Christ's advent was near, by the end of the twelfth century most Christians had ceased to believe that the Second Coming of Christ was imminent. Reading the prophetic books and the Gospel according to John, Joachim came to the conclusion that what was properly to be expected was not, immediately at least, the Second Coming of Christ but rather the Third Coming of God, the Coming of the Holy Ghost, sent by Christ just as the Father had sent Christ. The history of mankind, as Joachim saw it, falls into three main stages, each corresponding to a particular person of the Trinity.[2] The Age of the Father was the kingdom of law; the Age of the Son was the kingdom of grace. Still to come — one of Joachim's disciples, Gerard of Borgo, set the date more

1. Joachim of Flora: Expositio in Apocalipsim (1527), f. 3, cited by E. G. Gardner: "Joachim of Flora and the Everlasting Gospel" in Paul Sabatier et al.: Franciscan Essays, p. 58.

2. For further details see, apart from Gardner, F. E. Manuel: Shapes of Philosophical History (Stanford, 1965), pp. 35–45; Ernst Benz: Evolution and Christian Hope, trans. H. G. Frank (New York, 1966; reissued as Anchor Book, 1968), ch. III, pp. 35–48; and especially Gordon Leff: Heresy in the Later Middle Ages, Vol. 1, pp. 68–83.

precisely, as A.D. 1260—was the age of the Holy Ghost, the kingdom of grace abounding.

In the first two ages, so Joachim tells us, men have lived in servitude. In the kingdom of the Father they lived as slaves to the law, in the kingdom of the Son with "the servitude of sons." Now the time has come at which they are to be freed, enabled to confront God, not in fear, as in the reign of the Father, not with faith, as in the age of the Son, but with love, as "friends to God." The Church, Joachim was confident, would be reformed under the influence of a new élite, the spiritual monks—a role the Franciscans were only too willing to assume; the Bible would at last be fully comprehended, its symbols would be made plain and its message would conquer the world. Men would be granted spiritual understanding, perfection in holiness, and could thereby achieve, here on earth, the condition of angelic spirits.

The importance of Joachim's vision was that it encouraged men to anticipate the arrival of a long period of secular history, based on freedom and love, rather than a Last Judgement. Before Joachim, of course, there had been, as there still are, millennarians, convinced that Christ would come again and that after his advent the spiritual élite of all ages would be resurrected to rule with Christ over an earthly paradise. It was a novel view, however, that mankind *as a whole* was progressing towards a form of human society which would realize its ethical ideals.

More important still, there is an internal logic in the teachings of Joachim, a suggestion of dynamic processes inherent in human history itself, which is conspicuously absent in his predecessors. It is not just that, as for the millennarians, there is to be another Coming: the society which will succeed that Coming is already in gestation. "If Almighty God," Joachim writes, "wants to terminate the old to create the new, he allows persecution to arise within the Church. Then he abandons what he wants to terminate and protects that which he wants to live on. Thus we can say that the new and the good, which were hidden in the dark, can be brought to light when the opportunity arises."[3] Joachim tried to show in detail how one age prepares the way for another, not only by its virtues but, even more, by its defects. The corruption of the Church, for example, its lack of evangelical zeal, its avarice, were, on Joachim's interpretation of history, essential prerequisites for the appearance of a new, more spiritual age; they could not have been avoided, if God's plan was to be fulfilled. Only through struggle between the old and the new could the pattern of history be unfolded.

It is not surprising, then, that philosophers so different from one another and from Joachim as Lessing in the eighteenth century and Schelling and Comte in the nineteenth century have paid homage to Joachim as their predecessor. Lessing's three Revelations; Schelling's Ages of Fate, of Nature, of Providence; Comte's three stages of history—the religious stage, the metaphysical stage, the positive stage; Hitler's first, second and third Reich, all echo the Joachist tripartition of history.[4] Although Joachim himself, of course, took it for granted that the whole historical process was both God-governed and prophesied in Revelation, he at the same time left the way open for philosophies of history which, like Comte's, were devoid of all reference to God or to Revelation. For the historical investigation of a particular age, if Joachim was right, could detect in that age the seeds of the future, and the processes by which those seeds would spring to life.

The history of the Joachist movement foreshadowed problems which were to loom large in subsequent philoso-

---

3. Joachim of Flora: *Tractatus super quatuor evangelia*, publ. by E. Buonaiuti in *Fonti per la storia d'Italia, Scrittori sec. XII* (Rome, 1930), p. 43, 3 ff., as trans. in Benz: *Evolution and Christian Hope*, p. 47.

4. See Karl Löwith: *Meaning in History* (Chicago, 1949), Appendix I: "Modern Transfigurations of Joachim," pp. 208–13.

phies of history, controversies about the practical implications of historical prophecies. To Peter John Olivi, one of
Joachim's most ardent disciples, the situation was perfectly
clear: Joachim had shown what *must* happen; men should
now sit and wait until God chose to act in whatever way best
suited his plans. "The revivification of the spirit of Christ
and the reformation of the evangelical state," he wrote, "is
not a human matter; nor can it or should it be done by man,
but only by Christ."[5]

More revolutionary-minded Joachists, in contrast, saw in
Joachim's prophecies a blueprint for action. Indeed, it was
not long before Joachim's own writings came to be regarded
as a Third Revelation, thus adding yet another to the triune
antitheses of which Joachim was so fond: a Third Testament
for the Third Age. The Joachist Anabaptist, Thomas Münzer, was not the sort of man to sit back and wait, in humility,
for God's plan to be unfolded. The new age was at hand;
he was convinced that God meant him to help it along, not
merely, as Joachim had done, to preach the joys to come.
For God's reign to be initiated, the existing authorities had
first to be exterminated: that was God's order. In a letter of
May 12, 1525, addressed to Count Ernst von Mansfeld, Münzer informed the Count, his sovereign ruler, that God had
ordered the Anabaptists to remove him from the throne.
"For you are useless to Christendom. You are a pernicious
scourge of the friends of God."[6]

In the practical interpretation of Joachist teaching, then,
a new set of problems broke out, provoking controversies
which were more than reminiscent of the old Pelagian-

---

5. Quoted in Leff: *Heresy in the Later Middle Ages*, Vol. 1, p. 138 from L. Oliger, ed.:
"Petri Iohannis Olivi, De renuntiatione papae Coelestini V" in *Archivum Franciscanum His-
toricum*, 11 (1918), p. 370.

6. The whole letter, and comparable letters, can be read in Benz: *Evolution and Christian Hope*, p. 61. For Marxist accounts of Münzer see F. Engels: *The Peasant War in Germany*,
trans. M. J. Olgin (London, 1927), ch. II and Karl Kautsky: *Communism in Central Europe
in the Time of the Reformation*, trans. J. L. and E. G. Mulliken (London, 1897), pp. 106–54.

Augustinian debate. The question now in dispute is to what extent men, by deliberate effort, can affect the course of history. If the new age *must* begin in A.D. 1260, then, on the face of it, they have little or no capacity to do so. Whatever they do the date is fixed and unalterable. One might call this the "purely evolutionary" view. And it carries with it the risk, of which Pelagius was so conscious, that men will then do nothing to improve themselves, sitting back to wait for that new age which must, independently of their actions, set them on the path to perfection.

On a purely revolutionary, purely Pelagian, interpretation—which will have to abandon the idea of a fixed date, as it had to be abandoned, in any case, once the magic year had passed—Joachim had done no more than indicate the kind of perfect kingdom which men could, if they tried hard enough, construct by their own efforts. But on such an interpretation, there is no longer any guarantee that the third kingdom will in fact come about. It functions as a Utopia, as a reminder to men of what they might become; it serves as an inspiration to their efforts. But it is the success or failure of those efforts, whose success is by no means preordained, which alone can determine whether Utopia will be realized. (Just as the Pelagian, so Luther complained, has no guarantee that his efforts to secure salvation will be successful: at any point he may slip into sin and be damned.)

Or, finally, it might be argued that although in the long run God guarantees that the perfect kingdom will come about, this will only be as a result of human efforts which, by the degree of their energy, are able to advance or retard the beginning of the new age—an interpretation which corresponds, very roughly, to a theory of "co-operative" grace. The revolutionary, on this view, fights with God on his side but can aid or hinder God's plans. So, in the nineteenth century the anarchist P. J. Proudhon was to argue that even though "a revolution is a force against which no power, divine or human, can prevail" it may yet be "directed, moderated, delayed."[7] This, for obvious reasons, has been the most widely held of the three views, just as within Christianity the most widely-held view has been one which tries to incorporate free will and predestination into a single system of thought. But its difficulties are manifest.

Joachim's modern admirers, whatever view they took on this particular issue, were not prepared to found on Revelation their belief that history was the gradual unfolding of a divine plan. For the most part, they looked elsewhere for "the key to history," to metaphysics rather than to Revelation, and more specifically to a developmental metaphysics, based on the presumption that every potentiality must eventually be actualized. Such a metaphysics was first sketched by Leibniz.

Since every created thing must eventually actualize the perfections it potentially contains, it follows, according to Leibniz, that the universe as a whole must display a "perpetual and very free progress . . . such that it advances always to still greater improvement," as one thing after another attains to its individual perfection.[8] This does not imply, however, that the Universe will ever reach a static condition of absolute perfection. The Universe is infinitely complex; there is therefore no question of its ever realizing all its potentialities. Fresh perfections will always remain to be unfolded. And so, Leibniz concludes, progress will never come to an end. Men can look forward not only to a human history which constantly increases in perfection but, more than that, to a constantly perfected Universe. The progressive perfection of man, indeed, is a consequence of the progressive perfection of the Universe.

There are problems, on which we have already touched,

---

7. *General Idea of the Revolution in the Nineteenth Century,* trans. Robinson, p. 15. Proudhon fluctuated, cf. p. 184 above.

8. *De rerum originatione radicali* (1697) in *Die philosophischen Schriften von G. W. Leibniz,* hrsg. C. I. Gerhardt, 7 vols (Berlin, 1875–90), Vol. VII, pp. 302–8, as trans. in *Leibniz: Selections,* ed. Wiener, p. 354.

in understanding the Leibnizian view, problems which turn around his use of the word "perfection." On the face of it, all Leibniz is saying is that every potentiality must at some time be actualized; granted this extremely large assumption, these potentialities might turn out to be, one would think, potentialities for evil as much as for good. Perhaps, even, the potentialities which have still to be unfolded are all of them potentialities for evil. Unless Leibniz's view is coupled with another, even less plausible doctrine, viz. that evil is never "actual" but only the failure of a potentiality fully to be realized, it does not supply men with any real ground for optimism about their future.[9] But this crucial point was almost universally overlooked. Indeed, for a time, the "dynamic" side of Leibniz's philosophy exerted no influence—it must be remembered that much of Leibniz's work remained for long unpublished. The emphasis, at the hands of such system-ridden Leibnizians as Wolff, was on the other, static, side of Leibniz's teaching. Individuals, on this view, might progress, but the system of the Universe as a whole was fixed, in a way which necessitated the continued existence of evils. So Moses Mendelssohn, popularizing Wolff's ideas, laid it down that progress is open only to the individual. "That all mankind should always progress with the passage of time and perfect itself," he wrote, "this does not seem to me to have been the purpose of Providence."[10] Thus the standard Christian view was reinforced, in the name of a Leibnizian-style philosophy.

In his brief, but historically pregnant, *Idea of a Universal History from a Cosmopolitical Point of View*[11] Kant took over and developed the Leibnizian view that, in Kant's words, "all the

9. Compare Bertrand Russell: *A Critical Exposition of the Philosophy of Leibniz*, ed. cit., pp. 198–201.

10. Moses Mendelssohn: *Jerusalem*, quoted in Ernst Cassirer: *The Philosophy of the Enlightenment*, trans. F. C. A. Koelln and J. P. Pettegrove (Princeton, 1951), p. 195.

11. Kant: *Idee zu einer allgemeinen Geschichte in weltbürgerlicher Absicht*, in *Kant's gesammelte Schriften*, hrsg. v.d.K. Preuss. Akad. d. Wiss., 1 Abt.: Werke, Bd. VIII (Berlin, 1923); trans. in *Kant's Principles of Politics*, ed. and trans. W. Hastie (Edinburgh, 1891), pp. 1–29.

capacities implanted in a creature by nature, are destined to unfold themselves, completely and conformably to their end, in the course of time."[12] He felt the need, as Leibniz did not, of supporting this metaphysical presupposition by independent evidence. Leibniz, like so many of his predecessors, took for granted what Lovejoy has called "the principle of plenitude," i.e. the principle that whatever *can* exist must somewhere *actually* exist, since otherwise the potential creativity of God would not be fully realized.[13] In his first major publication— *The General History of Nature*—Kant had unreservedly accepted the principle of plenitude. "It would be absurd," he there wrote, "to represent the Deity as bringing into action only an infinitely small part of his creative potency."[14] But after the destructive endeavours of his *Critique of Pure Reason,* Kant could no longer enunciate such metaphysical principles with the same confidence. In his *Idea of a Universal History* Kant relies on arguments of a different sort, partly empirical, partly moral.

First, an argument from science: anatomy teaches us, Kant says, that there is a "contradiction" in the very idea of "an organ which is not to be used, or an arrangement which does not attain its end." If that argument does not satisfy us—our minds turn, perhaps, to the human appendix— Kant has another at his disposal. To reject the idea of inevitable progress is to be forced back, he says, on the "cheerless gloom of chance" as opposed to the idea of a nature governed by law.[15] If we still hesitate, doubting whether the "cheerfulness" of a doctrine is a good reason for accepting it, Kant appeals, in his more characteristic fashion, to our sense of duty: it is morally necessary, he says, that we should

12. *Idea of a Universal History,* First Proposition.
13. A. O. Lovejoy: *The Great Chain of Being,* p. 52.
14. Kant: *Allgemeine Naturgeschichte und Theorie des Himmels* (1755), Pt. II, ch. VII, as trans. in A. O. Lovejoy: *op. cit.,* p. 140. For the German text see *Kant's gesammelte Schriften,* ed. cit., Bd. I (Berlin, 1910), pp. 221–368. The only complete Eng. trans. is in *Kant's Cosmogony,* by W. Hastie (Glasgow, 1900).
15. *Idea of a Universal History,* First Proposition, as trans. Hastie, pp. 5–6.

believe in the perfectibility of human society, since to believe otherwise would weaken our moral efforts. The perfectibility of society is a "regulative idea" which must govern our conduct.

An obvious objection springs to mind. If all capacities are destined to unfold themselves, then the reason of every individual man must perfect itself; otherwise it does not "achieve its end." And this is clearly not the case. Men die, prematurely, or their minds are affected by disease, or they never meet with the circumstances in which their potentialities could unfold. To understand how every perfection can, in the end, be achieved, we have to concentrate our attention, Kant replies, not on the development of individual men, but on the development of mankind—of man as a species. We have to suppose that although each man must do what he can to perfect himself, this is only as a means to the perfection of mankind. "It is to be the happy fate of only the latest generations," Kant says, "to dwell in the building upon which the long series of their forefathers have laboured, without so much as intending it and yet with no possibility of participating in the happiness which they were preparing." [16] Christian millennarians had avoided this conclusion—why should later generations have all the luck?—by supposing that the élite would be resurrected to share in the rule of Christ on Earth. Kant held out no such expectation; individual men must, on his view, content themselves with the reflection that mankind, although not they themselves as individuals, will be perfected as a result of their efforts. For it is their moral duty thus to content themselves.

It is one of the most important features of Kant's essay that, like Pomponazzi, he thus shifts the emphasis from the perfectibility of the individual to the perfectibility of the human species. Scarcely less historically important is his suggestion that the outcome of men's struggles will be a per-

---

16. *Ibid.*, Third Proposition, as trans. Hastie, p. 9.

fect State. "The highest purpose of Nature will be at last realized," he writes of his ideal future, "in the establishment of a universal Cosmopolitical Institution, in the bosom of which all the original capacities and endowments of the human species will be unfolded."[17] The perfect "cosmopolitical" state, furthermore, will be a member of a Federation of States, a League of Nations.* For only within such a League can men achieve that "perpetual peace" which, to Kant, is an essential prerequisite of human perfection.[18]

Kant suggested, too, a particular mechanism of social change. "The means which Nature employs to bring about the development of all the capacities implanted in men," he writes, "is their mutual antagonism in society, but only so far as this antagonism becomes at length the cause of an order among them that is regulated by law."[19] With the help of this Joachim-like doctrine Kant hoped to solve a problem which is of central importance to him: to reconcile Christian pessimism about the nature of man with Enlightenment optimism about man's future. Although he rejected the orthodox Christian doctrine of original sin—describing it, indeed, as "the most inept" of all explanations of human evil—Kant is nevertheless at one with orthodoxy in maintaining that man's nature contains a "radical evil" which reveals itself as soon as men are capable of willing.† Man is not

17. *Ibid.*, Eighth Proposition, as trans. Hastie, pp. 24–25.

* As early as 1713 the Abbé de Saint-Pierre had published his *Projet pour rendre la paix perpétuelle en Europe* (3 vols, Utrecht, 1713–17) in which he set out a detailed plan for a league of European nations. Saint-Pierre was a typical product of the early Enlightenment: the inventor, so it is said, of the word *bienfaisance* and a perfervid exponent of the idea of progress. It was customary to laugh at Saint-Pierre as a visionary. But Kant respected his earnestness and his idealism and was extremely sympathetic towards his pacifist ideals.

18. *Ibid.*, Seventh Proposition. See also Kant's *Zum ewigen Frieden* (1795), trans. as *Perpetual Peace* by L. W. Beck in Kant's *Critique of Practical Reason and Other Writings in Moral Philosophy* (Chicago, 1949). For the German text see *Kant's gesammelte Schriften, ed. cit.,* Bd. VIII, pp. 343–86.

19. *Idea of a Universal History,* Fourth Proposition, as trans. Hastie, pp. 9–10.

† There is a tendency to think of Kant as a somewhat dry and humourless man. That view can certainly not survive, to mention only one example, the delicious footnote in

born naturally good, or naturally innocent. Nor is it true to say, with the Stoics, that although he has propensities which will lead him astray if they are not controlled by reason, reason can entirely conquer them. Evil, at least in the form of frailty and impurity, lies deep in the heart of human nature. This conclusion might well have led Kant, as it led so many of his predecessors, to deny that man is capable of making moral or social progress, except perhaps for short periods of time. Moses Mendelssohn had suggested that "the human race . . . has never taken a few steps forwards without soon sliding back with double rapidity to its former state."[20] But Kant was too deeply attached to the aspirations of the Enlightenment to take that view.

So what Kant rather argues is that the evil in man's nature is precisely what leads him along the path towards social improvement. "Thanks be then to Nature," he writes, "for this [man's] unsociableness, for this envious jealousy and vanity, for this insatiable desire of possession, or even of power!" Were it not for them, so Kant suggests, "all the excellent capacities implanted in mankind by nature, would slumber eternally undeveloped"—man would be content to live the life of an Arcadian shepherd.[21] It is only because men's spirit of emulation arouses them from their natural desire for a peaceful life that they are led into the politi-

---

which Kant ironically describes the traditional interpretations of "original sin." Kant's own view is that if any of us had been Adam we would have behaved as Adam behaved, and in our everyday life we make that fact apparent. "Original sin" is nothing more than the "frailty" of human nature, which prevents us from willing *what* we should will, and its impurity, which prevents us from willing *as* we should will, an impurity which leads us to act out of inclination rather than out of respect for law. To say that man has a "radical evil" in his nature is just to draw attention to these defects in his will. See on this point Kant's *Die Religion innerhalb der Grenzen der blossen Vernunft* (1792–93), Bk. I, Observations III and IV, trans. as *Religion within the Limits of Reason Alone*, by T. M. Greene and H. H. Hudson, rev. ed. (New York, 1960), pp. 27–39.

20. Moses Mendelssohn: *Jerusalem*, II. 44–47, quoted by Kant in *On the Saying, That a Thing May Be Right in Theory, but Will Not Hold in Practice* (1793), Section III, partly trans. by W. Hastie in *Kant's Principles of Politics*, pp. 65–76. The complete German text may be found in *Kant's gesammelte Schriften, ed. cit.*, Bd. VIII, pp. 275–313.

21. *Idea of a Universal History*, Fourth Proposition, as trans. Hastie, p. 11.

cal struggles which give rise to strong national States—the essential prerequisite, on Kant's view, for human progress. "One purpose," Kant writes in his *Perpetual Peace*, "shines manifestly through all her [Nature's] mechanical order: to use the discord of men for producing concord among them against their own will."[22] Men's struggles, their conflicts, not their peace-loving nature, are what keep them bent on progress, and especially on progress towards that "perpetual peace" so dear to Kant's heart. And their commercial instincts carry them in the same direction: the love of money, in itself deplorable, leads men inevitably to "honorable peace."[23] Mandeville's "private vices, public benefits" found in Kant an historical application, foreshadowing that Fichtean dialectic which Hegel and Marx were to turn to their own purposes.

Kant's doctrine of man, however, confronts him in a particularly acute form with a familiar problem. If it is a necessary condition of man's progress that he be controlled by a good ruler, where is that ruler to come from, given that all men have in their nature a radical evil? "The highest authority," Kant writes, "has to be just in itself, and yet to be a man. This problem is, therefore, the most difficult of its kind; and, indeed, its perfect solution is impossible. Out of such crooked material as man is made of, nothing can be hammered quite straight."[24] Yet Kant is not prepared to conclude that the road to perfection must therefore be closed. He admits no more than this: that the choice of a legislator will be the last problem to be solved, since it needs for its solution great experience and much good will. This solution is by no means satisfactory; to depend on man's good will is, in the light of Kant's theory of human nature, to display an optimism there is no way of justifying.

22. *Perpetual Peace*, Second Section, First Supplement. At this point I follow the trans. in Gabriele Rabel: *Kant* (Oxford, 1963), p. 275.

23. *Ibid.*, as trans. Beck, p. 329.

24. *Idea of a Universal History*, Sixth Proposition, as trans. Hastie, pp. 14–15.

It is not surprising, then, that when Kant had directly to confront Mendelssohn's denial that humanity makes progress, he fell back on his moral-pragmatic argument. He does not have to prove, Kant says, that man is actually progressing: he can take his stand on man's "innate sense of duty."[25] However strongly the argument from history may seem to bear against his hopes, Kant continues, it does not *demonstrate* that, as Mendelssohn had contended, man's progress can never be more than temporary. And so long as Mendelssohn's conclusion cannot be demonstrated, men have a duty, Kant says, to believe that they can act now to improve mankind's future. Kant did not admit that, in fact, mankind has made no progress; human progress, he confidently asserts, has been real, although limited and uneven. He has recourse, too, to the theological argument that unless men can some day advance beyond their present state it is impossible to "justify creation" for putting such a race of creatures in the world.[26] But the moral-pragmatic argument came to be more and more central in his thought. For if man is radically evil, it is impossible to understand how his case can be cured merely by strengthening a State which will be ruled, inevitably, by a corrupt human being.

This is only one of the difficulties which confront Kant's prediction that men will someday find perfection in a perfect State. Perfection for Kant, as for the Christian tradition, implies much more than mere conformity to law. To be perfect men must not only do "the right thing," they must act out of the right motive—on Kant's view, out of respect for the moral law. And although a perfect State might be able to compel all men to conform to the law it is quite another matter to suggest that any form of State action could ensure that men will act out of the right motive. In his *Idea of a Universal History* Kant tried to solve this problem by suggest-

---

25. *On the Saying, That a Thing May Be Right in Theory,* as trans. Hastie, p. 68.
26. *Perpetual Peace,* as trans. Beck, p. 340.

ing that the State is not merely a coercive but an educative agent. Once it no longer has to waste its resources and its energies on fighting wars, it will be able wholly to devote itself to the moral education of its citizens. Kant does not doubt that with the help of education the State can develop "the right mental disposition" in its citizens.[27]

Nine years later, however, in his *Religion Within the Limits of Reason Alone*, Kant took a rather different view. He there distinguishes between that condition—he calls it "juridico-civil"—in which men are governed by coercive laws and that far superior "ethico-civil" condition in which they are united by "laws of virtue" in an "ethical commonwealth," as contrasted with a merely "political commonwealth."[28] He still argues, no doubt, that an ethical commonwealth must rest on a political commonwealth; the two, however, are far from being identical. It is towards the coming into being of an *ethical* commonwealth, the suggestion now is, that men are morally bound to direct their efforts. Kant freely admits, however, that human effort does not suffice to create an ethical commonwealth. The ethical common-wealth is a Church, a "City of God," not a State; it must be governed by God, and only God can bring it into being. This does not absolve men, Kant still argues, from acting as if everything depended on them; only by so acting can they hope that God will crown their efforts. To use the language of a later day, the ideal of an ethical commonwealth which men can bring about by their own strivings is a myth, but a myth by which men ought to govern their conduct.[29] The commonwealth must finally come about, Kant is convinced, just because its coming into being does not depend on men's "crooked wills," or—unlike the ideal State—on

27. Compare, on this point, *Perpetual Peace*, Second Section, First Supplement, trans. Beck, pp. 322–29.

28. *Religion Within the Limits of Reason Alone*, Bk. III, Division I, §I; trans. Greene and Hudson, pp. 87–88.

29. *Ibid.*, Bk. III, Division I, §II–IV; in trans. cited, pp. 88–93.

their capacity to choose an ideal ruler, but on the grace of God, granted towards men who seek to bring about what he has willed. By shifting his emphasis from the ideal of a perfect State to the ideal of an ethical commonwealth Kant at once avoids the objection that men cannot be moralized by State action and the objection that in order to create an ideal State "radically evil" men would have to entrust their fortunes to a "radically evil" legislator. The cost of this shift, however, is the admission that men can perfect themselves only with the aid of infused divine grace, neither entirely by their own efforts nor as a result of the workings of impersonal, metaphysically necessitated, laws.

Faced with a similar problem, the nineteenth-century followers of the French socialist Saint-Simon had recourse to mysticism rather than to Kant's "rational theology." The ruler of the ideal society, on their view, will be a genius who simply "reveals himself"; he will be recognizable by the fact that the people will unanimously accept his authority.[30] Kant was no friend to this kind of mystical absolutism. But he raised in men the hope that they could attain to a perfect society without providing them with the mechanism for doing so. More secularly-minded perfectibilists, unable to believe that such a society can come about only by God's grace, were tempted to find a substitute for God in an "inspired ruler." Kant liked to draw attention to the way in which men's bad intentions can work for good; in the fate of Kant's own political philosophy we can see just as clearly the way in which men's good intentions can work for evil.

Kant's *Idea of a Universal History* is no more than an outline; he looks forward to the appearance of, but does not himself profess to be, a "Newton of history" who would reduce history to a science just as Newton had reduced physics to a science. His former pupil, Herder, had already set out

30. G. G. Iggers: *The Cult of Authority* (The Hague, 1958), p. 95.

to be such a Newton.* The two men agreed on a great many issues. (It is pointless to try to establish priorities; they inherit a common legacy.) Herder, however, would have nothing to do with a Providential plan which culminates in, or rests upon, a State, an institution for which, to say the least, he displays no enthusiasm. Sometimes (to the horror of his Idealist successors), he writes about "the costly machines of state" almost in the manner of an anarchist.[31]

"The State," he once wrote, "robs men of what is most important—themselves."[32] As for the view advocated by Helvetius and his followers, that nations can be civilized by a universally applicable "art of legislation" this was, to Herder, the height of absurdity; nations are civilized by strengthening their own "veins and sinews," not by imposing

---

* Herder's relationship to Kant is more than a little complicated. As Kant's pupil at Königsberg, Herder had been deeply influenced by him. At that time, however, Kant's lectures had mainly been devoted to physical science. The first volume of Herder's *Ideas towards a Philosophy of the History of Man* was published early in 1784; Kant's brief essay on the *Idea of a Universal History* was published later in the same year. Kant may well have been stimulated to write it by the appearance of Herder's work, which he reviewed, severely and not altogether fairly, in the following year. Herder, he thought, was altogether too optimistic in his estimation of man's character; he did not recognize that man has a radical evil in his nature and that, in consequence, he "is an animal which needs a master." Then, too, he placed altogether too much emphasis, for Kant's taste, on happiness—to say nothing of his fondness for "poetical eloquence," metaphors and allegories, when what is required is careful logical analysis. But even if Herder's first volume appeared before Kant's essay, the subsequent and more important volumes of Herder's *Ideas* are directed against Kant's *Idea of a Universal History:* that is the justification for discussing him after Kant, rather than, as is commonly done, as one of Kant's predecessors. Kant's review of Herder can be read in its entirety in *Kant's gesammelte Schriften, ed. cit.,* Bk. VIII, pp. 45–66. An extract is translated in Gabriele Rabel: *Kant,* pp. 143–46.

31. See F. M. Barnard: *Herder's Social and Political Thought* (Oxford, 1965), ch. VI and, for a typical example, Herder's *Ideen zur Philosophie der Geschichte der Menschheit* (1784–91), Bk. VIII, ch. V, pp. 223–24, from which the quoted phrase is taken. The trans. used throughout is that by T. Churchill: *Outlines of a Philosophy of the History of Man* (London, 1800; photo. repr. New York, 1966), but, as is usually done, I have used *Ideas* rather than *Outlines* as its short title.

32. Quoted in Isaiah Berlin: "Herder and the Enlightenment" in E. R. Wassermann, ed.: *Aspects of the Eighteenth Century,* p. 61, from J. G. Herder: *Sämtliche Werke,* ed. B. Suphan, 33 vols (Berlin, 1877–1913), Bd. XIII, p. 341. Berlin should be consulted generally on Herder's relationship to the Enlightenment.

upon them from outside an alien set of laws.[33] Furthermore, Herder was dissatisfied with Kant's view—Kant himself calls it a "mystery"—that men must be prepared wholly to sacrifice their present happiness in the interests of an ideal community which they will not live to see established. It must be possible, Herder thought, for men to achieve happiness and perfection in their own lifetime; to ask them to sacrifice everything to the future struck him as monstrous.

What then, if not the setting-up of an ideal State, is God's plan for man? Herder, so far like Kant, describes it in Leibnizian terms: God's plan is that man shall fully realize, by his own efforts, his "humanity." Unfortunately, however, the idea of "humanity" is as obscure in Herder's thought as it is central. At one point Herder defines it as "reason and equity in all conditions and in all occupations of men."[34] That brings it fairly close to what Kant was later to call an "ethical commonwealth." But elsewhere Herder defines it more widely as including "the noble conformation of man to reason and liberty, to finer senses and appetites, to the most delicate yet strong health, to the population and rule of the Earth."[35] In short, "humanity" is the realization of whatever forms of good man has it in himself to achieve.

What a man can achieve at one time and in one place, however, is very different from what he can achieve at another time and in another place. That is a point which Herder particularly emphasized. It is ridiculous, he argues, to judge primitive Red Indians as if they were trying, and failing, to be eighteenth-century Europeans, let alone members of an Ideal State. Each nation has the task of bringing to perfection whatever, situated as it is, it is capable of perfecting, as the Romans perfected eloquence and the Red

.

---

33. J. G. Herder: *Auch eine Philosophie der Geschichte zur Bildung der Menschheit* (1774), trans. as *Yet Another Philosophy of History* by F. M. Barnard in *J. G. Herder on Social and Political Culture* (Cambridge, 1969), pp. 202–3.

34. Herder: *Ideas*, Bk. XV, ch. III, p. 453.

35. *Ibid.*, Bk. IV, ch. VI, p. 98.

Indians perfected hunting.* The same is true of individuals. "What of Shakespeare?" Herder asks, "Had he no taste, no rules?" And he answers: "More than anyone else; but they were the taste of *his* time, the rules for that which *he* could accomplish."[36] To condemn Shakespeare for not conforming to "classical" standards is quite preposterous; he perfected his own kind of art. Mankind as a whole, on Herder's view, progresses not by men's setting before themselves as their objective the progress of mankind but by their perfecting a particular human potentiality. They can then hand over to mankind, as its possession for all time, that particular form of perfection.

The history of humanity is like a snowball, to use Her-

---

* A nation, to Herder, is a "Volk," a people united by ties of language and culture, an enlarged family joined together for mutual support and protection. In the light of subsequent history and the terrible ravages of totalitarian nationalism, we naturally look with suspicion on such ideals. Herder, no doubt, cannot be held responsible for totalitarianism. The totalitarian State conjoins the ideal of a "Volk" and the ideal of an all-powerful government; if Herder accepted the first, he no less strongly disowned the second. Kant's view, that "man is an animal which needs a master," Herder rejected as wholly untenable. Nor did he in the least degree sympathize with the doctrine that a particular "Volk" has a natural superiority over, and a right to enslave, other peoples. Against that kind of nationalistic arrogance his whole system of ideas is directed. He was, too, a hostile critic of racialism, incurring Kant's criticism for that reason. Language and culture, not race, were what mattered to Herder; a German Jew was still a German. When Nazi "philosophers" extolled Herder as one of their great predecessors they conveniently forgot these facts. Yet there can be no doubt that the ideal of a "Volk" can be as deadly to humanity as the ideal of centralized government, encouraging on the one side the view that all German-speakers, or all speakers of Slavonic languages, or all English-speakers, must "naturally" be united in one community and on the other side the view that a State is "unnatural" if, like Switzerland or the old Austro-Hungarian Empire, it is not mono-linguistic. As the post-war federations have broken down in one newly-developed country after another the "Volk" ideal has everywhere triumphed over the ideal of a centralized State, its size and character determined by economic and political rather than by linguistic or cultural considerations. Indeed, the spirit of Herder has never been so potent as in our own time. But to develop that theme in detail and to consider its implications would carry us too far afield. For a brief exposition of Herder's views see his *Ideas*, Bk. VII, ch. I. On racialism see Barnard's introduction to his *J. G. Herder on Social and Political Culture*, p. 41, and, for Herder and German Romanticism, *ibid.*, pp. 51–59.

36. Herder: *Ursachen des gesunknen Geschmacks bei den verschiedenen Völkern, da er geblühet* (Prize essay, 1773, printed 1775) in *Sämtliche Werke*, ed. cit., Bd. V, p. 653, trans. as *On the Cause of the Decline of Taste* and quoted in A. O. Lovejoy: *Essays in the History of Ideas* (Baltimore, 1948), p. 170.

der's own metaphor, which as it rolls along gathers up all that individual men and individual societies have achieved. The mechanism by which this "gathering up" is accomplished is "education," understood as the transmission of traditions from one generation to another. "The whole history of nations is to us a school, for instructing us in the course, by which we are to reach the lovely goal of humanity and worth."[37] When that goal is finally reached, after a long period of education, then at last, "wherever men dwell . . . will dwell men rational, just and happy."[38] What at any time they should seek, however, is not this absolute perfection but rather, as Tennant was later to argue, the *relative* perfection which their circumstances and the standards of their times permit—"Humanity and happiness, on this spot, in this degree, as this link, and no other, of the chain of improvement, that extends through the whole kind."[39]

Thus it is that Herder tried to overcome the problem which had beset eighteenth-century perfectibilists, of reconciling their indignant horror at man's past with their glowing hopes for his future. History was to them, as Gibbon put it, "a record of the crimes, the vices and the follies of mankind" or, as Voltaire no less trenchantly described it, "little else than a long succession of useless cruelties, . . . a collection of crimes, follies and misfortunes."[40] Herder himself had once felt the same way. Until he discovered the principles of his philosophy of history, history had appeared to him, he tells us, as "an abominable series of desolations on a sacred Earth." But now no longer. He has come to see that "only amid storms can the noble plant flourish" and that although the work of good men may seem for a time to be lost, it will, when "irrigated with blood," finally shoot

37. Herder: *Ideas,* Bk. XV, ch. I, p. 442.
38. *Ibid.,* Bk. XV, ch. V, p. 466.
39. *Ibid.,* Bk. IX, ch. I, p. 229.
40. Voltaire: *Works,* trans. T. Smollett, *et al.,* 25 vols (London, 1761–65), Vol. IX, pp. 142, 144, 152, as quoted in C. Frankel: *The Faith of Reason,* p. 108.

forth "an unfading flower." Revolutions, bloody as they may be, help to keep the world young: "the genius of humanity blooms in continually renovated youth, and is regenerated as it proceeds, in nations, generations, and families."[41]

Progress, that is, is not a matter of a lineal succession from the bad to the good, to the better, to the perfect. The idea of a "general, progressive amelioration of the world" Herder dismisses as a mere fiction: "a quiet progress of the human spirit towards the improvement of the world is hardly anything more than a phantom of our minds, and never the working of God in nature."[42] Once a society has accomplished all that it can accomplish, it must be destroyed, and it may be replaced by a society inferior to it in many respects. Roman civilization is no doubt infinitely inferior to the civilization of Greece; the Middle Ages is certainly inferior to Rome. But to say this is not to deny, according to Herder, that there is a divine plan in history, by which men are linked in a "golden chain of improvement."[43] Greece achieved what it could achieve, Rome achieved what it could achieve, the Middle Ages achieved what they could achieve, each in a fashion determined by the needs of the place and the time. So every age demonstrates, in its own particular way, what man can accomplish.

It is illuminating to compare Herder's with what may fairly be described as the "conventional" eighteenth-century account of Providential government, which Kant had been content to modify. According to that conventional account, evils are necessary as a means to goodness. So although, for example, the Roman Empire had, in Herder's phrase, "a bloody history," it was a necessary stage in human progress because it served the ends of God by diffusing the Christian religion. Herder will have none of this. God, he

---

41. Herder: *Ideas,* Bk. IX, ch. I, p. 231.
42. Herder: *Yet Another Philosophy of History,* Sections 1 and 2, as trans. in Barnard: *J. G. Herder on Social and Political Culture,* pp. 187, 195.
43. Herder: *Ideas,* Bk. IX, ch. I, p. 231.

argues, could have chosen other means; it still has to be explained why he chose bloodshed. The consequence, furthermore, of his using this particular means, if it is to be thought of as a means, was the birth of "a romish christian bastard . . . of which there are many who wish, that it had never been born."[44]

The rise and fall of the Roman Empire, that is, cannot be justified if it is thought of as a means towards the diffusion of Christianity. But the fact is, Herder argues, that the Roman Empire had its own energies, its own intrinsic perfection, just as Christianity has. If we want to understand why Rome rose and fell, we must look, as Gibbon looked, to secular causes, not to "final causes," not to ends to which its decline was a means—and Herder, Lutheran pastor though he was, is therefore ready to defend Gibbon against his clerical critics.[45] But if we ask why Rome *had to exist at all*, then the answer is that it demonstrated what man was capable of in the way of fortitude, of poetry, and of eloquence. That is one reason why Herder rejected Kant's view that it is men's duty to work towards the Ideal State or even towards an ethical commonwealth. When men take the future as their objective, they are liable to overlook their duty to the present, and it is by performing that duty, Herder thought, that they will most effectively hasten mankind's progress towards perfection. "To set goals beyond the grave harms rather than promotes the welfare of mankind."[46] Herder thus made of himself an apostle of the present, as opposed both to the view that all perfection lay in the past, in some remote golden age, or that perfection will come to pass only in the future, in some equally remote Utopia.[47]

44. *Ibid.*, Bk. XIV, ch. VI, p. 434.

45. *Ibid.*, Bk. XVII, ch. III, p. 516, fn.

46. Quoted in Barnard: *J. G. Herder on Social and Political Culture*, p. 43, from Herder's *Briefe zu Beförderung der Humanität* (1793–97) in *Sämtliche Werke, ed. cit.*, Bd. XVII, p. 120.

47. Compare what he says on this point in *Journal meiner Reise im Jahre 1769*, trans. as *Travel Diary* in Barnard, *op. cit.*, pp. 87–88.

Turgot worked out the "conventional" view in a way which brought him closer to Herder and yet which enables us to see in what the peculiarity of Herder's theory of progress consists. This was as early as 1751, in an unpublished "Plan for Two Discourses on Universal History." Turgot's principal thesis is that evil brings forth good. Thus although, he says, the wars by which clans were transformed into nations had as their motives greed and ambition and were fought cruelly and destructively, they were none the less essential if men were ever to learn to speak a common language and to build up, in that language, a body of knowledge. So far Turgot is working with that means-end picture of Providential action to which Herder so strongly objects— although there are places in which he falls back on it. But Turgot goes on to make a rather different point. "No change has occurred," he says, "which has not brought with it some advantage; for none has occurred that has not been fruitful of experience and without extending, or improving, or preparing the way for [man's] education."[48] That is much more like Herder's argument.

In the end, however, Turgot finds it impossible completely to reconcile the actual events of history with the view that they are, in detail, providentially determined. The rise and spread of Mohammedanism, he writes, "opposes the wall of superstition to the *natural progress towards perfection*."[49] So, it seems, the actual course of history does not coincide with history's "natural" progress towards perfection. Mohammedanism ought never to have been. Herder, in contrast, will not admit the possibility of any such conflict between the "natural" and the "actual." Since Mohammedanism exists, it is wrong, on his view, to dismiss it simply as "a superstition," although no doubt it *is* a superstition.

48. A. R. J. Turgot: *Plan de deux discours sur l'histoire universelle* (c. 1751), in *Oeuvres*, ed. G. Schelle, Vol. 1, p. 285.

49. *Ibid.*, p. 297 (my italics).

There must be something to be learnt from it; in his chapter on "Effects of the Arabian Kingdoms" Herder tells us at some length, indeed, just what Europe has learnt from its Arabian teachers.[50]

The question still remains, however, what grounds there are for believing that man is bound to learn from history—not by imitating the past but by deriving from it his conception of what is humanly possible—and in this way to proceed towards perfection. Herder lays so much stress on the rise and fall of civilizations that we naturally become doubtful, as we turn the pages of his *Ideas,* whether there can be any rise without a fall. This is the more so as he gradually abandoned the Augustinian view, to which he had adhered in his *Yet Another Philosophy of History*—published in 1774, some ten years before the first volumes of *Ideas*—that mankind can properly be compared to an individual man with, like any such man, a childhood, a youth and a maturity. He argues, rather, that at any given time there exist on the surface of the earth societies which are at different "biological" stages. As he puts the point in his *Letters for the Advancement of Humanity,* "on our terrestrial globe, all the ages of humanity continue to live and to act."[51] So we are left, on the face of it, with no good reason for believing that "mankind," as distinct from a particular man or a particular society, has any history at all, that it makes any sense to speak of mankind as moving towards perfection.

Confronted with the difficulty of guaranteeing that mankind, in spite of its rises and falls, is in progress, Herder looked for laws. It should first be observed, however, that there was no reason, on his theory of providence, why evils should not disappear. He did not believe in original sin. Man is, on his view, free to choose what is good; he is not corrupted, as Kant thought he was, by a "radical evil." In

---

50. Herder: *Ideas,* Bk. XIX, ch. V.
51. *Briefe,* Tenth Collection, Letter 122, in *Sämtliche Werke, ed. cit.,* Bd. XVIII, p. 287.

imitation of Pico della Mirandola, Herder describes man as "a god upon Earth" with his own fate in his own hands — even if he is also subject to "a wise Goodness" that "disposes the Fate of Mankind."[52] Nor does Herder suggest, as the conventional eighteenth-century doctrine of evil does, that evil must exist if good is to exhibit itself. That it had to exist, Herder admits, but not that it must *continue* to exist. By struggling to overcome evils, men learn how to perfect themselves, but once they have learnt how to act, what they have learnt can be passed on by education and the evil which gave birth to it allowed to disappear. So although, for example, "the pressure of the romish hierarchy was perhaps a necessary yoke, an indispensable bridle for the rude nations of the middle ages," the "romish hierarchy" could safely be overthrown once the "rude nations" had been brought into order.[53] The only question is whether there is any good reason for believing that such for-the-time-being-necessary evils *must* disappear. That is where Herder's "laws" come into the picture.

Of these "laws" the most important is that "all the destructive Powers in Nature must not only yield in the Course of Time to the maintaining Powers, but must ultimately be subservient to the Consummation of the Whole."[54] That such a "law" in fact operates can, so Herder argues, be clearly discerned through the study of history: "the progress of history shows, that, as true humanity has increased, the destructive demons of the human race have diminished in number; and this from the inherent natural laws of a self-enlightening reason and policy."[55] Note the phrase "a self-enlightening reason." We are not now far from the Hegelian

52. *Ideas*, Bk. XV, ch. I, p. 442; Bk. XV, ch. V, p. 462. On Herder's attitude to freedom, see also R. T. Clark: *Herder—His Life and Thought* (Berkeley, 1955), pp. 312–14.

53. *Ideas*, Bk. XX, ch. VI, pp. 631–32.

54. *Ibid.*, Bk. XV, ch. II, p. 443. On Herder's "laws" in general see Lewis W. Spitz: "Natural Law and the Theory of History in Herder," in *Journal of the History of Ideas*, Vol. XVI, 1955, pp. 453–75.

55. *Ideas*, Bk. XV, ch. II, p. 445.

conception of history as a process by which Reason comes to consciousness of its own powers.

Herder is not a consistent philosopher: two Herders struggle in a single breast—the Lutheran pastor and the philosopher.[56] But of the two, it is Herder the philosopher who is of consequence in our story; that is the Herder we have emphasized. For it is he who suggests that each historical epoch, however un-Christian, has something to offer in enabling us to realize what man can become, and it is he who suggests that human history is governed by empirically-detectable laws. And thus it is that, whatever the feelings of Herder the Lutheran pastor, the way is opened up for theories of history which see no need for the supposition that these "laws" are the work of Providence, rather than laws which operate and can be seen to operate at a purely secular level in human history. And the way is opened up, too, for theories which carried Herder's "historicism" to a point which would not permit Herder to exclaim as he does, with indignation, at, for example, the barbarities of the Roman Empire. Indeed, some of Herder's German successors—the historian Meinecke, for example—condemn Herder's emphasis in the *Ideas* on "humanity" as a retrogressive step. They greatly prefer the less mitigated historicism of *Yet Another Philosophy of History*.[57]

This is the kind of "historicism" against which, in the Inaugural Lecture he delivered at Cambridge in 1895, Lord Acton was moved to protest. "Opinions alter, manners

---

56. See particularly the introduction by Max Rouché to his collection of extracts entitled Herder: *Idées pour la philosophie de l'histoire de l'humanité* (Paris, 1962, French-German text) and Berlin: "Herder and the Enlightenment" in Wassermann, *op. cit.,* pp. 101–3. Berlin emphasizes, quite rightly, the points at which Herder was at odds with the Enlightenment.

57. For the tensions in Herder's own thought on this question, and the variation in his views between *Yet Another Philosophy of History* and *Ideas,* see G. A. Wells: "Herder's Two Philosophies of History," in *Journal of the History of Ideas,* Vol. XXI, 1960, pp. 527–37, and the note in Georg G. Iggers: *The German Conception of History* (Middletown, Conn., 1968), p. 293, n. 17.

change, creeds rise and fall," Acton told his audience, "but the moral law is written on the tablets of eternity"[58]—and it is by that moral law, on Acton's view, that men, past and present, must be judged. Acton rejected out of hand the contention that "a murderer was no criminal if he followed local custom, if neighbours approved, if he was encouraged by official advisers or prompted by just authority, if he acted for the reason of state or the pure love of religion . . ."[59] Acton was opposed to "historicism," amongst other reasons, because it made nonsense of the idea of progress. "The golden chain of improvement" has to be an improvement by *absolute* standards if Herder is to avoid the objection that a later age, using different standards, may come to condemn as retrogression what he thinks of as progress.

Herder attempted to protect himself against such objections by arguing that certain principles of equity and justice and rationality are engraved in the hearts of all men. Even the cannibal, Herder rather comically tells us, has a sense of justice: "for when he eats the flesh of others, he expects to be eaten in his turn."[60] So Herder felt entitled to condemn with moral fervour "the bloody history of Rome,"[61] because Rome did not live up to standards it should have recognized, and did in fact recognize, to be morally binding upon it. But his historicist successors were not to be convinced that the "heart" has any moral principles engraved upon it. If the artistic quality of Shakespeare's *Macbeth* is to be judged by the standards of Shakespeare's time, not of ours, why should not the morality of Macbeth's conduct, they asked, equally be judged by the standards of his bloodthirsty times?

The same tension between relative and absolute standards of moral perfection recurs in Marxism; morality is at

58. "The Study of History," Inaugural Lecture, Cambridge, 1895, in *Lectures on Modern History* (London, 1906), p. 27.
59. *Ibid.*, p. 25.
60. Herder: *Ideas*, Bk. IV, ch. VI, p. 102.
61. *Ibid.*, Bk. XIV, ch. VI, p. 433.

once determined by class-membership and yet supplies the Marxist with an absolute standard by which the bourgeoisie can be judged corrupt. Modern anthropologists find it no easier to reconcile their desire to "do justice" to primitive societies, to avoid any hint of patronage, with their inability not to think of, let us say, the life of a New Caledonian cannibal as a poor and miserable one.[62] This much is certainly clear: even if the most barbarous ages may unwittingly contribute to the perfection of mankind, and even if they can be excused for their barbarity on the ground that they knew no better, there must be some absolute sense of perfection if it is to be meaningful to assert that, as an absolute fact, man is gradually perfecting himself. Ethical relativism cannot, without inconsistency, be associated with a belief in the reality of progress.

In Herder's philosophy of history a developmental philosophy of history is oddly conjoined with an appeal to historical influences of a wholly empirical sort. On the one side, the whole of history is the gradual realization by man of the potentialities inherent in him; on the other side, the manner of that realization is profoundly affected by geography, by climate, by the crops and the animals at man's disposal, to say nothing of what, from a human point of view, Herder is prepared to describe as "chance." Merely from a consideration of man's nature, or a particular episode in his history, one could not hope, if Herder is right, to deduce the entire course of that history. One has to know not only man but geography in order to understand, let us say, the history of Athens.

It is true that geography is not, according to Herder, related in a purely accidental way to the history of mankind. Providence, he says, deliberately disposed the mountains and rivers and seas in such a way as to facilitate communi-

---

62. Compare Robert Redfield: *The Primitive World and Its Transformations* (Ithaca, N.Y., 1953), ch. VI: "The Transformation of Ethical Judgment."

cations between certain nations and to cut off others from one another. But the fact remains that although in order to understand history as a whole we need only know that it is an advance towards humanity, to understand why a particular advance occurred at a particular place and time the historian, Herder is willing to admit, has to rely upon his knowledge of quite specific and quite material historical factors.

To Herder's successors in the German Idealist tradition, Herder's dependence on the empirical, the actual, the material, was intolerable. His suggestion, for example, that the character of human rationality was profoundly affected by man's erect stature they condemned as the grossest form of materialism, not to be excused by the mere reflection that Providence bestowed that stature on man. One of his German critics, the Hegelian Eduard Gans, was to complain of Herder's *Ideas Towards a Philosophy of the History of Mankind* that they "contradict their title by not only banishing all metaphysical categories, but moving in an element of positive hatred to metaphysics."[63] No doubt, it is hard to be metaphysical enough to satisfy a German philosopher. But Herder's emphasis on man's erect posture unpleasantly reminded even a more sympathetic Scottish Idealist of La Mettrie's materialism.[64]

Kant, too, had tried to compromise. No doubt, history is, on his view, *a priori* in so far as its general nature and the objectives towards which it moves can be determined simply by considering what is implicit in the idea of "reason," without any reference to the actual course of history. On the other hand, it is by no means his intention, he tells us, to discourage empirical work in history—although he would like, by providing for it a metaphysical frame, to reduce the amount of detail in which it is involved. Both for

63. As quoted in Robert Flint: *The Philosophy of History in France and Germany* (Edinburgh, 1874), p. 378.
64. Robert Flint, *op. cit.*, p. 379. For the reaction of his successors to Herder see G. A. Wells: *Herder and After* (The Hague, 1959).

Herder and for Kant, one might say, to understand history as a whole is a task for philosophy, but to understand any particular slice of history is a task for the historian. The precise relationship between these two enterprises, however, is by no means apparent.

For Fichte, in contrast, any science, and the "science of history" therefore, begins from a single principle and proceeds by unfolding that principle. Herder had already condemned "the German disease of deriving everything, whether it really follows or not, from purely formal propositions";[65] in Fichte and his successors that disease was to rage with unprecedented virulence. Empirical history, Fichte no doubt admits, can serve to illustrate or to exemplify the nature of historical processes. Essentially, however, a science of history will demonstrate what the course of history *must* be, taking as its starting-point the nature of human activity. "The philosopher," so Fichte sums up, "must deduce from the unity of his presupposed principle all the possible phenomena of experience." When the philosopher takes history as his subject, according to Fichte, he "follows the *a priori* course of the World-Plan, which is clear to him without the aid of History at all; and the use which he makes of History is not to prove anything by it, for his principles are already proved independently of History; but only to illustrate and make good in the actual world of History, that which is already understood without its aid."[66]

What "the historical world-plan" is directed towards, Fichte agrees with Kant, is a life in which men govern all their relations freely but in accordance with reason. To reach this point, Man proceeds through five stages, each of which,

65. Herder: *Travel Diary*, as trans. Barnard in *J. G. Herder on Social and Political Culture*, p. 113.

66. J. G. Fichte: *Die Grundzüge des gegenwärtigen Zeitalters* (1806), trans. by W. Smith as *The Characteristics of the Present Age* in *Fichte's Popular Works*, 4th ed., 2 vols (London, 1889), Vol. II, Lecture 1, p. 3 and Lecture 9, p. 154.

Fichte tells us, is logically necessary.[67] He must from the beginning have been rational since otherwise he could never have become rational. But his rationality, so Fichte argues, was at first instinctive; primitive man accepts the customs and tradition of his community, subordinates his individual interests to them, without apprehending their rationality. From this primitive condition he falls away, in an age of authority, into a condition in which he thinks of authority as something purely external to him; he obeys, but only out of "blind faith and unconditional obedience." From such a condition of subservience he passes into a third stage, in which individualism is rampant and the claims of rational authority are wholly rejected—"the Age of absolute indifference towards all truth, and of entire and unrestrained licentiousness." That, so Fichte thought, was the age through which mankind had just been passing—the Enlightenment. (Although it was an *a priori* truth that human history had to pass through such a stage, it is an empirical question, according to Fichte, at what point human history now stands; Fichte himself vacillated on this matter.) The age of individuality, Fichte suggests, was coming to its end. Man—under the guidance of German idealism—was about to enter a fourth stage, the age of "Reason as Knowledge," in which reason, as exhibited in the State, should be consciously revered, in which men would freely place themselves at its disposal, as distinct from obeying it by instinct or out of fear. Beyond the age of conscious reason there lies a further stage still, conceived of in Joachim's fashion as a kingdom of perfect freedom, in which the idea of authority would wither away as unnecessary and man would convert himself into the very image of reason.[68] "If all men could be perfect, if all could attain their supreme final goal," Fichte writes, "they

---

67. For the contemporary setting of this theory of history see Xavier Léon: *Fichte et son temps*, 2 vols in 3 (Paris, 1922–27; repr. 1954–59), Vol. II, i, pp. 437–63.

68. *The Characteristics of the Present Age*, Lecture 1; *ed. cit.*, p. 9.

would all be absolutely identical; they would be one, one subject." Thus it is that "the final goal of society is the fusion of all, the unanimity of all the possible members."[69] This "final goal" is in many respects a reversion to the original state of man: humanity sets out to return to that condition of instinctive rationality into which it was created. But the journey is a necessary one; humanity has to learn not only how to be governed by reason but how consciously to participate in reason's work.*

We need no longer be perturbed that the history of man as it has so far progressed does not, on the face of it, encourage optimism about the history of man as it is yet to be. The past *had to be* torn asunder by conflicts; history proceeds "dialectically." Recurrent conflicts between, for example, the "thesis" of individuality and its "antithesis," authority, were essential to human progress. Only thus could society achieve a higher "synthesis," in which, by man's own free choice, authority and individuality will be at one. We need not worry, either, lest perhaps man never will be perfected: he is bound to be perfected, by the very logic of history. Granted only the original presupposition that history is the gradual self-revelation of mind, everything else,

---

69. Quoted from Fichte's *Das System der Sittenlehre nach den Principien der Wissenschaftslehre* (1798), trans. as *The Science of Ethics as Based on the Science of Knowledge*, by A. E. Kroeger, 2nd ed. (London, 1907), in J. L. Talmon: *Political Messianism* (London, 1960), p. 186.

* This is Fichte's version of the "fortunate fall." Man falls from his primeval Adamic innocence, but fortunately so; his fall induced God to take flesh and made possible in man a degree of spiritual sophistication of which he would not otherwise have been capable. So Milton's Adam in *Paradise Lost,* XII, 473–78:

> Full of doubt I stand,
> Whether I should repent me now of sin
> By me done or occasioned, or rejoice
> Much more that much more good thereof shall spring—
> To God more glory, more good will to men
> From God—and over wrath grace shall abound.

Compare A. O. Lovejoy: "Milton and the Paradox of the Fortunate Fall," in *Essays in the History of Ideas,* pp. 277–95.

so we are given to understand, logically follows. (Like Condorcet before him, however, Fichte is constrained to admit that the "natural" course of history is sometimes disturbed by "external influences.")

If we ask what form this perfection will take, Fichte's answer is that Nature will at last be conquered by spirit, or more accurately perhaps—Fichte's metaphysics is extremely complex and obscure—spirit will eventually reveal itself fully in Nature. The earthquakes, the volcanoes, the hurricanes which at present disrupt human life are nothing more than "the last struggles of the rude mass against the law of regular, progressive, living, and systematic activity to which it is compelled to submit."[70] Nature, that is, like human history, is still in process. It has not yet realized its perfect form; it is not yet subject to wholly regular laws; it still resists man's efforts. But it is destined in the end to provide him with a suitable dwelling place.

Nature, then, will be completely controlled. It will also be fully understood, as men come to see in it the workings of spiritual laws. Work will cease to be a burden, as men learn how to reduce mechanical toil. What are now savages will develop into cultivated and virtuous men, since otherwise "it is impossible to conceive of a purpose in their existence." All humanity will "unite itself into one single body, all the parts of which shall be thoroughly known to each other, and all possessed of similar culture." If it must be admitted that mankind, in respect of individual works of art and philosophy, has still not passed beyond "the aesthetic and intellectual culture of the ancient world," this is not, Fichte reassures us, because it is retrogressing, but because in its present stage what it has to do is to spread culture throughout the world. That once achieved, when "the

---

70. *Die Bestimmung des Menschen* (1799), Bk. III, Section II, trans. as *The Vocation of Man* by W. Smith in *Fichte's Popular Works*, 2 vols (London, 1873), Vol. I, p. 331. This work has also been translated as *The Destination of Man*.

existing culture of every age shall have been diffused over the whole inhabited globe," then it is that "without further interruption, without halt or regress, . . . humanity shall move onward to a higher culture, of which we can at present form no conception."[71]

Such a "higher culture," for Fichte, is not merely a goal towards which all men ought to strive. Fichte is prepared to write of it that "it shall, it must be realized" since the very existence of rational beings is unintelligible unless this is their purpose. If it is never to come into being, according to Fichte, then all human life is merely a "theatrical display for the gratification of some malignant spirit," and a rational man has but one course to pursue: to commit suicide. That "human life" might fall between these two extremes, as neither a stage on the way to absolute perfection nor yet "a mere theatrical display for the gratification of some malignant spirit," is a possibility Fichte does not so much as contemplate.[72] Such an all-or-nothing attitude to life is, indeed, characteristic of perfectibilists: they can endure the present—Fichte yields to nobody in denouncing his own times—only if they can think of it as a necessary stage on the way to the perfection of all men. It is not enough, for them, that life should continue to be a mixture of horror and exaltation, of pain and happiness.

There is always a particular danger in developmental "logically necessary" theories of perfection, comparable to the danger inherent in theories which lay all the stress on divine grace—the danger that men will think of their own actions as impotent. Fichte fully recognizes, as Kant had done before him, what Hegel was to call "the cunning of history." Good men, acting with virtuous intentions, may nevertheless work against the development of human so-

---

71. *Ibid.*, pp. 334–35.
72. *Ibid.*, pp. 340–41.

ciety. "The most despicable passions of men, their vices and their crimes, often forward, more certainly, the good cause than the endeavours of the virtuous man, who will never do evil that good may come!"[73] If, then, the attainment of an earthly paradise is "the whole object" of our existence, it looks as if, all the same, it is not something we can sensibly take as an end, for we can never know what will further and what will hinder its realization. "It seems that the Highest Good of the world pursues its course of increase and prosperity," so Fichte sums up this line of reflection, "quite independently of all human virtues or vices, according to its own laws."[74] To Fichte, with his intense belief in the importance of moral effort, such a conclusion is intolerable.

To avoid it, Fichte introduces the conception of a "transcendental" life over and above the "sensual" life—the equivalent of the Christian heaven but thought of, in a neo-Platonic manner, as a life in which a man can participate here and now. If man's end were entirely to be found in everyday, terrestrial, sensual life, then his free will, his virtue, his good intentions would have no point; the only question would be whether what he did, from whatever motive, advances or retards the progress of mankind. But there is another, more glorious end, so Fichte suggests, which men will come to know only in another life, a life in which God will "set before me some other purpose wholly incomprehensible to me here."[75] (At this point, in the characteristic Lutheran manner, Fichte appeals to "faith.") It is this life for which men prepare themselves when they follow their conscience, when they act as they ought to act, whatever the consequences of their action. And by this means they perfect *themselves* as distinct from perfecting human society. "I

73. *Ibid.*, Bk. III, Section III, p. 342.
74. *Ibid.*, p. 342.
75. *Ibid.*, p. 347.

am immortal, imperishable, eternal, as soon as I form the resolution to obey the laws of reason; I do not need to *become* so."[76]

As part of his argument to this conclusion, Fichte reinstates the older ideal of a final, absolute, perfection in contrast with the Enlightenment ideal of limitless perfectibility. "The generation which has once reached it," he writes, "can do no more than abide there, steadfastly maintain its position, die, and leave behind it descendants who shall do the like."[77] Fichte makes use of this fact, indeed, to argue that such earthly perfection, "conceivable, attainable, and finite" cannot be man's final end; by moving beyond it to a transcendental life Fichte hopes to avoid the conclusion that the progress of humanity eventually comes to a standstill.

Thus it is that, with a great deal of help from Kant's metaphysics, Fichte conjoins in a single system the secular aspirations—or certain of them—of modern perfectibilists and the godlike aspirations of the Platonic tradition; thus it is, too, that he tries to conjoin a belief in the logical inevitability of progress with a moral theory of the traditional sort, for which what counts morally is not the consequence of my act but its intention. It is every man's moral duty, according to Fichte, to act in such a way as is most likely to advance the progress of humanity, but the moral value of his action, its contribution to his own perfection, is quite independent of its actual consequences.

It is not surprising, of course, that the Fichtean variety of perfectibilism should be so different from the French variety, as illustrated, for example, in the writings of Condorcet. Fichte was a religious-minded professor of humble origin, living in a small community, with no developed middle class, and in a country where the Church was strictly under State control; Condorcet was a man of affairs, a mar-

76. *Ibid.*, p. 351.
77. *Ibid.*, p. 341.

quis, a mathematician, in a powerful country where commerce, however restricted by feudal institutions, was rapidly expanding, and the Church proclaimed its independence of the State. For Fichte to have grounded his case for progress on the weakening of the Church's power, or even on the weakening of existing State authorities, would have been, in the German context, ridiculous; so far as there had been progress in Germany it had come from above, from enlightened rulers, and so far as there could be further progress it depended on the unification of Germany, on that surrender by petty princelings of their powers and prerogatives which in his *Addresses to the German Nation* (1808) Fichte so warmly advocated. So Fichte envisaged progress as, in the first place, progress towards unification; only in a unified state, as he saw it, could men be free and rational.

The French and English Enlighteners, in contrast, had already experienced unification: they looked forward to commercial expansion beyond national boundaries, a commercial expansion which would bring with it, they correctly believed, the development of science, widespread prosperity, a growing tolerance of intellectual differences. Progress, in their eyes, lay in the development of new forms of human activity, human enterprise, and to this there was no end. To a German idealist it lay in the development of a national spirit and the surrender of individual interests to that spirit; by its nature it converged into an ever increasing degree of unity.

The old German mystical Christianity, with its emphasis on "union with God," on self-sacrifice, on the abandonment of individual interests, was united with the typical Lutheran emphasis on "vocation," so strong in Fichte, and called upon to sanctify the emergence of a national spirit. That, not the satisfaction of desires, was in Fichte's eyes the path to perfection. And it had a terminal point: it converged towards an absolute unity, towards a complete identification of interests, whereas French perfectibilism fanned outwards, commerce and science generating new desires in the very process of satisfying old ones.

In the philosophy of Hegel the idea of development is sharply separated off from the idea of infinite progress. Although Hegel, like Fichte, believed that what happens in history is a matter of logical necessity, he disclaimed all ability to predict the future condition of human society. The philosophy of history, on his view of the matter, consists in a "thoughtful consideration" of history as a "rational process" which is at the same time a revelation of "the wisdom of God" and the coming to "the consciousness of its own freedom on the part of Spirit."[78] That is the limit of the philosopher's achievement.

Of the perfectibilist aspirations which Fichte shared with Condorcet, there is in Hegel very little sign. It is true that in *The Philosophy of History*, Hegel accepts the doctrine of the perfectibility of man, if this is taken to mean what it meant for Rousseau, that man has within him the capacity to improve his position in the world. But this, he says, tells us nothing about the form which that improvement will take; the fundamental idea we need in order to understand history is development, not perfectibility. Hegel himself was more than satisfied with what had so far happened in history. Spirit had come to full consciousness of itself, he thought, at the political level in the Prussian State and at the intellectual level in his own philosophy. No doubt the "World Spirit" would go on working; indeed, Hegel went so far as to predict a great destiny for Russia and for the United States. "America," he wrote, "is therefore the land of the future, where, in the ages that lie before us, the burden of the World's History shall reveal itself."[79] But philosophy, on Hegel's view, cannot determine in detail what Spirit will

78. G. W. F. Hegel: *Vorlesungen über die Philosophie der Geschichte* (1837), trans. as *Lectures on the Philosophy of History* by J. Sibree (London, 1857; repr. 1905), pp. 8–9, 16, 20.
79. *Ibid.*, p. 90.

do next; it can do no more than help us to understand what Spirit has so far done.

Hegel applied to philosophy Herder's historicism, although in a way that Herder certainly did not intend. Herder had argued that men should seek the kind of perfection, the kind of happiness, possible to them in their own time and age. Hegel took a parallel view about philosophical understanding. "Whatever happens," he writes, "every individual is a child of his time; so philosophy too is its own time apprehended in thoughts. It is just as absurd to fancy that a philosophy can transcend its contemporary world as it is to fancy that an individual can overleap his own age." And the same applies to social projects: "if his theory really goes beyond the world as it is and builds an ideal one as it ought to be, that world exists indeed, but only in his opinions, an unsubstantial element where anything you please may, in fancy, be built." [80]

We drew attention, in discussing Herder, to the extreme difficulty of persisting in an ethical relativism, firmly adhering to a decision "to judge every community by its own standards": the very judgement that this is what we ought to do is an absolute, not a relative, one. Even more difficult is the attempt to maintain, as a timeless philosophical truth, that there are no timeless philosophical truths. Hegel, after all, is professing to show us something not merely about his own time but about the general forces in operation in history. It is not surprising that Hegel's disciples formed themselves into two groups, right-wing and left-wing Hegelians, the first accepting, the second rejecting, the view that philosophy cannot look beyond the present to the future.

Hegel's more faithful, "right-wing," disciples devoted themselves either to expounding his ideas or to detailed

---

80. *Hegel's Philosophy of Right,* trans. T. M. Knox (Oxford, 1942, corr. repr. 1945), Preface, p. 11. The German original was first publ. in 1821 under a double title: *Naturrecht und Staatswissenschaft im Grundrisse* and *Grundlinien der Philosophie des Rechts.*

work in the history of philosophy. In politics they were conservative. And they took Hegel's word for it that his philosophy was a defence of Christianity. The left-wing Hegelians,
in contrast, were not to be persuaded either that the Prussian State was the ideal outcome of history, or that Christianity had at last been rationally defended. Hegel's own
attitude to religion had been by no means consistent; like
Fichte he became more pious in his later years. He never
ceased to criticize, however, the God of traditional theology.
"Any one can see . . .", he wrote in his *Logic*, "that this most
real of beings, in which negation forms no part, is the very
opposite of what it ought to be and of what understanding
supposes it to be. Instead of being rich and full above all
measure, it is so narrowly conceived that it is, on the contrary, extremely poor and altogether empty."[81] To be metaphysically perfect, on Hegel's view, God must indeed be
one, but in a manner which enables him to include within
himself the diversity of Nature and of human history. He
cannot be "relegated to another world beyond" but must
be thought of as working in and through Nature. History
is God—or Spirit—at work. Where historians would ordinarily say that this or that man had produced a certain historical effect, to Hegel the "true agent" was Spirit, using a
human being as his vehicle.

To argue thus, however, may suggest a possible reversal
of the Hegelian position, a "standing of it on its head," in
Feuerbach's phrase. If "John Smith did that" and "God did
that" are two ways of describing precisely the same situation, why not conclude that the "true agent" is always man
rather than that it is always God? This is what Feuerbach
argued. Hegel's philosophy, he suggested, is the last refuge
of theology, the form which religion takes when it ceases

---

81. *The Logic of Hegel*, trans. from his *Encyklopädie der philosophischen Wissenschaften im Grundrisse*, Pt. I (a shortened and rev. version of his *Wissenschaft der Logik*), by William Wallace, 2nd ed. rev. (Oxford, 1892), p. 74.

to be superstitious and begins to reflect upon itself. But Hegel had not gone far enough. Further reflection shows that, properly understood, Christianity is no more than a confused way of talking about human beings and human social relationships: "God is nothing else than the nature of man purified from that which to the human individual appears, whether in feeling or thought, a limitation, an evil," and "Christ is the love of mankind to itself embodied in an image."[82]

Once more we hear the voice of Pindar. For Feuerbach's object, he says, is to change "the friends of God into friends of man, believers into thinkers, worshippers into workers, candidates for the other world into students of this world, Christians, who on their own confession are half-animal and half-angel, into men—whole men."[83] But Feuerbach goes much further than Pindar. If men are to "think mortal thoughts," this is because there are no other thoughts to think. No doubt men believe that it is their aspiration to be godlike, but in this they are simply mistaken: the aspiration which they thus describe is a human aspiration, the aspiration to live a life of "pure subjectivity," to separate off their consciousness from its setting in Nature, to take a moral holiday, in William James's phrase, from the demands that life makes upon them.[84]

The left-wing Hegelians, then, hoped wholly to destroy the supernatural and to describe man's growth to perfection in purely secular terms. So far they were carrying to its extreme limits the spirit of the Enlightenment. At the same time, they sought to preserve, and to convert to their own purposes, that metaphysical theory of "natural devel-

82. Ludwig Feuerbach: *Das Wesen des Christentums* (1841), trans. as *The Essence of Christianity* by George Eliot, with introductory essay by Karl Barth and foreword by H. R. Niebuhr, Harper Torchbook (New York, 1957), pp. 181, 268.

83. *Das Wesen der Religion* (1846), as trans. in the introductory essay by Karl Barth to *The Essence of Christianity*, ed cit., p. xi.

84. *The Essence of Christianity*, ed cit., p. 98.

opment" the lack of which made it so difficult for Enlightenment thinkers to justify their belief in the inevitability of progress. The confluence of the two streams is very obvious in Engels. "We want to remove everything," Engels writes, "that calls itself supernatural and superhuman and thus remove untruthfulness. For the pretences of the human and natural to become supernatural are the root of all lies." So far this is a radical version of the Enlightenment. But Engels goes on to explain why God can be deposed even from his role as Providential guardian of history. "To see the glory of human nature, to understand the development of the human species in history and its irresistible evolution, to realize its always certain victory over the unreasonableness of the individual," he tells us, "we do not have to call in the abstractions of a God to whom we attribute all that is beautiful, great, sublime and truly human."[85] The idea of an "irresistible development," the idea that it consists in the victory of the "species" over "the unreasonableness of the individual" Engels took over from German Idealism, but in a manner which entirely divorces it—here Feuerbach's influence was of the first importance—from its roots in the idea of a superintending Providence.

As for perfectibility, Engels completely rejected the classical idea of perfection. "A perfect society, a perfect 'state,'" he writes, "are things which can only exist in imagination."[86] It was Hegel's great mistake to suppose that in his philosophy thought had found a final resting-place. "The Hegelian system, in itself," so Engels maintains, "was a colossal miscarriage . . . suffering, in fact, from an internal and incurable contradiction."[87] This "contradiction" resides in the

85. Karl Marx-Friedrich Engels: *Gesammelte Schriften* (Stuttgart, 1902), Vol. I, pp. 484 ff., as quoted in E. Benz: *Evolution and Christian Hope, ed. cit.,* p. 90.

86. *Ludwig Feuerbach and the End of Classical German Philosophy* (Stuttgart, 1888), as trans. in Karl Marx-Friedrich Engels: *Selected Works,* 2 vols (Moscow, 1949; London, 1950), Vol. II, p. 328.

87. *Socialism—Utopian and Scientific* (Brunswick, 1878; first Eng. ed. 1892), as trans. in Marx-Engels: *Selected Works,* Vol. II, p. 122.

From Joachim to Marx 373

fact that on the one side Hegel described human history as a process of evolution which by its very nature cannot issue in the discovery of a so-called "absolute truth" and on the other side professed to have discovered "the very essence of absolute truth." What Marx did, according to Engels, was to take over "the revolutionary side" of Hegel's philosophy without its "idealist crotchets," constructing thereby a picture of the world according to which "the progressive movement from the lower to the higher . . . asserts itself through all zigzag movements and temporary regressions."[88] But where Hegel had seen the driving force of history in the "self-realization of the Idea," Marx saw it in class-struggles, arising at "particular historical phases in the development of production" and leading by way of "the dictatorship of the proletariat"—Marx's version of the millennarian "rule of the saints"—to "the abolition of all classes and to a classless society."[89]

In his earlier writings, Marx had expressed himself rather differently, in a way which links him more closely with the Leibnizian tradition. Man, Marx wrote in an early manuscript, "practically and theoretically makes his own species as well as that of other things his object."[90] Man concerns himself, that is, with "mankind" and with the development of mankind, with what Feuerbach had called "the human species." But under capitalism he is alienated from his fellow-men, and in consequence from his "human essence."[91] Private property alienates him; in his work, he is not, as he should be, producing out of joy in his creative powers, his control over nature. "The worker does not affirm himself in his work but denies himself, feels miserable

88. *Ludwig Feuerbach and the End of Classical German Philosophy*, ed. cit., pp. 349–50.
89. Karl Marx: Letter to J. Weydemeyer, 1852, as excerpted in *Selected Works*, Vol. II, p. 410.
90. "Economic and Philosophic Manuscripts" (1844), in *Writings of the Young Marx on Philosophy and Society*, ed. Easton and Guddat, p. 293.
91. For a critical discussion of this view, see Eugene Kamenka: *Marxism and Ethics* (London, 1969), pp. 19–30.

and unhappy, develops no free physical and mental energy but mortifies his flesh and ruins his mind."[92] Communism as "the complete and conscious restoration of man to himself" will free him from this alienation. "It is the true resolution of the conflict between existence and essence, objectification and self-affirmation, freedom and necessity, individual and species."[93]

Marx is not advocating the sort of communism envisaged in Plato's *Republic*, in which private property still exists, although as something possessed by the State and handed out to individuals; his is a communism in which the idea of private property is completely "overcome." Only in such a society, he says, can man achieve "the complete and conscious restoration of man to himself within the total wealth of previous development, the restoration of man as a *social*, that is, human being." With the abolition of private property, according to Marx, man can at last find himself as a social being, no longer in necessary conflict with his fellowmen. Then at last "the riddle of history [is] solved and knows itself as its solution."[94]

So far, Marx can fairly be regarded as subscribing to the perfectibility of man, as the eighteenth century and, even more, as Fichte understood it—man will finally become what he has it in himself to be, not a superman but a "true" man, not a mere functionary, dedicated to the pursuit of technical perfection but an all-round human being, living in a society from which "the enslaving subordination of the individual to the division of labour, and therewith also the antithesis between mental and physical labour, has vanished."[95] Marx was, however, extremely reluctant to describe in detail what Oscar Wilde called "the soul of man under socialism." He was contemptuous of Utopias, of any

---

92. *Writings of the Young Marx*, p. 292.
93. *Ibid.*, p. 304.
94. *Ibid.*, p. 304.
95. *Critique of the Gotha Program*, as trans. in Marx-Engels: *Selected Works*, Vol. II, p. 23.

attempt to draw up a blue-print for the future. There is no trace in him of that Utopian insanity which led Fourier to predict a future when the seas would run with lemonade. And he was, of course, highly critical of "bourgeois" theories of progress, which identify it with the satisfaction of individual wants.

It was, indeed, essential to his theory that we cannot predict, living as we do in a capitalist society, what new forms of culture, what kinds of "soul," would come into being in a very different society. He is prepared to describe the progress towards such a society, nevertheless, in Rousseau- and Fichte-like terms, as a return to that "natural" community from which men were, inevitably, estranged by civilization but to which they could now return, enriched by the intervening course of human history—a community which was "natural" in the sense that it did not depend for its continuance upon the exercise of State power, on force and fraud.

It will be, too, a free society. Negatively, it will be free of oppression; positively, it will be so organized that men can express their own nature in their labour and in their social relationships. "Men's own social organization," writes Engels, "which has hitherto stood in opposition to them as if arbitrarily decreed by Nature and history will then become the voluntary act of men themselves." Historical progress is the ascent of man from the kingdom of necessity to the kingdom of freedom.[96] Joachim's ambition reappears: a society without servility, which to Marx was the worst of all vices.

It is not surprising that the "Kingdom of Freedom" is left as vague as Joachim left his kingdom of the Holy Ghost. For what Marx and Engels bid us look forward to is a form of society which conjoins the creativity, the intellectual and artistic enterprise of classical Greece or modern Europe,

---

96. Engels: *Anti-Dühring*, Pt. III, ch. II, as trans. E. Burns (London, 1934; corr. repr. 1947), p. 311.

with the absence of fundamental conflicts typical, or so they believed, of "primitive communism." That such character-istics are in fact compatible, that the absence of social con-flict will not bring with it, inevitably, a decline in the quality and extent of social creativity, Marx and Engels are called upon to show but never do show. To attempt to describe in detail a society which is at once unified and creative would have brought to light the fatal contradictions inherent in the whole enterprise. It is only occasionally, as in Trotsky's *Literature and Revolution,* that a Marxist permits himself fur-ther speculations, allowing himself to assert positively, as Trotsky does, that "the average human type will rise to the heights of an Aristotle, a Goethe, or a Marx" and that "above this ridge new peaks will rise."[97]

The general understanding, however, is that after Com-munism has once come into being the possibility of im-provement is endless, even if the details are best left ob-scure. But it is by no means the sort of progress eighteenth-century perfectibilists envisaged, a gradual revision of already existing, already partly satisfactory, cultural and economic standards. For there is, according to Marx, "a fun-damental flaw in the civilized world": progress has so far not humanized but dehumanized men.[98] The "civilized world" —bourgeois society—must be overthrown, it cannot be amended. If Marx and Engels, then, reject the classical ideal of a final perfection, they are still committed to the Phoe-nix myth, the myth of a fresh start, a "breaking through" which will carry men if not to perfection then at least to a condition which permits of unlimited improvement.

It will by now be obvious that the doctrine of "natu-ral development" can take a great variety of forms. In its earlier versions it is reinforced by religion: in Joachim by

---

97. L. Trotsky: *Literatura i revoliutsiia* (Moscow, 1924), pp. 193–94, as trans. in Theo-dore Denno: *The Communist Millennium* (The Hague, 1964), p. 57, which should be con-sulted generally on this question.

98. Marx: *The Holy Family* (1844), excerpted in *Writings of the Young Marx,* p. 381.

prophecy, in Herder by his belief in Providence. But its tendency is towards rejecting religion, substituting for the belief in Providence a belief in immanent "laws" which determine the course of man's progress. The roots of this theory of immanent laws lie in Aristotle, or in Leibniz's version of Aristotelianism; they are laws of an "unfolding" by which man, or Spirit, or the Idea, or God, gradually comes to a full realization of his nature, achieving complete rationality and freedom—which are, so it is supposed, inherent in that nature—in a form of society in which rationality and freedom can fully express themselves. The disagreement amongst developmentalists turns about the nature of the immanent laws and the form of society in which they will finally issue. But it is generally agreed that some form of "antagonism," some kind of "dialectic," is essential to man's development, although not to his final condition.

TWELVE

PROGRESS BY NATURAL DEVELOPMENT: FROM DARWIN TO TEILHARD

When Darwin's *Origin of Species* first appeared in 1859, Engels was repelled by its "crude English method"—its deference to facts?—but welcomed it in so far as it helped to "smash theology."[1] Not only orthodox theology, indeed, but the concealed theology of Idealist metaphysics must yield, so Engels thought, to Darwin's arguments. "Darwin," Engels writes, ". . . dealt the metaphysical conception of Nature the heaviest blow by his proof that all organic beings, plants, animals, and man himself, are the products of a process of evolution going on through millions of years."[2] Whatever its usefulness in destroying God and metaphysics, however, Darwin's theory of evolution by natural selection did not, on the face of it, provide men with any ground for believing that History was on their side. Whereas in Herder's *Ideas* man had been represented as the crown of Nature, towards which all natural processes converged and beyond which, except through his perfection, no progress was to be expected, Darwin's "natural selection" has no special interest in man. A radical change in man's environment could result, if Darwin was right, in the total disappearance of the human species, just as the dinosaur had become extinct; a new species might arise, capable of taking over from man his present supremacy, or the world might be destroyed by a cosmic collision. Herder was quite sure that providential "Nature" would not permit a stray comet to destroy the

---

1. Karl Marx-Friedrich Engels: *Briefwechsel*, Vol. II (1854–60), p. 548 (Engels to Marx, December 12, 1859), quoted in Benz: *Evolution and Christian Hope*, ed. cit., p. 84.
2. Engels: *Socialism—Utopian and Scientific*, in Marx-Engels: *Selected Works*, Vol. II, p. 121.

earth, but natural selection has no control over the vagaries of comets.

At the very end of the *Origin of Species,* no doubt, Darwin expresses his confidence that ultimately all "corporeal and mental endowments" will, as a consequence of natural selection, attain to perfection. He wrote thus: "As all the living forms of life are the lineal descendants of those which lived long before the Silurian epoch, we may feel certain that the ordinary succession by generation has never once been broken, and that no cataclysm has desolated the whole world. Hence we may look with some confidence to a secure future of equally inappreciable length. And as natural selection works solely by and for the good of each being, all corporeal and mental endowments will tend to progress towards perfection."[3] But it does not follow from this that *man* must be perfected; the perfection of his "corporeal and mental endowments" may entail the evolution of man into a quite new species, just as the capacity of certain fish for moving over land could only be perfected by their ceasing to be fish.

The co-discoverer of the principle of natural selection, Alfred Wallace, was much more optimistic; he was prepared to predict that evolution would issue in an earthly paradise for men. Evolution, he said, in language very similar to the language Trotsky was later to use, must culminate in a condition in which the world is "inhabited by a single homogeneous race, no individual of which will be inferior to the noblest specimens of existing humanity." Government will die out, to be replaced by voluntary associations. Men will no longer permit themselves to be ruled by their passions, once they have discovered that "it was only required of them to develop the capacities of their higher nature, in order to convert this earth, which had so long been the theatre of their unbridled passions, and the scene of unimaginable misery, into as bright a paradise as ever haunted the dreams

3. Charles Darwin: *The Origin of Species,* ch. XIV (London, 1859), p. 489.

of seer or poet."[4] Paradise, then, lies within men's reach. Not only a spiritual élite, not only an elect few, but each and every man will "by the development of his higher faculties" enter into it, if not here and now, then at least within the history of this earth.

"The capacities of their higher nature" which Wallace expects men to develop include, it is interesting to observe, mystical and para-psychological faculties, which in their present form presage, so Wallace thinks, the powers of man in his earthly paradise. The expectation that man would, as a result of evolutional progress, develop "higher faculties" is by no means peculiar to Wallace. It is astonishing just how often "god-smashing" evolutionists have substituted for the ancient gods a new god—man as he is to be, with powers of a kind which had ordinarily been ascribed only to the divine. The time was not far distant when a Utopian novelist could tell his readers that "if humanity sprang from gorillas, from humanity gods shall proceed."[5] Some evolutionists, as we shall see, did not go quite so far: supermen rather than gods are, on their view, the final outcome of evolution. But the line of demarcation between these three views—that evolution will finally produce perfect men, that it will give rise to supermen, that its outcome will be the emergence of gods—is anything but a sharp one.

Darwin's and Wallace's hopes for the future rest, for the most part, on an inductive argument. So far "the ordinary succession by generation has never once been broken" and therefore, they conclude, progress in the future can confidently be expected, without fear of a total cataclysm. But Darwin, in the passage quoted above, also used another argument which, could it be sustained, would be

4. Alfred R. Wallace: "The Origin of Human Races and the Antiquity of Man Deduced from the Theory of 'Natural Selection,'" in *Journal of the Anthropological Society of London*, Vol. II (1864), pp. clxix–clxx.

5. Edgar E. Saltus: "New York from the Flat-Iron," a magazine article quoted in H. G. Wells: *The Future in America* (London, 1906), p. 43.

considerably more powerful. "All corporeal and mental endowments will tend to progress towards perfection" just because natural selection works "solely by and for the good of each being." What, we must now ask, is the justification for this last premise?

The arguments in its favour were more fully developed by Herbert Spencer, first of all in his *Social Statics*. Spencer had been an evolutionist before he met with Darwin's writings. The general idea of evolution was, indeed, in no sense Darwin's invention. To say nothing of earlier evolutionists, Darwin's grandfather, Erasmus Darwin, had combined a belief in biological evolution with perfectibilist hopes; the word "evolution" had been freely employed, too, by German metaphysicians, as the antithesis of revolution, to express their belief in the inevitable but gradual progress of the universe. In Spencer's eyes, as in the eyes of such metaphysicians, evolution is a general process to which the whole universe, not only the animal kingdom, is subject—a process which transforms the Universe, and every particular form of existence it contains, "from an indefinite incoherent homogeneity to a definite coherent heterogeneity."[6] But Spencer took over from Darwin the idea of natural selection, converted it into a theory of "the survival of the fittest," and applied it to ethics.

Evil, he argued, always results from a thing's failure to adapt to its environment. A camellia planted in calcareous soil will become sickly and die, because its present structure does not enable it to cope with lime. Just for that reason, Spencer concludes, evils tend to disappear; either the camellia learns to adapt or else it dies; in either case the evil of its sickliness is evanescent. And if it survives, Spencer thought, it will pass on this newly-acquired capacity to cope

---

6. H. Spencer: *First Principles*, 6th ed. (London, 1900), ch. XVII, p. 367. For a fuller account of evolutionary ideas in this period, see J. A. Passmore, *A Hundred Years of Philosophy, ed. cit.*, ch. II.

with lime to its progeny, so that not only its own sickliness but a weakness of the whole species will eventually be conquered.

From the fact that so many evils affect men living in society, we can therefore deduce, according to Spencer, that man has not yet adapted himself to social living. "His primitive circumstances," Spencer tells us, "required that he should sacrifice the welfare of other beings to his own; his present circumstances require that he should not do so; and in as far as his old attribute still clings to him, in so far is he unfit for the social state."[7] All the sins of man flow from this unfitness; he sins because he has not yet learnt to be altruistic, has not yet been fully converted into a social being.

To assert that men are morally perfectible is to assert, on Spencer's view, that they must eventually, by the process of adaptation, come to be wholly fitted for the social state. That this will happen, Spencer has no doubt. "As surely as a blacksmith's arm grows large," he writes, ". . . so surely must the human faculties be moulded into complete fitness for the social state; so surely must the things we call evil and immorality disappear; so surely must man become perfect."[8] The very nature of adaptation, that is, guarantees human perfection. "Evolution can end," as he elsewhere puts it, "only in the establishment of the greatest perfection and the most complete happiness."[9] And again: "Progress . . . is not an accident, but a necessity."[10]

In a footnote he added in 1891 to the revised edition of

7. *Social Statics,* Pt. 1, ch. II, §3; orig. ed. (London, 1857), p. 62. For a critique of Spencer's ethics see G. E. Moore: *Principia Ethica* (Cambridge, 1903; repr. 1948), ch. II, §29–35.

8. *Social Statics,* Pt. I, ch. II, §4; *ed. cit.,* p. 65.

9. *First Principles* (London, 1862), ch. 16, as quoted in P. B. Medawar: *The Art of the Soluble* (London, 1967), p. 49. This passage disappears from the sixth and last edition: Spencer was persuaded by the argument from entropy that the universe is running down. Compare Medawar, *op. cit.,* pp. 39–60 and Passmore: *A Hundred Years of Philosophy, ed. cit.,* p. 113.

10. *Social Statics, ed. cit.,* Pt. I, ch. II, §4, 65.

Social Statics, Spencer shows himself, however, more than a little uneasy about his earlier views. He had forecast "the evanescence of evil." For "evanescence," he came to think, he should perhaps have written "diminution." In bad habitats, he admits, men may prove unable completely to adapt. And as they approach nearer to perfect adaptation, so the strength of their impulse towards further adaptation diminishes. They can "get by" without perfect adaptation. Completely perfect adaptation, Spencer therefore concludes, would take an infinite time.[11] Once again, the ideal of infinite improvability has triumphed over the idea of an absolute perfection, once-and-for-all attainable.

Not all evolutionists were prepared to believe, with Spencer, that natural selection could safely be relied upon to perfect man's nature, or, indeed, that man could have been elevated to his present heights merely as a consequence of its operations. Thus, although Henri Bergson accepted the fact of evolution and did not try to defend the orthodox view that man was separately created by God, he sought to show that man's emergence on the earth—or, at any rate, the emergence of beings endowed with freedom—is nevertheless no accident of natural selection. Evolution, Bergson argued in his *Creative Evolution,* is the work of a vital impetus, an *élan vital,* which has succeeded in penetrating matter and has by this means given rise to living beings. This "vital impetus"—so far like Plato's Demiurge—is not free to do as it will: it is limited by the matter upon which, and the environment within which, it works. We are not to think of it, either, as having deliberate plans—the deliberate intention, for example, of creating man. In this respect it is quite unlike Plato's Demiurge. It radiates like a fan, trying to conquer matter in this way or that, until it finds that it can progress no further in a particular direction. Then it

---

11. *Social Statics, Abridged and Revised* (London, 1892), pp. 27, 31.

retreats to make the same attempt elsewhere. It created insects, for example, but failed in its task of imposing intelligence on them; the ant-heap and the bee-hive represent the highest levels of its achievement in that particular line of development.

In man, according to Bergson, evolution has satisfied itself; it has produced a being who possesses "the largest possible amount of indetermination and liberty."[12] No doubt some species other than man as we know him might have been produced by the "vital impetus"; perhaps such a species has in fact evolved on another planet. But evolution, so Bergson argues, was bound to produce either man or a being who is, as it were, man's "moral equivalent." It by no means follows, however, that man is an ideal being. He has been endowed with intelligence, certainly, but intelligence, according to Bergson, is a practical tool, designed to give man control over nature, permitting him to conquer the world; it does not enable him to penetrate to the true nature, the inward life, of things. For its own practical purposes, intelligence breaks up the fluid continuity of the Universe into sharply definite, easily manageable, conceptualized entities. In so doing, it falsifies the true nature of Reality. Only the mystic, Bergson maintains, and then by relying on intuition, not on intelligence, catches a glimpse of the essential nature of the Universe, its unity, its continuity.

In his *Creative Evolution* Bergson's argument, like Hegel's, was essentially retrospective. He tried to show how Nature produced man, and why in man it went as far as Nature could. In *The Two Sources of Morality and Religion,* he looked beyond that point. "A body compact of creative intelligence and, round about that intelligence, a fringe of intuition," he still says, "was the most complete thing nature had found it

---

12. Henri Bergson: *Creative Evolution*, trans. A. Mitchell (London, 1911), ch. III, pp. 264–86. The quotation is on p. 265. For a clear, brief account of Bergson's views, see T. A. Goudge: "Henri Bergson" in *The Encyclopedia of Philosophy*, Vol. 1.

possible to produce."[13] But in man, Bergson goes on to suggest, evolution developed a being who is endowed with the intrinsic power of growing further in that direction in which evolution has so far moved, if only he chooses to exercise that power. The Universe, Bergson goes so far as to say, is a "machine for the making of gods." But it depends on human effort whether that "essential function" of the Universe is exercised on this "refractory planet."[14]

In a curious manner, Bergson is reversing what had been the view characteristic of Christian mysticism, that although men must strive to make themselves fit, by purgation, to receive God, they can take the final steps towards the godlike condition only if they submit to God's grace. Human effort, Bergson is saying, plays no part in the first steps towards the godlike condition; the first steps are evolution's doing. From that point on, however, the initiative rests entirely in man's hands. What form such human effort must take Bergson leaves uncertain. Perhaps, he says, a great leader will arise, who will persuade his fellow-men to set out once more on the path towards perfection. Or perhaps psychical research will reveal to men what they have it in them to become and will thus encourage them to make themselves gods. But although the Universe is in some not very clear sense "on the side of" such human aspirations, it will not, by its own mechanisms, as distinct from human effort, lead them to human perfection. Once more we meet with that vacillation—between the view that men *must* in the end be perfected and the view that they will only be perfected if they arouse themselves to new efforts—which is typical of "developmental" varieties of perfectibilism and reflects in a new form the old Augustinian-Pelagian controversy.

One further detail is worth noting. To move forward,

---

13. Bergson: *The Two Sources of Morality and Religion* (first publ. Paris, 1932), trans. R. A. Audra and C. Brereton (New York, 1935; repr. 1949), p. 301.

14. *Ibid.*, p. 306.

Bergson suggests, men will first have to move back, returning to an earlier point in human history in order to fan out
again in a new direction. Our present life, Bergson complains like the anarchists before him, is moving in the direction of ever greater luxury and ever greater complexity.
It threatens to convert men, one might say, into sybaritic
ants. To become godlike, therefore, men must first return
to a simpler life. So in Bergson's scheme of salvation the old
ascetic impulse reasserts itself, once more allied both with
mysticism and with the belief that man can become godlike.

It is an important presumption of Bergson's theory of
evolution, in contradistinction from Darwin's, that at a certain point in the evolutionary process there has been a leap:
"man alone has cleared the obstacle." The animal kingdom
as a whole, whatever path it took, found it impossible to
make the leap into freedom.[15] This same doctrine of "a
leap" is to be found in the exponents of "emergent" as distinct from "creative" evolution. For the most part, emergent
evolutionists were anything but inclined to follow Bergson,
in whose writings, they complained, analogy is everywhere
substituted for reasoning, and rhetoric for evidence. Their
leader, Lloyd Morgan, was typical in his reaction when he
wrote of Bergson in his *Instinct and Experience* that "with all
due respect for M. Bergson's poetic genius—for his doctrine
of Life is more akin to poetry than to science—his facile
criticisms of Darwin's magnificent and truly scientific generalizations . . . serve seriously to hinder the progress of
biology."[16] Whereas Bergson's creative evolution is a metaphysics, his own theory, Lloyd Morgan tells us—although
many of his critics were sceptical on this point—is a serious
scientific hypothesis. But for all his admiration for Darwin,
Lloyd Morgan follows Bergson in opposing what he regards
as Darwin's exaggerated emphasis on the degree of conti-

15. *Creative Evolution*, p. 279.
16. Lloyd Morgan: *Instinct and Experience*, 2nd ed. (London, 1913), p. 180.

nuity in evolution. With man, Lloyd Morgan is confident, "something new" entered the biological scene.

Of course, one might be moved to reply, "something new" enters history with the first appearance of any species, or, for the matter of that, of any new mutation, and even more conspicuously "something new" enters history when birds first appear, or reptiles, or mammals. On the face of it, however, man is more closely related to the apes than birds are to reptiles; it seems odd, from a biological point of view, to think of man as "something new," in a very special sense of "something new" which contrasts him with the whole previous course of animal history.

The crucial fact, Lloyd Morgan would retort, is that with the appearance of man life takes on a quite new form, as "mind" or "consciousness." Consciousness involves, he would add, not merely those capacities for seeing, or hearing, or dealing intelligently with the world which man admittedly shares with the apes, but also, and now in distinction from the apes, a capacity for *self*-consciousness which enables man to look reflectively and critically at himself, at his powers, and at the course his evolution has so far taken. The appearance of this capacity was, according to Lloyd Morgan, a crucial step in the evolution of the world, as crucial as that earlier step by which physico-chemical processes developed the new property of life. At certain points in evolution, on his view, changes occur which are quite fundamental, in that what emerges is not only different from anything that has previously existed, as a bird is different from a reptile, but is "on a higher level than its predecessors" in a sense in which both bird and reptile are "on the same level."

Even orthodox Darwinians were sometimes driven to not dissimilar conclusions. In a lecture on "Evolution and Ethics," delivered on May 18, 1893, Thomas Henry Huxley vigorously criticized the Spencerian argument that "fitness" can be identified with "goodness," in the moral sense of that word. A species, he observed, may be "fit to survive" just in virtue of its brutality and violence.[17] Another Darwinian, if a more heretical one, G. J. Romanes, had already suggested that brutality and parasitism were, on the face of it, the best guarantee of survival. After millions of years of evolution, he had written, "we find that more than half of the species which have survived the ceaseless struggle are parasitic in their habits, lower and insentient forms of life feasting on higher and sentient forms; we find teeth and talons whetted for slaughter, hooks and suckers moulded for torment— everywhere a reign of terror, hunger, and sickness, with oozing blood and quivering limbs, with gasping breath and eyes of innocence that dimly close in deaths of brutal torture!"[18] Far from its being the case, Huxley argued in a similar spirit, that cosmic processes are on the side of morality, precisely the reverse is true. "The ethical progress of society depends," so he suggests, "not on imitating the cosmic process . . . but in combating it."[19] Man is on a "higher level" than his fellow-animals just because he can combat the cosmic processes which they must be content to endure.

As his critics were not slow to point out, however, Huxley's supposition that man can combat cosmic processes comes strangely from a Darwinian. For Darwin's principal thesis is that man is part of Nature and subject, therefore, to its "cosmic forces," in no sense standing outside or above them. In a note added to the printed version of his lecture Huxley substantially admitted the force of this criticism. "Strictly speaking," he there wrote, "social life, and the ethical process in virtue of which it advances towards perfection, are part and parcel of the general process of evolution."[20] He went on to grant that even in rudimentary forms

---

17. T. H. Huxley: "Evolution and Ethics" in T. H. and Julian Huxley: *Evolution and Ethics, 1893–1943* (London, 1947), pp. 81–82.

18. "Physicus" (G. J. Romanes): "Supplementary Essay in Reply to a Recent Work on Theism," *A Candid Examination of Theism* (London, 1892), p. 171.

19. *Evolution and Ethics*, p. 82.

20. *Ibid.*, Note 20, p. 101.

of human society "love and fear come into play, and enforce a greater or less renunciation of self-will" so that "the general cosmic process begins to be checked by a rudimentary ethical process, which is, strictly speaking, part of the former." "Strictly speaking" ethical progress is part of the evolutionary process, as Darwin had already maintained, and Huxley provides us with no good reason for speaking other than strictly.

Natural selection, the conclusion would seem to follow, has after all been responsible for man's ethical progress, even if it has chosen a somewhat deplorable method of bringing that progress into being. So much granted, argument is still needed to show that there is anything in natural selection to guarantee that ethical progress will continue. Perhaps it is no more than an accident that natural selection—in so far as it has done so—has encouraged the rise of morality. Huxley was certainly correct in emphasizing that the future victory of morality does not follow from the mere fact that natural selection "preserves the fittest."

Darwin himself, like many another progressivist, had been somewhat disturbed by the fact that "the intellectual development of the old Grecians" had not been matched by their successors during the centuries that followed. But this, he finally concluded, was a point in favour of Darwinianism as against the Lamarckian theory of the inheritance of acquired characteristics. "For in a state of anarchy, or despotism, or bad government, or after irruption of barbarians, force, strength, or ferocity, and not intellect, would be apt to gain the day." [21] But however favourable to natural selection, this consideration certainly tells against the inevitability of perfection—unless it counts as "perfection" when man becomes more brutal in order more effectively to cope with his enemies. If by "perfection" we mean something other

---

21. *The Life and Letters of Charles Darwin*, ed. Francis Darwin, 3 vols (London, 1887), Letter to C. Lyell, March 12, 1860, in Vol. II, p. 295.

than the better adjustment of a species to a new environment, if perfection be used in a sense which entails moral perfection, there is not the slightest ground for believing that such perfection will be ensured by the steady flow of evolution. The "fittest" might, in a particular environment, be the most bloodthirsty of parasites, the least ethical of monsters. In Hitler's Germany, S.S. guards were fitter to survive than the most moral of Jews. It may be that Hitler's Germany foreshadows the future of mankind. Granted that some men have now developed an ethical outlook which enables them to criticize the cruelties they observe in nature, this does not, on the face of it, serve to demonstrate that man is bound steadily to improve himself, morally and intellectually. Perhaps it is just these morally sensitive men who are destined to die out.

Even without the aid of a special metaphysics of emergence, some contemporary philosopher-biologists—T. H. Huxley's grandson, Julian Huxley, will serve as an example —try to meet such objections by laying great stress on what Huxley calls "the uniqueness of man" as distinct from his continuity with the animal kingdom. Man, Huxley argues, is different from the other animals in a way which guarantees his continuous mastery. He is, in the first place, enormously variable, and yet has kept his capacity to interbreed within the whole range of that variability. As a result of his habit of migrating and his relative willingness to ignore differences in, for example, colour when he mates, he has contained variability within a single species. Thus it happens that "the difference between a somewhat subnormal member of a savage tribe and a Beethoven or a Newton is assuredly comparable in extent with that between a sponge and a higher mammal."[22] And this gives man, Huxley points out, an im-

---

22. Julian Huxley: "The Uniqueness of Man" in *Man in the Modern World* (London, 1947; repr. 1950), p. 5.

mensely fruitful reservoir from which he can breed in order to advance the general level of the human species.

More important still, Huxley suggests, is the fact that with man a new type of evolution has entered upon the scene; for the first time acquired characteristics can be passed on. The human child has a long period of adult-dependence. The adults on whom the child is dependent pass on to him general concepts, tradition, a stock of information, in the manner which Herder had emphasized. So it comes about, Huxley goes on to maintain, that by the gradual increase in his scientific knowledge, man can substitute new methods of "effective, progressive change"—methods which are less dilatory, less wasteful, less cruel—for natural selection. He can deliberately bring about progress, he can deliberately impose upon himself and his planet what Huxley calls "the best and most enduring of our human standards."[23] Indeed, Julian Huxley is not, in the end, so far removed from his grandfather. For it would be easy enough to restate the thesis of Thomas Huxley's *Evolution and Ethics* in the following way: evolution has now produced in man a being who is critical, from an ethical standpoint, of natural selection, and who seeks to introduce other, more ethical methods, of producing biological changes. The difference is that Huxley thinks of the "uniqueness of man" as itself a product of evolutionary development; he is prepared to say therefore that there is within evolution itself a tendency to progress, not universally present but running as "a narrow thread . . . through the whole web of change." For evolution has produced man, and in man a being uniquely capable of progress.[24]

The difficulty remains, of course, which his opponents

23. *Ibid.*, p. 21.
24. Julian Huxley: "Thomas Henry Huxley and Julian Huxley: An Imaginary Interview" in *Man in the Modern World*, p. 209.

had urged against T. H. Huxley. If "natural selection" is in fact the mechanism by which biological characteristics are preserved, then to speak of man as substituting other methods for natural selection is, on the face of it, as absurd as it would be to speak of him as "defying the laws of gravity." When men travel to the moon they do so by relying on the "laws of gravity," not by defying them. When men breed new varieties, similarly, they do not, in so doing, "overcome" natural selection—and it makes no difference if the "new varieties" are new varieties of men. If the new varieties cannot accommodate themselves to the environment in which they find themselves, and have no way of changing their environment, then they will die out.

What should more accurately be said, it might be replied, is that natural selection has now produced a being who can deliberately breed for perfection and deliberately vary the environment so that the new varieties he breeds will survive. He does not "overcome" natural selection, if this entails that he can now breed without any longer worrying himself whether the new varieties might not, as a result of their environment, die out. But he can now, as natural selection could not, ensure that men will be perfected.

To argue thus, however, is to adopt the standpoint of genetic perfectibilism, with all its difficulties. There is no longer any guarantee in the mere course of natural history that man will be perfected. Everything now depends on the knowledge and the goodwill of the geneticists, imperfect men breeding for perfection—to say nothing of the technical question, raised by Medawar, whether the attempt to breed for perfection is not, for genetic reasons, self-defeating. Either evolution perfects *of itself* or else it can no longer be invoked to support a developmental, as distinct from a manipulative or managerial, perfectibilism.

Julian Huxley is not content, even, to suggest that men are, or can be, somehow "outside evolution." He wants to take matters still further. Men possess, he says, hidden powers whose nature they have not yet appreciated. Or if that is not quite true, these powers have only been appreciated, and then partly, by those Eastern mystics who, Huxley is prepared to acknowledge, have shown the world "what transcendent states of inner peace and unity of spirit the human personality is capable of."[25] Man, it therefore appears, has a future before him in which his uniqueness will be made more apparent; he will come into possession of spiritual powers the nature of which he is yet only on the verge of understanding, such powers as telepathy, extra-sensory perception, and Yoga concentration. On this question Huxley and Bergson are at one, in however improbable an alliance.

There is in several versions of evolutionary perfectibilism more than a hint, then, that man will develop into a being who is, by present standards, a superman. Such expectations had already been made explicit by the philosopher-economist Eugen Dühring. Under the conjoint influence of Darwin and Marx, Dühring had suggested that "humanity could eventually be transformed into a more perfect type of living being and would then look back upon the type of man whom we consider most highly developed as upon some extinct species of animal."[26] Man will evolve, that is, not only into a better man, but into a species higher than man. The most striking point about Dühring's superman is that he will at last have shaken himself free from religion. That liberation, according to Dühring, will transform man into superman; he will at last be free to realize his potentialities without fear of supernatural intervention and punishment. Joachim's age of the Holy Ghost, when men for the first time are fully free, is thus transformed by Dühring into an age without the Holy Ghost.

The idea of a "superman" is most commonly associated

---

25. Julian Huxley: *Evolution in Action* (London, 1953), p. 149.
26. *Der Werth des Lebens* (Breslau, 1865), trans. in Benz: *Evolution and Christian Hope,* p. 92, from the 3rd ed., 1881, p. 194.

with the philosophy of Nietzsche. Nietzsche liked to speak scornfully of Darwin. Darwin possessed, he says, "the intellect of a respectable but mediocre Englishman." A more damaging comment, from a German, is scarcely imaginable. And certainly Nietzsche did not believe that his superman will come into being by natural selection, as distinct from human choice. Nietzsche's attitude was, for the most part, Pelagian: he exhorted men to give birth to the superman by an exercise of will.

There are occasions, no doubt, on which he sounds like a Darwinian. In *Thus Spake Zarathustra* he addressed his fellow-men in post-Darwinian terms: "Ye want to be the ebb of that great tide, and would rather go back to the beast than surpass man? What is the ape to man? A laughing-stock, a thing of shame. And just the same shall man be to the Superman: a laughing-stock, a thing of shame."[27] But although in this passage Nietzsche writes as if the "tide" were moving in favour of the production of supermen, he is elsewhere only too willing to admit that what may rather emerge is that terrifying figure, the bane of the modern imagination, the "Last Man"—mass-produced man, a being so despicable that he is no longer capable even of despising himself. If the Superman is, according to Nietzsche, "the meaning of the earth," this is only to say that he is what the earth needs. Although he is "called for" it does not follow that he will come.

The belief in the inevitability of progress, Nietzsche argues in *The Will to Power*,[28] is nothing but the old religious way of thought, thinly disguised: progress, as we might put the matter, is Providence in his working clothes.* Indeed, Nietz-

27. Friedrich Nietzsche: *Thus Spake Zarathustra*, Pt. I, Prologue, §3, trans. Thomas Common in *The Complete Works of Friedrich Nietzsche*, ed. O. Levy, Vol. 11 (Edinburgh, 1909).

28. *The Will to Power*, Bk. IV, Aphorisms 1062–63, trans. A. M. Ludovici in *The Complete Works*, Vol. 15, 2nd ed. (Edinburgh, 1913), Vol. II, pp. 425–27.

* Lord Acton tells us that "this constancy of progress in the direction of organized and assured freedom, is the characteristic fact of Modern History, and its tribute to the

sche reacted so strongly against progressivism as to revert to the Stoic conception of an "eternal recurrence." The cyclical conception of history, he came to feel, is the only sure defence against the resurrection of God—that God who is now dead, since man has seen through him, but the relics of whose reign are not so easily disposed of. In thus separating the idea of the superman from any sort of evolution-based aspiration, Nietzsche, as so often, was unique.

George Bernard Shaw, under Samuel Butler's influence, pulled the two ideas together again. In the preface to his *Man and Superman* he is adamant that man as he now is has gone as far as he can go. "We must therefore frankly give up the notion that Man as he exists is capable of net progress." [29] For progress to be possible, then, man must be replaced by Superman. Man's only hope is his evolution into a higher species. By "evolution," however, Shaw means, in *Man and Superman,* deliberate breeding. Not until *Back to Methuselah* is his enthusiasm for "creative evolution" in full swing; that play is designed, he tells us, as the "beginning of a Bible for Creative Evolution." [30] The phrase is an interesting one: it is, indeed, only if evolution is conceived of in what are fundamentally religious terms, as the mode of operation of a Providential force, that it can provide any ground for the belief that man *must* turn into Superman.

Exponents of an evolutionary based progressivism have sometimes, we said, not been satisfied to predict the superman; evolution, on their view, has its eyes on something higher than the superman, something which can only be called divine. By the time Darwinism got under way, it was already a familiar view among German metaphysicians that human history can only be understood as part of the pro-

---

theory of Providence." (Inaugural Lecture in *Lectures in Modern History,* ed. H. Trevor-Roper, p. 26.)

29. Preface to *Man and Superman* in *The Complete Prefaces of Bernard Shaw* (London, 1965), p. 179.

30. Preface to *Back to Methuselah* in *Complete Prefaces,* p. 546.

cess by which God comes to be conscious of himself. The relation between God and the Absolute Idea in Hegel is no doubt obscure; sometimes Hegel writes, as Bradley does in *Appearance and Reality,* as if God is no more than an imperfect approximation to the true Absolute, sometimes, especially in his later writings, as if God and the Absolute were identical. This ambiguity explains why some of his disciples saw in him a critic of religion and others—as he saw himself—as its defender. In his *Philosophy of History,* however, Hegel was prepared explicitly to say that it was his task to "justify the ways of God to man" by demonstrating, in opposition to the common belief that Providence works in ways too mysterious for men to understand, that the works of Providence are visible in history—a Providence defined as "Wisdom, endowed with an infinite Power, which realizes its aim, viz., the absolute rational design of the World."[31] By 1811 Schelling could write without fear of contradiction, at least in Germany, that "it is now a customary idea to regard the entire history of the world as a progressive revelation of God."[32]

Ernest Renan, French-born but German-admirer, united the German concept of an evolving God and the French doctrine that the advance of science must bring progress in its train. By so doing, he gave birth to the first religion of science. In his *The Future of Science,* Renan divided the history of mankind, in Joachim's manner, into three stages: the age of myth, the age of analysis, the age of complete understanding. In the age of myth, he says, men project their dreams on to the world. The second age, the age of analysis represented by the Enlightenment, destroys the myths, without attempting to understand them; in so doing it impoverishes human life. But it has to undertake this work of destruction

---

31. G. W. F. Hegel: *The Philosophy of History,* Introduction, §111, as trans. J. Sibree, last rev. ed. with new introd. by C. J. Friedrich (New York, 1956), p. 13.

32. F. Schelling: *The Ages of the World,* trans. F. de W. Bolman (New York, 1942), p. 194.

in order to prepare the way for a third stage, in which it is for the first time understood that the world revealed by science is in itself miraculous. In this third age, which Renan thinks of himself as initiating, science and religion no longer appear as bitter opponents but as united in a system of ideas which is at once science and religion. Only after such a unification has been accomplished, according to Renan, can sages arise who, religious and scientific at once, are fit to guide mankind "by the light of reason along the path to perfection."

Man is to perfect himself, then, by coming to a fuller understanding of what he can be. The trouble with religions like Christianity, Renan argues, is that they have drawn a sharp distinction between the sacred and the profane. In consequence, they have identified perfection with *moral* perfection, to the exclusion of much that is of supreme value in human nature. A man is perfect, according to Renan, only if he conjoins in himself all that is valuable, not only morality, but curiosity, wisdom, poetry, passion. Renan reinstates, that is, the Renaissance ideal of "the universal man" harmoniously conjoining every variety of human perfection. "The perfect man," he writes, "will be he who is at the same time poet, philosopher, scientist, virtuous man, and that not by intervals or at distinct moments of his life; . . . he is indeed simultaneously poet and philosopher, philosopher and scientist, one in whom, in a word, all the elements of humanity are joined in a higher harmony, as in humanity itself." [33] And the actualization of the ideal, the perfection of man is, at the same time, so Renan tells us, the coming-into-being of God, God who exists as an ideal, but only as an ideal, until man perfects himself through science.

In a later work, his *Philosophical Dialogues*, Renan devel-

---

33. Ernest Renan: *L'Avenir de la science* (written 1848–49; first publ. Paris, 1890), in *Oeuvres complètes*, ed. H. Psichari, Vol. III (Paris, 1949), p. 736. For Renan's personal and political background see H. W. Wardman: *Ernest Renan* (London, 1964).

oped these ideas in a little more detail. For men to perfect themselves, he there says, they must first develop a new consciousness, higher than any they now possess but already adumbrated in nations or churches in so far as they behave as if they were individuals possessed of a single mind. As a result of this development of a "group mind," there will eventually come into existence, according to Renan, "a single being, summing up all the joys of the universe"—a being whose perfections all men will share in so far as they have helped to create him.[34] The whole universe is in travail for such a being: "let us console ourselves, poor victims: a God is being made with our tears."[35] Not, as Kant thought, a perfect state, not even an ethical commonwealth, but God is what human beings must by their efforts help to bring into existence.

Renan was not the only one who sought to bring together religion and science into a single harmonious whole and to base on their unity his confidence in the perfectibility of men; that, we might even say, was the most characteristic intellectual enterprise of the nineteenth century. At a more popular level, Henry Drummond's *The Ascent of Man* set out to show that "the God of Evolution," a God who gradually reveals his nature to man, "is infinitely grander than the occasional wonder-worker, who is the God of an old theology."[36] Evolution, according to Drummond, is progress towards the full revelation of a benevolent God of love. Properly speaking, he says, it should be called *in*volution rather than *e*volution; its meaning is given by what it moves towards, not by what it develops out of. There is no need, Drummond argues against Comte and Renan, of a new reli-

---

34. *Dialogues et fragments philosophiques* (1876) in *Oeuvres complètes,* Vol. I (Paris, 1947), p. 623.
35. *Ibid.,* p. 630.
36. Henry Drummond: *The Lowell Lectures on the Ascent of Man* (London, 1894), ch. X, p. 428.

gion to incorporate the revelations of evolution; Christianity can be such a religion. Christianity is the way in which evolution spreads abroad its message of love; Christianity shows men the path they must follow in order to reach that final consummation towards which all evolution is directed. Drummond's "nature" is a Nature infused by love, a Nature whose aim it is that man shall perfect himself—a far cry from Romanes' "Nature" with its preference for savagery and parasitism, a far cry, too, from Augustine's God.

In the twentieth century, the same hopeful note has been sounded by Teilhard de Chardin. Although a Jesuit, Teilhard is willing to agree with Renan that traditional Christianity has gone astray, although not that it needs to be replaced by a religion of science.* In the first place, he alleges, Christianity has been at fault in so far as it has wrongly supposed the Universe to be static; it has supposed, that is, that "the spirit is no longer under way, it is not going anywhere, it is simply hanging on; nature is complete." This erroneous supposition has forced it to conclude that "perfection can consist, for men, only in an individual ascent towards the supernatural." For Teilhard, very much in Renan's manner, perfection lies in the progress, not of individuals but of mankind as a whole, towards a unification with God which, if supernatural in character, is at the same time the "natural" outcome of evolution.[37]

The second mistake, Teilhard agrees with Renan, lies in Christianity's attempt to drive a wedge between the sacred

---

* Sometimes, however, in the manner of a Joachim or a Lessing he looks forward to the emergence of a new, and higher, form of Christianity. He developed a fondness for expressions with the prefix "super"—super-humanity, super-Christ, super-Charity—although he explained that he meant by these expressions to refer not to a difference in nature but "a more advanced degree of realization and perfection." See Pierre Teilhard de Chardin: *Science et Christ* (Paris, 1965), trans. as *Science and Christ* by René Hague (London, 1968), ch. X.

37. Teilhard de Chardin: Unpubl. "Notes sur la notion de perfection chrétienne" (1942), quoted in Emile Rideau: *Teilhard de Chardin*, trans. R. Hague (London, 1967), p. 37.

and profane. "There is a sense in which he [God]," writes Teilhard, "is at the tip of my pen, my spade, my brush, my needle, as well as of my heart and of my thought." Not realizing this, he says, "nine out of ten practising Christians feel that man's work is always at the level of a 'spiritual encumbrance'"—an attitude of mind which leads them to live "a double or crippled life." In contrast, Teilhard argues that "*nothing* here below *is profane* for those who know how to see." He looks forward to a time when "there will be little to separate life in the cloister from the life of the world." Only then, he says, will mankind "have attained the intended plenitude of its humanity." [38]

Teilhard does not realize, it would seem, that in taking this view he was adhering to an already-established Christian tradition, exemplified in Luther and in Francis de Sales, for which man's vocation is sacred. This is not altogether surprising; Teilhard shows few signs of having any close acquaintance with the Protestant tradition. And he was developing his ideas at a time when, in reaction against "modernism" and in terror of Communistic humanism, the Roman Catholic Church was anything but inclined to enter into an alliance with science or to extol the greatness of human achievements. As for Protestantism, under Kierkegaard's influence and in an attempt to turn back the rising tides of secularism, it had reinstated an attitude to the world not far short of Manichaeanism. Kierkegaard had written, for example, that "Christianity does not unite men, on the contrary, it separates them—in order to unite each single person with God"; he had been prepared to maintain that "to love God means to hate the world." [39] For Teilhard, in contrast, it is above all characteristic of Christianity that it *unites* men. And the "two great loves" which it has to reconcile,

38. *Le Milieu divin* (Paris, 1957), trans. B. Wall and others (London, 1960; Fontana ed. 1964, repr. 1967), pp. 64–67.

39. Søren Kierkegaard: *The Last Years, ed. cit.,* pp. 54, 130.

without the fusion of which "there can be no Kingdom of God," are the love of God and the love of the world.[40]

No one could be more remote than is Teilhard from Gnosticism or from that version of Christianity which bids men flee the world. Teilhard is willing to admit that "matter is the burden, the fetters, the pain, the sin and the threat to our lives," that "it weighs us down, suffers, wounds, tempts and grows old." But asceticism, he says, looks no farther than this: "and it recoils, exclaiming 'Flee!'" That, to Teilhard, is, in Dante's phrase, "the great refusal," not to see the creative, as well as the destructive, powers of matter. "What would our spirits be, O God, if they did not have the bread of earthly things to nourish them, the wine of created beauties to intoxicate them, and the conflicts of human life to fortify them?" The problem is "to contemplate the sphinx without succumbing to its spell."[41] Christ has assumed material form: that sanctifies the world. "Matter," so Teilhard addressed the world, "you in whom I find both seduction and strength, you in whom I find blandishment and virility, you who can enrich and destroy, I surrender myself to your mighty layers, with faith in the heavenly influences which have sweetened and purified your waters."[42]

When Teilhard speaks of "the love of the world" he is not referring, of course, to what is commonly called "worldliness"; he does not mean that men should devote themselves to the pursuit of wealth and reputation. Nor does he mean that they should love the world as an artist may love it, rejoicing in its diversity of form and its sensual texture. To love the world, for Teilhard, is to love it as something with which men can co-operate in its progress towards ever higher spiritual levels. (The influence of Bergson is

---

40. Teilhard de Chardin: Letter of 31 December 1926, quoted in Henri de Lubac: *The Religion of Teilhard de Chardin*, trans. R. Hague (London, 1967), p. 105.
41. *Le Milieu divin, ed. cit.*, pp. 106–7.
42. *Ibid.*, pp. 110–11.

obvious.) Man alone can love it in this way. With his evolution, according to Teilhard, something "quite new" has
come into existence, a being who was capable of becoming
conscious of himself as evolving, a being who can understand that "the World is constantly, even if imperceptibly,
emerging a little further above nothingness" and who can
help it to do so.[43] Christianity has treated the world, in Augustine's fashion, as something which has simply to be used.
For Teilhard, in contrast, the Christian's motto should be "to
heaven through fulfilment of earth"—a fulfilment which implies *co-operation* with the world. "The very notion of Christian perfection," he therefore writes, ". . . has to be revised
and overhauled."[44] It is because they shared this attitude
to the world that Teilhard and Julian Huxley, for all that
Teilhard was a Jesuit and Julian Huxley a humanist, could
recognize in one another kindred spirits.

In what direction is the world moving? In the first place,
so Teilhard argues, towards a society infused by mutual love,
an organized society in which men can live as ultra-human
beings. Teilhard has a passion for unity—"there is only one
Evil = disunity"[45]—for the bringing together of superficially
disparate ingredients into a single complex form of organization; his attitude towards unity, indeed, is the attitude of
a mystic, although a mystic who sees God in the universe
rather than above it. From childhood, he tells us, he had
"the passion for the Absolute."[46] "To be entirely happy," he
writes, "I needed to know that that 'Some One Essential
Thing' existed, to which everything else was only accessory
or even an ornament."[47] He carried over that same attitude

43. Teilhard de Chardin, quoted in Lubac, *op. cit.*, p. 23.
44. "Research, Work and Worship" (1955), as trans. in *Science and Christ*, p. 220.
45. "My Universe" (1924), as trans. in *Science and Christ*, p. 80, n.
46. As quoted in Lubac, *op. cit.*, p. 13.
47. Quoted from "Le Coeur de la matière" (1950, unpubl.) in Nicolas Corte: *Pierre Teilhard de Chardin*, p. 3.

into adult life: "The multitude of beings," he once wrote, "is a terrible affliction."[48]

However confused and incoherent the world might sometimes look to him he never lost his conviction that "this incoherence is the prelude to a unification."[49] It was not merely, Teilhard thought, that he possessed, what others lacked, a taste for unity. Questions of taste apart, there was evidence in evolution itself, he tried to argue, that it sought ever higher degrees of complex unification. Man could not stay as he now is, the "human" world could not remain for ever "a huge and disparate thing, just about as coherent, at the moment, as the surface of a rough sea."[50] To say that it could do so would be to deny, he maintains, the clear teachings of evolution or—as he liked, in Drummond's manner, to call it—"*in*volution."

Even if humanity is bound to be further unified in wider complex wholes, however, it is anything but clear that the resulting unified complex would be infused by love. But Teilhard thought that there were *moral* reasons for believing that such a love-infused society must be, at least, the object of men's strivings. For only in such a society could men love their neighbour as themselves. Teilhard's "two great loves," it will be remembered, were the love of God and the love of the World, not, as one might expect from so convinced a Christian, the love of God and the love of one's neighbour. Teilhard confesses, indeed, "that I have long been, and even now am, recalcitrant to the love of my neighbour"; he had, he tells us, a "sort of repugnance," a "feeling of revulsion" towards his fellow-men. He could not help seeing in them "the greatest threat we meet on the road our personality follows as it develops." Far from its being the case that men

48. *Le Milieu mystique* (1917), quoted in Lubac, *op. cit.*, p. 251.
49. Letter to the Abbé Breuil, 25 May 1923, in *Letters from a Traveller, 1925–1955*, trans. R. Hague and others (London, 1962; paperback ed. 1967), p. 34.
50. *Ibid.*

have a natural sympathy towards one another, they would, he thinks, if they were left to their own resources, respond to each other with mutual repulsion rather than with sympathy.[51] Teilhard had good friends, but it is extraordinary how little, in such writings as *Letters from a Traveller,* he has to say about the Chinese people amongst whom he lived and worked and how superficial his observations are. Scenery, yes, people as picturesque objects, yes. But he has none of that passionate interest in the diversity of human beings, their diversity in outlook, customs, beliefs, which mark the humanity-centred traveller. To Teilhard such diversity was but an obstacle to unification.

This attitude to his fellow-men is not, of course, peculiar to Teilhard. Rousseau, as we have already seen, had traced the source of all corruption to "the hands of men." But perhaps Kant, writing under Rousseau's influence, comes nearer than anyone else to Teilhard. In his efforts to achieve Christian freedom, man finds himself, Kant says, corrupted by other men, not because they are "sunk in evil" but because they inevitably arouse in him the spirit of emulation. "It suffices that they are at hand, that they surround him, and that they are men, for them mutually to corrupt each other's predispositions and make one another evil."[52]

It is not only evil communications, that is, but communications of any sort which corrupt. (The desert fathers, it will be remembered, held precisely this same view of human relationships.) The corruption now inherent in human relationships can, according to Kant, only be overcome in that "ethical commonwealth," that society based on "the laws of virtue"—i.e. on non-coercive laws—in which alone reason can find full satisfaction. Such a society, he further argued,

51. For the sources of these quotations and the full development of this theme, see Rideau, *op. cit.,* pp. 471–72.

52. Kant: *Religion Within the Limits of Reason Alone,* Bk. III, Introduction, as trans. *ed. cit.,* p. 85.

can never be complete until it is total, until it is a society of all rational men, ruled by God.

On Teilhard's view, something very like Kant's "ethical commonwealth" *must* come into being, but not because reason would otherwise be perpetually dissatisfied but because that is the direction in which evolution is moving. He thinks of it, too, as a society infused with love rather than, in Kant's typically moralistic fashion, with virtue. He agrees with Kant, however, on the vital point: only in such a society can men safely love their neighbours, seeing in them a helpful ally rather than a corrupting rival in their quest for perfection. Men can *begin* to love one another, Teilhard nevertheless suggests, as soon as they have "woken to an explicit consciousness of the evolution that carries them along, and begin to fix their eyes, as one man, on one same thing ahead of them."[53] Teilhard is like so many other scientists, then, in setting up as his ideal a society which is nothing less, in its spiritual atmosphere, than one great research team, dedicated to a single objective and working towards that objective by co-operative effort, under the leadership of Christ.

There was, Teilhard thought, empirical evidence—as well as the general principle that evolution always moves in the direction of greater organization—to suggest that men, here and now, were working towards such a form of society.* It was much easier for Teilhard to sympathize with Fascism

---

53. Teilhard de Chardin: *La Centrologie* (1944), No. 29, in *L'Activation de l'énergie* (Paris, 1958), p. 126, quoted in Rideau, *op. cit.,* p. 54.

* Once again we are reminded of Renan, of Renan's view that here and now men could discern that higher form of life of which they would eventually form part. What human beings are creating, Teilhard says in a note, is "a living organism"—a living organism which "encloses us." As evidence of what that "living organism" would be like, he refers to our experience in war-time when "wrested out of ourselves by the force of a collective passion, we have a sense of rising to a higher level of human existence" ["A Note on Progress," written 10 August 1920, first published in *L'Avenir de l'homme* (Paris, 1959), trans. as *The Future of Man* by N. Denny (London, 1964; paperback ed., 1969, pp. 21–22)]. In general terms, what Teilhard is trying to do is to *Christianize* Renan and, beyond Renan, German "developmental" philosophies.

or with Communism than with such of his fellow-Christians as were suspicious of new social orders or saw no reason for expecting that the future would be brighter and better than the past. He was almost completely indifferent, it would seem, to the loss of liberty Fascism and Communism entailed or to the suffering they brought with them. As one of his biographers has put it, Teilhard was "in a sense the least humanitarian of men."[54] He is quite unable to appreciate the feelings of those who wish that the atomic scientists had "destroyed the dangerous fruits of their invention." In his essay "Some Reflections on the Spiritual Repercussions of the Atom Bomb" he does not so much as mention Hiroshima or Nagasaki; it is enough for him that the atom bomb showed what could be accomplished by scientific team-work and that it would, so he thought, forward the internationalization of the world.[55] One is uncomfortably reminded of what the Countess Tolstoy once wrote to her husband: "Maybe you can remain above all feelings of affection for your own children, but mere mortals like me cannot. Or maybe it's that we don't try to justify our lack of any profound love by pretending to love the whole universe."[56]

Teilhard was prepared, indeed, to write with approval of Fascism that it "opens its arms to the future" in so far as it sets out "to embrace vast wholes in its empire"; he went so far as to maintain that it "may possibly represent a fairly successful small-scale model of tomorrow's world." What was wrong with Fascism, in his eyes, was that it is nationalistic, and so too narrow in its outlook. He has nothing to say against its illiberalism; he praises Fascism, indeed, because "it is more anxious than any other system to allow for the preservation of the élite (which means the

54. Robert Speaight: *Teilhard de Chardin* (London, 1967), p. 89.

55. Teilhard de Chardin: "Some Reflections on the Spiritual Repercussions of the Atom Bomb," first publ. 1946, in *The Future of Man, ed. cit.,* p. 145.

56. Letter of Countess Tolstoy, 3 February 1882, quoted in Henri Troyat: *Tolstoy,* trans. Nancy Amphoux (New York, 1967), p. 423.

personal and the Spirit) and to make good use of it."[57] Writing about the Communist forces in China, Teilhard suggests that the real struggle in the modern world is not, as Marx had thought, between worker and exploiter or, as so many Christians believe, between Christian and atheist; fundamentally the conflict is between the bourgeoisie "who simply wish to make the world a comfortable dwelling-place" and the representatives of what he elsewhere calls a "new substance," "*homo progressivus*," a species made up of such men as can only conceive the world as "a machine for progress—or, better, an organism that is progressing." This "new type of man" is most fully exemplified in "scientists, thinkers, airmen and so on—all those possessed by the demon (or the angel) of Research." Whatever their metaphysics, their politics, their religion, such men are, in Teilhard's eyes, the true "toilers of the Earth," the humanity of tomorrow, "the agents and elements of planetization." As for those who merely want to make the world more comfortable, they are "the cast-offs."[58]

There was not much love, one naturally objects, in Mussolini's Italy or in Stalin's Russia. And, of course, Teilhard would freely grant that neither Fascist Italy nor Communist Russia were, in detail, the society of which men are in search. The first was insufficiently "universalistic," the second insufficiently "personalistic." But he needed some evidence that mankind was now moving towards "the planetization of humanity," some evidence stronger than the inductive argument, for what it is worth, that up until now evolution had moved from a primitive disunity towards an ever higher degree of unified organization.

He somehow had to show, too, against humanists like Julian Huxley, that evolution cannot be content with man

57. Teilhard de Chardin: "The Salvation of Mankind" in *Science and Christ, ed. cit.*, pp. 140–41.

58. "The Planetisation of Mankind," first publ. 1946, in *The Future of Man, paperback ed. cit.*, pp. 142, 144.

as he now is, or man in an intellectually and morally improved form, that it is moving towards a type of organization
which includes but is higher than man.[59] Teilhard found
the evidence he needed, or so he thought, in the rise of
totalitarian social organizations. "The modern totalitarian
régimes," he wrote, ". . . are in line with the essential trend
of 'cosmic' movement."[60] (They scarcely afford, as we have
already suggested, any evidence that evolution was moving
towards what he called "amorization," the growth and diffusion of love.) Even as late as 1946, he was still prepared
to write that it was too early "to judge recent totalitarian experiments fairly," to make up our minds whether "all things
considered, they have produced a greater degree of enslave-
ment or a higher level of spiritual energy."[61]

Teilhard's primary interest, however, is in the perfecting
of the Universe; to this climactic event the perfecting of man
is only a preliminary. In the final culmination the individual
person, like everything else, is taken up into the mystical
body of the Universal Christ, a Christ who gathers to himself "not only the scattered multitude of souls, but also the
solid organic reality of the universe, taken whole and entire
in the extension and total unity of its energies."[62] (Teilhard
was profoundly influenced by Paul, especially the Epistle to
the Ephesians, according to which God will "in the fulness
of times . . . gather together in one all things in Christ, both
which are in heaven, and which are on earth.")[63] Man will be

---

59. There are many points of resemblance between Teilhard's views about the nature
of secular progress and the views expressed in F. S. Marvin's *The Living Past* (Oxford, 1913)
and *A Century of Hope: A Sketch of Western Progress from 1815 to the Great War* (Oxford, 1919).
The critical comments on Marvin in Robert Shafer: *Progress and Science* (New Haven, 1922)
have more than a little relevance to Teilhard.

60. Teilhard de Chardin: "The Grand Option," written 3 March 1939, in *The Future
of Man, ed. cit.,* p. 48.

61. "Life and the Planets," first publ. May 1946, in *The Future of Man, ed. cit.,* p. 123.

62. "La Parole attendue" (1940) in *Cahiers Pierre Teilhard de Chardin* (Paris, 1958),
No. 4, p. 27 as quoted in Rideau, *op. cit.,* p. 61.

63. Ephesians 1:10.

finally perfected, then, only when he is unified with Christ — so far Teilhard writes in the spirit of Christian mysticism. And at the end, he also agrees with the mystics, it is only by divine grace, human effort being at this point powerless, that the final consummation can come about. The movement towards perfection, if not the final state, can, Teilhard nevertheless argues, be described in purely scientific, secular terms and supported by scientific evidence, as distinct from the "intuitions" on which Bergson relied or the teachings of revelation on which Christians have ordinarily rested their confidence in the future.

If we still have doubts, if we still feel that it is an unjustified extrapolation from the scientific facts [64] to suggest that the entire Universe, and with it man, are moving towards perfection, Teilhard appeals to moral-pragmatic considerations. Men *must* believe that mankind is perfectible, since otherwise human effort will collapse.* " 'Positive and critical' minds," he writes, "can go on saying as much as they like that the new generation . . . no longer believes in a future and in a perfecting of the world. Has it even occurred to those who write and repeat these things that, if they were right, all spiritual movement on earth would be virtually brought to a stop?" And if it is, he goes on to add, "the whole of evolution will come to a halt — because we are evolution." [65] Never more ingenuously has it been argued at

---

64. For a lively criticism of Teilhard's astonishing claim that *The Phenomenon of Man* is a "scientific" work, see P. B. Medawar: *The Art of the Soluble*, pp. 71–84.

* Teilhard was not, of course, the first to take this view; we have noted it, in a weaker form, in Kant. It is more explicit in Benjamin Constant's *De la Perfectibilité de l'espèce humaine*, first published in his *Mélanges*, in 1829. If we do not accept the perfectibility of man then, according to Constant, "we ought to close our books, renounce our speculations, free ourselves from fruitless sacrifices, and devote ourselves completely to useful or agreeable acts, which would serve to make less insipid a life without hope and decorate for a moment a life without future." (Ed. P. Deguise, Lausanne, 1967, p. 42.) Yet the Greeks did not believe in the perfectibility of man and can scarcely be said to have "renounced speculation." Constant and Teilhard are giving expression to a queer modern attitude, not to a universal state of mind.

65. *The Phenomenon of Man*, trans. by B. Wall and others (London, 1959), pp. 232–33.

once that evolution, as Christ's work, must go on and that if men cease their efforts, it will cease to go on.

To an extraordinary degree, then, Teilhard built into a single system almost all the main forms of perfectibilism which we have so far distinguished from one another. He was a mystic: perfection consists in union with God. He was a Christian: perfection depends on Christ's working in man through evolution. He was a metaphysician: perfection consists in the development to its final form of that consciousness which is present, according to Teilhard, even in elementary electrons. He believed in perfection through science: scientific research is, in his eyes, the prototype of "working with God." He believed in perfection through social change: men are to be perfected through their participation in a society infused with love. He believed that Christianity shows us in what perfection consists: the New Testament, and especially Paul, reveal to us the nature of that final unity in which evolution must finally come to rest; the Incarnation, the sacrifice of the Mass, symbolize the unity of the material and the spiritual. He believed that science can demonstrate that humanity is moving towards such a perfection. He was Pelagian in his constant emphasis on human effort; he was anti-Pelagian in so far as he argued that God's grace is essential if mankind is to achieve its final perfection. If Teilhard had not existed, it would almost have been necessary to invent him, in order to weave together our diverse themes.

Let us now look back on the path we have taken in our discussion of progress by natural development. For Joachim, progress to a new age was guaranteed by prophecy, even if its manner of development can be empirically discerned in the course of history. Leibniz, in contrast, argued that the final perfection of all things is guaranteed on purely metaphysical grounds; everything *must* in the end achieve the perfection inherent in it, by a necessity inherent in the very nature of the Universe. Herder accepted the

Leibnizian metaphysics, but concerned himself more particularly with the perfection of mankind; mankind will perfect itself, he tried to show, in a form of society in which men can fully realize their "humanity"; they work towards that society by means of traditions, which are handed on from generation to generation by education. Kant looked forward, rather, to an ideal State, or, in his later writings, to an "ethical Commonwealth." Although he commits himself, at times, to a Leibnizian metaphysics, he also presents us with a moral-pragmatic argument; men *must* work towards an ideal society because nowhere else can the demand of their reason be satisfied. Hegel set out to understand past history rather than to forecast the future; he saw in history the gradual coming to full self-consciousness of an Absolute Idea, sometimes identified with God, by means of dialectical processes. His left-Hegelian followers rejected the view that this process of development had reached its final point in the Prussian State; the dialectic, they argued, is still under way; it is a dialectic which works, according to Marx, through class-struggles and will finally issue not in the State but in a class-less, State-less, society.

The rise of Darwinianism led to an even greater emphasis on the perfection of men by natural processes: in Spencer, the survival of the fittest was identified with the survival of the best, and the future perfection of mankind was deduced from the fact that evolution selects the fittest. Other philosophers rejected the view that natural selection is sufficient to guarantee the perfecting of mankind; evolution, they maintained, is the expression of a "life-force," which has finally produced in man a being capable of shaping his own social destiny.

In one way or another, indeed, there has been a growing insistence, in opposition to Darwin, that man, whatever his origins, is unique, unique in his freedom, unique in his power of co-operating with—or perhaps working against—the processes of evolution. Although he has developed out of lower forms of living organisms, the self-consciousness which makes him unique represents, it is argued, an "emergent" quality, not definable purely in terms of living processes and still less in terms of physico-chemical reactions. But if man has thus "emerged," the further conclusion is drawn, there is good reason for believing that something higher than man may yet be evolved, some form of superhuman being, with psychical powers we can yet only guess at, perhaps a God, perhaps gods.

There is no conflict, so a number of philosophers have sought to show, between religion and evolution. It has been a matter of controversy, however, whether evolutionary theory demonstrates the need for a new religion to include the new idea of an evolving Universe or whether nothing more is needed than a transformed—or for the first time clearly understood—Christianity. In Teilhard these various tendencies converged. Evolution, so he suggested, moves towards, first, the perfection of man in new forms of social organization and, then, ultimately, man's union with Christ —a union which evolution prepares us to expect, in so far as it involves the unification of all things, but to which revelation gives its specifically Christian content. So if Teilhard is right, the idea of perfection by natural development is identical with the idea of perfection by mystical union with Christ; science prepares the way for "the coming of Christ," as do human attempts to find a unified form of social organization in which men, at last, can love their neighbours as fellow-workers for Christ.

THIRTEEN

PERFECTION RENOUNCED:
THE DYSTOPIANS

No variety of perfectibilism has yet entirely vanished, killed outright by criticism or cast aside as obsolescent. Even the most fanciful extremes of Christian perfectibilist heresy still have their devotees; rashly to open one's door to the missionaries of some twentieth-century sect is, as often as not, to be engulfed in perfectibilist prophecy, millennarian, Manichaean. Christian mysticism, in the eighteenth and nineteenth centuries somewhat suspiciously regarded by Roman Catholics and Protestants alike, has in our own century won new admirers; never before, perhaps, have Buddhist and Hindu mystical perfectibilism attracted so many Western disciples. There has been a notable revival, even, of nineteenth-century ready-mix mysticism, which looks to drug-taking rather than to purgation for its "enlargement of consciousness."

Secular perfectibilism, in all its forms, is no less persistent. Genetic manipulation is still extolled as man's one chance of salvation from the ills of flesh and spirit; education and science and legislation are still warmly advocated as instruments of perfection. "I believe in the perfectibility of man," defiantly announces that twentieth-century Enlightener Erich Fromm—even if he is careful to add that it is not inevitable, but only possible, for the "New Man," at last perfected, to emerge as a fit inhabitant for the "One World" of the future.[1] Anarchists have not ceased to hope that they

---

1. Erich Fromm: *Beyond the Chains of Illusion: My Encounter with Marx and Freud* (New York, 1962), pp. 177–82.

can fertilize a new world with the ashes of the old. Combining the two perfectibilist threads, secular and religious, it is in our century, and in its middle decades, that Teilhard has produced his extraordinary amalgam of mystical and scientific perfectibilism. And no less extraordinary is the Freud-inspired perfectibilism of Norman Brown's *Life Against Death*—a mysticism which seeks to find "a way out of the human neurosis into that simple health that animals enjoy, but not man."[2]

Tempting as it is, then, to contrast in the sharpest possible way the scepticism and cynicism of the post-1939 world with the optimistic perfectibilism of the pre-1914 world, one can properly do so only with considerable reservations. That reservation applies even to the most optimistic form of perfectibilism, according to which the perfecting of man is guaranteed by the slow but sure operation of impersonal historical forces. "No reasonable person," a contemporary political theorist is no doubt prepared to write, "can today believe in any 'law' of progress. In the age of two world wars, totalitarian dictatorship, and mass murder this faith can be regarded only as simple-minded, or even worse, as a contemptible form of complacency."[3] But neither Teilhard nor the Marxists would admit to irresponsibility or simple-mindedness or complacency. Wars, dictatorship and mass murders are, on their view, but passing phases in the ever onward and upward progress of mankind. All that can correctly be said is that liberally-minded Western intellectuals have for the most part lost their belief in the inevitability of progress. Liberally-minded Western intellectuals represent, however, only a segment of the modern world—in numerical terms a very small segment.

On the other side, pre-1914 Europe was by no means

2. Norman Brown: *Life Against Death* (London, 1959; repr. 1960), Pt. VI, ch. xvi, p. 311.

3. Judith N. Shklar: *After Utopia: The Decline of Political Faith* (Princeton, 1957), Preface, p. vii.

unrelievedly optimistic. Although enthusiasm for progress was nowhere more marked than in France, the poet Baudelaire could still attack what he called the "infatuation" with progress as "a grotesque idea, flourishing on an earth made rotten by modern self-satisfaction" and the novelist Gautier could expostulate: "What a stupid thing it is, this pretended perfectibility of man they din into our ears."[4] Victor Hugo was by no means expressing the unanimous conviction of French intellectuals when in his *Plein Ciel* he composed a sonorous hymn to perfectibility.

Poets and novelists can be expected to go their own way. But nineteenth-century politicians, too, and especially conservative politicians, were far from universally convinced that it was man's destiny constantly to improve his condition. Lord Balfour, philosopher-statesman, chose the occasion of an address to undergraduates, delivered in 1891 in his capacity as Rector of Glasgow University, to express his doubts; his young audience, he fully realized, would listen to him with scepticism and impatience. There is no empirical evidence, he told them, to suggest that civilization—as Condorcet and after him Hegel had maintained—must always pass on from nation to nation; perhaps it will some day collapse, once and for all. The theory of evolution, he went on to say, does nothing to justify optimism about the future of mankind. Were the environment to alter, mankind might degenerate rather than improve. Art and Science, Balfour argued against the Fabians, would almost certainly decline in a society which runs more smoothly, which is less subject to conflict, than our own. As for the idea that man could be perfected by legislation, governmental action, he said, touches only the periphery of human conduct; its incidence is, even then, uncertain. "The future of the race," so Bal-

---

4. C. Baudelaire: "Exposition universelle de 1855," *Curiosités esthétiques* (Paris, 1923), p. 227 and T. Gautier: *Mademoiselle de Maupin* (Paris, 1927 ed.), Préface, p. 23, quoted in D. G. Charlton: *Secular Religions in France, 1815–1870* (London, 1963), pp. 157–58.

four summed up, "is thus encompassed with darkness: no
faculty of calculation that we possess, no instrument that we
are likely to invent, will enable us to map out its course, or
penetrate the secret of its destiny."[5]

His fellow-statesman, Disraeli, had more succinctly
summed up a not uncommon Conservative attitude when
he wrote that "the European talks of progress because by
the aid of a few scientific discoveries he has established a
society which has mistaken comfort for civilization."[6] Water-
closets and macadamized roads did not, that is to say, constitute moral progress. There were always those, in short, who
were convinced that moral progress was largely an illusion,
that human beings, and the civilizations they create, were
unlikely in the future to be substantially better, at least from
the point of view of moral perfection, than they had been in
the past. To suppose otherwise, merely because nineteenth-
century civilization, in certain limited respects, had reached
a new high water mark, was, they agreed with Dean Inge, to
"mistake the flowing tide for the river of eternity."[7]

But Balfour and Disraeli, Baudelaire and Gautier, were
consciously defying the "spirit of the age." Like the defend-
ers of progress in the seventeenth century, they were moved
to write as warmly as they did because the opposite view
was so strongly, and so widely, maintained. What particularly strikes us, indeed, is the unexpectedness of the pre-
1914 writers who express their conviction that men not only
could and should, but most certainly would, lift themselves
to higher and higher stages of perfection. "Men," wrote
that arch-amorist or arch-liar Frank Harris in his *My Life
and Loves,* "at least should grow in goodness and loving-

---

5. Lord Balfour: *A Fragment on Progress*, Rectorial Address, University of Glasgow,
1891 (Edinburgh, 1892); included in his *Essays and Addresses*, 3rd ed. (Edinburgh, 1905),
p. 279.

6. Quoted in W. R. Inge: "The Idea of Progress," Romanes Lecture, 1920, included
in *Outspoken Essays*, Second Series (London, 1922; repr. 1927), p. 179.

7. *Ibid.*, p. 169.

kindness, should put an end, not only to war and pestilence, but also to poverty, destitution and disease, and so create for themselves a Paradise on this earth." He went on to add, even more remarkably, that "man . . . must create not only a Heaven for men but for insects and plants, too, for all life, especially the so-called lower forms of it."[8] Man certainly need have no fear of his powers, if he can create an earth which will be at once a paradise for mosquitoes and a paradise for humanity.

The prevailing mood was slightly less ecstatically expressed in Winwood Reade's much-reprinted *The Martyrdom of Man*. First published in 1872, it illustrates very clearly the secular perfectibilism which then flourished, with its roots in the eighteenth century. "The Prince of Darkness," Reade was willing to concede, "is still triumphant in many regions of the world; epidemics still rage, death is yet victorious." But the God of Light—demythologized into science as the Prince of Darkness is demythologized into ignorance—is bound, Reade was fully confident, finally to conquer.*

Science will convert earth into a paradise. Hunger, let alone starvation, will be unknown; "none will be rich, and none poor." More than that; man will conquer his own nature. He will subdue not only "the forces of evil that are without" but, much more importantly, "the base instincts

---

8. *My Life and Loves*, orig. publ. Paris, 1922–27; ed. John F. Gallagher, 5 vols in 1 (London, 1964), Vol. IV, p. 843.

* Reade's metaphors derive in the long run from Zoroaster. His is, indeed, an unusually explicit version of the secular Zoroastrianism so characteristic of nineteenth-century perfectibilists. History is conceived of as a great drama in which the forces of progress fight against—and will finally destroy, thanks to the Messiah, Science—the forces of reaction, as represented especially by religion. Such a secular Zoroastrianism, rather than the elaborate metaphysical constructions of a Hegel or the economic analyses of a Marx, is the faith which sustained much everyday nineteenth-century secular perfectibilism. It lent itself to pictorial illustration: science was symbolized by electricity—for the late nineteenth century the prime example of scientific achievement—and expelled the forces of darkness in a quite literal sense. The battle between Electricity and Darkness was, on the continent of Europe especially, the stock-theme of anti-clerical pageants, the secular counterblast to Christian dramas of salvation. Compare Belloc's "The Benefits of the Electric Light" in *Complete Verse* (Duckworth, 1970), pp. 155–58.

and propensities which he has inherited from the animals below." The whole world, in consequence, will be "united by the same sentiment which united the primeval clan, and which made its members think, feel, and act as one." What God had been in man's imagination, man would become in reality. "Man then will be perfect; he will then be a creator; he will therefore be what the vulgar worship as a god."[9]

As late as 1922, H. G. Wells, a great admirer of Reade, could end his widely-read *A Short History of the World* on a similarly optimistic note. Man, he said, relying on an analogy which is by now only too familiar, is still adolescent; his troubles arise out of his "increasing and still undisciplined strength," not out of senility and exhaustion. "Can we doubt," he rhetorically concluded, "that presently our race . . . will achieve unity and peace, that it will live, the children of our blood and lives will live, in a world made more splendid and lovely than any palace or garden that we know, going on from strength to strength in an ever widening circle of adventure and achievement?"[10] Only too easily, many of Wells's readers would now reply, can we doubt whether our children will live in a world more splendid and more lovely than any palace or garden that we now know. At best they will live in an air-conditioned box, at worst they will not live at all, or will live in a hovel in a devastated world.

Wells himself, when in 1946 he revised his *Short History of the World,* expunged his optimistic predictions and added a new chapter, with a significant title: "Mind at the End of Its Tether." "*Homo sapiens,*" he there wrote, ". . . is in his present form played out. The stars in their courses have turned against him and he has to give place to some other animal better adapted to face the fate that closes in more and more swiftly upon mankind."[11] By the standards of later

9. *The Martyrdom of Man,* 9th ed. (London, 1884), pp. 512–15.
10. H. G. Wells: *A Short History of the World* (London, 1922), ch. LXVII.
11. *Ibid.,* definitive rev. ed. (Harmondsworth, 1946; repr. 1949), ch. 71: "From 1940

generations, however, Wells was still an optimist. He did not plumb the full depths of modern pessimism, the fear that not only man but every living species might be totally destroyed by a nuclear explosion.

The pessimism of modern liberals is by no means surprising: over the last half-century perfectibilists have experienced a long series of historical blows. To some former perfectibilists, as to Karl Barth, the First World War was enough to reveal how absurd it is to put any faith in men and, more particularly, in intellectuals, for the Enlightenment the great agents of perfection. At the first blast of the trumpets intellectuals, with few exceptions, had cast aside the cloak of internationalism and draped around their shoulders the national flag. Augustine, it will be recalled, was led by the Fall of Rome sharply to separate men's hopes for salvation from their hopes for social progress. Writing in 1917, the theologian P. T. Forsyth reacted in precisely the same way to the First World War. "You have grown up," he told his readers, "in an age that has not yet got over the delight of having discovered in evolution the key to creation. You saw the long expanding series broadening to the perfect day." But now, he went on, "every aesthetic view of the world is blotted out by human wickedness and suffering." Men must look to the Cross, so he concluded, to the symbol of salvation through suffering, not to evolution, to free them from their imperfection.[12]

For Sigmund Freud, the outbreak of the First World War was scarcely less significant. It is possible to read the early Freud—he has, indeed, often been read in this way— as essentially an Enlightenment perfectibilist according to whom man's troubles derive, purely and simply, from his

---

to 1944: Mind at the End of Its Tether," §2, p. 349. Wells also used the title *Mind at the End of Its Tether* for a short book which he published in 1945.

12. P. T. Forsyth: *The Justification of God: Lectures for War-Time on a Christian Theodicy* (orig. publ. 1917; repr. London 1948), p. 159, as quoted in John Hick: *Evil and the God of Love*, pp. 247–48. See Hick generally on this theme, especially pp. 242–50.

failure to realize the nature of his own impulses. Once bring into the clear light of consciousness what has so far been unconscious and, on this interpretation, all will be well. In a letter to his American disciple, James Putnam, Freud makes it perfectly clear that this is not in fact his view: "I do not agree with Socrates and Putnam that all our faults arise from confusion and ignorance."[13] But if Freud never fully shared those illusions about human beings which, so he argues in his *Thoughts Concerning War and Death,* were responsible, by way of reaction, for the widespread disillusionment provoked by the war, there can be no doubt that he, too, was profoundly shaken by it. "We are constrained to believe," he wrote, "that never has any event been destructive of so much that is valuable in the common wealth of humanity, nor so misleading to so many of the clearest intelligences, nor so debasing to the highest that we know."[14] The dark note in Freud's post-war writings, which not even the most casual reader could assimilate to the Enlightenment picture of man as a being free of all native impulses towards destruction, runs in important respects parallel to the Augustine-inspired pessimism of Karl Barth.

There were some, no doubt, for whom the First World War had produced an outcome so precious as to demonstrate, once more, that out of darkness light emerges—the setting up of the Soviet Union. But the ruthlessness the Soviet Union displayed in agricultural collectivization, the purges of the 'thirties, the treacherous manoeuvres of the Communist Party in the Spanish Civil War, the German-Soviet Pact, the Hungarian invasions, the Czecho-Slovakian interventions—one or the other of these events has de-

13. S. Freud: Letter to J. Putnam, July 7, 1915, quoted in Ernest Jones: *The Life and Work of Sigmund Freud,* ed. and abridged by Lionel Trilling and Steven Marcus (New York and London, 1961), Bk. 2, ch. 23, p. 342.

14. S. Freud: *Thoughts for the Times on War and Death* (1915), §1, in *Collected Papers,* Vol. IV (London, 1925; repr. 1948), p. 288.

stroyed the Soviet Union as a symbol of hope in the breasts of all but a very few Western intellectuals.

The Nazi régime was, for others, the death-blow of perfectibilism. As early as 1870, the French Socialist Blanqui, until that time an ardent proponent of the view that universal education would of itself destroy every trace of exploitation, had his faith in education shattered by the advance of well-educated but none the less brutal German troops into France.[15] The Prussian invaders, however, were still relatively civilized. The peculiar primitiveness of the Nazi régime, the extent to which a people who had prided themselves on their education and their culture degenerated into the lowest forms of barbarism—no less in the Nuremberg Rallies than in the concentration camps—was more effective than the familiar horrors of invasion in shattering the belief that human society could be perfected by education and gradual social progress.

The pessimism of the liberal intellectual in our times derives, then, from a variety of sources. Its intensity and its diversity are made particularly clear in what have come to be called the "dystopias," most notoriously exemplified in Aldous Huxley's *Brave New World* and George Orwell's *Nineteen Eighty-Four,* but assuming an even more terrifying form, perhaps, in Zamiatin's *We*—written in 1920 in the Soviet Union although, like so many great Russian works, published abroad. Dystopias, it is true, are not peculiar to our century; Mandeville's *Fable of the Bees* is a notorious eighteenth-century example. Mandeville there depicts a society which sets out to base itself entirely on the ideal of moral perfection and, in the process, destroys its civilisation. Dystopias now flourish, however, as never before.[16]

15. A. B. Spitzer: *The Revolutionary Theories of Louis Auguste Blanqui* (New York, 1957), pp. 54–55.

16. See Chad Walsh: *From Utopia to Nightmare* (London, 1962). Sir Thomas More himself intended "Utopia" to be read as a pun on "Eutopia"—a "nowhere" that is also a "good

The quotation from Nicolas Berdyaev which Huxley uses as an epigraph to *Brave New World* is particularly apposite to that work. "Utopias," says Berdyaev, "now appear to be much more realizable than we had previously thought. We find ourselves nowadays confronted with a question agonizing in quite a different way: How can we avoid their final realization?—Perhaps a new century is beginning, a century when intellectuals and cultivated men will dream about methods of avoiding Utopia and returning to a society which is not Utopian, less 'perfect' and more free." [17] Berdyaev, that is, is rejecting perfection as an ideal; perfection and freedom, he is suggesting, are antagonists. That is the principal theme of Huxley's and of Zamiatin's dystopias.

Classical Utopias, like Plato's *Republic*, criticized existing societies by contrasting them with a theoretically realizable ideal society. The conventional criticism of such Utopias, from Aristophanes' *Ecclesiazusae* onwards, has been that they are impracticable, inconsistent with human nature. Modern dystopias proceed quite differently: they criticize existing societies by constructing a nightmare society which, they suggest, is the inevitable outcome of existing social tendencies. The classical Utopians exhort men: "This is what you ought to try to bring about!"; the modern dystopians exhort men: "This is what you ought to try to stop!" Yet the fact remains that in content many of the modern dystopias are not so very different from the classical utopias: in essence, they are Plato's *Republic* transformed by modern technology. It is a tribute to the quality of Plato's imagination that his

---

place." A "dystopia" is a bad place; that it is, or will be, nowhere, Orwell and Huxley are less confident. On More's use of the word see M. I. Finley: "Utopianism Ancient and Modern" in K. H. Wolff and B. Moore, eds.: *The Critical Spirit: Essays in Honor of Herbert Marcuse* (Boston, 1967), p. 3. For earlier dystopias, see F. L. Polak: *The Image of the Future*, 2 vols (Leyden, 1961), ch. XVI, Vol. II, pp. 15–20. On the relations between Huxley, Orwell, Zamiatin and the early writings of H. G. Wells, see M. R. Hillegas: *The Future as Nightmare—H. G. Wells and the Anti-Utopians* (New York, 1967).

17. Nicholas Berdyaev: *The End of Our Time* (London, 1933; cheap ed., 1935), ch. IV, §11, p. 187. The translation, however, is my own.

ideal society still so influences men's minds, whether they contemplate it with delight or recoil from it with horror. Zamiatin and Huxley recoil from it with horror as a tyranny, the more dreadful for having been imposed out of good will and accepted without reservation by all but a very few of its victims. In a footnote to his *Behaviorism,* J. B. Watson remarks that "the behaviorist . . . would like to develop his world of people from birth on, so that their speech and their bodily behavior could equally well be exhibited freely everywhere without running afoul of group standards"—a state of affairs, which, in the main text, he entitles "behavioristic freedom."[18] Precisely such a "behavioristic freedom" is realized in *Brave New World*—a society in which everyone can say whatever he likes because nobody likes to say anything that will "run afoul of group standards." "That is the secret of happiness and virtue," observes Huxley's Director, "liking what you've *got* to do. All conditioning aims at that—making people like their unescapable social destiny."[19] At the very end of Orwell's *Nineteen Eighty-Four* the rebel Winston is finally conquered by the Party. The sign of its final victory is that now, in utter abasement, he sincerely loves Big Brother.[20] The condition to which Winston is finally reduced is the dystopic equivalent of "Christian freedom" when that "freedom" is defined as loving submission to God's will, just because it is God's, and to whatever God commands—even if it be the command, as Abraham was commanded, to sacrifice one's own son or, as Winston was commanded, to betray one's beloved. Winwood Reade, it will be recalled, looked forward, like Fichte before him, to a time when "the whole world will be united by the same sentiment which united the primeval clan, and which made its members think, feel and

18. J. B. Watson: *Behaviorism, ed. cit.,* pp. 303–4.
19. Aldous Huxley: *Brave New World* (first publ. 1932; Penguin ed., Harmondsworth, 1955, repr. 1968), p. 24.
20. George Orwell: *Nineteen Eighty-Four* (first publ. 1949; Penguin ed., Harmondsworth, 1954, repr. 1968), p. 239.

act as one." Such a society Huxley and Orwell and Zamiatin fear above all others.

No doubt their dystopias differ greatly in character. One can easily enough imagine someone saying: "But I should *like* to live in Huxley's brave new world."* That is a world, for most of its inhabitants, of peace and stability, of sensuality and drug-induced contentment—like the book-burning world of Truffaut's dystopian film *Fahrenheit 451*. It is much harder to imagine anyone confessing that he would like to live in Orwell's dystopia—which is not to say that its blind worship of power, its violence, its mindless discipline, its Puritanical austerities, might not represent a great many secret dreams.†

The inhabitants of Huxley's and Zamiatin's dystopias are, almost all of them, completely contented, and their so-

---

* In his *From Utopia to Nightmare* Chad Walsh reports that an occasional college student has reacted in precisely this way (p. 25). The "Orgy-Porgy" scene in *Brave New World* is an extraordinary anticipation of the "participating theatre" of the 1960s or the Pop concerts which preceded it. Or perhaps not so extraordinary when one realizes that what Huxley has done is to use modern techniques of sound and light to recapture the spirit of a Dionysian ceremony. As usual, what represents itself as "advanced" is in fact primitive. It is interesting to observe that in Huxley's own later writings—notably in *Island*, which he first published in 1962—Huxley takes over into what is now represented as a genuine Utopia much that in *Brave New World* he had described with horror, especially the use of drugs.

† Huxley remains convinced that he was right and that Orwell was wrong. Even the Soviet Union, he argues in his *Brave New World Revisited* (London, 1960), is gradually moving towards a situation in which it "manages" people rather than governs them by force. De Tocqueville long ago predicted that society would develop a new kind of servitude which "covers the surface of society with a network of small complicated rules; through which the most original minds and the most energetic characters cannot penetrate . . . it does not tyrannize but it compresses, enervates and stupefies a people, till each nation is reduced to nothing better than a flock of timid and industrious animals of which government is the shepherd" (*Democracy in America*, ch. xxxiv, p. 580). In other words, Benthamite or Fabian perfection made manifest. "It will be," he says, "a society which tries to keep its citizens in 'perpetual childhood'; it will seek to preserve their happiness but it chooses to be the sole agent and the only arbiter of that happiness" (p. 579). Compare F. A. Hayek: *Studies in Philosophy, Politics and Economics* (London, 1967), p. 225, where he quotes this passage from de Tocqueville along with a passage from an English social worker describing the "regulation-bound" lives of young English workers. Grateful as we are that we are still not living in a totalitarian state, we can easily overlook the degree to which we have lost freedoms which before 1914 were taken for granted, freedom to travel without passports, freedom from secret police, to take only two examples.

ciety is technically perfect. This is certainly not true of *Nineteen Eighty-Four*, in which the shabbiness and bureaucratic incompetence of the twentieth-century Communist State are faithfully reflected. Orwell's "proles," furthermore, are not brought under full control; they are permitted to live under conditions of Dickensian squalor. The gloominess of Orwell's dystopia, interestingly enough, is a reflection of the fact that his pessimism does not run as deep as Huxley's or Zamiatin's. He still believes that the Enlightenment ideals were realizable in an "earthly paradise"; such a paradise was not brought into being, on his view, only because power was seized by a "new aristocracy."[21] Huxley's and Zamiatin's criticism is much more far-reaching. They set out to show that the Enlightenment Paradise would, if realized, be a Hell.* Even Orwell, however, rejects as instruments of

---

21. Compare the long document included by Orwell in *Nineteen Eighty-Four*, Pt. II, ch. 9. The phrases quoted are in *ed. cit.*, p. 164.

* The dystopians do not have to go back to the eighteenth century to encounter the Enlightenment ideas they were attacking; these ideals had been reaffirmed by H. G. Wells, who influenced the dystopians in extremely complex ways. Wells was a disciple of T. H. Huxley; he began by arguing, in Huxley's manner, that evolution was by no means on the side of "human progress," that in the end it would discard man. And at the same time he suggested—especially in *When a Sleeper Awakes* (London, 1899)—that capitalism was evolving towards a state of society in which individual freedom would be entirely sacrificed to the needs of the machine. In many respects, these early writings *anticipate* the dystopias. (Zamiatin, it is worth noting, wrote a book on Wells.) From about 1905 on, however, Wells took up the other side of Huxley's teachings; man could, by an exercise of will, impose his own ethical ideals on Nature. In a series of Utopias—orderly, tidy, élite-governed, mechanical—Wells set out to show what a society would be like in which those ideals were realized. He envisaged, without fear, a society in which every detail about every human being is known to a central authority: provided only that the government is a "good" one, he argues, no harm could possibly come of this, and it is a necessary prerequisite for a tidy, orderly, well-governed society. He has complete trust in government by intellectuals; in *The Open Conspiracy: Blue Prints for a World Revolution* (London, 1928) he reverts to the old dream of a social revolution which will unite enlightened businessmen and intellectuals. Wells was never to react against these ideals; what in the end he came to doubt was that men had enough "goodwill" to bring them into being. His last word to humanity is summed up in the 1941 preface to *The War of the Worlds* (London, 1898)—"I told you so, you damned fools." It is astonishing to what a degree Wells anticipated the science-fiction to come, perfectibilist and anti-perfectibilist. Compare, for example, *The Fate of Homo Sapiens* (London, 1939), pp. 308–10 with Edgar Pangborn's *Davy* (New York, 1964). On Wells himself see M. R. Hillegas: *The Future as Nightmare* along with David Lodge's review of that book in "Utopia and Criticism," *Encounter*, Vol. 32, No. 4, April, 1967, pp. 65–76.

tyranny what had been, for the Enlighteners, agents of perfection.

Thus, for example, whereas Enlightenment perfectibilists based their hopes for man on his malleability, in *Nineteen Eighty-Four* it is the arch-villain O'Brien who lays down the principle that "men are infinitely malleable."[22] That same assumption is the ruling factor of Huxley's "brave new world" and Zamiatin's "united state": that men can be moulded into any desired shape by a combination of eugenic measures and training, both of them brought by modern technology to a level of efficiency which Helvetius could not envisage. Why is the malleability of man, in the eyes of the dystopians, a ground for despair rather than, as Hartley and Helvetius had assumed, for hope?*

---

22. *Nineteen Eighty-Four*, Pt. III, ch. 3; *ed. cit.* p. 216.

* I have nowhere faced head-on the question how far man is in fact malleable. There are a great many similar questions, extremely relevant to our theme, which I have only skirted, e.g. whether God exists. In each case for the same reason: the points at issue are so large that they would demand a book to themselves. It is enough to remark that even if man is malleable it does not follow that there is any prospect of perfecting him, and that even if God exists, it does not follow that he is in the least degree interested in perfecting men. But if it be true, as a great many recent writers have suggested, that man is by nature aggressive and that any society has to provide opportunities for that aggression—thought of as "a beast within"—to be satisfied, then certainly, neither individual man nor human society is perfectible. In order to establish a connexion between malleability and perfectibility it is necessary to argue not only that there are no true propositions of the form "All men are aggressive"—understood as meaning that however men are trained their aggression will demand some outlet—but, a much more difficult affair, that there are no true propositions of the form: "If men are trained in certain ways, certain consequences will inevitably follow," e.g. if they are crowded closely together with their fellow-men, they will *become* aggressive. For if any propositions of the second sort are true, they limit what can be done with man, just as "if there is full employment, there will be inflation" limits the degree to which the economy can be controlled. There are two metaphors about the development of human beings which have dominated our thinking about them: the metaphor which looks upon the child as a blank sheet (malleability) and the metaphor which looks upon him as an acorn (natural ends: the realization of potentialities). Both metaphors ought, I should say, to be abandoned. The child is neither born entirely without a "programme," in the sense of a set of ways of dealing with, and reacting to, the world, nor is he "programmed" to seek happiness or freedom or the vision of God or any other end. If he comes to be happy or free, this will be an achievement, an achievement resulting from the interplay between himself and his environment, and, as the Greeks were keenly conscious, a fragile and temporary achievement: it is no more "natural" for him to be free

We have already noted that there is a yawning gap between the doctrine that man is malleable and the conclusion, so often immediately deduced from it, that man is perfectible. That gap the Enlighteners filled by presuming that social agencies can be set up which will perfect, rather than pervert, malleable man. There now exists, they thought, a class of men—the intellectuals—who, although themselves not yet perfect, have reached a level of development at which, once entrusted with power, they can set their fellow-men on the long uphill path towards perfection. By his very nature, they supposed, the intellectual is incorruptible, devoted to the public welfare, uninterested in power or in status for its own sake. "Scientists, historians, philosophers—," so Denis Brogan has formulated this view, "they were supposed, on the one hand, to be above the mere party battle and, on the other, to be capable, because of their training, of distinguishing the true from the false without being blinded by political or religious passion."[23]

Consider, in the light of this confidence, the composition of the ruling "Party" in *Nineteen Eighty-Four*: "bureaucrats, scientists, technicians, trade-union organizers, publicity experts, sociologists, teachers, journalists, and professional politicians."[24] Precisely the sort of people, that

---

than it is natural—as Comte thought—for him to be servile and dogmatic. What sort of human being he becomes, free or servile, happy or unhappy, will depend, very largely, on the circumstances of his life, which vary enormously from man to man. That is the truth behind the malleability doctrine, in opposition to the view that there is a fixed "human nature." But the "very largely" is an important addendum: it is a highly implausible view that it makes no difference whatsoever what kind of brain, or nervous system, or hormonal balance a man inherits. We know that the very same drug can act as a stimulant to persons of a particular constitution, as a depressant to others. On the face of it, something similar is true of any kind of training; in the most primitive, the most uniform, societies, there are occasional rebels. It would be very strange if, although in order to explain the behaviour of everything else we have to take account both of its own character and of its environment, in the case of a human being we need only take account of his environment.

23. Denis Brogan: "The Intellectual in Great Britain" in H. M. Macdonald, ed.: *The Intellectual in Politics* (Austin, Texas, 1966), p. 62.

24. *Nineteen Eighty-Four*, Pt. II, ch. 9; *ed. cit.*, p. 164.

is, in whom the Enlighteners placed such faith—their own kind. Nor does this list reflect an eccentric Orwellian prejudice: there is nothing eccentric, nowadays, in blaming scientists and intellectuals, in an unholy alliance with bureaucrats, for all the ills of the world. "Let us build," writes Aldous Huxley ironically in the foreword, dated 1946, to the 1950 reprint of *Brave New World*, "a Pantheon for professors. It should be located among the ruins of one of the gutted cities of Europe or Japan, and over the entrance to the ossuary I would inscribe, in letters six or seven feet high, the simple words: SACRED TO THE MEMORY OF THE WORLD'S EDUCATORS."[25]

From Aristophanes onwards, conservatives have condemned intellectuals for introducing innovations, stirring up discontent, weakening the unity and stability of the social system. But now the accusation is very different. The typical intellectual, nowadays, is the scientist and scientists, the suggestion is, are heartless, inhuman. Professing to be disinterested, they are in fact uninterested—uninterested in human beings as such, except as statistical items in some grand experiment, some total plan. Pretending to absolute objectivity, they in fact seek to secure their own position in society; they will serve any government, acquiesce in any form of social arrangement, whether it be capitalism, communism or the Third Reich, provided only that it will provide them with the funds they need for their experiments. They disclaim all responsibility—like the Inquisition handing over heretics for burning to "the secular arm"—for applications which they know quite well to be inevitable.[26] More than that, they are hungry for power and status, for public recognition, for influence. Mankind means less to them than a Nobel Prize. "As far as science is concerned," Karl Popper has written, "there is no doubt whatsoever in

---

25. *Brave New World*, Foreword; *ed. cit.*, p. 8.
26. See, on this theme, Edmund Leach: *A Runaway World?* (London, 1968), ch. 1.

my mind that to look upon it as a means for increasing one's power is a sin against the Holy Ghost."[27] He is very conscious, however, that this sin is only too often committed. The Universities, so the contemporary indictment continues, have surrendered their ancient traditions of independent research and open publication to satisfy the insatiable demands of their scientists for new equipment, bigger research teams, higher status. In so far as the Universities have continued to educate—as distinct from serving as the research branch of government and industry—they now, so it is alleged, have no objective except to turn out, in order to satisfy the requirements of government and large corporations, an unfailing stream of docile, amenable, technically perfected, executives—"highly skilled, but politically and economically *dumb* 'personnel.' "[28]

The dystopians, then, reflect a wider disquiet about the influence of intellectuals, not now as radical innovators, but rather as agents of the "industrial-military complex" and the governments that complex so powerfully influences. Even in the eighteenth century Kant had argued against Plato that intellectuals ought not to be rulers since, he maintained, "the possession of power inevitably corrupts the untrammelled judgement of reason."[29] The question, nowadays, is how far collaboration, as distinct from actual rule, has the same effect.* When young radicals of the more

27. Karl Popper: "The Moral Responsibility of the Scientist," in *Encounter*, Vol. 32, No. 3, March, 1969, p. 56.

28. Paul Jacobs and Saul Landau: *The New Radicals* (New York, 1966; Pelican ed., Harmondsworth, 1967), p. 228. Most of the accusations summarized above can be found in this volume.

29. Kant: *Perpetual Peace*, Second Section, Second Supplement, as trans. L. W. Beck, *ed. cit.*, p. 330.

* Collaboration is one of the most important moral problems of our century, but it has been singularly little discussed. Looking up "collaboration" in the Library of Congress subject index I found nothing but "collaborationist, see traitor." That is far too simple-minded an attitude. The problem whether a man should collaborate, and how far he ought to collaborate, with an authority to which he is opposed, if there is no other means by which he can keep alive or foster the types of activity he cherishes, is not to be lightly dismissed. Undoubtedly, collaboration ties his hands; then, too, his association with it may

uncompromising kind refuse to accept the offer of well-meaning administrators to permit them a greater share in University government their elders are often genuinely puzzled. What the young fear, however, is that once they participate in the mechanism of power, they, too, will begin to think like bureaucrats, they will start looking at things from "a sensible point of view": they will take over a standpoint, that is, according to which ease and efficiency of management, a smooth-running organization, is all important, even when the organization is no longer securing the objectives towards which it is ostensibly directed. In their own radical groups, such rebels fear above all else the emergence of hierarchical structure, leadership from above. Official leaders, they believe, "inevitably develop interests in maintaining the organization (or themselves) and lose touch with the immediate aspirations of the rank and file."[30] So much has been made apparent, they think, from the history of the Soviet Union.

If the new radicals are right, if, that is, not only power but collaboration with power inevitably corrupts, that fact is highly germane to our theme: it is then quite ridiculous to suppose that men can ever be perfected from above, by legislation or by an education which is imposed upon

---

lend respectability to a bad government; the activity he *actually* fosters may turn out to be very different from the activities he hoped to foster; he may acquire the habit of being silent when he ought to speak out, he may come to love the trappings of power. Yet, on the other side, there may be no other way in which he can exert any influence, or save his own people. The Jews faced this problem during the Roman Empire and, characteristically, sought to cope with it by laws. See D. Daube: *Collaboration with Tyranny in Rabbinical Law* (Oxford, 1965). Democracy depends on compromise; to refuse ever to work with people with whom one disagrees is fanaticism. "As soon as a man begins to treat of public affairs in public," as de Tocqueville puts it, "he begins to perceive that he is not so independent of his fellow-men as he had at first imagined, and that, in order to obtain their support, he must often lend them his co-operation" (*Democracy in America*, 1835–40, Eng. trans. Henry Reed, of same dates; abridged version, London, 1946, ch. XXIV, p. 371). The question always is—and there is no rule by which the issue can be settled—how far can compromise and collaboration be safely carried?

30. Jacobs and Landau: *The New Radicals, ed. cit.*, pp. 39–40, quoting Tom Hayden, past president of S.D.S.

them. But even if the extreme position of the new radicals is mistaken, even if power does not inevitably corrupt but, as Acton thought, only *tends* to corrupt, there is certainly nothing in our experience to suggest that whenever an intellectual rules, freedom, justice and equality must flourish. Lenin and Salazar are powerful enough evidence to the contrary—to say nothing of Oxford-bred African dictators. The Enlightenment attitude to the "mob" still persists among contemporary intellectuals.* Intellectuals in power can readily persuade themselves, therefore, that they "know what is good" for the population at large, what men "really want," and how to protect them from the propaganda which, weak-minded as they are, might lead them to suspect the ever-virtuous intentions of their rulers. Only too easily do intellectuals—not all of them but enough of them to make the indictment plausible—come to share the sentiments of Ballas in Vaclav Havel's play *The Memorandum:* "When the good of Man is at stake, nothing will make us sick."[31]

Rule by intellectuals is not the only Enlightenment recipe for perfection on which the dystopians have cast doubt. One of the leading presumptions of the Enlighteners was that if once man could discover a perfect language his troubles would largely be over. The rulers in Orwell's dystopia are in the process of constructing such a language, a language without ambiguity, which it is impossible to misunderstand, since "every concept that can ever be needed, will be expressed by exactly *one* word." And this, it turns out, is one of the ways in which they tyrannically control the thoughts of men. "In the end," says Orwell's Syme, "we shall

* Compare H. G. Wells: *Men like Gods* (London, 1923), Bk. III, ch. 2, §6: "You have never seen a crowd, Crystal; and in all your happy life you never will"—the crowd he describes as a "detestable crawling mass of unfeatured, infected human beings" (p. 265). Huxley tells us that *Brave New World* began as a parody of *Men like Gods.*

31. Václav Havel: *The Memorandum,* trans. from the Czech by Vera Blackwell (London, 1967), p. 43.

make thoughtcrime literally impossible, because there will be no words in which to express it."[32]

There is a fuller treatment of the perfect language theme in Havel's *The Memorandum*. The artificial language of that play, Ptydepe, is so constructed as "to guarantee to every statement . . . a degree of precision, reliability and lack of equivocation, quite unattainable in any natural language."[33] (In a manner only too characteristic of our age, this precision is in the interests neither, as for Leibniz, of religion, nor, as for Condorcet, of science, but of bureaucracy: Ptydepe is to be the language of interoffice memoranda.) In Havel's eyes, the new language is a symbol of the totalitarian outlook, yet another way of ensuring that it will be at all times clear exactly what every human being is doing and saying. It destroys, in the process, the very possibility of irony, one of the few forms of freedom which a totalitarian ruler cannot be quite confident he has wholly brought under control.

This brings out the fact that the "imperfections" of everyday language are precisely what permit it to be used as an instrument of human freedom, as a way of introducing new ideas, new attitudes—allowing Freud, for example, to speak of "unconscious mind" when "mind" had commonly been *defined* as consciousness, or Wittgenstein to describe as "senseless" sentences which, judged by ordinary criteria, certainly have a meaning.* Admittedly, these very same "imperfections" allow men to talk nonsense, to confuse, to deceive, to corrupt. It is quite easy to understand, in consequence, why well-intentioned men have been so attracted by the ideal of a perfect language. A society in which lan-

---

32. *Nineteen Eighty-Four*, Pt. I, ch. 5; *ed. cit.*, p. 45.
33. *The Memorandum, ed. cit.*, p. 24.
* Interestingly enough, H. G. Wells recognized this: the inhabitants of his *A Modern Utopia* (London, 1905) speak an internationally comprehensible, but not a perfect, language. Their tongue is, indeed, an "animated system of imperfections" (ch. I, §5). The reason is that otherwise language would not adjust to new discoveries, changes of thought. Wells's Utopia is not fixed and unchanging, as the dystopias set out to be.

guage can be used ambiguously, or to deceive, distort and illicitly influence, will never be a perfect society. So much the worse, the dystopians have concluded, for perfection.

As for the closely connected Enlightenment doctrine that the mathematization of social relationships will be the salvation of mankind, this is bitterly satirized in Zamiatin's *We*. Life in his dystopia is mathematically perfect.* The central character D-503—numbers have, of course, replaced personal names—sums up the faith the "United State" lives by thus: "there are no more fortunate and happy people than those who live according to the correct, eternal laws of the multiplication table." (Compare the society depicted in François Truffaut's *Fahrenheit 451*, where books are not only banned but burned. The time thus saved at school is devoted to teaching children the multiplication tables for high numbers.)[34] Morality in the "United State" is now at last completely scientific—"based on adding, subtracting, multiplying, and dividing."[35] Music is composed by mathematically-designed machines. And the effect is the complete bureaucratization of all human relationships.

In the popular mind, a mathematically-organized world has now come to be associated with a computerized world. For the "new radicals" the ultimate indignity is to "be an

---

* Zamiatin's main line of attack had been anticipated as long ago as 1846 by that virulent critic of the Enlightenment, Dostoievsky. In his *Letters from the Underworld* Dostoievsky attacks the characteristic Enlightenment view that once men understand the laws which govern them, they will at once be enabled to manage their lives more adequately. He goes on satirically to contemplate the construction of a "calendar" in which "all human acts will . . . be mathematically computed" and, once computed, entered into a logarithmic table. By this means wrong-doing will be banished from the world. As for economic problems, they too will yield to mathematics. "In a flash all possible questions will come to an end, for the reason that to all possible questions there will have been compiled a store of all possible answers." The ideal computer, in fact! See Feodor Dostoievsky: *Letters from the Underworld*, trans. C. J. Hogarth, Everyman's Library (London, 1913, repr. 1929), pp. 29–30.

34. Truffaut's film is based on the novel of the same name by Ray Bradbury. This detail, however, does not appear in the novel.

35. Eugene Zamiatin: *We*, trans. Gregory Zilboorg (New York, 1924; paperback ed. 1952), pp. 4, 64, 14.

IBM card"—the modern equivalent to what used to be called, significantly enough, "being a cipher," a number with no meaning outside mathematics. The computer, in the eyes of the new radicals, is the symbol of faceless power, the most terrifying of all those many modern devices which "break down communication and destroy community in the interests of efficiency."[36] And the computer does no more than express mechanically a mathematically simplified world. It is not only—though this, too, is feared—that the computer may replace men, may make their technical tasks superfluous. The fear of the computer goes deeper than this: that it will destroy human relationships.

The mathematician and the computer expert will no doubt condemn these reactions as ill-informed and ridiculous. Mathematics, the mathematician will rightly point out, is not to be identified with practical calculating devices: it is one of the great imaginative constructions of the human mind. As for computers, they represent, their designers are confident, a triumph of the human intellect, the conquest of mere toil, opening up to man quite new prospects of alleviating his miseries. The dystopians, they would say, are responding in the manner only to be expected of panicky literary men, afraid of what they do not understand, and still responding as unthinkingly as they did as schoolboys to the intricacies of mathematics.

Yet it is easy to understand why mathematics and computers are so feared. "Evil," Sartre once wrote, "is the systematic substitution of the abstract for the concrete."[37] Mathematics, by its very nature, is abstract. Groups and relationships, not individuals, are its starting-point: in its statistical applications it is interested only in the behaviour of large numbers, not in individuals.

36. Jacobs and Landau: *The New Radicals, ed. cit.,* p. 14.
37. Quoted from Sartre's *Saint Genet* in Susan Sontag: *Against Interpretation, and Other Essays* (New York, 1966), p. 97.

No one has brought out the nature of a computer-run society more clearly than E. M. Forster, in a story "The Machine Stops" which he wrote as long ago as 1912, as a reply to Wells's Utopias, although it was not published until 1928. He depicts a society entirely run by a centralized machine. Only through the machine do human beings communicate one with another, and the machine, like Havel's ideal language, does not "transmit *nuances* of expression." It is content to give a "general idea of people"—quite enough, so it is said, for ordinary purposes. One of the characters finds her bed too large for her tastes; it was useless to complain— beds were the same size all over the world and "to have had an alternative size would have involved vast alterations in the Machine." Although scarcely anybody travels, there are still regular airlines; it was too troublesome to abolish them. In short, the whole society is ruled by one principle: what will it cost for the machine to alter its own programming?[38] If this is perfection, Forster is suggesting, let us abandon the ideal of perfection, while there is still time.

If their critique of the Enlightenment ideals of a perfect language and a perfectly mathematical society are readily intelligible, it is at first sight more surprising that the ideal of happiness, too, does not go unscathed in the dystopias. Adam and Eve, so R-13 suggests in Zamiatin's *We,* had a choice: the choice between freedom and happiness. They chose freedom.* Now at last it has become clear, he continues, that Adam and Eve were wrong: the "United State" takes men back beyond the Fall, to a world of perfect hap-

---

38. E. M. Forster: "The Machine Stops," in *The Collected Tales of E. M. Forster,* Modern Library ed. (New York, 1968), pp. 148, 151, 155–56.

* The source of this doctrine, too, is Dostoievsky, in this case *The Brothers Karamazov.* "Men," says Ivan, "were given paradise, they wanted freedom, and stole fire from heaven, though they knew they would become unhappy." The "Grand Inquisitor" claims it as a merit for himself and his Church that "at last they have conquered freedom and made men happy" (trans. Constance Garnett, Pt. II, Bk. V, ch. IV, V). Dostoievsky's "Grand Inquisitor" is "the love of humanity" personified.

piness.[39] At the culminating point of Zamiatin's novel, the last remaining obstacle to man's complete happiness is surgically removed: a compulsory operation cuts away man's imagination, the source of all those anxieties which had so far proved irremediable.

Huxley's *Brave New World* has happiness always ready at hand, in the form of the drug *soma:* "one cubic centimetre cures ten gloomy sentiments."[40] Those major sources of human unhappiness, unsatisfied sexual desire and sexual possessiveness, are in the dystopias no problem. In Jean-Luc Godard's film *Alphaville,* as in Mahomet's heaven, sexually attractive women are at all times available; in *Brave New World* sexual relationships are so ordered as to reduce to a minimum the interval between "the consciousness of a desire and its fulfilment."[41] The more bureaucratic society of Zamiatin's *We* is slightly more formal—one needs a pink ticket and sexual relationships are only permitted at certain hours—but they still involve, it is presumed, no element of frustration. As for *Fahrenheit 451,* the women in that film live in a perpetual state of narcissistic gratification.

Truffaut's book-burning firemen justify their book-burning in similar terms: books make people unhappy. And indeed when the rebel fireman reads aloud a passage from *David Copperfield* to a group of television-moulded wives this accusation is shown to be justified. One of them weeps, reminded of past sorrows. You can have your choice, the assumption is: literature or happiness, but not both. The controller of *Brave New World* makes a similar point. The literature of the new world, he admits, is intrinsically inferior to Shakespeare's *Othello.* But a happy people will not be able to understand *Othello:* the envy, the jealousy, which is its motivating force will be totally unintelligible to them.

---

39. *We,* Record Eleven; *ed. cit.,* p. 59.
40. *Brave New World, ed. cit.,* p. 53.
41. *Ibid.,* p. 46.

Happiness *or* freedom, happiness *or* art, happiness *or* pure
science—for pure science, as distinct from controlled technology, is forbidden in *Brave New World*—these, it is now
suggested, are the choices before man. "People are happy";
the Controller is confident, "they get what they want, and
they never want what they can't get. They're well off; they're
safe; they're never ill; . . . they're plagued with no mothers
or fathers; they've got no wives, or children, or loves to feel
strongly about; they're so conditioned that they practically
can't help behaving as they ought to behave." Why, he goes
on to ask, should anyone throw all this away "in the name of
liberty"?[42] The Enlighteners, in contrast, presumed that art,
science, freedom, justice, equality, happiness were not ir-
reconcilable alternatives but different facets of human perfection.

The dystopian criticism, it might therefore be argued—
as Erich Fromm, for one, argues—has nothing to do with
happiness, rightly understood. No doubt, the dystopias
offer men freedom from suffering and the immediate gratification of impulses but this, according to Fromm, is not
happiness. Drugs like *soma* can bring with them placid content, but happiness is very different from contentment. Man
can be happy, Fromm somewhat portentously observes, only
when he "has found the answer to the problem of human
existence: the productive realization of his potentialities."[43]
On this view, there can be no clash between freedom and
happiness: freedom is a necessary condition for happiness.
As for literature and science, they are special forms of happiness.

There are no doubt, as Fromm is suggesting, definitions
of happiness—e.g. as enjoyable activity—in which it is far

---

42. *Ibid.*, p. 173.
43. *Man for Himself* (London, 1949), p. 189. See the discussion of this whole issue in
J. H. Schaar: *Escape from Authority* (New York, 1961), ch. 2, pp. 81–158. The variety of ways
in which the concept of happiness has been employed is made evident in V. J. McGill: *The
Idea of Happiness* (New York, 1967).

from being incompatible with freedom. But the dystopians are not arbitrarily introducing a new use of the word "happiness": happiness as they understand it is happiness as the Utilitarians understood it—the maximization of pleasure and the minimization of pain. And they are emphasizing that men might be free of pain and frustration in a society in which liberty is lost, art and science are dead, and love is abolished. The possibility of creating such a society has become less remote as medical science has proved itself able to relieve anxiety and depression by drugs. Freud thought that anxiety and depression could be alleviated only by the patient's becoming free, by his overcoming what Freud significantly called "repression." But now, it seems, men can be relieved of anxiety and depression not only without in the process becoming freer men but, in the sharpest possible contrast, by becoming drug-dependent.

The dystopian attack on ideal languages, on mathematized social relationships and on the technological manipulation of human beings in the interests of their happiness, is directed, fundamentally, against the identification of perfection with technical perfection. And, what goes with that, against the conception of society as a great machine, perfect in virtue of its order, its stability, its harmony, a machine in which everyone has a place, everyone knows what that place is, and everyone keeps to that place—the old Platonic ideal. "We gave each man," so Plato sums up the ideal society he sketched in the *Republic,* "one trade, that for which nature had fitted him. Nothing else was to occupy his time, but he was to spend his life working at that."[44] Plato's ideal State won new admirers in the nineteenth century, especially amongst the disciples of the French socialist Saint-Simon, including Comte. A perfect society, according to Comte, would be one in which the "spiritual powers" —Comte's substitute for Plato's philosopher-kings—would

44. *Republic,* Bk. II. 374, as trans. Lindsay, p. 55.

allocate each person to the functions for which he is best suited. This is the social programme which J. S. Mill, not unjustly, described as "the completest system of spiritual and temporal despotism which ever yet emanated from a human brain."[45]

Modern society, in the eyes of its critics, is steadily moving in the direction of precisely such a spiritual despotism, in the name of technical perfection. "Our civilization," wrote Paul Valéry in 1925, "is taking on, or tending to take on, the structure and properties of a machine. . . . This machine will not tolerate less than world-wide rule; it will not allow a single human being to survive outside its control, uninvolved in its functioning." In short, it is moving towards that unified "world-community" which Wells and Teilhard, in their own different ways, saw as the one hope of human perfection. Valéry goes on to describe this world-to-come in terms which even more clearly relate it to the world of the dystopians: "It cannot put up with ill-defined lives within its sphere of operation. Its precision, which is its essence, cannot endure vagueness or social caprice; irregular situations are incompatible with good running order. It cannot put up with anyone whose duties and circumstances are not precisely specified." If it encounters such people, Valéry goes on to say, it tries either to eliminate them or to force them to undertake regular and specified tasks.[46] Thus Plato's—and Saint-Simon's—dream is Valéry's nightmare. The picture of the world he so grimly paints is precisely the world as the young rebels now see it becoming—a world in which the eccentric, the individual, is not allowed to exist, not even as a despised drop-out.

45. *Autobiography*, ch. VI; *ed. cit.*, p. 213. For the Saint-Simonians as a whole see G. G. Iggers: *The Cult of Authority*.
46. Paul Valéry: "Remarks on Intelligence" (1925) included in P. Valéry: *The Outlook for Intelligence*, trans. D. Folliot and J. Matthews, originally publ. as Vol. 10, Pt. 1 of *The Collected Works of Paul Valéry*, ed. J. Matthews, Bollingen Series XLV (New York, 1962; Harper Torchbook repr. 1963), p. 81.

Western civilization as we now know it is not, of course, the world which Valéry describes. It is far from being the case that the world is a single uniform community, it is far from being the case, even, that nobody in modern times can live "an ill-defined life," that there are no longer any "irregular situations." Were this true, indeed, such phenomena as the "hippie" communities could not for a moment survive. Specialization, too, is not complete; all men are still called upon to vote, to be soldiers, to be members of juries. But the preoccupation of so much contemporary literature with the "outsider," the drop-out, with "ill-defined lives" and "irregular situations," can only be understood as an attempt to stem what so many writers, especially, dread as an all but irresistible movement towards a tidy, specialized world. Not, of course, that the "outsider" is a new phenomenon, as the case of Rimbaud sufficiently reminds us. In modern society, however, "outsiders" create a peculiar unease—very similar, in many respects, to the unease created by the Brethren of the Free Spirit in Medieval Europe, whom the hippies resemble in so many ways. No one knows how to cope with them; they challenge the principle of order on which the society is constructed, the principle, in the modern case, that everybody should have a regular job, be a member of a small family group, and devote himself to his personal advancement through the technical perfecting of his special skills.

Furthermore, it is only too easy to envisage, in the light of contemporary tendencies, a society in which even warfare and politics and judicial decisions are, all of them, left entirely to technicians. Freedom is then wholly subordinate to "perfection," to individual perfection defined as technical expertness, to social perfection defined in classical aesthetic-metaphysical terms as permanence, stability, order, harmony. The dystopias present such a society as a realized fact. In Zamiatin's *We* the ideal is to become "perfect like a machine"; in *Brave New World*, men are deliber-

ately bred to fit them for a specific task. "Ninety-six identical twins working ninety-six identical machines! You really
know where you are." This is the means by which Huxley's
dystopia lives up to its great motto: "Community, Identity,
Stability."[47]

Confronted with the spectacle of ninety-six identical
twins, the visiting primitive retreats behind a palm in order
to vomit. The only possible comment, we may feel. But are
we merely being sentimental, as Skinner accuses his critics
of being sentimental?[48] Human society has, in important
respects, progressed as a result of the division of labour and,
what is related to it, the careful choice of particular types of
individuals for particular types of task.* Romanticists may
continue to yearn for a simple, agricultural society, where
everybody turns his hand to whatever task needs to be done;
such a society, in which perfection is conceived of not as
technical but as moral perfection, the practice of virtue, and
technical perfection is dismissed as an unnecessary refinement, has been the stuff of a great many Utopias, ancient

---

47. *Brave New World, ed. cit.,* p. 18.

48. B. F. Skinner: "Utopia and Human Behaviour" in Paul W. Kurtz, ed.: *Moral Problems in Contemporary Society* (Englewood Cliffs, N.J., 1969).

* The classical defence of specialization is in Emile Durkheim's *De la division du travail social* (Paris, 1893: trans. George Simpson as *The Division of Labour in Society,* Glencoe,
1933). Durkheim begins (p. 42) by quoting from the Swiss philosopher, Charles Secrétan,
a passage which expresses the ideal of technical perfection in an unusually uncompromising way: "To perfect oneself is to learn one's role, to become capable of fulfilling one's
function." The only alternative to specialization, Secrétan suggests, is an "affected dilet-
tantism." As a representative of the opposite extreme, Durkheim quotes de Tocqueville:
"In so far as the principle of the division of labour receives a more complete application,
the art progresses, the artisan retrogresses" (p. 44). In other words, technical perfection
dehumanizes. In reply to de Tocqueville, Durkheim sets out to show that the division of
labour, at least in its "normal" forms, is a socializing and moralizing agent, that, for example, human affection as we now know it depends upon the specialization of sexual roles,
so that the destruction of specialization would actually be dehumanizing. The truth of the
matter, I am suggesting, is that everything depends upon the extent to which specialization is pushed: it can be dehumanizing but so can the attempt to live one's life without
ever concentrating on particular forms of achievement. Both specialization and versatility
can be forms of cowardice: in the former case, a fear of venturing beyond a narrow field
in which one can comfortably think of oneself as an expert, in the latter case a fear of
showing up one's defects in capacity and judgement by venturing beyond superficiality.

as well as modern. A patriarchical, rural society, however, is entirely devoid of what may fairly be regarded as the greatest of human achievements, in literature, in science and in philosophy. And the assumption that, by way of compensation, moral virtue flourishes in a patriarchal setting cannot survive the most casual reading of the Old Testament.

Suppose, in contrast, it is possible to construct a society in which every person is engaged in a highly specific task, so chosen as to suit his capacities—a task he has been bred and trained to perform willingly and with the utmost efficiency. Suppose that in his leisure hours, he is supplied with entertainment which fully satisfies his wants. Suppose he is governed by experts who ensure that society runs smoothly, in an organized fashion, that men's health is maintained at a high level, that their anxieties—in so far as they still have any—are instantly tranquillized. Everybody, that is, is technically perfect in the performance of a task, he is content, he lives in an orderly peaceful society. What more, one might ask, could anyone want?

Such a society, the reply would often come, is "dehumanizing." That is why Marx rejected it. The division of labour, Marx willingly conceded, was a necessary stage in the growth of human society; it made possible the development of towns, and in towns the emergence first of bourgeois culture and then of that industrial proletariat in whose hands, according to Marx, the future lies. But in a "real community," he nevertheless maintains, each individual will "cultivate his talents in all directions."[49] Versatility, not specialization, will be the rule. And only in such a community, he says, will man be "truly human." This same view—that there is something inhuman about specialization—is even more vigorously maintained by those twentieth-century French philosophers whom it is customary, against their will and as an

49. "The German Ideology" in *Writings of the Young Marx on Philosophy and Society*, ed. Easton and Guddat, pp. 457–58.

ironic exemplification of exactly what they object to, to classify as "existentialists." "Travelling on the Underground," writes Gabriel Marcel, "I often wonder with a kind of dread what can be the inward reality of the life of this or that man employed on the railway—the man who opens the doors, for instance, or the one who punches the tickets. Surely everything both within him and outside him conspires to identify this man with his functions—meaning not only with his functions as worker, as trade-union member or as voter, but with his vital functions as well."[50]

One ought certainly to regard with an initial suspicion such expressions as "truly human" and "dehumanizing." The accusation that the technologically perfect society is dehumanizing is often levelled, but seldom made sufficiently precise. Often enough, such phrases as "truly human" are used quite illicitly, as polemical devices, to suggest that certain particular forms of human activity, those of which the writer approves, are somehow "in accordance with man's nature," or "truly human," whereas other forms of human activity are, in some obscure way, not really human at all, for all that they are undoubtedly characteristic of many human beings. So in the present instance, some men are versatile, while others, by choice or necessity, concentrate all their attention on a single task, perhaps narrowly conceived, in the manner Plato advocated. To say of the specialist that he is not "truly human," to lay it down that to be "truly human" one must be versatile, is, on the face of it, quite arbitrarily to pick out what is only one type of human being in order to proclaim him, and him alone, "truly human."

The same criticism can be applied more generally. Cruelty and envy are peculiarly human forms of behaviour; to

---

50. Gabriel Marcel: "On the Ontological Mystery" (1933) in *The Philosophy of Existence*, trans. Manya Harari (London, 1948), p. 2. Compare J. A. Passmore: *A Hundred Years of Philosophy, ed. cit.*, ch. XIX.

assert of someone who is cruel or envious that he is not "truly human" is undeservedly to compliment the human species. It takes a human being to be a Marquis de Sade, to construct the concentration camps at Auschwitz, to wage war, to lie, to betray, to hate. Man is never less an animal than in the depths of his depravity. To describe a state of society as "dehumanizing" merely because it encourages men to deceive, to lie, to be cruel is, on the face of it, arbitrarily to admit as human only what is good.

The word "humanize," however, is ambiguous. It can mean not only "to make human"—as when cow's milk is "humanized"—but also "to make humane." And this latter also, like the Roman *humanitas,* in either of two senses: to make more sympathetic, kindly, considerate, or to make more civilized.[51] In this latter sense, it is not uncommonly associated with a rather narrow conception of "civilization," dating from a time when a civilized, humane man was one who devoted himself to the study of the Greek and Roman classics, presumed to be the sole repository of human achievement. But without too great a strain on the concept of the "humane," we can extend it so as to include every form of imaginative civilized achievement, in science, in technology, in industry, as much as in the arts. Then we can argue thus: a form of society, an ideal, is "dehumanizing" if its effect is either to make men less considerate, less gentle, less sympathetic, or else to cut at the roots of civilized human achievements.* In order to demonstrate, then, that a society organized on the principle of technical

---

51. Compare the *Shorter Oxford English Dictionary* on "humanity."

* There are other important ways of defining "dehumanizing"; a man is dehumanized, it might be said, when he is robbed of his freedom or when he is treated as a thing, rather than as a person. It will emerge, in what follows, that these are closely related to the criteria here suggested; to destroy freedom is to destroy civilized human achievements, to be inconsiderate is to treat men as objects. But I have preferred to approach the question by keeping close to everyday usage, in a way which does not immediately involve the philosophical problems raised by the concept of freedom and by the ideal of "treating as a person."

perfection is "dehumanizing" we do not need to show that it somehow "destroys the essence of man" or is not "truly human" but only that it weakens the influence of, or destroys, a certain type of man—the type we call "humane," the type we call "civilized." This is substantially what is suggested in the dystopias of Zamiatin or Orwell and Huxley—and suggested, too, by critics of our own society who condemn it as dehumanizing because it is dominated by the principle of specialization and the associated ideal of technical perfection.

Our own society, of course, has not been deliberately founded on the ideal of technical perfection, as Plato's republic was. It has developed into a specialized society as a result of economic pressures; so far as it can be said to be dominated by an ideal it is the ideal of material prosperity, or economic growth, rather than an ideal of perfection. But in the interests of the ideal of maximum output, it has taken over as a sub-ideal the concept of technical perfection, of efficiency; it judges men by their fitness for jobs, not jobs by their fitness for men. And for that reason we can think of modern industrial civilization as exemplifying the dehumanizing effects of the ideal of technical perfection.

By treating men as machines, whose perfection is to be equated with their technical perfection, it helps to destroy sympathy, compassion, kindliness. Such judgements as "he's a nice chap"; "he is quite without malice and envy"; "he would never let you down" come to seem irrelevant; the sole question of importance becomes: "Is he efficient?" Sympathy, compassion, even friendliness are condemned as destructive weaknesses, destructive of efficiency; friendship generates loyalties which may cut across technical efficiency, limit mobility, reduce a man's willingness to economize labour.[52] If, then, when it is said that the ideal of a

---

52. Compare on this theme W. H. Whyte: *The Organization Man* (New York, 1956).

society founded on technical perfection is dehumanizing what is meant is that it weakens men's "humaneness," the accusation* seems to be thoroughly justified.

It may be replied that industrial societies, even if they were once inhumane, have now given birth to the Welfare State. Before we condemn too fiercely the inhumanity of modern Western industrial societies, we have certainly to remember that they do not leave people to die of starvation in the streets. Those many critics of Western societies who accuse them of lacking "true humanity" but who themselves display the utmost callousness towards their own fellow-men remind us once more how accusations of "inhumanity" can serve as nothing more than expressions of prejudice; indeed, Western societies are sometimes described as cold and inhumane for no better reason than that their officials are not readily subject to bribery and corruption.

Yet the fact remains, as the familiar simile "cold as charity" reminds us, that the distribution of alms, in however scientifically ordered a form, is no substitute for humane relationships in everyday life. The tendency of industrial society is to suppose that it is: pension schemes and the like are used to salve its conscience—to say nothing of their practical effects in reducing the mobility of labour. But pensions do not compensate for loneliness, and welfare benefits do not contribute to the development of humane relations

---

* Here again, however, one has to be careful not to sentimentalize the past. Unremitting toil is also dehumanizing; in some cases at least, technological advances have freed men from toil and left them time and energy for human relationships. Men's complaints about the dehumanizing character of modern social relationships are in large part a product of ideals that we have only come, since the Enlightenment, to take for granted: neither the medieval serf nor the brutalized eighteenth- or nineteenth-century workman was commonly regarded as a human being. In different societies, different classes of men are dehumanized, and in different ways. It does not follow that we ought therefore to acquiesce in dehumanization as an inevitable effect of social organization; particular dehumanizing factors have in the past been abolished, or reduced in importance; there is no reason why we should acquiesce in those which persist, or are increasing in strength, in the present. What we have always to watch is that, however admirable our intentions, we do not, in trying to abolish a particular form of dehumanization, substitute others even worse and more widespread. That is precisely what has happened in the case of Communism.

when their recipients, as is all but inevitable, are regarded with watchful suspicion, as men and women who will quite certainly cheat the State if they can discover a method of doing so.

Let us look now at the other side of the idea of "humanity," in which it connotes "civilized achievement." Such achievements depend, above all else, on man's "perfectibility," in Rousseau's sense of the word, his ability to innovate, to react in novel ways to new situations. The innovator, however, must in the first place be discontented, he must doubt the value of what he is doing or question the accepted ways of doing it. And secondly, he must be prepared to take fresh paths, to venture into fields where he is by no means expert. This is true, at least, of major forms of innovation; they make it possible for other men to be expert, but are not themselves forms of expertise. Freud was not an expert psycho-analyst; before Freud wrote there was no such thing; he created the standards by which psycho-analysts are judged expert. Neither was Marx an expert in interpreting history in economic terms nor Darwin an expert in evolutionary biology. If a man is trained, purely and simply, to be expert and contented in a particular task he will not innovate; Freud would have remained an anatomist, Marx a philosopher, Darwin a field-naturalist.

That is why classical Utopias, and the modern dystopias which ironically incorporate their ideals, are static. "The ideal . . . is to be found," as the narrator remarks in Zamiatin's *We*, "where nothing *happens*."[53] Innovations, as in Plato's *Republic*, are discouraged, or permitted only when they tighten the grip of the State over the individual. The technically expert citizen is expert only in his allotted task; for him to think about the value of that task is for him to pass completely beyond the limits of what is permissible.

In Utopias like Skinner's *Walden Two*, the situation is

---

53. *We*, Record Six; *ed. cit.*, p. 24.

rather different. Innovation is not only permitted, but encouraged. But it is left to experts. Experts alone are to determine what innovations are to be introduced, they will train, or re-train, men to cope with the new tasks which arise out of them. To accept this policy, however, is greatly to limit the sources of innovation. In our own society—although only in the last decades—there has emerged, admittedly, a class of professional innovators, dedicated to, and supposedly expert in, the discovery of innovations. But they are by no means the only source of innovation. Innovations result from public protests, from discontent with things as they are, from the ingenuity of workmen and amateurs. Often enough, too, they win recognition in spite of experts rather than with their encouragement, as the history of art, science and technology only too clearly reveal.

Such innovations, it will no doubt be objected, are liable to be harmful; innovations, social or technological, should all of them, so the argument will then run, arise out of designed experiments and be introduced more widely only if the experiments are successful. At this point we are brought face to face with what is the leading presumption in the ideal of a perfect society based on technical perfection, namely that as well as experts in carpentry and experts in mathematics, there are experts in determining what-ought-to-be-done. Plato was convinced that there were such experts. His philosopher-kings, in virtue of their knowledge of the form of the good, know in detail what policy ought to be adopted, whether in relation to politics or the arts or science or industrial production.

Suppose, however, we consider a particular issue, one which has constantly arisen in the history of perfectibilism: should men be permitted to marry for love? It is certainly true that psychological and sociological experiments are relevant in discussing this question. But it is quite another matter to say that there is some expert or class of experts whose investigation can finally decide the answer to it—in the sense in which they might decide, for example, whether men who marry for love are more or less likely than those whose marriages are arranged to have children whose intelligence quotient is higher than the average intelligence quotient of their parents. Yet unless all such questions are "matters for expert decision," it at once becomes apparent that at the very heart of a "technically perfect" society—in its decision upon what functions shall be exercised and who shall exercise them—there lies not the technical perfection of an élite but the exercise of despotic power. And the effect of bowing to the commands of such an élite is to destroy such major forms of innovation as art, where the pretence that there are "technical experts" who can decide how, and what, the artist ought to be allowed to paint can only issue, as it has issued in the Soviet Union, in an art which is merely a display of expertise, not an opening up of new human horizons. "There can be a real literature," Zamiatin once wrote, "only when it is produced by madmen, hermits, heretics, dreamers and skeptics and not by painstaking and well-meaning officials."[54] From Plato on, the setting up of a technically perfected State entails, indeed, that artistic innovation is simply not to be permitted.

There are, then, good grounds for believing that a society which is entirely based on the ideal of technical perfection will be "dehumanizing." But the phrase "entirely based on" is crucial. There is nothing "dehumanizing" in the ideal of technical perfection, or in specialization. Specialization is not "instinctive" with human beings, as it is with ants or bees. Men have learnt to specialize: this is one of their greatest achievements. At the opposite extreme from the fully-specialized dystopia lies the Arcadian ideal, the ideal of a society where there is no specialization, where everyone grows his own food, forges his own tools, makes his own

---

54. Quoted by Merle Fainsod: "The Role of Intellectuals in the Soviet Union" in H. M. Macdonald, ed.: *The Intellectual in Politics*, p. 89.

clothes. It, too, has a perennial appeal. Marx, describing a communist society without specialization, depicts it as one in which man hunts in the morning, fishes in the afternoon, rears cattle in the evening, and exercises his critical powers at night.[55] That is hard enough to envisage. But even more unimaginable is an ideal society in which a man would be a physicist in the morning, a painter in the afternoon, a biologist in the evening and a philosopher at night: the fact is that these forms of activity, taken at all seriously, inevitably preoccupy—they cannot be picked up and dropped at will. Many an intellectual, in search of Arcadia, has discovered, as did Nathaniel Hawthorne,[56] by harsh personal experience how impossible it is to reconcile intellectual achievement with unremitting physical labour.

The value of specialization is not to be underrated. In some ways, indeed, modern society is not specialized enough. It demands from its citizens a type of versatility which is incompatible with the highest sort of achievement, or even with the exercise of humane virtues; it expects everyone, however ill-fitted for such tasks, to drive a car, to care for his property, to be a good husband and a good parent. In many respects, too, there is in contemporary society too little competence, too little efficiency, too little urge for perfection in the conduct of a task. Not everybody who extols the virtues of efficiency is himself efficient, as the visitor to the United States is very rapidly made aware. To take a pride in doing one's work as well as one can, whether it is the work of a philosopher or of a waiter, of a shoe-black or of a hotel keeper, is by no means dehumanizing.

It is dehumanizing, however, for a man to be placed in a situation in which he has no opportunity of displaying any kind of enterprise in his work, as must be the case where the nature and conditions of that work are absolutely pre-

---

55. "The German Ideology," *ed. cit.*, pp. 424–25.
56. See Nathaniel Hawthorne: *The Blithedale Romance* (Boston, 1852).

determined in detail. Specialization is dehumanizing, too, if it holds men rigidly to a particular task, preventing them from following an activity, or an argument, wherever it leads them because to do so is to move into "someone else's field." Or if it so structures men's tasks that they are encouraged to think of their fellow-workers not as collaborators, but as rivals, rivals to be regarded with suspicion, hostility and envy. Or finally, if it governs a man's whole life, as distinct from some section of it; if he simply becomes, in the manner of a machine, "that which performs a particular function." Not specialization as such, but specialization in the interests of a total scheme based on the ideal of perfect social order, is the enemy to be feared.

Galbraith has described in his *Affluent Society* the ways in which "practical heartlessness" has been justified as "serving the public good"—a "good" which, it is presumed, can be identified with maximum output, maximum technical efficiency. One can add that if the same ideal of maximum output is allowed to determine the policies of universities, of science, of the arts, it will destroy not only humane feelings but the highest achievements of civilization. When it—and the cognate idea of "technical perfection"—encroaches into universities the effect is that a scholar is judged by his output rather than by its quality, and by the technical expertness of what he produces rather than by its capacity to illuminate. But what is wrong, once more, is neither the ideal of technical perfection, nor even the ideal of scholarly productiveness. Rather, it is the total subordination to those ideals of other ideals which are very much more important, if less precisely definable.

Considering, then, the criticisms which the dystopians have directed against both Enlightenment and Platonic ideals of perfection—ideals which converge at many points—we see that they consist, in general terms, in rejecting, as dehumanizing, the ideal of technical perfection and the connected ideal of "aesthetic" perfection through a total ordering of society. To attempt to perfect society through the application to it of a total plan in which everybody has his place, is, the dystopians argue, destructive both of personal relationships and of literary and scientific achievement. It must culminate, as the social tendencies of our own time clearly reveal, either in a society which is grim and grey, in which the ideal of perfection is but the disguise of power — this is Orwell's *Nineteen Eighty-Four* and the Communist societies of Eastern Europe — or, alternatively, in a society in which men achieve contentment only because they are conditioned to be contented and are drugged or sensually gratified as a way of reinforcing that conditioning. This, some of its critics argue, is modern Western civilization. In either case, so the suggestion is, human relationships are subordinated to an alien ideal — to orderly perfection and the technical efficiency of a machine.

FOURTEEN

MYSTICISM AND HUMANITY

The dystopian criticism of technical perfectibilism rests on a fundamental assumption, namely, that certain forms of human relationship and certain forms of human achievement are intrinsically valuable. "Dehumanizing," the dystopians do not for a moment doubt, is a condemnatory, dyslogistic adjective. This is what the Stoic, the mystic, the Buddhist, all question; to attain to perfection, they argue, man must first *renounce* his "humanity." In the place of "humanity"—tender human relationships and human achievements—they set up the ideal of a mystical union, whether with God, or with the One, or with the Universe as a whole. Only through his participation in such a union, on their view, can man reach perfection.

The mystical perfectibilist's attack upon "humanity" is two-pronged—moral and metaphysical. The *moral* criticism, very characteristic of Christianity, is that human relationships are all of them infected by such vices as pride, selfishness, ambition, vanity. The *metaphysical* criticism is that purely human relationships are by their very nature impermanent, transitory. The loved one dies; the cause to which a man devotes himself turns out to be a failure; the work of art, the technological achievement, the scientific theory are all of them liable to pass away, perhaps outmoded, perhaps deliberately destroyed in a new wave of barbarism. Only by becoming, or by uniting himself with, or by fixing all his affections upon, a Being who is eternal, simple, unchanging, wholly self-sufficient, can man, so the mystics conclude, find true peace of mind, true happiness, true perfection. "I have seen all the works that are done under the sun; and behold, all is vanity and vexation of spirit."[1] Ecclesiastes here sums up that critique of human activity which mystical perfectibilism takes as its starting-point.

Up to a point, the mystical criticism of "humanity" can scarcely be gainsaid. That there is no object of human affection which is not, in some degree, a source of anxiety, that no human action, however admirable, is wholly free from such motives as pride, ambition, vanity—these are conclusions which, if not quite indisputable, are at least highly plausible. As for the transitoriness of human achievements, although we like to claim that a Shakespeare or a Newton is "immortal," a few hundred years is a long way from immortality. It takes a bold man to presume that Newton and Shakespeare will still be familiar names ten thousand, to say nothing of ten million, years hence. The more modest achievements of the ordinary philosopher, scientist, artist, technologist, industrialist, are unlikely to survive his own decease, if they endure so long.

The real question, however, is whether such objections matter. Or, at a deeper level still, whether the attempt to substitute for ordinary human relationships and human achievements a supposedly "higher" relationship and "higher" achievement—union with God, or with the One, or with the totality of things—does not issue in what is actually a lower form of life, inferior to what human beings daily accomplish in their ambitious, proud, anxiety-ridden way. Is it so obvious that to attain to union with an undifferentiated unity—the typical mystical ambition—is a higher achievement than it is to succeed in loving a woman, or writing a poem, or cultivating a farm?

Consider in this light the perfectibilist's moral criticism of "humanity." Then we might first wish to challenge the traditional Christian view that pride is a vice, and that humility,

---

1. Ecclesiastes 1:14.

resignation, self-surrender are virtues. As Zamiatin suggests in his *We*, the Christian view anticipates, at this point, the moral outlook of a totalitarian state. "The greatness of the 'Church of the United Flock,'" he writes of the Christians, "was known to them. They knew that resignation is virtue, and pride a vice; that 'We' is from 'God,' 'I' from the devil."[2] The refusal of an artist or a scientist to accept the judgement of State or Church that his work must be suppressed contains within it, no doubt, more than a touch of pride. But his conviction of the value and importance of what he is doing, his refusal to be brow-beaten by authority, to submit, to obey, many of us, certainly, would refuse to characterize as vicious.

There are, however, many different forms of pride. For our present purposes, three are particularly important. Let us call them, respectively, aristocratic pride, Pelagian pride and, in a somewhat extended sense of the phrase, pride in workmanship. "Aristocratic" pride is pride in one's status —spiritual, social, or economic. It, quite certainly, is dehumanizing, ruling out, for those who are obsessed by it, certain kinds of human relationship and certain kinds of human achievement as "beneath their dignity." The aristocratically proud cannot love those who fall outside their own class, their own caste, or their own sect of élite Christians. Their relationships with such "outsiders" must be maintained at an impersonal level; the "chosen ones" can be charitable towards outsiders, relieving their sufferings, but they cannot enter into tender relationships with them, as friends or lovers. Nor can they embark upon such tasks, whether manual work or commerce, as are "unfitting" for members of the "aristocracy." Often enough, as Wesley observed, "aristocratic pride" has been encouraged rather than discouraged by Christianity. It has been encouraged,

2. *We*, Record Twenty-Two; *ed. cit.*, p. 121.

at least, whenever Christianity has drawn a sharp distinction between a spiritual élite—an elect, God's anointed, the One True Church—and the unregenerate masses.*

"Pelagian" pride lies in some respects at the opposite extreme from "aristocratic" pride; it is pride in being a "self-made" man, in being what one is entirely as the result of one's own efforts. This is the kind of pride against which the Christian doctrine of grace is particularly directed. In so far as man can do anything that is good, so Calvin argues, it is entirely God's, not his own, doing. No one is a "self-made" man; man is made what he is by God. Within Christianity, as we have seen, the controversy between Pelagians and Augustinians continues, and is likely to continue as long as Christianity survives. If we translate this controversy into secular terms, however, there can be little doubt that the secular Augustinians have the best of the argument. It is ridiculous for anybody to think of himself as "self-made"; if a man achieves anything at all this is very largely as a result of "grace," of gifts which are not bestowed upon him as a consequence of his merit but which are, in a broad sense of that phrase, "a matter of luck."

Consider a very minor example—the writing of a book. This is made possible only by a series of "graces," gifts from others, gifts the author has done nothing to deserve. These graces are manifold, and highly diversified in their origin—the great mistake of Augustinianism is to suppose that there is a single source of grace, an omnipotent being. In the case of a learned work they would include the tradition of scholarship which the author inherits; the encouragement, the criticisms, the suggestions, of teachers, pupils and col-

---

* Aristocratic pride can take the most extraordinary forms. The nun in Kawalerowicz's film *The Devil and the Nun* is proud of being possessed by the devil; the only option she is prepared to consider is to become a saint; to be exorcized would make of her a "merely ordinary" person. Similarly, the young are sometimes proud of their youthfulness: they think of themselves as forming a superior caste and regard affectionate relationships with the elderly as demeaning. Drug-takers are no less proud of their drug-taking and condemn relationships with non-drug-takers as unworthy of the initiated.

leagues; the contributions of his predecessors. It is not an author's own doing, not a reward for his merit, that he lives in a country and at a time when he is free to write as he will, and that is the greatest grace of all.

For an author to feel proud of himself for what he has done would therefore be absurd. In relation to any single one of these graces he is, no doubt, a co-operator: no one of them, by itself, explains why he has written as he has written. To that extent, he can rightly speak of "his contribution" in relation to, let us say, the existing tradition of scholarship or the culture of his country; he can think of himself as "saying something original," so long as he realizes that his "originality" is, in relation to what he has learnt from others, extremely slight in extent. A deeper exploration of the situation, however, soon reveals how dependent even that "originality" is on other sources of grace, on genetic inheritance, on upbringing, on the accidents of history. When Christians complain that humanists turn men into God, that they make men proud when they should be humble, their complaint is not entirely without justification—at least when, like Pico della Mirandola or Jean-Paul Sartre, humanists are enticed into the excesses of secular Pelagianism. "There but for the grace of God go I" has more humanity in it than "There, but for my own efforts, go I"—even if, or so I have suggested, what should properly be said is "There, but for the grace of other men, go I."

But there is a third kind of pride, only too often, but wrongly, identified with Pelagian pride, viz., a man's pride in what he is doing, in his work, as distinct from pride in himself for having done it. That is the sort of pride exhibited by Socrates before his Athenian accusers. Socrates displayed no sign of aristocratic pride; he would talk freely to anybody, to statesman, to workman, or to slave. Nor was he proud of himself; he did not think of himself as a "great man." But he took pride in what he was doing. When he was called upon to desist, he refused to do so, even in the face of death. What mattered, to Socrates, was not himself but his work—and this we may properly think of as the "classical" attitude, in opposition to the Romantic, Pelagian, emphasis on "originality" and "genius."

"Classical" pride, pride in workmanship, is the very stuff of civilization. Often enough, no doubt, it is objectively unjustified: men may take pride in what they are doing, persisting in the face of every obstacle, when what they are doing is intrinsically worthless. If "humility" means nothing more than the capacity to learn from criticism, then it has an undoubted value; but if "humility" means a willingness to submit to authority—to abandon or to modify what one is doing merely because it does not accord with the teachings of the Bible or the thoughts of Chairman Mao—then it is death to the spirit: the proper name for it, indeed, is "servility."* In so far as mystical perfectibilism seeks to destroy pride in workmanship, to convince men that no human task is worth while for its own sake, it carries dehumanization to its extreme point.

Pride in one's work carries with it a determination to accept the demands imposed by that work: in the case of philosophy to follow the argument where it leads, in the case of history to discover what actually happened, in the case of literature to explore to its depths a particular theme. In consequence, this sort of pride demands freedom: it has to be laid low in any authoritarian State. The historian, in such a system, has to conform to official interpretations of the past, the philosopher to dogmas, the writer to stereotypes of human action, the craftsman to "production-schedules."

---

* It is interesting to observe that Socrates and Jesus are the stock-types of humility. Yet neither was prepared to abandon what he took to be his proper work because the authorities—whether political or ecclesiastical—condemned it as worthless or dangerous. William Blake's *The Everlasting Gospel* (written about 1810) is largely devoted to this theme. Jesus, he says, "acts with honest triumphant pride." (Section V, 1.30 in *The Poetical Works of William Blake*, ed. John Sampson, Oxford Standard Authors, London, 1913; repr. 1958, p. 150.)

More subtly, attempts are made to lay pride low in a con-
sumer's society: the film-director, the novelist, the craftsman are called upon to produce "what will sell" at whatever
cost to their pride in workmanship. (Nothing could be more
opposed to pride in workmanship than "built-in obsoles-
cence," the ideal of a throw-away society for which everything is replaceable.) Indeed, better novels may come out
of an authoritarian state in which the author writes without
any expectation of being published than out of a society in
which he has one eye constantly fixed on "the market." In
the long run, however, the quality of a society will be largely
decided by the degree to which it encourages and facili-
tates pride in workmanship; a society in which that pride is
humbled will be a shoddy, second-hand, society.*

Pride, then, need not be an imperfection. But although
the anti-human perfectibilist particularly directs his criticisms against pride, the attack on pride is not essential to
his case. Let us grant, for the sake of argument, what the
critics of "humanity" allege: that in man's most dedicated
and devoted acts, the dedication and devotion are always
flawed, since the eye of the moralist can always detect an
element of possessiveness in love, of self-seeking in courage,
of self-display in science and in art. What is really striking,
even then, is not that such a degree of Pelagian pride and
self-centredness persists but, rather, to what heights of disinterested dedication and devotion, of courage and of love,
men—not only famous heroes but quite ordinary men and

* In his study of pride, Robert Payne concludes that it is the great disease of the
West: "Through the whole of Western history," he writes, "there rings the continual im-
placable cry: *Non serviam*." In the manner characteristic of contemporary mystics, Payne
sets against Western pride the self-abnegation of the East. I am suggesting, in contrast,
that "Non serviam," the refusal to obey, to submit, is the great glory of humanity, the fount
of human creativity, the guardian of freedom. But the pride inherent in this attitude, I
am also saying, is not pride in status nor is it the pride of the "self-made man": simply, it
is the conviction that what men can achieve has its own independent value. See Robert
Payne: *Hubris: A Study of Pride* (New York, 1960), p. 305. This is a revised edition of a book
first published in London (1951) as *The Wanton Nymph: A Study of Pride*.

women—have managed to attain. Those who reject human achievements as valueless because they are morally flawed are themselves, in that very act of rejection, offering testimony to the standards men have come to take for granted, the degree to which they have conquered self-satisfaction. But they are also testifying to the depths of absurdity into which men can be driven by their perfectibilist aspirations.

If ambition is a vice, one might finally add, it is certainly nowhere better illustrated than in the writings of the mystics. No Newton, no Einstein, has ever gone so far as did Angela of Foligno when she claimed that "the eyes of my soul were opened, and I beheld the plenitude of God, whereby I did comprehend the whole world, both here and beyond the sea, and the abyss and all things else."[3] If it be objected that Angela does not claim to have achieved this knowledge by her own efforts but only by God working in her, the claim to have become one with God is, to say the least, scarcely the extreme of humility.* Here ambition does not take its harmless, indeed desirable, form—the desire to create something worth while—but rather its dangerous form, to exercise control over the world.

In our own time, the doctrine of a "moral flaw" sometimes takes, under Freudian inspiration, a somewhat different form. And although Freud himself used this doctrine as a way of criticising secular perfectibilism, it has recently been invoked in support of a new variety of mysticism. "What appears in a minority of human individuals," Freud writes, "as an untiring impulsion towards further perfection can easily be understood as a result of the instinctual

---

3. *Book of Divine Consolation*, trans. M. G. Steegmann, p. 172, quoted in Sidney Spencer: *Mysticism in World Religion* (Harmondsworth, 1963), p. 238. Compare Robert Payne on the pride of John of the Cross and of Pascal in *Hubris, ed. cit.*, pp. 113, 193.

* There are a great many examples to illustrate this point in Robert Payne's *Hubris*, especially in his chapter on "The German Agony" (pp. 147–67) which is devoted to the German mystics. Here, for example, is Angelus Silesius: "I must myself be the Sun, and with my rays Stain the discoloured Sea with my divinity" (p. 160).

repression upon which is based all that is most precious in human civilization."[4] So far, then, as man perfects himself through his civilization he does so, if Freud is right, only at the cost of repression, a repression for which he has to pay a price, in neurosis, in aggression, in suffering. Complete perfection, in consequence, lies beyond man's reach: he may, in some measure, improve his condition in science, in art, in civilization, but what he can achieve is always limited by the very psychological circumstances which make such creative achievements possible. For him to be at once entirely free, entirely happy and entirely civilized—the typical ambition of secular perfectibilists—is by the very nature of the case impossible.

Were men wholly free, Freud argues, they would seek immediate instinctual gratification: they would not submit to that delay in gratification which is the foundation of civilization. They would not work, they would not produce, they would not create. Instinctual repression, and that alone, makes possible the transition from a gratification-seeking animal, entirely governed by what Freud calls "the pleasure principle," to a reasonable, socialized, civilized, human being. This repression is made necessary, Freud tells us, by scarcity. Men cannot support themselves without toil; were they always to seek the immediate gratification of their instincts, the human race would soon die out. Repression and scarcity, then, are the foundations of "humanity"; by their very nature, nevertheless, they limit and warp the "humanity" they make possible. Perfection is not to be expected. The repressed always returns, whether as a nightmare to trouble the repose of civilized man or as a war which destroys his illusions of peaceful, perpetual, progress.

The Freudian doctrine that civilization inevitably rests on repression has been diversely deployed for controver-

4. *Beyond the Pleasure Principle*, as trans. J. Strachey in *The Standard Edition of the Complete Psychological Works of Sigmund Freud*, Vol. XVIII (London, 1955; repr. 1957), p. 42.

sial purposes. Most often, perhaps, it is invoked in defence of repression, sexual repression in particular. Since civilization rests on repression, it is then suggested, sexual permissiveness must be destructive of civilization. To permit or to encourage freer sexual relationships would be to destroy, as Freud himself suggests, "all that is most precious in human civilization."[5]

But in, to mention only one example, Norman Brown's *Life Against Death,* Freud's doctrine is taken as the starting-point of a critique of civilization, or of some of its most notable achievements, and used to defend a new variety of mystical perfectibilism. Freud himself, at the very end of *Civilization and Its Discontents* had raised the question whether civilization is worth the instinctual sacrifices it entails. We must think the worse of civilization, Brown more confidently affirms, if it is based on instinctual renunciation. So whereas the classical mystics argued that men's passions must first be destroyed if they are to reach perfection, the new mystics argue that, on the contrary, their passions must be freed from the inhibitions which now restrain them. Yet the astonishing fact, as we shall see later, is that in their ultimate objectives the new and the old mystical perfectibilism almost wholly coincide: the dispute is about means.

If we turn now to the "metaphysical" critique of human achievements, the question is whether what the metaphysical perfectibilist, from Plato on, condemns as a defect in human relationships, their transitoriness, has the importance he attaches to it. Aristotle long ago pointed out, arguing against Plato, that a white thing which lasts forever is no more white than a white thing which lasts only for a short time. Everything we love, no doubt, will pass away, perhaps tomorrow, perhaps thousands of years hence. Neither it nor our love for it is any the less valuable for that reason.*

---

5. J. D. Unwin: *Sex and Culture* (London, 1934).
* This does not imply that artists, in the manner of some contemporaries, should

The opposite feeling—that nothing is worth while unless it lasts for ever—runs, however, very deep in human thinking. We must try to understand it, however absurd, once coolly considered, it may look. At this point, mystical perfectibilism links up with teleological perfectibilism, and especially with the idea of a "happiness" which is man's final or ultimate end—a happiness taken to consist, as the Epicureans took it to consist, in an absolute and total peace of mind. The search for such an absolute and total peace of mind is only too intelligible; there is no difficulty in understanding why so many human beings have looked with longing towards a state of affairs, individual and social, in which they would be entirely free from anxiety, or care, or concern. Interestingly enough, they have often constructed for themselves a legend of a time when that condition was satisfied, in the Golden Age or the Garden of Eden. And perhaps it once was satisfied, not only in legend but in fact. In their mother's womb, or in sucking her breast, in childhood play, men may have known a condition of unalloyed enjoyment without the intrusion of care.

Mystical perfectibilism takes as its ideal such a state of unalloyed enjoyment. It is no accident that the language it employs to describe the mystical state is so often sexual, that when we read a mystical poem by John of the Cross we should certainly read it as a poem of sexual love were we

---

deliberately design works of art so that they will be self-destructive, or that authors should confine themselves to ephemera and teachers to the contemporary scene, or that men and women should begin from the presumption that their love for one another will not last. That is a totally absurd, but only too characteristic, reaction to the discovery that nothing will last for ever. There are works of art, buildings, ideas, which human beings can continue to enjoy over long periods of time and which lend continuity to civilization. The ambition to create such objects is both potent and desirable. But it does not follow that only what lasts for a long time is valuable. The world is a better place for every love, every example of clear thinking, of devoted workmanship, of courage, which occurs within it, even when it passes unnoticed by all but a very few. One finds it hard to decide which is the more distasteful: that vulgar Philistinism for which "out-of-date," "nineteenth-century," "old-fashioned" and the like function as dismissal-terms or that inhuman complacency which waves aside whatever is lively and experimental in the present on the ground that it is "only a passing phase."

not told to read it otherwise, or that the Song of Solomon was for so long interpreted as a mystical paean. For what the mystic is seeking is a form of union, of unalloyed enjoyment, which is most easily exemplified in sexual terms.* It is sometimes said that while this may be true of the "ecstatic" mysticism of a Teresa—whom Bernini's famous statue depicts in a state of orgiastic satisfaction—or of a John of the Cross, it is certainly not true of "intellectual" or contemplative mysticism. And no doubt the mystical emphasis on unalloyed enjoyment is somewhat concealed when the mystical relationship to the One is described as a form of "vision."

The fact remains that "vision," in this context, is a form of unalloyed enjoyment, the consciousness of an object in a manner which is devoid of anxiety—a seeing without striving, without concern, without care. When a human being looks at anything, it is, for the most part, with "care." He looks at the sky and sees it as promising or as threatening; only rarely does he simply contemplate it as an object, to be enjoyed for its own sake. "The mere looking at a thing," Goethe once wrote, "is of no use whatsoever. Looking at a thing gradually merges into contemplation, contemplation into thinking, thinking is establishing connexions, and thus it is possible to say that every attentive glance which

---

* Puritanical Christians have sometimes tried to drive enjoyment out of the Garden of Eden, but Aquinas, for one, was quite convinced that Adam and Eve enjoyed sensual pleasures far greater than anything fallen men can experience. The element of direct sensual enjoyment in the idea of the Greek Golden Age has never been concealed; it is made particularly manifest in Agostino Caracci's painting *The Golden Age* and the chorus at the end of Act I of Tasso's *Aminta*. That popular English Utopia the fourteenth-century poem *The Land of Cockaygne* is no less unabashed in its description of a world where "All is sporting, joy and glee." For Aquinas, see *Summa theologica*, Pt. I, q. 98, 2; for Caracci and Tasso see Wayland Young: *Eros Denied*, 2nd ed. (London, 1967; paperback ed., 1968), plate 22 and ch. 26. For *The Land of Cockaygne* see A. L. Morton: *The English Utopia* (London, 1952; paperback ed., Berlin, 1968), p. 280. On Paradise and the womb, Simon Magus is said to have argued that the Garden of Eden is but a symbol for the uterus, and to have explained in detail how the two correspond. Compare Wilhelm Fränger: *The Millennium of Hieronymus Bosch* (trans. E. Wilkins and E. Kaiser, London, 1952), p. 50 n.

we cast on the world is [ultimately] an act of theorizing."[6] That is the typical "humanist" attitude.* But the mystic is not interested in theorizing: he is in search of a "looking" which can be enjoyed for its own sake, without the difficulty, the care, which is inherently involved in theorizing, in the tracing of connexions. Leibniz set out to rebut the charge that the vision of God would be an essentially boring experience—did not the fallen angels tire of it?—by suggesting that God's infinite attributes left the mind always with something to contemplate. But God, by his very nature, cannot be explored; he sets, to a transfigured mind, no problems; he cannot be worked upon, investigated, in the manner of a scientific problem. And that is even more obviously so when God is defined, in the typical mystical fashion, as a "Primordial One" or an "undifferentiated unity."

That pure vision and pure enjoyment are somehow linked is brought out in the ideal of a "beatific vision," the mode in which, in classical theology, the enjoyment of God and the vision of God are run together. Now we can understand why, too, there has been so much emphasis on the passivity of the mystic in his relationship to God: he is looking for a condition in which he no longer has to act, but simply to enjoy, or in which he no longer has to take care.[7]

6. J. W. von Goethe: *The Theory of Colours,* Preface, quoted in Erich Heller: *The Disinherited Mind* (Cambridge, 1952), p. 19.

* Contrast Wordsworth, describing his childhood:

The mountain and the deep and gloomy wood
Their colours and their forms, were then to me
An appetite, a feeling and a love,
That had no need of a remoter charm
By thought supplied, or any interest
Unborrowed by the eye.

Wordsworth is here describing one of the purest forms of play, the direct visual delight in natural scenery. But the mystics seek a delight which is at the same time the revelation of truth: "Man was created to contemplate truth directly, *without labour*" (A Benedictine of Stanbrook Abbey: *Medieval Mystical Tradition and Saint John of the Cross,* p. 18).

7. For the passivity of mysticism see pp. 132–33 above.

The word "care" has, of course, more than one meaning. Consider, as well as "take care!", "he takes good care of her"; "he cares for nothing else but his work"; "he doesn't care"; "he is full of care"; consider, too, the difference between being carefree, being careless, and being uncaring. The mystic is prepared to admit as permissible a form of "care" which, he tells us, is simply love, but he is looking for a love which is devoid of anxiety,* which no longer needs to "take care." We are suggesting, rather, that it is no accident that the word "care" conveys—like the German "Sorge"—both love and wariness, or anxiety, or sorrow. The Stoics were right; to care for anything is no longer to be carefree; the man who cares will not be careless. Where there is no care there is no love; the mystic's "love" is no love at all, but only passive enjoyment.

Most typically, as Heidegger has emphasized, man's care is directed towards the future.[8] British epistemologists have tended to think of consciousness as an optical device, recording what immediately surrounds it and generalizing these records by means of reasoning. On such a view consciousness records, let us say, "there is something green at time t_1," "there is something tall at t_1." This is then mysteriously combined into "there is a green tree at time t_1," and even more mysteriously compounded, with other such records, into the generalization "all trees are green." To think of consciousness in such a manner is at once to divorce it from the general flow of nature—to which it is related, on this view, only as an observer—and completely to misunderstand the nature of man's ordinary attitude to the world.

---

* The word "anxiety" is very commonly used—as in "anxiety neuroses"—to suggest a state of affairs one would certainly wish to be free of, a degree of solicitude which inhibits love. But if an excess of anxiety is destructive of love, some measure of anxiety, solicitude, care, is, I am suggesting, essential to love—just as, which is more and more recognized, it is essential to learning.

8. See J. A. Passmore: *A Hundred Years of Philosophy*, 2nd ed., ch. xix, pp. 476–516. The corresponding chapter in the first ed. is unsatisfactory.

Man is not a recording demi-angel, but someone who has to make his way in the world, to cope with it, who finds in it promises of help and threats of frustration. Generalization is man's natural attitude to the world, because only by means of generalization can he confront the future; memory is important to him because it suggests generalizations; imagination is crucial because it anticipates the future; error is inevitable because the future is not identical either with the present or with the past. Man is a generalizing animal, a rational animal, an imaginative animal, a disappointed animal, a triumphant animal, because he is an animal whose "principal home," as Paul Valéry puts it, "is in the past or in the future."[9] To say to him, then, "take no thought for the morrow" is to say to him: "Cease to be conscious—cease to be human."

No doubt, as we have already suggested, care is not the only human attitude to the world; there is also unalloyed enjoyment. But enjoyment is, in man's "humane" relationships, always conjoined with care. "He that hath wife and children," as Bacon tells us, "hath given hostages to fortune."[10] More generally, he who loves anything at all—persons, places, activities—has "given hostages to fortune." That is a principal point of difference between love and simple enjoyment. Enjoyment, as such, gives no hostages. To love is to care about, to care for, to take care of; to enjoy is to delight in what is immediately present. A love devoid of enjoyment is not love at all, it is what Cudworth called "slavish imposition," duty masquerading as love. But a love devoid of care, equally, is simple enjoyment pretending to be love.

Let us appropriate the word "play" for what I have been calling "simple" or "unalloyed" enjoyment, defining it, in a classical manner, as "pure activity, without past or future,

9. Paul Valéry: *The Outlook for Intelligence*, ed. cit., p. 97.
10. The quotation is from his essay *Of Marriage and Single Life*.

and freed of worldly pressures and constraints."[11] "Play" includes, to take our examples from perception, gazing at something as distinct from looking at it, hearing instead of listening, touching rather than examining with the hands.[12] When we handle a cup, for example, we are at the same time taking care of it, being wary; this is no longer pure play. But to stroke its surface is to enjoy it, purely, in a tactile way. To gaze, similarly, is a form of play, as distinct from looking which is an active attempt to "make something of" what surrounds us, to see whether it threatens or promises us anything. Play may take strange forms: the child twirling himself around to become giddy is playing, and so is the adult who makes himself drunk, or the vandal in the enjoyment of destruction—when his destruction is wholly purposeless and not, for example, a deliberate revolt against authority.

A child is engaging in play, in this limited sense of the word, when he touches or sucks a block. If, however, he uses his blocks to build a tower, although he is still playing, he is no longer *simply* playing: he is playing a game.* For he

11. This is Roger Caillois' summary, in his *Man, Play, and Games,* trans. Meyer Barash (New York, 1961), p. 163, of the position taken up by Karl Groos in *The Play of Animals* (New York, 1898).

12. Cf. I. A. Sikorski: "L'évolution psychique de l'enfant," *Revue philosophique,* XIX (1885), p. 418.

* Most of the classical writings on "play" and "games" fail to make this distinction, perhaps because many of them are written in the German language; in German the words "spielen" (to play) and "Spiel" (game) are so closely allied that German writers are inclined to presume that whenever a child is playing, he must be playing a game. Partly in consequence, the definitions such writers offer—attempting as they do to bridge every type of play and every type of game—are quite unsatisfactory: most often, they define "game" as if what they were defining were "play," missing the element of *seriousness* in a game, or alternatively, they define "play" as if they were defining "games," ascribing rules to direct sensuous enjoyment. It will be obvious, of course, that I am myself using the word "play" in a way which is not wholly in accord with common usage. But there is, I think, a very important distinction to be made at this point—even if, like most distinctions, it is not sharp at the edges—and the words "play" and "game" lie ready to hand as a fashionably quadriliteral way of making it. The distinction between "play" and "playing games" is made by P. H. Nowell-Smith in "Morality, Religious and Secular" (*Rationalist Annual,* 1961, p. 10). It is at least suggested in Jean Piaget's study of the game of marbles, contained in his *The Moral Judgment of the Child* (London, 1932).

is no longer acting "without past or future": the order in which he acts is now essential. Nor is he any longer free of "worldly pressure and constraints"; what he is building is not a tower unless it satisfies certain objective criteria, in relation to which his tower-building is successful or unsuccessful. In other types of games, the element of constraint takes a different form. Sometimes, the game is governed by formal rules, to which the child must conform in order to win or lose: sometimes the element of constraint—as in "playing doctors"—lies in the need for conforming to certain pre-existing modes of behaviour. "Playing Indians" is very different from "playing doctors"; in either case, however, there is an element of constraint, of care. A child cannot play even the simplest of games, like *ring-o'-roses* or *snakes and ladders*, without submitting in some measure to discipline, without taking care.

A game, indeed, can become nothing but a form of care, it can turn into *toil*. "What used to be a pleasure," as Caillois puts it, "becomes an obsession. What was an escape becomes an obligation, and what was a pastime is now a passion, compulsion, and source of anxiety."[13] A compulsive gambler is no longer playing. But equally a child is not "playing chess" if he moves the pieces at random merely out of physical delight in pushing them across the chess-board. (Playing with chessmen is very different from playing chess.) Play is direct, unalloyed, enjoyment of what is immediately present; a game is enjoyment—with care; toil is care without enjoyment—an activity undertaken merely out of a sense of duty, or merely for the sake of money, or status, or wholly under compulsion, internal or external. Most characteristically, "games" become toil when the outcome of the game—the gratification which success brings, in the form of money, or reputation, or status—comes to be more important than the

13. *Man, Play, and Games,* p. 44.

game itself. But a game can also become a form of toil because a person is obsessed by it, or because he finds himself in a position in which he has to engage in the game out of a sense of duty, or because—as in the case of a schoolchild—he is compelled to engage in it.

Human activities which are not ordinarily regarded as games can nevertheless be "treated as games." We can say of someone: "He treats science as a game"—or love, or politics, or commerce, or philosophy. To treat such activities as games is, positively, to enjoy them and seek, with care, to be successful in them but also, negatively, not to care about the object towards which that activity is characteristically directed. Let us suppose, for example, that a man "treats love as a game." Then he enjoys his relationships with women, he takes pride in the skill and care with which he flirts with, or seduces, them, but he does not care for, or about, the women as such. For the libertine, the woman in relation to whom he judges himself successful or unsuccessful is replaceable; should she die, or move elsewhere, he is only momentarily disconcerted. It is not that such a games-player cares for nothing except victory over women; they are not, to him, merely a means of acquiring wealth or status, or satisfying a compulsion to dominate. There are Don Juans for whom relationships with women are compulsive, a form of toil, not a game: they derive no joy from their relationships with them. The man for whom "love" is a game is not like that: he enjoys his sexual relationships; he likes women and prefers them to be witty and attractive. Simply, he is not prepared to take care of the woman, nor is he concerned with her future development; he does not *cherish* her. She exists for him only in the present, as a companion at table or in bed.

Parallel attitudes are sometimes to be met with in politics, in science, in art, in philosophy. Some philosophers and some scientists are quick-witted, clever, but not really interested in arriving at conclusions. They enjoy science and philosophy just as they might enjoy a crossword puzzle, as an exercise of ingenuity. "The mathematician," writes Adam Ferguson, "is only to be amused with intricate problems, the lawyer and the casuist with cases that try their subtilty." He goes on to suggest that human happiness largely depends on man's capacity thus to turn his occupations into "games," or, as he calls them, "amusements." [14] In our own society, it is rather disreputable for anyone to admit that he is in business except as a way of earning money,* just as in that Calvinist Edinburgh in which Ferguson was writing it was rather disreputable for him to admit that he was in business except in order to fulfil a God-bestowed vocation. But Ferguson is certainly right; a man is more likely to enjoy his life if he can treat his work as a "game"—one does not have to watch Polynesians at work on a Pacific island to realize that fact; watching an enthusiastic bricklayer will do as well. What Sartre calls "serious people" will no doubt find this attitude objectionable; they cannot shake off the feeling, so powerful in Genesis, that work is a punishment for sin, that to treat business as an enjoyable occupation rather than as the pursuit of profit is like singing in a prison cell— an insult to the majesty of the Law. Indeed, to "save their face" in the eyes of "serious people" men often *pretend* that they are acting out of duty, or out of necessity, or in order

---

14. *An Essay on the History of Civil Society* (1767), Pt. 1, Section VIII; *ed. cit.*, p. 50.

* Attitudes on this question are very complex. Many businessmen are in fact much more interested in status than in money, but it is more respectable to be interested in money. Most Americans, according to David Riesman, will insist—at least in certain moods —"that they act only out of self-interest" even when they are conspicuously *not* doing so. At the same time, he draws attention to the growth of a convention amongst Americans to speak of their work as "good fun" (David Riesman: *Individualism Reconsidered*, Glencoe, 1954, pp. 294, 319). This is a natural reaction from Puritanism. But "fun" suggests play rather than "games," as I have described them—or at the very least "games" in which the element of care is at a minimum. Business, in contrast, requires the exercise of enterprise and intelligence: it is more like chess than it is like a day at Luna Park. "Business is fun," in short, over-reacts against Puritanism.

to achieve some external end, rather than because they enjoy what they are doing. To answer the question "Why are you doing this?" with "Because I enjoy it" has come to seem improper. But the "serious people" have run the world for too long, the world "has grown grey at their breath." If our society does not permit men to enjoy their work, so much the worse for our society.

Games, in the broad sense of the word, are, then, by no means to be despised.* We need, all the same, to differentiate between games and a somewhat more complex form of activity, distinguished from games by its special relationship to the object towards which it is directed. Let us call that more complex activity "love." A judge may enjoy-with-care, as a game, the subtleties of legal debate, but we expect of him, above all, to "love the law"—to care about the outcome of his decisions, the situation which arises out of them, as distinct from enjoying his ingenuity in applying the law to an unfamiliar case. Similarly, although these phrases

---

* I mean, of course, that *games as such* are by no means to be despised. Flirtation can be cruel when one of the parties to it takes it seriously. Indeed, cruelty, malice, deception can all be enjoyed with care, they can all be "games" in my sense of the word. (We often speak, in such circumstances, of someone as "playing with" his victim.) Eric Berne in his *Games People Play* (New York, 1964; Pelican edition, Harmondsworth, 1967) uses the word "game" to describe those forms of stereotyped behaviour which men employ to disguise their real motives; a "game," as he describes it, is "basically dishonest"—to treat politics as a game would mean being in politics only for what one can get out of it (Pt. I, ch. 5, § 1). That this use of the word "game," rather than its older use as "amusement, fun, sport, diversion" should now come so strongly to the fore—as if the typical games-player were the cheat—reflects the cynicism of a society which has good grounds, no doubt, for its cynicism. I need hardly explain that this is *not* the sense in which I am using the word "game"; what Berne calls a "game" I should prefer to describe as a "ploy," a special form of toil. Concealment of motive can, of course, occur during the course of a game of football, or chess; both parties can enjoy with care the deception and the attempts to see through it. But such "ploys" are not designed *finally* to deceive, nor are they essential to all games. Some American writers on this subject, amusingly enough, have taken Stephen Potter's "gamesmanship" seriously. Potter cuts through the pretence that whenever anyone is playing a game he is "playing the game," in the English idiomatic sense. But that idiomatic sense is not itself a form of hypocrisy. There is an earlier, now classical, distinction between play and games in G. H. Mead: *Mind, Self and Society*, ed. C. W. Morris (Chicago, 1934), pp. 150–64. Mead's concerns are different from mine, and he substantially restricts games to team-games.

now sound pretentious and are undoubtedly in some respects downright misleading, we expect a serious artist—as
distinct from someone who simply "makes a game" of painting—to "love beauty," a scientist to "love truth," a statesman
to "love his country."*

What is meant in such contexts by "love"? To "love" is to
take delight in the continuing existence of an object, to find
it beautiful, to rejoice in its qualities and structure, and—
when this lies within our power—to help it to survive and
to develop. (This is not, by any means, a complete analysis
of the concept; but these, at least, are some of the things
it entails.) It involves enjoyment of the object as it now is—
love without enjoyment, with no element of play in it, is,
as I said, no longer love but toil. However, it goes beyond
play, as it goes beyond the enjoyment of the activity directed
towards an object.† What we call "the appreciation of art,"

---

* I should explain, perhaps, that I am not suggesting that all "loves" are good—the
love of money, the love of power and the love of glory are sufficient evidence to the contrary. I should also explain, in case anyone supposes otherwise, that I am not setting out
to offer a complete classification of human activities. There are, for example, "hatreds" as
well as "loves"—Philistinism is one form of hatred, racialism another. Hatreds, far from
cherishing, seek the destruction of the object towards which they are directed.

† The word "love," especially in the language of everyday discourse, is often used
in an extremely broad sense, to cover any case where there is enjoyment. ("I simply love
chocolates.") There is an element of stipulation, admittedly, in my restriction of it to that
range of activities where the lover cares about the continued existence and the growth
of the object towards which his activity is directed. But "love," I think, is the proper, if a
somewhat open-textured, word for what I have in mind. The verb "cherish" in its older
sense—it is now mostly used in the phrase "cherish the idea"—might serve as an alternative, but the noun "cherishment" is a dictionary-word, if ever there was one. It is certainly
vital to keep it in mind that "love," as I am using the word, refers to an activity, and that
it is not a synonym either for "enjoy" or for "like." At the same time, it entails both enjoying and liking. A child, it should be observed, cannot love his parents until he is able,
in some measure, to care for them, to take account of their interests when he acts. The
baby's relationship with his mother is a play-relationship; play only gradually gives way to
a love-relationship, marked by the decline of selfish possessiveness. (It may, of course, be
replaced not by love, but by fear, or even by hatred.) Theocentric Christianity treats the
love of child for parent as the typical relationship and urges us to become as little children. It will be obvious that, on the contrary, I think of love as typically a relationship
between adult human beings or between adult human beings and the objectives which
they foster. Of course, what happens in childhood can determine whether, and what, a

and reckon as part of humanity, is much more than a merely sensuous enjoyment of colour, of sound, or tactile surface, but it is not always displayed, either, by the trained critic. A critic may enjoy his own activity in dissecting a painting, in pointing to its defects and virtues. But he may still not love the works of art he is dissecting. What he enjoys is the game of criticizing, not the paintings. His work seeks to arouse in his readers an admiration for his talents, not for the works of art he is discussing; he may be read with pleasure, talked about, even by those who never venture into a gallery. The critic who loves works of art would be completely dissatisfied with this situation. Nor would a judge who loved justice be content merely because the cleverness of his judgements is greatly admired, if the effect of these judgements is to bring law into contempt. When a man loves a woman he does not merely like looking at her, or enjoy his own relationship with her: he cares about her as an individual, he suffers and re-joices with her. A scientist who loves science cares about the extension of human knowledge, as an activity which he not merely enjoys but would fight for. (Love, it should be ob-served, is far from being a merely sentimental expression of feeling; the lover needs courage.) Such a scientist could no more imagine abandoning science for administration, at least while he still has something to offer to science, than a mother could imagine exchanging her child for another, at least while he still needs her care.

In describing any individual case, we no doubt meet with problems. Only too often, we find on closer examination that love, in spite of professions to the contrary, is directed not towards the object of an activity but only towards the agent himself. We can properly speak, in such cases, of "self-love." The mother who at first sight seems to love her chil-dren may in fact love nobody but herself: her children are

human being learns to love. But to learn to love is at the same time to learn no longer to be a child.

but an extension of herself; their successes are *her* successes, their failures are *her* failures. An artist, similarly, may be interested in works of art only when he can think of them as "expressions of his own personality"; his love of the objects he creates is but a love of himself; if he is a writer, he does not write novels but only thinly disguised egoistic autobiographies, designed to make plain his "genius," not to expose objectively and critically the kind of person he is.

It has sometimes been argued, as part of the critique of humanity, that all loves are of this kind, self-love in disguise. But there are ways of distinguishing object-loves from self-love: object-love is marked by a generosity and freedom which is not to be found in self-love. A mother loves herself rather than her children if she will not grant them freedom, if she tries to force them into a predetermined shape, if she is jealous of any influence upon them other than her own. (Just as if she would like them never to change, her relationship to them is a play-relationship, not love.) "If we be distrustful or jealous," writes Adam Ferguson, "our pretended affection is probably no more than a desire of attention and personal consideration, a motive which frequently inclines us to be connected with our fellow-creatures. . . . We consider them as the tools of our vanity, pleasure, or interest."[15] An artist loves himself rather than his art if he cares only for his own work, is jealous of the work of other artists, and resents all criticism of his work as a form of personal attack. He loves himself rather than his work, too, if he is prepared to accept outside directives as to what he should do, and how he should do it, directives he accepts because they will increase his income or improve his status. Love is closely connected with taking pride in one's work, as distinct from being proud of oneself as its creator. Pure cases of love, we must admit to the critics of humanity, are rare; love and self-love, pride in workmanship and Pelagian pride, are

---

15. *An Essay on the History of Civil Society,* Pt. I, Section VIII; *ed. cit.,* p. 54.

usually so intertwined that it is easy to confuse them, as are games and "ego-games." But the distinction between them is nevertheless both real and important.

The very same type of activity, it must always be remembered, can be for one person a game, for another a form of love, for yet another a form of toil. Take, for example, building a boat. A skilled carpenter can enjoy building a boat even though he does not love boats; he would equally enjoy any other intricate task, e.g. building a jewel-cabinet. For him, building a boat is, in my broad sense of the word, a "game." But it is also possible for building a boat to be, as we say, "a labour of love"; then the builder not merely enjoys what he is doing: he cherishes the boat he is making. Finally, a man may be building a boat quite without enjoyment, merely to obtain some external end—to earn money, to gain prestige, to fulfil a promise. For him, boat building is toil. This is a crucial fact: it is of the first importance to realize that what we ordinarily call work can sometimes be a "game" and sometimes a form of "love," just as what we ordinarily call a "game" can sometimes be "toil," and what is ordinarily called "love" may be either a "game" or "toil." A man can be described by the world as a "scientist" who neither enjoys its ingenuities or loves its objectives; science, to him, is "just a job." "Love," as we have already seen, can be for a certain type of man a form of toil, for another a game. It is not wholly arbitrary thus to cut across ordinary usage; this is the best way of bringing out exactly what is wrong with the mystical—and a good many other—criticisms of everyday human life. Such phrases as "a labour of love," and "tennis isn't a game to him: all his interest is in winning," will perhaps help to break down any initial resistance to what is admittedly a somewhat disconcerting redeployment of everyday distinctions.

To return to the main theme. Mystical perfectibilism, we can now say, is an attempt to find a way of life which is purely play, devoid of care.* It rejects as valueless both games and love, rejects them on the ground that they are imperfect, flawed by self-love, flawed by care. It permits toil, but only that species of toil which is a stage in the progress towards the mystical union. Or else it thinks of toil as the proper way of life only for the Marthas of this world, for those who are not fit for the higher kinds of spirituality.

Very commonly the mystic sets out to free himself from care by denying the existence of the future. Time, he suggests, is unreal, an illusion; in reality, there is only the present, the "Everlasting Now." There is no future for men to care about. If men fasten all their affection, the mystic tells us, upon that "Everlasting Now"—given such names as God, the One, the Universe as a Whole—they will no longer have any need for care. It is the only object which men can love without giving hostages to fortune. They can unite with it without any fear that it will change, because it is immutable; there need be no fear that it contains secret threats which will only later be revealed, for it is absolutely simple; there is no risk that it, and through it those who love it, will suffer, for it is impassible. So man's relationship with the Everlasting Now can be unalloyed enjoyment, entirely care-free. Thus it is that the supposedly "higher" mystical love turns out to be identical with the elementary relationship

---

* That is why the "One" of mysticism replaces the "God" of everyday religious practices, and why, too, all forms of mysticism, Christian, Buddhist, Hindu, drug-taking, converge in their description of their supreme objective. Mysticism, as has often been pointed out, has no special connexion with any particular religion—or, indeed, with any religion at all. For Luther, it is far from true that man's relationship with God is a form of "play"; it is, indeed, unremitting toil. In the religious life of Italian peasants, it is more like a "game"—which, somewhat unexpectedly, Plato tells us it ought to be. Only mysticism converts man's relationship with God into a form of play. For Plato see his *Laws,* 803; *ed. cit.,* pp. 187–88. [After completing this book, I set about writing a review of *Selected Critical Writings of George Santayana,* ed. Norman Henfrey (Cambridge, 1968). There I read: "Changeless pleasure without memory or reflection . . . is just what the mystic, the voluptuary, and perhaps the oyster, find to be good" (Vol. II, p. 168). See also Santayana's essay on "The Philosophy of Bergson" (Vol. II, pp. 122–60).]

of uncaring enjoyment. "Joy," as Nietzsche puts it, ". . . does not want heirs, or children—joy wants itself, wants eternity, wants recurrence, wants everything eternally the same."[16] In short, "joy"—the spirit of play—wants, and in mysticism professes to have found, the One, the Eternal Now. We need no longer be surprised that the German mystics are so fond of the word "Spiel"—play—and its derivatives.[17]

16. Quoted in Norman Brown: *Life Against Death*, Pt. III, ch. viii; *ed. cit.*, p. 108.
17. J. Huizinga: *Homo Ludens*, trans. R. F. C. Hull (London, 1949), p. 38.

FIFTEEN

THE NEW MYSTICISM: PARADISE NOW

Mystics of the traditional sort, Christian or Hindu or Buddhist, would for the most part deny, with some acerbity, that there is any "real" resemblance between direct enjoyment and mystical union. The sexual language in which mystics delight, they would assure us, is only "symbolic"—although why the mystic should turn so naturally to the symbol of the passive bride remains to be explained. Contemporary mysticism—as exemplified in the "body-mysticism" of Norman Brown's *Life Against Death*—is bolder; it deliberately identifies mystical experience and sensual enjoyment. It is not unique in so doing; in some forms of Eastern mysticism, in Tantric Buddhism, for example, the two are also identified.[1] The "new mystics," however, think of themselves as inheriting the tradition of Christian, as well as Buddhist and Hindu, mysticism, even if they are particularly attracted by the religious attitudes of India, Japan and Tibet.*

---

1. In this case, too, it is sometimes argued that—except in perverted or vulgarized forms—the sexual references are only symbolic. See, for example, Anagarika Govinda: *Foundations of Tibetan Mysticism* (London, 1960; paperback ed., 1969), Pt. IV, ch. 4, pp. 140–43.

* I suggested that what happened in the eighteenth century could be described as the Confucianization of Europe; what is happening now, one might say in the same sense, is the Buddhization of Europe. In one of his *Letters to Leontine Zanta* Teilhard remarks: "We could perhaps learn from the mystics of the Far East how to make our religion more 'Buddhist' instead of being over-absorbed by ethics, that is to say too Confucianist" (trans. B. Wall, London, 1969), p. 58. It never seems to occur to the new mystics to ask themselves whether the societies in which mysticism and drug-taking have flourished are in any sense "more perfect" than Western societies, whether love is more widespread in them, or a sense of community, or compassion, or courage—to say nothing of creative achievements in art and literature. But since a French convert to Buddhism, André Migot, is prepared to argue that Tibet—as it was in the time of the lamas—and Upper Mongolia are the best governed people in the world, I suppose someone might also claim that they have the best

In most respects, certainly, they enunciate familiar themes, but from a new, bodily, point of view. Take the case of timelessness. Freud once remarked, although without much relying on the doctrine, that "there is nothing in the id which corresponds to the idea of time."[2] And in a sentence he jotted down at the very end of his life he also wrote: "Mysticism is the obscure self-perception of the realm outside the ego, of the id."[3] We might put the same point, in the terminology we have so far been deploying, thus: in direct enjoyment there is no reference to the past or the future; mysticism is an attempt to go back beyond repression to a state of uncaring enjoyment or "play."

Brown argues, quite specifically, that the very idea of time is a product of repression. "Time," he says, ". . . is . . . neurotic."[4] So too, he maintains, are such human achievements—or what we should ordinarily take to be achievements—as formal logic, quantified science, industrial production. As against all such "achievements," Brown sets up as his ideal the "insights" of mysticism, Romantic poetry, the childlike, playful attitude to life, direct sensuous enjoyment, unconfined, unrepressed. The traditional mystics, he says, in a passage to which we have already referred, "take seriously, and traditional psycho-analysis does not, the possibility of human perfectibility and the hope of finding a way out of the human neurosis into that simple health that animals enjoy, but not man."[5] Freud presented a dilemma: either civilization, which rests on repression, or unrepressed enjoyment. When it came to the point he preferred civilization, if with some misgivings. Brown, in the typical mystical fashion, chooses the other horn of the dilemma.

---

philosophers, the best scientists and the best artists. Compare André Migot: *Caravane vers Buddha* (Paris, 1954; Eng. trans. by Peter Fleming: *Tibetan Marches*, London, 1955).

2. *New Introductory Lectures on Psycho-Analysis*, XXXI, as trans. J. Strachey in *The Standard Edition of the Complete Psychological Works*, Vol. XXII (London, 1964), p. 74.

3. Standard Edition, Vol. XXIII (London, 1964), p. 300.

4. *Life Against Death*, Pt. V, ch. xv; *ed. cit.*, p. 274.

5. *Ibid.*, Pt. VI, ch. xvi; *ed. cit.*, p. 311.

Freud's own teachings, Brown argues, are badly affected by repression. This is why—most clearly, perhaps, in his "Analysis Terminable and Interminable"—Freud was led to reject the view that it is ever possible fully to free a person from internal conflicts, to "perfect" him. "Our aim," Freud wrote, "will not be to rub off every peculiarity of human character for the sake of a schematic 'normality,' nor yet to demand that the person who has been 'thoroughly ana- lysed' shall feel no passions and develop no internal con- flicts."[6] The object of psycho-analysis, he rather says, is to secure the effective operation of the ego, the "I" of everyday life. Brown, like the classical mystics, is completely dissatis- fied with this everyday "I," and, more generally, with Freud's anti-perfectibilist conclusions.

For Freud, although the child is "polymorphously per- verse," civilization rests on genital heterosexuality. So far as this is so, Brown concludes, civilization is grossly imper- fect. The perfected human being will delight "in that full life of all the body which [he] now fears"; his sexual enjoy- ment will no longer be flawed by an anxiety lest it overstep the permissible limits of sensuality.* The concentration on genital sexuality is, Brown says, "unnatural" and constitutes "the bodily base of the neurotic character disorders in the human ego."[7] We need not pause to ask whether this is so: Brown's ideal is what interests us, the ideal of an enjoyment which is immediate and absolute, which refuses nothing in the way of immediate experience.

As for science, that has value, Brown argues, only if it

6. *Analysis Terminable and Interminable,* as trans. J. Rivière in *Standard Edition,* Vol. XXIII, p. 250.

* Recent investigations into sexual life in the United States have made it clear that in that country what Brown sets up as an ideal is in fact being largely realized: sexual relationships, to a rapidly increasing degree, are taking an anal or oral form. See the inves- tigations reported in Charles Winick: *The New People: Desexualization in American Life* (New York, 1968; paperback ed., 1969), pp. 319–23. The new mysticism, in this and in other respects, may be responding to a general social change, as distinct from advocating an eccentric ideal.

7. *Life Against Death,* Pt. VI, ch. xvi; *ed. cit.,* p. 308.

can be transformed into a "non-morbid" form in which it would be "erotic" rather than "sadistic," seeking, that is, "not mastery over but union with nature."[8] It would then be a type of "erotic exuberance," no longer an attempt to replace the world we enjoy by a set of laconic formulae. Goethe's theory of colours, in which, in opposition to Newton's mathematico-physical analysis, colours are objects of immediate enjoyment, is for Brown, as for so many German or German-inspired thinkers, the paradigm of "true," non-morbid, science.

Doctrines very like Brown's are to be found in much of the literature of the 1960s, especially in novels originating in the United States. In an underground novel first published in 1966, Richard Fariña's *Been Down So Long It Looks Like Up to Me,* drug-taking, with its object the destruction of time and care, sexual promiscuity, which does not involve any care for what is enjoyed, and mysticism, which cares nothing for any merely human achievements, run together in harness with nostalgia for the television serials of the children's session and, of all things, the writings of A. A. Milne. Scenes of sexual enjoyment are interlarded with extracts from *Winnie the Pooh;* one of the characters is named "Heffalump"—another, equally characteristically, is called "Gnossos," to suggest gnosticism.

That "Bible of the hippies," Henry Miller's *Tropic of Capricorn,* no less freely deploys all the old mystical themes. "There is only one great adventure," writes Miller, "and that is inward towards the self, and for that, time nor space nor even deeds matter." To embark on that "adventure," men must not go forward but backwards, according to Miller, into a super-infantile realm of being—to that life of early childhood which "seems like a limitless universe."[9] The

---

8. *Ibid.,* Pt. V, ch. xv; *ed. cit.,* p. 236.
9. Henry Miller: *Tropic of Capricorn* (London, 1964; Panther paperback ed., 1966), pp. 11, 117.

"hipster," Norman Mailer writes in a similar spirit, lives "in that enormous present which is without past or future, memory or planned intention."[10] The ideal of John Barth's *Giles Goat-Boy*, characteristically, is "only to Be, always to Be, until nothing was . . . but one placeless, timeless, nameless throb of Being"—and "Be" is used as a synonym for sexual enjoyment.[11]

Indeed, the demand for carefree, child-like enjoyment is what, at least in its "Romantic" form, "the revolt of the young" is about.* The society of their elders—to a degree exaggerated by the Depression and the war which followed —placed its emphasis either on success or on security, and, in either case, looked to the future. "Everything," writes Henry Miller, describing the household of his childhood, "was for tomorrow, but tomorrow never came."[12] In gen-

10. Norman Mailer: *Advertisements for Myself* (London, 1961; Panther paperback ed., 1968), Pt. 4, The White Negro, §2, p. 271.

11. *Giles Goat-Boy*, Vol. I, First Reel, ch. 5; *ed. cit.*, p. 35.

* Many of the young revolutionaries—very obviously in Czecho-Slovakia but in some degree also in the democracies—are still working within the liberal tradition. What they are seeking is an extension of democratic rights, greater access to representative institutions, a higher degree of personal freedom. They may be mistaken in believing that a particular right will give them greater freedom, but this is a mistake about the facts. There is certainly nothing undemocratic, for example, in opposing conscription. The "Romantic" rebels, on the contrary, are not interested in democratic institutions or in democratic processes. In the manner of the anarchists before them, they would like to replace institutions by "community." Although the two types of revolt are, in practice, interconnected in complicated ways, in their pure forms they stand in complete opposition one to another. This is very clearly brought out in Yves Ciampi's semi-documentary film *A Matter of Days* (1969). The young French "Romantic" revolutionary heroine is bored and exasperated by the Czecho-Slovakian student revolt; to her, it is merely an attempt to set up that sort of bourgeois society against which, in France, she has been rebelling. The contrast between the risk-taking revolution of the young Czechs and the theatrical gestures of the "Romantic" revolutionaries is only too manifest. But that is not to say that the "Romantic" revolutionaries have absolutely no ground for their revolt, however ill-defined may be their objectives and however unpalatably childish some of its manifestations may be. (Violence, I said, can be a form of play: and the faecal preoccupations of some of the more depressing American young are typical of childish scatology—although it has to be added that both violence and obscenity can be a reaction of helplessness. It has also to be added that neither violence nor obscenity is peculiar to the young. What their elders see, abstractly, as authority, the young experience concretely as violence.)

12. *Tropic of Capricorn, ed. cit.*, p. 11.

eral, modern life is extraordinarily dependent on time. No doubt, there are still areas of freedom. We have not yet reached the point described in J. G. Ballard's story "Chronopolis,"[13] in which, to avoid traffic problems, every detail of everyone's daily life is governed by a rigid time-table. The narrator of Zamiatin's wholly time-dominated *We* can look back with astonishment to our own era as one when men were still free to walk in the streets, or to have sexual intercourse, at times of their own choosing. But the fact remains that whereas not until the late Middle Ages were there town-clocks, modern life would be unimaginable without what the English language significantly calls "a wrist-*watch*." It is by no means surprising, then, that the ideal of timelessness—of inhabiting a world in which nobody ever says "you'll be late"—should have its appeal.

Nor is it at all surprising that the ideal of pure enjoyment should be resuscitated. For a great many people, life in our society—as, admittedly, in any other society—has been sheer toil, not at all a "game," let alone an exercise of "loves." This is perhaps particularly true of the executive classes, from the ranks of whose children the new mystics are so largely recruited. As for play, simple carefree enjoyment, that has threatened to vanish. Forced to postpone enjoyment, the middle-aged generation, as the young can see for themselves, find it unattainable when at last they "have time" for it. They seek for enjoyment, no doubt, but what they find, often enough, is only a new form of toil. Even games in the narrower sense of the word have come to be reserved for those who play them well; and merely to play, as distinct from playing games, is thought of as undignified, unworthy of the "serious man." (There is an extraordinary contrast, at this point, between the attitude of the Japanese—in so far as they are still not wholly converted to

13. Included in J. G. Ballard: *The Four-Dimensional Nightmare* (London, 1963; paperback ed., Harmondsworth, 1965).

Western ways — and the attitude of the West; the idea of re-
laxation as "play" still survives in Japan. But it is conjoined,
it would seem, with an attitude of mind for which work is
mere toil, not enjoyment with care.) [14]

If the old Puritanical attitudes to sexual play have broken down — this has happened only in part — they have often
been replaced by new forms of anxiety, deriving from "sex
manuals" — anxieties about "sexual adequacy," anxieties
about inhibitions. Whole books are now written on "the
sexual responsibility" of the man or of the woman. Sex has
become almost as serious a matter, as little spontaneous,
as business. "Sexual play" is now, at its best, a "game," but
at its worst, dutiful toil, no longer the spontaneous flower-
ing of tender sensuality, but an applied technique. The intentions behind such manuals are often humane; they are
attempts to turn sexual activity into a form of love which
involves the cherishing of each sexual partner by the other.
Many of them take as their starting-point a growing concern for women, the refusal to regard them as mere objects of enjoyment. But every "love," like every "game," can
easily be converted into a form of anxiety-ridden toil. "We
turn lovemaking into a compulsory sport," writes the novelist Stephen Vizinczey in his *In Praise of Older Women,* "an
etiquette of technique or a therapeutic prescription." And
then in reaction from this, as he goes on to point out, we
"haste to succumb to joy"; we take the libertine as our hero.[15]
(The libertine lives in an "Everlasting Now" by deliberately
refusing to pay any attention to the future of the woman he
seduces.) That kind of love which is neither a game nor a
form of toil, which rests on enjoyment with care but cherishes its object is what seems to lie beyond our capacities.

One can only too easily understand why, when "loves"

---

14. David and Evelyn Riesman: *Conversations in Japan* (New York, 1967), pp. 188, 195.
15. Stephen Vizinczey: *In Praise of Older Women* (London, 1966; Pan Books ed., 1968),
pp. 181, 185.

are understood as "toil," the new mystics reject every form of "love," along with every form of toil, in favour of an immediate anxiety-free enjoyment, Paradise now, to be obtained by drugs, if in no other way. Their spokesmen, for the most part, fail to make the crucial distinctions on which we have been insisting. They distinguish, merely, between "games" and "non-games"—defining games as "behavioural sequences defined by roles, rules, rituals, goals, strategies, values" and counting as non-games only "physiological reflexes, spontaneous play, and transcendental awareness."[16] But roles, rules, goals, strategies, values are as characteristic of toil as of games: such a definition entirely overlooks the element of *enjoyment* in games—perhaps because it is being assumed, as it is so often assumed, that "care" and "enjoyment" are incompatible. As a consequence, it is made to appear that man has to choose between toil and play.*

Closely associated with the rejection of loves as too onerous is the rejection of freedom and responsibility in favour of the mystical ideal of "unity." The young generation respond, so we are told, "to the sense and sound of friendship and community, to the exultation they feel when thousands of people link hands and sing 'We Shall Overcome.'" They are prepared to sacrifice everything to "that feeling of community, of life," they are not to be deterred

16. Timothy Leary, Richard Alpert and Ralph Metzner: *The Psychedelic Experience* (New York, 1964), p. 13, quoted in Lewis Yablonsky: *The Hippie Trip* (New York, 1968), pp. 311–12.

* It may be argued that the best human society can do for most men is to provide for them intervals of play in a life of toil. In his *Laws* (653) Plato suggests something of this kind: the Gods, he says, out of pity for men's toil have set up festivals, to offer them relief. The "carnival"—a period of irresponsible enjoyment—is a familiar feature of traditional societies and has survived, in a reduced and modified form, into the modern world. Puritanism, with its ideal of a wholly toil-dominated life, sought to destroy festivals; the contemporary fascination with "orgies" reflects, perhaps, a self-conscious attempt to reinstate them. It is worth observing that not only the essentially totalitarian Plato but also Dostoievsky's Grand Inquisitor suggest that a life which alternates between toil and play is the one which makes men easiest to control. When men enjoy their work they also demand the freedom to innovate within it; toil plus play is a recipe for tyranny, enjoyment in work entails freedom.

by "nineteenth-century rhetoric about democracy and freedom." [17] This, of course, was the Nazi attitude; if the young
have come to mistrust "nineteenth-century rhetoric about
freedom and democracy"—not surprisingly when one re-
calls how often this "rhetoric" is used by those for whom
"freedom" means the despoliation of natural resources and
"democracy" the use of the State to suppress minorities—
they have still not learnt sufficiently to mistrust twentieth-
century rhetoric about "community and life."*

Their attitude, however, is understandable. Modern democracy, which pretends to be pluralistic, daily becomes
more atomistic. Universities, for example, threaten to become stock-piles of experts, who in no way cherish either
the traditions of the University to which they belong or, except in an accidental way, their colleagues and pupils. The
Stoical ideal of self-sufficiency has in part been realized:
the effect is that men feel isolated, powerless against the
State, lonely. Often enough, especially in America, loneliness is described as if it were the human condition. But the
themes of human loneliness, separation, isolation, are typi-

---

17. Jacobs and Landau: *The New Radicals, ed. cit.,* p. 15.

* I do not mean to suggest that the "Romantic rebels" are Nazis in jeans; they have
an almost pathological mistrust of the "leader principle." Fundamentally, they are Dionysians, in Nietzsche's sense of the word. Indeed, Nietzsche's description of the Dionysians
sums up their ideals admirably: "Now the slave is free; now all the stubborn, hostile bar-
riers, which necessity, caprice or shameless fashion have erected between man and man,
are broken down. Now, with the gospel of universal harmony, each one feels himself not
only united, reconciled, blended with his neighbour, but as one with him; he feels as if the
veil of Maya had been torn aside and were now merely fluttering in tatters before the mysterious Primordial Unity. In song and in dance man expresses himself as a member of a
higher community . . . from him emanate supernatural sounds. He feels himself a god, he
himself now walks about enchanted, in ecstasy, like to the gods whom he saw walking about
in his dreams. He is no longer an artist, he has become a work of art: in these paroxysms
of intoxication, the artistic power of all nature reveals itself to the highest gratification
of the Primordial Unity." There could be no better description of the world of pure play.
Nietzsche, too, was no Nazi. But the fact is that the attempt to construct a society wholly
based on "play" and "community" leads either to total collapse or to tyranny. If not the
God Dionysus, then an earthly, and less amiable, surrogate, has to sustain it. See *The Birth
of Tragedy from the Spirit of Music,* trans. C. P. Fadiman (1926), and included in *The Philosophy
of Nietzsche,* introd. W. H. Wright, Modern Library (New York, 1937). The reference is to
pp. 173–74 of the separately paginated text of *Ecce Homo* and *The Birth of Tragedy.*

cal of the industrial age, not of literature as a whole, where loneliness is represented, rather, either as something to be sought—"I wandered lonely as a cloud"—or as a condition to which a few, but only a few, human beings are subjected by chance. Adam Ferguson saw this clearly, even in the eighteenth century. It is, he suggests, only in the "commercial state"—although he adds "if ever"—"that man is sometimes found a detached and a solitary being: he has found an object which sets him in competition with his fellow-creatures, and he deals with them as he does with his cattle and his soil, for the sake of the profits they bring."[18]

The young are rebelling, in part, against the atomistic tendencies of modern society. But they have reacted, in the manner only too typical of human beings, by reverting to the old perfectibilist, and in the end tyrannical, ideal of a total unity rather than the admittedly more complex ideal of a plurality of intersecting communities. It is very natural to argue thus: the experience of belonging to a community is essential to "humanity," therefore the best of all possible worlds would be a total community to which everyone would belong. But this conclusion by no means follows. If communities can be stimulating, encouraging, the source of "graces," they can also be stifling, discouraging, destructive of love. A man can be born into a community which does not suit him, from which he has to break loose if he is ever to enjoy his particular loves. One great virtue of democracy, so long as it continues to be a network of communities, is that it is always possible to leave one community and join another, with different rules, different habits, devoted to different pursuits.

This implies, however, that not *everybody* does so; otherwise, there will be no community to join; the value of a community depends on its possessing a degree of stability, of continuity. (Admitting, of course, that the birth of new com-

18. *An Essay on the History of Civil Society*, Pt. I, Section III; *ed. cit.*, p. 19.

munities and the death of old communities is also a part of the democratic process.) Too considerable a degree of mobility destroys community, it generates what Durkheim called "anomie." A university teacher, for example, is unlikely to cherish his university, his colleagues, his students, if he is perpetually poised, ready to move anywhere which offers him more money or a higher status. He may try to substitute his professional associations for his university, but the professional association provides relatively few personal contacts: it cannot serve as a substitute for a face-to-face group. And it leaves his students, not yet "professionals," with no sense of belonging, in their university, to a genuine community.[19] These are just the circumstances in which one would expect to encounter a sense of loss, issuing in a demand for a total community, in which one would be "at home" wherever one moved. To react thus, however, is to miss the point that a community needs to be small and adapted to the special interests of its members—"available," up to certain limits of size, to those who share these interests, but certainly not providing a suitable "home" for everybody. A "total" community would be so diluted as to be no longer a community: concretely, indeed, it would coincide with that completely atomistic society which, abstractly, is its opposite extreme. It is easy enough to see this in the history of universities. The attempt to include all forms of activity within the university destroys the university; it becomes pointless, from the standpoint of "community," to be a member of it. Everyone begins to pursue his work in isolation from his fellows. So the "total" community—the "multiversity"—ceases to be a community at all, and the advantages which previously excluded persons and activities

19. There is, of course, an enormous literature on this subject. The major lines of controversy are sketched in Ferdinand Tönnies: *Community and Society* (1887), trans. and ed. C. P. Loomis (East Lansing, 1957; paperback ed., New York, 1963). On the special case of universities see T. Roszak: "On Academic Delinquency" in T. Roszak, ed.: *The Dissenting Academy* (New York, 1967; paperback ed., Harmondsworth, 1969).

were supposed to gain from membership of it no longer exist—just as when an attempt is made to "let everybody enjoy" the peace and quiet of a mountain valley by opening a four-lane highway to it. The student, often enough, feels that he belongs to a "real community" only when he joins in revolutionary activity; the "sit-in" is a community, as the university itself is not.*

In Marshall McLuhan's *The Medium Is the Massage*—McLuhan, it is worth observing, is a warm admirer of Teilhard de Chardin—the ideas of timelessness and of "community" are explicitly run together. "Ours," he says, "is a brand-new world of allatonceness. Time has ceased, space has vanished. We now live in a *global* village . . . a simultaneous happening. . . . We have begun again to structure the primordial feeling, the tribal emotions from which a few centuries of literacy divorced us."[20] Considered as an account of what is actually the case, this is utter nonsense; men live as much

---

* Communities differ in character, however. A university is not, and cannot be, anything like a "sit-in." Terrible confusion has been caused by the confluence of a number of factors: the ridiculous habit of describing the university as "a community of scholars" rather than as, at best, a community of scholars and pupils, the educational dogma that education must be "problem-oriented" rather than "subject-oriented," the over-emphasis in universities on the contemporary, the breaking up of educational sequences into disordered "units." (All of these factors have been particularly influential in faculties of arts and social sciences.) Together, they generate the conclusion that the ideal university would be one in which students and teachers, on equal terms, sat around discussing whatever "problems" happened to be currently fashionable. The fact is that students entering a university are ignorant; what they need is to be introduced to consecutive and ordered subjects. As pupils they have rights in the community, and they can reasonably complain when their masters ignore them, teach them badly, or not at all, and refuse to allow them to participate in the university's government. But a university is not, cannot be, and ought not to be, a community of equals: it could become such only by destroying scholarship, abandoning learning, forgetting that its task is to *teach*, which implies that there are learners, and to advance knowledge, which implies that knowledge is something one only gradually acquires. Once again, the remedy proposed by the "Romantic rebels" is even worse than the disease. The demand that their teachers be constantly at their beck and call, for example, displays a complete incapacity to understand the conditions necessary for scholarly work. But, on the other hand, a pupil needs to do a great deal more than merely to "audit" a course—that revealing American expression; he needs to participate in courses of studies as distinct from simply "hearing" what is said to him.

20. Marshall McLuhan and Quentin Fiore: *The Medium Is the Massage* (New York, 1967; paperback ed., Harmondsworth, 1967), p. 63.

in time and space as they ever did, and in a manner by no means global. Television, on which McLuhan lays so much stress, does not carry the world to the sitting-room; on the contrary, much more than a book, it carries the sitting-room to the world. Men still judge what they see in the light of where and what they are. They are not brought into human relationship with one another merely by looking at the same television programme. If, however, McLuhan is misreporting what is actually the case, he is not misreporting what a great many of the younger generation like to think is the case: that only the present counts, and that the present is the same everywhere—a belief which is no doubt encouraged by the illusion of "prescience" and "contemporaneity" which television offers its devotees. The "Everlasting Now" is ready at hand for all men. To see, as Angela of Foligno did, "the whole world, both here and beyond the sea" they stand in no need of ascetic disciplines; they need only buy, or rent, a television set.

"Timelessness" and "community" are by no means the only perfectibilist ideals to which the "Romantic" rebels revert. The word "beat" in the phrase "the beat generation" is not, as might easily be supposed, a way of referring to those who have been beaten by life; it is an abbreviation for the "beatific," those who have experienced the beatific vision. The old perfectibilist demand for absolute purity of motive has once more raised its head. So the Californian "Diggers"—a "Hippie" group—will accept gifts "only if they are given with love," as distinct from charity.[21] ("Charity" no longer means the love of God but, rather, a patronizing "hand-out"; thus, by an interesting twist of language, acting "out of charity" has come to be identified with acting out of impure motives, whereas to Christians charity was the only pure motive.)

Even the most bizarre "Romantic rebel" behaviour can

21. Yablonsky: *The Hippie Trip*, pp. 283–84.

turn out, indeed, to have its roots in a long-standing mystical perfectibilist tradition. Take, for example, unisexuality. According to Genesis, God first of all created Adam; he did not create Eve directly, as a pure expression of his creative power; he made her out of Adam's rib. Man and woman, according to Genesis, are "one flesh." The implication was not lost on mystical perfectibilists: in the state of perfection, they tell us, there will indeed be only one flesh. In the apocryphal Gospel according to the Egyptians Jesus tells Salome that the final secrets will not be unveiled until "ye have trampled on the garment of shame, and when the two become one, and the male with the female is neither male nor female." In the so-called "Second epistle of Clement" this becomes: "When the two shall be one and the outside (that which is without) as the inside (that which is within), and the male with the female neither male nor female." [22]

The sixteenth-century mystic, Jacob Boehme, was convinced that imperfection entered the world with Eve's creation. No longer were all created things direct emanations of God—Eve was the prime exception. The German mystically-inclined poet, Gottfried Benn—at one time an enthusiastic follower of Hitler—took as his ideal that "pre-logical" stage of human consciousness, when religion reflected "the original monosexuality of the primitive organism, which performed seed-formation, copulation and impregnation within itself." [23] In many Indian sects, male and female are but different aspects of the one deity. "Margot"—one of the "hippies" in Lawrence Lipton's *The Holy Barbarians*—has been told by her male associates that "the gods were conceived of in their pure primitive form as androgynous . . .

---

22. *The Apocryphal New Testament*, ed. M. R. James (Oxford, corrected ed. 1955), p. 11.

23. Gottfried Benn: "Provoziertes Leben," first publ. in *Ausdruckswelt: Essays und Aphorismen* (Wiesbaden, 1949); trans. as "Provoked Life: An Essay on the Anthropology of the Ego" in *The Psychedelic Reader*, sel. from *The Psychedelic Review*, ed. G. M. Weil, R. Metzner and T. Leary (New York, 1965), p. 42.

hermaphroditic." [24] To be godlike, it follows, one must first ignore the differences between the sexes. In search of "Paradise Now," men and women must dress alike, act alike, and in their sexual relationships be indifferent to the sex of their partner.

That is one of the striking features of the "tribal-love rock musical" *Hair.* (Note the typical "community" reference to "tribal-love"; the young American rebels are "playing Indians," rejecting the traditional view that the true hero was the individualistic, aggressive, tribe-destroyer, pioneering cowboy.) In the sharpest possible contrast to the traditional "musical," which has always emphasized sexual differentiation, *Hair* makes it hard to distinguish which of the characters are men and which women. And the sexual actions which are casually simulated appear to be determined only by proximity, indifferently directed towards male or female.*

24. Lawrence Lipton: *The Holy Barbarians, ed. cit.,* Pt. I, ch. 3, p. 81.

* It is women who suffer from this identification, as is very clearly brought out in *Hair.* Women are mere "hangers-on," no longer sexually necessary. Girls are dressed as boys rather than—for all their long hair and decorative garb—boys as girls. The sexual relationships suggested and simulated are not, for the most part, of a genital kind: they are anal and oral relationships, for which women are not necessary. What we are perhaps witnessing, in the name of "community," is a revolt against women—but a revolt in which women themselves participate because it can be represented, as by Simone de Beauvoir, as a revolt against the conception of a "feminine role." It is Eve, not Adam, who must vanish if the "original state" of perfect humanity is to be regained; she must take her old place, in Adam's rib, no longer separate flesh. This is not the first time that a class has participated in a revolution of which, in the end, it is the victim. On the unisexual tendencies in the United States see, although with considerable reservations, Charles Winick: *The New People.* The themes of nakedness and unisexuality played a prominent part in the Adamite sects, to which Augustine refers, and were also conspicuous in the teachings of certain of the Brethren of the Free Spirit. Sects of this kind have of course—like the "hippies" of our time—always been a small minority. But the reappearance of these ideas at such crucial stages in the history of civilization is of more than passing interest. See particularly Wilhelm Fränger: *The Millennium of Hieronymus Bosch,* trans. Wilkins and Kaiser, ch. 2. In the light of recent developments, Fränger's interpretation (p. 121) of Bosch's notorious "anal flower" may have to be reconsidered; the interpretation he rules out, that the Brethren of the Free Spirit thought every erogenous zone permissible, may well be the correct one.

Unisexuality is a reversion to early childhood, to a point before sex-roles were made apparent by differentiation in clothing and behaviour. At the same time, it is a special application of the mystical search for total unity, for a total community in which, as in Fichte's and Winwood Reade's dream, all mankind thinks and feels as one. So long as the role of the sexes is sharply distinguished that total community remains inaccessible. It is no accident that in Mao's China, too, differentiation between the sexes is reduced to a minimum.

Hair is notorious for its naked scene rather than for its unisexuality. But the nakedness, also, is presented as a mystical revelation, a revelation which makes unimportant, in the act of revealing, the difference between the sexes. More significantly, it suggests a ritual sloughing-off, a purification, through the casting away of "inessentials," mystical and perfectibilist in its inspiration. Adam and Eve, in the familiar Genesis story, "were both naked, the man and his wife, and were not ashamed." God knew that Adam had sinned, when he saw he had covered his nakedness. Unselfconscious nakedness, an unawareness of sexual difference, belongs, in other words, to Paradise; self-consciousness about nakedness only to man after the Fall. Orthodox Christianity took as its point of departure man in his fallen state; in medieval sculpture, therefore, the naked figure is a "huddled body cowering in consciousness of sin."[25] Metaphorically, however, nakedness continued, as we have seen, to play its ancient role. The mystic must "strip himself naked" before he can unite himself with God. In the Syrian monasteries, as amongst Eastern mystics, physical nakedness was by no means uncommon as a sign of sanctity.*

25. Kenneth Clark: *The Nude* (London, 1956), ch. VIII, p. 303.
* At the same time—a fact of which the Nazis made full use in their concentration camps— *compulsory* nakedness can be a powerful weapon of humiliation, as also can be that replacement of names by numbers which is a feature of mathematically perfect societies.

With the Renaissance painters nakedness is once more linked with Paradise; later writers and painters have developed the association between nakedness and perfection still further. In the eighteenth century the conception of the Pacific as an idyllic Paradise inhabited by noble savages was strengthened by the nakedness of those "savages." E. M. Forster's "The Machine Stops" presents the hero, Kuno, as rebelling against the atomistic life of his machine-governed Utopia. Trying to make his way to the outer world, he reflects thus: "I felt that humanity existed, and that it existed without clothes. . . . Had I been strong, I would have torn off every garment I had, and gone out into the outer air unswaddled."[26] The inhabitants of the most attractive of Wells' Utopias, *Men like Gods,* go unselfconsciously naked; that the visitors from our planet are horrified, or tantalized, by their nakedness is, as Wells represents the situation, the clearest possible sign of their imperfection. So when the cast of the "Living Theatre" strip themselves naked for their performance of *Paradise Now* they are reverting to an ancient theme. (Of course, the desire to shock is also an ancient one; but it would be a mistake to suppose that this is all that is involved in apocalyptic nakedness.)

The road to Paradise, one might conclude, is simple: it does not involve a prolonged agony through a dark night of the soul; all one need do is to take off one's pants. That would not be quite fair. The dropping of pants is a symbol for the dropping of inhibitions. The "new mystic," as we have already seen, rejects Freud's own view that inhibitions are essential to civilization. Man, he believes, is naturally good; and any society which rests on inhibitions is but an artificial

---

By making himself naked, as by scourging himself, by starving himself, by prostrating himself, by submitting without question to authority, the ascetic mystic voluntarily makes use of precisely the dehumanizing mechanisms the totalitarian state uses to impose its will on its victims.

26. E. M. Forster: "The Machine Stops," in *Collected Tales, ed. cit.,* p. 170.

civilization—a "plastic" substitute for a genuine inhibition-less community, in which man's natural goodness will express itself in love and tenderness.

Drug-taking is another instance in which ancient mystical ideals reappear in a more explicitly physical guise. Again and again, in describing the effects of drugs, addicts use language which compellingly reminds us of mysticism and of Stoicism.* Hashish, a nineteenth-century addict wrote, offers to men "a sense of detachment from oneself, of loss of all impulse towards action, and of widespread indifference to other persons as to all worldly ties."[27] Describing his feelings under the influence of mescalin, a contemporary poet uses such expressions as "I know everything"; "there is no Time"; "I am without care, part of all."[28] The resemblances between drug-inspired and mystical experience have been most throughly explored by Aldous Huxley and Alan Watts—who first established his reputation as an exponent of Zen Buddhism. Under the influence of mescalin, Huxley reports, "visual impressions are greatly intensified. . . . Interest in space is diminished and interest in time falls almost to zero. . . . The mescalin taker sees no reason

---

* Many drug-takers, in flight from "humanity" and the care inherent in it, turned first to mysticism. So when they took drugs, the language of mysticism was at their disposal to describe their experiences; they taught that language to new converts. But the fact remains that the old language seemed to them to fit their new experiences like a glove. It is very important to recognize that drug-taking has now—as for centuries past in other cultures—taken on the character of a religion: it has zealous converts, who seek to convert others. Like any other religion, of course, it also serves as a source of profit to "drug-pushers." But this should not be allowed to conceal the manifest sincerity of a great many drug-takers and drug-recommenders. "LSD," Marx might now have written, "is the religion of the intellectuals." On this point see especially Richard Blum and associates: *Utopiates: The Use and Users of LSD* (London, 1965), p. 134. For a criticism of the attempt to relate drug mysticism to classical mysticism—a criticism directed especially against Huxley, see R. C. Zaehner: *Mysticism: Sacred and Profane* (Oxford, 1957), which particularly insists on the point made in chapter IV, above, that Christianity stops short of the idea of an *absolute* unity between the mystic and God.

27. Quoted in "The Search for Ecstasy," *Mind Alive*, Vol. I, No. 4, p. 100. The source is not given.

28. Mike McClure: "Peyote Poem," from *Semina 3*, quoted in Lipton: *The Holy Barbarians, ed. cit.*, pp. 172–73.

for doing anything in particular and finds most of the causes for which, at ordinary times, he was prepared to act and suffer, profoundly uninteresting."[29] In other words, he no longer cares and no longer cherishes.

Watts adds that drugs revive a sense of community. By breaking down that defensiveness which inhibits physical tenderness, they help men and women to enter into "associations with others based on physical gestures of affection," associations which take the form of "rites, dances, or forms of play which clearly symbolize mutual love between the members of the group."[30] In the normal life of modern industrial societies, men and women are inhibited from these relationships; they are unable to permit themselves any erotic contacts—touching, for example—which fall between the extremes of purely verbalized contacts and full genital sexuality. But, by destroying inhibitions, drugs make such contacts possible, and in so doing, it is argued, promote community.

To the traditional Christian it is, of course, an intolerable suggestion that there is any resemblance whatsoever between "spiritual" and drug-taking mysticism. But, as Huxley points out, the classical mystics did in fact produce bodily changes in themselves—by starvation, by flagellation, by the perpetual muttering of prayers. All of these give rise to physical changes in the body, precisely the sort of changes which from our knowledge of bio-chemistry we should expect to produce "mystical experience."[31]

These observations do not, of course, suffice to demonstrate that the mystics were mistaken in what they reported, that they were wrong in supposing that they had

---

29. Aldous Huxley: *The Doors of Perception* (London, 1954; publ. together with his *Heaven and Hell* in 1-vol. paperback ed., Harmondsworth, 1959, repr. 1969), p. 23. For criticism of the view that Christian and drug-taking mysticism have any connection one with the other, see R. C. Zaehner: *Mysticism: Sacred and Profane* (Oxford, 1957).

30. Alan W. Watts: *The Joyous Cosmology* (New York, 1962), p. 92.

31. A. Huxley: *Heaven and Hell*, Appendix II; *ed. cit.,* pp. 117–22.

been granted a vision of God. Huxley himself believes that the taking of drugs can now accomplish what it once took starvation and flagellation to bring about. It so affects the chemistry of the brain that the brain no longer acts in its normal fashion as an inhibitor, allowing us to experience only what is practically important, and so permits what Huxley calls "Mind at large" to flow through its filters.*

The question what we are to make of reports of mystical experience is, of course, a large one, not lightly to be settled. One thing is obvious: whenever the mystics—"spiritual" or "bodily"—make claims which can be empirically tested, they are false. Angela of Foligno tells us that she was lifted up so that she could see all the countries of the world; it follows that in her mystical vision the world was flat. Had we asked her to describe then-undiscovered Australia it is not a mere guess that she could not have done so accurately. If, similarly, a drug-taker tells us that, now he has taken LSD, he "feels like Einstein" it will certainly be pointless to expect from him some new contribution to the unified field theory. He is in exactly the same position as the alcoholic driver who is convinced that he is now in a fit state to win the Grand Prix. William James has told us how under the influence of ether he was convinced that he was thinking great thoughts; writing them down he discovered them, in

---

* The title of Huxley's principal book on drug-taking is *The Doors of Perception*. His epigraph is from Blake: "If the doors of perception were cleansed everything would appear to man as it is, infinite." (The quotation is from *The Marriage of Heaven and Hell;* I have corrected Huxley's version to make it conform to the text in the Oxford Standard Authors edition of Blake's *Poetical Works*, p. 254.) In Blake, very many of the themes we have just been developing are clearly announced: the emphasis on infancy, "nestling for delight In laps of pleasure" (p. 290); the attack on Newtonian-type science and abstract reasoning (p. 381 and *passim*); the praise of "the naked Human Form Divine" (p. 157); the hostility to "the two Impossibilities, Chastity and Abstinence, Gods of the Heathen" (p. 429). Note as well, what is very typical of the "Romantic Rebels," Blake's Christianity without God—"God is Jesus" (p. 430)—and his hostility to societies of "wheel without wheel, with cogs tyrannic Moving by compulsion each other" as contrasted with Eden whose "wheel within wheel, in freedom; revolve in harmony and peace" (p. 388). In short, Blake forcibly reminds us just how much of what the "Romantic rebels" teach derives from a long tradition.

his waking moments, to be absolute nonsense, of a pseudo-metaphysical kind. Not every drug-mystic, unfortunately, is a William James, capable of recognizing nonsense when he sees it.

As for the view, again an empirical claim, that drug-taking encourages a "sense of community," no one can read the pitiful story of American "hippie" communities and still believe that drugs encourage "community," as distinct from vague feelings of "togetherness." A genuine community has common interests and is able to work together in a common life: out of its common interests affection develops. Touching is not a substitute for love—which is not, by any means, to deny that physical contacts of this sort can have their value. (In "The Machine Stops" E. M. Forster treats it as characteristic of the dystopia he there describes that its citizens cannot bear any kind of physical contact one with another: our own society has perhaps been approaching that point.)

Nor is there any ground for believing that drugs and spiritual exercises "enlarge the consciousness." Science *does* enlarge men's consciousness: it enables human beings to range more freely through space and time; it reveals to them a variety of objects about which they would otherwise be entirely ignorant. Art, too, "enlarges the consciousness"; it creates new objects, objects we can enjoy with care; it helps us to appreciate the shapes and forms, the modes of life, which lie around us. Drugs and mystical exercises, on the contrary, deliberately set out to destroy consciousness, governed as it is by care; they seek to carry men back to the world as they experienced it before they were capable of thinking, a world without structure and order, in which contours and forms float free, the world of "pure experience" as Bradley and James described it, in which even the distinction between men and the world around them does not exist. Becoming a human being consists, precisely, in learning how to reduce to order that primitive chaos of experience—to which we sometimes revert under conditions of fever or extreme fatigue. The mystic wants us to forget everything we have learnt: in short, no longer to be human.*

This, it might be argued, is only in order to deal more effectively with the world; mysticism retreats only in order to advance. Classical mystics, it is sometimes said, recognized that "this is the life that counts, and that the state of self-transcendence is a means, not an end in itself."[32] As a generalization about "spiritual" mystics, this is false. But some mystics, certainly, have sought in transcendent states a form of spiritual refreshment, which would prepare them to live the religious life on earth.† Equally, nineteenth-century opium addicts sometimes believed that opium-taking would

---

* Even more obviously is this true of Zen Buddhism. The Zen monk seeks to go back even beyond childhood, to think of himself as if he were a rock or stone. The typical Zen stone-gardens are made of unchanging rocks: the seasonal changes of the Western garden play no part in them. The living is excluded, because the living involves care, change, death. Such gardens undoubtedly have their attractions as a moral holiday, a respite from the attempt to grasp and cope with a changing world—the same sort of respite which can be obtained in a mountain range.

32. Sidney Cohen, as reported in Yablonsky: *The Hippie Trip*, p. 250.

† The claim that mystical experience, whatever its origins, makes its devotees better persons is hard to test—if only because there is often very little agreement between the mystics and their critics about what constitutes a better person. But so far as there is agreement on this point, the evidence suggests that although drug-takers, at least, *feel* they are better men after their drug-taking, independent observers often disagree with them. Eighty per cent of the drug users examined in Blum's *Utopiates* (p. 104) thought their fellow drug-takers had changed for the better: sixty-nine per cent of observers who did not take drugs thought they had either not changed at all or changed for the worse. The fact seems to be that the breaking down of inhibitions by any means improves some people and makes other people worse; no one who has observed the effect of alcohol will be surprised by this observation. As for the view that the taking of LSD improves the functioning of the intellect, I can only beg the reader—to take one case—to read Timothy Leary's "The Religious Experience: Its Production and Interpretation" in *The Psychedelic Reader*, pp. 191–213. Intellectual irresponsibility is there exhibited at its very worst. Zen Buddhism positively prides itself on its moral and political irresponsibility; a leading representative of the contemporary Zen movement found no difficulty in becoming a convinced Nazi. Compare on this point Arthur Koestler: *Drinkers of Infinity* (London, 1968), pp. 287–91. In his *The Myth of the Twentieth Century* Alfred Rosenberg traced back the ideas of the Nazis to German mystics, especially Eckhart. This, no doubt, is too hard on the mystics, but it is not entirely without justification. Contemporary hippie-mystics are often convinced that they are the recipients of a special divine grace; they display that fanaticism, "aristocratic" pride and antinomianism which Wesley so feared, setting themselves above all kinds of moral restraint.

offer them "spiritual experiences" which would enable them the more effectively to express themselves in poetry—even if the actual effect, in most cases, was to evoke nothing more productive than "the intention but failure to write a great philosophical work."[33] Contemporary mystics, in contrast, often drop out of the world in intention as well as in effect; they are the modern equivalent of the fourth-century hermits in the Syrian desert—even if their desert is not Syria but California and what they are mourning is not so much the worldliness of Christianity as the worldliness of Civilization.

The fact remains that even when the mystic believes that he has an obligation towards his fellow-men which his temporary retreat from the world will enable him, in the long run, more effectively to perform, he does not find perfection in that human relationship but only in his relationship to the One. And although it be true that, as a result of mystical withdrawal, he finds it possible to act in ways in which he could not otherwise act, this does nothing to demonstrate that the withdrawal is itself anything but a form of play. Other men feel the need for orgies, whether sexual orgies or orgies of destruction, for bouts of drunkenness, or for violent physical exercise, to achieve the same catharsis.

To speak of the mystical ideal as one of unalloyed enjoyment is, it might be objected, an absurd misinterpretation of the situation: how can it possibly be said that the mystic is longing for a life of unalloyed enjoyment when he endures such austerities? But two points arise here. First, we have come to be somewhat suspicious of austerities. As little as half a century ago Baron von Hügel could relate with every expectation of approval the story of a nun who, on learning that a favourite pupil had become the mistress of a wealthy man, told her that until the relationship was terminated, she would scourge herself daily so that she stood in a pool

---

33. Alethea Hayter: *Opium and the Romantic Imagination* (London, 1968), ch. I, p. 27.

of her own blood. Such spiritual blackmail has nowadays lost much of its moral appeal. But even apart from that, the nun's motives would now, very commonly, be regarded with suspicion; the sexual complications of such self-scourging are only too familiar. Scourging can be a form of sexual play. The practices of famous medieval ascetics are described in detail in the case-histories of Krafft-Ebing's *Psychopathia Sexualis.*

As well, and more fundamentally, mystical austerities are commonly represented, as we have often had occasion to remark, as a "stripping off" to the point of nakedness. It is a constant theme of perfectibilists that men need to return to an earlier state, to become as little children, to find their way back to unity with Nature, to the undifferentiated whole they experienced before they began to think, to primitive community. Difficulty, struggle, toil, are needed only in order to find the way back. That the mystic is forced to toil, to struggle, does nothing to demonstrate that what he is seeking to achieve at the end of his struggle is something other than a state of absolute unalloyed enjoyment. The old mystic differs from the new mystics only in believing that to achieve that state he must first toil, not in his definition of what he hopes to achieve. (The danger attaching to LSD, the fact that it may, often does, produce suffering—a "dark night" of depression and horror—is part of its attractiveness to some of its devotees; it links them more closely with the mystical tradition.)

At the opposite extreme from the play-ideal lies Puritanism, that Puritanism, so potent in the United States, but widespread also in Europe, against which the new mystics are reacting* and which has to be taken into account if their

---

* Obscenities are a rebellion against the euphemisms of the "comfort-station" and the "powder-room"; nakedness against an extreme body-Puritanism, for which even to show the navel was wicked: unisexuality against a rigid distinction between masculine and feminine roles, panic-stricken by homosexuality; dirtiness and, more particularly, carelessness about faeces against the exaggeration of hygiene and toilet-training; pacifism

attitudes are to be comprehensible. "Play of whatever sort," a German educator once wrote, "should be forbidden in all evangelical schools, and its vanity and folly should be explained to the children with warnings of how it turns the mind away from God and eternal life, and works destruction on their immortal souls."[34] "Play," in this context, has of course, the widest possible application: any form of enjoyment, whether it be play, game, or love, "turns the mind away from God." Life should be wholly devoted, according to the Puritan, to toil. Secularists have sometimes adopted a not dissimilar attitude. Anxious not to be condemned as pagan hedonists they—some of the Fabians for example—have so strongly emphasized the importance of duty, of service, of seriousness that, in their practical attitudes to life, they could scarcely be distinguished from the most pious of Puritans. There is certainly nothing playful about George Eliot, or about the Webbs.

Up to a point, in reacting against the Puritan attitude to life, the exponents of "Paradise Now" are saying no more than what is said in those somewhat trite but extremely pertinent lines of the Georgian poet W. H. Davies:

What is this life, if full of care
We have no time to stand and stare?[35]

Looking back on his own past life, so serious a philosopher as Herder was led to comment adversely, as many of us might do on looking back at our own life, on its absence of play. "The sense of touch and the world of sensuous plea-

---

against the cult of violence and gun-carrying; the ideal of "community" against a viciously competitive individualism; the ideal of play against an intense seriousness of purpose, wholly hostile to wit, irony or any kind of secret smile; the "return to Nature" against savage industrial despoliation; mysticism and ritualism against a moralistic version of Christianity.

34. The pietist Töllner, quoted in K. Groos: *The Play of Man, ed. cit.,* pp. 398–99, from K. A. Schmid: *Geschichte der Erziehung,* 5 vols (Stuttgart, 1884–1902), Vol. IV, p. 282.

35. The poem is entitled "Leisure."

sures," he writes, ". . . these I have not enjoyed. I see and feel *at a distance.*" We have all lost, he goes on to suggest, "the noble sensuality of ancient times, especially in the East"; he himself had suffered in later life, he came to think, because he had failed, in his youth, to live the life "of images, of sensations, of upsurging delight."[36]

In so far as contemporary mysticism develops this theme, in so far, that is, as it is a reaction against a life too "full of care," one does not have to be a mystic to appreciate its attractions. J. M. Keynes was certainly no mystic; but even he complained that men have looked too much to the future; in the language of the nursery, they have placed too much stress on jam tomorrow, too little on jam today.[37]

There is certainly room in life for play, room for "moral holidays," more room than our society has permitted. Herbert Marcuse has particularly emphasized that the "scarcity" which is used to justify the postponement of gratification is, in modern industrial societies, largely artificial; ideas like "economic growth" and a "higher standard of living," used to justify more and more toil, have become absurd fetishes.[38] When Freud argued that civilization can only be founded on repression, because human resources are so limited that immediate gratification would destroy civilization, he was reflecting the ideas of a pre-technological age. Much human toil, nowadays, is directed towards the obtaining of possessions and status which are simply not worth having: which, having, one does not enjoy; which are possessed only to be cast aside in favour of objects which are more "up-to-date" and can be purchased only by additional toil.*

36. Herder: *Travel Diary,* as trans. Barnard in *J. G. Herder on Social and Political Culture,* pp. 69, 83, 78.

37. J. M. Keynes: *Essays in Persuasion* (London, 1931; pop. ed. 1933), p. 370.

38. Herbert Marcuse: *Eros and Civilization* (Boston, 1955; paperback ed., London, 1969).

* If violence increases to a point at which every citizen has to buy a double lock for every door and add a room to his house as an armoury, this will contribute to economic

But this is not to say that we should take as our ideal a world which is without past and future or entirely devoid of care. Brown is certainly right: if men were not "full of care," they would have no sense of time—as children at first have not, or that kind of adult who is ordinarily condemned as "irresponsible"—they would have no logic, no history, no quantified science, no technology, no system of production. One can go much further than this; they would have no art, no friendship, no stable human relationships. No doubt, these points are disputable. The attempt to turn art into a "happening" is, one might say, precisely the attempt to create an art without "care," which is to be enjoyed once and for all as it happens and which is to be in its creation entirely spontaneous, the expression of an immediate enjoyment.* And this is only the Romantic conception of art carried to its

---

growth. A country may have a high national income only because it is busy producing weapons of war; its standard of living may be statistically reported as "high" only because unscrupulous salesmen are successful in selling shoddy goods by fraudulent methods to customers who get no enjoyment out of what they are persuaded into buying. For more on the topic of economic growth see, allowing for his idiosyncrasies, E. J. Mishan: *The Costs of Economic Growth* (London, 1967) and on national income see, for example, C. S. Shoup: *Principles of National Income Analysis* (Boston, 1947), pp. 269–70. It is interesting to note that although he is a fundamentally conservative thinker Mishan agrees with the "Romantic rebels" on at least two crucial points: the need for recreating a sense of community and the need for living more fully in the present. The conventional "left" and the conventional "right" are still squabbling about who is to get what, and by what means; the Soviet Union and the United States are equally committed to the fetish of economic growth. That is one major reason why the conventional divisions between political parties now seem to many people quite irrelevant: the basic conflict, only gradually emerging, is between those who are still wholly committed to the ideal of economic growth and those who are uninterested in economic growth, except where there is clear evidence that—as it sometimes has done, and in many countries still could do—it improves the quality of men's lives, diminishes mutual suspicion, enables men to devote themselves more freely to their loves, offers them opportunities for creative enterprise, or, in short, does what the Enlightenment hoped it would do.

* It can also be an expression of discontent, a wilful—as distinct from a playful—destruction of established forms and practices, directed against their authoritarian character, or what is presumed to be such. In this respect the "happening" in Heinrich Böll's novel *The End of a Mission* may be more typical than it at first sight appears to be. Anarchism is an attempt to turn political action into a "happening," and in anarchism there is a peculiar mixture of rational criticism and mystical aspiration. It is only to be expected that the boundary lines I have been drawing will be ill-defined and often crossed. (Böll's novel has been translated into English by Leila Vennewitz, London, 1968.)

extremes; in a fashion characteristic of Romanticism it encourages Pelagian pride, pride in one's "creativity" or originality, discourages pride in work.

Art, however, is not simply play, it is a form of love—
enjoyment with care, cherishing an object. So is science.
A "science" which was "erotic exuberance," which did not
try to generalize, to economize, which sought only to enjoy each individual object for itself as distinct from cherishing the growth of knowledge would simply not *be* science.
What we may question, indeed, is whether the ideal of a life
wholly devoted to enjoyment is even conceivable. The baby
must, eventually, withdraw its lips from its mother's breast;
the sexual embrace cannot last forever. Only if the mystic is
right, only if there is an "Everlasting Now" to which one can
be eternally attached, is perpetual enjoyment possible. And
the idea of such an "Everlasting Now" to which a temporal
being can somehow attach himself cannot stand up to philosophical criticism; it "saves" itself only by retreating into unintelligibility, as the doctrines of the pseudo-Dionysius will
sufficiently illustrate.

For all its virtues, then, play is not enough. Theatrical
"happenings"—except when they are interspersed, as they
so often are, with boring, sentimental and witless dialogue
—can be exciting, in their primitive way; they may represent
the return of a not-undesirable Dionysian element into our
art. To suppose, however, that a society would be more perfect whose theatre despised Shakespeare and concentrated
on "happenings" is as clearly absurd as to suppose that a
society would be more perfect whose art consisted only of
propaganda for approved ideals.*

---

* In discussing *Hair* we have already noted some of the ways in which the experimental theatre of the 'sixties is allied to mysticism. And whether or not *Hair* "lasts" is irrelevant
to its interest as a cultural phenomenon, as giving expression in the twentieth century to
old, but for long submerged, mystical ideals. Much recent theatre seeks to break down
the distinction between audience and performer, to make of them a "single community,"
and to arouse in the audience physical sensations rather than to offer them occasion for
thought. Like advertising, it seeks to kill thought, not to arouse it, by making a direct

The fact is, or so I am suggesting, that there is nothing better than "loves." Some measure of "play" is certainly desirable. "Games" can be enjoyable and can contribute a great deal to the vigour and vitality of a community. Toil is in some measure unavoidable; self-sacrifice, action out of duty, unenjoyable work are bound up with—and can be justified by reference to—our loves. But the quality of a society depends on the quality of the loves it exhibits and fosters.* Quite certainly, if the loves it fosters are the love of power, of money, and of status, it is a low-grade society. Yet even these loves are relatively harmless compared with the "cos-

---

onslaught on its audience. It refuses to count a thinking audience as a participating audience; to "participate" is, the presumption runs, to be physically involved, to be touched, showered with confetti, moved amongst, fondled, or sat upon. (Admittedly, a good many traditional theatre audiences neither think nor participate in any other way; but whereas Shaw tried to break down the lack of participation by making his audience think—and could only do so by thinking himself—thinking by no means suits the contemporary style.) Taking up the suggestions of Antoine Artaud, theatrical productions and experimental films have sought to "explore our nervous impressionability with rhythms, sounds, words, resonances and vocalizations." Theatre has abandoned the traditional stage for open halls reminiscent, in Artaud's words, "of certain temples of Upper Tibet." [For Artaud see "Le théâtre et la cruauté" (*c.* 1935) and "Le théâtre de la cruauté—Premier manifeste" (1932) included in *Le théâtre et son double* (Paris, 1964; the passages quoted are on pp. 133 and 146).] It is worth noting, once more, just how reactionary the new mysticism is. Such dramatic forms as comedy and tragedy gradually emerged out of ceremony and ritual, they became drama precisely by doing so. But the suggestion now is that the theatre ought to revert to the religious ceremony it once was—just as Heidegger would have human thinking revert to its pre-philosophical and pre-scientific stages. The current revival of interest in astrology, magic, the occult, witchcraft, is no less intellectually reactionary in character; it involves abandoning those habits of thinking scientifically and critically which men have slowly and painfully built up. Its recrudescence demonstrates just how little scientific thinking has penetrated our society, particularly, perhaps, the feminine segment of our society. (The women's journals are the great propagators of occultism.)

   * "Man only plays," Friedrich Schiller once wrote, "when he is in the fullest sense of the word a human being, and he is only fully a human being when he plays." For "plays," in this passage, one should rather read "loves." Schiller is conscious of this in so far as he adds that "with beauty man shall only play, and it is with beauty only that he shall play." The "play" Schiller has in mind is a play in and through cherished forms. I should rather say, adopting for the nonce Schiller's style: "Man only loves when he is in the fullest sense a human being, and he is only a full human being when he loves; his loves man shall enjoy; these are not the only things he should enjoy, but they are the enjoyments in which he shows himself at his best." See Friedrich Schiller: *On the Aesthetic Education of Man*, Fifteenth Letter, Sections 9, 8: ed. E. M. Wilkinson and L. A. Willoughby (Oxford, 1967), p. 107.

mic loves"—the activities which describe themselves as the love of God and the love of Humanity. These are the "loves" —on my view, the pseudo-loves—in the name of which human beings persecute, torture, censor, kill. Sometimes, of course, people describe as "the love of God" or "the love of Humanity" what is in fact love for persons: there are doctors, nurses, clergymen, men and women in every walk of life, whom one might in this sense describe as "loving humanity" and who might think of themselves as loving God. Again, we know what Wittgenstein is driving at when he tells us in the foreword to his *Philosophische Bemerkungen* that, except that he knows he would be misunderstood, he would like to say of his work that it is written for the "greater glory of God"; he goes on to add that in so far as it has been written not out of this motive but out of vanity, it ought to be condemned. To act out of love for God, or for the glory of God, can mean nothing more than to seek to make a contribution to human life, as distinct from satisfying one's vanity—love as distinct from self-love is sometimes thus described as "the love of God."

But often enough, as we have seen, men have sought to demonstrate their love for God by loving nothing at all and their love for humanity by loving nobody whatsoever. These are the men to be feared above all others— the Robespierres who "love humanity," the Inquisitors who "love God." The loves which determine the quality of a society are not such pseudo-loves as these but what, relatively speaking, might be called the "little loves"—the love of one's work, of one's friends, of works of art, of scientific and technological achievements, of justice, of political freedom, of one's community, one's wife, one's children.*

---

* Another "cosmic love" is the "love of Nature." Man's relationship to Nature exemplifies the contrasts I have been emphasizing. It may be a relationship of toil: Nature is then an object to be exploited in the interests of profit. Or Nature may serve, as it does to the yachtsman and the mountaineer, as the opponent in a game. Or, finally, men may be

What of "love for one's neighbours"? It is quite misleading to use the word "love" in this context. The appropriate attitude to a neighbour—to another human being merely as such—is not love but that quite different relationship which one might call "consideration." It consists in treating a neighbour as another human being, taking his interests into account, coming to his aid if he is in difficulties, admitting his right to live his own life in his own way. Love, when it is a love for persons, includes consideration but goes much beyond it: it is a special relationship to other persons, which implies taking a peculiar interest in their growth and development.

A principal objection to the view that we ought to love our neighbours, love them as brothers, is that it is presumptuous to do so. They may properly resent any attempt on our part to take a peculiar interest in them, merely in virtue of their being our neighbours. We certainly do not wish to be loved by everybody: why should we imagine that everybody wishes to be loved by us? Affection—personal love—always carries with it some degree of intimacy, loss of privacy. Nowhere is there more talk about "the brotherhood of man" than in the Soviet Union: there it is used to justify the total rejection of the right to privacy, the denunciation of neighbours one by another, constant interference in one another's lives. That is why Orwell called his supreme ruler

---

said to "love" Nature. But two quite different attitudes are covered by this phrase. Nature may be loved as a farmer, a conservationist, a forester, loves it—as something to be cherished. Or it may be "loved" in Wordsworth's manner, as a purely sensual object; in my terminology, that is, man's relationship with Nature may be simply "play." In this latter form, significantly enough, it is often associated with mysticism. The "lover of Nature" feels himself "at one" with it, indistinguishable from it, in a kind of swooning enjoyment, not necessarily interpreted in religious terms. Even in this form, the "love of Nature" is perhaps the least harmful form of pseudo-love although one often finds it serving as a substitute for the love of care-creating human beings. Hermits often built their hermitages in settings of great natural beauty, and it would be difficult to excel, in this respect, the surroundings of Hitler's Berchtesgaden. But it is certainly the active form of love which is now called for, if this is to be a world worth living in.

"Big Brother." And precisely the same phenomenon has occurred in rigidly Christian communities like, for example, Puritan New England or sixteenth-century Spain.

If, with these reservations, we think of "love" as the highest form of human activity we have still to grant to the perfectibilist that "loves," even the best of them, are not perfect in any of the classical senses. "Care" is essentially involved in them, discontent, anxiety, dependence on others, disunity, opposition, unhappiness. Herder sums in his characteristically metaphorical fashion: "No where upon Earth does the rose of happiness blossom without thorns: but what proceeds from these thorns is every where and under all its forms, the lovely though perishable rose of vital joy." [39] Lovely, perishable, joyous—such are the best human loves. But full of thorns.

To write a book, for example, can be a "vital joy," but a joy which is inevitably united with the thorns of anxious care. It is not a contribution to perfection, as perfection is classically understood. To write anything worth writing is to arouse opposition, controversy—writing does not promote the classical perfectibilist ideals of unity and harmony or contentment; it is to abandon all hope of self-sufficiency, to make oneself dependent on a multitude of other human beings, to surrender one's peace of mind, to stir up one's passions, to struggle with time. Love for persons is no less "imperfect" in the classical sense of the word.

On the other side, or so I have suggested, the classical ideals of perfection banish care only by dehumanizing. No doubt they can be so interpreted as not to be destructive of humanity. Art and science have their own orders, the artist and the scientist seek particular forms of harmony: to that extent the love of order need not be dehumanizing.

---

39. Herder: *Ideas*, Bk. VIII, ch. V; *ed. cit.*, p. 222. Compare D. H. Lawrence on Melville in *Studies in Classic American Literature* (London, 1924), ch. X. Lawrence particularly attacks the mystical conception of a love which is "thornless" in virtue of the fact that lover and beloved are identical.

If "simplicity" is interpreted to mean no more than "Do not unnecessarily complicate your life with possessions!" — it is an ideal any humanist would do well to adopt. Science, though itself a passion, must certainly be "dispassionate"; if freedom from passion means nothing more than objectivity, disinterestedness, it is certainly not a dehumanizing ideal. Man needs to think of himself as "at one with the world," as the perfectibilist urges him to do, if this is to be contrasted with setting himself above, or apart from, the natural world. "Self-sufficiency" is vitally important to humanity, when it means no more than a capacity to do without such solaces as reputation and status.

But classical perfectibilists go a great deal further than this. They set out in search of a total order, a total harmony, and neither science nor art, as Plato saw and the dystopians have seen after him, could be freely operating loves within such a total order; science and art are by their very nature revolutionary, destructive of established orders. Perfectibilists tell us not only to abandon our possessions but to abandon our loves; to be not merely dispassionate but, what is very different, without passion; to seek a kind of unity which is destructive of that diversity which is the glory of the world and the secret of all man's achievements; to be self-sufficient in a sense which does not permit of love. That is precisely why perfectibilism is dehumanizing. To achieve perfection in any of its classical senses, as so many perfectibilists have admitted, it would first be necessary to cease to be human, to become godlike, to rise above the human condition. But a god knows nothing of love, or science, or art, or craft, of family and friends, of discovery, of pride in work. And can we really count as perfection a condition which excludes all of these, for the sake of eternity, of order, or of unalloyed enjoyment?

In spite of these reflections, which might lead us to reject perfectibilism in any of its forms, it is very hard to shake off the feeling that man is capable of becoming something much superior to what he now is. This feeling, if it is interpreted in the manner of the more commonsensical Enlighteners, is not in itself irrational. There is certainly no *guarantee* that men will ever be any better than they now are; their future is not, as it were, underwritten by Nature. Nor is there any device, whether skilful government, or education, which is certain to ensure the improvement of man's condition. To that extent the hopes of the developmentalists or the governmentalists or the educators must certainly be abandoned. There is not the slightest ground for believing, either, with the anarchist, that if only the State could be destroyed and men could start afresh, all would be well. But we know from our own experience, as teachers or parents, that individual human beings can come to be better than they once were, given care, and that wholly to despair of a child or a pupil is to abdicate what is one's proper responsibility. We know, too, that in the past men have made advances, in science, in art, in affection. Men, almost certainly, are capable of more than they have ever so far achieved. But what they achieve, or so I have suggested, will be a consequence of their remaining anxious, passionate, discontented human beings. To attempt, in the quest for perfection, to raise men above that level is to court disaster; there is no level above it, there is only a level below it. "To be man," Sartre has written, "means to reach towards being God."[40] That is why he also describes man as "useless passion." For certainly man is a "useless passion" if his passion is to be God. But his passions are not useless, if they help him to become a little more humane, a little more civilized.

40. Jean-Paul Sartre: *Being and Nothingness*, trans. Hazel E. Barnes (New York, 1956; London, 1957), p. 566.

SUBJECT INDEX

Absolute flaws, 16
Absolute perfection, 19, 163, 201, 241, 357–58, 366, 383
Action, as embodied contemplation, 92–93
Adamite sects, 493 n.
Adaptation, 382–83
Aesthetic perfection, 24–25, 26, 39, 163, 233
Aggression, 426 n.
Albigensian heresy, 212
Alienation, 373–74
Allegorical method, 86, 86 n.
Alms-giving, 131
Ambition, 460
American Unitarians, 136
Anabaptists, 203, 335
Anarchism, 264, 272–89, 294, 413, 505 n.
Anchoritism, 65, 176, 177, 179–80
Anomie, 489
Anti-Christ, 221
Antinomianism, 123 n., 172, 209, 211, 212, 214, 218, 219 n.
Anti-Pelagians, 155, 163, 166, 200
Anxiety, 466, 466 n.
Arab civilization, 312
Arcadian ideal, 449–50
Aristocratic pride, 455, 456 n.
Aristotelianism, 58, 60 n., 63
Asceticism: Apostle Paul and, 123 n.; Buddhism and, 188–89; John Cassian on, 178–79; Judaism and, 176; mysticism and, 53–54, 189, 201, 495 n.; Plato on, 49; Puritanism and, 187–88; sexual enjoyment, 502; vs. Stoicism, 82
Associationism, 255–56, 261, 295, 328; English, 296; French, 297
Ataraxia (peace of mind), 65
Atom bomb, 406
Atonement, 210
Augustinianism, 82, 134–35, 166–71, 235, 456
Auschwitz, 444

Beatific vision, 465. *See also* Vision, of God
Beauty: Augustinian account of, 134; Platonic account of, 47–48, 52, 114
Béghards, 219
Behaviorism, 256–58, 261, 423
Biblical prophecies, 327
Biblical space, 112, 147
Bienfaisance, 236, 341 n.
Bodhisattva, 189
Body-mysticism, 479
Boethian era, 41 n.
Boundless, the, 35–36, 35 n., 38
Brethren of the Free Spirit, 121, 215–17, 440, 493 n.
Brook Farm, 281
Buddhism, 74, 244 n.; ideal of disengagement, 21; mysticism, 189; sphericity, 39 n.; theory of grace, 142 n.; transmigration, 45

Calculus of probabilities, 315–17, 327
Calvinism, 204, 237, 247
Cambridge Platonists, 237, 244, 328 n., 330
Capitalism, 373, 425 n.
Care, 466–67, 469, 477, 505, 510
Caritas, 153
Carnival, 486 n.
Caste system, 6 n.
Catharism, 121, 212–13, 214
Charity, 131, 180, 239, 491
China, 244 n., 302 n., 494
Chosen people, 117–18
Christianity: and aristocratic pride, 455–56; ascetic, 130, 178; attitudes toward marriage, 122 n.; attitudes toward perfectibility, 27–28, 80–81, 120, 124; attitudes toward the flesh, 121–23; and contemplation, 65; criticism of Stoicism, 73; disputes about perfectibility, 17; early perfectibilism, 96 n.; egocentric, 130; and evolution, 405, 408–10,

Name and Title Index

Abbadie, Jacques, 248 n.
Abelard, Peter, 105
Abraham, 36, 83
Acton, John E. E. D. Acton, 1st baron, 286, 356–57, 394 n., 431
Adam, 126–28, 144, 158, 308, 464 n., 492, 493 n., 494
Addison, Joseph, 240, 300
Addresses to the German Nation (Fichte), 367
Aeschylus, 31, 33, 34
Affluent Society (Galbraith), 451
Agamemnon (Aeschylus), 31, 34
Agricola, Johannes, 218
Alembert, Jean le Rond d', 266, 298–99
D'Alembert's Dream (Diderot), 234
Alphaville, 436
Alvarez, Balthasar, 193
Ambrose, 126
Aminta (Tasso), 464 n.
Analysis of the Phenomena of the Human Mind (James Mill), 270
Anaxagoras, 30
Anaximander, 35, 35 n., 38
Angela of Foligno, 181, 190–91, 460, 491, 498
Angelus Silesius, 460 n.
Anselm, 115
Anthony of Padua, 119
Anti-desperation (Arnold), 105
Antiquities of the Jews (Josephus), 125 n.
Apology for the Religious Orders (Aquinas), 186
Apology for the True Christian Divinity (Barclay), 206
Appearance and Reality (Bradley), 396
Aquinas. *See* Thomas Aquinas
Aristides the Just, 232
Ariston, of Chios, 76
Aristophanes, 66
Aristotle: on the Boundless, 35; civic humanists and, 227; on contemplative life, 46, 63–65, 91–92; on contrast between philosophical and civic goodness, 63–64; on health and wealth as goods, 77; on nature of God, 62–63; neo-Platonists and, 60; on progress, 305; on sphericity, 39–40; theory of perfection, 9, 12–13, 58–65; on transitoriness, 462; on truth, 112
Arles, Synod of, 146
Arnold, Matthew, 105
Artaud, Antoine, 507 n.
The Ascent of Man (Drummond), 398–99
Athanasius, 126
Athena, 30
Athenagoras, 214
Augustine: anti-Pelagian tracts, 140–41; on charity, 233–34; on contemplative life, 185; doctrine of original sin, 126, 128; on evil, 13, 219; on human perfection, 133–35, 220, 224; on love of God, 131–32; monasticism, 180; mystical visions, 115 n.; on nature of God, 99, 113–14, 116; rejection of cyclical theory of history, 306–7; theory of grace, 142–44; view of progress, 307–8, 419
Avicenna, 198

Babeuf, F. N., 268
Back to Methuselah (Shaw), 395
Bacon, Francis, 309, 313, 314, 467
Bain, Alexander, 255
Bakunin, Michael, 286–88, 302
Balbus, 39, 70
Balfour, A. J., 1st earl, 415–16
Ballard, J. G., 484
Barclay, Robert, 206
Barth, John, 200, 483
Barth, Karl, 6, 97, 166, 168–71, 202, 419, 420
Basil, 176, 177–78, 180, 183

The typeface for this book is New Baskerville, which is based on the types of English type founder and printer John Baskerville (1706–75). Baskerville is the quintessential "transitional" face: it retains the bracketed and oblique serifs of "old-style" faces such as Caslon and Garamond, but in its increased lowercase height, lighter color, and enhanced contrast between thick and thin strokes, it presages "modern" faces.

This book is printed on paper that is acid-free and meets the requirements of the American National Standard for Permanence of Paper for Printed Library Materials, Z39.48-1992. ∞

Book design by Chitra Sekhar,
Stevens Point, Wisconsin

Typography by Tseng Information Systems, Inc.,
Durham, North Carolina

Printed and bound by Edwards Brothers, Inc.,
Ann Arbor, Michigan